The Joan Palevsky Imprint in Classical Literature

In honor of beloved Virgil—

"O degli altri poeti onore e lume . . ."

—Dante, *Inferno*

The publisher gratefully acknowledges the generous contribution
to this book provided by Joan Palevsky

The School of History

Studious *arete:* Athenian grave relief of youth reading book- roll, ca. 400. Grottaferrata abbey, Rome. Photo courtesy of the Deutsches Archäologisches Institut, Rome, neg. no. 61.173.

The School of History

Athens in the Age of Socrates

Mark Munn

UNIVERSITY OF CALIFORNIA PRESS
Berkeley Los Angeles London

University of California Press
Berkeley and Los Angeles, California

University of California Press, Ltd.
London, England

Library of Congress Cataloging-in-Publication Data
Munn, Mark Henderson.
The school of history : Athens in the age of Socrates / by Mark Munn.
p. cm.
Includes bibliographical references and index.
ISBN 0-520-21557-5 (cloth : alk paper)
1. Athens (Greece)—Civilization—Political aspects. 2. Greece—History—Athenian supremacy, 479–431 B.C. 3. Democracy—Greece—Athens—Historiography. I. Title.
DF277.M86 2000
938′.04—dc21 99-046451

Manufactured in the United States of America

08 07 06 05 04 03 02 01 00 10 9 8 7 6 5 4 3 2 1

The paper used in this publication meets the minimum requirements of ANSI / NISO Z39.48-1992 (R 1997) (*Permanence of Paper*). ♾

For my parents,
Robert Henderson Munn and Ethel Marie Bianucci Munn,
with love and thanks
for the best of beginnings

CONTENTS

LIST OF ILLUSTRATIONS x

ACKNOWLEDGMENTS xi

MAPS xiii

Introduction 1

PART I THE SPIRIT OF DEMOCRATIC ATHENS, 510–415

1 The Past of Democratic Athens 15
The Past and the Truth / The Origins of Democracy / Choral Songs and Tragedies / Praise in Song / Enacting the Immanent Past / Performance and Public / The Dead and the Living / Everyman's Past / Witnesses to the Past

2 The Aristocracy of Democratic Athens 46
The Privileges of Empire / The Best of the Athenians / The Public Display of Private Arete */ Prowess in War / The Impression of Power / The Best of the Greeks*

3 Servants of the Athenian Democracy 64
The Power of Numbers / Slaves of Slaves / Friendship with Foreigners and Loyalty to the Demos */ The Sycophants / The Demagogues / The People's Money / The Tyranny of the* Demos */ The Sophists / The Speech-Writers / Victory, the Measure of Virtue / The Oracle Mongers / The Expertise of* Syngrapheis */ The Conspirators*

PART II THE CRISIS OF ATHENS, 415–403

4 The Expulsion of Alcibiades, 415–413 95
Alcibiades / Sicilian Ambitions / Antiphon the Sophist / Spoiling the Moment / Athens Turned Inside Out / The Conspiracy of the Mysteries / Alcibiades' Defense / The Destruction of Alcibiades / Hearing the Testimony of History / The Limits of Power / The Will of the Gods / Alcibiades in Flight / The Flight of the Birds

5 Rationalizing Oligarchy, 413–411 127
On the Boundaries of Asia / Saviors and Phantoms / Sage Advice / The Ancestral Constitution / The Best Laid Plans / Desperate Straits / Moderation and Accommodation

6 A Procession of Victories, 411–408 152
Victory at Cyzicus / Immutable Change / The Generals and the Men of Athens / Realizing Vision / Alcibiades Triumphant / Alcibiades and the Laws / Beloved of the Mother of the Gods

7 The Limits of Democratic Imperative, 408–405 175
Lordship of Asia / The Eclipse of Alcibiades / Victory at Arginusae / The Trial of the Generals / Playing on Reason / Finding the Right Perspective / To Humor the Lion

8 Surrendering to Sparta, 405–404 195
The Friendship of Cyrus / The Battle of Aegospotami / Conon, Cyprus, and the New King / The Siege of Athens / Negotiating With Sparta / Theramenes' Secret / The Surrender of Athens / The Agents of Oligarchy / Again, the Ancestral Constitution / Breaking the Back of the Democracy / Pulling Out the Roots of Empire

9 The Athenian Civil War, 404–403 218
Freedom and Slavery / The Thirty "Establishers of the Laws" / Social Engineering / More Ancient Virtues / Those Who Are In and Those Who Are Out / Beating Out the Lion / The Return of the Exiles / War Between Piraeus and Athens / The Spartan Settlement

PART III RESURRECTING ATHENS, 403–395

10 The Laws of Athens, 403–400 247
Sources / The Few and the Many / The Restoration of a Democracy / The Heroes of Piraeus / True

Athenians / Andocides and the Laws / The Work of the Nomothetai */ The Laws of Athens*

11 Eliminating Socrates, 401–399 273
The Case Against Nicomachus / Amnesty and Remembrance / Ominous Reminders / Socrates' Offense

12 Athenian Democracy and History, 399–395 292
A New Past for a New Beginning / A Passion for Books / Socrates and the Laws / Remembering the Spoken Word / The Account Compiled by Thucydides / Thucydides in Exile / Thucydides in Athens / Why Thucydides Wrote / The Unfinished Condition / The Beginnings of Posterity

APPENDIX A. EPIGRAPHIC CHRONOLOGY 331

APPENDIX B. EURIPIDES' *HELEN* AND ARISTOPHANES' *THESMOPHORIAZUSAE* 333

APPENDIX C. CHRONOLOGY OF THE EVENTS OF 410–406 335

APPENDIX D. THE SURRENDER OF ATHENS AND THE INSTALLATION OF THE THIRTY 340

ABBREVIATIONS 345

NOTES 347

BIBLIOGRAPHY 441

GENERAL INDEX 469

INDEX LOCORUM 495

ILLUSTRATIONS

Grave relief of youth (frontispiece)

1. The tyrant-slayers 19

2. The Albani relief 53

3. Nike relief from the parapet of the temple of Athena Nike 84

4a–b. Attic-style tetradrachm with satrap's portrait and Athenian owl 164

5. Seated statue of the Mother of the Gods 173

6. The Lenormant relief 182

7. Fragment of the calendar of sacrifices 228

8. Reconstructed view of the southwest corner of the Athenian Agora, ca. 400 270

9. Panathenaic prize amphora 312

10. Fragment of an oinochoe showing the tyrant-slayers 313

11. Grave relief of Dexileos 314

ACKNOWLEDGMENTS

This book originates in my desire to understand the achievement of Thucydides. It is in part a reaction to the view, held by many admirers of Thucydides and articulated by Jacqueline de Romilly at the end of her masterful *Thucydides and Athenian Imperialism,* that "Thucydides is, in a way, outside the main stream of intellectual relationships which allow us to follow the influence of different minds on one another" (de Romilly 1963, 357). My endeavor has been to find what Thucydides had *in common* with his contemporaries that enabled him to produce so remarkable a piece of writing. Those who accept his unique genius as a sufficient explanation of his achievement might see my work as tending to undermine Thucydides' special claim to fame. I can only hope that most readers will feel, after reflecting on the main stream of events and influences described here, that his reputation is undiminished, and that we can continue to admire him with a greater appreciation of "the influence of different minds on one another."

The tools for this inquiry, and the inspiration to use them, came directly from my mentors in graduate school, first and foremost, Michael Jameson. He will, I hope, recognize here the influence of his teachings on Thucydides, on the Athenian empire, and on Greek religion. I am also indebted to Donald Lateiner, who first drew my attention to the abiding questions that surround the ending of Thucydides' work and its continuation by Xenophon, and to Martin Ostwald, who made me consider the relationships in thought among Thucydides, Plato, and Aristotle.

This book began to take shape during a year as a junior fellow at the Center for Hellenic Studies (1992–1993), and took its first written form with the benefit of a grant from the Research and Graduate Studies Office of the College of Liberal Arts, Penn State University (1996). Since then it has been transformed through the advice and guidance of Lynda and

Theodore Chenoweth, Mary Lou Zimmerman Munn, Martin Ostwald, Kurt Raaflaub, and an anonymous reader for the University of California Press. Though they have by no means all indicated agreement with my choices, by giving encouragement and withholding it as appropriate, each has contributed immensely to the form and content of the resulting book. The patience and profound good sense of my wife, Mary Lou, deserve more heartfelt thanks than words can express, not least because she has helped me bring so many half-formed thoughts into clearer focus.

The book has also benefited at various stages from the contributions, advice, and wise words of Aileen Ajootian, Deborah Boedeker, Paul Cartledge, Mortimer Chambers, Carolyn Dewald, David Engel, Garrett Fagan, Robert Frakes, John Graham, Mogens Hansen, Timothy Howe, Lisa Kallet, Margaret Miles, Jonathan Price, Antony Raubitschek, Eric Sanday, Doyle Stevick, Sanford Thatcher, Victoria Wohl, and Randy Wood. Some of the themes of this book have developed under the influence of discussions with students and colleagues in the Penn State seminar in Ancient Mediterranean Studies: Rangar Cline, James Dorwart, Russell Egan, Baruch Halpern, Paul Harvey, Julie Kim, Danielle Knerr, Gerald Knoppers, Eugene Shaw-Colyer, Thomas Shields, Jeffrey Veenstra, John Waterstram, and Raina Weaver. The libraries of the Center for Hellenic Studies and of the Pennsylvania State University have been invaluable resources. The vision of Mary Lamprech and Kate Toll and the editorial patience of Cindy Fulton and Elizabeth Ditmars have made possible the appearance of this book with the University of California Press. To all I owe thanks.

MAP 1. Mediterranean and western Asia

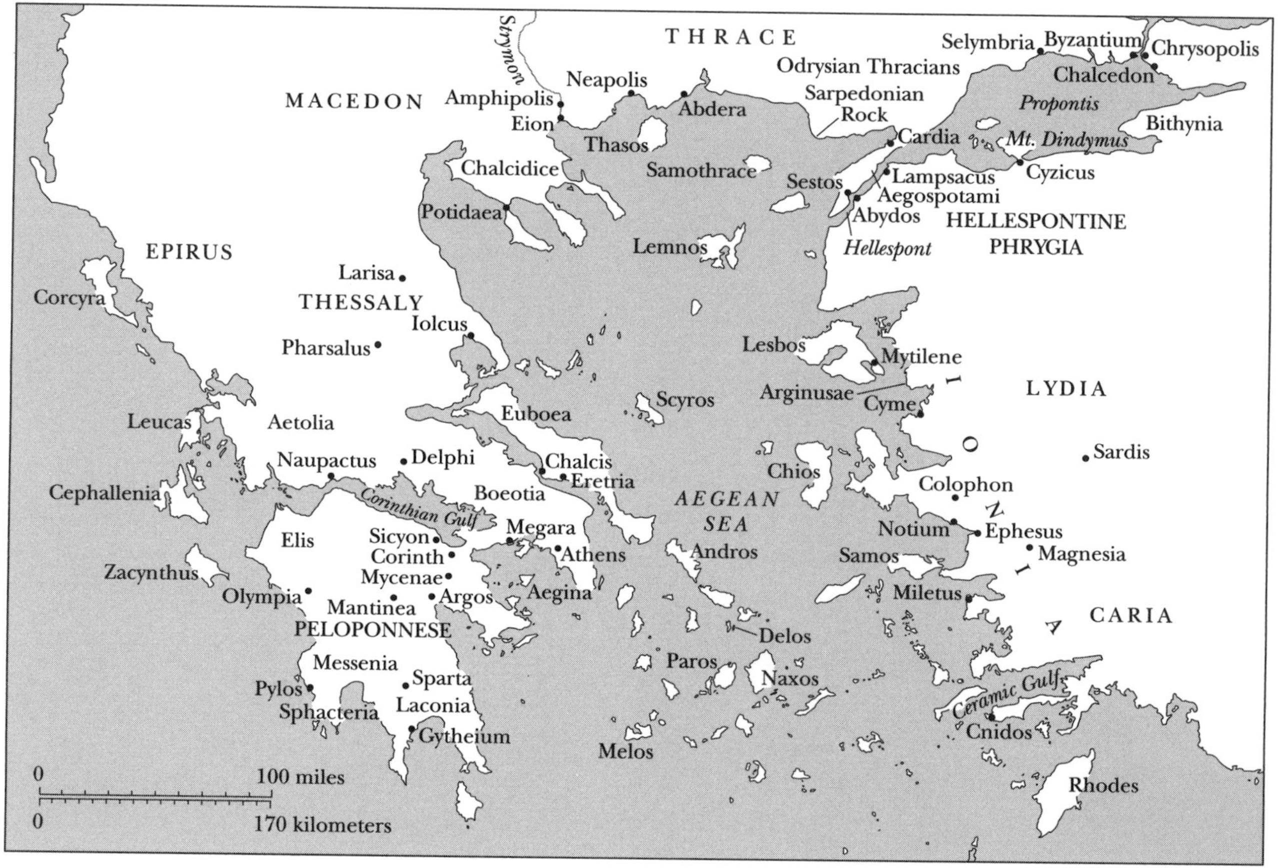

MAP 2. Greece and Asia Minor

Artemisium
Oreus
Scyros
Thermopylae
LOCRIS
EUBOEA
PHOCIS
Orchomenus
Chalcis
BOEOTIA
Aulis
Eretria
Tanagra
Thebes
Asopos
Oropos
Mt Parnes
Plataea
Decelea
Oenoe
Phyle
Marathon
Eleusis
ATTICA
Carystus
Megara
Athens
Sicyon
Piraeus
Salamis
Corinth
Isthmia
Nemea
Orneae
Aegina
Mycenae
Epidaurus
Sounion
Keos
Argos
Oenoe
ARGOLID
Hysiae
Troizen
Thyrea
Hermion
0
50 Miles
0
80 Kilometers
Prasiae

MAP 3. Attica and central Greece

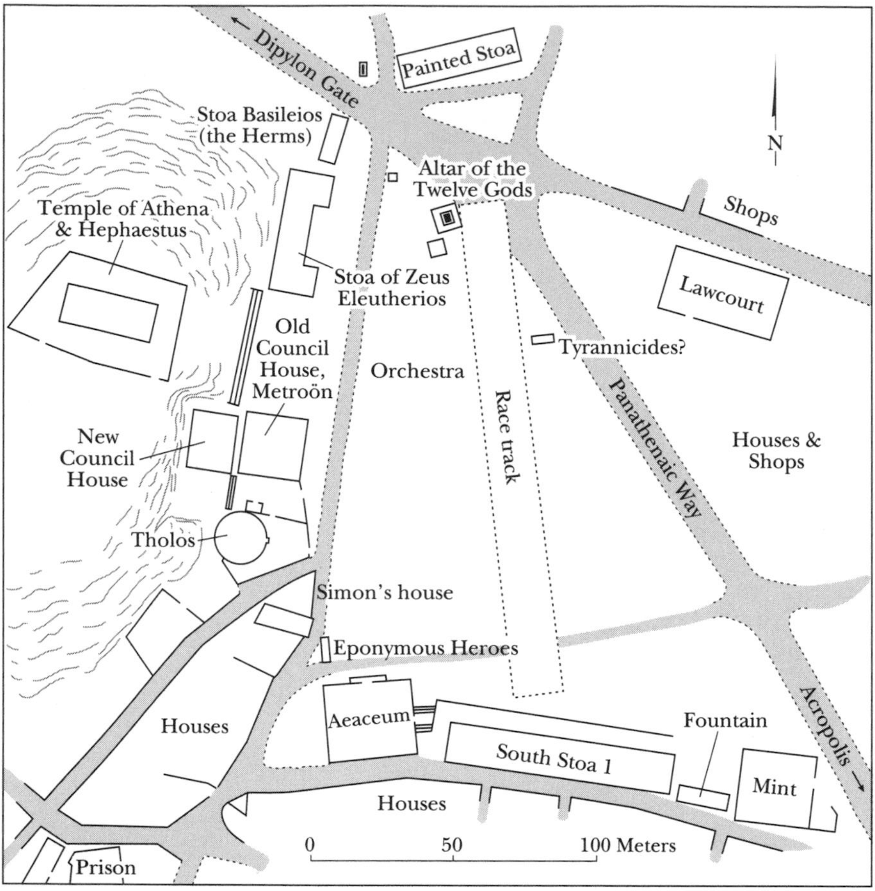

MAP 4. The Athenian Agora, ca. 400. Adapted from plans by J. Travlos and W. B. Dinsmoor, Jr.

Introduction

THE SUBJECT

In less than a century (between 478 and 404 B.C.E.*) Athens gained and lost an empire. Among ancient empires bordering the Mediterranean, the Athenian empire was impressive neither for its size nor for its durability. But as the creation of a democratic state it was unique. No dynasty or ruling oligarchy controlled the instruments of power at Athens. Political, judicial, and military power were directed by means of public debates in which skilled speakers tried to sway the majority against their rivals' efforts to do the same. Because power was publicly constructed, contestants for political influence at Athens developed the means to appeal to wide audiences, and to guide popular approval or condemnation not so much according to narrow, sectional interests, but by casting their arguments in terms of transcendent principles. Over the course of the Athenian experience with empire, the use of writing to hone the skills of debate and to express the principles that made arguments memorable gave rise to new habits of discourse and standards of judgment. These habits in turn provided the foundations of rhetoric, political philosophy, constitutional law, and history.

Writing had long been employed among the Greeks, especially as an aide-mémoire for poetry and to give voice to monuments, but in the course of the fifth century it became increasingly the medium for other forms of expression, particularly in prose. Athenian democracy encouraged habits of literacy, both for the creation of public records and memorials and in the personal use of writing as one of the tools to sharpen and amplify rhetoric. The consequences of this trend were various and profound. Poetry at

*Unless otherwise noted, all dates are Before the Common Era.

Athens was enriched by the absorption of rhetorical and eulogistic style and content. In this period the public conscience was both entertained and at the same time informed about underlying meanings and ironies within contemporary events through the allegories of tragedy and the farces of comedy, all created and preserved in writing. The enrichment of literary description and rhetorical argument achieved by writers versed in a growing literary heritage enabled critical history to be written, first by Herodotus and then by Thucydides. And many of the same motives that sharpened rhetoric and critical history stimulated the reflective and analytical skills of political philosophy, best known in the person of Socrates and represented in the writings of Plato.

A surprising amount of the foregoing is represented in the literary products specifically of the generation that saw the Athenian empire come to an end, in 404, as the final outcome of the Peloponnesian War. Aristophanes was of that generation, and although Sophocles and Euripides both died in 406 and did not live to see the defeat of Athens by Sparta, they did experience and respond to the convulsions that preceded the final fall. Within that period the *Histories* of Herodotus were written, and Thucydides, although he was writing after the fall of Athens in 404, began to gather material for his account when the war with Sparta began in 431. Pericles, who died in 429, left no written speeches of his own, nor did any of his contemporaries. But within the following generation, Gorgias, Antiphon, Thrasymachus, and other sophists circulated treatises displaying their rhetorical skills. Increasingly, texts of actual speeches were collected and studied, and by 400 a great number of contemporary speeches were in circulation. Plato was born and educated in these final decades of the fifth century, in the most influential period of his mentor, Socrates. Although Plato's works belong to the generation after the Peloponnesian War, the event that inspired Plato to write was the trial and execution of Socrates in 399. The same year marked the publication on stone of a substantial body of the laws of Athens. The compilation of these laws, beginning in 411, resulted in the creation of the first known centralized state archive and marked the beginnings of research into constitutional history.

It is not a mere quirk of fortune that such a literate legacy should survive from the last three decades of the fifth century, and not, to any comparable degree, from earlier decades. The habits of reading and the applications of writing burgeoned specifically in the late fifth century, and testimony to the phenomenon is evident in the immediately following generations. Within the fourth century, written works of rhetoric and history, and studies of poetry, laws and institutions, and political philosophy proliferated. All such works referred directly to literary predecessors or implicitly reveal the influence of earlier works. The wide-ranging writings of Aristotle exemplify the tendencies of fourth-century authors to thrive on the works of their predecessors. Yet amidst all this attention to works of the past, as the citations by Aristotle attest, the vast bulk of the literary heritage available to fourth-century authors is traceable to works no earlier than the last third of the fifth century.[1]

The Athenians were well aware that their city was the home of this literary revolution. Athens was the "school of Hellas," as Thucydides reports the famous claim of Pericles. There is an apparent danger of circularity in accepting this testimony, since Athenian rhetoric naturally praised Athens. But such praise is neither the sole nor even the chief support for this judgment. Much of the political commentary of late-fifth and fourth-century Greece was openly critical of Athenian policies and institutions. Yet it confirms that Athens, in the final decades of its domination of an Aegean empire, was the central focus of tracts of rhetorical polemic, of reflective drama, of philosophical criticism, and of historical analysis out of which emerged the intellectual tools by which human achievements then and ever afterward have been more keenly judged and compared.[2]

What were the conditions that brought standards of criticism and debate to so high a pitch? Part of this inquiry must seek to establish the objects of criticism and debate at Athens, and part must seek to establish *when* debate at Athens reached such a threshold of intensity that it yielded a lasting record in writing. Put in these terms, an investigation into the conditions that placed Athens at the center of an intellectual and literary revolution must become a historical investigation of the time in which this revolution took place, and particularly of the intersection between political and intellectual culture at that time. The present book is a historian's investigation of this subject.

THE PROBLEM

The investigation begins with a survey of how the Athenians recorded their past between the birth of classical Athenian democracy in the late sixth century and the era of the Peloponnesian War nearly a century later. Some of the themes of popular struggle celebrated by later generations of Athenians can be traced to the origins of democracy in the overthrow of tyranny. But we do not encounter scrutiny of the contemporary practices of democracy and empire or critical reflection on the traditions of the Athenian past until we arrive at the generation that experienced the Peloponnesian War (431–404) and witnessed the destruction of the Athenian empire as its outcome.

Themes of social and political division within Athens are already recognizable close to the time of the death of Pericles in 429. Over the following generation these divisions led to a series of progressively more violent political convulsions, and eventually to revolution and civil war. At each stage, we find Athenians looking to their past to find guidance through troubled times. And at each stage, just as communal stability seemed at hand, renewed crisis called present wisdom into question and prompted deeper reflection on the meanings of a past that was ever growing in complexity.

Our investigation thus comes to focus on the period that Thucydides chose to write about, the Peloponnesian War. It is even possible that our interest in identifying the origins of critical historical analysis has much in common with Thucydides' motives for writing history. Having lived through this period of ever-intensifying crises, Thucydides was surely responding to the challenge of explaining the destruction of the Athenian empire. But his history never reached that point. Having set out to narrate "the war" that began in 431 and that lasted, as Thucydides notes in 5.26, for twenty-seven years until the surrender of Athens, his work ends abruptly in the midst of its twenty-first year (411/10). Thucydides' narrative was later continued by others, so we are able to follow the events that Thucydides had in view when he wrote. But the incompleteness of his work is problematic for present purposes, because we lose contact with Thucydides' intellectual project as it approaches the very time in which it was formed.

Before the abrupt termination of his narrative, Thucydides reveals some of his judgments in view of the outcome of the war. His views are always nuanced, and they likely would have become even more so had he gone on to narrate a further six or seven years of the career of the Athenian empire. But without his judgments on the events accompanying the final defeat of Athens we are hard put to evaluate his meaning in the several passages where he fully contextualizes events but goes on to affirm superlative instances like, "[These were] certainly the best men... who perished in this war," (3.98.4); "a disaster more complete than any..." (7.29.5); "... a man who, of all the Hellenes in my time, least deserved to come to so miserable an end" (7.86.5); "... the greatest action that we know of in Hellenic history" (7.87.5); and "... a better government than ever before, at least in my time" (8.97.2). We simply do not know how Thucydides would have dealt with the ecstatic highs and bewildering lows that lay in store for the Athenians and their foes in the final six years of the war, or in the civil war at Athens that followed.[3]

Thus as we approach the climax of the story of the greatness of Athens and her fall, we lose the perspective of the man who drew our attention to the subject. Xenophon, whose continuation of Thucydides' narrative is our chief source for the events after 411, is not up to the task of evaluating the many implications of events according to the standards set by Thucydides. He was a young man at Athens in these years, and probably an eye-witness to several of the episodes he narrates. But Xenophon told the story after the passage of at least twenty and possibly more than forty years, and he offers a selective and comparatively simple, linear narrative. Xenophon invests his talents chiefly in details that evoke a strong picture of individual character. We lack, however, the depth-perception of Thucydides that allows us to see shadings of motive and the contingencies of events.[4]

The shadings of motive and the cross-purposes of protagonists that pitched events into unexpected directions all became pronounced, in Thucydides' narrative, in his eighth and final book. This tells the tale of events following the Athenian disaster in Sicily, in 413, through the first overthrow of democracy at Athens in 411. Book 8 contains many changes of stylistic and narrative habits, by comparison with the previous books of Thucydides' account, and these changes have usually been explained as a feature of incompleteness. The absence of speeches and the frequency of authorial judgments and conjectures, it is thought, would all have been edited out if Thucydides had lived to finish his work (death being thought the most plausible explanation for the sudden end of a project so clearly conceived and thus far forcefully executed). It may well be, however, that the very complexity of events accounts for the change in style, and possibly even the abrupt ending, of Thucydides' history.[5]

This was the dénouement for Athens, the point at which war, for them, truly became

> a stern teacher; in depriving them of the power of easily satisfying their daily wants, it brings most people's minds down to the level of their actual circumstances.... To fit in with the change of events, words, too, had to change their usual meanings.... Any idea of moderation was just an attempt to disguise one's unmanly character; ability to understand a question from all sides meant that one was totally unfitted for action. Fanatical enthusiasm was the mark of a real man....[6]

These are the terms in which Thucydides characterizes the effects of *stasis,* factional conflict and civil war, that first struck Corcyra in 427 and that eventually convulsed "practically the whole of the Hellenic world" (3.82.1). *Stasis* struck Athens in 411, and again more violently in 404–403. Before and between those events, in Thucydides' own narrative and in other sources, we can detect the effects of fanaticism within the politics of Athens. It would seem that by 411 the changing quality of the story of the war was sufficient to account for the changes in Thucydides' narrative style. Given his ambitious goal of providing a "clear account" *(to saphes)* of events, Thucydides may have been overwhelmed by the complexities imposed on him, in times when words themselves were changing their customary meanings. It was a task that could only be dealt with by the simplified choices of Xenophon, and through the haze of time elapsed.

This hypothesis suggests that the fall of Athens and the civil war of 404–403 were the eye of an epistemological storm that, paradoxically, may have both prompted Thucydides to write history and prevented him from completing it. If so, then there is a functional link between the eventual failure of narrative by Thucydides' exacting standards and the failure of Athenian democracy and empire. The present book will seek to justify this hypothesis and its corollary, namely, that Thucydides' writing was only possible with the return of democracy and of renewed hopes for empire after the passing of the storm of 404–403.

This book will also examine other intellectual progeny of the storm of internecine brutality at Athens in 404–403 and the subsequent restoration of democracy. Those events were the background to the trial of Socrates in 399, and this, in turn, was the source of disillusionment with Athens that impelled the young Plato away from politics and into a life devoted to philosophy. Plato's writings and those of other Socratics, among whom Xenophon is the only other whose works survive, were retrospective accounts of significant encounters in the life of Socrates from the 430s until his execution in 399. They deal with almost exactly the same period that Thucydides defined as the appropriate subject of political history. Although there is very little direct overlap of subjects treated in the works of the Socratics and in Thucydides' history, they have in common the underlying conundrum of finding reason within a community where all decisions are subject to the approval of a sovereign popular assembly.

For a generation Socrates had been close to the center of a tradition of thought critical of Athenian democracy. His trial was therefore in part a review of a generation of Athenian political experience, seen through the distorting lens of 404–403. Socrates was charged, however, not with political misdeeds, but with impiety. His trial thus pitted his personal devotion to abstract ideals against a pragmatic, public consensus on the appropriate forms of piety. This public sense of piety was given strong expression, in the year of Socrates' trial, by the publication of a comprehensive calendar of public sacrifices. Scholarship to date has not made much of this conjunction of evidence, however, for none of our sources treat either this or any other explicit connection between the trial of Socrates and renascent democratic ideology. But affirmation of the supremacy of democratic consensus was clearly the issue upon which the trial of Socrates turned. To Plato, the condemnation of Socrates was a sign that Athenian democracy would remain as obtuse to the rule of reason as it had been, in the judgment of Socrates and his circle, before 404. While Plato chose, as a result, not to subject himself to the rule of public consensus, at close to the same time we find Thucydides offering an artifact of reason as an antidote to popular ignorance.

To recognize the links between the trial of Socrates and the intellectual project of Thucydides requires an appreciation of the larger matrix of both subjects, namely, Athens at the transition between the fifth and fourth centuries. The task requires a narrative account of the political transformations of Athens in these years, for one of the features that renders the period so problematic is that Athens itself was a dynamic concept, and never so unstable and violently changeable as it was in the last decade of sovereignty over its empire. To trace such a narrative will also require us to confront a problem that is the most explicit, though enigmatic, link between the interests of both Thucydides and Socrates, namely, the career of Alcibiades.

From Thucydides' narrative, and in the historical and biographical traditions that later looked back on these events, no personality has evoked stronger reactions and more perplexity than Alcibiades. He rose to the forefront of Athenian politics in the generation after Pericles, displayed moments of captivating brilliance in a turbulent career, and left a reputation clouded by the disasters that led to the collapse of the Athenian empire and to the subversion of Athenian democracy. Alcibiades was prominent among those who, from time to time, kept company with Socrates, and this fact was one, though by no means the most remarkable, sign of the ambiguous relationship between Alcibiades and the democracy of Athens.

Fascinating though he is, within scholarship of the past half-century Alcibiades has not been a favorite focus of historians chronicling classical Athens, her democracy, or her empire. Students of Athenian democracy tend to overlook him as an aberration, and focus instead on the features of democracy established by Pericles and his contemporaries or on the institutions of the more stable democracy of fourth-century Athens, rebuilt from the rubble of the civil war in 404–403 that marked the end of Alcibiades' life. The aversion is not entirely a modern phenomenon. Aristotle's *Constitution of the Athenians* surveys in detail the political turmoil at Athens in the last decade of Alcibiades' life and never mentions him. Xenophon cannot avoid him, but scarcely probes beneath the surface of his public acts—Alcibiades certainly provided no model of character worth an extended portrayal, according to Xenophon's standards. But Thucydides, in confronting the deeds of Alcibiades, is repeatedly drawn into penetrating judgments. Thucydides' most trenchant statements about the nature of Athenian politics and the fate of Athens were made with Alcibiades clearly in mind. The nuances, in these instances, that Thucydides reads into contemporary Athenian political culture are by no means all unfavorable to Alcibiades.[7]

The enigma of Alcibiades is underscored in the picture that emerges from the Socratic writings of both Xenophon and Plato. Alcibiades was the only man for whom Socrates admitted a temptation to yield to the power of Eros. The tribute affirms the well-known charms of Alcibiades in physical appearance and charismatic presence. But it also points to an essence underlying these qualities that Socrates, that most powerful deconstructor of character, wished to confront and experience. Plato's portrait of the relationship between Socrates and Alcibiades in the *Symposium* is rich in detail and implications, but it is hardly a transparent window into the political virtues, whatever they may have been, that Socrates saw in Alcibiades. Elsewhere, in the *Alcibiades* 1, *Protagoras,* and *Gorgias,* Plato provides further context for Socrates' fascination with Alcibiades, but these do not prepare us to understand how Socrates' relationship to Alcibiades was, as Xenophon relates in the *Memorabilia,* one of the chief reasons why Socrates was condemned to death by a jury in 399.[8]

In the century following their deaths, both Socrates and Alcibiades were cast in the light of ignominy that generally surrounded the men connected in 404–403, in one way or another, with the fall of empire and the deepest crisis of democracy at Athens. So Aeschines the orator could remind a jury that "Socrates the sophist" had been put to death, "because he was shown to have been the teacher of Critias, one of the Thirty who put down the Democracy." In view of these circumstances, Plato and Xenophon's Socratic dialogues may be seen, in part, as a concerted effort to rescue the memory of Socrates from the simplistic, popular characterizations that followed complex and controverted times. Alcibiades had his apologists too, although they engendered no cult of personality so coherent as that which grew up around the memory of Socrates. The most influential of them were Plato and Thucydides.[9]

The political turmoil of Athens in the late fifth century collapsed the customary definitions of community that the Athenians had so artfully constructed over a century's experience of democracy. The very force and rapidity of that collapse, coming in stages no more than a few years apart, generated powerfully creative reactions from among those experiencing it. Among those with a talent for eloquence, the challenge to find meaning in agony, anxiety, and unbearable loss yielded works of inspiration, transforming forever the standards of literary expression and critical judgment. The art of Euripides represents this in tragedy; Aristophanes expressed the genius of comedy, and captured the yearning of the era most memorably in his *Frogs.* These artists spoke for the community as a whole, for the Athenian *demos* too was, collectively, a political actor. As Athenians reconstructed their civic identity after 403, those among the survivors who had been connected with the shifting circles of leadership were compelled, sometimes by the processes of law, to offer closely reasoned justifications of their actions in previous years. Some preserved documents from the times as witness to their political convictions, in the belief that time would reveal the honor of their intentions and the wisdom of their deliberations. Some, like Thucydides earlier in this period, and Xenophon and Plato later on, sought refuge abroad and then turned to writing as part of their personal reconciliation with Athens.

Yet for all the array of documentary evidence that survived these years of crisis, for all the rhetorical incision displayed, or dialectic subtlety employed, no account of these times succeeded in presenting more than a highly partial, and in that respect historically inadequate, analysis of the course and causes of events. In fact, only Thucydides set himself the task of providing a comprehensive account. Employing the skills and the sources at his disposal, he established a magisterial presence in setting forth a reasoned historical narrative. But for some reason he stopped short of the conclusion.

In contemplating the story left unfinished by Thucydides, we are drawn to consider the relationship between the times and Thucydides himself. For his project was clearly both a product of his times and timeless in its insights. Much the same can be said of Plato, among other distinguished coevals of Thucydides. Taking the relationship between times and the decisions made by those living in them as a problem for investigation, I set out in this book to study, through the diverse partial accounts that survive, the times in which these men lived. By examining through a narrative of events the impact of experience on critical thought, I offer a new understanding of the conditions that gave birth to the luminary skills of both Plato and Thucydides.

THE BOOK

In studies of Athenian history, or Greek history generally, it has been nearly universal practice to treat the events of 404–403 as a great divide. The Athenian empire came to an end, and with it the Athenian democracy, in the regime of the Thirty inaugurated in 404. In 403 the Thirty were overthrown and Athenian democracy was reborn, to remain more or less stable until Aristotle's day. But the lasting consequences of the events leading up to 404–403 were not fully manifested until after the democracy was restored, and the vision of empire as a goal of Athenian policy did not die forever in 404. We must recover, therefore, the perspective of those who lived through the crises of 411 and 404–403 in order to recognize the unique impact of those events on the later shape of Athenian democracy, and upon enduring habits of reflection and standards of critical judgment about the past.[10]

To appreciate the lessons of history as they were experienced from an Athenian perspective, preexisting conditions must be established. This is the purpose of Part I of this book. Analysis here is discursive and topical, designed to frame issues that reemerge in subsequent chapters. Chapter 1 opens on the question of how the past was known to Athenians, and to Greeks generally, before the emergence of historical thought honed by Herodotus and Thucydides. From the very birth of their classical democracy, with their celebration of the memory of the tyrant-slayers, Harmodius and Aristogeiton, the Athenians developed distinctive ways of relating past experience to their present concerns. Monument, song, dance, drama, and eulogy were the chief forms in which knowledge of the past was preserved and, as revealed in subsequent chapters, reinterpreted as occasions demanded. The following two chapters focus on the relationship between the Athenian empire and democracy on the one hand, and the self-perceptions of the Athenian aristocracy on the other. Empire promoted elitist ideals among Athenians, and this in turn fostered a latent tension within democratic Athens between those who counted themselves among the *kaloi k'agathoi,* the "beautiful and the good," and the less affluent majority of Athenians who constituted the sovereign authority of the Assembly and the law courts of Athens. Elitist ideals could coexist with democracy as long as Athens and her empire were prosperous and successful. But war against Athens and her empire brought on by Sparta and her allies changed these conditions. The Peloponnesian War, commencing in 431, compelled the sovereign *demos* of the Athenians to enforce its authority even over its own elite by harsh measures. New forms of democratic leadership and new ways of articulating elite ideals, some supportive and some critical of democracy, were the result.

With Part II, the book becomes a historical narrative in six chapters, tracing the movements of Athens from the height of her power before the Sicilian expedition of 415 through defeat and surrender in 404 to civil war and reconciliation in 403. Although Thucydides' masterful narrative of the stages that led the Sicilian expedition to its destruction in 413 is not recounted here, Part II of the present book does appraise significant military events in the years that followed, and offers solutions to problems of chronology bequeathed to us by the termination of Thucydides' carefully measured account. The guiding purpose of chapters 4 through 9 is to assess the effects of war on political culture at Athens. Reflections of contemporary concerns in tragedy, comedy, and Socratic literature are introduced alongside the usual sources of historical narrative, with results that transform our understanding of events and of the sources themselves. Among the features developed here to a greater degree than in most accounts of this period is an appreciation of the often ambiguous but ultimately decisive influence of the Persian court on the politics of the Aegean.

Part III, comprising the last three chapters, continues the narrative from the reconstitution of democracy in 403 through the year of Socrates' trial in 399, and looks ahead to the renewal of war between Athens and Sparta in 395. In this period, both the events and our sources lend themselves to a more topical narrative, while thematic links between one chapter and the next build a new understanding of this transformational decade. Chapter 10 examines the reemergence of democracy and its relationship particularly to the project to revise the laws of Athens, resumed after 403. Chapter 11 relates the emerging definition of the laws of democratic Athens to the concept of public piety. The condemnation of Socrates on a charge of impiety, in the same year as the publication of a revised calendar of public sacrifices, thus becomes intelligible as an assertion of a new form of democratic authority over the realm of communal identity. This was one means by which the Athenians hoped to avoid repetition of the catastrophes of the recent past, blame for which was being placed on visionary leaders, inspired by obscure forms of private knowledge. Finally, chapter 12 examines the forms of knowledge about the past, especially the recent past, that were accessible to Athenians after 403, and the uses and abuses of that knowledge encouraged by the Athenian democracy. From among the various practices deployed and criticized by orators like Lysias and Andocides, by the followers of Socrates and by his critics, it becomes possible to recognize the conditions that made it both possible and desirable for Thucydides to write history.

The view that Thucydides' account was largely composed at one time, after the fall of Athens, has been a minority view for some time, advocated most cogently in the works of John Finley. A wider acceptance of Finley's arguments has been undermined by a common misconception about Thucydides' relationship to the events he describes. Thucydides states at the opening of his work that he began to write as soon as the war broke out, in 431. Later in his narrative, he states that his exile in 424 allowed him to gather information from both sides of the conflict. The common assumption has been that, throughout this period, Thucydides had in mind the composition of a historical treatise.

Here it is argued that this idea did not occur to Thucydides until well after his return to Athens in 404. His claim to be writing as early as 431 can be understood in the context of Athenian political culture of that period. Political leadership depended upon the mastery of rhetorical skills, and this produced a fascination for rhetoric noticeable already in the early 420s. As an aspirant to political prominence in those years, Thucydides must have engaged in the attested practice of taking notes on speeches as they were delivered and sharing such notes among friends in discussions of key moments of judicial or political decision-making. In the same manner, memorable conversations or lectures delivered by illustrious sophists of the day formed the basis of the dialogues of Socrates later reported by Plato. Plato provides our most important testimony to the process of transmitting the spoken word through notes and edited texts.

Contrary, therefore, to the prevailing opinion that Thucydides' speeches were largely creative reconstructions of what could only be dimly remembered words, it is likely that written notes underlay most if not all of the speeches reported by Thucydides. The question of how close the Thucydidean rendition might be to the original words remains, but the scope of the question, which lies at the heart of Thucydides' claim to objectivity, is fundamentally transformed by this realization. The increased reliance on written texts, and the close inter-reference of texts and spoken words, attested in a variety of ways in the generation of the Peloponnesian War, is one of the keys to understanding the intellectual refinements achieved by that generation.

This book concludes that new standards of critical thought emerged from the experience of history, as individuals attempted to guide and advise the Athenians in difficult times, and as they sought ways to avoid the failings of the past. The writings of Plato are the expression of a personal quest begun under these conditions. The writing of Thucydides represents a more focused and immediate response to the same set of conditions. In Thucydides' case, the very immediacy of his work provides clues to the unique relationship between events and the writing of his history. The concept of Thucydides' entire work, and many of his distinctive analytical and narrative choices, derive from circumstances at the time of composition. This can be precisely placed, as I argue here, in 396–395. At that time the Athenians were hoping to recover their empire, and as a result were again contemplating the renewal of war with Sparta. Thucydides wrote for an audience poised between desire and uncertainty, looking to the past for guidance. As Thucydides conceived it, history was the school of a democracy struggling to comprehend its future.

PART ONE

The Spirit of Democratic Athens, 510–415

CHAPTER ONE

The Past of Democratic Athens

In investigating past history, and in forming the conclusions which I have formed, it must be admitted that one cannot rely on every detail which has come down to us by way of tradition.

THUCYDIDES 1.20.1*

THE PAST AND THE TRUTH

Every generation learns from its stories of the past. Stories that claim to instruct usually assert that they are "true." The "truth" told in stories can be understood as an aspect of communication involving both speaker and listener in cognitive harmony. It depends upon a common key, a base of reference, or a source of authority, which the speaker invokes and the listener accepts.

Divine inspiration was an ancient sanction of truth. But inasmuch as truth is always a matter of assertion and can be contested, we find that from the beginnings of Greek literature, Homer and Hesiod spoke to audiences mindful of the fact that gods can inspire men to speak "many falsehoods that were like true sayings." Some three centuries and more after Homer and Hesiod, Thucydides, in the quote above, gave himself critical distance from stories of the past that were told in his day. Was Thucydides an innovator in this respect? What were the standards by which the Greeks in his day and before were prepared to recognize the truth?[1]

The currency of a story was perhaps the most fundamental test of which story, among less credible accounts, deserved to be treated as "true." That which is *alethes,* "true" in Greek, is, etymologically, that which is "unforgettable." That which has proved itself memorable, therefore, is *alethes.* Such a subjective construction of truth gave first place to the test of time, a criterion that the ancient stories of the Homeric epics could easily satisfy. This explains what seems to us to be a naive acceptance of the myths and legends that pervades Greek thought. Even Thucydides, with his critical stance, has

*Translated by R. Warner. Translations elsewhere, unless attributed, are by the author.

disarmed modern commentators with his candid treatment of the "facts" about Agamemnon's army at Troy. Critical scholarship about the past, among Greeks both before and after Thucydides, was less concerned with systematic criteria for separating the verifiable past from legend than it was with determining which legends deserved credence, according to the largely subjective standards of prevalence, and which ones had been distorted. This was the concern expressed by Hecataeus of Miletus, writing around the end of the sixth century, in the opening lines of his work on genealogies: "I write what I believe are truths *(alethea),* because many stories of the Greeks, as it seems to me, are absurd."[2]

However much a teller might invest his stories with reason and plausible detail, truth and significance were ultimately qualities to be affirmed by audience acceptance. Public approval required the skillful combination of the familiar with both novel and pleasurable elements—a combination most effectively managed in song and performance. But familiar stories full of significance for one audience might seem odd or contradictory to the "common knowledge" of other audiences. The resolution of these contradictions and the articulation of the prevailing "truth," something sensible to the majority of listeners, was at the center of the artistry of all Greek poets who hoped to achieve more than local distinction, and of all learned men, like Hecataeus, who hoped to show themselves to be judicious arbiters of truth.[3]

Truth, as one approached recent events, had to be gauged differently. An event that had not passed through the filters of communal telling and retelling could not be measured by the standards of consensus. A reliable account of recent events depended upon the established wisdom and veracity of the source or informant. Hecataeus, and perhaps also the so-called Seven Sages of an earlier generation, men like Solon of Athens, probably relied upon their reputations for wisdom about things far away in time and space to establish their authority in matters of immediate concern. That authority was a matter of practical concern, for all of the so-called Sages were statesmen, as was Hecataeus, who appears in Herodotus' history as a wise advisor in the affairs of his native Ionia during the crisis of war against the Persians. As far as we know, none of these men wrote anything resembling a historical account of their own times.[4]

History was born when Herodotus and Thucydides each ventured the ambitious task of creating treatises that would simultaneously demonstrate their discriminating wisdom and apply it, Herodotus to the recent past, Thucydides to the immediate past. On subjects of wide interest and concern, they both were aspiring to define what popular consensus *should* be as, and even before, it formed. In the process, a new and more exacting standard of truth about the past was established.

This standard was the truth that each author claimed "to know," and that each encouraged their readers to accept by engaging them in the complex web of reason and circumstantial detail that was their history. Their endeavor thus to construct a *historical* truth required them to disavow what they did not or could not "know" as beyond the reach of reason or evidence. Their authorial standpoint therefore involved a potential challenge to prevailing notions of truth and a tension with public opinion that their texts do not often reveal, but which never lay far below the surface of their narratives.[5]

What notions of truth about the past prevailed at Athens before Herodotus and Thucydides set down their versions of the formative years of Athenian democracy and empire? How, more particularly, was the Athenian past known to Herodotus, Thucydides, and their contemporaries? The remainder of this chapter considers the ways the past was told, from the late sixth until the second half of the fifth century, and how the particular character of the Athenian public and its institutions influenced the stories of its past.

THE ORIGINS OF DEMOCRACY

Gazing at the paintings on a wall of the Stoa of Zeus Eleutherios, "The Liberator," in the Agora of Athens (map 4), the literary travel-guide, Pausanias, identified the figures of Theseus, Democracy, and Demos ("The People"). The painting was probably created in the 340s, some 500 years before Pausanias wrote. "It shows Theseus," Pausanias reports, "as the establisher of political equality for the Athenians." He goes on:

> There is also a popular tradition that Theseus transferred sovereignty to the people and that from his time on they were a democracy, until Peisistratus came to power as tyrant. But in fact many similar things that are not true are said by most people who are uneducated in history, who believe what they have heard since childhood in choral songs and tragedies; and one such falsehood is told of Theseus, who in fact himself ruled as king, and his descendants as well, for four generations after the death of Menestheus. And if I wanted to recite genealogies, I could even enumerate all those who were kings after Melanthus until Cleidicus the son of Aesimides.[6]

Pausanias' commentary on truth and history displays an agonistic pride in learning that characterizes the authorial voice in Greek literature as far back as its beginnings with Homer and Hesiod. Like these archaic poets, Pausanias could claim authority by displaying an expertise that his audience would recognize because it treated familiar themes in knowing detail. But unlike the audiences of oral performance for which poets composed, Pausanias was addressing a learned readership. His was an audience that would recognize, from the few names he dropped, that he was in command of the scholarship that had recorded royal genealogies, and that he could thus show that Theseus the King was the founder of a line of kings, not of popular sovereignty as represented in the paintings before him.

Yet, as Pausanias' comments show, learned scholarship was powerless to correct traditions still deeply entrenched in monument, song, and ceremony. The needs of civic identity dictated what was acceptable to audiences educated in choral songs and tragedy. Tradition, when the paintings on the stoa were created, held that democracy was an Athenian trait, and therefore it must have been so from the time of its legendary founding hero. It was not useful to have history correct that tradition.[7]

Public celebration of Democracy was an even more recent development at Athens than Pausanias thought. Celebrations in the name of Democracy were no older than 403, at the earliest. The term *demokratia,* "rule of the people," is not firmly attested as a description of the Athenian form of government until the last third of the fifth century. Within those years, the term was referred back to "the ancestral laws that Cleisthenes established when he introduced *demokratia.*" The reforms of Cleisthenes in 508 are in fact now commonly accepted as the most fundamental event in the development of classical Athenian democracy. But it is only a matter of conjecture among scholars that the term *demokratia* is as old as the reforms of Cleisthenes. The evidence favors the conclusion that *demokratia* gained currency ca. 460, close to the time of Ephialtes' reforms and the strengthening of popular sovereignty that became the classical democracy in the age of Pericles.[8]

Whatever the true origins of *demokratia* may have been, it is clear that the Athenians themselves, by the late-fifth and fourth centuries, advanced several accounts of the foundation of their democracy, tracing it back variously to Cleisthenes, to Solon, and to Theseus. When we understand that Athenian democracy was an evolving process and not a fixed entity, it is not remarkable that its origin should be ambiguous and subject to contested interpretations. In fact, from an early date Athenian civic identity was more closely tied not to democracy, but to the liberation of Athens from the tyranny of the Peisistratid family, an event that took place in 510, close in time to Cleisthenes' reforms. The overthrow of tyranny was celebrated in song and monument not more than two years after 510, and these commemorations were perpetuated in long-lived institutions. But by the late fifth century the nature and significance of the overthrow of tyranny had become hotly disputed, especially in the divide between learned and popular traditions.

Popular tradition linked the liberation from tyranny to the assassination in 514 of Hipparchus, member of the ruling Peisistratid family, by Harmodius and Aristogeiton. The tyrant-slayers lost their lives in the act, but gained immortal fame. Five years later, and soon after the actual fall of the tyranny, statues of Harmodius and Aristogeiton (figure 1) were erected at a

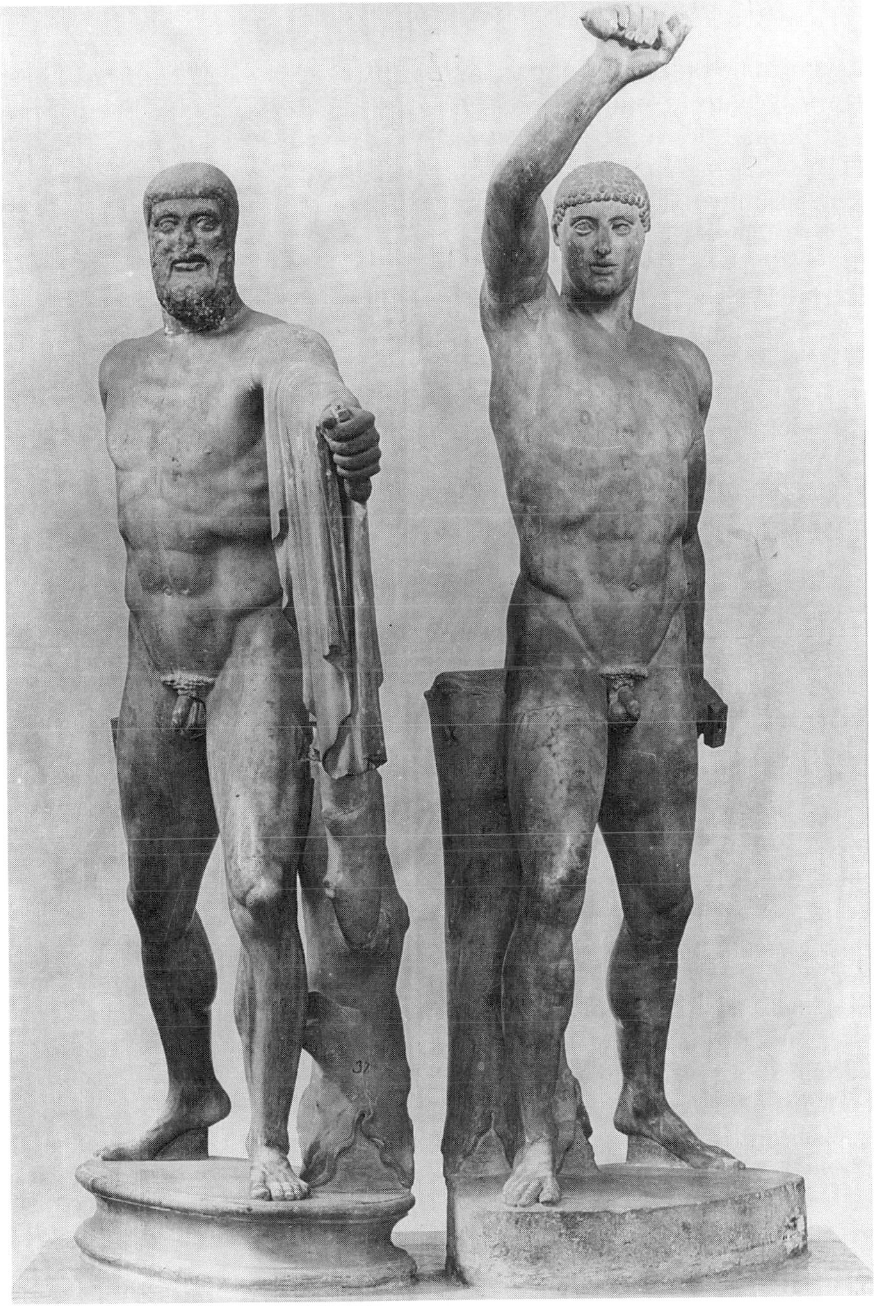

FIGURE 1. Celebrating the tyrant-slayers: Roman copies of the statues in the Athenian Agora depicting Harmodius (right) and Aristogeiton (left) in the act of striking down Hipparchus. Naples, Museo Archeologico Nazionale no. 44825. Photo courtesy of the Deutsches Archäologisches Institut, Rome, neg. no. 58.1789.

central point in the Agora of Athens, probably close to where the assassination took place. An inscription, echoed in drinking songs, praised the two for "slaying the tyrant," and bestowing liberty, or equality, upon Athens. Probably at the same time that the statues were erected, public offerings were instituted at their graves outside the Dipylon gates of Athens in an area that later became the burial ground of many illustrious Athenians. An inscription from the second half of the fifth century lists the descendants of Harmodius and Aristogeiton among public figures entitled to the regular honor of dining in the Prytaneum on state occasions, and the maintenance of this honor is well attested throughout the following century.[9]

The learned tradition, represented in the narratives composed by Herodotus and Thucydides roughly a century after the events, and still later by Aristotle, pointed out that Harmodius and Aristogeiton did not put an end to Peisistratid rule by the murder of Hipparchus. Hippias, his elder brother and leader of the Peisistratid clan, held power for four more years, and was not deposed until a Spartan army defeated his supporters and forced him into exile. The celebration of Harmodius and Aristogeiton's act completely overlooked this aspect of the end to tyranny at Athens.[10]

The reaction against popular tradition is strongest in Thucydides, who singles out this episode, near the beginning of his history, to illustrate how mistaken popular opinion can be. Later in his work he returns to the story to explain the motives for the assassination. Harmodius, the beloved of Aristogeiton, had spurned the amorous advances of Hipparchus and had in turn suffered insults to his family's honor. The assassination of Hipparchus was revenge for this affront, and far from freeing Athens from tyranny, it actually turned Hippias' regime from benevolent despotism to suspicious oppression.

Aside from his introductory chapters, Thucydides' digression on the murder of Hipparchus in Book 6 is his most revealing criticism of popular tradition and pointed demonstration of his superior method of ascertaining the facts. He cites inscriptions and refers to authoritative sources (unfortunately unnamed) for information that refuted the persistent belief that Harmodius and Aristogeiton were the liberators of Athens. There will be occasion to consider the reasons for Thucydides' remarks later, in chapters 4 and 12. Here we should note that Thucydides' vehemence makes it clear that when he wrote the public at large still held Harmodius and Aristogeiton to be the greatest mortal benefactors of the Athenian political order.

CHORAL SONGS AND TRAGEDIES

The fervor of Athenian attachment to the memory of Harmodius and Aristogeiton seems paradoxical both because it reached such a high pitch soon after their deaths and because it was blind to important events that actually accounted for the end of tyranny at Athens. The Athenians who had lived through the death of Hipparchus and overthrow of Hippias knew full well why Harmodius and Aristogeiton slew Hipparchus, and what its consequences had been. But the tale of lovers' revenge made no difference to the transcendent meaning that the Athenians collectively invested in Harmodius and Aristogeiton. Their impassioned act of personal revenge was too useful a symbol of the overthrow of tyrannical autocracy to be explained away by any misplaced concern for factual accuracy.[11]

The need for a symbol of Athenian self-determination, as soon as the Spartans withdrew, may explain the swift heroization of Harmodius and Aristogeiton. Their statues were erected in the Agora, according to Pliny, in 509—the first men to be so publicly honored, according to Aristotle. Coincidentally, another civic event was inaugurated in the Agora at Athens at about the same time. The first competitions of dithyrambic choruses were held probably in the Agora at the Dionysia festival of spring 508. No source explicitly links this custom to the fall of the Peisistratids, to the commemoration of Harmodius and Aristogeiton, or to Cleisthenes' reforms, but the close coincidence of all these events impels us to seek such a connection.[12]

The annual competitions of dithyrambic choruses were a civic event, and the competing choruses each represented one of the ten Athenian tribes. These tribes were the creation of Cleisthenes' reforms. The area known as the orchestra, or "dancing-floor," of the Agora, near the altar of the Twelve Gods, was probably the original location of these competitions (map 4). The orchestra is also named as the location of the statues of the tyrant-slayers. Preserved songs from dithyrambic song-and-dance performances tell of deeds of legendary heroes, such as Theseus, and make topical references to the occasion of performance. Dithyrambs were clearly adaptable to momentous occasions, for Aristophanes depicts a poet offering choral dithyrambs in the manner of Simonides to the founders of a new city.[13]

The victorious dithyrambic poet of 508, Hypodicus of Chalcis, is no more than a name to us, and the subject of his winning song is not attested. But the occasion called for veneration of the new heroes of Athens, Harmodius and Aristogeiton, and a song linking their heritage to the destiny of Athens. Hypodicus may well have been uniquely qualified to sing about the ancestry of Harmodius and Aristogeiton since his own heritage, like theirs, was Euboean. Herodotus reports that the clan of the Gephyraei, to which Harmodius and Aristogeiton belonged, traced its origin to Eretria on Euboea. But he goes on to report an alternate version of the clan's lineage, according to which the Gephyraei had come to Athens after being expelled by the Boeotians from Tanagra, along the lower reaches of the Asopos river north of Attica.[14]

The lands along the Asopos were a contested frontier between Boeotia and Attica, and the Athenians and Thebans had recently been at war over them. If Hypodicus wove together in song these recent events with the experiences of Harmodius and Aristogeiton and those of their ancestral clan, then the destiny of Athens and of the Gephyraei would become one. Both were victims of Boeotian aggression. The ancient victims, the ancestors of Harmodius and Aristogeiton, had been recipients of Athenian compassion. Now, by striking the first blow against tyranny at Athens, Harmodius and Aristogeiton more than repaid that ancestral favor. Poetic reckoning could thus urge the Athenians to honor their memory and repay the debt to the tyrant-slayers by striking a blow against their common ancestral enemies, the Boeotians. Within two years of the celebrations of 508, the Athenians were again fighting the Boeotians, on Tanagran ground, and won a victory that Herodotus later described as the truest proof that the recently-won political equality *(isegoria)* of the Athenians was the source of their new strength.[15]

It would be satisfying if it could be proven that the public performance of 508 so thoroughly tied the distant and recent past to the present, steeling the resolve of the Athenians in the face of potential dangers of the future. There must have been *some* articulation of the glory of Harmodius and Aristogeiton that captured a wide audience at that early date, and Herodotus' accounts of preceding and subsequent events, and the history of the Gephyraei themselves, give the clue to a unifying theme. It is a shame that we have no trace of the text of Hypodicus' performance such as we have of some of his more famous successors. But perhaps, in the martial enthusiasm of the newly liberated Athenians, we see its effects.

Tragedy too could take up contemporary themes under the nascent Athenian democracy. Phrynichus is the earliest tragedian whose artistry is known to us before the surviving works of Aeschylus. He is best known to history for the impact of his play, *Sack of Miletus.* The play dramatized the fall of the chief city of Ionia to the Persians at the end of the Ionian revolt of 499–494. In the early years of the revolt, the Athenians had accepted appeals to the Ionian kinship they shared with the people of Miletus and had supported the revolt and participated in the sack of Sardis, the Persian satrapal capital. But soon thereafter the Athenians withdrew their support and left the Ionians to confront the massed response of Persian-led forces alone. The capture of Miletus by the Persians in 494 was the event that broke the Ionian rebellion. In Phrynichus' play the horrors of men butchered and women enslaved, so often told of the fall of Troy, were brought home to the Athenians with an unsettling immediacy. Phrynichus was censured and fined for being the cause of public grief.[16]

It is commonly assumed that Phrynichus' play was performed in 493, when the mood of the Athenian public was still sensitive to the distressing news from Miletus. But his play could have had its effect at any moment when the Athenians had reason to fear Persian vengeance. Rather than an ill-considered aggravation of recent grief, Phrynichus may have intended the emotional impact of his play to rouse the Athenians to preparatory action. Between the end of the Ionian revolt and the arrival of Xerxes in 480, another Athenian, Themistocles son of Neocles, is known to have urged the Athenians, in the face of some indifference, to take defensive measures in anticipation of a Persian attack. Themistocles was responsible for commencing the fortification of the harbors of Piraeus, and for the massive ship-building program that gave the Athenians the navy that allowed them successfully to confront the forces of Xerxes in 480. It is tempting to see in these events evidence of a collaboration between Themistocles, the ambitious statesman, and Phrynichus, the poet.[17]

Collaboration between politician and playwright is certain a few years later, when Themistocles dedicated a monument to his victory in the Dionysia of 476 as the producer of the plays of Phrynichus. This production probably included Phrynichus' *Phoenician Women,* a dramatic telling of Xerxes' defeat in the sea-battle at Salamis in 480. Because of Themistocles' decisive role among the leaders of the Greek naval forces, this victory over the Persians secured Themistocles' place in history. In view of other indications that Themistocles used piety as a means to promote his own achievements, it is altogether probable that he used Phrynichus' artistry, once again, to shape the memory of recent events as he wanted to have them imprinted on the public mind.[18]

PRAISE IN SONG

The telling of recent memorable deeds in song was ever the goal of poets aspiring to please audiences with novelty, truth, and skill. So even in the *Odyssey,* Homer depicts the singers in the great houses of Ithaca and Phaeacia diverting their audiences with songs of the Achaeans at Troy, and especially of their recent homecomings, sad though they may be for some to hear, "for men give more praise to the song that is the latest to circulate among listeners."[19]

Men proud of their deeds and singers proud of their art were the chief wellspring of Greek poetry. The many varieties of Greek poetry can be accounted for by the various social circles that patronized praise in song, from the friends and family of a champion athlete to the political community celebrating the triumphs of their common purpose. Poets who could adapt their songs of praise to suit these various audiences won the widest fame for themselves. Prize-winning contests in various forms of song had gained prominence across Greece in the sixth century, so that poetry itself became an ever more eminent field of achievement. Praise, in Themistocles' day, was reaching its most refined expression in the specially commissioned and highly paid poetry of Simonides, Bacchylides, and Pindar.[20]

Themistocles patronized the poetry of Simonides, who sang of his incisive counsel before the battle of Salamis in a poem that may have been prompted by one of the many occasions when he was honored for his leadership at Salamis. Most famous was the occasion at Sparta, where Themistocles was entertained with high honors, and given a prize for wisdom and an honor-guard to escort him to the borders of Spartan territory, something, Herodotus notes, that the Spartans granted to "him alone of all men known to us." Elsewhere, at the convocation of Greek commanders at the Isthmian sanctuary of Poseidon, and later at the games of Olympia, Themistocles was "all the talk."[21]

Themistocles seems to have sought out, or at least taken full advantage of, the various public occasions when both talk and song could manufacture fame. At Isthmia certainly, and probably at Olympia as well, his status as a distinguished commander and representative of the Athenians entitled him to host banquets attended by illustrious guests. Such banquets were customarily the occasion for song, both impromptu and prepared solo performances. At Athens, song and celebration must have accompanied his dedication of a new shrine to Artemis Aristoboule, "Of the Best Counsel" (his own special attribute), as it surely did when he sponsored the restoration of the family shrine of the Lycomidae. Song made the stories memorable, and the fact that they were sung in some cases by so illustrious a poet as Simonides was itself a sign of distinction.[22]

Of all Greek commanders in the war against Xerxes, Themistocles was the most successful at associating victory with his personal genius. But he had rivals for the honors of victory. Herodotus frequently notices the competition for honor in war, not so much between opposing sides as within the allied Greek camp. The point is made by analogy in the famous phrase attributed to Themistocles in council with his fellow-commanders, when he remarked that "those who start the race late win no prizes." The point is more direct in the vignette of a named Persian officer interviewing some Greek deserters. They informed him, shortly after the Persian victory at Thermopylae, that the Greeks were preoccupied with the games going on at Olympia. When they added, in response to his questions, that the prizes of the contests were olive wreaths, the officer exclaimed to his commander, "Oh, Mardonius! What kind of men are these that you have brought us to fight against—men who compete with one another for no material reward, but only for honor!" As apocryphal as this utterance seems, it was no mere Hellenic conceit. It depicted a driving force that found concrete expression, after the victory at Salamis, in the vote of the Greek generals, solemnly taken at the altar of Poseidon, for the individual award of *aristeia,* prizes of supreme excellence. The vote resulted in no acknowledged winner—every commander had voted for himself. But the overwhelming preference for Themistocles as runner-up was the beginning of his fame at Salamis.[23]

The personalized quality of *aristeia* identified the excellence of victorious athletes with the excellence of victors in war. Outside of single combat, however, war produces no self-evident individual victors, so the honors of *aristeia* in war were open to contention, and could be accorded only by common acclaim. But why, it may be asked, was it so important to identify and hail the bearers of *aristeia?* Was it more than a matter of pride?

Victory, athletic or martial, was the indisputable mark of the favor of the gods. In battle, athletic victors were revered by their comrades-in-arms as talismans of divine favor. Decked out in their victor's ribbons, they gave courage to friends and struck fear in foes. Those who could boast that they had slain a great athlete in battle, as Sophanes of Decelea did, had still more right to be proud. In addition to Sophanes and several athletic champions, Herodotus draws attention to numerous examples of personal prowess, all of which were probably made memorable by songs of praise and monuments.[24]

A victory, witnessed and acknowledged by all, endowed the victor with an immanent quality, *kudos* ("glory"), that might imbue also those who honored him. So victorious athletes and warriors were cherished by their kin and community, and by publicly praising the victor the community sustained the *kudos* he had achieved in the moment of victory and thereby became partners in the manifestation of divine favor. Conversely, if there were no acts of praise and commemoration, the *kudos* of the victor would evaporate, and would benefit no one. Formal recognition of victory was thus essential, and praise was to be sought.[25]

As Athenian general and statesman, Themistocles moved in circles of influential men from throughout Greece who included in their number the celebrated victors of the day and their equally celebrated praise-singers. To command the esteem of his peers, Themistocles was obliged to claim his share of the honor due from the phenomenal victory at Salamis. But it was almost impossible for a military commander to distinguish his personal achievement from the communal effort he represented. Themistocles, however, had a special distinction in his recognized counsel before the battle of Salamis. Once this was formally acknowledged by others, in the crown "for wisdom" *(sophia)* granted him at Sparta, and in the praise of his "clever judgment" *(deinotes kai gnome)* sung by Simonides, Themistocles had an established claim on personal achievement. His Spartan counterpart, Pausanias, victorious commander at the battle of Plataea, was less successful in distinguishing personal from communal achievement. He was censured by Spartan authorities for placing his own name as "Leader of the Greeks" on the victory offering dedicated to Apollo at Delphi.[26]

In the aftermath of his great victory, our sources depict Themistocles repeatedly demanding the respect due to his proven foresight, sometimes in his own right and sometimes in the name of the Athenians collectively. But, striving so hard to convert his fame into political capital, he could not avoid also becoming the focus of envy. Plutarch quotes from several poems of Timocreon, an exile from Rhodes who once courted favor with Themistocles, unsuccessfully, and who thus reviled the Athenian for being corrupted by the bribes of others. Timocreon took pride chiefly in his reputation as a victorious pentathlete, and his contempt for Themistocles stemmed in part from his confidence in his own indisputable excellence and Themistocles' failure to acknowledge it. Timocreon is the earliest preserved source to accuse Themistocles of venality, and to praise by contrast Themistocles' colleague in generalship, Aristides, as "the choicest man from Athens." It may be that Aristides' reputation as "the Just" Athenian was created in part by people like Timocreon who could no longer endure the self-promotion of Themistocles and who therefore diverted the credit due for the great achievements of Athens to others.[27]

In the end it was the Athenian public that decided his fate. In sharp contrast with the custom prevailing within the fellowship of warriors of acclaiming the *aristeia* of individuals, the Athenian civic community granted no such marks of esteem to its military leaders. Equality, expressed as *isonomia,* "equality before the law," and *isegoria,* "equality of speech," was the leitmotif of the early democracy. After the overthrow of the tyrants, the Athenians could not welcome the vaunting of a man who had bested the king of Persia in battle. Thus the praise due for his unique achievements conflicted with his obligation to acquiesce to civic equality, and this in the end proved to be his undoing.[28]

Rivals decried the arrogance of Themistocles, and critics declared that his celebrated foresight—the only element of victory he could claim as truly his own—was stolen from others. Less than a decade after his triumph at Salamis he was ostracized from Athens. A few years later evidence was produced to show that his greatness entailed the greatest arrogance—he was linked with Pausanias in a conspiracy to betray Greece to Xerxes. True or not, the fate of Themistocles was a clear warning to any who aspired to the highest pinnacles of fame as a war-leader. The Athenians preferred to have Themistocles' *kudos* superseded by a more inclusive, less personalized vision of the greatness of Athens.[29]

Public celebrations of the defeat of Xerxes at Athens acknowledged no living individual above any other. Success was bestowed by divine favor on all Athenians alike. The first sea-battle in which Themistocles commanded the Athenians against the Persians was at Artemisium, and credit for destruction of enemy ships afterwards was given to Boreas, the north wind. Simonides wrote a choral song, possibly commissioned for the occasion of the dedication of the altar of Boreas, that told of Boreas' kinship with the Athenians: long ago the god had seized Oreithyia, a daughter of the Attic King Erechtheus, and had taken her to Thrace as his wife; he fathered two sons on her, wind-spirits, and these had come to the aid of the Athenians before the battle of Artemisium. Mythical kinship thus suffused all Athenians with the glory of victory.[30]

Praise of the Athenians collectively was more direct in the poetry of Pindar, who, in a choral dithyramb commemorating the same battle at Artemisium, celebrated "the sons of Athens," who "laid the brilliant foundations of liberty." Likewise, the city itself was the object of effusive praise in another fragment of a dithyrambic chorus by Pindar, this time referring to the Athenian role at Salamis: "O glistening, violet-crowned, and renowned in song, the pillar of Greece, famed Athens, the divine city..." The verse had a long life in the popular memory, for it gave the Athenians an almost tangible foundation for their collective pride. Its phrases were used by suppliant ambassadors to Athens in later years, and, according to Aristophanes, had the effect of making the easily-flattered Athenians "sit up on tippy-butt at the mention of 'crowns'; and if someone were to call Athens 'glistening,' he'd get all he wanted just for saying 'glistening'—a better description for sardines than for a city." The Athenians enjoyed this notion that they were, collectively, crowned victors, and they favored especially those leaders who brought them this distinction without intruding themselves into the contest for honor.[31]

ENACTING THE IMMANENT PAST

God-favored leaders were essential to winning the god-given gift of victory. But, bowing to the force of political equality and growing democratic sentiment, Athenian commanders after Themistocles deferred such honors to heroes of legend. The icons of Athenian greatness had to become, like Harmodius and Aristogeiton, creatures of popular imagination.

Cimon son of Miltiades was a younger contemporary of Themistocles who began an illustrious career as a commander, in 476/5, leading Athenian forces in the north Aegean. On the borders of Thrace, by the mouth of the Strymon river, Cimon captured the town of Eion from Persian forces. Sometime later he added the island of Scyros to Athenian possessions after driving out the "pirates" who inhabited it. Cimon's popularity was assured when, obedient to an oracle, he was able to recover on Scyros the bones of Athens' greatest ancestral hero, Theseus. The miraculous discovery of the bones of Theseus and their conveyance to Athens gave Cimon's triumphs in the north Aegean a transcendental significance. The ancient king, champion of Attic unity and hero of labors in many lands, was back among his people. The event confirmed the transformation of Theseus into the king of democratic Athens. Under Cimon's auspices, Theseus' bones were installed in a shrine below the Acropolis, and art and song began a new stage in the celebration of Theseus.[32]

Out of this movement emerged several representations of Theseus as defender of Attic soil against barbarian invaders. The story of Theseus' defeat of the Amazons found wide expression and became closely linked in the Athenian mind with the triumphs of Athenians over the Persian invaders. The most memorable depiction of this union of myth and history that animated the bones of the hero was in the murals decorating the Painted Stoa in the Athenian Agora (map 4).[33]

Built a decade or more after the return of Cimon and Theseus, the Painted Stoa may have been the product of booty from one of Cimon's successful campaigns, though this is far from certain. It was originally known as the Peisianactian Stoa, after Peisianax, brother of Cimon's wife, suggesting that a connection with Cimon was popularly perceived. Two of the panels displayed on the walls of the stoa showed Theseus saving Attica from the Amazons, an earlier invasion of barbarians from the north, and Theseus rising from the underworld to fight in the forefront of the Athenians against the Persians at Marathon. Not only were Cimon's victories against barbarians in the north thus secured, in popular esteem, by a heroic patron, but so too were the deeds of his late father, Miltiades, the famed commander at Marathon in 490, whose career had previously been clouded by accusations of tyrannical pretensions.[34]

The heroic deeds of Theseus thus accounted for the remarkable deeds of the recent past by showing how recent deeds conformed to an ancient paradigm. More than this, they also established the moral framework for the unfolding of Athenian destiny. For the events of Cimon's day were radically transforming the familiar universe of Athenian politics from the realms of Athens and Attica to the wider realm of the Greek and non-Greek peoples of the Aegean and beyond. There must have been many among the Athenians, as evidently there were among the Spartans, who felt anxious or uncertain about their rightful role in this wider universe. Depictions of the outrageous deeds of the barbarians, whether they were Persians or Amazons, or, as elsewhere, centaurs or Trojans, gave the Athenians the moral incentive to wage war against outrageous aggressors. Song, ceremony, and art made them mindful of the need to live up to the deeds of their mythic ancestors.[35]

The same blends of historical and mythical paradigms were still more subtly woven in contemporary tragedy. In the spring of 472, Aeschylus' *Persians* was performed in a trilogy produced by Pericles son of Xanthippus, another politically ambitious young man of a distinguished family. The *Persians* represents an updated perspective on the story of the victory at Salamis told four years previously in Phrynichus' *Phoenician Women,* when Themistocles was at the apogee of his fame. Aeschylus' *Persians,* produced at about the time when Themistocles was ostracized, encouraged Athenians to see their deeds as their own, and not the gift of a uniquely talented man, as Phrynichus may have suggested. We can be more confident about another aspect of Aeschylus' play that could not have been so strongly present in Phrynichus' at its earlier date. Aeschylus' play depicted Athens as due heir to the dominion in Thrace and Asia Minor, and even among Ionian Greeks, previously held by Xerxes but lost through his folly and arrogance.[36]

The play opens with the appraisal, by the Persian elders, of the likely course of events in faraway Greece. Given the best of preparations by King Xerxes, enumerated in detail, reason gives them confidence in victory (lines 65–106). But the outcome remains uncertain. Atossa, the mother of Xerxes, is troubled by foreboding dreams and questions the elders about Athens, the object of her son's vengeance. Because of her high standing, her misgivings must be taken seriously. After proposing ritual responses, the elders begin to concede that the evidence of past encounters with the Athenians does not justify so confident a forecast. A messenger arrives with news of the disaster, told in convincing detail. Knowing now that her foreboding was divinely guided, Atossa consults the ghost of her dead husband, Darius, to learn the cause of this disaster, where blame lies, and what can be done. Xerxes is the sole bearer of blame, but as king he is irreproachable before his subjects. At last Xerxes himself arrives, to verify in person the report that has already come. He can offer no consolation, but can only confirm in grim detail the magnitude of the losses and formally commence the lamentations that are the only response possible for the Persians.[37]

Thus, in outline, the play tells the story of the a monarch's overweening pride and his great failure when confronted by the defenders of freedom. But in telling this story, Aeschylus provided the Athenians with more than a cautionary tale about empire or the pleasures of seeing the misery of one's foes. The catastrophe, portended in dreams, foreseen from the past, described by living messenger, explained by the ghost of Darius, and verified by Xerxes himself, conveyed by growing stages a powerful message of affirmation for its Athenian audience. The "hateful memory of Athens" (286–87) was in fact the enactment of the memorable glory of Athens. For the inverse of the Persian catastrophe was the destined path of Athenian greatness.[38]

The complete defeat ("as by a single blow," line 251) of Xerxes and the Persian host is attributed to a sequence of agents beginning with Salamis and Athens (lines 284–86), to the gods and men of Athens (lines 345–54), and to Greeks generally (lines 402–405), and finally to the agency of the Ionian Greeks in particular (lines 562, 950–54, 1011, 1025). Throughout the play, the element of Athenian might, the sea, is the element in which the Persians meet death (lines 274–77, 302–481), especially as divine punishment for daring to enslave the sea by laying chains across the Hellespont (lines 722–24, 744–50, cf. 905–906). The role of "the Dorian spear," i.e. the Spartan-led infantry, in completing the destruction of Persian forces at Plataea is noticed (lines 796–820), but it is Athens above all (lines 474–75, 823–26, 975–77) that deals this cataclysmic turn of fate to the Persians.[39]

The play envisions a seamless, even simultaneous continuity between the battle of Salamis in 480 and the expansion of the Athenian maritime alliance of Ionian states, the Delian League, created in 478/7. The victory at Salamis was won by Ionian hands (line 562), was the work of Ionian Ares (lines 950–54), and was within view of Athens (lines 975–77). Athens is at once the champion of Ionian liberty (lines 584–97) and heir to the dominion, previously given willingly to Persia, of the Thracian and Ionian coastlands of the Aegean, and of islands as far as Cyprus, with its significantly homonymous city, Salamis (lines 852–906). In the same way that the fate of Miletus depicted earlier by Phrynichus was "their own suffering," the Ionian deeds recounted in the play by Xerxes were one and the same with the deeds of Athens. Aeschylus perhaps takes advantage of the fact that "Ionia" *(Yauna)* is the Persian name for "Greece." The words of the Persians themselves, then, grant authority to the Athenian vision of themselves as the chief seat of all Ionians and the proper agent for Ionian vengeance. This vision was only possible after 476, when the Ionian states led by Athens had begun to "plunder the land of the king in retribution for what they had suffered," as Thucydides later described the purpose of the League. According to Aeschylus' play, the Athenian empire was born, like Athena from the head of Zeus, in the moment of triumph at Salamis.[40]

The *Persians* was the middle play of the trilogy staged by Aeschylus and Pericles in 472. The first was *Phineus,* the third *Glaucus at Potniae,* of which nothing but a few lines survive. With little direct evidence to go on, modern commentators have been reluctant to see any programmatic connection between the *Persians,* a "historical" play, and the other two, dealing with mythological themes. But enough is known of their subjects to make it likely that the vision of destiny created out of the recent past at Salamis in the *Persians* was complemented in mythical teleologies in the other two plays, and that the coherence of the three tragedies was such that the *Phineus* alluded to the earlier battle at Artemisium, in 480, and, in a rather different manner, the *Glaucus at Potniae* alluded to the later land battle at Plataea, in 479.[41]

Phineus was a king of Thrace who married a daughter of Boreas and Oreithyia. Like the god of the north wind himself, Phineus was thus a kinsman of the Athenians. He had offended the gods by blinding his sons from this marriage, and was himself punished by being blinded and by having his food constantly stolen by harpies. Despite his crime, in what must be the crux of Aeschylus' tragedy, Phineus was delivered from the harpies by his brothers-in-law, the sons of Boreas. These same Boreads, grandsons of Erechtheus, were the wind-spirits praised in the hymn on the battle of Artemisium by Simonides, a hymn that was sung often afterwards, on the occasion of the festival of Athena, as an invocation of the winds to accompany the Panathenaic ship in its procession to the Acropolis.[42]

Like Theseus, the Boreads were miraculous comrades-in-arms of the Athenians against the Persians. In addition, as denizens of Thrace and merciful deliverers of Phineus, they served to establish for the Athenians an ancestral claim to dominion in the north. Simonides had located their birth on "the Sarpedonian rock," a promontory of the eastern Aegean coast of Thrace. Pindar, in a poem composed a decade after Aeschylus' play and probably reflecting its allusions, gives their home as mount Pangaeum, overlooking the Strymon river in western Thrace. This was gold-mining territory, a region that attracted Athenian settlers following Cimon's capture of Eion on the Strymon in 475, and that caused the outbreak of war with Thasos a decade later. Like the Ionian empire of the *Persians,* Aeschylus' *Phineus* revealed Athenian dominion in Thrace to be a working out of a destiny beyond the ken of any mortal Athenian leader.[43]

Glaucus at Potniae dwelt on a story not so popular in later tradition, but sufficiently clear in its main features to see that it illustrated the tragic consequences of overweening pride, this time among Greeks. Glaucus was the son of Sisyphus and king of Corinth, who fancied winning the greatest honors among the heroes of his day, Heracles, Jason, and the Argonauts among them, in the chariot race at the funeral games of King Pelias at Iolcus. Pelias' son Acastus had invited the heroes of Greece to prove themselves in contests that, according to one version of the story, inspired an oath of unity and the foundation of the Olympic games. Glaucus had incurred the anger of Zeus, however, possibly for his practice of feeding his horses on human flesh, as a measure, perhaps, to give them supernatural strength. He pastured his horses at Potniae, near Thebes in Boeotia, and there divine retribution led his horses to drink from a spring, or to eat poisonous grass, that would drive them mad. In the race at Iolcus, his team threw Glaucus from the chariot, tore him to pieces, and ate him.[44]

The contest at Iolcus and, if it was in Aeschylus' tale, the pledge taken by the heroes united there alluded to the battle of Plataea and the pledge of unity made among the Greeks before it. Glaucus' fate was an allegory for the foredoomed pride of the Peloponnesian leaders at the battle of Plataea. The fields of the Asopos where the battle was fought were the pasture-lands of Glaucus' horses; the spring at Potniae, a little south of Thebes, was the chief spring in the area of the great Persian camp, on the north bank of the Asopos. Stories of its power to inspire madness must have led the Greeks to hope for beforehand, or to see afterward, a similar divine hand working on Mardonius, general of the Persians, or perhaps Masistius, his cavalry commander. Most of all, however, this allegory was meant to remind Aeschylus' audience of the hubristic pride of other Greeks.[45]

First among these were the Corinthians, "the countrymen of Glaucus," as they were named in Simonides' elegy on the battle of Plataea. Although Simonides had praised the Corinthians for bravery at Plataea, the Athenians favored the account later reported by Herodotus, that the Corinthians had fled the battle in panic. Whatever the reasons for this Corinthian-Athenian animosity may have been, it was clearly latent in 472, for within a decade after Aeschylus' play the two states were at war in the first open manifestation of what Thucydides called "the great hatred" of Corinth for Athens.[46]

The most famous example of overweening pride at the battle of Plataea, however, was Pausanias, the Spartan commander-in-chief of the Greek allies. Within a year or two of the battle of Plataea, Pausanias had been censured for a tactless victory dedication, and had been recalled to Sparta from his command at Byzantium after protests against his behavior by the Athenians and Ionians. He was later reinstated at Byzantium, but again fell afoul of his Greek allies. By 472 Pausanias was probably in the midst of the scandal that would lead to his condemnation for collaboration with the Persians.[47]

In sum, Aeschylus' tragic trilogy of 472 depicted the predestined success of Athens in struggles that brought others low. The *Phineus* showed the justice of Athenian claims to the Thracian coast of the north Aegean. The *Persians* showed the Athenians as the rightful protectors of Greek freedom violated by Xerxes. And the *Glaucus at Potniae* showed the rot at the core of rival claims to leadership among the Greeks. Where Glaucus' lust for glory literally consumed him, in the hippodrome of Iolcus, the champions from Attica won fair prizes. For Aeschylus almost certainly capped the trilogy by portraying the victories at Iolcus that legend attributed to the Boreads.[48]

Aeschylus' trilogy was itself crowned with the victor's prize in 472. Like the several murals on the walls of the Painted Stoa, the shrine of Theseus, and other Athenian monuments of the middle decades of the fifth century, Aeschylus' trilogy played creatively with an array of stories that all served to affirm the "rightness" of Athenian goals. The empire that was to be the product of their labors was not yet perceived as such, even though some of the acts of conquest and retribution that Thucydides later described as the beginnings of empire had already taken place. But its domain, and their rightful claim to be its champion, were clearly laid out in Aeschylus' trilogy. The persuasiveness and pervasiveness of these affirmations of purpose, in story and in art, created the ethical climate in which democratic institutions could sustain the creation of an empire. For these were the underpinnings of the famous Athenian daring, a distinctive and, to many, a disturbing characteristic, spoken of by Athenians and non-Athenians by the time of the outbreak of the Peloponnesian War.[49]

PERFORMANCE AND PUBLIC

Aeschylus' *Persians* is unique among surviving examples of Greek tragedy in being a "historical" play. Yet, as the foregoing illustrates, plays that dealt only in characters of myth were equally charged with "historical" meanings, in the sense that all provided cogent instruction based on "events" of the past. All manner of performance poetry, whether tragic drama, dithyrambic chorus, elegy, or victory hymn, constructed significance around the moment of performance. In that moment, through the transport of Dionysian make-believe, past events from myth or recent memory are made to converge on the audience, creating a vivid impression of meanings coming from beyond the boundaries of normal experience. The living Persian king, or his dead predecessor, an ancestral hero, or even a god, speak before the audience and inform them of causes and purposes that shape their present moment and orient them toward the future.[50]

The past is thus, in a sense, timeless, and the eternal present is everything, always carrying with it the significance of the past. From this perspective, events of the past are not evaluated from the standpoint of the figures of the past except insofar as they might be identical with the interests of the present. So, for example, it mattered not a bit to the spectators of the first Dionysian dithyrambs praising Harmodius and Aristogeiton that these assassins of Hipparchus had neither the intention nor the effect of creating a new political order. The meaning of their act was an artifact of popular perception, shaped by the needs of the moment. In 510 the Athenian public demanded a symbol of autonomous self-determination, and found in the deed of these two men the supreme rejection of tyrannical autocracy.[51]

The Athenian public was thus no passive audience, but participated in shaping the messages that it witnessed and celebrated. The regulation of dramatic and choral performances on their appointed occasions in the city's religious calendar was a civic responsibility of the highest priority for the archons of Athens, customary already in the time of the Peisistratids and evolving without interruption with the festival institutions of the new democracy. The chief Athenian magistrate, the eponymous archon, was regularly charged with the annual selection of poets and producers to sponsor the choruses and dramas that would be staged in the city's festivals. The archon thus served as the primary mediator between art and public sentiment, and in democratic Athens he was accountable to the public.[52]

The authority of public sentiment is clearest in the case of Phrynichus. His bold experiment in the *Sack of Miletus* demonstrated the power of his art over the emotions of his audience, but his civic audience in turn made it clear that he had abused the privilege of his unanswered theatrical monologue. Later dramatists regularly chided or guided their audience and its political spokesmen. But, except when comedy pressed this role to its limits, dramatists did so indirectly, through archetypal examples, and never again confronted the audience with "their own" tragedy. The practice of screening dramatic productions, in the *proagon,* before they were enacted in public, may have emerged as a consequence of Phrynichus' experience, adding another level of public accountability.[53]

Dramatic and dithyrambic performances at Athens were prize-bearing competitions, adding a further level to the influence of public approval. The Great Dionysia, the oldest and most prestigious of the dramatic and dithyrambic festivals at Athens, was the most important ceremony of self-representation for the Athenians, both to themselves and to foreigners, whether they were resident aliens, visitors, or official emissaries. By the mid-fifth century the Athenians were using this occasion, in the spring of each year, to display Athenian prowess in the form of the tribute collected from their allies, and in the parade of the sons of Athenian war-dead, trained and armed at state expense. These proofs of sacrifice, piety, and power, together with the splendor of the performances themselves and the crowns awarded to the victors, put all in mind of the divine favor that graced this Athenian convocation.[54]

Immediately after the dramatic contests the Athenians held an assembly both to review the conduct of the festival and to transact public business befitting this moment of heightened civic pride. In times of war this was a most portentous time of year, for the sailing season was just beginning, and decisions would be made then that would determine the objectives of that year's expeditionary forces. So, on one such occasion, more than dramatic plot prompted the invocation of Athena's protection for the alliance between Athens and Argos, for friends in Egypt, and for partners in Thessaly, in Aeschylus' *Eumenides,* the last tragedy of his trilogy of 458. Athenians were fighting in Egypt, and later that summer they would rely on Argives and Thessalians to aid them in battle at Tanagra against the Spartans and Boeotians. A generation later, the assembly after the Dionysia was the occasion when the Athenians formalized agreements with Spartan ambassadors, whose presence in Athens through the festival will have been required in order that proposed terms could be drafted in council beforehand. By so inviting the muses of poetry to speak on their behalf, the Athenians could hardly have contrived a more effective manner of imbuing political transactions of the highest importance with inspired expressions of their civic ideals. Its effects are apparent in several aspects of the overlapping spheres of poetry and politics.[55]

Drama and politics involved persuasive performances before much the same audiences. The language of the theater, both in style and in content, could influence political oratory, and the opposite influence is likely too. Ion of Chios described Cimon's public demeanor as "muse-inspired... like a dramatic production." His meaning was that, in addition to the gravity of the tragedies, Cimon also possessed a touch of levity, like the satyric play that capped a poet's presentation. Pericles, on the other hand, was more serious and profound, his words like "awesome thunderbolts delivered by his tongue," and he himself was dubbed "Olympian" by comic playwrights poking fun at this image. Pericles' reputation in this regard calls to mind that of Aeschylus, who won Aristophanes' nostalgic contest of poets in the *Frogs* by demonstrating how "mighty thoughts and designs must give birth to appropriate words; the language of demigods is rightly more lofty." Prominent or aspiring political figures were occasionally dramatic sponsors, as noted above, and vice-versa. Sophocles was elected *hellenotamias,* one of the curators of the tribute collected by the Athenians, and later he was one of the ten Athenian generals during the Samian War of 440–39.[56]

Those who approached the Athenian *demos* on the occasion of the Dionysia, treating as allies or as foemen, were also affected by the experience. In the later 420s, ambassadors from Catana in Sicily came to Athens to appeal to the Athenians to send back to them the military force that had recently been withdrawn. Justin describes their appeal:

> The ambassadors appeared before the assembly in mourning: filthy clothes, unkempt hair and beards, and a generally miserable appearance designed to excite pity. Tears accompanied their entreaties, and such was the compassion they aroused in the people by their appeals that a motion was passed condemning the generals who had withdrawn the reinforcements from them.[57]

The Catanians were clearly employing devices familiar to the stagecraft of Euripides to win boons from the same audience that was fascinated by the pathetic realism of that playwright. And if Euripides was not often awarded first prize himself by the Athenians, his reputation is said to have done them inestimable service. For some of the Athenian captives at Syracuse, after 413, are said to have been spared

> for the sake of Euripides. For the Sicilians, it would seem, more than any other Hellenes outside the home land, had a yearning and fondness for his poetry.... [Some Athenians reported that] they had been set free from slavery for rehearsing what they remembered of his works; and some that when they were roaming about after the final battle they had received food and drink for singing some of his choral hymns....[58]

Plutarch, who recounts these stories, elsewhere reports that all Athenians owed Euripides a greater debt of gratitude shortly after the poet's death. When the Spartans and their allies were deliberating over the fate of Athens, after her surrender in 404,

> Some say that in very truth a proposition to sell the Athenians into slavery was actually made in the assembly of the allies.... Afterwards, however, when the leaders were gathered at a banquet, and a certain Phocian sang the first chorus in the "Electra" of Euripides... all were moved to compassion and felt it to be a cruel deed to abolish and destroy a city which was so famous, and produced such poets.[59]

We may doubt, as will be discussed later, that the fate of Athens hung by so delicate a thread, but there is no reason to doubt the tribute to the wide impact of Euripides' dramatic poetry. For at the end of a century of poets striving to show Athenians their destiny in the world beyond Athens, Euripides had succeeded in making part, at least, of that world treat Athens as its own. The theater of Dionysus was Athens' heart.[60]

THE DEAD AND THE LIVING

Outside of deliberative assemblies and the theater, extended orations to the Athenians regularly took place on one further occasion, at the end of the ceremonies commemorating the Athenian war-dead. Perhaps inspired by the return of the bones of Theseus to Athens in 475, the Athenians adopted the practice of conveying back to Athens the cremated remains of those killed in battle for a communal funeral outside the Dipylon gates, along the road to the grove of the hero, Hecademus (later Plato's Academy). Thucydides described the practice as the customary treatment of all Athenian war-dead, except for those who died at Marathon, whose special honor deserved a burial monument on the battlefield. As scholars have noted, however, burial on the field of battle was a well-established custom, and the Athenian ceremony of conveyance to a common grave outside of Athens was the innovation. Not until after Xerxes' invasion would the Athenians have realized that the rapidly widening field of war required them to make explicit decisions about how and where they would conduct their observances of those who had fallen in battle abroad for Athens. Their conveyance back to Athens was a powerful reminder of the links that bound Athenians to those battlegrounds across the seas.[61]

The funeral itself was a further demonstration of civic identity being transformed by the institutions of democracy and nascent empire. The cremated remains of the fallen were brought to their common gravesite in communal coffins, one for each of the ten Attic tribes. Individual identities were thus physically subsumed by group identities within the structures of Athenian citizenship. Individuals were named on the monument erected over their grave, but without further indication of patronym or family affiliation. The names of the dead, grouped by tribe, were listed under a heading typically in the form: "Of the Athenians, the following died at. . . . " Aside from noting the ranks of officers, few further distinctions were made among the names listed, but the exceptions are revealing. The occurrence of subheadings for "barbarian archers" and, in one instance, "servants," as well individuals identified by non-Attic ethnics, suggests that these honors for supreme sacrifice in service of Athens were deemed appropriate for the construction of a wider definition of "Athenians" than the group of individuals who, in practice, exercised the rights of citizenship. The indications of inclusiveness represented in the surviving fragments of these lists, however, are inconsistent. It is likely that what was deemed appropriate, over the several decades covered by these lists, varied as much among the Athenians as it has among the modern scholars commenting on them.[62]

Appropriating for itself a share of the observances due from the families of the deceased, the state thus solemnified its unity as a supra-kinship group, embracing in equal honor wealthy and poor, citizens and foreigners, free men and even slaves—all, by meeting death in battle, as glorious Athenians. This was the preeminent moment for a eulogy of Athens and her greater domain, and the task was assigned by the Athenian Council "to a man," Thucydides says, "who is considered not to be lacking in intellectual distinction, and who enjoys an excellent reputation." Among those reported to have been selected for this honor was Gorgias of Leontini, a non-Athenian, but one known to have been widely admired at Athens for his oratory. Although scholars have denied that foreigners could deliver the eulogy over the war-dead of Athens, the ancient testimony points the other way. Nothing, in fact, could confirm the eminence of Athens in the world better than to have their heroes eulogized by distinguished foreigners. Like the occasions for dramatic and choral poetry, when foreign and Athenian poets alike competed, the institution of the funeral oration was a central one in articulating the image of an Atheno-centric universe.[63]

Plato, in the character of Socrates, describes the effects of this institutionalized "praise of Athenians to Athenians" in humorous but not insincere terms:

> In every conceivable form they praise the city, and they praise those who died in war, and all our ancestors who went before us, and they praise ourselves who are still alive, until I feel quite elevated by their laudations, and I stand listening to their words, Menexenus, and I become enchanted by them, and all in a moment I imagine myself to have become a greater and nobler and finer man than I was before. And if, as often happens, there are any foreigners who accompany me to the speech, I become conscious of having a sort of triumph over them, and they seem to experience a corresponding feeling of admiration at me, and at the greatness of the city, which appears to them, when they are under the influence of the speaker, more wonderful than ever. This consciousness of dignity lasts me more than three days, and not until the fourth or fifth day do I come to my senses and know where I am—in the meantime I have been living in the Islands of the Blessed. Such is the art of our rhetoricians, and in such manner does the sound of their words keep ringing in my ears.

Plato singles out Pericles as the most memorable of speakers on these occasions. But given the conventional nature of these addresses, he goes on to point out, even pupils of inferior instructors in rhetoric and in music could do a creditable job.[64]

Like tragic drama, the funeral oration was a vehicle for conveying a sense of purpose from out of the past to the present moment—in this case an occasion for real grief, fear, and uncertainty. To be effective in this context, the

Athenian past had to be reduced to a limited set of recognized, repeatedly enacted, and therefore inexorable themes: Athens stood for fairness and equality; in the name of these goals it championed the weak against the oppression of the strong; its mission, like its people, was aboriginal, and this divinely sanctioned link to native land was not to be broken by any invader, nor supplanted by allegiance to any authority other than to the time-honored customs and laws of Athens. These goals justified the ultimate sacrifice of its citizens and of their allies in battle, and this sacrifice in turn justified the heroic honors paid, collectively, to those who had fallen in the continuing struggle to achieve Athens' mission. Speakers could choose to give greater or lesser emphasis to any of these themes, but nearly all of them are represented in each of the Athenian funeral orations that survive. The orations were thus, in part, reviews of the Athenian past, but as such they were rather unreliable guides to Athenian history. For funeral orations were bound to elide the particularities of past events into equal steps in the same monumental stairway.[65]

One of the most peculiar effects of this tendency, from our perspective, is the claim that the funeral oration itself was sanctioned by a *patrios nomos,* which can be translated either as "ancestral law" or as "ancestral custom." All accounts touching the history of this practice, including Plato's example in the *Menexenus,* acknowledge that the interment and commemoration of war-dead at Athens was a new institution, established after the invasion of Xerxes, and belonging to the era of widening Athenian involvement in warfare far beyond the confines of Attica. It was, in other words, a feature of the emergent Athenian empire and of the democracy of the Cimonian and Periclean era. In what sense could such a recent institution be described as "ancestral"?

The answer lies in the knack of the Athenian myth-historical imagination (not, to be sure, a uniquely Athenian gift) for investing innovation with the dignity of ancient tradition, as illustrated in the examples of Theseus and the Boreads, in which legendary precedents were found for emergent concerns. In the case of the return of the war-dead to Attica, the charter myth was the story told by Aeschylus in the *Eleusinians,* later retold by, among others, Euripides in the *Suppliant Women:* the Athenians of yore had been the protagonists of a Greek custom, a *Hellenikos nomos,* also called an unwritten statute of the gods, in championing the recovery of the fallen Argives from before the gates of Thebes and giving them an honorable burial in Attica. From this seminal act the Athenians would ever afterward uphold the supreme obligation to honor their *own* fallen, in victory or defeat, by recovering them and returning them to Attic soil. The founder of this practice was, of course, Theseus.[66]

EVERYMAN'S PAST

Athenian civic life was rich with images of the past and references to memorable events, both distant and recent. But in order to comprehend the diverse realities of past experience and their polysemantic potentials for the future, the focus on the past in public monument and memorial was always extremely diffuse. From the century before the Peloponnesian War only three events emerge as truly distinct landmarks in this haze: the overthrow of the Peisistratid tyranny, the battle of Marathon, and the battle of Salamis. These were often recalled as unique and transformative events, defining forever the beginning of a new era—but only inasmuch as they were fresh proofs of the revival of ancient Athenian virtues. In making durable icons of these episodes, as we have seen, even the recent past was quickly simplified.[67]

Other events were recorded in word and monument with even less attention to detail, circumstances, and individuals. Victories of the post-Peisistratid democracy, over Greeks and barbarians alike, were celebrated in almost generic terms. The deeds of the victors were analogous to those of ancient heroes—Menestheus and the Athenians fighting at Troy, according to one monument—and thus Athens' contemporary champions were assimilated to an ideal of heroism that was both communal and eternal, and an ideal that every generation could strive to replicate.[68]

An instructive instance is found in the defeat of the Boeotians and Chalcidians a few years after the expulsion of the tyrants, commemorated by trophies and a brief epigram displayed on the Acropolis. Herodotus describes this episode, mentions the monuments, and recites the epigram. Archaeological discoveries have shown that the inscribed base seen by Herodotus was a second monument, erected roughly half a century after the original, which had presumably been damaged by the Persians. Replicating, with only slight variations, the original dedication, this second monument was probably prompted by one of the occasions, near the middle of the fifth century, when the Athenians were again fighting Boeotians and Euboeans. Herodotus' account of the late sixth-century victory, moreover, reads like an excerpt from an Athenian funeral oration, with its catalogue of past conflicts, and its summation in a eulogy of the merits of freedom from tyranny; it is tempting to believe that his account—our only narrative source to describe these events—derived from just such a retrospective oration at the end of another year of battle with the same foes.[69]

The obscurity of the contemporary referent was often deliberate even in the case of memorials to recognized events. So, anonymous monuments commemorated Athenian victories over the Persians at Eion in Thrace, at the Eurymedon River in Pamphylia, and in Cyprus, and over the Spartans at Oenoe in the Argolid. None of these monuments, in verse on stone or, in the last case, a scene depicted in the Painted Stoa, bore the name of a contemporary Athenian or any indication of date. As a result, the exact chronology of *all* of these events remains uncertain now as it already was in Thucydides' day, at the end of the fifth century. Only Cimon's personal celebrity rescued his role in the victories at Eion, Eurymedon, and Cyprus from obscurity. The battle of Oenoe, on the other hand, can be connected with no known individuals, and only conjecturally related to other events. It would be completely unknown to us were it not for Pausanias' description of the painting at Athens and notice of a related Argive monument at Delphi.[70]

As these examples illustrate, monuments and orations sponsored by the Athenian democracy had no need for chronology, avoided exaltation of individuals, and offered no explanation of events beyond affirming irreproachable qualities of excellence. Within a past viewed in such terms, the difference between recent "historical" events and those of the mythic past was meaningless. As much as recent events embodied a heightened sense of truth because they were within the living memory of many, such truth was problematic, because recent events had many implications and had been variously experienced. The more distant past was more useful for civic ideology because it had long been thoroughly processed into simpler, more widely-recognized truths about the past. Public poetry, and especially drama, was created out of the rich semantic opportunities that lay between a community involved in complex contemporary experiences and their "known" past. Public oration, especially funerary eulogies, began the process of rendering recent, often powerfully affective events into a sensible part of the "known" past that the community could henceforth carry with it.

One feature of the communal construction of recent events deserved specific record. This was the geography of exploits, of victories, and of death in battle. Commemoration of the geography of events established an eminent domain of the Athenians over other lands. Similarly, the record of the native origins of those who joined Athenians in the exploits, victories, and in death, demonstrated that the impetus to contribute to the Athenian destiny transcended the boundaries of citizenship. We may call such commemorations imperialist, and demonstrations of empire, but to do so casts a historicizing eye over them that was not appropriate to their moments of creation. For the Athenians were constructing a view of their place in the world that was not finite and bounded, but open to new potentials. Although in documents of practical record terms like "the allies," or "the cities," or eventually "the subjects" and even "the cities that the Athenians control" gave definition to their empire, in commemorative rhetoric as in drama, such concrete terms were rarely admitted.[71]

The past told in this manner produced a meaningful account, but one whose meaning was completely subjective, and was constantly retold to sustain the process of integrating present experience with the past. It was meaningful especially because it served the purpose of renewing, for each generation, the prototypes of civic devotion, and for recording the territorial landmarks of Athenian endeavor that each generation should strive to maintain or exceed. It is probably the case, and may be stated here as a hypothesis, that a radically different way of rendering meaning out of the past emerged only as it began to become apparent that the eminent domain of Athens was not limitless.

WITNESSES TO THE PAST

Until Herodotus completed his history of the Persian Wars, no earlier than the 420s, there was no account of the recent past of Athens apart from the essentially oral traditions of public history as they were conventionally constructed and popularly construed. The need that Herodotus felt to present an account of the Persian Wars, "lest events fade through time from human memory," was just as urgent for the half-century between the Persian and Peloponnesian Wars. Thucydides expresses outright pessimism when confronting the poverty of information available to him about the era of his own youth when he remarks, at the beginning of his history, that "it was impossible, because of the passage of time, to find out accurately about events before [the Peloponnesian War]...." In different ways, Thucydides and Herodotus both drew attention to the subjective and shifting quality of knowledge about the past prior to their accounts. Their viewpoint in this regard was widely shared within the intellectual community that made Athens its crossroads in the last third of the fifth century.[72]

When Herodotus' work appeared, Thucydides was also writing on some aspect of the war then underway between Athens and Sparta. Hellanicus of Lesbos, among other works, compiled a chronicle of Athenian, or properly, Attic events, from the mythical past to his own day, that appeared shortly before Thucydides put his account in order, after the end of the war in 404. In addition to these works, and all roughly within the span of 430–400, the list of Athenian eponymous archons was published in an inscription giving names starting in 683/2; Hippias of Elis compiled the list of Olympic victors that began in 776; Antiochus of Syracuse wrote about southern Italy and Sicily from early times to his day; Glaucus of Rhegium composed his *On the Ancient Poets and Musicians,* comparing the artistry and establishing the chronologies of poets from the early seventh century until at least the time of Phrynichus and Aeschylus; and works of erudition on comparable subjects were produced by Ion of Chios, Stesimbrotos of Thasos, Damastes of Sigeum, and Charon of Lampsacus, as well as others who are known to us for the most part only from passing references to their works.[73]

Posterity has affirmed that the achievements of Herodotus and Thucydides stand far above the rest in this crowd, but the point of interest here is that there was a *crowd.* While not all might deserve, retrospectively, to be called historians, they were all busy converting their research and wide learning about the past into prose treatises, and were doing so at very close to the same time. There were forerunners, such as Hecataeus of Miletus and Pherecydes of Syros. But there is no indication that their earlier works inspired the great *proliferation* of writings about the past that took place in the late fifth century. And no forerunners can explain Herodotus' and Thucydides' transformation of the critical inquiry into the past through their focus on recent events.[74]

From amidst this gathering crowd, Herodotus introduced a work that promised the familiar and produced something profoundly different from other chronicles of the past. Herodotus presented his account of the Persian Wars, he announces at the head of his work, "lest events fade through time from human memory, and lest great and amazing deeds displayed both by Greeks and by barbarians should lose their glory, and especially to show the reason why they fought one another." Herodotus' first phrases echo the formulae of epigrammatic monuments that stand before their viewers as durable reminders of the glory of those honored. Like the praise of victory-songs, the lists of genealogists, and the chronicles of landmark events in a community's past, these displays do not explain, they only affirm. For affirmation of an ancient pattern, like that given in a funeral oration, is sufficient reason in itself. Herodotus' last phrase, on the other hand, evokes the milieu of ancient epic and contemporary tragedy, for only there were stories told to explain *why* things happened.

Here lay the remarkable vision of Herodotus. For deeds celebrated in praise and eulogy were the tokens of immortality, born of the hope that some essential and infallible quality, be it *kudos* or *kleos* (both "glory") or *arete* ("excellence"), would inhere in the deeds of an individual or a community, however fallible and mortal they otherwise were. Their message to posterity was a summons to perpetuate their memory and to strive to surpass them. But tragedy had another message. The stories of tragic drama gripped the imagination precisely because they showed how elusive these tokens were, and how evanescent they could become as great men and women found themselves crushed by a fate larger than they had comprehended.[75]

The implications of tragedy were the opposite of eulogy. The Athenians were able to cultivate both to so high a degree only because, after Phrynichus' unsettling experience, they firmly maintained the boundary between "*our* inexorable destiny" and "the unforeseen fate of *others*." The fate of others, to be sure, was always at some level an allegorical warning to the audience that they should not thus mistake the tokens of their own doom. This added to the appeal of tragedy, for it excited a sense of danger to a highly emotional pitch. But that experience was tolerable through the release the audience could seek in the knowledge that this doom was not, in fact, their own.

Herodotus knew well the lesson of Phrynichus, since he is our source for the story. He knew well, too, the importance of the events Phrynichus had enacted in his *Sack of Miletus,* since they had been the consequence of "the beginning of evils for Greeks and barbarians," namely, the support of the Ionian revolt by Athens and Eretria. And that event, in turn, had been the consequence of the Athenians' accepting and acting upon a vision of their own destiny, as fatherland of Ionians, presented to them by Aristagoras of Miletus. Herodotus tacitly reminded his audience that the doom of Miletus, so fearful to the Athenians, was later visited upon Athens itself, sacked by Xerxes. Xerxes in turn had been humbled, at least in Greek eyes, and the story of these wars achieved a sort of closure following the final defeat of his army of invasion.[76]

But the story went on, as Aeschylus had portrayed it in the *Persians,* with the Athenians rightfully inheriting part of his former dominion. Tragedy brought out the unexpected in events in part by choosing different points in time to mark the beginning and the ending of a tale. The importance of this device of tragedy to Herodotus' story is brought out from his opening narrative of the fate of Croesus. Starting with this thematic precedent, his *Histories* are replete with stories of how the mighty had mistaken the warnings of their doom for the tokens of their destiny. We must ask, therefore: before an Athenian audience in the 420s and 410s, could Herodotus' tale of empire and its limits be taken as the tale of the fate of others and not *also* as a vivid warning about their own? In what sense had "the beginning of evils for Greeks and barbarians" reached fulfillment? For as of 431, the Athenians were at the center of "the greatest disturbance in the history of the Hellenes," as Thucydides described it, "affecting also a large part of the barbarian world, and indeed, I might almost say, the whole of mankind." In such a context, the Greeks, and especially the Athenians, could not seek release from the warnings implicit in the tragic structures of Herodotus' *Histories* because the events he told were, in fact, their own. This inescapable tension must underlie the anecdote that Thucydides cried when he heard a reading of Herodotus' *Histories.*[77]

The tears of Thucydides are emblematic of what Herodotus must surely have intended in writing the *Histories*—to reflect on the dangers inherent in the power enjoyed by Athens in the 420s and early 410s. There is universal recognition that Herodotus finished his work no earlier than the 420s, but the question of how long his work had been in preparation and when his "publication" is to be placed are contested. I align myself with those who see the work as a whole to be the product of a life of learning but no more than a few years of composition. Passages at 6.98 and 9.73 indicate that the reign of Artaxerxes I (464–424) and the Spartan invasions of 431–425 had both come to an end by the time these passages were written. Herodotus wrote, I would argue, in view of the great swings of emotion and reason that prevailed at Athens after 425, when peace with Sparta was foreseeable, possibly even in hand, but its implications for the destiny of Athens were still hotly contested.[78]

Thucydides provides our most important insights into the nature of opinion at Athens from the victory of Cleon at Pylos in 425 to the death of Cleon at Amphipolis in 422. Among other passages, the tenor of public sentiment at Athens in this era is portrayed at a significant juncture in the narrative of Thucydides, in the summer of 424. In that summer, the Peace of Gela settled war among Sicilian states and led to the withdrawal of an Athenian force from Sicily. The generals responsible for the withdrawal, however, were thereafter placed on trial and banished or fined for having neglected to exploit opportunities to the best interests of the Athenians (the same event recalled in the passage from Justin, quoted above, page 35). Thucydides comments:

> Such was the effect on the Athenians of their present good fortune that they thought that nothing could go wrong with them; that the possible and the difficult were alike attainable, whether the forces employed were large or wholly inadequate. It was their surprising success in most directions which caused this state of mind and suggested to them that their strength was equal with their hopes.

This, I believe, was the audience to which Herodotus directed his moral, delivered to King Croesus from the mouth of the Athenian sage, Solon: "Look to the end, no matter what it is you are considering. Often enough God gives a man a glimpse of happiness, and then utterly ruins him."[79]

The past animated public policy, and Athens of all places had the most numerous and well established of institutions for reenacting the past before a wide public. Under the Athenian democracy, especially from the era of Pericles on, Athens had the most developed institutions for converting public animus into state policy. Herodotus' project was a logical outgrowth of this milieu, placing his own wide learning and that of his predecessors and contemporaries, especially the Greeks of Ionia who had endured other forms of tyranny and remembered other forms of empire, into an account that comprehended the most potent Hellenic icon of the past, the Persian Wars down to the creation of the Athenian empire. Thucydides was among those Athenians who experienced the disturbing consequences of political power driven by, among other things, this very icon. Among the ways in which Athenian intellectuals of this era chose to come to grips with the profound changes of their time, Thucydides chose the model pioneered by Herodotus. But in doing so, he attempted a radical departure from the mode of Herodotus' discourse. Herodotus assembled truths that converged from all directions, including from myth and fable, on the world as seen by Greeks of his day. To Thucydides, such accounts partook too much of "stories of the past that people ... uncritically accept from each other," or that "poets have sung with exaggerated embellishments," or that "speech-writers composed with more attention to persuading their listeners than to telling the truth." His exacting standards constrained him to write, he claimed, only about events that he or his informants had experienced directly, and that were therefore not subject to any of the filters of official or popular recollection.[80]

The remainder of this book is an examination of the audience that Herodotus addressed, and of the circumstances that impelled a member of that audience, Thucydides, to further refine his critical approach to the past. The inquiry will lead, by the final chapter, to a new argument about Thucydides' means and motives for writing history. To reach that point, we need to follow an analytical narrative of events down to the time that Thucydides wrote, particularly bridging the gap between the point at which, in 411, Thucydides left his history unfinished, and the point from which, after the surrender of Athens in 404, Thucydides attests that he wrote. The next two chapters examine prevailing conditions, especially ideological conditions, at Athens in the 420s, when Thucydides participated in Athenian politics before his banishment in 424/3. The fourth chapter begins, in Part II, the thread of narrative from the point at which the aspirations of 424, described above, were at last put in motion in the scheme to conquer Sicily.

CHAPTER TWO

The Aristocracy of Democratic Athens

"The admiration of the present and succeeding ages will be ours, since we have not left our power without witness, but have shown it by mighty proofs. . . . "

PERICLES, IN THUCYDIDES 2.41.4*

THE PRIVILEGES OF EMPIRE

Athens at the height of its empire, by the middle of the fifth century, was a community endowed like no other of its day with opportunities for it members to enjoy both material prosperity and communal glory. The opportunities extended to all echelons of Athenian society. Munificence in the form of public pay for a wide range of duties and services, and land for settlement in conquered territories, radically transformed the lives and livelihoods of the poorer citizens. It also fueled the quest for individual distinction within a sizable class of comparatively well-to-do Athenians. Empire was the source of the power and the revenues, at a scale previously unheard of among Greek states, that made this possible. More than any other subject, the business of empire pervaded the assemblies of Athens in all their political, judicial, festival, commemorative, and military varieties, and provided Athenians with a common political purpose.[1]

The empowerment of the less affluent majority of citizens through democracy and empire was the most remarkable achievement of fifth-century Athens. A tradition of citizenship that embraced rich and poor alike had long been affirmed by the laws of Solon and confirmed by the aristocratic patronage of the Peisistratids and Cleisthenes. Political empowerment of the entire citizenry reached its most developed level within the democracy that grew from the reforms of Ephialtes in the late 460s and the liberal policies promoted by Pericles in the following decades. This empowerment was connected to the reliance of Athens on its navy, where many poorer Athenians gained their pay, and through which the revenues

*Translated by R. Crawley.

of empire were assured. By constant reminders that their toils secured their own benefits, the majority of Athenians were encouraged to identify their democracy with their empire.[2]

Among the well-to-do of Athens, empire was also widely perceived as a prize worth defending, for it was both a source of material enrichment and an arena for the construction of personal prestige. As the poor benefited from territories acquired abroad, the wealthy benefited still more, for they had the capital to make their personal income grow. Those with real holdings could secure income by leasing out property or agricultural land, both in Attica and abroad. Those with surplus income could multiply it by astute investment in such areas as agricultural futures, tax-farming, mining concessions, and mercantile ventures. Such opportunities, while not exclusive to the wealthy of Athens, were more accessible and secure to Athenians within the orbit of lands, harbors, and trade routes dominated and protected by the navy, and the law courts, of Athens.[3]

The empire also provided a less tangible but no less potent incentive to channel the energies of the well-to-do and the ambitious. For imperial Athens was as rich in the currency of praise and esteem as it was in material opportunities. Although public commemorations of a myth-historical Athenian past tended to suppress the glorification of individuals, each day the pursuit of the people's business afforded opportunities for the ambitious to distinguish themselves in living fame as champions of the political agenda of the democracy, as war-leaders of the empire, and as patrons of the festivals of Athens.

Pericles, whose leadership spanned the apex of the empire, best articulated the complex union of personal and collective aspirations that defined the Athenian imperial democracy. The ability of Pericles to embrace all alike in a vision of communal glory was recalled by Thucydides in his funeral oration, represented in the quote at the head of this chapter, as it also was by Plato in his portrayal of the transports of rhetoric in his *Menexenus,* quoted in the previous chapter. Even at the height of his career, however, Pericles was not without his detractors. But after 450 the only sign of a rival vision of the destiny of Athens emerged briefly in the debate with Thucydides son of Melesias over the use of imperial revenues for the Parthenon and the great building program advocated by Pericles in the 440s. Even this debate might have been submerged beneath the memory of time had it not been for the opening of a deeper division within the social fabric of the Athenian democracy toward the end of Pericles' career.[4]

The split opened in the debate over the Spartan demand, in 432, that the Athenians make unilateral concessions to the grievances of the friends and allies of Sparta. In the name of rightful dominion and the preservation of Athenian liberty, Pericles advised the Athenians to refuse the Spartan demand. The war that followed was the first serious and sustained challenge to the Athenian vision of empire. The Peloponnesian War opened a rift between those Athenians who saw war as the proving ground for the strength of imperial democracy and those who saw war as the descent into the insatiable maw of a mindless rabble. The division was not so much between rich and poor Athenians, although this was the dimension in which it became most apparent. The battle was fought in political contests among those of the well-to-do who contended for positions of authority and leadership in the Athenian democracy. Its eventual effect was the overthrow of democracy.[5]

This and the following chapter trace the development of this division within the Athenian upper class in the first decade of the Peloponnesian War. The development is discussed here not so much in chronological terms as it is synoptically, in terms of the ideals that had, for a generation and more, largely united Athenians of all social standings, but which began to divide them under the acute pressures of war in the 420s. The motive at the core of this rupture was an ancient one. It was the competitive quest for distinction among those who considered themselves, both publicly and privately, to be among the *aristoi,* "the best," of the Athenians.

THE BEST OF THE ATHENIANS

Aristocracy is a blend of habitual and consciously asserted behavior, the result of an individual's upbringing, the privileged material conditions that support it, and the group of like-behaving, like-minded individuals with whom one associates. The naturally endowed conditions of birth and kinship are clearly essential features of aristocracy, as they play fundamental roles in upbringing, material conditions, and group formation. But conscious choice plays an equally essential role in defining an aristocracy. Birth and kinship are the results of marriage unions, created and sustained in response to peer approval. Often enough, deliberate choices so transform the relations of individuals that even natal unions do not remain dominant factors in upbringing, material conditions, and group association. Aristocratic ideology, however, tends to disguise such purposefully modified relationships, for it is characteristic of an aristocracy to claim that the qualities that it prizes are endowed by birth and by nature.

Aristocracy is thus both a generalized ideal and the sum of the shifting individual circumstances of those who claim to partake of it. To understand the historical dynamics of the aristocracy of democratic Athens, we must appreciate not only the relationship between aristocratic and democratic ideals, but also something of the variety of the individual circumstances of those who aspired to be included among "the best" of the Athenians. Above all, we must recognize the manner in which the democracy and empire of Athens provided roles that served the aspirations of the Athenian upper class, and how those roles changed in the course of events.

The picture of the Athenian aristocracy developed in this chapter is a composite drawn from a variety of sources that comment on the relationship between ideals and individual aspirations. Although the singular examples of prominent men like Pericles, Nicias, and Alcibiades stand out in this account, a richer and perhaps more representative context emerges from the incidental details of relationships among men who gathered on various occasions in the company of Socrates, as known to us above all from the writings of one of his youngest associates, Plato.[6]

Plato was born in 428/7 to a well-connected but only moderately endowed Athenian family. His father, Ariston son of Aristocles, was said to be a descendant of the ancient Neleid kings of Athens. At the time of Plato's birth, Ariston's property consisted of a landholding, or cleruchy, granted to him by the Athenian state on the island of Aegina, where Athenians had been settled in 431 following the expulsion of the Aeginetans. Plato's mother, Perictione daughter of Glaucon, was from an equally distinguished but more prosperous line praised in the poems of Solon, Anacreon, and others, and whose living members included Perictione's cousin, Critias son of Callaeschrus. Plato's older brothers, Glaucon and Adeimantus, later distinguished themselves in battle at Megara, probably in 409, and were celebrated in an elegiac poem that began, according to Plato: "Sons of Ariston, whose race from a glorious sire is godlike...." Ariston did not live to see his sons' moment of glory, however, for he had died when they were young, and their mother remarried. Her second husband was her own maternal uncle, the wealthy Pyrilampes, an associate of Pericles according to comic poets, and well known for his service as ambassador to the Persian court. Plato's older step-brother, Demus, also distinguished himself as an ambassador, while his younger half-brother, Antiphon, was known to occupy himself with horse-keeping. Among the attributes of an aristocracy, according to Aristotle, is the nobility of those with recognized high standing combined with wealth, both sustained over generations. By this standard, Plato was on the cusp of nobility, and was well positioned to contend for recognition among the aristocracy of Athens.[7]

Nobility was personified in the youthful beauty and cultivated intellect of Perictione's brother and Plato's uncle, Charmides son of Glaucon, as depicted in the dialogue bearing his name set a few years before Plato's birth. An object of pride to his older cousin, Critias, Charmides' striking beauty made him instantly the center of attention of his age-mates and admired by older men like Socrates, who looked forward to his company in the private wrestling-ground of Taureas where friends met to work out and to talk. Past the age of elementary education in writing, athletics, and music, Charmides was already a respectable poet and pursuer of wisdom. He was regarded as a paragon of *sophrosyne*—a subtle concept, describing temperate behavior. His gifts entitled him to display them appropriately, always with deference to his elders. In sum, Charmides had the tact and talent and the network of influential relatives and friends that would enable him to rise in esteem and would entitle him to seek, with maturity, a prominent place in the politics of Athens. He achieved this goal briefly at the end of his life, as a protagonist with his cousin Critias of the second oligarchic revolution at Athens. The tension between his aristocratic ideals and the democratic political order in which he grew up marks the great fault line in the social foundations of political power at Athens that was building pressure throughout the youth of Plato.[8]

The vignette preserved by Plato of Charmides at the prime of his youth is symptomatic of a preoccupation with the complex of traits that defined *arete,* "excellence," discernible among privileged Athenians in the decade of Plato's birth. These traits included nobility of birth *(eugeneia),* upbringing *(paideia),* and wealth *(ploutos).* Debate about the comparative importance of birth and education, the teachability of virtue, and the relation of wealth to merit, is well attested in the circles of influence with which Plato identified himself. Although these topics already had a long tradition in Greek literature by Plato's day, they were taken up with unprecedented interest in both private circles and in public discourse, as seen in Plato's Socratic dialogues and in contemporary tragedy and comedy, at Athens in the era of the Peloponnesian War.[9]

The cultivation of *arete* was the pursuit of reputation. Reputation was malleable, shaped by those who spoke of it and always subject to the buffeting of envy. There were few ways beyond deeds and demeanor by which an aspirant for good repute could influence talk. But it was a great advantage if talk had to take account of a prevailing favorable opinion about one's family and ancestors. Among peers, where rivalries were keenest and even slight advantages were treasured, it helped immeasurably in the pursuit of distinction if one could cite notice of one's ancestors in the verses of a famous poet, as Critias and Charmides could. Having one's own reputation embedded in poetry was so much the better. Although the days of public praise-singing for great Athenians had passed with Themistocles, the tradition was kept alive in private circles, as attested in the elegy in praise of Plato's brothers, cited above. Composing poetry was itself a competitive art, and giving praise well in poetry was praiseworthy itself, as Pindar had been fond of noticing. So Charmides and Critias were themselves poets, as was Plato in his youth. In favoring prose expression in his mature years, Plato nevertheless took the opportunity to affirm discreetly his own nobility by referring in his writings to the traditional tokens of the poetic esteem granted to his kinsmen.[10]

The occasions for such mutual exchanges of esteem were the gatherings of friends and peers such as we find in the works of Plato and his age-mate, Xenophon son of Gryllus. These gatherings might be associated with a display of physical or intellectual excellence by an acknowledged virtuoso, as portrayed in Plato's *Laches, Protagoras, Gorgias, Hippias* 1 and 2, and *Euthy-*

demus. Or they might develop impromptu, as in the wrestling-ground of Taureas, or in the similar settings depicted in Plato's *Lysis* and *Euthydemus*, when friends gathered to admire the emergent excellence of youths. Likewise they might follow from public gatherings, like the festival of Bendis as depicted in the first book of the *Republic*, where athletic competitions impelled the admirers of beauty and prowess to gather. Plato is said to have been drawn into Socrates' company when the two met on the occasion of the Dionysia, the dramatic festival, in which Plato hoped to compete. The interplay of esteem was most active in the privacy of the dining room, when friends and invited guests dined and toasted a triumphant champion, as in the dinner celebrating the tragic poet Agathon's victory at a dramatic competition, depicted in Plato's *Symposium*. In Xenophon's dialogue of the same name, a similar gathering is shown at the dinner hosted by the wealthy Callias son of Hipponicus, to celebrate Autolycus son of Lycon for his victory in the boys' athletic competitions at the Panathenaic festival.[11]

These, in the memory of Plato and Xenophon, were natural occasions for the celebration of *arete*. Such gatherings tended to define a community of men of leisure, busy with the pursuit, or in observing the pursuit, of *arete*. These were gatherings of men who had achieved some sort of standing in the culture of esteem, and of still more young men who were eager to learn and to make their marks in these circles, and together they constituted a sub-community within the greater community of all Athenians. They were private groups, not public gatherings, although public occasions often provided the incentive for them to convene. By their reverence for excellence they spurned the commonplace, and affirmed all that made their members better than common folk.

As long as *arete* was perceived to be the quality of individuals striving to outshine one another, it was no threat to the pan-Athenian ideology of excellence that had prevailed in public discourse since the time of Themistocles. The glory of Athens, in the view of Pericles shared by most Athenians, was constantly renewed by the demonstrations of the *arete* of its best citizens. But when Athenian preeminence was put to the test in war against Sparta in 431, and the fallibility of the Athenian *demos* began to appear, it became possible to question the identification of *arete* with Athenian democracy. Although this challenge from within did not manifest itself politically until 415, its growing presence is revealed by new expressions of behavior and thought displayed, beginning in the 420s, by those Athenians who regarded themselves "the best."

THE PUBLIC DISPLAY OF PRIVATE *ARETE*

By the early 420s, a variety of new terms and concepts gained currency to express and to make visible new forms of group identity, all of them implicitly at odds with the egalitarian ideal of Athenian democracy. The societies depicted in the Socratic dialogues named above were cultivating a form of elitism constructed around highly personalized and explicitly *not* pan-Athenian traits. This pursuit had a new name, *kalokagathia,* or the fellowship of the *kaloi k'agathoi,* the "beautiful and the good." Although rooted in ancient concepts, the specific terminology of *kalokagathia* first appears in the 420s, in Aristophanes and in Herodotus, confirming its appropriateness in Plato's dialogues set in that decade. Fascination for the manifest excellence and captivating power of physical beauty was the most salient trait of these groups of privileged Athenians. Plato depicts Socrates both sharing this fascination and probing its implications for the meaning of excellence.[12]

Visible beauty as the sign of transcendent excellence was also commemorated at this time in a renewed interest in the display of private funerary monuments by the well-to-do of Athens and Attica. The "end of restraint, c. 425 B.C.," as Ian Morris terms it, has been most frequently noticed for the introduction, after a hiatus of more than a half-century, of elaborate funerary sculpture. The idealized human form perfected in the sculptures of the Parthenon was now appropriated for the representation of deceased Athenians whose families could afford such lavish displays (see frontispiece and figure 11 on page 314 for examples dating close to 400). The reason for this "end of restraint" has long seemed problematic and obscure, but it is surely to be explained as a manifestation of the *kalokagathia* that began to preoccupy the Athenian elite with the commencement of war in 431.[13]

More than a decorative phenomenon, the "end of restraint" as observed by Morris entailed a systematic change in the burial practices of the wealthy. Not only did sculpted monuments once again evoke personalized affections for departed individuals, as rich archaic monuments once had done, but families now more visibly asserted their identities by the clustering of monuments and the erection of conspicuous enclosures around family graves. The archaeological evidence in some cases demonstrates that these were embellishments added to family burial grounds that had been in use for many generations. One such instance of continuity in the Kerameikos cemetery was marked by what Morris describes as a "self-consciously 'Homeric' cremation" and elaborate burial of an adult male in the 420s.[14]

Where, for half a century, ostentatious burial rites had been reserved only for the communal funerals of Athenian war-dead, elite display now returned. It did not displace the public memorials, however, for they too became grander and more elaborate (see figure 2). But private identity, using some of the same symbols that the state had previously monopolized, now openly competed with communal identity.

The assertion of *kalokagathia* by mutual affirmation within elite society and in publicly displayed monuments beginning in the 420s was in part a

FIGURE 2. Heroic *arete* in battle: the Albani relief, showing an Athenian cavalryman striking a fallen enemy, possibly from a public monument for the war-dead at Athens, usually dated ca. 430–425. Rome, Villa Albani no. 985. Photo courtesy of the Deutsches Archäologisches Institut, Rome, neg. no. 62.696.

reaction to the suppression of the most important traditional outlet for the display of aristocratic *arete:* the martial valor of the warrior class. The Periclean policy of avoiding battle with the Peloponnesian invaders of Attica, beginning in 431, was one of more explicit signs of the subordination of aristocratic values to democratic policies under wartime conditions. The tension that this generated will be discussed in the next chapter. Here we will note the vitality of the yearning among Athenians who sought, on the eve of the Peloponnesian War and throughout its course, to impersonate the heroism of Homeric warriors whenever and wherever the opportunity presented itself.

PROWESS IN WAR

Esteem privately cherished was most valued when it was gained before the widest public. Capable Athenians could pursue reputation in a variety of public endeavors, but the prospect of emulating ancestors by winning glory in war was especially enticing to the ambitious, most of all to those who had not yet had the opportunity to prove themselves. War on the frontiers of empire provided a suitably grand setting to rival the deeds of legend. The revenues of empire made large-scale warfare possible, when sanctioned by the will of the *demos.*

On the eve of the Peloponnesian War, the revolt of Potidaea in Thrace provided the "best" of the Athenian hoplite soldiery the chance to prove themselves in battle. Arrayed against them were troops led by the Corinthian Aristeus, son of the reviled Adeimantus whom the Athenians had accused, along with his countrymen, of cowardice at the battle of Salamis. In 432, after these two sides met in a sharp but inconclusive battle, the campaign against Potidaea settled into a grueling two-and-a-half-year siege. Yet even under such inglorious conditions the Athenians maintained their forces at a rate of pay that befitted the self-esteem of men of honor. Sailors of the fleet supporting the siege were receiving a drachma a day—a handsome wage—for year-round service, while the Athenian hoplites received two, one for themselves, Thucydides explains, and one for their servants. Such a subvention for the infantry service of a slave-owning class was never heard of, before or after the siege of Potidaea. Three thousand hoplites and some six thousand sailors were maintained in this way for the duration of the siege, with substantial occasional reinforcements. By the time Potidaea surrendered, in the winter of 430/29, the siege had cost the Athenian treasury two thousand talents. This was far more than the cost of the Parthenon, and probably the equivalent the entire expenditure for the Periclean building program of the 440s and 430s.[15]

Socrates had fought at Potidaea, and the opening of the *Charmides* describes the occasion of his homecoming, where the first topic of his conversation among the *kaloi k'agathoi* at Taureas' gymnasium was news of the war. Prominent among the exploits that Socrates had to tell of was the heroism of young Alcibiades son of Cleinias, ward of Pericles. Making his debut in battle at the age of 18 or 19, Alcibiades made a brave showing but had fallen wounded. After the battle he was awarded the *aristeion,* a prize of a panoply of armor, for his bravery.[16]

Such a formality evoked a Homeric sense of prowess and encouraged others to aspire to display skillful panache in single combat. Two of Plato's dialogues take, as a point of departure for the discussion of teachable virtues, the example of instructors in the arts of dueling in armor who frequented the gymnasia of the well-to-do, offering their services for hire. Those who sought out training in such skills might hope to be honored like Alcibiades and to achieve, with him, the fame of the winners of *aristeia* in the Persian Wars, and possibly even to rival the storied feats of the Achaeans at Troy. Contemporary testimony confirms that Homeric imagery pervaded the thoughts of many of Alcibiades' peers. In Xenophon's *Symposium,* Niceratus son of Nicias, the distinguished general, recounts, "My father was so anxious that I should prove myself a good man *(aner agathos)* that he compelled me to learn all of Homer. And now I can recite the entire *Iliad* and the *Odyssey* by heart."[17]

Emulation of Homeric heroes went hand-in-hand with the thirst for splendid armor, helmets, crests, and shield-blazons. Such tokens of individuality were extravagances of the well-to-do in an era when service as a heavily-armed hoplite infantryman required little more than a serviceable shield, a stiff felt cap, a set of spears, and a short sword as side-arm. Aristophanes, in his comic celebration of *Peace* at the Dionysia of 421, makes fun of the arms manufacturers who will be put out of business by peace. Aside from the spear-shaft scraper, whose trade depended on volume, those most distraught are the dealers in status items: the helmet-seller, the crest-maker, and, treated with greatest comic effect, the maker of expensive body-armor. Immediately after dismissing these arms dealers, significantly, Aristophanes' protagonist has to dissuade members of a boys' chorus from singing warlike verses from Homer and other traditional poets.[18]

It is hardly likely that either the passion for Homer or the manufacture of prestige emblems ever actually languished. The urge to display martial excellence certainly contributed to the enthusiasm for the Athenian decision to invade Sicily in 415. Thucydides describes the exceptional preparations made on that occasion for the dispatch of "the finest-looking force of Hellenic troops that up to that time had ever come from a single city." It even outstripped, he notes, the forces mobilized at the high point of the Potidaea campaign.

> The fleet was in a high state of efficiency and had cost a lot of money to both the captains and the State. Every sailor received a drachma a day from the Treasury, which also provided empty ships . . . all manned with the best crews available. The captains, too, offered extra pay, in addition to that provided by the State . . . and they went to great expense on figure-heads and general fittings, every one of them being as anxious as possible that his own ship should stand out from the rest for its fine looks and for its speed. As for the land forces, they had been chosen from the best men who were liable for calling-up, and there had been much rivalry and much pains spent by everyone on his armor and personal equipment. It therefore happened that there was not only all this competition among the Athenians themselves, each in his own particular area of responsibility, but to the rest of Hellas it looked more like a demonstration of the power and greatness of Athens than an expeditionary force setting out against the enemy.[19]

In the second year of the Sicilian campaign, the general Lamachus son of Xenophanes, famous for his splendid crests and gorgon-faced shield-blazons, ended his life outside of Syracuse in an encounter that could have been choreographed by a Homeric rhapsode, though the glory is all in the telling. As Thucydides narrates it, Lamachus led a counterattack across a ditch in front of Athenian lines with a few men and was cut down by the enemy cavalry. Plutarch adds details that likely come from the contemporary and possibly eyewitness account of Philistus:

> One of the most redoubtable and daring of the Syracusan officers, named Callicrates, called out Lamachus to single combat. The Athenian general accepted the challenge, came forward and received the first thrust, but succeeded in closing with his adversary and returning the blow, so that he and Callicrates fell together. The Syracusans gained possession of his body with its armor and carried it off....[20]

Lamachus died as he had lived, seeking the singular moment of encounter that would raise him to the company of the legendary heroes who fought at Troy. To carry on the tradition, he left behind him a son with a suitably Homeric name, Tydeus.[21]

Such examples show men of privilege among this generation of Athenians ever mindful of the glory to be won by deeds of personal valor in war. More than poetry fed this longing, for among the monuments marking the common graves of Athenian war-dead outside the city, Athenians could also contemplate the graves of celebrated individuals of the recent past, like Sophanes of Decelea, slayer of the Olympic pentathlete, Eurybates of Argos, or Pythion of Megara, whose grave stele at Athens boasted that he "slew seven men and broke seven spears in their bodies." Somewhere in their company was the grave of Tellus, who long ago had "achieved the fairest of deaths" turning back the foemen of his city in battle, and leaving behind him sons who had already grown to esteem among the *kaloi k'agathoi.* Not all the wealth of Croesus, as Herodotus told the story to approving listeners at Athens, could give a man greater happiness than that enjoyed by Tellus.[22]

THE IMPRESSION OF POWER

The competitive quality of *arete* made it an exceptionally useful social force, motivating not only bravery in battle but also various forms of public service. The Athenian state controlled access to the chief roles through which capable Athenians could gratify their personal ambitions. Pride was most directly displayed by the victors in public games and contests, for they and their fellow tribesman were authorized to celebrate personal *arete* in public monuments to their victories. Appointment to office was also a matter of pride, even when offices were awarded by allotment, since all appointments had to pass peer review. Many a public officer had his name inscribed on either a dedication commemorating his term of office or on a public inscription recording official transactions during his tenure of office. Personal abilities were most closely connected to military offices, which, in view of the skills required, remained elective.

The drive for competitive distinction was especially valuable, in democratic Athens, when it motivated private expenditure for public causes. By performing *leitourgiai,* liturgies or "works for the people," wealthy individuals managed many aspects of the Athenians' most costly recurring military and religious enterprises. In both areas, expenditures from public funds assured that minimally acceptable standards were maintained, but private expenditure and liability were considerable. Those capable of bearing these responsibilities could justly claim inclusion in the class of social elite who called themselves *dunatoi,* the "capable ones," or *chrestoi,* the "useful" or "worthy ones," or *plousioi,* the "wealthy."[23]

From a later generation, it was possible for the aging Isocrates to reminisce about the competitive pride of "the capable" Athenians of his youth in the 420s:

> When I was a boy, to be wealthy was thought to be so secure and dignified that practically everyone pretended to have more wealth than they actually had, since they wanted to enjoy the prestige it gave. Now, however, a man has to be ready to defend himself against the charge of being rich as if it were among the greatest of crimes, and he must keep a sharp watch if he is to save himself. For it has become far more dangerous to be thought of as a man of means than to commit blatant crimes.

Isocrates' perspective was not merely the bitterness of old age. His parents' generation had enjoyed an era of burgeoning opportunities for Athenians. Many had sought to build prestige through displays of munificence, and to do so they had availed themselves of the increasingly common means of converting one's resources into cash, especially through loans. In the process, the archaic image of "being wealthy," *to ploutein,* as possessing the produce of one's own land or a store of goods in kind, gave way to the more fluid notion of "having means," *to euporein.* Wartime, however, both drove the demands for liquid capital higher and rendered its securities, especially in rural land, overseas holdings, and mercantile ventures, less stable. Some of those who struggled to make their means meet their ambitions were caught in the press, and were ruined. Isocrates expresses the cynicism of an age that matured quickly in the late fifth century, where those struggling near the threshold of wealth faced the dilemma of exposing their vulnerable means to the demands of public service. Investments might fail and make fulfillment of public obligations impossible. Under such conditions some might choose to keep their private revenues from public view.[24]

Those who succeeded conspicuously in the business of moneymaking found it difficult to escape the jealousy of their less fortunate peers. Plato frequently acknowledges the widespread preoccupation of his peers with moneymaking, but insinuates that this kind of success was not a mark of true worth. In the face of such cynicism, those who could afford to do so struggled all the more to convert their personal prosperity into irreproachable forms of meritorious and magnificent public service.[25]

The most prestigious military liturgy was the trierarchy, or the management of a warship for a year. The ship and its gear were provided by the state, as was basic pay for the crew, but the trierarch had to maintain the ship, hire the crew, and make good on all essential expenses, even, as need arose, those for which the public treasury was liable. The trierarchy could be a repeated and sometimes an exceedingly costly undertaking. Those who could afford to make a splendid showing of their ship took especial pride in this display, but few could sustain the expense.[26]

Sponsorship of a festival chorus, or *choregia*, was another opportunity for the ambitious and the proud to seek public affirmation. As a rule, a *choregia* in a particular festival was assigned to a liturgist only once in his lifetime for any given category of performance. Liturgists therefore offered themselves as candidates for selection by the archon when they were best prepared to provide their tribal dance or theatrical troupe with lavish ornaments and costumes and to hire the best actors and accompanists money could buy. With only one opportunity to make their mark in each competition, those with the highest political ambitions went to great lengths to have their prominence confirmed in festal competition.[27]

Nicias son of Niceratus was a man ambitious for public distinction in the 420s and able to pursue it with the fortune he made as a contractor of slave gangs in the Attic silver mines. To augment the successes of his military career, Nicias relied on his wealth to compensate in popular esteem for what he lacked in charisma as a speaker. Among his many choregic victories and public displays the most memorable was his sponsorship of a *theoria*, a sacred embassy and chorus, sent to Apollo's shrine at Delos. The occasion probably marked the purification of Delos in 426/5, when the Athenians gave thanks to Apollo and Artemis for the abatement of the plague that had ravaged Athens for much of the previous four years. Representing imperial Athens in an assembly of Ionians, and demonstrating to all the undiminished capacity of Athenians to offer proud and pious display, Nicias' *theoria* surpassed all precedent in its magnificent procession and choreography, in its generous public feasting, and in its monuments, including an endowment to perpetuate the offerings and feasts in Apollo's name. These benefactions were all the more memorable for Nicias' supreme misfortune later as commander of the doomed Sicilian invasion. Yet even in tragedy (or perhaps because of it) he succeeded in winning the honorable recognition he aspired to in life. After reporting his execution by the Syracusans, Thucydides remarks that Nicias, "of all the Hellenes in my time, least deserved to come to so miserable an end, since he was completely devoted to earning a reputation for *arete*."[28]

Magnificence displayed at personal initiative was essential to projecting the greatness of the Athenian state. But magnificence too highly personalized, as Themistocles learned, could turn public admiration to fear and hostility, and arouse personal rivals to acts of spite and malice. Nicias' deferential and pious character made his useful magnificence tolerable to most Athenians. His sometime rival, Alcibiades, on the other hand, devoted his gifts of noble birth, beauty, wealth, and charisma to building an unrivaled reputation through the customary honors of office, public service, and competition for prizes at Athens and abroad. Replacing Nicias' all-encompassing piety with an opportunistic boldness, Alcibiades became the most admired and the most feared Athenian of his generation.

The opening of Alcibiades' speech advocating the invasion of Sicily, as portrayed by Thucydides, is the most powerful argument for the communal value of personal *arete* outside of the poetry of Pindar:

> Athenians, I have a better right to command than others—I must begin with this as Nicias has attacked me—and at the same time I believe myself to be worthy of it. The things for which I am abused bring fame to my ancestors and to myself, and to the country profit besides. The Hellenes, after expecting to see our city ruined by the war, concluded it to be even greater than it really is, by reason of the magnificence with which I represented it at the Olympic Games, when I sent into the lists seven chariots, a number never before entered by any private person, and won the first prize, and was second and fourth, and took care to have everything else in a style worthy of my victory. Custom regards such displays as honorable, and they cannot be made without leaving behind them an impression of power. Again, any splendor that I may have exhibited at home in providing choruses or otherwise is naturally envied by my fellow citizens, but in the eyes of foreigners has an air of strength as in the other instance. And this is no useless folly, when a man at his own private cost benefits not himself only, but the city: nor is it unfair that he who prides himself on his position should refuse to be on an equality with the rest.[29]

The envy of fellow citizens accompanied Alcibiades throughout his years of prominence and was only encouraged by his custom of responding to any affront by an ever bolder assertion of his indomitability. On the occasion of one of his choral liturgies, according to later accounts, a rival challenged the legitimacy of a member of Alcibiades' chorus. Alcibiades responded by slapping the competing choral sponsor on the head. He then went on to win the victory prize in the contest, and the affront went unpunished, even unremarked except by his rival and that man's friends. The man so treated was Taureas, a kinsman of Critias and a second cousin of Andocides son of Leogoras and the owner of the gymnasium in which Plato depicted the meeting of Charmides and Socrates.[30]

Alcibiades' greatest formal prize was won through competition in Panhellenic games. As his son later boasted, Alcibiades did not compete in gymnastic contests, "for he knew that some of the athletes were of low birth, inhabitants of petty states, and of mean education." Rather, he contended in the four-horse chariot race, "which is the occupation of those most favored by fortune, not to be pursued by one of low estate." Following victories in preceding years at the Pythian and Nemean games, at the Olympic festival of 416 Alcibiades entered an unprecedented fleet of seven chariots drawn by twenty-eight horses and, as he boasts in the speech quoted above, he swept nearly all honors.

One of the teams that Alcibiades entered at Olympia, according to some the winning team, was paid for by a friend, Teisias son of Teisimachus, who afterward came to resent that Alcibiades had claimed the team as his own entry. In light of later events, this issue became grounds for a legal suit. At the time, however, no such quibble stood in the way of Alcibiades' quest for fame. Like other Athenian victors at the Panhellenic games, Alcibiades was entitled to receive the honor of public hospitality alongside the descendants of Harmodius and Aristogeiton on any occasion when distinguished guests were entertained in a state banquet at Athens. Although he himself did not remain in Athens long enough to enjoy this perquisite often, he saw to it that his presence was remembered in one of the most famous banquet halls at Athens. In the banquet room in the Propylaea of the Acropolis, Alcibiades dedicated two paintings of himself commemorating his equestrian victories. These were perhaps the first examples of self-commissioned portraiture at democratic Athens.[31]

THE BEST OF THE GREEKS

Such singular examples stand out in any account of personal achievement among the Greeks, but an estimate of the overall number of Athenians who could commit their private means to public services is the primary basis for the claim that the *aristoi* of the Athenians were indeed the "best" of the Greeks.

By the beginning of the Peloponnesian War, every year 300 of the wealthiest Athenians assumed individual responsibility for maintaining a trireme and its 200-man crew. By no means all trierarchs saw active duty in a given year (250 in service in 428 was reported by Thucydides as an exceptionally high number), but the actual number of men available to serve as trierarchs had to be much larger than 300. The expense of a year of trierarchic service entitled one to a year of exemption, and at some point during the Peloponnesian War this became two years of exemption. Moreover, in recognition of the mounting expenses of prolonged naval campaigns, within the last few years of the war it became possible for two men to jointly finance a single trireme. No firm numbers of Athenians liable for trierarchy can be derived from this information, since among other variables not all

Athenians eligible for exemptions claimed them (it was a matter of pride for the wealthy to boast of uninterrupted trierarchic service); but some useful approximations can be worked out.

With up to 250 ships potentially in service, at least 500 Athenians had to be capable of trading off year-to-year trierarchic duties; a two-year exemption and the joint-trierarchy meant that considerably more than 500 could be counted on to command Athenian ships. Vincent Gabrielsen has estimated that Athens had some 900 eligible trierarchs in the last years of the fifth century, but since this estimate uses the unique maximum of 250 in active service and assumes that all trierarchs exercised their full rights to exemptions—both conditions demonstrably untrue during the difficult final years of the Peloponnesian War—this number is probably too high. Perhaps 700 is nearer the number of Athenians who shared among themselves the most expensive of the burdens of military service.[32]

In addition to the trierarchy, approximately 100 festival liturgies had to be fulfilled each year, and these too entitled their bearers to exemption from consecutive service, as well as from simultaneous trierarchic service. The expense of sponsoring a tragic or dithyrambic chorus at the Dionysia, with costumes, accompanists, and, in the event of success, a victory monument, could be comparable to that of a trierarchy, but the majority of choral or gymnastic liturgies and other public entertainments were less expensive. Notionally, some 200 Athenians had to be available to trade off annual festival liturgies in addition to those rotating through the duties of the trierarchy. But since those eligible for the trierarchy made up a much larger pool of candidates that overlapped those liable for festival liturgies, it would be reasonable to take 800 as a rough minimum for the number of individuals who were capable of undertaking all the liturgies that implied wealth and brought public distinction at Athens in the late fifth century.[33]

Many more than these 800 Athenians might claim to be wealthy individuals, however. Those called upon to pay, the liturgists, were heads of household who controlled their family estates. Family property known to have supported liturgies in the past was both a token of ancestral excellence and an incentive to its heirs to sustain an established reputation for public service. The importance of this incentive was the reason why the primary judicial duties of the eponymous archon, the most honorable executive officer of the state, concerned the disposition of inheritances. Most men who possessed estates of liturgical status (women or orphaned minors temporarily in control of an estate were specifically exempted from liturgies) and who were over 50 years of age will have had adult sons or sons-in-law who only became liturgists when they inherited the family estate or, as sometimes happened with exceptionally large estates, when they received a share of their patrimony from their father. A demographic model, derived from early modern pre-industrial population statistics and applied to classical

Athens by Mogens Hansen, indicates that men 50 years old and older made up approximately 21.4 percent of the male population above the age of 19 (when eligibility for liturgy began). Using this percentage, we may estimate that 170 of the 800 liturgists were at least 50 years old. If each of these men had an adult son, natural or adopted, or a son-in-law, then there were at least 170 additional adult males who could be considered wealthy by lifestyle and family connection, but who were *not* themselves liable for liturgy; Plato and his brothers, the stepsons of Pyrilampes, are examples of this group. Our number of notionally wealthy Athenians thus approaches 1,000; but in fact it is even larger.[34]

From shortly before the Peloponnesian War, 1,000 Athenian men of more than moderate means kept themselves and a horse in shape for service in the cavalry of Athens. Horse-rearing was widely recognized as an aristocratic distinction, and although the Athenian state provided a loan for the purchase of a suitable mount and paid an allowance for fodder while a cavalryman was in active service, Athenian cavalry required a certain level of personal wealth as well as the leisure to tend a horse. Candidates also had to pass an examination of their qualifications for service that was certainly influenced by such factors as ancestry, attendance to duty, and moral character. Cavalry service entailed exemption from liturgies for those who were otherwise qualified for liturgical service, although most cavalrymen were probably below this rank of wealth. Adding the Athenian cavalry and a modest number of eligible replacements (including the sons of liturgists) brings this tally of the late fifth-century Athenian aristocracy up to a minimum of 2,000.[35]

In fact, considering that each year members of the Athenian upper class filled the offices of archons, treasurers, military commanders, priests, and many of the seats among the 500 members of the Council, to say nothing of ad hoc commissions such as ambassadors, the number of *aristoi* needed for continuing service in all of the above categories must have been well above 2,000. How much above this number is impossible to say, because there was no fixed threshold for entry into the status of the *aristoi*, the *chrestoi*, and the *dunatoi*. A fluid balance between means, ambition, and peer-pressure determined who would participate in the competitive culture of reputation at Athens.[36]

Despite the scarcity of hard data, some notional calculations can be made. Out of a total adult male citizen population between 40,000 and 60,000 at the outbreak of the Peloponnesian War, somewhere in the range of five to ten percent possessed some measure of the material and ideological qualifications to display the attributes of an aristocratic lifestyle. Still more Athenians, men like Socrates, fell well below the material threshold but embraced the ideology of aristocratic society. To place this calculation in comparative terms, those Athenians able to contend at some level for personally distinct public honors facilitated the operations of what was by far the largest navy deployed by any Greek state; they patronized the most celebrated artists of the day and filled the busiest festival calendar of any Greek community with lavish public displays; and they fielded a cavalry force far larger than any maintained in the Peloponnese, roughly a match for the assembled cavalry of all Boeotian towns, and exceeded only by the assembled cavalry of Thessaly, when it was united. Athens was a great city, and insofar as its greatness arose from the recognized endeavors of individuals, it was the paragon of aristocracy. *En Athenais panta kala,* "All's fine at Athens," was a Peloponnesian aphorism with a touch of irony but plenty of respect.[37]

CHAPTER THREE

Servants of the Athenian Democracy

"Our master is a country-minded, bean-eating, quick-tempered, hard-of-hearing, grumpy old man—Demos resident in Pnyx by name. Last month he bought a new slave, a tanner named Paphlagon, the biggest crook and liar in the world. This tanning-Paphlagon, as soon as he figured out the old man's habits, started cringing before the master and coddling, wheedling, flattering, and deceiving. . . . 'O Demos,' he would say, . . . 'would you like something to eat?' Then he'd grab whatever some one of us had prepared and treat the master to it."

DEMOSTHENES AND NICIAS, AS CHARACTERS IN ARISTOPHANES' *KNIGHTS* 40–45

Democracy turned proud aristocrats into its slaves, according to Aristophanes' *Knights,* and forced them to turn on each other in their rivalries to please their master. The comedy parodied conditions widely recognized among Athenians in 424, when the *Knights* was staged. Such a relationship between the assembled people and their most talented leaders and advisors became especially pronounced under the conditions in which Pericles led the Athenians to war in 431. This chapter examines the tensions inherent in this relationship, as they are revealed especially in the circumstances of war in the 420s.

THE POWER OF NUMBERS

With the offices of leadership and the instruments and symbols of power at Athens in the hands of a large and comparatively affluent aristocracy, it was perplexing to outsiders and annoying to many of the Athenian elite that political power at Athens was ultimately not in their control. Among the conservative oligarchies that dominated much of Greece outside of Athens, only individuals with a certain measure of real property could share in government. But even the poorest Athenians, the *thetes,* had long-established rights of participation in sovereign deliberative assemblies and jury-courts, and the political self-assertion of this class was greatly encouraged by the growth of the Athenian maritime empire over the middle decades of the fifth century.

Sovereignty in all matters lay with the Athenian *demos,* the forty to sixty thousand adult male citizens (whose numbers, after 431, were being whittled away by war and intermittent plague). The votes of the majority in the Assembly dictated the tasks to be carried out by the officers of the state, while majority votes in the jury-courts imposed penalties on those who failed to carry out the people's will. More than half of the Athenian *demos* were laborers, craftsmen, or tradesmen with little or no landed property or substantial fixed assets. This echelon of Athenian society was largely dependent upon the urban economies of Athens and Piraeus, and upon the economic conditions generated by empire. These conditions had enabled growing numbers of poorer Athenians to identify materially with the middle class, and in the process the traditional distinction between the class of *thetes* and the largest Athenian census group known as *zeugitai,* the hoplite class, was becoming blurred. War, in 431, reinforced all of these trends, by further concentrating the populace in the urban area, and by mobilizing still more of the financial resources of the democracy in the form of steady pay for garrison troops and sailors. Thus the numerous middle and lower classes became aware that their economic interests were at stake in the defense of their empire, and in their control of the agendas of government.[1]

The Athenian upper class, who, for all the reasons described in the previous chapter, enjoyed a disproportionate share in the privileges of office-holding, found themselves outnumbered in the sovereign courts and assemblies by a majority of Athenians who were not like themselves in manners and habits. Those like Pericles who prized the benefit to all Athenians of a united body politic minimized these differences and celebrated the egalitarian ethic of *isonomia,* equality before law, for all Athenians. But those who despised this ethic as a debasement of their own innate excellence looked to peers outside of Athens who cherished the same elitist values. It was not difficult for them to find more appealing alternatives to their own political system. In a Mediterranean peopled by kingdoms, chiefdoms, and a variety of oligarchically constituted federations and states where power emanated from the top down, the remarkably inclusive structure of Athenian citizenship defied all norms in the social construction of political power.[2]

SLAVES OF SLAVES

The anonymous treatise entitled *Constitution of the Athenians,* written in the 420s and traditionally but incorrectly included among the works of Xenophon, attempted to explain this anomaly to non-Athenians who could not comprehend how the Athenian elite could be bent to the will of the masses of the poor and the undistinguished. After the author, known today as Pseudo-Xenophon (or sometimes "the Old Oligarch"), avows that things are not as they ought to be at Athens, he goes on to explain the compelling logic behind the Athenian constitution, beginning with the following observation:

> The poor and the *demos* there [at Athens] are right to have more than the well-born and the wealthy for this reason: it is the *demos* that rows the ships and that endows the city with power; the steersmen, the callers, the first mates, the bow-watchers, and the shipwrights—these are the ones who endow the city with power far more than the hoplites, the well-born, and the worthy.[3]

The justification of democracy expounded in this treatise is couched throughout in a tone of strong disapproval. This attitude is conveyed in the contrast between the terms used to describe the "worthy" *(chrestoi),* "well-born" *(gennaioi),* and "best" *(aristoi, beltistoi),* and the terms of contempt—the "mean" *(poneroi),* the "rabble" *(ochlos),* the "inferior," *(cheirous),* and the "raving lunatics" *(mainomenoi anthropoi),* who "lack education" *(apaideusia)* and are filled with "ignorance" *(amathia)*—that describe the poor and the *demos.* What the poor and the *demos* "have more" of was a share of the Athenian *politeia,* the constitution of Athens. Access to offices and the freedom to advocate their own interests before all such bodies gave the poor and the common citizens their advantage in the Athenian political order. But even though a certain logic justified the supremacy of the *demos,* this advantage, according to the terms of social and moral approbation employed throughout the treatise, was unnatural, perverse, and, by implication, illegitimate.[4]

No argument was necessary here to make the point that Athenian democracy was a perversion of the proper order of things. This was a given, according to the aristocratic prejudices common to the author and his non-Athenian, probably Spartan, addressee. The Athenian author did, however, have to explain to his counterpart some of the peculiar consequences of this "acknowledged folly," as democracy was later called by another Athenian speaking to Spartans. The most outlandish practice observable at Athens was the license allowed to resident aliens, the metics, and to slaves:

> Now among the slaves and metics at Athens there is the greatest uncontrolled permissiveness; you can't hit them there, and a slave will not stand aside for you. I will explain the reason for this peculiar practice. If it were customary for a slave, a metic, or a freedman to be struck by one who is free, you would often hit an Athenian citizen by mistake on the assumption that he was a slave. For the people there are no better dressed than the slaves and metics, nor are they any better looking. If anyone is also surprised by the fact that they allow their slaves indulgences there and let some of them live in grand style, it would be clear that they even do this for a reason. For where there is a naval power, it is necessary from financial considerations to be slaves to the slaves.... Where there are rich slaves, it is no advantage in such a place for my slave to fear you. In Sparta my slave would fear you; but if your slave fears me, there will be the chance that he will give over his money so as not to have to worry anymore. For this reason we have set up equality between slaves and free men, as well as between metics and citizens, since the city needs metics in view of the many different trades and the fleet.[5]

Where, in other communities, aristocratic presumption held that men worthy of the esteem of citizens could be recognized by their looks and refinements, at Athens such prejudices were misplaced. Slaves and metics were indistinguishable from the mass of Athenian citizenry. For the sake of the skills they possessed, for the money they generated, and, in the case of the *demos,* because of the political power they commanded, the insolence of all such despicable brutes had to be tolerated. For the "worthy" and the "well-born," to suffer such license was like being "slaves to slaves." To those of aristocratic sensibilities, this was the very essence of *kakonomia,* a political order governed by "bad laws." "For the people do not want good laws under which they themselves are enslaved; they want to be free and to rule. Bad laws are of little concern to them. What *you* consider to be the lack of good laws is the very source of the people's strength and freedom."[6]

In such a sharply polarized account of Athenian democracy, it was easy to reduce the agenda of the *demos* to the unprincipled pursuit of financial gain, "for poverty tends to draw them to disgraceful actions." What especially galled the author of this treatise and his like-minded peers was that the Athenian *demos* relied on members of the Athenian upper class, as liturgists and holders of high offices, to manage and provide for the interests of the Athenian people as a whole. "Respectable" Athenians thus became the tools of the "disgraceful actions" of the *demos.*[7]

FRIENDSHIP WITH FOREIGNERS AND LOYALTY TO THE *DEMOS*

Much of the administration of the empire, particularly its finances, was handled by officers elected from among Athenians of the highest standing. Such men were the generals, the ambassadors, and the curators of imperial revenue, the Hellenotamiae. In dealings with representatives of other states, whether they were ambassadors of rival powers like Sparta or the representatives of Athenian allies and subjects, these men generally dealt with their peers in social and economic standing. Not infrequently, official transactions were facilitated by personal ties of friendship among such men. In some cases these ties were ancestral, having been formalized long ago in the rituals of *xenia,* "guest-friendship."

The archaic practice of *xenia* was traditionally marked by the exchange of gifts and the less tangible interchange of hospitality and other services that defined latent and even hereditary bonds of friendship between distant families. Such formalities of mutual esteem among members of the social elite throughout the Greek world had long given loose definition to a community of peers that cut across the political boundaries of localized citizenship. Spartan leadership in particular operated through this community of aristocratic peerage. By supporting the social and political conditions that assured the economic advantages particularly of land-owning elites, the Spartans secured loyal allies among the traditional aristocracies of Greece.[8]

Athenian democracy of the fifth century was the most powerful construction of localized identity to challenge this pan-Hellenic aristocratic peerage. Commanding the resources of empire and defining a community whose interests were not dominated by a land-owning elite, the Athenian *demos* could defy many of the norms that underlay the aristocratic construction of esteem. In so doing, however, the Athenian democracy was not seeking to uproot and eliminate this traditional system of relationships, but to dominate it. To this end, the Athenian *demos* assumed a corporate role in the formalities of *xenia*. The *demos* granted *proxenia*, or formal recognition of favored standing, to foreign benefactors of the Athenian state. Foreigners honored as *proxenoi* of the Athenians are first attested, by Herodotus and later literary sources, at the time of the Persian wars. Contemporary inscriptions attest that grants of *proxenia* became an increasingly common practice of Athenian policy in the 420s and afterward. The formalities of state-sponsored hospitality to foreign dignitaries, also called *xenia*, are likewise best attested from the 420s and afterward.[9]

As the state bestowed *proxenia*, it also required personal ties of *xenia* to be subordinated to the public interest. With the onset of war in 431, Pericles displayed the priorities appropriate to the Athenian elite under democracy, not by renouncing his ties of *xenia* to the Spartan king, Archidamus, but by publicly bequeathing his landed estates in Attica to the Athenian *demos* in the event that Archidamus, at the head of the army of invasion, should display the favoritism characteristic of aristocratic *xenia* and spare Pericles' property from devastation. A decade later, the ties of *xenia* established between Nicias and the Spartan king Pleistoanax were instrumental to the negotiation of peace in 421. At about the same time, *xenia* between Alcibiades and leading Argives was instrumental in the alliance between Athens and Argos that led shortly to renewed war with Sparta.[10]

Even in the shadow of the *demos*, then, members of the Athenian elite continued to compete for the prestige that personal ties of *xenia* might bring, and foreigners were ready to seek influence at Athens through such ties. Purely personal ties of *xenia* thus not only retained their importance, but were even enhanced in value whenever they touched the interests of the Athenian *demos*. Most of the business of empire officially transacted in the Athenian Council, introduced as resolutions to the Athenian Assembly, or litigated in Athenian law courts, was prepared as far as possible beforehand in private negotiations between influential members of the Athenian elite and their foreign counterparts. The formal adjudications of tribute assessments, for example, were preceded, in some cases at least, by private negotiations. At issue in these negotiations of private and public interests were alignments of favor that might win the highest prizes: the prestige of decisive influence over policy; the possession of property; even life and liberty in cases of capital importance.[11]

The revolt of Mytilene from Athens in 428 provides a glimpse into the intricate tangle of private and public concerns in the affairs of empire. The revolt was precipitated, Thucydides tells us, after Mytilenean *proxenoi,* motivated "by a private feud," persuaded the Athenians that actions by certain of their fellow Mytileneans posed a threat to other allies and to the Athenians themselves. Aristotle provides additional details:

> In the case of Mytilene, a feud over the marriage of heiresses was the origin of many ills and of the war with Athens in which Paches captured their city. A certain Timophanes, an affluent man, died leaving two daughters. Dexander, attempting but failing in his suit to have them married to his sons, began the feud and incited the Athenians to act, since he was their *proxenos.*[12]

From these beginnings Dexander brought about the destruction of his personal enemies, rivals for the inheritance of Timophanes. But by the time Mytilene surrendered after nearly a year of hard fighting and siege, the Athenian *demos* was in no mood to trifle over distinguishing good Mytileneans from bad and passed a resolution to put to death all adult males and to enslave the women and children. The day after this awful decision was taken, a general mood of uneasiness spread among the Athenians. "Observing this," Thucydides reports, "the deputation from Mytilene which was in Athens *and the Athenians who were supporting them* approached the authorities with a view to having the question debated again." Thus again by private initiative the matter was placed on the agenda for reconsideration by the Assembly, and as a result of the second debate the order for mass execution at Mytilene was rescinded.[13]

The final episode of this private feud was played out in an Athenian law court, and resulted in the destruction of Paches, the Athenian general who had brought the rebellion of Mytilene to an end. In the course of a review of his conduct in office, Paches was convicted of charges so injurious to his honor that he drew his sword and committed suicide in court. Paches was driven to this extremity by Hellanis and Lamaxis, two Mytilenean women who accused Paches of rape and the murder of their husbands. At least this is how, centuries later, the fate of Paches was told in song and remembered in the funerary monument of the two women at Mytilene. Hellanis and Lamaxis must be the daughters of Timophanes, whose dowered properties, as Aristotle reports, were the reason for the feud at Mytilene. In the end, the disposition of property on Lesbos fell to the Athenian *demos* to decide. It is most likely that the lethal accusation against Paches turned on evidence that the Athenian general had profited illicitly from his command. Evidently, Paches, as executor of the imperial might of Athens, lost his balance amidst the conflicting forces of personal honor, private interests, and loyalty to the *demos*.[14]

THE SYCOPHANTS

By the time of Paches' trial, the *demos* had become adept at asserting its authority. Decrees of the Athenian Assembly passed in the 420s proclaimed severe legal sanctions against anyone obstructing the authority of the Athenian *demos*, especially in its business of collecting tribute. But the harsh tone of imperialism, it should be noted, was directed primarily at *Athenians*. The officers of the Council responsible for the agenda of public business were subject to explicit penalties if they delayed or deferred essential items of business, or if they introduced contrary measures. Beyond discouraging inefficiency, such statutory injunctions were designed to combat the potentially insidious effects of favoritism. If unchecked, those who managed the busy schedule of the Council could easily serve covertly the interests of Athenian or foreign friends by delaying or halting the progress of vital business. In addition to putting its own officers on notice, the *demos* also pronounced general warnings against anyone, Athenian or ally, who might be guilty of punishable wrongdoing or treasonous offense. To put teeth in the measures, anyone, Athenian or ally, who might know of such offenses was invited to indict the malefactors. The *demos* thus turned natural envy among peers into a tool to secure the public interest against private arrangements.[15]

By long-standing practice, many matters of public concern at Athens were left for *ho boulomenos*, "anyone who wishes," to initiate action before the appropriate executive or judicial bodies. As of the 420s, however, the stark realities of a state at war encouraged an accumulation of statutory mandates to deal with perennial or recurring concerns. In the absence of public prosecutors, the job of assuring that malefactors were stopped still required *ho boulomenos* to come forward with specific accusations wherever evidence of subversion of the people's interest might emerge. In the highly charged atmosphere of tension between the public interests of the Athenian *demos* and the private interests of Athenian elite, this practice gave rise to one of the most distinctive stereotypes of the era, the sycophant, or self-appointed professional informer.

Their role was vital to democratic processes, but because our sources overwhelmingly reflect the views of those who resented such individuals, the stereotype of the sycophant is an odious one. Most of those dubbed sycophants were probably on the social threshold of the upper class and used their access to or intimacy with the wealthy for the benefit of the people, or, as their enemies claimed, for their own benefit. Athenian sycophants became notorious for their ability to ruin wealthy notables, especially among the tributary allies, by characterizing their dealings in a way sure to win a condemnation in an Athenian popular court. From this ability arose their further reputation as blackmailers, happily enriching themselves through the fear inspired by their threats of prosecution.[16]

The fear of embarrassing prosecutions was felt by wealthy Athenians as well. Nicias' great wealth and pursuit of public honors, combined with his reputation for avoiding dangers and difficulties whenever possible, made him the butt of jokes about what an easy mark he was for sycophants. He would gladly pay them off, as Plutarch quotes a contemporary comic poet, to avoid any embarrassment to his public image. By the same token, Nicias feared being held publicly accountable in more serious matters. The lesson of Paches' fate, Plutarch relates, was one that encouraged Nicias to avoid difficult commands, for he saw how destructive slanderous prosecutions afterward could be. Although such a capital case is not normally thought of as the province of sycophants, in practice there was no line between charges of misdemeanor and of offenses that might warrant the ultimate penalty.[17]

A case in point, where an evidently distorted charge resulted in capital punishment, took place possibly in the early 420s, when the entire board of Hellenotamiae was accused of misappropriating funds. A speech composed by Antiphon for a Mytilenean aristocrat on trial at Athens in the 410s refers to the condemnation of the Hellenotamiae as an example of how an emotionally charged case had once led to a notorious miscarriage of justice:

> Anger swept reason aside, and they were all put to death save one. Later the true facts became known...and it was shown how the money had disappeared. The man who had already been handed over to the Eleven for execution was rescued by you the *demos;* but the others had died entirely innocent. You older ones remember this yourselves, I expect, and the younger have heard of it like myself.

Whatever the circumstances of this case may have been, its example served as a chilling reminder that, true to the language of its decrees, the Athenian *demos* would brook no incompetence or willful resistance, *especially* where its money was concerned.[18]

THE DEMAGOGUES

The unexpressed irony underlying these developments was that the *demos* was incapable of acting, even to enforce its own will, without aggressive leadership. Such leadership came not from elected or allotted officers, who essentially discharged routine duties, but from volunteer specialists among *hoi boulomenoi.* Like the so-called sycophants who specialized in rooting out malfeasance through the courts, popular leaders were those who regularly came forward to speak in the Assembly, before the Council, or before any other board of public officers that had to deliberate on matters in the people's interest. Inasmuch as their leadership was not dependent on any formal office, such volunteer speakers were not accountable for specific conduct. Their power lay in their ability as speakers to persuade the majority to vote as they advised.

Leadership of this sort invariably came from the ranks of those who were, or could claim to be, the worthy, capable, and wealthy—members of the Athenian upper class. But some, at least, of those who were proud of their aristocratic distinctions regarded it as unseemly for their peers to cater to the masses. Pseudo-Xenophon considered them as sinister traitors to their class:

> There are some who are not by nature men of the people but who truly are on the people's side.... But whoever is not a man of the people and yet prefers to live in a democratic city rather than in an oligarchic one has readied himself to do wrong and has realized that it is easier for an evil man to escape notice in a democratic city than in an oligarchic one.[19]

Pericles had enjoyed what by any standard was a successful career of leadership under the Athenian democracy, often serving as an elected general, but more often appearing in the self-appointed role of advisor for the people's interest. Comedy in his lifetime and after paid tribute to his authoritative presence in the Assembly by giving him epithets like "Olympian," "Thunderer," and "Lord" *(anax)*. Thucydides summarized the era of his leadership by claiming that, by his skillful advice to the *demos,* "in what was nominally a democracy, power was really in the hands of the first citizen." He had "given the people what was theirs" in the form of pay for public duties and, more generally, had vigorously articulated policies that benefited the largest numbers of Athenian citizens. By setting such standards for successful public leadership, Pericles had delineated a model that his successors would strive to match or outdo. Around the time of his death in 429, this model of leadership had been given the name *demagogos,* demagogue, or "leader of the people." It was applied to the man who was indeed striving to surpass Pericles' reputation as spokesman for the masses, Cleon the son of Cleaenetus.[20]

Born to a family that owned a profitable tanning business and that had already achieved liturgical status, and rising to a career of public preeminence, Cleon achieved the most spectacular military success of any Athenian general of the 420s, led the Athenians in negotiations with the Spartans, and ultimately died in battle at the head of his troops, in 422. He might have been remembered as an outstanding example of nobility at the service of his state were it not for the fact that his popularity was built on the explicit denial of traditional aristocratic pretense and a readiness to attack any Athenian who presumed that personal *arete* was more valuable than unconditional loyalty to the Athenian *demos.*[21]

Thucydides, who was witness to most of Cleon's career, introduces him as "the most violent of citizens," since he above all others had unleashed the full force of the people's will against his opposition. His public demeanor likewise violated prevailing standards of decency in the circles of leadership, for Cleon, according to Aristotle's Athenian constitutional history: "was the first who shouted on the speaker's platform, who used abusive language and who spoke with his cloak hitched up around him, while all others used to speak in proper dress and manner."[22]

In 424, Aristophanes used Cleon's contempt for aristocratic manners to comic effect in his *Knights,* as reflected in the quote at the head of this chapter. Two good and true slaves of old man Demos, Nicias and Demosthenes, are worried that they will suffer from the influence of Demos' newest slave, the outlandish Paphlagon (a most barbarous slave ethnic used as a pseudonym for Cleon). This comic Cleon is extremely jealous of his master's affections, so Nicias and Demosthenes are reduced to desperate measures to undo Cleon's influence. They elevate a greasy sausage-seller of the marketplace into a rival demagogue to outdo Cleon. The sausage-seller is at first incredulous that he, an uneducated menial *(poneros),* and by no stretch of the imagination one of the *kaloi k'agathoi,* could rise to a position of power in the state. But his qualifications are perfect, Nicias and Demosthenes affirm, for "demagoguery is not for a man of culture or refined manners, but for the ignorant and despicable!"[23]

Although sources like Pseudo-Xenophon, Thucydides, Aristotle, and Plutarch echo similar pejorative judgments on the social merits of Athenian demagogues, we are badly misled if we take Aristophanes' caricature for fact. Demagoguery was not for the low-born and ignorant, but for the savvy and bold. The violence of the times required leaders who would speak the unvarnished truth to the *demos.* Those who blamed the demagogues themselves for the character of wartime politics at Athens were expressing nostalgia for an era that had passed away when Pericles persuaded the Athenians to reject Spartan demands and go to war to preserve their empire.

THE PEOPLE'S MONEY

The basis of Cleon's popular leadership, Aristophanes has to admit, was what he could do for the people, especially in matters concerning money. Challenged by the upstart sausage-seller to a contest for the affections of his master, Demos, Aristophanes has his comic version of Cleon begin to plead: "How could any citizen love you more than me, Demos? I was the first, when the rest were giving you advice, to show a profit for the state, twisting these, squeezing those, and claiming a fair share from others, never minding anyone's private interests if I might please you."[24]

Private interests were trampled under the financial demands of the state in a new way, in 428, when the mounting costs of the war prompted the Athenians to levy an *eisphora,* or property tax, on the wealthiest Athenians and resident aliens. Direct taxation of Athenians to defray the expenses of the democratic state was an exceptional practice, and Thucydides notes that the *eisphora* of 428 was "the first time" such a measure was enacted. By this measure the private wealth of Athenians was placed at the disposal of the *demos* not, as in liturgies, for services that also benefited the reputation of those who spent the money, but for expenditure on needs decreed by the democracy (mostly public pay for rowers, soldiers, and office-holders).[25]

Liability for the *eisphora* could be imposed on individual estates on the basis of any evidence for qualifying wealth. Before the *eisphora* was introduced, all public measures of wealth conveyed honor as well as public responsibility. Past liturgical service was the chief evidence of wealth among Athenians. In addition to this, the *lêxiarchika grammateia,* or "office-selection registers" kept by local deme officials, listed property-holdings of individuals above the census-class of *thetes,* presumably for the purposes of establishing eligibility of individuals for allotment or election to the various grades of public offices at Athens. With the introduction of the *eisphora,* the pursuit of honor through liturgical service or office-holding brought with it a new sting of liability. Cleon, and other demagogues who followed in his path, could use the public demand for tithing of the wealthy as another means of intimidating Athenians with any pretense at public prominence, as Aristophanes again reveals in another outburst of his comic Cleon against his rival: "You'll get a fair judgment by me—crushed by *eisphorai!* For I'll make sure you are registered among the wealthy!"[26]

Imposed, as this passage implies, more than once in the few years between 428 and 424, the *eisphora* was resented by propertied Athenians, who mustered enough popular sympathy to pass a resolution forbidding the proposal of an *eisphora,* on pain of death, unless an enabling resolution justifying the measure was first passed. The enabling resolution, or *adeia,* probably had to be formulated as a proposal of the Council, so the requirement would temporarily transfer the initiative for such a measure from the open Assembly to the quieter deliberations of the Council. This process, also applied to protect other privileged sources of money, impeded the recklessness of the *demos* and its demagogues in their reliance on the *eisphora.* It was possible to do so only because another source of money was at the command of the *demos,* the tributary allies of Athens.[27]

In the same year in which the *Knights* of Aristophanes was staged, the Athenians conducted a systematic reassessment of all tribute, effectively doubling the total revenue due to Athens from the maritime states under her control. The increase was achieved by a combination of strict adherence to established quotas of tribute due from individual states, and by demanding tribute from many communities not previously assessed (cities in the Black Sea, for example, appear for the first time on the list). This extraordinary measure has been plausibly ascribed to the policy of Cleon, although his name is not directly associated with it. Two names that *are* connected with the reassessment reveal the sorts of associations formed in pursuit of the people's business.[28]

The proposer of the decree of reassessment was Thudippus, a well-to-do Athenian who probably at about this time became a son-in-law of Cleon. Although Thudippus' ancestry is unknown, members of his family continued to serve the state in various capacities for over a century. Another associate soon made a greater name for himself in Athenian politics, for among the board of ten Assessors selected to set the new tribute quotas was Alcibiades. As former ward of Pericles and member of one of the most distinguished of Athenian families, it is likely that Alcibiades was familiar with the ways and means of the allies. Soon after he came of age, Alcibiades is said to have accompanied his uncle Axiochus on a voyage to Abydus, a key town on the Hellespont. No firm facts are known about their business there, but it is probable that Axiochus, who was later associated with other diplomatic affairs in the north Aegean, was involved in state business and was introducing his promising young nephew to the circles of influence in this most strategic quarter of the empire. Now, some six to eight years later, Alcibiades was a logical choice as one of the Assessors who negotiated with—or dictated to—the representatives of the allied states who had been summoned to Athens to participate in the reassessment of tribute.[29]

Since the persona of the radical demagogue was hostile to the interests of all parties except the Athenian *demos,* no demagogue could be an effective intermediary between the Athenians and any other state. This remained the domain of those Athenians who took pride in their connections with leading men abroad. But these Athenians had to negotiate their loyalties between their foreign friends and the Athenian *demos* with the utmost care. In the reassessment of 425/4, Alcibiades seems to have won distinction in the discreet manner used earlier by Cimon, by placing his own work and that of his colleagues under the protective aegis of an Athenian hero of the past. For this was probably the occasion when Alcibiades led the Athenians in honoring the memory of Aristides, "the Just," who was revered especially for the fairness of his assessment of tribute from the allies of Athens upon the formation of the Delian League in 478/7. Alcibiades proposed a resolution that awarded income and a large grant of land on Euboea to Lysimachus son of Aristides. As a public bequest, like the honors accorded to the descendants of Harmodius and Aristogeiton, the people expressed their gratitude for the enduring benefit that they received from the wisdom and fairness of his father's assessment. By implication, and against critics in some quarters, Alcibiades secured the same public gratitude for the work he and his colleagues had accomplished. A few years later, "the tribute fixed by Aristides" was affirmed as the accepted standard during treaty negotiations with the Spartans in 421, and it must likewise have been the guiding principle of the Assessors of 425/4.[30]

THE TYRANNY OF THE *DEMOS*

From Aristides to Pericles and to the generation of Alcibiades, the Athenian state had forged an imperial identity for itself that sought to endow all Athenians with pride and a communal sense of *arete.* As a consequence of that inclusiveness, however, the majority of participants in the Assembly and jury-courts came to be those who, although they might admire many aspects of aristocratic excellence, were aware that their own social and economic realities were different from those of the aristocracy. This difference was tolerable to the majority as long as aristocratic ideals served the interests of the majority. But the war against the Athenian imperial identity commenced in 431 by Sparta and her Peloponnesian allies compelled the *demos,* under the guidance of its leaders, to become increasingly jealous in the defense of its interests. In words used by both Pericles and Cleon and echoed by Aristophanes, the Athenians were called upon to exercise *tyrannis,* "tyranny," over their empire. Those who felt the burden of this tyranny most heavily were those most capable of threatening the interests of the *demos.*[31]

Such a burden was laid upon the landed aristocracy of Athenians at the very outset of war, in 431, when Pericles advised the Athenians to withdraw within the walls of the city and to allow the Peloponnesians to ravage their fields and country homes in Attica. Pericles' refusal to fight the full strength of the Spartans and their allies was essential to his vision of Athens as the leader of a maritime empire, impervious to the demands of the Spartans. But his strategy, barely supported by the majority in the Assembly, fired an anger of frustration, an *orge* as Thucydides describes it, that burned in the hearts of those who shared the warlike self-image of the *kaloi k'agathoi,* especially the young among them, who yearned to prove their prowess in war. "Everyone knows," says Pseudo-Xenophon,

> that all is not well with the hoplite infantry at Athens; they [the *demos* of the Athenians] have made it so, since they regard their infantry as inferior to the enemy and fewer in number—but they are stronger even on land than those of their allies who pay tribute, and they consider their hoplite infantry to be adequate if they are more powerful than their allies.[32]

Pericles' ability to sustain his policy, despite an emotional opposition, was one of the chief justifications for Thucydides' judgment that Athens, "though a democracy in name, was in fact coming under the rule of its best man." Although Pericles' foresight was confirmed many times over, in the generation of war that followed, Athenian hoplites were ever keen to find an outlet in which to prove their prowess. In the end, the desire to fight like Spartans proved to be the downfall, in the civil war of 404–403, of those Athenians who cherished the ideals of archaic aristocracy above all else.

Those who *did* carry the honor of the Athenians into battle outside the walls of Athens in 431 were the Athenian cavalry (represented in figure 2 on page 53). Able to concentrate quickly wherever the enemy was vulnerable, the cavalry probably succeeded in limiting the depredations of Peloponnesian invaders in Attica. But without substantial support from the hoplite infantry, the cavalry could do no more than skirmish. Their effectiveness, therefore, was questionable, and within the first four of five years of war in Attica they had to defend themselves from a new enemy, Cleon.[33]

In all likelihood, Cleon argued that the subventions provided by the state to the cavalrymen for the cost of horses and for fodder was wasteful of public money: the *demos* was paying to support the pride and self-esteem of horse-riding pretty-boys who did little or nothing to benefit the state. By 425/4, thanks to Cleon, the Athenians were able to use the Spartans captured on Sphacteria as hostages, and by threatening to execute them they put an end to Spartan-led invasions of Attica. So by the time the *Knights* was staged in 424, Cleon's attacks on the cavalry had new vigor. This was the context in which Aristophanes, bringing his sausage-seller into a duel of demagoguery with Paphlagon/Cleon, gives him the support of these outraged cavalrymen:

> *Sausage-seller:* And who will be my ally? For the wealthy fear him, and the poor folk are terrified.
>
> *Demosthenes:* But there are the cavalrymen, a thousand good men *(agathoi)* who hate him, and they will come to your side; and the *kaloi k'agathoi* among the citizens as well, and any of the audience who is quick-witted *(dexios),* and I with them; and the god will take part....[34]

As Aristophanes suggests, the cavalrymen had to rely on help from any quarter to make their case against hard-nosed assaults on their usefulness to the Athenian *demos.* Reference to the fact that the cavalrymen were glad to see "Cleon cough up those five talents" suggests that, on one occasion, the argument was won by an orator skilled in rhetorical accounting, who showed that Cleon's accusation of unwarranted financial drain was nullified by the discovery of resources overlooked, or mismanaged, by Cleon elsewhere. The salvation of the Athenian cavalry corps seems to have depended more on lawyers and accountants than on prowess on the field of battle.[35]

THE SOPHISTS

One of the consequences of the pressures of war, the tyranny of the *demos,* and the railing of demagogues was a heightened urgency to define the *arete* that some claimed was the birthright of all Athenians, and that others claimed was what separated "the best" *(hoi aristoi)* from "the rest" (or *hoi polloi,* "the many"). Although pursued with greatest intensity within intellectual circles among the leisured well-to-do, this debate also had wide currency in the public at large, as speeches from the dramatic theater and from the Assembly show. What combination of wisdom, courage, justice, and temperance constituted the perfection of *arete?* What share of these virtues could the common citizens actually possess, compared to the wealthy, who had so much the greater opportunity to study such matters? Yet again, were these virtues inherited at birth or acquired by study?[36]

Such questions became especially pointed in the presence of men who professed to teach *arete* in one or another of its various forms. Like the great poets and performers from all parts of Greece in all ages, the teachers of poetry, of music, and of various forms of graceful and athletic movement had a long history of courting the patronage of the wealthy. By the generation of Socrates and the era of the Peloponnesian War, a new species of such teachers was being drawn to Athens to seek patronage amid the unique construction of pride and affluence to be found there. These teachers were the *sophistai,* the sophists, or exponents of "wisdom," as *sophia* is usually translated.

The term *sophia* comprehended knowledge, aesthetic and ethical discretion, and proficiency. Poetry was traditionally the preeminent form of verbal expression of *sophia,* and poets could also be called sophists. Poetry was the common medium for knowledge of all sorts, both on public occasions and, especially, within the private circles of the elite. So Parmenides and Empedocles among those later known as the "Pre-Socratics" in Greek philosophy wrote in verse, and Protagoras is quoted as claiming that "the most important part of a man's education is to become an authority on poetry." But as the Athenian experience with democracy and empire attracted speculative thought increasingly to the challenge of defining the nature of the political community, masters of *sophia* adapted their teachings and writings to the subject of politics and to its medium in another form of artful expression: persuasive non-poetic speech.[37]

Between the mid-fifth century and the 420s, Protagoras of Abdera established a reputation for articulating a form of political *arete* that he claimed was naturally endowed in all of mankind. This native virtue consisted of a rudimentary sense of justice and mutual respect essential to any community of equals. Protagoras' expositions of this subject provided an ideological basis for the democratic construction of *arete* that Pericles championed. Protagoras conceived that, for a community to succeed, the native *arete* of all individuals had to be cultivated through the guidance of just laws. Thus he allowed a role for himself as a teacher, and for the likes of Pericles as a practitioner, in the art of formulating just laws and policies. Protagoras' own lectures exemplified how persuasive speech achieved the desired ends of effective deliberation by refining and realizing the collective *arete* inherent in the assembled people.[38]

Protagoras' fame as an exponent of these ideas and skills was evidently at its height around the time of the outbreak of the Peloponnesian War. A rapidly growing fascination with the skills of persuasion at that time probably accounts for his reputation as the first to advertise instruction in such political skills for hire. The fascination with persuasion also accounts for the fundamental transformation of the aims of Protagoras' younger contemporaries. After 431, the polarizing pressures of war tended to reduce the pursuit of intellectual *arete* to the pursuit of rhetorical skill itself. Because it was the key to preeminence in the Council, in the Assembly, and in the jury-courts of Athens, the persuasive power of rhetoric became the chief object of the teaching of the sophists in the 420s.[39]

The year 427 stands out in the history of rhetoric, "the art of making clever speakers," as Plato identifies this form of sophistry. That year Gorgias of Leontini, the celebrated Sicilian wordsmith, arrived in Athens on an embassy and enthralled the Athenians with his eloquence. The popularity of his displays encouraged him to stay in Athens as a teacher, and won for him the public honor of delivering one of the annual orations over the Athenian war-dead. Frequenting other states as well as Athens over the following four decades, Gorgias achieved a reputation as a highly paid teacher rivaling that of Protagoras.[40]

Already in 427, Gorgias' audience was well prepared to judge virtuoso performances. Earlier in the same year, Aristophanes' first production on the comic stage, his *Banqueters,* featured a debate between two brothers, one brought up by his father with old-fashioned virtues, and the other trained by fashionable teachers of rhetoric. The speaking styles of the sophist Thrasymachus of Chalcedon and even of the young Alcibiades are parodied in the contest which led, in Aristophanes' play, to the same unsettling conclusion about the merits of new intellectual fashions that Aristophanes depicted a few years later in his more famous satire of sophistry, the *Clouds.*[41]

This year also saw the Athenians debate the punishment they would inflict on the rebellious Mytileneans. In reconsidering the resolution to execute the Mytileneans, the opposing speeches of Cleon and Diodotus reported by Thucydides both open with lengthy warnings about the present state of decision-making. Cleon complains about speakers more interested in displaying their own verbal dexterity than in offering sound advice, and ends his preamble by chastising the Athenians for their fascination with the performance aspects of oratory:

> It is obvious that anyone who is [now going to advise you on how to deal with the Mytileneans] must either have such confidence in his speaking abilities that he thinks he can prove that what has been finally settled was, on the con-

> trary, not decided at all, or else he must have been bribed to put together some elaborate speech to lead you off the track. But in competitions of this sort the prizes go to others and the state takes all the danger for herself. *You* are the ones to blame, for stupidly instituting these competitive displays! You have become regular speech-goers, and as for action, you merely listen to accounts of it; if something is to be done in the future you estimate the possibilities by hearing a good speech on the subject, and as for the past you rely not so much on the facts that you have seen with your own eyes as on what you have heard about them in some clever piece of verbal criticism. Any novelty in an argument deceives you at once, but when the argument is tried and proved you become unwilling to follow it; you look with suspicion on what is normal and are the slaves of every paradox that comes your way. The chief wish of each one of you is to be able to make a speech himself, and, if you cannot do that, the next best thing is to compete with those who can make this sort of speech by not looking as though you were all out of your depth while you listen to the views put forward, by applauding a good point even before it is made, and by being as quick at seeing how an argument is going to be developed as you are slow in understanding what in the end it will lead to. What you are looking for all the time is something that is, one could say, beyond ordinary experience, and yet you cannot think straight about the facts of life that are before you. You are completely at the mercy of the pleasure of listening, and are more like spectators gathered around sophists than those deliberating affairs of state![42]

Two points stand out in Cleon's diatribe against current fashions in rhetoric. The first is that it is a fine piece of rhetoric itself. No assembly of the *demos* could decide an issue, especially in the increasingly complex and far-flung affairs of empire, based solely on direct experience. Debate was essential, as Protagoras had recognized, for the *demos* could only exercise its collective power of discrimination after listening to wise guidance (and increasingly, as will be seen below, the guidance of specialists). So Cleon's complaint that the Athenians prefer to rely on "a clever piece of verbal criticism" rather than trusting to "the facts that you have seen with your own eyes" was, like his allegation of bribery, merely an effort to shut the ears of his audience to the voice of opposition. Just so his challenger, Diodotus, defended the need to let well-chosen words rather than fear and anger guide policy, and suggested that the state would be better off if men who silenced their opposition by accusations of corruption were themselves silenced.[43]

The second point is the remarkable assimilation between audience and orator evident in this passage. As spokesman for the people, Cleon is at one with his audience through the medium of rhetoric. Unity of purpose between audience and orator was the aim of Protagoras' "art of politics" *(politike techne),* and Cleon's efforts to become the voice of the Athenian commons attest the affinity of his practices to Protagoras' teachings. But when Cleon's audience rejects his advice, he must disparage the web of rhetoric that binds his audience to other speakers. By depicting his audience as misled would-be orators, Cleon reveals the prevailing fascination for sophistic rhetoric that characterized the politics of Athens in his day.[44]

The practice of politics was a competitive art, and the ear of the *demos* was attracted by novelty. Sophists and their Athenian students were associated with a variety of artful and studied manners of speaking, characterized by distinctive turns of phrase or newly-coined words. Gorgias captured audiences with highly wrought phrases in almost poetic cadences. Alcibiades affected a contrived, dissembling style accompanied by a lisp that many found endearing. No one style held sway, and every debate, as Cleon remarked, had become like a formal contest to see who would prove the most persuasive at the moment.[45]

Cleon, in the Mytilenean debate, suggests that his opponent must be a sophistically skilled speaker, ready to subvert common sense by a facile argument, and that those in the audience who might be taken in were more interested in rhetorical display than in substantive advice. Though Cleon's claim was surely exaggerated for the sake of argument, there was some truth to it. Part of the fascination with sophistic rhetoric was due to the desire among the *aristoi* of Athens to find political leaders to their liking, capable of displacing Cleon and his fellow demagogues. This, after all, was the plot-line of Aristophanes' *Knights,* although there the quest took a comic turn when the distinguished statesmen, Demosthenes and Nicias, had to look to the *poneroi* rather than to the *kaloi k'agathoi* to find their champion.

Reducing the opposition to a vulnerable stereotype was a regular device of both rhetoric and comic satire. Cleon managed to play upon a widespread public sentiment that the patrons of the sophists, and especially of sophistic rhetoric, were ultimately up to no good. Aristophanes, even while lambasting the demagoguery of Cleon, echoes this sentiment. In the *Knights,* Aristophanes depicts such rhetorical enthusiasts as young men misusing their leisure by avidly dissecting the modes of expression employed in a recent speech in court that had won the decision for the defendant. In the *Clouds,* a father desperate for help with legal difficulties sends his son to the sophists to learn some skills useful for pleading in court, and gains instead an initiate of the sophists ready to prove that it is lawful for sons to beat their fathers. In the *Wasps,* a young sophisticate takes running notes on the speech of a devotee of Cleon and then bests him in debate.[46]

The last example reveals a significant detail of the passion for study and analysis of the spoken word. Along with the written demonstration-texts of the sophists, written notes on actual debates before the Assembly and the jury-courts seem to have become a common medium of study among the up-and-coming, hyper-engaged listeners blasted by Cleon and parodied by Aristophanes. Thucydides was a member of this crowd, and this phenomenon in due course had important implications for the writing of the history of this era. More immediately, however, studied rhetoric had its most pervasive impact, at once exciting and unsettling to the educated, in the popular law courts.[47]

THE SPEECH-WRITERS

Athens in the 420s was a vortex that sucked in the revenues of far-flung commerce, of a naval empire, and of its own wealthy. The handling of the people's money, as it was assessed and as it was spent, generated a nearly continuous flow of judicial hearings. Regular audits of officers responsible for public funds were legally mandated. Although testimony from *hoi boulomenoi* was always admitted where there was evidence that crimes had been committed against the public interest, when any hint of financial wrongdoing required legal investigation the state deployed specialists to handle the case. These public prosecutors were the *synegoroi,* or *syndikoi,* who were appointed to assist the financial auditors of the Council whenever a case came before a jury.[48]

Under these circumstances, prominent men involved in the people's business among the Athenians and their subject-allies were liable to find themselves brought under unwelcome public scrutiny, defamed by accusers claiming to act in the public interest, threatened with fines, or worse. Skillful speakers were able, "like tyrants, to put to death any man they will, and deprive of their fortunes and banish whomsoever it seems best," according to the bold claim of the sophist, Polus, in Plato's dialogue on rhetoric named after Gorgias. Whatever their motives, orators and prosecutors were now especially distinguished by, and feared for, their command of the art of persuasion.[49]

To match the skill of an interested prosecution, if a well-to-do defendant could not buy it off, or did not chose to do so, he could hire a professional speech-writer, a *logographos,* to prepare a suitable defense. Although supporting speakers, *synegoroi* or *syndikoi,* could also plead for the defense, defendants had to speak on their own behalf. In the increasingly competitive environment of forensic rhetoric in the 420s, memorizing a prepared speech became an essential preparation for a contest in the courts. It is no accident that the earliest examples of Greek forensic speeches, as well as comic parodies of their rhetoric, come from Athens in the 420s and 410s. For this was the era when studied rhetoric first became absolutely essential to a public career.[50]

Anyone hoping to rise to public prominence in almost any capacity had to become acquainted with current fashions in public speaking, and to become facile with the sorts of arguments—especially the sorts of bottom-line financial reckonings—that commanded the attention of the Athenian citizenry. Public money and who controls it was, for example, the crux of the great debate between the old devotee of Cleon and his sophisticated son in Aristophanes' *Wasps,* staged in 422. Eight years earlier, Pericles had been fined for misappropriating funds after losing a debate of this nature, probably to Cleon. Before a popular audience it mattered more to be able to put the right spin on one's accounting—or to avoid rendering accounts before a hostile jury, according to the advice that Alcibiades is supposed to have given Pericles—than to engage in complicated calculations.[51]

To be able to provide an effective speech on such occasions to friends in need was an estimable quality, but the mercenary aspect of writing for hire could stigmatize successful speech-writers. Not only was such work for profit an ignoble use of *sophia,* but it also reinforced the reputation of sophistic rhetoric as an amoral tool. The well-known assertion of sophists of being able to teach a skill that "brings freedom to mankind in general and to each man dominion over others in his own country," as Plato has Gorgias describe his art, was easily reduced to the claim that "these men will teach—if one gives them money—a speaker how to win both just and unjust cases," as Aristophanes parodies their practice.[52]

Fascination with rhetoric's promise of total success thus ran up against the unshakable common sense that not all arguments deserve to win. For those, like Socrates, who chose to plumb the depths of *sophia,* the political success of studied rhetoric seemed to indicate the fallacy of measuring truth, justice, and wisdom by success in persuading the uneducated masses. But confirmation of such a fallacy required indisputable evidence that truth, justice, and wisdom had failed. Personal failures in court, like setbacks in the political arena, provided grievances to individuals and their friends, but no proof of a systematic flaw in the premises of democracy. As long as the *demos,* collectively, was successful in its endeavors, there could be no intellectually coherent challenge to the politics justified by Protagoras and practiced by Pericles and his followers.

VICTORY, THE MEASURE OF VIRTUE

Victory over others in sport or in war, as discussed in chapter 1, was its own justification and a proof of *arete.* But victory in a deliberative debate was *not* the equivalent of victory in a prize-bearing contest, even though successful speakers were inclined to treat it as such. Guiding the deliberations of the assembled *demos* was fundamental to realizing the *arete* of the community, Protagoras' "political *arete,*" but this collective quality became manifest only through the outcome of the community's resolution, not in the moment of arriving at a decision. Yet the equation of personal victory in debate with a more transcendent, Athenian *arete* was encouraged by the long-reinforced notion of the infallibility of the *demos,* and by the Athenian trait, remarked more than once by Thucydides, of regarding their resolutions as all but achieved the moment they were made.[53]

War heightened the tensions underlying all of these assumptions. The hard pragmatics of wartime politics made victory the only defensible standard of

FIGURE 3. The charm of victory: Nike holding a helmet, the prize of victory, in a fragment from the parapet of the temple of Athena Nike on the Acropolis, usually dated ca. 415. Athens, Acropolis Museum nos. 1013 and 1001. Photo courtesy of the Deutsches Archäologisches Institut, Athens, neg. no. 68/146.

behavior, but to seek victory too quickly was to court disaster. The heightened urgencies of war placed increasing strain on those, like Pericles at its outset, who wished to argue that immediate hardships were justified by long-term benefits. Wherever the odds did not seem overwhelmingly favorable for victory, it became ever more difficult to sustain a policy based on reasoned argument. For this reason, Pericles' prestige was severely eroded in the first years of the war, the last years of his life. For this reason too, Nicias was circumspect in his undertakings, almost to the point of timidity. Victory was chiefly for those who knew when to seize the moment. For this reason, both Cleon and later Alcibiades were bold, though not without circumspection. Whenever victory was achieved, it deserved the highest celebration (see figure 3).[54]

But because success, sometimes even victory in battle, could not always be recognized at once but only some while after the event, those who were adept at argument could sometimes persuade others that a setback was in fact not a failure, or that it was an unavoidable jolt on the rough road to eventual success. For this reason, Athenians who trafficked in the affairs of war had to be quick-witted speakers.[55]

An important part of the arsenal of such argumentation came from lessons of the past. The privations suffered by Athenians under the leadership of Themistocles and Aristides provided a useful precedent. This was the lesson of the past recalled by Pericles in his last speech to the Athenians reported by Thucydides: "You must not fall below the standard of your fathers, who not only won an empire by their own toil and sweat, without receiving it from others, but went on to keep it safe so that they could hand it down to you."[56]

Potentially more powerful, however, were arguments that relied on greater antiquity, and that appealed to more pervasive forces than the imperial power created by the previous generation of Athenians. Privation and hardship could be endured if it could be seen that these things came from the gods, and would lead in due course to a desirable outcome, as revealed in ancient oracles. To understand this evidence, and to take due account of it in the formulation of policy, required the advice of a good soothsayer. Every Athenian statesman knew the importance of this domain of expertise, especially in wartime.

THE ORACLE MONGERS

Cleon recognized the value of oracles for justifying policies. According to Aristophanes, he had a whole box full of oracles, to be deployed whenever the occasion required support or guidance from a higher authority. To be sure, it is for farcical effect that Aristophanes depicts the demagogue's reliance on oracles, from the beginning of the *Knights* to its climax in the duel of the demagogues. But farce relies on the familiar, and in this as in much else, Aristophanes was exploiting the humorous potential of what his audience knew to be a serious matter.[57]

The attitude of Athenians toward oracles and oracle mongers, *chresmologoi*, can only be described as skeptical credulity. Thucydides himself, generally regarded as the epitome of rational skepticism, embodies this paradoxical attitude of his contemporaries. He sometimes mentions oracles to make the point that they were unreliable, or, as a speaker in his work claimed, even deceptive guides, "which, encouraging hope, lead men to ruin." Yet more often he mentions ancient oracles and their fulfillment without a hint of skepticism, and notes the fulfillment of several oracular predictions within the war that he narrates. So, for instance, in Book 2,

Thucydides challenges the popular interpretation of a Delphic utterance banning settlement on the ground called "Pelargikon" at Athens:

> In my opinion the oracle was fulfilled in a way quite contrary to the sense in which people accepted it; for the city's misfortunes did not, I think, befall her because of the forbidden settlement; it was rather that the necessity for the settlement was caused by the war, and the oracle, without naming the war, knew in advance that houses would never be built on the Pelargikon in furtherance of prosperity.

Interpretations may be contested, but there is no skepticism here about whether or not an oracle could legitimately be "fulfilled," nor doubt that Delphi's oracle "knew in advance" a truth of considerable importance to the Athenians. In Book 5, Thucydides reveals a similarly nuanced perspective when he affirms the unity of the period of twenty-seven years as the overall duration of the war he narrates.

> For those who made any firm assertion on the strength of oracles, here is one solitary instance of their having been proved accurate. I myself remember that all the time from the beginning to the end of the war it was being put about by many people that the war would last for thrice nine years....

The skepticism he expresses here about the utility of oracles, again, does not challenge the validity of paying them serious attention; rather, it casts doubts on the ability of most people, aside from this one instance, to arrive at the right interpretation of oracles.[58]

In this respect, oracles were like any other objective evidence that Athenians had to take into account as they debated policy and made decisions (and from the hindsight of Thucydides, the Athenians were no wiser in understanding oracles than they were in deliberating other matters). Oracles were, however, a domain of knowledge where the judgment of some individuals commanded more respect. Diopeithes and Lampon, both famous expounders of oracles mentioned by Aristophanes, in the *Birds* of 414 and in numerous other passages, are both attested as proposers of decrees in the Athenian Assembly in the 420s. Their advice typically concerned matters of religion, but the oracles that they and others expounded for the edification of all Athenians touched on all aspects of Athenian policy.[59]

The clearest instance of this comes again from Thucydides. In a passage that suggests that the interpretation of oracles was a more routine activity in the Assembly than he otherwise indicates, Thucydides describes the reaction of the Athenians to the news, in 413, of the destruction of their forces in Sicily. "They were angry with the orators who had joined in promoting the expedition, just as if they had not themselves voted it, and were enraged also with the reciters of oracles and soothsayers, and all other omenmongers of the time who had encouraged them to hope that they should conquer Sicily."[60]

In the era of the Peloponnesian War no less than in the Persian War, when Themistocles advised the Athenians of the true meaning of the oracle of the "wooden walls," a fair-sounding oracle was useful to an argument on state policy. Matters of grave concern always encouraged men to seek divine guidance, and the war, and especially the plague that befell Athens early in the war, gave the Athenians every incentive to scour the books of oracular utterances, and to listen to those who professed to understand such things. But the *demos* was ever at risk of being fooled by the most beguiling orator or oracle monger, as both Aristophanes and Thucydides show. Herodotus, too, was reminding his listeners in the 420s that the misinterpretation of oracles could be the surest avenue to destruction for those who commanded great wealth and power. Expert guidance was called for, so that the *demos* could deliberate on such matters with as much objectivity as possible.[61]

THE EXPERTISE OF *SYNGRAPHEIS*

One of the premises underlying Socrates' lifelong pursuit of *sophia* was the observation that certain types of knowledge could be mastered by experts. Masters of technical skills were widely recognized for their expertise, and in some cases were even honored by having their expertise consulted by the Athenian *demos.* So Socrates opens his challenge to Protagoras, in Plato's dialogue of that name, with a paradox. Some forms of honored expertise are teachable, but the most important domain of knowledge and skill, Protagoras' *politike techne,* seems to elude that quality:

> Now when the Athenians meet in the Assembly, then if the state is faced with some building project, I observe that the architects are sent for and consulted about the proposed structures, and when it is a matter of shipbuilding, the naval designers, and so on with everything which the Assembly regards as a subject for learning and teaching. If anyone else tries to give advice, whom they do not consider an expert, however handsome or wealthy or nobly born he may be, it makes no difference; the members reject him noisily and with contempt, until either he is shouted down or desists, or else is dragged off or ejected by the police on the orders of the presiding magistrates. That is how they behave over subjects they consider technical. But when it is something to do with the government of the country that is to be debated, the man who gets up to advise them may be a builder or equally well a blacksmith or a shoemaker, a merchant or shipowner, rich or poor, of good family or none. No one brings it up against any of these, as against those I have just mentioned, that here is a man who without any technical qualifications, unable to point to anybody as his teacher, is yet trying to give advice. The reason must be that they do not think this is a subject that can be taught.[62]

Socrates' account characterizes the difference between open debate and formal consultation, but it overlooks a form of expertise that was also consulted by the *demos* on a variety occasions, including in matters of state. This was expertise in the form of commissioned reports, or memoranda, referred to as *syngraphai*. These were usually composed by a committee whose members could be referred to as *syngrapheis*. Their memoranda could define the terms of treaties and the oaths that bound parties to a treaty. *Syngraphai* also appear in public decrees dealing with the practical aspects of religious and cultic affairs, including building designs that might also call for the advice of architects. The texts of legislative proposals could also be referred to as *syngraphai*.[63]

Like the inscriptions that attest the majority of known *syngraphai*, the evidence for such commissioned reports is fragmentary, but it is sufficient to suggest their growing importance as a new form of expertise in democratic Athens. Beyond the applied expertise of architects and, presumably, the received expertise of priestly officiants, the commissions composing *syngraphai* seem to have derived their authority from the consultation of existing documents, such as treaties or oaths, or the texts of religious laws and regulations. Such documents, analogous to collections of venerable oracles, were regarded as authoritative in and of themselves, but uncertain in their application to current concerns. The interpretation of such sources, for legislative or executive action, therefore became the charge of specially appointed committees. *Syngraphai* were thus the product of applied research. They represent a procedure by which the *demos*, evidently with increasing frequency after about 430, derived authoritative guidance from past precedents as they formulated policy for the future.[64]

One publicly sponsored research report of singular historical interest is the publication on stone of the list of Athenian archons extending from the early seventh century down to the mid-420s. Only small fragments of this list survive, and none of them from its heading, so we are not informed about the purpose or occasion of its compilation. The need to record the passage of time in official documents is self-evident only for a limited number of transactions, the most significant of which are financial. The increasing stringency, from 428 on, of financial administration in wartime Athens may have been an impetus for publishing a list of annual archons by which the passage of time on arrears of tribute, loans, taxes, and fines due to the state or to the gods could be publicly observed, but this cannot explain why the archon-list reached so far into the past.

This interest in distinguished names from the past most likely originated from the same source that originally prompted those archons to record their own names on dedications and monuments, and that likewise prompted their kinsmen to remember them: namely, the honor accruing to themselves, to their descendants, and through them to their community. That this register had significance to Athenian families in the 420s is indicated by the fact that seven out of the eleven names that are readable with fair probability, representing archons from the early sixth to the early fifth century, come from families with living descendants in the 420s (two of the remaining names are Peisistratids, whose direct line had been eliminated). The archon-list might, then, have served as a testimony to the long—and still living—legacy of *arete* at Athens.[65]

These considerations, however, are only possible attendant motives for the compilation of the archon-list. We have to admit that the specific occasion justifying its publication remains obscure. But whatever initiative led to the proposal to inscribe such a list, its existence is evidence for a significant development: it was the publicly sanctioned product of erudite, historical research. No such list existed before the 420s, although a host of individual monuments known to us from their remains or from citations by Thucydides and later authors could have provided material for this research project.[66]

Similar projects of the 420s and later were the product of sophistic research. The compilation of the list of Olympic victors by Hippias of Elis was one such, and so were works by his contemporary, Hellanicus of Lesbos, who compiled a list of victors at the Spartan Carnea, a chronographical treatise on *The Priestesses of Hera at Argos,* and one on the history of Attica referred to by Thucydides as Hellanicus' *Attike syngraphe.* Like these works, the Athenian archon-list was almost certainly a *syngraphe,* or perhaps a *syngramma katalogaden,* "systematic compilation." Even though it must have been commissioned by a public resolution, it tapped the same reservoir of talents and interests that produced sophistic *syngraphai.* All are examples of the *akribeia,* "accuracy," an attribute of *sophia,* that the learned class applied to various forms of documentary composition in the final decades of the fifth century, and that the Athenian *demos* summoned to instruct its resolutions.[67]

THE CONSPIRATORS

As long as expertise was at the service of the people, it was held in high public regard. This was as true of verbal artistry, as illustrated by the celebrity of Gorgias, as it was of any of the politically useful skills that could be taught by sophists. But while expertise could be publicly deployed, it had to be privately cultivated, and in the competitive social and political culture of Athens, patronage of the many skills of the sophists most often seemed to be, and was, privately motivated.

In the virulently democratic culture of Athens in the 420s and later, anyone in a position of high responsibility was liable to be accused by political rivals of mismanaging the people's business, or embezzling the people's money. Small matters could be blown out of proportion before the public, especially if the evidence in question was originally supposed to be confidential. To guard against such attacks, and to be sure that one's political confidants would not abuse private trust for political advantage, and also to be sure of the selfless devotion of a group of loyal friends, many among the well-to-do who pursued their interests in politics formalized their association in groups called *hetaireiai,* "fellowships." These emulated the Homeric image of a band of *hetairoi,* "comrades," the devoted followers of a great chieftain, for their association was highly personalized, usually as the following of a distinguished individual. They were also more commonly called *synomosiai,* "sworn associations," after the oaths of allegiance that bound them together. Generally committed to the elitism of the *kaloi k'agathoi,* the *synomosiai,* Thucydides tells us, "existed in Athens for mutual support in lawsuits and elections." A similar description is given in Plato's *Apology,* as Socrates describes his disdain for what he, disingenuously, includes among the habits of "most" Athenians:

> I did not care for the things that most people care about—making money, having a comfortable home, high military or civil rank, and all the other activities, political appointments, secret societies [*synomosiai*], party organizations [*staseis*], which go on in our city. I thought that I was really too strict in my principles to survive if I went in for this sort of thing. . . .[68]

Such groups represented a formalization, for purposes of political support, of the bonds of affection and shared aristocratic values that Plato characterizes in the various gatherings that Socrates frequented. Any or all of those gatherings might either have been identical with a *synomosia* or *hetaireia,* or might have contained elements of one or more such sworn societies among their number. But according to Socrates' avowal, the true philosopher did not compromise his principles with the sorts of concessions to expediency that might dictate the political actions of such groups, so Plato offers us no insight into that aspect of these societies. But Aristophanes shows us, in his *Knights* and *Wasps,* how ready some speakers were to allege the political influence of such groups whenever rival speakers or public officers could be said to be behaving in a manner not in the best interests of the Athenian *demos.*

Allegations of conspiratorial private interests were especially common whenever personal contacts and negotiations were underway between members of the Athenian elite and their foreign counterparts. When matters that might affect public business were being discussed behind private, closed doors, it was almost impossible for the wider public to distinguish motives through the welter of innuendo that might be stirred up. So suspicion was a weapon hurled against his challenger by the blustering Paphlagon/Cleon, in Aristophanes' *Knights* of 424. The sausage-seller himself was so base and despicable that he was below reproach, and thus out of harm's reach in this attack. But his allies, the Athenian cavalrymen, were prime targets:

> I'm going straight to the Council to denounce the *synomosiai* of the lot of you: your night-time meetings in town and your sworn dealings with the Medes and the King, and all that cheesy business with the Boeotians!

Talk of conspiracy also figures in the *Wasps* of Aristophanes, of 422. In that play, staged on the eve of the Peace of Nicias, allegations of conspiracy ranged between anti-democratic collaboration with the Spartans and plots to establish "the tyranny of Hippias." In either case, as the comic satire would have it, the devotees of Cleon were ready to believe that *someone* was out to subvert the people's government.[69]

The inflammatory rhetoric of demagogues relied on such fears of subversion to command the attention of the Assembly and the jury-courts. Although we may be inclined to dismiss this evidence, when it comes from Aristophanes, as comic exaggeration, there is good reason to believe that the bluster became especially serious at crucial moments of decision, when the Athenian Assembly had to evaluate most critically all of its informants and their motives. For personal motives were always at play, sometimes at cross-purposes, when statesmen were advocating the people's business.

At such moments of decision, when the future was most uncertain, the certainty that seemed to reside in knowledge of the past assumed all the more importance. Especially then did the Athenian *demos* look to expounders of the past for secure guidance. Such was the case in the spring of 415, as the Athenians contemplated their boldest military venture, the conquest of Sicily. Appeals to the terms of treaties, to the history of empire, to ancient ties of kinship, and to oracular predictions were all used to assure that enthusiasm for the project would check the anxieties felt by some. But anxieties were aroused still further by the appearance of undeniable signs of a conspiracy.

PART TWO

The Crisis of Athens, 415–403

CHAPTER FOUR

The Expulsion of Alcibiades, 415–413

"You perhaps think that your empire extends only over your allies; I will declare to you the truth. The visible field of action has two parts, land and sea. In the whole of the one of these you are completely supreme, not merely as far as you use it at present, but also to what further extent you may think fit. . . . "

PERICLES, IN THUCYDIDES 2.62.2*

In Part I it was suggested that the concepts of historical inquiry inaugurated by Herodotus and refined by Thucydides were the product of rapidly changing conditions bought on by a war, beginning in 431, that threatened to destroy the Athenian empire. By 415, the Athenians were both at the height of confidence in the strength of their empire, and were reduced, by bizarre events, to the depths of perplexity about the future. In that year, as will be argued in this chapter, Herodotus' work was in the process of becoming known by an Athenian public craving reasoned guidance, and accustomed to seeking it in accounts of the past. Certain features of Thucydides' narrative, it will also be argued, reflect this search for guidance from the past. Aristophanes' farce, in the *Birds* of 414, reflects both the perplexity of these bizarre times and the yearning of the Athenians for enlightened leadership to show the way.

The year 415, which saw the launching of the Sicilian expedition, also marks the beginning of an especially convulsive sequence of events that threatened both the Athenian democracy and its empire. Over the following decade, in both the strategies of war and the practices of government, the Athenians experienced optimism and catastrophe in rapid succession. Each catastrophe left the Athenians questioning previously accepted wisdom, and, purged by failure, they looked to a residual core of what seemed to be more reliable truth. Yet, in each case, the lessons of failure were soon repeated, until, by 404, the Athenians had lost both their empire and democracy. The Athenians then had to endure their greatest catastrophe, civil war.

*Translated by R. Crawley.

Part II traces the course of these events and reflects on how the Athenians sought, especially in political practice and in drama, to give order and meaning to their experiences as they unfolded. Complexity and ambiguity are the salient characteristics both of these events and of their reflections in contemporary sources. Since the accounts of our narrative sources were given only after some passage of time, the causal connections between events have often been obscured or recast to suit later perspectives. Of necessity, then, the interpretations I offer here are at times more speculative than others have been, especially in treating subjects only skirted allusively in our sources. But even in instances where specific proof is lacking, my approach will be justified if the questions it raises draw attention to the nature and effects of the deepening quest for meaning and reason that the Athenians themselves experienced in these years.

ALCIBIADES

In the public eye since he came of age, as a battlefield hero, in 432, Alcibiades lived to unite his personal *arete* with the manifest *arete* of Athens. He embodied the exhortation to all Athenians of his guardian and mentor, Pericles, to

> fix your eyes every day on the greatness of Athens as she really is, and fall in love with her. When you realize her greatness, then reflect that what made her great was men with a spirit of adventure, men who knew their duty, men who were ashamed to fall below a certain standard. If ever they failed in an enterprise, they made up their minds that at any rate the city should not find their *arete* lacking. . . .[1]

As an advocate of imperial policy in the period of Cleon's leadership, Alcibiades gained a reputation as the quintessential ambitious young man. Shortly after Cleon's death in 422, his influence reached its apex as he became the chief critic of Nicias' policy of rapprochement with Sparta. In 420 Alcibiades succeeded in aligning Athens with Argos as the core of a new movement to challenge Spartan dominance in the Peloponnese. In 418 this alliance gave the sons of Marathon, the Athenian hoplites, the chance to prove themselves on the battlefield against the Spartans at Mantinea. More senior commanders, Laches and Nicostratus, led the Athenians and lost their lives in the hard-fought Spartan victory. In its aftermath, Alcibiades was able to use his connections in the Peloponnese in ways that continued to benefit Athens and himself.

The summer of 416 saw Alcibiades' unprecedented feats of victory in the Olympic games. This moment of glory was followed, at the end of the next winter, by a moment of peril for Alcibiades. For this was most likely the time when the Athenians decided, on the advice of the demagogue Hyperbolus, to hold an ostracism in which it was expected that either Alcibiades or Nicias would be expelled. But by the connivance of these two influential men, the vote for exile fell instead on Hyperbolus. In the spring of 415, the triumphant Alcibiades was poised to lead an Athenian expedition to aid allies in Sicily, with the destruction of Syracuse and the conquest of the island clearly in mind.[2]

The launching of the Sicilian expedition was pivotal to the careers both of Alcibiades and of imperial Athens. Alcibiades' sudden fall from favor, examined in this chapter, was harbinger to the destruction of the Sicilian expedition, the single greatest catastrophe suffered by Athens before her final defeat. Sharing a view commonly expressed in the years after 415, Thucydides identified Alcibiades as the key figure in determining the fate of Athens. Although the implications of Thucydides' judgment on this point are contested, there can be no doubt that Alcibiades had a greater impact on the fate of Athens and her empire in its final decade and a half than any other individual.[3]

The extraordinary story of Alcibiades' movements among the Spartans, the Ionians, and the Persians, of his instigation and then repudiation of revolution at Athens, and of his eventual triumphant return to Athens, has since antiquity been regarded as the tale of an exceptionally agile personality. Plutarch, probably following Theopompus, likens him to a chameleon—able to make himself agreeable wherever he went and having no scruples to hinder his self-aggrandizement. His chief accomplishments during his exile are, for the most part, beyond doubt (that he fathered a son on Timaea, wife of the Spartan king Agis, must remain in the realm of intriguing uncertainties). Explaining his achievements is an abiding challenge. Ancient biographical tradition, preserving more than a tinge of the powerful slander generated by his foes, focuses on the unique qualities of Alcibiades' personality. In this light, the events he had a hand in are seen as lying on or beyond the bounds of human norms, as if shaped by the genius of good and evil. Like Aristotle's *politikon zoön,* Alcibiades strove to achieve perfection within his political community; but, fallen from it, he was rendered like Aristotle's *apolis,* the man beyond law and community, who must be either a beast or a god.[4]

However unparalleled Alcibiades' deeds may have been, and whatever their moral value, they were achieved by skillful negotiation of prevailing norms and circumstances. Alcibiades' career thus reveals dimensions of social and political relations normally obscured by the rhetoric of democracy and patriotism. Transcending boundaries that defined more conventional political careers, the deeds and experiences of Alcibiades became the touchstone for many a debate on political leadership in the turmoils of his lifetime and afterward. They are our best window into the heart of turbulent times.

SICILIAN AMBITIONS

The vision of Sicilian states paying tribute to the Athenian empire was neither the brainchild of Alcibiades nor the whim of a moment. It was a prospect that had animated public resolutions, alliances, military expeditions, and judicial proceedings at Athens for at least a generation. In the heyday of Pericles and on the eve of the Peloponnesian War, alliances in Sicily were made with the expectation that Athenian might would follow. Between 427 and 424 continuous military operations in support of the Sicilian and Italian allies at war with Syracuse had been sustained on the presumption, Thucydides reports, that they would "bring Sicilian affairs under their control." In the *Knights* of 424, Aristophanes even made fun of a grandiose scheme of Hyperbolus to launch an expedition against Carthage, as if Sicily were already in hand. But by the end of 422, when the Athenians were ready to make peace with Sparta, expectations in the west remained frustrated. A series of generals who had commanded Athenian forces in Sicily were made to account for popular disappointment before the courts, and at least three were found guilty of punishable offenses.[5]

Two of the most prominent Athenian commanders in Sicily in the 420s, Laches and Phaeax, are known to have been personal enemies of Alcibiades. It is not improbable that their enmity arose in the context of trials over their direction of Sicilian policy. Already by 425, Alcibiades had a reputation as one of a number of shark-like prosecutors seeking easy prey in the courts. In Aristophanes' *Wasps* of 422, Laches is depicted as ripe for prosecution for his alleged illicit gains made during his Sicilian campaigns. Cleon is Laches' prosecutor in the mock-trial depicted by Aristophanes. Although Alcibiades is not named in this context, his support of causes championed by Cleon is well attested, and Aristophanes does allude, in the course of Laches' mock-trial, to earlier trials where Alcibiades had a role. From the beginnings of his political career, then, it seems that Alcibiades had openly aligned himself with the interests of the *demos* in an aggressive Sicilian policy.[6]

Although Thucydides does not say so, it is likely that Alcibiades shared this commitment to achieve dominion in Sicily for many years with Hyperbolus, Cleon's leading successor as champion of the *demos*. As we will see further below, much of the popular enthusiasm for the expedition of 415, and the scandals that immediately preceded its departure, are better understood when it is recognized that Hyperbolus, the demagogue, had a leading role in promoting the project. But Hyperbolus was suddenly removed from the scene by ostracism, almost certainly at the beginning of spring 415. Thucydides makes no mention of this event until much later, when he describes the murder of the exiled Hyperbolus in 411. His narrative of the final deliberations over the expedition therefore begins, in 6.8.1, immediately after the ostracism of Hyperbolus, at the time when the Athenians received the last of a series of embassies from their Elymian allies at Segesta in Sicily. We will follow Thucydides' account from this point, and introduce evidence from other sources, including evidence for the circumstances of Hyperbolus' ostracism, as it becomes essential to clarify points left unexplained by Thucydides.[7]

At the beginning of spring 415, the Assembly voted to appoint Alcibiades, Nicias, and Lamachus as generals with full powers *(autokratores)* to command the expedition to Sicily requested by their allies at Segesta. The force, Thucydides notes at another point in his account, was to be the largest ever sent to Sicily by the Athenians. How large was to be determined by expert advice. Nicias, appointed to command against his will, argued on the basis of practical considerations—undue risk for uncertain gain—against this undertaking. But Nicias' speech had an effect opposite to his intentions, Thucydides notes, for its reasoned arguments only spurred the Athenians on to further measures to remove risk. Encouraged by Alcibiades, Athenian confidence in their ability to achieve their goals was at a peak. In a striking phrase, Thucydides summarizes the urge that had seized hold of both young and old: "A passionate desire [*eros*] to set sail fell upon all alike" (6.24.3).[8]

A few, according to Thucydides, did not share the enthusiasm of the vast majority, but, "through fear of being thought unpatriotic for voting against them, kept quiet" (Thucydides 6.24.4). Aside from the logic of Nicias' cautious advice, neither Thucydides nor any other source explains the reason for the opposition of the few. In view of the disastrous outcome of the venture, no later account required an explanation to justify the foreboding that some felt. As Plutarch notes, the truth was foreseen by the likes of Socrates the philosopher, relying on his *daimonion,* or "divine inspiration," and by Meton the astronomer, "who was fearful for the future either through reasoned reckoning or by some form of divination." Whatever the nature of the misgivings of these individuals, Thucydides and Plutarch give clues to a source of apprehension on the part of some that arose not from fears that Alcibiades' cause would fail, but that it would succeed.[9]

Immediately prior to noting the quiet apprehensions of the few, Thucydides observes that "the general masses and the average soldier himself saw the prospect of getting pay for the time being and of adding to the empire so as to secure permanent paid employment in future." Perhaps it was this prospect of unlimited opportunities for pay for the masses that unsettled a certain element among the Athenian elite. Further evidence confirms this impression.[10]

In the years and months immediately prior to the Sicilian campaign the Athenians were conducting military operations around the Aegean, supporting allies at Argos, attempting to recapture Amphipolis on the Strymon, and, most recently, conquering the island of Melos. These actions were small in scale and duration, and were largely intended to consolidate the authority of the Athenian empire within what had become its customary sphere of influence, no doubt much to the benefit of the established members of the Athenian leadership. The Sicilian venture on the other hand was grandiose, with seemingly limitless potential to enrich Athens and Athenians, and especially those Athenians with little to lose and everything to gain. Vested interests in Aegean affairs meant practically nothing in this venture. The possibilities were almost revolutionary.[11]

Although the personal pretenses and successes of Alcibiades had surely long turned the eye of jealousy upon him, it was his mastery on this occasion of the aspirations of the mass of Athenians, not to mention of the allies and hired mercenaries as well, that instilled fear in those of his peers who did not stand with him. There was also a substantive sting that prompted quiet resentment against the measures championed by Alcibiades.

To assure success and to safeguard Athens from enemies at home while a large force was away, the Athenian Assembly had enacted a series of decrees describing the procedures to be followed for the launching and sustaining of the expedition. Among the provisions, which were recorded on stone and displayed on the Acropolis, were details about the numbers and classes of fighting men to be maintained at public expense both for the expedition and for home defense, and stipulations about how the state was to meet these expenses. The surviving fragments of these inscriptions reveal that the Athenian Assembly gave prior approval to the assessment of any necessary *eisphora,* or tax on propertied Athenians, should tribute or other revenues prove insufficient.[12]

Such an open-ended commitment to provide sustained pay was without precedent, and to place the personal wealth of the Athenian aristocracy at the disposal of an enthusiastic mob entranced by the figure of Alcibiades was too much for some to bear. What was more, the measures even prescribed the provision of arms to seven hundred Athenians too poor to own them already, so that they could join the ranks of the hoplite corps. Pay for military service during the previous decade of war had already had the effect of blurring the traditional distinction between the hoplite middle class who could provide their own weapons and the propertyless, wage-earning class of *thetes.* Now, not only was pay to be given generously, but the state was to underwrite, possibly for the first time, the very tokens of esteem that marked the social elevation of poor Athenians into the ranks of "the hoplites, the well-born, and the worthy."[13]

This provoked a reaction in conservative circles, to judge by the traces of a speech by Antiphon preserved in much later sources. The phrase, "to make all the *thetes* hoplites," is attributed to Antiphon's *Against Philinus,* and the circumstances of 415 provide the most likely occasion for this reference. A late and uncritical biographical sketch of the orator's life mentions among his outstanding achievements Antiphon's service in "arming men of military age" *(tous akmazontas hoplizon)* and in manning sixty triremes. This is surely a reference to the measures adopted for sending the fleet to Sicily, where sixty was the number of triremes that the Athenians originally resolved to send out, before Nicias' speech prompted them to increase the number. Known for his oligarchic views, Antiphon would certainly not have been a supporter of the expedition, nor would he have endorsed the elevation of *thetes* to hoplite status. This biographical note, then, must be a garbled inference drawn, at second or third hand, from some discussion of the subject of arming *thetes* and manning a fleet in a speech by Antiphon. In all probability, the speech attacked the legality of an innovative policy of arming poor Athenians through a liturgy imposed upon the wealthy.[14]

Such a conclusion derives support from a remark by Plutarch that, in the debate with Alcibiades, Nicias' few supporters included wealthy men *(euporoi)* who withheld their opinions in public because they were afraid to be accused of "trying to get out of their liturgies and trierarchies." Normally, the trierarchy would have been the *only* personal liturgy borne by a wealthy Athenian at the outset of a military expedition. In this case, the implication of Plutarch's words is confirmed by the fragmentary decrees of 415: wealthy Athenians faced additional and unwelcome financial impositions at this time. It is entirely in keeping with what is known of Antiphon's sentiments and strategies that he would have used the courts to oppose such a measure as a violation of Athenian custom.[15]

ANTIPHON THE SOPHIST

Antiphon son of Sophilus of Rhamnous, active in the 420s and 410s, was the first Athenian known to later tradition as a composer of commissioned speeches. His talents were displayed, in the manner of foreign sophists like Gorgias, by exemplary speeches that showed how to argue a case, even how to argue both sides of a hypothetical case. He also composed treatises on aspects of law, education, knowledge, social psychology, and politics. By these he came to share, in the opinion of his peers and successors, the ambiguous space between sophist and philosopher also occupied by Socrates. Because his talents in speech-writing were placed at the service of others, he was snubbed as a money-grubber and as an inferior intellect by Plato, among others. Yet he was respected by many influential Athenians in his day and much admired by Thucydides in particular:

> Antiphon was an Athenian second to none of his contemporaries in *arete.* He had a powerful intellect and was well able to express his thoughts in words; he never came forward to speak in front of the assembly or willingly competed in

> any other form of public life, since the people in general mistrusted him because of his reputation for cleverness; on the other hand, when other people were engaged in lawsuits or had points to make before the assembly, he was the man to give the best and most helpful advice to those who asked him for it.[16]

Antiphon's helpful advice was based in part on his mastery of the many and varied legal documents that guided deliberative and judicial procedure at Athens. His exceptional proficiency in this field makes it likely that he was influential in the development of a legal device later commonly employed to oppose political measures, the *graphe paranomon.* First attested in 415, the *graphe paranomon* was a written denunciation of a measure as being either in substance or procedurally "unconstitutional," that is, in violation of existing laws. The determination of applicable statutes, however, was itself a matter for dispute, and the effect of the written injunction was to suspend a given measure until a law court was able to hear arguments and render a decision. Clearly, proficiency in citing statutes, and in finding statutes of the highest authority possible, was essential to the successful application of a *graphe paranomon.* This was Antiphon's forte.[17]

Although he did not quote directly from documents, as later orators often did, Antiphon displayed his facility in arraying documentary evidence: "The law runs as follows..." (6.36); "But when the *Basileus* read them the law..." (6.38); "The laws which apply to each one of these charges differ..." (5.10); "the law concerned applies to the custodians of malefactors..." (5.17). In Antiphon's work, too, we find appeals to high antiquity as affirming the validity of laws and customs. A case in point is his reference to the laws of Draco, which still applied in his day in cases of homicide:

> It would be unanimously agreed, I think, that the laws which deal with cases such as the present are the most admirable and righteous *(kallista kai hosiotata)* of laws. Not only have they the distinction of being the oldest in the land, but they have changed no more than the crime with which they are concerned; and that is the surest token of good laws, as time and experience show mankind what is imperfect. Hence you must not use the speech for the prosecution to discover whether your laws are good or bad: you must use the laws to discover whether or not the speech for the prosecution is giving you a correct and lawful interpretation of the case.

This passage is repeated verbatim in two speeches by Antiphon, indicating the importance of a historical perspective to Antiphon's forensic technique. Fragments of his other works contain similar appeals to the sanctity of established tradition: "Justice consists in not transgressing the customs of the city in which one enjoys citizenship..." (from *On Truth*); "...and knowing that your laws were handed down from ancestors *(patroön)* and were ancient..." (from an unknown work).[18]

Antiphon thus had at his disposal the tools by which to oppose any measure that could readily be labeled as a violation of tradition. A proposal that established a precedent for making "all the *thetes* hoplites" was certainly such a measure, especially if it did so by allocating to the poor the private property of well-to-do Athenians. For it confounded the distinction between the ancient census classes of *thetes* and *zeugitai,* a distinction supported by the venerable authority of Solonic and Draconic law. Publicly sanctioned research into these laws began only a few years later, in connection with the oligarchic movement of 411, a movement in which Antiphon was a leader. Some of the fruits of this research were summarized a century later in Aristotle's *Constitution of the Athenians,* where it is stated that the possession of arms was the essential qualification for the full rights of citizenship in the time of Draco. The evidence for this statement is not clear, and it is now generally accepted that Aristotle's so-called "constitution of Draco" was the invention, or at least the distorted concoction, of oligarchic propagandists in the late fifth century. The evidence of Antiphon's scholarship and partisan interests makes it possible to suggest that this ideological interpretation of early Athenian law first gained recognition in the hearing of a *graphe paranomon* challenging the practice of arming *thetes* bound for Sicily.[19]

The battle, for the time being, was inconclusive. Seven hundred *thetes* were armed and set sail. But at a time when the archaic status of *thetes* was becoming meaningless in practical terms, the fact that *thetes* remained a legal category represented a victory of sorts for the conservative agenda.

SPOILING THE MOMENT

The legal acumen of the aristocracy, epitomized in Antiphon, provided one avenue of attack against what some saw as the unconscionable indulgence of the poor masses that Alcibiades now championed. But this attack was slow, and its effects were not immediately felt, although within a few years it became the basis of a systematic effort to do away with democracy at Athens. Events might well have turned out otherwise, however, if Sicily had been brought under Athenian dominion under the leadership of Alcibiades. This prospect clearly terrified some among the Athenian elite. If Alcibiades' bold venture succeeded, the confidence and power of the *demos* would be greatly increased, and those who had no share in bringing these good things to the *demos* would suffer by seeing their rivals rise above them. A more drastic attack against Alcibiades and his supporters had to be launched, immediately.

One morning, not many days before the expedition to Sicily was to depart, the Athenians discovered that most of their Herms, their traditional statues of Hermes, had been vandalized. The phallus-bearing piers that stood by public and private entryways in and around the city had had their erect phalluses smashed or knocked off. Alcibiades may well have come to mind as Athenians contemplated this outrage. Years earlier Aristophanes had remarked that Alcibiades had been "born in the archonship of Phallenius," joking about a conspicuous aspect of Alcibiades' pride; a few years after the affair of the Herms, Alcibiades again was featured in Aristophanes' play, *Triphales,* or "He of the Triple (or, All-Powerful) Phallus." The act may thus have symbolized to some the docking of the pride and power of Alcibiades. But it also had other, more ominous levels of significance.[20]

The most solemn of public and judicial oaths at Athens were taken while standing on the severed genitals of sacrificial animals, as an imprecation of an analogous fate upon him who swears falsely. Destruction of the most public virile members of Athens may have been construed as symbolic fulfillment, or as a deceitful aversion, of the imprecations recently made in the oaths of office taken by certain officials, Alcibiades among them. The act was a warning that men entrusted with the greatest powers were capable of escaping even the most powerful vows of loyalty to the *demos.* In this light, it is surely significant that the greatest concentration of Herms lay beside one of the entrances to the Agora, in front of the Stoa Basileios, also known as the Stoa of the Herms (map 4). Before this stoa lay a venerable stone upon which the Athenian Archons and other officials customarily stood while taking their oaths of office after *tomia,* the symbolic severed members, had been placed on the stone. The oath-stone probably received a generous offering on the night of the *Hermokopidai,* or "Herm-choppers," as the conspirators soon came to be called.[21]

Although interpretation of this outrage was far from straightforward, one self-evident conclusion was that this act of vandalism against a deity who protected wayfarers was a menacing omen for the fleet about to depart. To understand the impact of this sacrilege on the attitude of the public, the remarks of a man defending himself against a charge of murder in an Athenian court not more than a few years before this incident are instructive:

> In cases of this nature the signs sent by the gods must also influence your verdict. It is upon them that you chiefly depend for safe guidance in affairs of state, whether in times of crisis or tranquillity...I hardly need remind you that many a man with unclean hands or some other form of defilement who has embarked on shipboard with the righteous has involved them in his own destruction....[22]

The prospect of launching a major sea-borne expedition with such an unatoned defilement upon the city, even with the perpetrators possibly among those embarking, checked enthusiasm for the venture. Oracles and portents were always taken seriously. On this occasion, Plutarch reports, Alcibiades had seen to it that his proposal to sail was supported by soothsayers and readings from ancient oracular books, while Thucydides notes the anger of the Athenians with these soothsayers and oracle mongers two years later, when the destruction of their forces in Sicily became known at Athens. The appointment of Nicias to share command with Alcibiades and Lamachus was probably favored by many on account of Nicias' scrupulous piety as much as for political reasons. Alcibiades himself, as Thucydides reports, urged the Athenians to see the virtue of combining his own energies with Nicias' celebrated good fortune. By these means, Alcibiades was probably concerned to allay fears raised by his opponents about the ancient curse of the Alcmaeonid clan, to which Alcibiades belonged through his mother. To rekindle these fears was at least part of what the *Hermokopidai* intended.[23]

Although some were prepared to dismiss the affair as a drunken prank, and others thought that it must have been done by the Corinthians, allies of Syracuse, the need to *know* who committed this offense overwhelmed all other public concerns. A Commission of Inquiry was appointed by the Council, and the Assembly authorized a reward for anyone who could identify the perpetrators. In the mood of the moment, it was also decreed that anyone, citizen, foreigner, or slave, who would come forward with information about *any* impious act would be immune from prosecution. This much, perhaps, was foreseen by the conspirators, for it opened a line of attack against Alcibiades himself.

Among other allegations that were soon made in response to this decree, a slave was produced to testify that he had witnessed Alcibiades and others enacting the Mysteries at a private house. These were rites of initiation sacred especially to the Eleusinian goddesses, Demeter and Persephone. All Athenians, and even all Greeks, could participate in these rituals, but only under the officiation of hereditary priests, and only within the enclosure of the goddesses' temples; they were not to be spoken of, or revealed, outside of those boundaries. A private enactment of such rites was as outrageous an affront to public piety as was the defacement of the images of Hermes.[24]

Alcibiades spoke at length in the Assembly against the accusation and demanded that the issue be settled by a trial before he set sail for Sicily, knowing that the goodwill of most Athenians, and especially of those preparing to embark with him, was still on his side. But the unresolved fears of sacrilege and conspiracy unleashed by these events had created an issue that Alcibiades could not control. His rivals and enemies appreciated this fact immediately, and directed public sentiment so as to remove Alcibiades, step by step, from his position of paramount influence.

For the moment, the Commission of Inquiry declared that a proper investigation would take time. In the meantime, Alcibiades' enemies, according to Thucydides, "introduced other orators who said that he should sail now and not delay the departure, but that upon his return he would stand trial within a set number of days.... And it was resolved that Alcibiades should sail" (6.29.3). The game was well afoot, and Alcibiades must have known that his opponents would do everything possible to prevent his return as a conquering hero. In fact, within two months of his departure they had secured his indictment for desecration of the Mysteries and had removed him from command.

ATHENS TURNED INSIDE OUT

The Commission of Inquiry and the Council, which was given authority by the Assembly to make arrests in these matters, wielded great power but could aim it only as its informants directed. In the weeks following the departure of the expedition to Sicily the Commission received accounts of several private performances of the Mysteries, some of them involving Alcibiades, some not, as well as various lists of men involved in the mutilation of the Herms. Hundreds of men were allegedly involved in these incidents. Even after cross-examination discredited some informers, the numbers of men who stood accused was alarming. A brother of Nicias, Diognetus, who was a member of the Commission of Inquiry, was denounced for participating in an illicit performance of the Mysteries and thought it wisest to flee into exile; another brother of Nicias, Eucrates, was arrested as a mutilator of the Herms on the authority of another informer, but released when the informer's testimony was later discredited. Many feared being named in the widening circle of blame and retribution.[25]

The effects of the inquisition were manifold. The arrests and ongoing investigation allayed fears of divine retribution through the sense that the contamination was being contained and would be thoroughly expunged once the inquisition reached its conclusion. Regarding the motives of those accused, however, consternation was on the increase. The alleged principals were men of high social standing; many of them, like Alcibiades himself, were identified with the potentially subversive "young" intellectuals, members of *synomosiai* or *hetaireiai;* all of them were men who met, in their several groups, to perform secret acts by night. They conformed, therefore, to the demagogue's stereotype of anti-democratic conspirators.

The outrages attested in the depositions gathered by the Commission of Inquiry thus gave substance to long-standing apprehensions fostered by the demagogues that the aristocratic *hetaireiai* were devoted to the subversion of the Athenian *demos.* As the most influential Athenian aristocrat, Alcibiades easily became the focus of denunciations. But how could the mutilation of the Herms, which upset the cause of Alcibiades, be connected with the enactments of the Mysteries involving Alcibiades? And how could outrages against pious sensibilities be so directly equated with political conspiracy? To answer these questions we begin by probing the significance of the action alleged most directly against Alcibiades himself, the profanation of the Mysteries.

From the evidence adduced and summarized in our sources, there can be no doubt that Alcibiades, among others, had engaged in acts that were now being treated as punishable offenses. But we are hard put to understand precisely what these acts were, why they were performed, and how they came to be so roundly condemned. The scandal produced a highly polemical interpretation of their religious and legal significance, and we are only given a summary of the official response and of the public opinion on which it was based; nowhere are we told what Alcibiades said publicly in his own defense. On a subject so much talked around, but so little talked about, we must rely on inferences. Close attention to terminology and circumstances, however, enables us to aim some converging conjectures into the heart of the affair of the Mysteries.

What Alcibiades and others did has often been described as a parody, or mockery, of sacred rites. Although "parody" and "mockery" could translate the terms *apomimesis* and *hubrisma,* used to describe the acts, they lead to the impression that what was done was done in jest, and that the scandal of the profanation of the Mysteries was, in essence, making light of a serious matter. The impression is abetted by the description of Plutarch of these acts accompanied by the influence of wine. In this case, however, Plutarch is referring simultaneously to the mutilation of the Herms, which other sources ascribe to a drunken revel; there is no independent support for the notion that the profanation of the Mysteries was performed purely as a drunken prank.[26]

Apomimesis and *hubrisma,* at a more essential level, mean "imitation" and "arrogant act," the first a descriptive term, the second interpretive. That these meanings better suit the accumulated testimony is borne out by the explicit description of these acts in a speech composed by Lysias for a contemporary of these events: "This man donned a ceremonial robe, and in imitation of the rites he revealed the sacred things to the uninitiated, and spoke with his lips the forbidden words. . . . " According to the terms of those who denounced these events, what Alcibiades did was not parody or mockery, but enactment. His was not the arrogance of disrespect, but the arrogance of appropriation. He took upon himself, for the benefit of his own circle of friends, powers otherwise vested in an ancestral priesthood, to be exercised for the benefit of the Athenian community as a whole. The political dimension of the accusation of impiety is affirmed by the account of Alcibiades' son, years later, in the course of defending his late father's reputation:

> Since [his enemies] knew that in matters pertaining to the gods the city would be most enraged if any man should be shown to be violating the Mysteries, and that in other matters if any man should dare to attempt the overthrow of the democracy, they combined both these charges and tried to bring an action of impeachment before the Council. They asserted that my father was holding meetings of his fellowship *(hetaireia)* with a view to revolution, and that these men, when dining together in the house of Poulytion, had given a performance of the Mysteries. . . .[27]

A second and most important clue to the significance of the profanation of the Mysteries is that this was not a single event, nor one in which Alcibiades was in every case involved. The denunciations implicated Alcibiades in these acts on at least two occasions, at two different houses, and implicated at least two other groups on occasions that did not involve Alcibiades. The Lysian speech quoted on page 10, although it describes acts that other sources attribute to Alcibiades, is in fact a description of what Andocides son of Leagoras, kinsman of Critias and Taureas, is supposed to have done at about the same time as Alcibiades. We therefore are dealing with a pattern of deliberate behavior, not a spontaneous act of indiscretion. It was a pattern in which several aristocratic groups were involved, and it was a private behavior in which many had voluntarily participated, but now, in the turmoil of the inquisition, a revealed and condemned behavior in which many feared implication.[28]

The *hetaireiai* of Alcibiades and others, as noted in chapter 2, were also called *synomosiai,* "sworn fellowships," and oaths were always taken in the name of patron deities and accompanied by acts of solemnification. It is probable that, in this as in so many of his other endeavors, Alcibiades had moved these solemnities to a higher plane by adopting the ritual forms of mystic initiation to give heightened sanctity to the oaths that bound members of his *hetaireiai* to himself and to each other. Several archaic kinship groups in Attica had long enjoyed the practice of exclusive rites of communion at private shrines. Alcibiades and his peers no doubt viewed their own rites, novel though they were, as commensurate with these established practices. But those who participated in the ceremonies of the Lycomidae and the Gephyraei, to name two known kinship groups celebrating private rites, did not pretend to identify their communion with the leadership of the Athenian state, Alcibiades did. As an unrivaled Olympic victor in 416, Alcibiades had achieved a level of distinction that made him, like the archaic heroes of yore, a talisman of victory, god-favored, and imbued with a power that all around him sought to share. To be initiated by Alcibiades as *hierophant,* "revealer of the sacred things," was the closest that any of his associates could come to sharing his numinous power. By so intensely personalizing and sanctifying the quality of leadership, Alcibiades and his followers, and the others groups implicated in these acts, pushed the boundary between personal loyalties and the paramount loyalty to the state to the breaking point.[29]

THE CONSPIRACY OF THE MYSTERIES

The occasion for these solemn acts, and the impetus for several aristocratic groups to become involved, must have been the preparations for the ostracism of the demagogue, Hyperbolus. Contemporary accounts affirm that the ostracism of Hyperbolus was a remarkable event. "Not for the likes of him was ostracism devised," declared a character of Plato the comic poet. His meaning was that the burden of ostracism was a badge of honor, to be borne by men like Aristides, Cimon, and Thucydides son of Melesias, but not Hyperbolus. Thucydides the historian vents his feelings about demagogues in the strongest terms when he mentions "Hyperbolus, a wretched character, who had been ostracized, not because anyone was afraid of his power or prestige, but because he was a thoroughly bad lot and a disgrace to the city." Such denigration of Hyperbolus is nearly unanimous in our sources. Yet, in expounding the baseness of Hyperbolus, in both his lives of *Nicias* and *Alcibiades,* Plutarch reveals that Hyperbolus *did* command a sort of power and prestige that *did* strike fear into his rivals:

> Hyperbolus of the deme Perithoedae [was] a man whose boldness was not due to any influence that he possessed, but who came to influence by reason of his boldness, and became, by reason of the very credit which he had in the city, a discredit to the city.... [Hyperbolus] was unmoved by abuse, and insensible to it, owing to his contempt of public opinion. This feeling some call courage and valour, but it is really mere shamelessness and folly. No one liked him, but the people often made use of him when they were eager to besmirch and calumniate men of rank and station.[30]

Hyperbolus clearly had the ear of the *demos* and was every bit as fearful to "men of rank and station" as Cleon had been before him. In the 420s, Hyperbolus had been a champion of an aggressive policy in the west, and so, in all likelihood, he was a supporter of the mission under discussion with Segestan envoys in 415. The ostracism of 415 was proposed by Hyperbolus, we are told, with the expectation that it would remove one of the "men of rank and station" who were his chief rivals. Alcibiades was certainly the most likely target, but Nicias was also at risk, and so was Phaeax.[31]

Plutarch affirms that the surprising reversal of Hyperbolus' plan came about when "the followers of Nicias and Alcibiades, mindful of the baseness [of Hyperbolus], communicated with each other in secret, and after uniting and harmonizing both their factions, won the contest.... " Such secret coordination *was* a conspiracy. At one point, Plutarch states that it was Alcibiades in particular who "brought together the factions," and implies that the number of these factions *(staseis)* was not limited to two. Hyperbolus posed a threat to all prominent "men of rank and station." So a conspiracy against him was formed in the name of aristocratic solidarity. To transcend the rivalries that usually pitted aristocratic groups against each other, this solidarity was given expression in rites of mystic initiation. Inspired by Alcibiades, the secret movement thus united for a single purpose groups who were otherwise divided.[32]

As soon as its purpose was achieved, the existence of the movement was revealed and the *demos* was immediately alarmed. As Plutarch notes, "The people were incensed at this for they felt that the institution [of ostracism] had been insulted and abused, and so they abandoned it utterly and put an end to it." The insult, according to Plutarch, was that the honor of ostracism had been abased by its use on so lowly a victim. But this interpretation is predicated on the aristocratic bias against Hyperbolus. It disguises the true source of alarm that many among the *demos* must have felt—the alarm at seeing their champion so unexpectedly removed.[33]

Alcibiades stepped into the void left by the ostracism of Hyperbolus. Leadership of the Sicilian expedition, it is true, was vested in three men: Alcibiades, Nicias, and Lamachus. But leadership of the popular movement formerly championed by Hyperbolus was now taken up by Alcibiades alone. Alcibiades' very persuasiveness among the aristocratic factions thus converted him almost instantly into a new, possibly even more fearful, champion of the *demos*. The passionate devotion to a cause that had so effectively removed Hyperbolus immediately animated some among the aristocratic factions to undo Alcibiades himself. The game was dangerous, however, for to reveal or denounce the deeds of Alcibiades was to risk being implicated in them. The immediate result was the mutilation of the Herms; the unfolding revelation of the wider mystic conspiracy was the inevitable consequence.

ALCIBIADES' DEFENSE

Once the fear of conspiracy had begun to consume the attention of the public, his enemies lost no time in portraying Alcibiades' personal ambitions as offensive to rites of communion that gave all Athenians a special place in divine favor. By eliciting testimony from outsiders, in particular from uninitiated slaves who had been present during these ceremonies, his enemies showed that Alcibiades and his ilk had misappropriated Eleusinian rites. These potent acts secured for all Athenians and for all humanity the blessings of the goddesses, gods, and heroes who had brought forth, at Eleusis, the very sustenance of life, family, and community. Alcibiades' mimicry violated the sanctified secrecy of the Eleusinian Mysteries, and so threatened to bring upon all Athenians the curse of the goddess' anger.[34]

When Alcibiades spoke in the Assembly against his accusers, he must have denied that he had performed Eleusinian rites. Acts resembling mystic initiation had been performed on the comic stage, after all, and as long as they did not reveal specific deeds or words, they were not sacrilege. Alcibiades probably appealed to such a distinction in his case. But his acts were solemn, and not performed for comic effect. Alcibiades must therefore have also pointed out that his was a communion with a different divinity, one known to all, and more ancient even than the Eleusinian goddesses—Eros. An elemental power, Eros was both a primordial force of nature, according to Hesiodic and Orphic theogonies, and the spirit of passionate affection that bound all men and women, citizen and foreign, to the service of Athens, according to Periclean rhetoric. Piety, patriotism, and plausibility would all have been served by such an argument, and both circumstantial and specific evidence suggests that it did, in fact, play a part in Alcibiades' defense.[35]

It was not difficult to make the case that Alcibiades' patron deity was the all-conquering god of desire and attraction. Eros was ever-present with Alcibiades, courted as he was by powerful men in his youth, and as a man, in Xenophon's words, the prey of respectable women. Alcibiades made no secret of his erotic jealousy when his lovers turned their eyes toward others, according to Plato's Socrates. And Alcibiades advertised his devotion to his divine champion with a singularly appropriate shield-blazon: Eros striking, Zeus-wise, with a thunderbolt.[36]

Speaking publicly in his own defense, then, Alcibiades probably sought to involve the assembled *demos* in a vision of devotion to Athens through communion with Eros. Such an appeal would justify his private acts of devotion by attaching them to the highest ideals of democratic Athens. Whatever the exact terms of his defense, his apology won the battle but lost the war. Alcibiades further charmed those already under his spell and satisfied the majority that the case of sacrilege was not self-evident. But he provided his enemies with a theme that they could amplify in a new key; Eros was a fickle god, and had his unseemly side. Above all, Alcibiades' well-known identification of personal glory with the glory of Athens had now, through ceremonies of initiation attested by witnesses and confirmed, in some respects at least, by his own mouth, brought him to the threshold of self-proclaimed mystic communion. To claim that his personal realization of divine favor was in the interests of all Athenians was to transform the highest personal aspirations into the ultimate public pretense—it was tantamount to tyranny.

THE DESTRUCTION OF ALCIBIADES

To the delight of his foes, the impetus of Alcibiades' own design, to command the expedition to Sicily, removed him from Athens at the moment of his greatest crisis. In his absence, the fervor of denunciations and the ongoing inquisition melted away the force of his defense. Weird and upsetting events had just occurred, and the Athenians were still far from resolving their anxieties when the fleet sailed. Testimony gathered over the two months following the departure of the fleet, shaped by orators determined to bring Alcibiades down, resulted in an indictment of Alcibiades for offending the Eleusinian goddesses. Here, and in the following two sections, an assessment is offered of the emotional and intellectual bases of the allegations that succeeded in removing Alcibiades from command and driving him into exile.

When the expedition was still under discussion, Alcibiades had offered an immodest justification of his leadership. When allegations against him arose following the mutilation of the Herms and the first allegations concerning the Mysteries, Alcibiades had defended himself in terms that we can only conjecture, but, in the spirit of the moment and the spirit of the man, we can be sure were as immodest as ever. Alcibiades' professed ambitions showed his enemies a line of argument that the public would most readily accept as the explanation for the disturbing developments under investigation:

> Making a great hue and cry, they claimed that both the affairs of the Mysteries and the mutilation of the Herms had been done in order to subvert the people, and that none of these things had been done without his connivance, alleging as evidence all of his other exotic and perverse habits.[37]

To make the indictment of Alcibiades compelling, his personal habits were compared, in speech and in writing, to historical precedents in order to demonstrate that he conformed to the ultimate anti-democrat, the would-be tyrant.

An invective against Alcibiades composed by Antiphon exemplifies the campaign to defame Alcibiades, and reveals a probable source of many of the scurrilous anecdotes found in the later biographic tradition. Excerpts from Antiphon's tract and from other sources allege that Alcibiades was already violent and disrespectful of authority and even of human life as a youth; his first travels abroad enabled him to learn the ways of dissolute foreign women; he falsely imprisoned free men; he used violence and threats to extort money from the most honorable of Athenians; he abused his own wife; he indulged in incest; and he had a long career "as an adulterer, as a stealer of the wives of others, as a perpetrator of lawless acts of violence in general."[38]

Alcibiades' wife, Hipparete, was the daughter of Hipponicus, at one time reputed to be the wealthiest man in Greece, and the sister of Callias. Bearing his father's fortune and hereditary title, Callias was *dadouchos,* or "Torch-Bearer," an officiant of the Mysteries of Demeter at Eleusis. He was thus one of the men, by virtue of both his priestly duties and his personal prominence, who was obliged to condemn publicly Alcibiades' violation of Demeter's rites. His close relationship to Alcibiades compelled his denunciation to include personal details that would make his repudiation convincing. We can believe, therefore, a diatribe against Alcibiades that refers to the following public announcement:

> In order to possess himself of Hipponicus' estate, he [Alcibiades] planned the assassination of Callias. Callias himself accused him of it before you all in the Assembly, and, for fear that his wealth would cost him his life, made over his property to the state in the event of his dying without issue.

Violence, the appropriation of other men's property, the corruption or abuse of other men's wives and daughters, and incest were all elements in the stereotype of the tyrant. This image, as exemplified in Callias' reported speech, was produced for consumption by the Athenian Council, jury-courts, and Assembly. Antiphon's tract provides important evidence for how this invective was disseminated and, moreover, how it survived its immediate use as propaganda and entered historiographic tradition.[39]

Antiphon's invective against Alcibiades is an early example of the use of a written tract to amplify the impact of forensic rhetoric. A surviving quotation shows that the speech addresses Alcibiades in the second person, as if he were present to hear its slanderous accusations. The much-anticipated trial of Alcibiades for the illicit performance of the Mysteries is the context in which such unbounded libel would have been most favorably received by an Athenian audience, and it is most likely that Antiphon's work represents a speech prepared for this event. Alcibiades never stood trial at Athens, however, so this speech was never delivered in court. But like other speeches that were circulated but never actually spoken, Antiphon's invective may have served its purpose best by becoming known before Alcibiades was summoned back to Athens.[40]

The slanderous nature of the invective against Alcibiades is remarkable but entirely in keeping with the habits of Athenian judicial procedure, and particularly suitable to the unique nature of this case. By custom and institution, especially in the numerous annual scrutinies of candidates for state office, the Athenians were habituated to passing judgment on individuals based solely on the evidence of character. In a case such as this, once informants had established the grounds for proceeding on a specific charge, testimony to character mattered as much as, or even more than, the "facts" of the case, especially when the defendant was a high official entrusted with the well-being of the state. Furthermore, in a matter of this magnitude, calumny of Alcibiades had the wider purpose of establishing guilt by association among his friends and followers. For connection to Alcibiades was the only basis for the charge of conspiracy. On these circumstantial grounds the case flourished in the frenzy of accusations and denunciations that followed the mutilation of the Herms. Its resonance was still felt in Athenian juries twenty years later, when a prosecutor attacking Alcibiades' son reminded his audience that the defendant was the scion of the most notorious of those men who have:

> most of them been whoring, while some have lain with their sisters, and others have had children by their daughters; and others again, have performed Mysteries, mutilated the Herms, and committed profanity against all the gods and offenses against the whole city, showing injustice and perversion alike in their public treatment of their fellow-men and in their behavior to each other, refraining from no audacity....[41]

HEARING THE TESTIMONY OF HISTORY

Allegations of this nature were convincing in 415 because they were shown to correspond to the pattern of outrages committed by tyrants in the past, and in particular to the precedents set by the Peisistratids. Thucydides demonstrates the importance of this lesson from the past in an observation at the beginning of his account of the process leading up to the indictment and recall of Alcibiades:

> The people knew from what they heard how oppressive the tyranny of Peisistratus and his sons had been in its later stages, and, further, that it was not because of themselves and Harmodius that it had come to an end, but because of the Spartans. They were consequently in a constant state of fear and took everything suspiciously.[42]

Just as one or more written texts underlay the indictment of Alcibiades, indirect but compelling evidence indicates that a prepared text was also behind the history of the Peisistratids that guided the deliberations of the Athenians at this time.

In the passage quoted above, Thucydides refers to the people's understanding *(epistamenos gar ho demos)* obtained by hearing (*akoei,* 6.53.3). The passage has usually been interpreted as a reference to common opinion derived from oral tradition. But this interpretation has led to considerable confusion about Thucydides' point, since the understanding he goes on to attribute to the Athenians was at odds with the traditional account of the tyrant-slayers. The Athenians, as Thucydides points out, were now correctly informed that it was the Spartans, and not Harmodius and Aristogeiton, who had delivered Athens from tyranny. The key element in Thucydides' phrase is *epistamenos,* "understanding," which describes secure knowledge and not mistaken opinion. By contrast, traditional accounts passed on by poets and orators were the basis of what people "accept uncritically from each other" (*abasanistos par' allelon dechontai* 1.20.2), "think incorrectly" (*ouk orthos oiontai,* 1.20.3, cf. 1.20.2, 6.54.2), and "say without accuracy" (*akribes ouden legontas,* 6.54.1). In the passage under examination above, Thucydides' language reveals that he is describing a precise understanding gained by the Athenians, in the summer of 415, through hearing an authoritative account—now for the first time—of the end of the Peisistratid tyranny.[43]

The account heard and understood by the people at this time amounted to a radical revision of the popular story of Harmodius and Aristogeiton. Their assassination of Hipparchus had long been equated with the liberation of Athens from tyranny. Now, however, the Athenian people were challenged to view their received traditions critically. Speakers out to denounce Alcibiades cited the proof of history to demonstrate to the Athenians, first of all, that Alcibiades possessed traits that portended the worst aspects of tyranny; next, that tyranny, once it had taken root, could not be shaken off without assistance from outside powers; finally, that the misdeeds of Alcibiades and his ancestors might bring divine vengeance upon the Athenians.[44]

The account that conveyed this information to the Athenians was an expert historical treatise. It resembled the *syngraphai* that customarily guided deliberations on matters involving both divine and human affairs. It also had much in common with Thucydides' own later historical treatise, which could be called a *syngraphe* (Thucydides repeatedly refers to it as the work that he *synegrapse,* "compiled"). In common, too, with the expert testimony received by the Athenians in 415, Thucydides' work was something to be received by hearing (*akroasin,* 1.22.4). And like it, Thucydides conceived of his work as something that would be

> useful for those who will want a clear understanding of the past as well as of the future which at some time or other, as far as human nature is concerned, will occur in much the same way.

This was the sort of authoritative information that, coming from an unnamed account, guided the Athenian *demos* by instructing them in the facts of the Peisistratid tyranny.[45]

The authority alluded to by Thucydides can only be the account of Herodotus. Herodotus' *Histories,* by this time, were becoming an element of the *sophia,* in particular, the *akribeia,* in which the educated took pride. A dominant theme of Herodotus' work was to underscore the peril of ignoring the "wise advisor," one whose wisdom derived either from personal experience or from his knowledge of the past. If ever there was a moment in Athenian history comparable to Croesus' fateful decision to attack Cyrus, or Xerxes' decision to invade Greece, it was the Athenian decision to invade Sicily. The scandals that came in the wake of that decision brought to the fore another theme woven through the fabric of Herodotus' work, namely, the dangers of tyranny. Both ideas, the conquest of Sicily and the fear of tyranny, had been in the air at Athens since the 420s. Herodotus' work placed both themes in a larger historical context. Now, at the peak of crisis in 415, his work was introduced as expert testimony to aid the deliberations of the Athenian *demos* and its Council.[46]

In the course of the inquisitions of that summer, a familiarity with Herodotus' research would have enabled a speaker to make a number of striking points regarding Alcibiades and tyranny. First of all, Herodotus reminded the Athenians of the sexual perversions of tyrants, of their arrogation of the property of others, and of their unbounded ambitions. Secondly, Herodotus' account emphasized how easily Peisistratus had gulled the Athenians into welcoming their tyrant. Thirdly, like Peisistratus, Alcibiades had a large force of Argive soldiers loyal to him. The former Argive force was instrumental in bringing the tyrant to power; in Alcibiades' case, the Argives had come to Athens to join the Sicilian expedition, and Alcibiades' influence with them was said to be one reason why his enemies were anxious to have the expedition depart before proceeding with the inquisition. Like Peisistratus' son, Hippias, Alcibiades was reputed to have the support of foreign powers who were prepared to establish the tyrant in Athens by force. Hippias was supported in two unsuccessful attempts to return to power, the first being an aborted project of the Spartans, and the second being the Persian landing at Marathon. In 415, soon after the departure of Alcibiades for Sicily, a Spartan force crossed the Isthmus and joined a Boeotian force on the frontiers of Attica, causing alarm in Athens fed by the rumor that these developments were part of a plot by Alcibiades to establish himself and his friends in power. Thus did the investigations of Herodotus provide warnings from the past that the Athenians should not mistake the signs of their present peril.[47]

Amidst the turmoil of scandal, sacrilege, conspiracy, and threats from hostile forces, the Athenians craved clear and informed guidance. Some informants were found to have given false testimony and were punished with death. Witnesses who were deemed reliable were rewarded by the Athenians. So, after nearly three months of denunciations, arrests, and counter-denunciations, the unrefuted testimony of a slave and a foreigner were honored at the summer's Panathenaic festival with the monetary rewards that had been publicly offered. Another informer and confessed partner in the conspiracy to mutilate the Herms, Andocides, was granted release from custody along with some his closest relatives in exchange for his testimony against the rest of the conspirators in that affair. As a result, somewhere between fifty and a hundred men were convicted of involvement in one or both of the scandals that were regarded as proof of conspiracy against the Athenian *demos*. Many of these were executed, although the majority escaped into exile.[48]

Resolution of the crisis was possible only when the Athenian *demos* felt that they were as safe as foresight could provide from the ill effects of human design and divine will. Safety, then, came from understanding these agents of their fate, and from taking action against the individual most capable of working harm on the Athenians and their destiny. Guided by history, the Athenians sought resolution in the indictment of Alcibiades for profaning the Mysteries of the goddesses of Eleusis. The indictment was registered as the proposal of Thessalus, grandson of Miltiades who had defeated the Persians at Marathon and ended Hippias' last bid to return as tyrant at Athens.[49]

Alcibiades was recalled from Sicily, summoned home with others indicted along with him, to stand trial at Athens. Knowing the changed mood that he would confront at home, Alcibiades and his companions escaped. At Thurii in southern Italy, they eluded their escort and in short order made their way to the Peloponnese. After the months of inquisition at Athens, the flight of Alcibiades into exile was almost anticlimactic, for it seemed to confirm what many Athenians now felt they "knew" about these affairs.[50]

But knowledge, in the aftermath of these proceedings, proved disturbingly uncertain, and probably for this reason the testimony of Herodotus is not directly linked to the condemnation of Alcibiades in any account that has come down to us. But the report found in the late chronographical tradition that Herodotus "was honored by the Athenian Council for reading his books to them" is probably to be explained by Herodotus' role as an expert witness in 415. Plutarch reports, on good authority, that the Athenians voted to give a monetary award to Herodotus on the proposal of the orator, Anytus. Neither the date nor the reason for this honor is stated, but since Anytus began his career as a statesman in the later 410s, the circumstances described here are chronologically plausible. The case is strengthened by a reference from Aristophanes.[51]

Five years after the affair of the Herms, when retrospect showed these events in a different light, Aristophanes made a sharp joke at Anytus' expense. During an interlude on the theme, "Women are better than Men," the chorus of the *Thesmophoriazusae* names a series of virtues, all of them grammatically feminine, that clearly top a series of men whose recent achievements have been less than honorable. When they come to *Euboule,* Good-Counsel, the chorus alludes to the shame of the previous year's councilors, who yielded their office to others, and remark: "not even Anytus will say one of them is better than Her." Apparently, by 410 Anytus' reputation for recognizing good advice had been called into question.[52]

For a brief while, in the summer of 415, the Athenians felt that they had been saved by *Euboule,* and Anytus had stood forward to direct public gratitude toward Herodotus for the definitive guidance the Athenians had received from his research. In time, though, the Athenians thought the better of their debt to history, and they were happy to let Anytus appear the fool for speaking on record on that occasion. There were many regrets after the summer of 415.

THE LIMITS OF POWER

The affair of the Herms had released upon the Athenians a spasm of fear and officially sanctioned violence that was without precedent in the memory of the democracy. The violence was the product of the power over property, liberty, and life exercised by the Athenian jury-courts directed, through rhetoric and demagoguery, primarily by members of the Athenian elite against other members of the elite. Improbably in some respects, but predictably in others, Alcibiades had become the chief scapegoat by which the fears of the moment were lifted. Targeted by an array of enemies and political rivals, he was made the victim of the popular stereotype of the would-be tyrant, as demonstrated by persuasive *tekmeria,* "evidence," from his public and private life, all interpreted on analogies from the past. We might find this evidence circumstantial and inconclusive if we were to judge the case against Alcibiades as it was presented to the Athenian *demos.* But the inductive reasoning that led to his conviction was persuasive to Athenians because it played on themes that, over the previous decade and a half, had become thoroughly familiar to them through political rhetoric, drama, and the testimony of respected experts. The logic by which Alcibiades was judged to be a manifest danger to the Athenian state was the logic of the nature and limits of power.

The logic of power as construed by the Athenians of 415 was the specific product of habits and precedents established by the Athenian imperial democracy of the late fifth century. Before resuming the narrative of Alcibiades' expulsion it will be valuable to outline some of the salient characteristics of these Athenian habits of thought. For the themes that came to the fore in 415 were to reappear in various forms over the next tumultuous decade and a half.

Under the leadership of Pericles and Cleon, the Athenians had become accustomed to identifying their power with their collective will. Empire required the assertion of sovereign authority over a domain to be limited only by the judgment of the Athenian *demos.* The decisions of a free and sovereign *demos* thus defined both their empire and their democracy. To accept limits declared by others would be an admission of weakness, and would be the beginning of the end of empire and of democracy. The Athenians had gone to war against Sparta and her allies precisely in order to keep their power free and unbounded. For, as Pericles argued, if the Athenians gave in to Spartan demands, they would be accepting slavery. To exercise power without limits, on the other hand, was for the Athenians to exercise their collective tyranny.

This striking metaphor had been used by Pericles and Cleon, as reported by Thucydides, not to chasten or restrain the Athenians but to exhort them to embrace their construction of empire. There was, by this reasoning, no middle ground for compromise with other powers in the administration of the empire of democratic Athens. Thus we find Aristophanes, at the height of Cleon's influence in the 420s, praising the power of the tyrannical empire of Athens as an essential quality of the Athenian *demos*.[53]

Like Aristophanes' depiction, in the *Knights,* of Demos as an individual whom "all men fear as a tyrant," the metaphor of the *tyrannis polis,* "tyrant-city," treated the qualities of a state as analogous to the qualities possessed by an individual autocrat. As with other equally collective or individual qualities, the metaphor of the tyrant could be applied freely in either direction. Thucydides demonstrates the double force of this metaphor most clearly in the mouth of another Athenian speaker:

> When a man exercises tyranny or a state controls an empire, nothing that is beneficial is unreasonable, and kinship means nothing unless it is absolutely reliable. Circumstances determine who is a friend and who is an enemy.

Thus Euphemus, an Athenian ambassador in Sicily at the end of 415, argues that circumstances assure the people of Camarina of a mutually beneficial friendship with the Athenians, although he has no qualms about admitting that, under different circumstances elsewhere, the Athenians do in fact use harsh measures to assure the loyalty of their allies and kinsmen. Just as a tyrant suffers no objections to his will, no law can prevent the Athenians from ruling as they will where they can. Only circumstances dictate the limits of Athenian power, and it is up to the Athenian *demos* to discern those limiting circumstances.[54]

The most famous demonstration of this logic, besides the debate over the expedition to Sicily, occurs in Thucydides' account of the culmination late in 416 of the campaign to force the islanders of Melos to submit to Athenian rule. Despite Athenian efforts over the previous decade to subdue them, the Melians had preserved their independence until they were finally broken by the siege of 416. In that year, the Athenians demanded that the small island community submit to Athens or face destruction. The Athenians alleged no grievance, only the imperative that no weaker state should be left independent when it was within their power to rule over them, for otherwise, present subjects would interpret this as a sign of Athenian weakness and be encouraged to rebel. The matter is set forth in a point-counterpoint debate between Athenian representatives and a small group of Melian officials. To the Melian claim that justice is on their side, the Athenians observe the following:

> . . . you know as well as we do that justice, as a matter of human reckoning, is something to be decided between equals, while those who are more powerful do what they are capable of doing, and the weak accept what they have to accept.[55]

By the terms of this argument, those who can objectively be deemed more powerful than others are beyond the bounds of equality with them, and therefore justice does not obtain as a consideration between them. Congruent logic would therefore draw disturbing conclusions from the personal claim of Alcibiades to "have a better right to command than others," especially since the verb "to command," *archein,* also means "to rule." His claim, made in the speech of 415 quoted in chapter 2, was based on the personal distinctions which were his by birth and by his exceptional achievements, all of which, as Alcibiades pointed out, convey "an impression of power." Alcibiades strove to identify his personal greatness with the interests of Athens, but in so doing he pressed the limits of *isonomia,* the equality before law that was the essence of the democratic community of Athens. So Thucydides reports his words in 415:

> And this is no useless folly, when a man at his own private cost benefits not himself only, but the city: nor is it unfair that he who prides himself on his position should refuse to be on an equality with the rest.

Some would say—did say—that Alcibiades placed himself beyond the bounds of *isonomia.* For it was his very greatness, Thucydides notes, as measured by his personal *paranomia,* "lawlessness," and by the scope of his ambitions, that eventually persuaded the majority of Athenians that Alcibiades aspired to tyranny.[56]

Alcibiades was not indicted for attempted tyranny, however, but for offending the Eleusinian goddesses. Alcibiades could justify a pride that offended his peers, but he could not justify such arrogance before another element of the Athenian community, the gods of the Athenians.

THE WILL OF THE GODS

As noted in Part I, the Athenians were acutely aware that the gods were implicated in their political community. Custom was ever the safest guide to behavior in the presence of the gods, but the effects of their involvement in public affairs was an uncertain matter, especially in times of war. An underlying tenet of public piety was that the gods upheld a system of justice that transcended justice by human reckoning. In concept the two systems should be congruous, with human justice imperfectly striving to conform to the divine model. Although a wrongdoer might evade human justice, divine retribution would bring redress in the end. Skeptics might question whether divine justice moved on a scale that could be perceived in a human lifetime, but it was more difficult to find objective reasons to deny that human prosperity, on a larger scale, shifted according to divine sanction. The underlying thesis of Herodotus' *Histories,* in fact, was to affirm through the testimony of the past that the prosperity of communities responded to divine will. Regardless, therefore, of personal skepticism, the common interests of the Athenian *demos* demanded that, in all public matters, due and customary attention be paid to the affairs of the gods.[57]

Within a public receptive to such views, it was imperative to bring the administration of justice into accord with what present portents or past experience indicated was "right." Justice therefore responded as much to an unfolding sense of "what was right" in a given situation as it did to any statutory guidelines. Difficult circumstances might cloud judgment with emotions or doubt, but in concept the transcendent standard of justice upheld by the gods remained ever present, to be discerned by the keen mind. Euripides gave voice to this concept in a prayer placed in the mouth of the captive Trojan queen, Hecuba, who uttered it before the Athenians in the spring of 415:

> You who bear the earth and are enthroned on the earth, whoever you may be, hard to reach through knowledge, Zeus, whether force of nature or human intelligence, to you I pray. For in a silent way you guide all mortal affairs according to justice.[58]

The play, *Trojan Women,* depicts the utter desperation of captives witnessing the methodical dismemberment of their community after foreign conquest. The manifest powerlessness of the women of Troy is shown to the Athenians in the context of a larger fate. In one direction, unforeseen suffering and death lie in store for the conquering Achaean chiefs, as foretold at the opening of the play by Poseidon and Athena, patron deities of Attica. In the other direction are the events that long before set the seal of doom on Troy.

The *Trojan Women* was the third play of Euripides' trilogy performed in the Dionysia of 415. The first play, the *Alexander,* told of the recognition of the foundling Alexander, better known as Paris, the darling of Aphrodite. When King Priam held games in honor of his supposedly long-dead son, this adopted cowherd's son came, and, to the astonishment the best of the Trojans, won all contests. Recognizing him, Priam and Hecuba embraced their lost son, and with him the doom long ago foretold in the oracle that had compelled them to expose him as an infant. Fate lies in the hands of the powerful, the poet says, although in the flush of success they may mistake the seeds of destruction for what seems to be the greatest blessing.[59]

These tales were spun before the Athenians as plans for the expedition to Sicily were about to be finalized. At the Dionysia of 415, ambassadors from Segesta in Sicily were probably already in Athens, accompanied by the Athenian commissioners who had been sent to confirm that conditions were favorable for the military venture advocated by Alcibiades, among others. Alcibiades, meanwhile, had been recently marked as a favorite of the gods by great success in the games, and the Athenians collectively had also savored the rare taste of total victory with the destruction, the previous winter, of the Melians. Euripides' offering that spring was surely calculated to encourage the Athenians to reflect upon the nature of their power, and to be mindful of signs that might portend its limits.

The capture of Melos, the execution of its men, and the enslavement of its women, had been an exercise in tyranny that would weigh, as first among several, on the minds of Athenians as they were to contemplate retribution in future moments of crisis. In Thucydides' account of the reasoning that led to the destruction of Melos, the Melians claim that the gods will uphold the justice of their resistance. To this the Athenians reply:

> Regarding the favor of the gods, we do not think we will be at any disadvantage. Our aims and actions are perfectly consistent with the beliefs men hold about the gods and with the principles that govern their own conduct. Our opinion of the gods and our knowledge of men lead us to conclude that it is a general and necessary law of nature to rule whatever one can.... We are merely acting in accordance with it, and we know that you or anybody else with the same power as ours would be acting in precisely the same way.[60]

Thus the Athenians accounted for their actions according to a universal principal. Power included the need to dominate.

In view of this understanding of the nature of power and the limits of justice, the open ambitions of Alcibiades could be seen as a sign of danger. When, in the spring of 415, deeds came to light that made it impossible to neglect the danger of divine displeasure that attached to Alcibiades, it is noteworthy that one of his accusers, Teisias son of Teisimachus, was one of the generals who had conveyed the Athenian ultimatum to Melos the previous year. Teisias was brother-in-law to Charicles, member of the Commission of Inquiry of 415 and a prime mover in the condemnation of Alcibiades. The following year, Charicles was an elected general and represented Athens in dealings with Argos, where Alcibiades had previously been influential. Teisias himself was the man who, in 416, had assisted Alcibiades in the purchase of the prize-winning chariot team from Argos, and who, after 415, remained locked in an inconclusive but symbolic lawsuit that claimed that the winning team at Olympia in 416 belonged to him and not to Alcibiades. The events of 415 encouraged many to believe that the power of Athens could only be preserved if it were no longer identified with Alcibiades. His power was to be dismembered, and its pieces appropriated by others.[61]

ALCIBIADES IN FLIGHT

But Alcibiades himself was not destroyed, and in exile he was able to recreate a base of power among the enemies of his enemies, with surprising consequences. Alcibiades was invited to Sparta by his Spartan friends as man of honor and standing seeking vengeance on his enemies in Athens. Alcibiades was precisely the sort of agent through whom the Spartans could hope to work in bringing the Athenians to terms. By the combination of armed force and insider influence, the Spartans had lately been attempting to convert Argos from foe to ally. They had recently secured their interests by similar means at Mantinea and Sicyon. In view of various hostile actions by the Athenians and their allies, and with the Syracusans and their Corinthian kinsmen now appealing to the Spartans to renew the war against Athens, the time to attempt the same strategy against the Athenians was at hand.[62]

Alcibiades' speech to the assembly of the Spartans in the winter of 415/14, as reported by Thucydides, touched on no point of strategy not already under consideration by the Spartans. He advised them to support the Syracusans and to fortify a base at Decelea in Attica, and so through a demonstration of strength attract more Greeks to the Spartan side. Of more interest is the manner in which Alcibiades, in supporting this plan, presented his credentials to an audience bound to be critical of his motives. Alcibiades' own name was Spartan, indicating a tie of kinship that might have been ancient or the product of closer relations between Athens and Sparta in the recent past, when his ancestors had been *proxenoi* representing Spartan interests at Athens. Alcibiades himself had made efforts, beginning with the care of Spartan prisoners at Athens after 425, to renew the obligations of *proxenia* himself. He claimed that he had been humiliated when the Spartans had negotiated the peace of 421 through Nicias, his enemy, rather than through him; thus any injury he had caused the Spartans by his dealings with Mantinea and Argos was justifiable. His personal score with Sparta was even, and both he and they should now look onward to their mutual interests. As to his and his family's prominence in a democratic state, their leadership of the people was always exercised in the name of opposition to tyranny, and always aimed at moderating the excesses of popular government. But others had led the mob on in wicked doings, and men of this sort had driven Alcibiades into exile. Wronged by such men, Alcibiades could best prove his patriotism by sparing no effort to attack his real enemies in control at Athens.[63]

So far, Alcibiades showed that his personal motives were aligned with the strategic objectives of Sparta by the coincidence of circumstances. But his finale sounded a more idealistic chord. By preventing further Athenian conquests and by bringing her present power low, the Spartans could achieve something that the Athenians, through their naked imperialism, have long forsaken: leadership by virtue of the grateful goodwill of all of Greece, not through force. What was not expressed directly, but was understood implicitly, is that the strength of such goodwill resided only in the honor of men like Alcibiades. To secure it, control of affairs must be taken from the shameless mob and its opportunistic leaders and placed in the hands of men of quality. This, if it were to be spelled out, was the creed of the Spartans and their allies.[64]

Alcibiades did not devise Spartan strategy in 415/14, but he was an accurate judge of possibilities and consequences. Following the assembly at which Alcibiades spoke, a Spartan commander, Gylippus, was sent to Sicily to rally the Syracusans. In little more than a year, by summer 413, the Athenian expedition and all of its reinforcements were destroyed. The consequent swell of petitions for alliance with Sparta, including many covert contacts from among Athenian subjects ready to revolt, must have made the vision of Sparta's leadership by the willing acclaim of the Greeks seem to be coming true. Alcibiades may have facilitated this process by a diplomatic tour through central Greece and Thessaly on behalf of Sparta in 413, upon the establishment of the garrison at Decelea by King Agis. Over the following winter of 413/12, Alcibiades certainly contributed to the formulation of Spartan policy in an area where the Spartans had most to gain from his expertise, the establishment of relations among the Greeks of the Aegean coast.[65]

The effects of Alcibiades' influence within the Athenian dominion in the Aegean will be traced in the next chapter. In closing this chapter we turn to evidence for Athenian attitudes toward Alcibiades at the beginning of his exile. Neither his formal condemnation nor his outspoken opposition to Athenian policies at Sparta could turn Alcibiades into a complete villain in the eyes of the Athenian populace. His resurgent popularity at Athens a few years later is well known. What has not been generally recognized, however, is the powerful hold Alcibiades had on the Athenian imagination from the beginning of his exile. For while he was busily reconstructing a base of power among the Spartans, his visionary politics and theology were being played out in the Athenian theater.

THE FLIGHT OF THE *BIRDS*

In the early spring of 414, Aristophanes staged his most elaborate fantasy, the *Birds*. The story reveals much of the mood of the time. Two Athenians, Peisetaerus (Companion-Persuader) and Euelpides (Good Hopes), leave their city to flee the juggernaut of Athenian jury-courts. There is a hint that they owe money to someone, or perhaps to the state, but this is incidental to their fear of informers and Gorgias-like fast-talking prosecutors. Such dangers have prompted them literally to "go to the crows," voluntarily complying with what must have been the parting wish of many a would-be prosecutor as their victims slipped across the borders of Attica—the equivalent of "go to hell!"

Our heroes go to find their distant kinsman, the legendary Tereus, who was long ago turned into a hoopoe-bird, and with him they form a plan to found a new city, "not greater [than Athens], but more agreeable." The plan is to unite all birds in a fortified city that will regain for them the control of their natural domain, the sky. Thus they can blockade the gods by cutting off their access to sacrificial odors from earth below, force the gods into submission, and assume dominion over mankind. Tereus' fellow-birds are naturally suspicious of the humans, longtime foes of the birds. But after Tereus points out the advantages of having humans on their side, Peisetaerus calms their fears in an oration weaving myth, legend, and contemporary custom into a demonstration that the right of the birds to rule was more ancient than the supremacy of the gods. So the project is embraced, and, after many an amusing episode, it is crowned with success.

The relevance of this fantasy to contemporary events has been doubted, but doubt is warranted only if one looks to the wrong set of events. The war underway in Sicily is far from view; the play looks instead to the topsy-turvy affairs of Athens. The opening of the play is full of puns likening the protagonists, two well-meaning and steadfast *hetairoi,* to birds taking flight at the frightful commotion in the jury-courts. The metaphor calls to mind flocks of *hetairoi,* friends and associates, fleeing into exile at the first sound of their denunciations in the affairs of the Herms and the Mysteries. Punning allusions to allegations of impiety, and a pun on *epoptes,* "mystic initiate," provided by *epops,* "hoopoe-bird," show the audience the direction of the fantasy from the start. As a result, the audience is ready to recognize the consummation of the bird-fantasy revealed in the hymn to Eros, the golden-winged god, born from an egg, sung by the chorus as they celebrate their collaboration with the persuasive Peisetaerus in his scheme to gain dominion over gods and man. The scheme and the fantasy allude to the grandiose plans of Alcibiades, and to his remarkable profession of allegiance to the primordial god of love, Eros.

From his entry as a pitiable fugitive, Peisetaerus does not immediately strike the modern reader as the perfect likeness of Alcibiades, but the fantastic transformations of this protean character clearly embody much of what astounded the Athenians about Alcibiades in 415/14. He is the consummate persuader of his *hetairoi;* he seeks refuge from his own countrymen among inveterate foes; and he has persuaded this alien species that together they can share an even greater destiny. His name, Peisetaerus, is a pun on the name of Peisistratus, lately also much on the lips of Athenians. His city in the clouds, *Nephelokokkygia,* "Cloud-Cuckoo-Land," is the fanciful concoction of Alcibiades' scheme of an Argive alliance, for the cuckoo was the bird of Hera of Argos. Through the force applied by his devoted followers, and through wit and forceful argument, he bends the very gods to his will. By the end of the play Peisetaerus is triumphant, and is hailed as *tyrannos* as he ascends, winged and wielding Zeus' own thunderbolt and bearing his bride, Basileia, "Sovereignty," all to the chorus of praise of his new-found kinsmen, the birds. Peisetaerus is the perfect ruler. He is Eros incarnate, and, like that all-powerful deity, "supreme of all *daimones,*" emblazoned on Alcibiades' shield and praised in the play's closing line, he is Alcibiades.[66]

CHAPTER FIVE

Rationalizing Oligarchy, 413–411

It was not surprising, therefore, that an undertaking carried out by so many intelligent men should have moved forward, however monumental a task it was; for it was no easy matter, about 100 years after the tyrants were put down, to deprive the Athenian demos of its liberty. . . .

THUCYDIDES 8.68.4

Even in exile, Alcibiades defined the scope of the crisis that confronted the Athenians following the collapse of their venture to Sicily in 413. More adept than his rivals, he saw their curses and condemnations rebound upon themselves, while he himself gained recognition for what he had proclaimed himself to be, the brightest hope for Athens' future. But until his deeds showed him to be as brilliant as the hopes he inspired, Alcibiades could not return home.

At Athens, Alcibiades was alternately opposed and promoted by a shifting array of political leaders, the most effective of whom, by 411, had come together to form the revolutionary oligarchy of the Four Hundred. These men were united by the effort to devise a reasoned response to the crises at hand. That all their efforts failed was due, in large part, to their inability to comprehend the influence of the Persian empire on the affairs of the Aegean.

ON THE BOUNDARIES OF ASIA

The status of the Greeks of Asia Minor was multifaceted and complex. Most of them were tributary subjects of Athens, their allegiance justified by their liberation from Persian rule following the defeat of Xerxes and maintained by the fact of Athenian naval superiority. The towns of the Asian coast, however, occupied an intermediate position between the Athenian domination of the sea and the Persian dominion of the continent, and despite the ideal of independence from Persia, the Greek communities were confronted with the practical necessities of dealing with neighboring Persian satraps and their henchmen.

The political divisions characteristic of Greek communities made for various arrangements of mutual advantage between local Persian lords and factions in some Greek towns. A notable example is the alliance of Colophon with Pissouthnes, the satrap of Sardis, following civil war in 430. By the same token, divisions of allegiance that characteristically accompanied the establishment of a successor on the Persian throne made for arrangements of mutual advantage between Persian satraps and the sources of manpower in the Greek world. Sometime after the death of Artaxerxes I and the outcome, by 423, of more than a year's struggle by Darius II to secure the throne, Pissouthnes declared his independence from Darius. He pitted his Greek mercenary army against Tissaphernes son of Hydarnes, kinsman by marriage to the king, and the man sent by Darius to establish rule in the king's name over the satrapy of southwestern Asia Minor. Athenian involvement in these murky circumstances was no doubt behind Aristophanes' quip, in the *Knights* of 424, about conspiracies in aristocratic circles involving "sworn dealings with the Medes and the king," as well as the negotiation of eternal friendship between the king and the Athenians claimed by Andocides as an achievement of his uncle, Epilycus.[1]

In the end, Pissouthnes was deserted by his mercenaries and their Athenian commander and fell into the fatal grasp of Tissaphernes and Darius. Little else is known about Persian–Greek affairs before 412, but by that time it emerges that Pissouthnes' son, Amorges, was still maintaining his independence from Darius, making war on Tissaphernes, and, most remarkably, was doing so with Athenian support. Tissaphernes had been charged by Darius with exacting the tribute due to the king from his domain, and the Athenians had prevented him from carrying out this charge in the Greek cities. Evidently, eternal friendship with the king did not extend to compliance with the demands of his satrap at Sardis, and this conflict made it inevitable that the Athenians would coordinate their resistance to Tissaphernes with Amorges.[2]

To the Ionian Greeks, the continuing conflict between Athens and Persia promised only to grind away on themselves. The tribute demanded by Tissaphernes probably seemed, to men of property and influence, a more moderate imposition than the invasive imperial rule of the Athenians. In the winter of 414/13 the Athenians replaced their tribute assessments with a five percent tax on all maritime trade within their empire, a measure that immediately shifted the burden of tribute from the landed elite to the mercantile class and to entrepreneurial tax-farmers. Thucydides reports that this innovation was designed to generate more revenue in order to stem a financial crisis brought on by the Sicilian campaign and the Spartan occupation of Decelea. It also had the effect of generating *immediate* revenue from the sales of tax-rights in all the chief harbors of the empire, and it may also have been intended to mollify the landed class among the subjects.[3]

But the destruction of Athenian forces in Sicily in the summer of 413 had a more profound effect upon Athenian allies. The prospect of the collapse of Athenian power in the Aegean encouraged many of the monied elite among the allies to look to the Persians for support. The Ionian Greeks from Chios southward appealed to Tissaphernes, while Greeks from Lesbos north to the Hellespont appealed to Pharnabazus, satrap of Hellespontine Phrygia. Each of these satraps with their respective Greek supporters sent emissaries to Sparta, competing to secure the strongest alliance against Athens. Recognizing the potential for rapid results, Alcibiades urged the Spartans to respond first to embassies from Tissaphernes and the Ionians, and to begin dismantling the Athenian empire by supporting the revolts of the Greeks of the Ionian coast, and to do so by sending him as spokesman for their cause in the first wave of Spartan naval forces.[4]

With Alcibiades announcing the impending collapse of Athenian power and with influential oligarchs ready to act, rebellion spread quickly in the summer of 412. A few days after instigating the revolt of Chios, the most powerful of the Aegean allies of Athens, Alcibiades was present at Miletus on the mainland, where Spartan authorities formalized their agreement with Tissaphernes. Quoted by Thucydides, the draft text was a declaration of mutual support in a joint war against Athens combined with the recognition of the Persian king's legitimate dominion over all land and cities in his control or previously in the control of his predecessors. The agreement conceded all to Persian claims, and must have done so with the understanding that Persian suzerainty was acceptable to the propertied and influential classes at Miletus and elsewhere in Ionia, and that the king would bear the cost of defending his own domain. Both expectations were reasonable, and the latter point was made explicit in a second draft treaty drawn up at Miletus at the beginning of winter, after Tissaphernes had captured the rebel Amorges with the support of the Spartan fleet.[5]

But by the winter of 412/11, the war against Athens in Ionia was not proceeding smoothly for the Spartans and their new allies. Against expectations, the Athenians had managed to launch sufficient ships to match the Spartans at sea and to stem the spread of rebellions. Chios was even placed under siege, while a large Athenian naval force based at Samos maintained a threat against Miletus. Pay did not flow freely enough from Tissaphernes to salve the wounds of battle, and setbacks divided the counsels of Spartan commanders. They began to blame each other for the lack of success on various fronts and to find fault with the agreement that had been reached with Tissaphernes. Since arriving in Asia Minor, Alcibiades had established himself in the company of Tissaphernes, acting initially as a go-between on behalf of the Spartans, but ingratiating himself with Tissaphernes by placing his counsel at the service of his new host. In a climate of souring relations between Sparta and Tissaphernes, Alcibiades knew that he would be viewed by the Spartans as an expendable scapegoat. To escape arrest as powerful men again turned against him, he stayed in the company of Tissaphernes, whose cause he had benefited most.

Alcibiades advised Tissaphernes that it was in the king's best interest to allow the Spartans and the Athenians to wear each other down, while, in the long term, the king would find the Athenians to be more suitable allies than the Spartans. Always thinking in cosmic terms, Alcibiades developed an argument that became influential because it was both comprehensive and harmonious with immediate goals and past traditions: the Athenians held a maritime empire, while the king's dominions were continental; a balance between them would be natural. These two powers had previously treated each other on terms of friendship. So they could again, and mutual accommodation over the status of Ionian Greeks was more likely to be reached with the Athenians than with the Spartans, whose announced cause was the liberation of the Greeks from any form of domination. Alcibiades' advice may well have persuaded Tissaphernes, who, as Thucydides notes, in any event acted in accord with it. According to a more cynical and equally plausible view, Tissaphernes recognized that it did not matter which Greek was his ally as long as the king's will was served. It was in either event to Tissaphernes' advantage to let Alcibiades' influence be known, for this stance could become useful leverage in his further dealings with the Spartans. For Alcibiades, his presence at the side of Tissaphernes, even acting as his spokesman to Greek delegations, elevated his importance as a key player in the ambiguous game of Ionian politics.[6]

SAVIORS AND PHANTOMS

The possibility of a rupture between Tissaphernes and the Spartans generated excitement among the Athenian forces in Ionia over the winter of 412/11, for it was common knowledge that the build-up of the Spartan navy was enabled by the pay he provided, and that this pay was, for a time at least, more generous than what the Athenians could manage for their own navy. The cost of maintaining the Athenian fleet was especially worrisome when operations in force were crucial and regular sources of revenue were suddenly in jeopardy. By the winter of 412/11, the Athenian navy relied more upon funds raised in the area of operations than on money from Athens, and gaps between income and essential expenditures had to be filled, in the final analysis, from the means at the disposal of individual commanders and trierarchs. As it had seemed to the Peloponnesian commanders and to their allies among the Ionian aristocracy, access to the seemingly limitless resources of the Persian king seemed an enticing solution to the crisis at hand.[7]

A popular fantasy thus took root among Athenian servicemen at Samos while their commanders began to devote attention to the means of realizing this idea. Through personal intermediaries, Alcibiades showed Athenian officers at Samos the way to win the cooperation of Tissaphernes and the king. The essential condition, Alcibiades let it be known, was that the influence of his political enemies over the fickle Athenian populace should come to an end, and that political leadership should be in the hands of men who could deal honorably with Persian officials and the king. Alcibiades' standing with Tissaphernes, and the evidence of his influence on the affairs of Ionia, seemed to be proof that the right men, in collaboration with Persian authorities, could exercise insurmountable power. Alcibiades was thus the key to this plan, but the price for success, it was recognized behind closed doors, was a curtailment of democracy.[8]

The idea discussed and generally endorsed among the circles of Athenian commanders at Samos spread quickly to the *hetairoi* of these influential men at Athens, where it resonated on the fears and hopes of the Athenian aristocracy. In this time of military setbacks and financial stringency, they were the ones who bore the burdens of *eisphorai* and the expenses of trierarchy, and they were the ones who took the blame before an angry *demos* whenever anything went wrong. But, when so much already had gone wrong and the might of Persia was potentially arrayed with their enemies, the very existence of Athens was at stake. It seemed the height of folly to defend the privileges of democracy to the detriment of all else. The Athenian aristocracy had long recognized the benefits of empire, and now came to believe that democracy had to be sacrificed, and Alcibiades embraced, to save the empire.

At the same time that oligarchy was privately mooted, the seductive vision of reconciliation with Alcibiades was taking hold of the Athenian public. There were still those who felt that his execration was justified—for the condemnation of Alcibiades had been a religious act, supported by priestly authorities who had affirmed that Alcibiades' attested deeds were offensive to the gods. There were those, moreover, like Phrynichus son of Stratonides, one of the generals at Samos, who felt that Alcibiades was merely an opportunist and ought to be opposed. But the public at large had come to feel differently. Aristophanes had produced his *Birds,* in 414, for a public willing to see Alcibiades as the victim of a destructive frenzy. Now, almost four years later, time and especially the disaster in Sicily had inclined many to doubt the authority of the priesthood that had condemned him, just as many now felt angered and aggrieved at the oracle mongers who had encouraged their former intentions to invade Sicily. The execration of Alcibiades had *not* averted divine wrath, and many signs, including Alcibiades' personal ascendancy in Asia, suggested that the Athenians had been misled. Perhaps the deeds for which they had condemned Alcibiades were *not* what they had seemed to be; perhaps Alcibiades' self-defense before the departure for Sicily *had* been just; perhaps it was time for Alcibiades' odyssey to end in a homecoming.[9]

Reflection of this popular sentiment in the spring of 411 was seen again in dramatic metaphor, in the *Helen* of Euripides. The play is the most remarkable of a long tradition of exculpations of Helen, she whose beauty had launched the most destructive expedition known to Greek legend. In Euripides' play, the warriors who had sailed to Troy had been misled by a phantom created as an agent of divine anger; the true and guiltless Helen had been carried by Hermes to Egypt and to the protective custody of its king, Proteus. As the play opens, Helen laments her past, "accursed, and held to be traitor to my own lord, and inciter of a great war for Greeks" (lines 54–55), as well as her present fate, for now she is the object of the unwanted affections of her new host, the young successor to the deceased Proteus. Soon she meets another luckless wanderer, her shipwrecked husband, who introduces himself as

> Menelaus, famed for my chariot-team, leader of the greatest expedition—and this I say not in boast—that sailed overseas against Troy; no tyrant I, who compelled men to war, but leader of the willing young men of Greece. Some among these are no longer to be counted among the living; others, thankfully, have escaped the sea, and bear the names of the dead back home... [lines 392–99]

Divinity presides over their moment of meeting, "for God," Helen remarks, "is the recognition of those dear to you" (line 560). But it requires the divinely inspired wisdom of the virgin seer, Theonoë, to consummate their reunion in an escape from barbarian shores. Their escape commences to the accompaniment of a choral hymn invoking the mountain-dwelling Mother of the Gods, who is identified with Demeter (lines 1301–68). Both goddesses were famed for visiting punishment on humanity in their grief over lost loved ones, the Mother of the Gods, or Cybele, for her lover Attis, victim of her own vengeance, and Demeter for the rape by Hades of her daughter Persephone. Both goddesses, in overcoming their grief, assured the future prosperity of those who made the prescribed propitiatory offerings. Euripides' chorus closes by asking of Helen,

> Did flame unconsecrated of rites unhallowed in your chambers shine? And so did you draw the wrath of the Mighty Mother? Was it you, O child, who irreverenced the sacrifices of the Goddess?...Did you trust in your charms alone?[10]

The chorus' anxious query is not directly answered. But the success of their escape, supported at the end of the play by divine providence sent from

Zeus, reveals that, if pride had misled Helen, her atonement was complete and her homecoming was assured.

Was the *Helen* an elaborate allusion to Alcibiades? Some modern commentators have thought so, though most have left the question unasked. Yet the plights of Helen and of Alcibiades and the ambivalent turnings of their ways back home are strikingly consonant, and ancient testimony supports the identification. Speaking of his sojourn at Sparta, where Alcibiades behaved as a Spartan, Plutarch remarked that one could have said of him that Alcibiades "is the same woman as ever." The reference, from Euripides' *Orestes,* was specifically to Helen and her irrepressible vanity. Comic poets too played with the erotic splendor and omnivalent sexuality of Alcibiades. Eupolis depicted him as a transvestite devotee of the Thracian goddess Cotyto in the *Baptae;* Pherecrates is quoted as saying, "For though Alcibiades is not a man, as it would seem, yet he is today the one man of all women." Euripides' *Helen* itself was lampooned the next year in Aristophanes' *Thesmophoriazusae,* where some have seen Alcibiades again called to mind among the effeminates and transvestites invading the women's preserve at the festival of Demeter Thesmophoros. Euripides himself is depicted as the target of women's anger for having abused the reputation of women in his productions. Perhaps Aristophanes' satire takes its chief point from the view of those who felt that to liken the divinely-endowed Helen to Alcibiades, always advertising his gifts, was the crowning insult to the reputation of Helen.[11]

Recognizing Alcibiades in Euripides' *Helen* accounts for many of the singular aspects of that play. In particular, it accounts for the pivotal role of one of Euripides' invented characters, Theonoë, daughter of Proteus and voice of divine reason, through which Helen and Menelaus find salvation. Theonoë has been seen as an allonym for Theano, famed as the priestess who, alone of Eleusinian officiants, publicly refused to curse Alcibiades at the time of his execration. In his reshaping of the story of Helen, Euripides surely intended this and other associations to be recognizable to his audience, although, as with all divinely guided voices, he spoke in ambiguities. Menelaus too embodies qualities of Alcibiades as war-leader and sovereign; it would probably be more faithful to the intent of Euripides' allusions to say that Helen and Menelaus together, in their reunion, embodied both the idea of Alcibiades and his reunion with Athens.[12]

Noteworthy too, in the *Helen,* is the allusion in this reunion to a reconciliation between Sparta and Athens. Helen and Menelaus were, after all, queen and king of Sparta, and their return marks the end of sufferings brought by war to Greeks. Alcibiades had made much of his kinship with Sparta in his two-year sojourn among the Spartans, and a strong part of his appeal to Athenians, early in 411, must have been not only that he could restore and preserve the strength of Athens, but that he could reconcile

Athens and Sparta. His jealousy over Nicias' prominence in that role a decade earlier was public knowledge, while the reaction against Alcibiades among the Spartan leadership, over the winter of 412/11, may not have been. In any event, his presence among the barbarians was known to be working toward a balance of forces between Athens and Sparta.

In keeping with these aspirations, also early in 411, the Athenians honored Dionysus with the staging of Aristophanes' *Lysistrata,* a comedy that made reconciliation of the warring Athenians and Spartans its central theme. The vehicle of reconciliation, significantly, was a woman who acted as a man. Her name, Lysistrata, "Army-disbander," was another pun on the name of Peisistratus. Like the tyrant, Lysistrata took power by seizing the Acropolis. And her power to compel reconciliation came, significantly, from denying the gifts of Eros to the Athenians, in fact, to all Greeks.[13]

SAGE ADVICE

Visions of reconciliation with Sparta and mutual accommodation with the Persian king, all brought about by a moderation of the litigious and belligerent democracy, represented a massive communal mood-swing away from the frenzy of demagoguery of 415. The mood strongly favored appeals to the image of stability represented by the past. This was reflected in the rhetoric used to discuss the crisis, in the individuals to whom the Athenians turned for inspiration and guidance, and in the reforms they adopted.

Immediately following the news from Sicily, in the autumn of 413, the Athenians had established a standing committee to serve as an advisory board to the Council and Assembly. The crisis required a continuity of deliberative wisdom to moderate the waves of congregational hysteria liable to sweep over the Athenians as each dispatch from their officers abroad confronted them with a new predicament. To fill this role, they elected ten *probouloi,* Advisors, all men over forty years old, who had the authority to convene the Council and with it to prepare the agenda for the Assembly. Such a body hearkened back to the role of the Council of the Areopagus, the council of elder statesmen who were credited, on the eve of another catastrophe, with providing the Athenians sound guidance and the financial means to man the fleet that had won the battle of Salamis. Two *probouloi* known to us by name exemplify the sort of men to whom the Athenians wished to entrust their affairs. One was Hagnon, the founder of Amphipolis on the Strymon, a colleague in generalship with Pericles and one of the signatories of the Peace of Nicias in 421. Hagnon, father of Theramenes who rose to prominence at this time, was at least in his 60s when he was appointed to this office. Another was the poet Sophocles, who had also served Athens under Pericles as a general and as a treasurer of imperial revenues.

Now in his 80s, Sophocles was a living link with the generation of Athenians that had created the empire.[14]

In imagination too, the Athenians were summoning heroes of the past to save them. Probably in 412 the comic poet Eupolis staged his *Demes,* in which a delegation of dead Athenians return from the underworld to set the affairs of their descendants in order. The play is known only from fragments and citations, but its main line of action is clear. Solon, Miltiades, Aristides, and Pericles are to accompany their leader, the general Myronides, back from the dead. Civil harmony, victory over barbarians, a just empire, and a strong democracy are thus represented as coming in the train of the hero who had twice rescued Athens from the grips of defeat. When, probably in 459, the bulk of Athenian forces were abroad, Myronides had led the youngest and oldest Athenians at home to victory against attacking Corinthians; a year later, following a great defeat at Tanagra, Myronides had rallied the Athenians to victory over the Boeotians. Such a hero was needed again, so that the accomplishments of the rest might survive. This sort of wishful thinking is understandable in the context of the setbacks of 412. But a deeper anxiety over the nature of leadership and power seems to have been present in the *Demes:* several citations attest that Peisistratus was hailed as tyrant and king in Eupolis' play, although to what effect we do not know. Whatever the role of Peisistratus may have been, the citations reveal another element of the historical imagination of the Athenians in this time of crisis, lending color to the statement by Thucydides that, "In the panic of the moment, as is the way with a democracy, the Athenians were ready to be as prudent as possible."[15]

While the mind of the public at large was thus animated, over the winter of 412/11 men of influence gathered their friends and *hetairoi* to discuss the nature of public prudence and how it might be institutionalized through constitutional reform. As among the Athenians generally, a focus on the Athenian past provided the rhetorical tools that enabled a sense of common purpose to emerge from competing personal agendas within the circles of the aristocratic *hetaireiai.*

A recurrent theme of Athenian political debate was the contrast between the revolutionary radicalism of youth and the stable conservatism of age. For two decades this theme had been exploited by demagogues to warn against sophistically trained young aristocrats. Reinforced in drama, the theme was so ingrained in political rhetoric that when at last, in 411, aristocratic intellectuals were gaining control of public debate, they had to make their message of purposeful change acceptable within this paradigm. A portion of a speech said to be composed by the sophist Thrasymachus of Calchedon opens on this theme. Aided by the desperation of conditions of 411, the theme is quickly converted into a justification for raising longstanding grievances of the aristocracy against the ways of the democracy:

> I wish, Athenians, that I belonged to that ancient time when silence sufficed for young people, since the state of affairs did not force them to make speeches and the older men were managing the city properly. But since our fortune has reserved for us this later time, in which we submit to [the government of] our city [by others] but [bear] its misfortunes ourselves, and of these the greatest are the work of neither the gods nor of chance but of the administration, one really has to speak. . . .[16]

Aristophanes was already parodying tags of Thrasymachus on the tongues of young men in the early 420s, so it is unlikely that Thrasymachus could represent himself as young in 412 or 411. But it was not the sophist who delivered this speech. The unknown speaker who commissioned it, moreover, need not have been any younger than Alcibiades; in drawing attention, perhaps in the presence of the venerable *probouloi,* to his comparative youth, he was playing on an established theme. Beginning, in unstable times, with the theme of the instability of youth, he utilizes the reputation of young intellectuals for adaptable expertise to move his audience through the confusion of conflicting advice toward a vision of an inevitable and already latent solution provided by the past:

> I shall begin by showing that in speaking against each other those of our politicians, and others too, who are at odds with each other, have undergone what inevitably happens to people who try to win without thinking. They think they are saying the opposite to each other, and fail to realize that they are pursuing the same policies and that their opponents' arguments are included in their own. Just consider, right from the start, what each of them is after. To begin with, our ancestral constitution troubles them, though it is very easy to understand and is what all our citizens have most in common. But surely, whenever anything is beyond the scope of our own judgment, we must abide by what our elders have said; and whatever the old-timers saw for themselves, we must learn of from those who beheld it. . . .[17]

Two authorities emerge here. One is the testimony of elders and old-timers, be it the living, as with the *probouloi,* or the written testimony of poetry, published laws, and decrees. More fundamental authority, but nebulous and therefore malleable, comes from the appeal to the ancestral constitution, *patrios politeia,* of the Athenians.

THE ANCESTRAL CONSTITUTION

The *politeia,* or constitution of the Athenians, was the system of relations among their *politai,* or citizens, as defined by the practices of office-holding and the exercise of lawful authority. Although certain formative acts and institutions were remembered or recorded in various ways, the Athenian *politeia* was embodied in no document, and had as yet no systematically described developmental history. In fact, the perspective of popular memory and public commemorations preferred to emphasize ancient continuities, and to explain changes, like the Peisistratid tyranny, as aberrations that, in time, were corrected by the restoration of ancestral practices. Their *politeia* was, above all, a way of life in which habits, customs, and laws blended seamlessly. It was an ideal that orators had long woven into the self-consciousness of all Athenians on occasions exemplified most famously in the funeral oration spoken by Pericles in the second book of Thucydides. Thus, the popular perception of the Athenian constitution evoked in the Thrasymachean speech held that it was the thing "that all our citizens have most in common," both now and in the past. According to this concept, all that was required to remedy the present crisis was to recognize the authentic, and ancient, core of the Athenian *politeia* and restore it by doing away with aberrant accretions.[18]

The accretions to be eliminated by the oligarchic movement were the measures adopted over the previous half-century that encouraged and enabled the poor majority of Athenians to participate in sovereign deliberative and judicial processes. These developments were within the memory of "old-timers," some of whom, under the circumstances and by a universal habit of human nature, were bound to give testimony to how much better things had been in the old days. Pay for office-holding, and especially for jury duty was the mainstay of the innovations witnessed by this generation, for it enabled "those who on account of their poverty would sell their city for a drachma," as Theramenes, one of the oligarchic leaders of 411, put it, to form the decisive majority in political and judicial assemblies. Degeneration in Athenian government brought about, it was argued, by concessions to such craven greed could be put right by restoring the *patrios politeia*.[19]

The legitimation of revolutionary action required that the authority of the past be made as explicit as possible. So the first official step toward the creation of an oligarchic constitution, in the spring of 411, included a historiographic exercise. Aristotle quotes a resolution submitted to the Assembly to create a commission of thirty *syngrapheis*, to be formed by electing twenty men to join the ten *probouloi* already in office, who were to draw up proposals for the security of the state; to this resolution an addendum was attached by Cleitophon:

> Those elected are also to conduct research into the ancestral laws that Cleisthenes enacted when he established the democracy, so that by hearing about these too they will take the best counsel.[20]

No source records the historical findings of these *syngrapheis*, and the comparatively brief space of time, a matter of days, before their report was submitted probably allowed for no more than the affirmation of the salient point already under discussion in ideological circles: the archaic Athenian state did not provide salaries to office-holders.

When the appointed day came for the Assembly to hear the report of the commission, Thucydides reports that

> the *syngrapheis* submitted no other proposal than this: that it be possible for any Athenian to make any proposal he liked with impunity; and they imposed heavy penalties on anyone who would indict a speaker for illegal proceedings, or who would injure him in any other way.

A series of specific proposals were then made and approved without opposition. Revenues were to be spent only for the war effort, and salaries for nearly all public offices were to be abolished. For the duration of the war the government was to be in the hands of 5,000 Athenians best able to benefit the state in financial and personal service.[21]

Imprecise though this description was, the creation of the so-called Five Thousand amounted to the establishment of a property qualification for citizenship. Since the time of Solon and earlier, the Athenians had described eligibility for certain offices in terms of wealth, but no precedent from Athenian history justified the imposition of a property qualification as the criterion for excluding free Athenians from *all* participation in government. Such criteria were the basis of contemporary oligarchies elsewhere, however. In the Athenian context, the designation of 5,000 men of means as the sovereign body represented an inclusive estimate of the number of *dunatoi,* those "capable" of getting things done financially, who could also be reckoned as ideologically aligned with the *aristoi,* the "best," since they were not beholden, like the poor, to whoever could provide them the means for their next meal.[22]

Pending the official registration of those Athenians who were to comprise the Five Thousand, all administration was to be in the hands of an interim council of 400. This council, soon to be known as the Four Hundred, was nominated by a procedure controlled by the ideological leaders of the oligarchic movement. "It was no easy matter," Thucydides comments, "about 100 years after the tyrants were put down, to deprive the Athenian *demos* of its liberty, since the *demos* not only was unused to submission, but for more than half this time it had been accustomed to exercise authority over others." But liberty, authority, and submission were fluid and circumstantial. So too was the nature of the Athenian *demos.*[23]

One of the factors enabling the oligarchic movement to surface at Athens in 411 was a progressive demographic shift among the Athenian citizenry, a consequence of the plague of the 420s, of losses in war, and especially of the Sicilian disaster. Conservatively estimated, between nine and ten thousand Athenians were killed or died in captivity as a result of the expedition of 415–413. More than two-thirds of the Athenians lost in Sicily were from among the poorest Athenians who, along with foreign hired labor, manned the oars of the fleet. The depletion of the numbers of poorer

Athenians was intensified by the commitment of manpower, in 412 and afterward, to the naval war in Ionia. Given earlier losses, the numbers of propertyless Athenian laborers by the beginning of 411 can hardly have been enough to provide one-third of the crewmen needed to man the nearly 140 Athenian triremes then in service. As a political presence, the poorest class of Athenians that twenty years earlier had roughly equaled the numbers of citizens of middling or better means was now reduced to virtually nothing.[24]

The depletion of poor laborers from among the urban citizenry left Athenian demagogues without the most committed element of their constituency. The battle for the allegiance of the largest remaining group of Athenians, the owners of moderate property, was likely to be a draw in purely ideological terms, since as many of them were likely to admire and aspire to the qualities of the aristocracy as would stand firm against them in the name of an all-inclusive democracy (the designation of 5,000 as the number of Athenians suitable for an oligarchy seems in fact to divide this middle class roughly in two). The Ionian revolts of 412–411, however, and the rumors about Alcibiades, decisively tipped the balance in favor of the aristocratic, oligarchic agenda.

Thucydides reports that for some time before the oligarchic revolution the partisans of the aristocratic groups, the sworn members of *hetaireiai,* monopolized public debate in the Council and Assembly, "and no one spoke in opposition to them, so fearful were the rest of the numbers of those in the movement." Their fear was fed by assassinations of outstanding opponents of the movement, "and no one tried to investigate such crimes or take action against those suspected of them." *Hetaireiai* whose influence seemed on the rise were attracting zealous young men eager to prove their worth and loyalty by acts of daring against the enemies of the *hetairoi.* So Androcles, a leading demagogue and foremost among those who had denounced Alcibiades in 415, was assassinated by "a clandestine band of young men... who wanted to ingratiate themselves to Alcibiades, whom they supposed was going to return and bring with him the friendship of Tissaphernes." A few weeks later, Hyperbolus, living in exile at Samos after his ostracism four years earlier, was murdered by a like-minded conspiracy among the Athenians at Samos, with the help of Samian collaborators.[25]

Another demagogue, Peisander, recognized the impact of changing conditions and took a different turn. Peisander had been foremost among the Commissioners of 415 who had propelled the investigation of the mutilation of the Herms into a hunt for subverters of the democracy. In 412/11, he was among the Athenian commanders at Samos who began negotiations with Alcibiades and became a leading advocate of oligarchic revolution. Peisander's reputation as a spokesmen for the people did much to make credible the claim that the oligarchic movement was the sole salvation of

Athens. It also enabled Peisander to take the high ground above the group rivalries of aristocratic politics.[26]

When the decisive day had come to hear the report of the thirty *syngrapheis,* the oligarchic planners made doubly sure that they played to a receptive audience by holding the Assembly not in its customary meeting place on the Pnyx hill overlooking the heart of Athens, but a mile outside the walls of Athens, in the enclosure of Poseidon Hippios at Colonus. Thucydides, who reports this detail, offers no explanation, but it has been commonly assumed that such a meeting place outside the walls, with the enemy at Decelea some twelve miles away, would have been attended by the Athenians under arms. If so, it was a method for assuring that those who could arm themselves were chiefly represented at the decisive assembly. The occasion also saw the mobilization of armed guards and scouts, particularly members of the cavalry, to whom Poseidon Hippios was especially sacred. Those attending the meeting would have to pass under the watchful eyes of these armed men, reinforcing the intimidation that had already accompanied the oligarchic movement. These circumstances, the depleted condition of the urban poor, and possibly also the constraints of space available within the sanctuary of Poseidon, all conspired to render this meeting of the *demos* an assembly of those Athenians most likely to comprise the Five Thousand, whose official creation Peisander himself proposed on this occasion.[27]

The resolutions of the Athenians assembled at Colonus were thus deemed to be the first acts of the Five Thousand, even though the official registration of the Five Thousand was still to be carried out. Aristotle, who provides a wealth of detail on the constitutional measures passed in 411, reports that a commission authorized by this assembly to draft constitutions for the Five Thousand and for the interim administration of the Four Hundred was elected by the Five Thousand, but elsewhere he also makes clear that the official register of the Five Thousand was never published. Revolution at Athens was thus brought about under conditions that had brought together a group of citizens who viewed their relationship to each other and to lawful authority far differently from assemblies formerly addressed by Pericles, Cleon, and Alcibiades. For a moment, the designs of the intellectual leaders of the oligarchic movement and the aspirations of a significant number of Athenians were in harmony.[28]

But by the time the Council of the Four Hundred took the place of the democratically allotted Council of 500, a few days after the assembly at Colonus, the conditions under which the revolution had begun were changing. Shifting currents in the politics that linked Athens to Asia Minor and the Peloponnese soon made it impossible for the authoritarian Four Hundred to govern effectively, and the regime of the Four Hundred collapsed after barely four months. Ironically, the concept of government by the 5,000 best Athenians remained vital precisely because it was never definitely realized. The idea of effecting change in the interest of the most qualified Athenians became, with the revolutions of 411, a potent stimulus for political action. But following the experiences of 411, political action in the name of the rightful, ancestral constitution of the Athenians could succeed only so long as leaders were mindful that their designs could be but one element in the web of circumstances enmeshing the Athenian community. The most drastic changes in 411 and in the years to come resulted from the failures of Athenian leadership to fix Athenian interests securely within the changing balance of external interests and powers affecting the Aegean, the Mediterranean, and southwest Asia.

THE BEST LAID PLANS

As the spring of 411 was approaching, the Athenian delegation to the court of Tissaphernes led by Peisander failed to reach an agreement with the satrap. Blame was placed on Alcibiades, who conducted the negotiations on behalf of Tissaphernes; it is impossible to say whether or not he was responsible for the unacceptable demands he conveyed from Tissaphernes, although he must have known that they would be refused. The Athenian emissaries were prepared to make many concessions to allow Darius to exercise authority over the Greeks of Asia Minor, but they would not agree to allow the king to build and man a fleet in the Aegean. Such a concession would threaten the basis of Athenian imperial power. From Tissaphernes' perspective, an agreement could be made with whichever party would yield most to the king. The Athenians might eventually prove compatible allies, as Alcibiades argued, but they were not yet sufficiently compliant. Immediately after the departure of the Athenian embassy, Tissaphernes contacted Spartan authorities and negotiated his third and most explicit treaty with the Spartans, an agreement that sanctioned the operation of the king's fleet in the Aegean.[29]

The oligarchic coup at Athens was thus consummated despite the failure to bring Tissaphernes to the Athenian side. Inasmuch as the leaders of the movement included not a few men who, like Phrynichus and Antiphon, had shown themselves to be bitter enemies of Alcibiades, these must have felt personally encouraged that Alcibiades would now have no part of their achievement. But without Persian funding the authorities in Athens could not support the fleet that defended their empire. The Athenian fleet, concentrated at Samos, had been maintained from practically the beginning of its operations in Ionia by the ability of its commanders and trierarchs to extract funds from Athenian subjects and allies, and by plundering their foes. The fleet had thus become financially independent of Athens, and remained an instrument of Athenian policy only by virtue of the personal allegiance of Athenian commanders and the compliance of the sailors to their orders. The Athenian revolutionaries attempted to broaden the basis of their support by appealing to the aristocratic inclinations among leading men in the states subject to Athenian rule. But in the interval of revolutionary transition, when personal loyalties and practical means were all put to the test, the self-interest of the "best" men proved to be the weakest link among the bonds of common purpose.

Immediately after the breakdown of negotiations with Tissaphernes, Peisander and his fellow oligarchic emissaries met on Samos and decided to implement a plan, long under discussion, to establish oligarchies in the states still loyal to Athens. In principle, the suppression of popular governments would enable men of means everywhere to act for the common good. The community of aristocratic interests spoken of in Pseudo-Xenophon's tract, eulogized by Alcibiades among the Spartans, and assumed by *kaloi k'agathoi* in and out of Athens, would thus be liberated from the tyranny of mob rule. The result, it must have been felt, would be a natural order of the "best" men, cooperating for their mutual benefit under the enlightened leadership of Athens.

Speaking out among the oligarchic conspirators, Phrynichus had previously pointed out that there was little reason to believe that the empowerment of the wealthy men of the Aegean would persuade them that Athens stood for the common good. The suppression of democratic government would merely, in his view, free powerful men to pursue their private interests unchecked. But Phrynichus' cautions were not popular among the oligarchic conspirators. Following the breakdown of negotiations with Tissaphernes, Peisander and his fellow emissaries had only their ideological program to guide them. So, as Peisander returned to Athens to put an end to the democratic government at home, the emissaries divided themselves into groups to carry out their mission around the Aegean. The scheme to convert the Athenian empire into a union of oligarchies quickly went awry, beginning at Samos.[30]

In the wave of rebellions from Athens spread by Alcibiades and the Spartans in 412, the arrival of Athenian ships at Samos had encouraged the Samian *demos* to act decisively against a movement among Samian aristocrats to join the anti-Athenian uprisings. Some 200 Samian aristocrats were executed and 400 were exiled. Through resolutions publicly inscribed at Athens, the Athenians gave official support to the dealings of the Samian democracy with these traitors to the empire, and rewarded the Samians, who had been reduced to the status of conquered subjects after a revolt in 440/39, with a grant of autonomy. By this decree, the Samians replaced the Chians in the place of honor as trusted allies and partners of Athens in empire.[31]

Independence in internal government (the essence of *autonomia*) was, on the one hand, a specious bit of propaganda at a moment when the Athenians were making Samos into their chief base for naval operations in Ionia. But it was highly effective, for it promoted close cooperation between Athenians and the Samians whose political leadership depended most upon the alignments of power maintained by the Athenian navy. The benefit was certainly mutual, since the Samian democracy, in possession of the confiscated property of 600 of its wealthiest families, had the means to provide essential support to the Athenian fleet during the months in which funding from Athens was drying up.

Close as the relationship between Samians and Athenians was, the beginnings of the oligarchic conspiracy among the Athenian commanders at Samos over the winter of 412/11 inevitably influenced Samian politics as well. While Peisander was bringing the oligarchic council of the Four Hundred into power at Athens, a conspiracy with leading Samians was supposed to convert Samos into one of the loyal oligarchies of the new Athenian empire. But the Samian *demos* proved too strong to be thus undone, precisely because of its symbiotic ties to the Athenian fleet. When plans for the coup became known in high circles, popular Samian leaders and a group of Athenian officers opposed to oligarchy made preparations against the conspiracy on Samos, and used Athenian forces to defeat the Samian oligarchs when they attempted to act. Ringleaders were executed or exiled, while the larger body of their followers were encouraged to become loyal to the Samian *demos*. The reaction against oligarchy thus began with the conspicuous victory of the Samian democracy, and the part played by Athenians in the fleet at Samos galvanized their identity as defenders of democracy and opponents of oligarchy. When word of the creation of the Four Hundred reached Samos shortly after these events, the Athenians of the fleet elected new officers who were known champions of democracy, chief among them Thrasybulus and Thrasyllus, and bound themselves and the Samians by oath to stand together in opposition to the Four Hundred.[32]

Athens and Samos were thus set on separate courses, and the resources available to the Athenian fleet at Samos proved the more durable. To the men at Samos, the failure of Peisander's negotiations meant only that Tissaphernes would not support the oligarchy at Athens. Despite Tissaphernes' agreement with the Spartans, the alignment of Persia remained an ambiguous issue for all Greeks. The treaty still required ratification from Darius, and Alcibiades let it be known that the king might yet be persuaded to change partners. In the meantime, Tissaphernes found various pretexts to defer providing pay to the Spartan fleet, deepening the frustration of Sparta and her allies. The Athenians on Samos, meanwhile, had reasons to feel hopeful. Alcibiades was known to be their advocate with Tissaphernes, and even if Alcibiades was not yet able to close the grand deal between the king and the Athenians, they believed him able to influence the affairs of the Ionian Greeks to the benefit of the Athenians at Samos.[33]

Having alienated the oligarchs at Athens, Alcibiades was soon embraced as a savior by the men of the democratic fleet. By formal resolution the Athenians on Samos granted Alcibiades immunity from prosecution on the charges that had led to his exile, and he was escorted from the court of Tissaphernes to Samos by his leading supporter, Thrasybulus son of Lycus. Reunited with Athenian forces, Alcibiades delivered a long speech recounting the wrongs he had suffered and the great hopes he had for the future, after which he too was elected general by the men of the fleet. In the euphoria of the moment there was strong sentiment that Alcibiades should lead the fleet to Athens and depose the illegitimate government of the Four Hundred, about whose regime tales of terror had been circulating at Samos. Always with a wider perspective in view, Alcibiades discouraged this movement and persuaded the assembly to send him to negotiate officially on their behalf with Tissaphernes.[34]

The uncertainty that surrounded the councils of Tissaphernes gave rise to much speculation, reflected in Thucydides' account, about what Tissaphernes intended and what Alcibiades actually achieved. A Phoenician fleet had been mobilized on the authority of King Darius, and in the course of the summer it advanced as far as Aspendus on the Pamphylian coast of Asia Minor. Tissaphernes made promises to the Spartans to bring this fleet into operation on their behalf, while Alcibiades declared to the Athenians at Samos that he would persuade Tissaphernes to bring it to the Athenian side, or not to use it at all. The last is what in fact happened, much to the disgust of the Spartans and their allies. The reasons for this outcome, however, involved more considerations than those mentioned by Thucydides.

The year 411 was particularly troublesome for the Mediterranean affairs of King Darius. The Phoenician fleet had been mobilized in response to rumors of a secret alliance between the Egyptian king and a king of the Arabs, who were said to be planning jointly to seize the coastlands as far as Phoenicia. Possibly at the same time, an uprising also took place on the island of Cyprus, where the Cypro-Greek Euagoras seized the lordship of the important town of Salamis from the Phoenician dynast, Abdemon of Tyre, called "friend of the King of the Persians" by Diodorus. With any or all of these events underway, Darius had more pressing needs for his fleet along the Levantine coast and in Cyprus than he did in Ionia.

Close to Tissaphernes, Alcibiades had been in a position to observe the demands on the resources of Darius. Before he left the court of Tissaphernes, Alcibiades may have been involved in negotiations with Euagoras. The friendship of Euagoras with Athens and with Tissaphernes, and his allegiance to Darius, are all attested within a few years. Foundations for these relations must have been laid at the time that Euagoras secured his power. It was surely with an eye to these matters that Alcibiades persuaded the Athenians on Samos to send him with a squadron along the Lycian coast, in the waterways between the Aegean and Phoenicia. Alcibiades had penetrated farther than any other Greek into the tangle of motives that dictated Tissaphernes' actions, and he knew the importance of maintaining a show of strength on this front.[35]

DESPERATE STRAITS

The oligarchs at Athens, meanwhile, were struggling for position within a smaller universe. Estranged from the fleet at Samos, they had at their disposal manpower barely sufficient to defend Athens and Piraeus. In their ship-sheds they may have had as many as sixty triremes, about half the number serving in Ionian waters, and they could man only about twenty. With little prospect of gathering imperial revenues or Persian money, their financial hopes were pinned on the personal fortunes of the putative Five Thousand who were to govern. It was not long before the regime of the Four Hundred proved incapable of defending even this resource.

Some among the oligarchs, like Phrynichus, did not expect to repair the breach with Alcibiades and the fleet at Samos in the near future. These men especially will have encouraged the sentiment among the *kaloi k'agathoi* for rapprochement with Sparta, since only the respect and support from a wider community of honorable men could give them strength. As a result, contacts with Sparta developed into close negotiations over the course of the four months that the Four Hundred had held power. The price for respect and support, it became clear, would have to be concessions particularly to the neighbors of Attica on the subject of disputed territories, such as the border communities of Oropos, Oenoe, and the island of Euboea. Negotiating such concessions placed the oligarchs, the self-proclaimed saviors of Athens, in a perilous position.[36]

Negotiation could proceed only from a position of strength, so, despite misgivings, the Four Hundred recognized the need to attempt to reconcile the men of the fleet to the new government at Athens. When an embassy came to Samos claiming to represent the government of the Five Thousand at Athens, Alcibiades sent a reply urging the Five Thousand to depose the Four Hundred and reinstate a council of 500, and, above all, "to hold out and make no concession to their enemies, for as long as they preserved the state, there was great hope for unity." This was probably the occasion on which, as Plutarch reports, Alcibiades "advised the Athenians to hold onto their land," reminding them of the oath taken by young Athenian men come of age, the ephebes, to defend the boundaries of Attica. By thus denouncing negotiated concessions to the enemies of Athens, Alcibiades knew that he could drive a wedge between the many Athenians who, on the one hand, still hoped for a miraculous recovery, and his personal foes among the Four Hundred on the other.[37]

This shrewd move proved fatal to the hopes of the committed oligarchs, Antiphon, Phrynichus, and now Peisander among them. For by depriving them of any support for their negotiations with Sparta, it forced them to literally turn inward and to prepare to use violence against Athenians in order to gain a dependent alliance with Sparta. Under such conditions, these men ordered the construction of a fort at the mouth of the Piraeus harbor, on the promontory called Eetionia, nominally to guard the harbor from attack, but in fact to provide a Spartan garrison with a base from which to assure Athenian compliance to the terms of a foreseeable settlement.[38]

For the sake of government by the right people, then, plans were afoot that would put Athens into the hands of the Spartans. But public sentiment, even within the war-distorted cross section of citizenry present at Athens, would support no such movement. Publicly, the council of the Four Hundred maintained their role as interim agents for the legitimate government of the Five Thousand. But growing disaffection for this pretense, and fear of the hidden agenda of the Four Hundred, gave rise to open opposition. Echoing Alcibiades' call to the Athenians, Theramenes son of Hagnon and Aristocrates son of Scellias, both men of high standing among the Four Hundred, espoused the cause of the Five Thousand and used the fort under construction at Eetionia as evidence of the treacherous intentions of their opponents.[39]

Out of the ensuing crisis a subtle but significant shift took place in the public platform of the oligarchy. The Five Thousand had originally been described as those "best able to benefit the state in financial and personal service." These qualifications had never been precisely defined. On the one hand, it had been left to the discretion of a committee of distinguished gentlemen, elected when the Four Hundred were empowered, to compile a list of eligible Athenians. This committee of Registrars, we learn from a speech later defending one of its members in a democratic court, had been quite inclusive in its compilation. It excluded no one who wished to be registered, in some cases to avoid arousing a dispute, and in other cases to do a favor for technically unqualified individuals. As a result, we are told, the register of the Five Thousand, the notional "best" of the Athenians, came to include 9,000 names. Publication of this list, on the other hand, was repeatedly deferred, and never actually achieved. The Five Thousand were an idea that meant different things at different times, and in the interests of the prime movers among the Four Hundred they were best left undefined. But changing interests required a new meaning to be given to the idea of the Five Thousand.[40]

By the time that Theramenes, Aristocrates, and their followers began publicly to challenge the intentions of the treacherous clique among the Four Hundred, they had to appeal directly to a self-evident constituency. These they found in the bodies of citizen hoplite soldiers that had been assembled on the authority of the Four Hundred for various tasks, most notoriously for the construction of the fort at Eetionia. They appealed to these men in the name of finally empowering the Five Thousand, and they let it be known that the Five Thousand were to include all Athenians who could equip themselves with hoplite arms. The many Athenians under arms in response to the threat from the Spartans encamped at Decelea and hovering, as it happened, in ships off their coast, were responsive to this appeal. Significantly, the appeal provoked activism even among the allied and mercenary troops of the *peripoloi,* the patrols of the watch, that formed a key element in the defense of the urban perimeter.

In a daring act of solidarity with the cause of Alcibiades, a group of these mercenary guardsmen assassinated Phrynichus upon his return from an embassy to Sparta. The aftermath of this affair prompted Theramenes and Aristocrates to lead soldiers in opposition to the Four Hundred, arresting one of their generals and dismantling the fortifications on Eetionia. The movement thus underway among the mass of Athenian soldiery was about to converge in a decisive assembly in Athens, to confront the spokesmen of the Four Hundred with the voice of the Five Thousand, when a military alarm was sounded. The Spartan fleet in the Saronic Gulf was sailing past Attica to attack Athenian forces defending Euboea.[41]

Euboea was a valuable resource to the Athenians, both individually and publicly. Agricultural land and much livestock owned by wealthy Athenians was concentrated on this large, nearby island. During Cleon's heyday, Athenian control of Euboean land had been the basis for a dole of grain to all citizens. Thucydides reports that, when the Peloponnesians began their invasions of Attica in 431, the safeguarding of Euboea had been a high priority of the Athenians, who regarded it as "worth more than Attica itself." The protection of Euboea likewise became a leading concern following the Sicilian disaster, and its rebellion was one of the first priorities of the enemies of Athens. The Spartans had put off this operation only when the more appealing plan to join forces with the Persians in Ionia was presented to them.[42]

After midsummer 411, with the Ionian war momentarily at a standstill, the Spartans and their allies sent a fleet past Attica to challenge an Athenian squadron defending Euboea. Despite hasty reinforcements from Athens, the Athenians were defeated in a sea battle in the straits between Attica and Euboea, and the island was lost to them. News of the battle for Euboea, according to Thucydides, was the cause of even greater panic at Athens than the Sicilian disaster. It was closer to home, it exhausted the small naval reserve still under the control of the regime at Athens, and it came at a moment of heightened uncertainty when the Athenians feared that their city was about to be betrayed to the Spartans by elements of their own leadership. The attack probably occurred because the enemies of

Athens perceived the weakness and division within the Athenian leadership. Thucydides goes on to remark that it was the greatest good fortune for the Athenians that the Spartans and their allies did not realize just how vulnerable the Athenians were at this very moment, and press their attack against Athens itself.[43]

MODERATION AND ACCOMMODATION

In the air of emergency that followed the Euboean disaster the Athenians assembled, for the first time since before Colonus, in their accustomed place on the hill of the Pnyx. By virtue of the fact that they met to vote on public business, they became the government. In this and in the frequent series of meetings subsequently convened on the Pnyx, this assembly officially disbanded the council of the Four Hundred and legitimized itself as the sovereign body of Athens, the assembly of Athenians *ek ton hoplon,* as determined by the bearing of arms. The council and officers elected by this body were once again representatives of the sovereign citizenry and were not the handpicked creatures of a clique that the Four Hundred had been.[44]

Thucydides, followed by Aristotle, calls this the government of the Five Thousand, indicating that in some sense this was regarded as the constitution originally ordained at Colonus, finally brought to power after the calamitous interlude of the Four Hundred. The abolition of pay for officeholding, a central tenet of the oligarchic revolution, was reconfirmed. And true to the vision of this as an opportunity to mend the ills of Athenian politics, Thucydides affirms that this government was a sane and fortunate episode in Athenian political history:

> For a period the political conduct of the Athenians seems to have been the best it ever was, in my lifetime at least, for a spirit of moderate compromise prevailed among the few and the many, and this enabled the state to begin recovering from its wretched condition.[45]

The clearest indication that the Athenians regarded the period following the overthrow of the Four Hundred to be the next stage of an ongoing process of constitutional reform was their election of a committee of *nomothetai,* "establishers of the laws." Mentioning the *nomothetai,* Thucydides adds that the Athenians "voted all other measures to form the constitution [*politeia*]." Unfortunately, he gives no further description of the acts of these *nomothetai* or of the measures enacted in the "many assemblies held afterward." But precedents from earlier in 411, and legislative enactments over the following decade, make it possible to describe the probable nature and purpose of this commission.[46]

The *nomothetai* of 411 almost certainly carried on the charge of the thirty *syngrapheis,* the commissioners appointed before the creation of the Five

Thousand and the empowerment of the Four Hundred, to research and reconcile the various ancestral laws of Athens, beginning with the earliest laws still preserved in written form, the statutes of Draco and Solon. Like the celebrated archaic lawgivers, the task of these *nomothetai* was to derive regulations applicable to issues of the moment from the principles intrinsic to past traditions, and to embody them in written form. Their essential duty was to command access to venerable authority; abstracting this authority into new or revised texts was a more creative aspect of their duties. Hence *nomothesia,* the process of carrying out their duties, is often translated "lawgiving." Appropriate to the conditions of late fifth-century Athens, authority for the process of *nomothesia* was not to be vested in any one supremely qualified individual, but in a committee.[47]

This committee proved to be the longest-lived institution of the period of crisis and reform commencing in 411. Their composition, like their duties, was essentially the same a decade later, in 403/2, when they become better known to us. At the latter date, a decree quoted by Andocides describes the legislative procedures to be initiated by a committee of *nomothetai* elected by the Council. These *nomothetai,* probably numbering thirty like the earlier *syngrapheis,* draft legislative documents that are to be ratified after deliberation by a second committee, numbering 500 and also called *nomothetai.* This committee of 500 was composed in the same manner as the Council of 500, and it is reasonable to assume that it was created specifically to assume the legislative duties of the Council of 500. The Council of the Four Hundred had previously had the authority to ratify laws under the oligarchy. The democratic Council that replaced the Four Hundred must have carried on this task. But probably within a year or two of the reconstitution of the Council of 500, the burden of ongoing legislative review became so great that the committee of 500 *nomothetai* was created to take it over.[48]

Although not previously recognized in these terms, archaeological evidence helps to verify the institution of 500 *nomothetai* sometime in the first half of the last decade of the fifth century. Within that period, the construction of a new Council-House in the Agora left the old Council-House available for a separate, standing committee of 500. With this transition, the old Council-House became known as the repository for state archives. Such archives were the working material of the *nomothetai,* whose long deliberations over texts and documents must have transpired in this building.[49]

Despite the fact that the lawgiving of the *nomothetai* did not spare Athens from further internal convulsions (Solon's work was no more successful in the short term), their codifications provided a foundation for the administration of justice, of religious affairs, and of affairs of government for generations to come. It is perhaps ironic that these lawgivers remain comparatively obscure in the view of posterity, but the reason is not hard to find. To a degree previously unprecedented, their task was to harmonize not only the conflicts and contradictions of contemporary practices, but also the accumulation of written documents, the published decrees and statutes, left by earlier generations. Their work required democratic consensus, which could be achieved only after legislation passed through review and revision by many hands. In the end, the validity of their work depended upon the authority of the sources they consulted, and so it was the names of these authorities, Draco, Solon, and Cleisthenes chief among them, that were affirmed for posterity.

Although the machinery of legal reform proceeded for many years after its initiation by the Five Thousand, the Five Thousand themselves quickly drop out of view in our narrative accounts. Thucydides' approval of the moderation that prevailed when they came to power hints that circumstances soon changed. Elsewhere he refers to the government immediately following the collapse of the Four Hundred as "the democracy." Echoing Thucydides' praise of the Five Thousand, Aristotle, in the historical treatise on the *Constitution of the Athenians,* tersely remarks that "the *demos* soon took over political affairs from them." We must regret the discontinuation of Thucydides' history in the midst of the events of 411, since Aristotle's brief comment is the only ancient reference to the end of the government of the Five Thousand. Just as Thucydides was able to regard the government of the Five Thousand as, in essence, the return to democracy, so Aristotle, later in his work, fails even to notice the Five Thousand in an otherwise comprehensive list of revolutions and shifts in the form of the Athenian constitution. How could the memory of the Five Thousand have so quickly evaporated?[50]

By the time they became a sovereign body, the Five Thousand were defined by terms that would hardly exclude any able-bodied citizen in Athens. Even before the crisis commencing in 413, the Athenians had augmented their fighting forces by providing hoplite arms to members of their lowest census-class, the *thetes.* Seven hundred *thetes* had been so armed to serve as marines during the Sicilian expedition, for example. The near-total mobilization of the fleet in 412 had drawn off much of the thetic class, while for over two years, with the enemy threatening from Decelea, the remaining Athenians ("*all* Athenians," Thucydides twice emphasizes) had been under arms on the walls and on patrol. The overthrow of the elitist Four Hundred had been facilitated, moreover, by the widespread impression that the call to empower the Five Thousand was tantamount to a call to re-empower the *demos.* And so in practice the distinction between government by those who could perform military service with their own hoplite arms and government by the Athenian *demos* was insignificant. Thus, in Aristotle's enumeration of changes in the Athenian constitution, "democracy again" was the immediate successor to the Four Hundred.[51]

Still, as Thucydides' appraisal implies, the initial phase of the government of the Five Thousand was not quite democracy as usual. After the fear and uncertainty fomented by the divisive leadership of the Four Hundred, the resolve shared by "the few and the many" facing a known enemy accounted for much of the cooperative spirit noticed by Thucydides. Unable, in their straits, to act against the enemy beyond the walls, the newly elected Council quickly channeled popular determination to resist Sparta into the prosecution of leading members of the Four Hundred. Antiphon and a colleague were arrested, brought to trial, and condemned to death for their treasonous dealings with the Spartans. Other leaders of this clique, among them Peisander, fled to Decelea and into exile before they could be arrested. The acts of the Four Hundred were thus repudiated not because they had abrogated democratic forms of government, but because they had attempted to betray Athens and Attica to the enemy. Only thus could Theramenes, Aristocrates, and other members of the Four Hundred who had opposed the pro-Spartan clique, survive politically. Continued survival required a reconciliation with the Athenian forces based at Samos, the champions of democracy, and this would inevitably reintroduce a contentious element into politics at Athens. How this would be achieved, and the effect it would have on the concept of political reform at Athens, depended upon circumstances.[52]

CHAPTER SIX

A Procession of Victories, 411–408

Wherever he stood, victory took his side, and amazing reversals of fortune attended him.

JUSTIN 4.5.12

Opinions vary on whether Alcibiades' success in battle came more from skill or luck. Nearly all agree, however, that he was a master of negotiation. Between late 411 and late 408 Alcibiades enjoyed great success in battle, and that success was magnified by his talents in negotiation. The effect was an almost irresistible attraction felt by the Athenians to bring themselves within his aura of providence and good fortune. The present chapter describes the growth of this attraction, despite opposition, and its culmination in Alcibiades' triumphant homecoming.

VICTORY AT CYZICUS

At the end of summer 411, the center of activity in the Ionian war shifted north to the strategic waterway of the Hellespont, the avenue of the Black Sea grain to Athens and Greece. Tissaphernes' failure to bring the Phoenician fleet west of Aspendus finally induced the Spartans to accept the invitation of Pharnabazus son of Pharnaces, satrap of Hellespontine Phrygia, to collaborate with him in making war against the Athenians. The Spartan fleet thus transferred its main base from Miletus in the south to Abydos on the Asiatic side of the Hellespont, and the Athenians responded by gathering their forces at Sestos on the opposite shore. The transition resulted in several encounters between the Spartan and Athenian fleets in the autumn, the most significant of them in the waters between Sestos and Abydos, resulting in two victories for the Athenians. These successes made their subjects more responsive to Athenian fundraising expeditions, and the news was welcomed at Athens as a sign that with Alcibiades in command, even without Persian support, the Athenians could still hope to defeat their enemies.[1]

As news of the first of these victories reached Athens, Theramenes stepped to the forefront of the cause of reconciliation with the Athenians of the fleet. On his proposal the Assembly at Athens passed a resolution recalling Alcibiades and others with him who had been exiled. The victorious commanders, Thrasybulus, Thrasyllus, and Alcibiades, had all been elected as generals by the fleet in defiance of the regime of the Four Hundred, so Theramenes' gesture was essential to bridging the rift between Athens and the fleet. News of the second victory off Sestos was brought to Athens by Thrasyllus, who requested reinforcements be sent to the Hellespont. Theramenes, who had been a general under the Four Hundred and so had the greatest personal stake in the process of reunification, saw to it that he was elected to command the reinforcements. For when these men arrived in the Hellespont, they would be the first to reunite the forces of the city and the fleet.[2]

That winter, Theramenes led a force of twenty ships from Athens. Prestige required him to arrive as a successful commander when he joined the company of Alcibiades and his colleagues. Opportunities to raise money and to plunder enemy holdings were open to Theramenes, thanks largely to the unsettled conditions in the Aegean over the winter of 411/10. Beginning on Euboea and proceeding into the islands of the central Aegean, Theramenes laid waste to land formerly protected by Athenian ships. Retracing the course that Peisander and his colleagues had taken when they were encouraging oligarchies among Athenian subjects, he brought as many allies back into cooperation with the Athenian democracy as he could. Fundraising was especially efficient at this moment, when the Athenians could confront known oligarchic sympathizers in the name of protecting the freedom of the people.[3]

Over the winter of 411/10 the Athenian fleet remained dispersed by the necessities of fundraising, and had to avoid confrontation with the Spartan fleet at Abydos. Toward the end of winter, news that Mindarus, the Spartan admiral, was preparing to put out from Abydos prompted the withdrawal of the Athenian squadron from Sestos to Cardia, outside of the Hellespont. From there urgent messages went out to Athenian commanders in various quarters: Theramenes was summoned from Macedon, where he had been supporting King Archelaus; Thrasybulus came from the Thracian coast and operations against the oligarchs on Thasos; Alcibiades, recently again in the company of Tissaphernes, made a timely arrival with a squadron brought from Lesbos. The Athenians, with 86 ships, now slightly outnumbered the Spartans with 80, but their advantage would be lost if the Spartans could avoid engaging them, since the Athenian needs for funding and supply would soon force them again to disperse. Recognizing this weakness of his foes, Mindarus had decided to base his force at Cyzicus in the Propontis. There, on the coast of Hellespontine Phrygia, the Spartan fleet could more easily be supplied by Pharnabazus, whose land forces were also close at hand.

Alcibiades and his colleagues resolved to hazard a direct attack against Mindarus, rather than to allow time to turn the balance in Sparta's favor. The Athenian fleet used the cover of night to pass Abydos in the Hellespont and to land at the island of Proconessus, where plans were made to attack Cyzicus, some thirty miles distant, on the following day. The morning of the attack was blessed with foul weather, as storm clouds hovered about Mount Dindymus on the headland above the approaches to Cyzicus. Through a rainstorm, separate units of the Athenian fleet managed to approach, undetected, positions for a coordinated attack on Cyzicus. In clearing weather, Alcibiades with twenty ships showed himself in the bay in front of Cyzicus, to draw the Spartan fleet. The bait was taken, and by the time that Mindarus realized that his own ships had been surrounded and were being engaged by a superior Athenian fleet, it was too late. Routed, Mindarus went ashore to give himself a Spartan warrior's death fighting in front of his men. Victorious on land and sea, the Athenians captured the entire Spartan fleet, and Cyzicus surrendered.[4]

After the disaster in Sicily, the victory at Cyzicus in early spring 410 marked the high point of Athenian fortunes in their war for empire. Not only did it yield a windfall of booty, and the compliance of still more former subjects among the Greek towns of the Propontis, but, under Alcibiades' leadership, it enabled the Athenians to secure steady revenues in the form of a ten percent tax on all shipping coming out of the Black Sea. This was achieved by the construction of a fortified base at Chrysopolis on the Asiatic shore of the Bosporus. Even though Chalcedon, in whose territory the base was located, and Byzantium across the way had rebelled from Athens and remained aligned with the Spartans and with Pharnabazus, the Athenians with thirty ships in the Bosporus commanded by Theramenes and a colleague could control all maritime traffic. Alcibiades and his fellow commanders meanwhile took advantage of the unprotected coast of Hellespontine Phrygia to add further to Athenian revenues, at the expense of Pharnabazus and his allies. Naval supremacy paid handsome dividends.[5]

Years of sacrifice borne of adversity gave way to celebration at Athens, and public debate shifted from the hard arguments of necessity to a tone of confidence based on success. The Spartans, realizing that fortune had abruptly turned away from them, sent an embassy to Athens to offer peace on the conditions that they would abandon Decelea in Attica and the Athenians would abandon Pylos in Messenia, garrisoned by the Athenians since 425, and otherwise each side would keep what they controlled. After the anxiety brought by the fall of Euboea, it must have been sweet pleasure for the Athenians to hear such an offer from the mouth of a foeman. But

Diodorus, who reports the speech, shows also the stick that the Spartan ambassador brandished as a reminder to the Athenians:

> For us the richest king to be found in the inhabited world defrays the cost of the war, for you the most poverty-stricken folk of the inhabited world.... When we make war at sea, we risk losing only hulls among resources of the state, while you have on board crews most of whom are citizens. And what is most important, even if we meet defeat in our actions at sea, we still maintain without dispute mastery on land...but you, if you are driven from the sea, contend not for the supremacy on land, but for survival.[6]

Conjecture was mixed with truth in these words, since King Darius was not yet securely pledged to the Spartans. Pharnabazus had made it his personal undertaking to bring this about, and in the meantime he was more generous with his personal resources on the Spartans' behalf than Tissaphernes had been. But Alcibiades ever held out the prospect that he could bring to the Athenians what the Spartans hoped for. It may also have been appreciated that the king's resources could not in any event be made liberally available to the Spartans, since he had to remain concerned about the loyalty of Egypt, and more seriously, he had to confront an uprising in Media. To an informed critic, the Spartan stick did not seem unbreakable. The rest, though starkly exaggerated, was essentially accurate.[7]

Many considerations led the Athenians to reject this offer. Their fortunes were on the upswing, and to settle now with the Spartans would be to give up the many former allies and subjects who might still be brought under Athenian control. It would also compel the Athenians to relinquish the profits of plundering enemies, Greek and barbarian, that largely sustained their naval strength. The revenues of an Athenian empire at peace under present conditions would leave the Athenians dangerously weak and their enemies intolerably strengthened. Such arguments, we may conjecture, were among the points made by Cleophon son of Cleippides, "the greatest demagogue of the time," who spoke at length against the Spartan overture. The Athenians were led on, according to Diodorus, by the inflated opinion of their own military prowess encouraged by Cleophon's rhetoric; above all, Diodorus summarizes:

> ...the Athenians, being elated by their successes and entertaining many great hopes because they had Alcibiades as the leader of their armed forces, thought that they had quickly won back their supremacy.

Encouraged by Cleophon, sustained by Alcibiades, this vision in fact proved to be a reliable forecast of Athenian fortunes for five years to come, and commitment to this vision from the moment the Spartan embassy was sent away also explains why, from the spring of 410 until the surrender of Athens six years later, "democracy again" prevailed at Athens.[8]

IMMUTABLE CHANGE

This development confronts us with some paradoxical circumstances not directly addressed in any of our sources. With no formal measures identified as either the end of the Five Thousand or the refoundation of democracy, we must ask how the agenda of reform begun in the name of the Five Thousand could coalesce with the reemergence of democracy. The abolition of pay for office and the concept of restricting political rights to those capable of serving with their own arms were distinctly un-democratic measures of the reform movement, and there is no explicit evidence that they were ever rescinded. The paradoxes untangle, however, when we follow the manner by which these restrictions were adapted to facilitate the reassertion of popular sovereignty. The key to this creative process lay in the facility of popular leaders at finding new ways to use the people's money.

The Great Panathenaic festival at midsummer 410 was an appropriate occasion for celebrating the restoration of Athenian supremacy. Coming every four years, the festival and games of Athena had been the occasion for announcing the official assessments of the *phoros,* the imperial tribute to be paid by Athenian subjects. Assessment of the *phoros* had been suspended with the onset of crisis in 414/13, but several sources indicate that in 410 the Athenians once again announced the liability of their subjects to the traditional payment of tribute. This declaration required the backing of naval force before it could bear fruit, in the following spring, and it did not entail abolition of either the universal five percent harbor tax or the newly established ten percent tax on Black Sea commerce. But with liability for tribute added to these imposts, Athenian forces had several avenues by which to justify their exaction of funds from around the Aegean and beyond. With optimism again a keynote, it was appropriate for the Athenians to reconsider how their anticipated resources would be distributed.[9]

In the month after the Panathenaea, the treasurers of imperial revenue recorded the first disbursement of the *diobelia,* or two-obol payment, an institution that lasted from this time until the fall of Athens in 404. Created by Cleophon, the *diobelia* was a modest stipend, the equivalent of a day's meal-money made available to Athenian citizens. Fourth-century sources treat the *diobelia,* and the reputation of Cleophon and other politicians connected with it, as a prime example of demagogues buying the favor of the masses, for this was a measure that appealed chiefly to the poor. Our sources, hostile to its memory, do not explain the terms and conditions of its distribution. Much later sources conflate the *diobelia* with jury-pay, Assembly-pay, or with the *theorikon,* a festival-stipend known to have been distributed to Athenians in the fourth century; but such direct identifications are unlikely. The dominant view among modern scholars is that it was simply a stipend given to relieve Athenians impoverished by the effects of the war.

There is probably an element of truth to all of the above accounts, but to understand how these elements were related to the concept of the *diobelia* requires a close look at the circumstances in which it was introduced.[10]

Cleophon and his supporters justified the institution of this stipend by the argument previously used by Pericles: what belongs to the Athenian *demos* should be given to them. Pericles had used this argument to justify pay for office-holding, most notoriously jury-pay. But since the elimination of jury-pay was a primary objective of the aristocratic reform movement, it is unlikely that Cleophon's proposal was simply a reinstatement of such salaries. The fact that it was not called *misthos,* "salary," suggests that his proposal deliberately skirted this identification. The most appropriate time to distribute a general stipend to eligible citizens, however, would have been the occasions when they gathered in official capacities, to sit on juries or in the Assembly, for these were occasions when officers of the state would in any event have to assure that non-citizens were excluded. If the *diobelia* were made available, on request, on such occasions, it would have the same political effect as jury-pay and the later Assembly-pay. Furthermore, by such a stipend the champions of democracy could frustrate the aristocratic agenda of using wealth as a means of excluding poor Athenians from political participation. Although two obols a day was a meager subvention for traditional hoplite status, the standards for equipping the rank and file fighting men of Athens were being stretched downward, as shown by other evidence discussed below. The exercise of empire both required and enabled the service of all able-bodied Athenians.[11]

Although practical reasoning, along democratic lines, favored the *diobelia,* Cleophon must have adduced the ancestral rights of all Athenians when he argued for its establishment. Tradition was always a factor in political debate, but arguments based on historical precedent were probably all the more important in a period of tumultuous change such as the Athenians were experiencing in 411/10. With the commission of *nomothetai* involved in the review of all *nomoi,* laws and customs, of the Athenians, respect for *ta patria,* ancestral ways, was paramount. We may be sure, then, that Cleophon's rhetoric paid due respect to tradition. Although the evidence is indirect, it is possible to suggest how he made the case.

Justification for the *diobelia* probably came from another dole of the recent past, a dole that was claimed as an ancient right and privilege of the Athenian democracy because it originated with Theseus. The privilege was bound up in the relationship Athenians claimed to land on the neighboring island of Euboea.

The loss of Euboea in 411 had been a grievous blow to all Athenians, among other reasons, because Euboean land had been the source of an occasional dole of grain for all Athenians. The largesse, attested in the 420s, may have been justified by the conquest of land from Chalcis on Euboea in the first great war of the Athenians after the overthrow of the Peisistratids. The humbling of Chalcis had been a boon for Eretria, friend and ally of Athens at the end of the sixth century. The early years of the Athenian democracy saw close harmony between Eretrians and Athenians, reflected in their collaborative support of the Ionian rebellion from Persia in 499, as well as, symbolically, by the installation of Theseus as one of the central heroes in the pedimental sculpture on Eretria's great temple of Apollo Daphnephoros. Theseus' legendary ties to Eretria were established through Elephenor, the Abantid lord of Euboea. Although details of their relationship are now lost to us, Elephenor was evidently under obligation to support the kingship of Theseus at Athens. For when Menestheus drove Theseus from Athens and usurped the kingship, Elephenor gave refuge to the sons of Theseus, Acamas and Dempohon, enabling them eventually to reclaim their patrimony. Elephenor's obligation must have been seen by the Athenians as an ancestral bond to the house of Theseus, for the Athenians felt justified in appropriating Euboean land beginning with their sixth-century defeat of Chalcis and continuing until the revolt of 411. To Theseus, then, the Athenian people owed all favors they inherited from Euboea.[12]

Cleophon probably employed an appeal to this tradition to argue that the dole of Euboean grain should be replaced by a cash stipend—until, he may have added, Euboea was reconquered. For at the beginning of winter 410/9 the imperial treasurers recorded a payment made in kind (probably out of plunder from Euboea) to a general, Eucleides, "from Eretria," where the Athenians maintained a fortified base. The plunder of Euboea, converted to cash, was probably the original basis for the *diobelia*. It maintained a benefit that the Athenians had come to regard as their own, and kept alive, for a short while at least, the hope of reclaiming their ancestral rights on Euboea.[13]

Recognizing that Cleophon's rhetoric had conferred such an ancestral origin on the *diobelia,* we can better appreciate a joke by Aristophanes on the payment claimed by the most menial of laborers. In the *Frogs,* performed in the winter of 405, Hermes instructs Dionysus that Charon, the lowly ferryman of Hades, will require two obols fare to convey him by boat into the Underworld:

> *Dionysus:* Wow! What a demand there is for these two obols everywhere! How come *he* gets to have them?
>
> *Hermes:* Theseus established the practice....[14]

Tradition, as ever, was at the service of the politically powerful, and by the summer of 410 the powerful were those, like Cleophon, who conducted the *demos* to the familiar strains of demagogic politics. Skeptics could treat their manipulations of tradition with wry humor, as in Aristophanes' passing jab, or they could insinuate that he who boasted of restoring the heritage of the Athenians had no claim on this birthright himself, as the comic poets did in asserting a foreign parentage for Cleophon. But none of this could confute his ascendancy in the political arena. Thus, even though the appeal to tradition had been a device of reactionary reform a year earlier, under changing conditions the movement to restore *ta patria* could be made to serve Cleophon's vision of Athenian heritage.[15]

Likewise, the legislative reforms of the *nomothetai* took a decidedly democratic turn beginning in 410. In the previous year, the oligarchic Council of the Four Hundred had made arrests, carried out executions, and conducted negotiations with Sparta, all on its own authority. In 410 or 409, the *nomothetai* authorized the republication of a collection of older laws defining and limiting the powers of the Council. Surviving portions of the inscription displaying these regulations specify that war cannot be made or ended, that no death penalty can be inflicted, and that no fine of a certain type can be assessed, *aneu tou demou tou Athenaion plethuontos,* "without a full meeting of the Athenian people." Anachronistic terminology and other peculiarities in the inscribed text make it clear that these regulations were scrupulously transcribed from an older, imperfectly preserved text. Whatever the original date of these regulations, in the early fifth century or earlier, it is noteworthy that through them the resurgent democracy of ca. 410 was making prominent use of the authority of the past to affirm the powers of the democratic Assembly and to limit the Council to its probouleutic, advisory, functions.[16]

Another product of the *nomothetai,* in the month preceding the Panathenaea of 410, was the promulgation of a law against tyranny containing an oath for "all Athenians to swear over intact sacrificial animals, by tribes and by demes ... before the opening of the Dionysia." Submitted for the approval of the Council and the Assembly by Demophantus, probably one of the *nomothetai,* this law stipulated that anyone who overthrows the Athenian democracy, holds any office after the democracy has been overthrown, works to become a tyrant, or supports a tyrant can be slain with impunity. Andocides, whose quotation of this law has preserved it for us, calls it a law of Solon. It is possible that the injunction to uphold the rights of the *demos* and abjure tyranny had a Solonic precedent, but the oath as drafted by Demophantus refers to the honors accorded to the families of Harmodius and Aristogeiton, who became heroes almost a century after Solon, and goes on to annul oaths previously sworn "at Athens, in the camp [i.e. at Samos], or anywhere else, against the *demos* of the Athenians." Whatever ancient authority there may have been for this "customary oath" *(nomimos horkos),* it was adapted to the circumstances of 410.[17]

There were many in Athens and abroad who had held office when the democracy was in abeyance, Theramenes and Aristocrates for example, and more who had sworn to work together for the cause of oligarchy. Yet no one was prosecuted on this account, for to do so could provoke civil strife and destroy the ascendancy now enjoyed by all Athenians. The oath had more to do with rallying the Athenians behind leaders committed to strengthening the democracy than it did with punishing the former partisans of oligarchy. If there was anyone against whom demagogues like Cleophon felt they had to strengthen themselves, it was Alcibiades.

THE GENERALS AND THE MEN OF ATHENS

Among the anomalies of this transitional episode was the fact that the city and the Hellespontine fleet remained administratively separate. The popularity of Alcibiades among his troops assured his continued leadership in the field, but he was not elected general at Athens. It is not certain that either of his chief colleagues in generalship, Thrasybulus and Theramenes, were elected either. Yet Alcibiades and his colleagues were in control of a fleet of nearly ninety ships with crews and fighting men loyal to them, and in the wake of Cyzicus no general sent from Athens would have any credibility before these veteran troops if he dared to come and claim command on authority from Athens.[18]

Among those who were elected generals at Athens in the spring of 410, Aristocrates son of Scellias and Anytus son of Anthemion were political figures, not known for military exploits. The most experienced general elected in Athens was Thrasyllus, who had returned from the fleet at Sestos the previous winter. In the early summer of 410, following the rejection of the Spartan peace offer, Thrasyllus won respect among the Athenians by successfully arraying his forces, citizen and foreign mercenaries, outside the walls and forcing the Peloponnesians to withdraw when King Agis had brought them down from Decelea on a plundering raid.[19]

In the summer of 410, Thrasyllus was charged to take a force of a thousand citizen hoplites, a hundred cavalrymen, and thirty ships to expand the Athenian military presence along the Ionian coast. With no strong Spartan fleet to oppose them, the Athenians expected to live by plundering their foes and to conquer by their ability to move by sea and to strike in large numbers. Vestiges of a Spartan navy were harbored at Chios, under the watchful eye of an Athenian squadron at Samos. With the forces available to Thrasyllus, the Athenians probably expected him retake Chios. For in addition to taking ships and men at Samos under his command, the Athenians further strengthened Thrasyllus' force by providing his crews, some five thousand men, with weapons so that they could reinforce the hoplites and cavalrymen.[20]

Xenophon calls Thrasyllus' armed sailors *peltastai* after the type of lightweight, usually wickerwork, shield *(pelte)* they carried in place of the heavy round shield carried by regular hoplites. Javelin-throwing peltasts were a distinctive type of skirmishing warrior in Thrace and northern Greece, but these peltasts were probably spearmen. Like the armament of *thetes* bound for Sicily, they were intended to augment the regular hoplite infantry formation, although in this case with less expensive (and less effective) equipment, in a manner that had become common practice especially among the naval forces operating in Ionia. As with the opportunities of 415, the needs of 410 furthered the process of compressing the social gap between poor and middle class traditionally displayed in arms and the solidarity of fighting units.[21]

Thrasyllus' expedition was a disappointment to all who had hoped for success for the forces from Athens. After scoring several minor victories and gathering plunder from the Lydian domain of Tissaphernes, Thrasyllus was decisively defeated in his boldest venture, an attack on Ephesus. Although he carried on with operations on Lesbos and was able to send captives home to Athens, he achieved no significant advantage for the Athenians.[22]

At the beginning of winter 410/9, the treasurers of imperial revenue at Athens recorded a payment of over 57 talents to unnamed Athenians at Samos. This was by far the largest transaction of the year, and it is clear that the record was merely a bookkeeping entry for funds paid at Samos out of funds raised at Samos. The amount, roughly enough to pay Thrasyllus' force for four months' work, evidently represented a settling of accounts to date for Thrasyllus' expedition, probably paid for out of the booty it had taken in. Behind this record lay the unpleasant reality that there were no profits to be shared at home. With the onset of winter and a large army to feed, Thrasyllus recognized the practical necessity of uniting his force with the command of Alcibiades in the Hellespont, where the only reliable revenues were being generated.[23]

Athenian forces elsewhere were equally luckless. In the fall of 410, Anytus was sent with thirty ships to break up a Spartan siege of the Athenian fort at Pylos. Unable to round Cape Malea in Laconia because of bad weather, the relief expedition failed, and Pylos fell in the course of that winter. Pylos had been the chief bargaining chip held by the Athenians for negotiations with Sparta, and Anytus' failure might have ended his career were it not for his political dexterity. Anytus was tried for treason, and would have been convicted, we are told, had he not been able to divert the jury's attention with some sort of financial inducement.[24]

The case is cited, in a review of the history of jury-pay in Aristotle's *Constitution of the Athenians,* as the first example of a public figure to corrupt *(dekazein)* a jury. Later sources, followed by modern scholars, have translated this simply as "to bribe" a jury, and have treated the incident as testimony to Anytus' wealth. But personal largess does not make the best sense of Aristotle's account, which discusses not bribery but the morally reprehensible effects of jury-pay, that encouraged people "other than the decent sort" to make themselves available for jury duty. Nor is "bribery" the literal meaning of *dekazein,* which is "to make into one's cronies" (*dekas* = "company" or "band," nominally of ten, but figuratively of any close-knit group). Taking into account the conditions at Athens at the time of Anytus' trial, a better explanation of his escape from punishment can be offered.[25]

Anytus' act must have involved some abuse of public funds in the interest of the Athenians who made up the jury. Jury-pay per se did not exist at this time, but the closely related *diobelia* was in its first year of distribution. Payment of the *diobelia* was dependent upon the flow of revenues to Athens, and by the winter of 410/9 there is reason to believe that Athenian officials were hard put to distribute this dole. Anytus' connivance with his jurors, we may conjecture, involved his promise that upon his acquittal he would find them the means to get their *diobelia.* A ready means would be to assess an *eisphora* upon wealthy Athenians and to use these revenues, all or in part, for the *diobelia. Eisphorai* were levied at Athens only on two occasions between 411/10 and 404/3, and Diodorus, referring to what must have been the first of these two occasions, reports that profits from plunder gathered by Alcibiades in the Hellespont over the winter and spring of 410/9 were used specifically to alleviate the burden of *eisphorai* at Athens. The levying of a property tax must have been a politically difficult measure in hard times and especially in the afterglow of the agenda of the Five Thousand to eliminate needless expenditures. But championing this measure to satisfy a *demos* once again demanding its due was what saved Anytus' skin on this occasion. The friends of Alcibiades could soon point to the proper way to meet the needs of the Athenians, by plundering their enemies and not their own best citizens. Anytus' memory was thus stigmatized, among the "decent sort," for this bit of self-serving demagoguery.[26]

REALIZING VISION

Military success in this year attended only Alcibiades and his colleagues. In the months following the battle of Cyzicus, they had captured Lampsacus on the Hellespont, plundered widely in the territory of Pharnabazus, and gained support from the Thracians on the European side of the Propontis in their expanding war against the allies of Sparta. No risky ventures were attempted, however, for Alcibiades knew the importance of securing the conquests he had made. Above all, he knew that long-term security depended upon relations with Persia.[27]

In the winter before the battle of Cyzicus, Alcibiades had approached Tissaphernes again, this time, our sources note, "bearing gifts of friendship and accompanied by a lordly retinue." He no doubt hoped to benefit by the Spartan switch of allegiance from Tissaphernes to Pharnabazus, but he found instead that Tissaphernes had decided to demonstrate his devotion to Sparta by arresting Alcibiades. He was a month in custody at Sardis before making his escape, secretly facilitated, so he claimed, by Tissaphernes himself. Perhaps the satrap realized that, while it was well to be seen arresting the enemy of the Spartans, it was also well to let the Spartans experience some pain as a consequence of their collaboration with Pharnabazus.[28]

So events transpired, and by the winter of 410/9 Alcibiades welcomed the reinforcements with Thrasyllus as an opportunity to mount greater pressure on the enemy. At first, however, the troops under Alcibiades disdained Thrasyllus' men, for they brought the taint of defeat to an army still treasuring its aura of victory. But shared successes in expeditions along the Asiatic shore of the Hellespont eventually enabled the consolidation to take hold, and by the spring of 409 the expanded force commenced two sieges, the first of Chalcedon, and the second of Byzantium, towns dominating opposite coasts of the Bosporus. The siege of Chalcedon on the Asiatic side, sustained in part by Alcibiades' arrangements with the Bithynian Thracians of the interior, was the latest and perhaps greatest of several blows to the prestige of Pharnabazus, and it finally brought him into negotiations with Alcibiades.[29]

In his dealings with Pharnabazus over Chalcedon, as in his military operations at Selymbria and Byzantium also begun in 409, Alcibiades displayed an unparalleled flair for gaining his ends by recognizing where brute force should yield to mutual interests. The siege of Chalcedon was lifted and other hostilities against Pharnabazus' domains ceased on condition that Pharnabazus pay the Athenians twenty talents, that he convey an Athenian embassy to the king, and that he swear that the Chalcedonians would resume their payments of tribute and other money owed to Athens. The treaty of Chalcedon signified the beginning of a wider entente with Pharnabazus that might yet realize Alcibiades' vision of an imperial alliance between Athens and Persia.[30]

As long as negotiations with King Darius were in progress and tribute was being paid to Athens, the treaty secured Chalcedon from Athenian intervention. It was in effect a grant of autonomy within the Athenian empire under terms similar to those established for certain towns of the Chalcidice by the Peace of Nicias in 421. In this case, the agreement signaled the coexistence of Persian and Athenian authority over this Asiatic Greek town, and the understanding was probably extended to all Greek towns formerly controlled by Athens within the domain of Pharnabazus (the coinage combining Persian and Athenian symbols represented by the unique example shown in figures 4a–b was probably issued as a consequence of the treaty of Chalcedon).[31]

More significantly, the embassy to Darius appointed by Alcibiades and his colleagues represented a plan to bring about a comprehensive settlement to

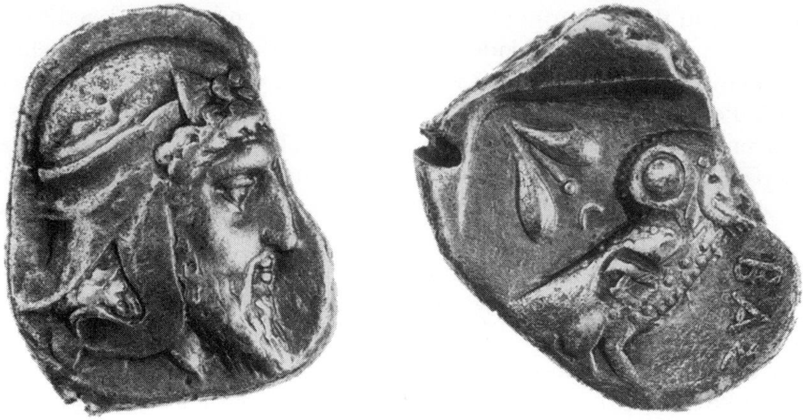

FIGURE 4A–B. The union of Athens and Asia: Attic-style tetradrachm with a satrap's portrait and Athenian owl, inscribed "(of the) King," possibly an issue of Pharnabazus, ca. 409–405. Photo © The British Museum, inv. no. 1947–7.6.4, neg. no. PS 128101.

the war in Greece, if we may judge by its composition. For it included high-ranking Spartans, representatives from Argos, and Syracusan exiles. All of these men were staking their futures upon rapprochement among all warring parties, and none of them more clearly than Alcibiades. Xenophon reports that the exchange of oaths, through intermediaries, between Alcibiades and Pharnabazus was solemnified not only in the name of Persian and Athenian sovereignty, "but also by personal pledges to one another."[32]

In the fall of 409, the embassy created by Alcibiades met Pharnabazus at Cyzicus and set out under his conduct for the court of Darius. The progress of this mission was impeded, the following spring, by developments at the Persian court, and, after being detained for two further years, the embassy was dissolved without achieving its goal. We will return in the following chapter to the circumstances that deflected Alcibiades' goal of creating a new balance of interests between Greece and Persia. But Alcibiades' vision, as we shall see in the course of the two succeeding chapters, did not die with that embassy.[33]

ALCIBIADES TRIUMPHANT

In the winter of 409/8, Alcibiades and Theramenes coordinated a surprise assault upon Byzantium, resulting in the defeat of the Spartan-led garrison and the reconciliation of that strategic city to Athens. The return of Byzantium to Athens greatly reduced the threat of Spartan interference in the Propontis. Only Abydus in the Hellespont remained in Spartan hands, and it was placed under close blockade. Thereafter, Alcibiades and his colleagues could concentrate their attention on matters in the Aegean, and Alcibiades especially could contemplate a return to Athens as a conquering hero.

Following the success at Byzantium, Thrasybulus took thirty ships into the north Aegean to bring over towns still in rebellion from Athens. His paramount concern was to press more closely the siege of Thasos, now in its second year. With the approach of spring 408, Alcibiades went to Samos and took twenty ships to Caria to conduct a profitable fundraising campaign. Thrasyllus, meanwhile, set sail for Athens with the remainder of the Attic fleet, along with prisoners and prizes.[34]

Alcibiades, by Xenophon's account, gathered a hundred talents in the Ceramic Gulf in Caria to bring with him to Athens. Such a large sum gathered in a specific location, probably in a fairly short period of time, was not likely to be the result of a campaign of plunder or forced contributions. After the ransomable prisoners had been sent to Athens with Thrasyllus, Alcibiades probably had a great mass of captives to dispose of, men from enemy ships and garrisons taken in the course of the previous year. It was probably by selling these men into slavery, at a market that served the demands of Cyprus, Phoenicia, and Egypt, that Alcibiades raised his hundred talents in Caria.[35]

Alcibiades made his way back to Athens, according to Xenophon, only by stages. From Caria he returned to Samos, and from there sailed with his twenty ships and hundred talents to the island of Paros. Samos and Paros were links to strongholds of the Aegean that were resisting Athenian dominion. Samos was the link to Chios, where a moderate regime had recently moved away from dependence on Sparta; Paros was the link to Thasos, were a moderate regime had also moved in the same direction. Both of these movements had probably been encouraged by Alcibiades, and both were in flux and susceptible to pressures from the great powers contending in the Aegean. It was essential for Alcibiades to have a clear assessment of the challenges that lay ahead in these directions before he ventured to advise the Athenians in imperial policy. From Paros Alcibiades sailed to Laconia and made a reconnaissance of the Spartan shipyards a Gytheium to see what force the enemy might launch in the near future. All the while, according to Xenophon, Alcibiades was awaiting news "of how the city was disposed toward him" before making the homeward journey.[36]

The Athenians, in the meantime, had been induced by a stream of favorable reports, and especially by the revenues that were reaching them from the Propontis, to look favorably upon the return of Alcibiades. In the summer of 409, after a period of financial stringency (above, pp. 161–62), the Athenians were sufficiently confident of their restored imperial income that they were able to resume work on the temple of Athena Polias, the

Erechtheum, on the Acropolis. For this they had Alcibiades to thank. Their gratitude was expressed, sometime before the spring of 408, by a formal resolution of the Assembly again recalling Alcibiades from exile. The measure, repeating the resolution that Theramenes had proposed in the fall of 411, was needed to affirm that, despite the resurgence of demagogic politics in the meantime, Alcibiades' popularity was strong. This time the proposal was made by Critias son of Callaeschrus, who, eager to fix himself to a rising star, even celebrated his role as the harbinger of Alcibiades in an elegiac poem. Finally, in the spring of 408, before the arrival of Alcibiades or any of his colleagues conveying home the prizes of victory, Alcibiades was elected general at Athens for the first time since he was deposed in 415.[37]

Before Alcibiades returned, Thrasyllus, possibly accompanied by Theramenes and other colleagues, arrived at Athens with the bulk of the plunder from the previous year's campaigns. Xenophon offers no tally of the booty, but all other accounts agree that two hundred enemy triremes were represented, either towed into Piraeus by Thrasyllus or accounted for by their severed rams and stern ornaments, all prominently displayed. Peloponnesian prisoners were brought in large numbers; Athenaeus says more than five thousand, although perhaps this sum represents the total of two years of victories, many of whom had been sent to Athens previously. In addition, the garlanded Athenian ships were decked out with trophies, and horse transports were piled high with booty and captured Spartan and Peloponnesian arms. This great display of prizes was surely calculated by Alcibiades to bring enthusiasm for his achievements to a peak for the moment that he himself would return.[38]

The return of Alcibiades himself at the beginning of summer 408 aroused passionate feelings among all who came to see it, and few willingly missed the spectacle. "The greatest number thronged to the harbors," Diodorus recounts in words paralleled in other sources, "so that the city was entirely deserted, free men vying with slaves." Given Alcibiades' keen sense of timing, and the importance of a dramatic entrance, there is no reason to doubt, as Plutarch does, the account of Alcibiades' arrival given by Duris of Samos. Carried home on a purple sail by the winds themselves, Alcibiades' trireme made the entrance of the Piraeus harbor without human effort; at the mouth of the harbor the oars were run out, and the half-mile across the great harbor was traversed to oarbeats called by Callipides, a tragic actor, accompanied by the ship's *aulos*-player, Chrysogonus, a Pythian victor, both artists dressed in their performance costumes. Even the routine sounds of the busy harbor were a matter of remark, Aristophanes tells us. The effects of sight and sound, in this natural theater lined with echoing colonnades, were surely not overlooked on this occasion, not by Alcibiades.[39]

Despite popular enthusiasm, Alcibiades was not playing to an entirely friendly audience. He was a feared personal enemy to not a few politically ambitious Athenians. Seven years earlier, when public anger had been stirred up against him, some of these men out of opportunism, others for self-preservation, had made public demonstrations of their contempt for Alcibiades. But the events of 411 had seen the destruction of his most outspoken enemies, men such as Androcles, Antiphon, and Phrynichus. But a considerable number of others, men like Callias son of Hipponicus and Teisias son of Teisimachus, remained. Their attitudes were insupportable in the present mood, and they kept quiet.

According to Xenophon, who was probably an eye-witness to the event, Alcibiades was apprehensive about the latent hostility felt by some toward him. Following Xenophon in this and other details, Plutarch also stresses Alcibiades' circumspection, describing him as fearful for his person and not disembarking to meet the throng gathered dockside in the Piraeus until he could see a coterie of friends and kinsmen ready to escort him. Xenophon also underscores the mood of foreboding with which some regarded the event, noting that Alcibiades' arrival coincided with the day of the *Plynteria,* on which the old cult image of Athena Polias was disrobed, covered, and given a ceremonial cleaning. This venerable but not celebratory ritual found the patron goddess temporarily deprived of her throne and splendor. "Some thought this to be unpropitious both for him and for the city," Xenophon states, "for on that day no Athenian would dare take up any serious business."[40]

By contrast, the attitude of the vast majority was an unrestrained adulation. Justin describes the feelings of the crowd in a rhetorically stylized, but nonetheless believable passage, representative of several accounts:

> It was on him that the whole community fixed its eyes, on him it gazed in suspense, on him people looked as if he were sent from heaven and as if he were the personification of victory.... The man to whom they had once refused any kind of human assistance they now wanted to set in heaven, if that were possible.

The basis of this awe and adoration was the undeniable experience of the Athenians over the previous seven years. With his absence, they reflected, Athens had known only disaster; the might of Athens barely extended beyond their city walls. Under his leadership their forces had enjoyed uninterrupted success, and "their enemies could withstand them neither by land nor by sea," as Nepos states in his biography of Alcibiades. The resurgence under Alcibiades of Athenian might "by land and by sea" is a phrase repeated with variations in all narratives except Xenophon's, and is even found in the annual financial records of the Treasurers of Athena inscribed probably shortly after the arrival of Alcibiades.[41]

The first order of business for Alcibiades upon his arrival, as so many times already, was to give an account of his circumstances that would resolve doubts and concerns about his purposes and his loyalties. Surrounded by close friends, Alcibiades made his way directly to the city to address first the Council and then the Assembly.

In his speech, Alcibiades had to affirm his own constancy in the face of the errant opportunism of his enemies. In Athens as at Sparta, we may be sure that Alcibiades referred to the real enemy as worthless men who had led the Athenians astray. His case was easy to make, for wherever he had a hand in the circles of leadership, success followed; those who drove him away sooner or later suffered catastrophe. Alcibiades' intrinsic merit was thus manifest by the favor of the gods. As for divine favor, the charge of impiety was an invention of unscrupulous enemies, who, unwilling to perjure themselves, could produce no credible witnesses, but only a slave and a woman, the one intimidated and the other deceived into testifying against him. Alcibiades was preaching to the converted, for the Athenians had already signaled their change of heart by also allowing the return of a number of men who had been condemned along with him, among them Adeimantus son of Leucolophides, who was now also an elected general, and Axiochus son of Alcibiades, uncle of the hero.[42]

Despite the opportunity for personal invective, Alcibiades' defense was marked, according to Diodorus and Plutarch, by a conciliatory tone. The *demos* that had convicted him, in error, had since atoned for its lapse by condemning the likes of Antiphon and Phrynichus. Alcibiades also excused the mistreatment he had experienced, Plutarch adds, as the doings of a certain "envious spirit" *(phthoneros daimon)*. This evil spirit had the nasty habit of following him, and it might yet work its nefarious influence if ambitious men were to try again to bring him down to their level. Conceding nothing, Alcibiades thus appealed to his audience to commit themselves to his cause for the good of Athens and to aid him in restraining this "envious spirit," if ever again it reared its ugly head. Thus the mistakes of the past could be avoided.[43]

Following this speech, and Alcibiades' forecasts for the future, popular enthusiasm was irrepressible. All public decrees passed against him as a result of the inquisition of 415 were ceremoniously revoked, his confiscated property was restored to him, and he was elected general *autokrator,* empowered to make command decisions at his own discretion. This was a privilege he had held before he was deposed in Sicily, though shared then with two colleagues; it was a recognition of the supremacy he already exercised among his colleagues in generalship.[44]

Although he had finally rebutted the charges of impiety, Alcibiades knew that more was needed to still the fears of divine displeasure kept alive by his enemies. Among the public resolutions passed on his behalf was an order that the curses pronounced against him by the priestly clans of Eleusis be revoked. But one of the Hierophants, or initiatory High Priests, Theodorus, refused to perform any act in response to this charge. "If Alcibiades does no wrong, then I invoked no evil upon him," Plutarch quotes him. Alcibiades made a grand gesture, therefore, to prove his pious devotion and the gods' acceptance of it.[45]

Shortly before his return to the field in the fall of 408, he commanded Athenian armed forces to escort the procession from Athens to Eleusis and back again for the celebration of the Great Mysteries of Demeter and Persephone. Ever since the Spartans and their allies had taken up permanent station at Decelea, this procession, Plutarch relates, had been conducted "with no splendor at all by sea; and sacrifices, choral dances, and many of the sacred ceremonies performed along the road... had of necessity been omitted." Now Alcibiades could affirm his piety, make a show of military strength, and preside over the festival of the deities that his enemies claimed that he had offended.

The gesture far transcended the mere performance of a festival liturgy. Plutarch, always interested in manifestations of traditional piety, narrates the episode in some detail. The terms in which he describes the popular response to Alcibiades' procession are significant:

> He made of his generalship such an august and devout spectacle that those who were not smitten by envy called it his High Priesthood *(hierophantia)* and his Guiding of Mystic Initiates *(mystagogia)*.... At this he was exalted in spirit himself, and exalted his army with the feeling that it was irresistible and invincible under his command. People of the humbler and poorer sort he so captivated by his leadership that they were filled with an amazing passion *(eran erota thaumaston)* to have him for their tyrant, and some proposed it, and actually came to him and urged him to know that he was superior to envy, and that he could do away with decrees and laws and the petty thinkers who were ruining the city, so that he might act and conduct affairs without fear of malicious prosecutors ("sycophants").[46]

Just as the reference to his triumph over Envy *(phthonos)* echoes the words of Alcibiades' recent speech, as Plutarch reports, so must the approval of Alcibiades' sacerdotal functions and the power of Eros (translated "passion" here) reflect Alcibiades' own justifications of his past actions. The terms in which Alcibiades' tyranny was envisaged likewise reflect highly circumstantial concerns. To "do away with decrees and laws and the petty thinkers who were ruining the city" was a reference to the politicized process of collating and recodifying the mass of legal and executive documents underway at that time, under the authority of the *nomothetai*. Their work was to guide and to constrain political action, and in light of the all-encompassing enthusiasm for Alcibiades' leadership, many felt such constraints to be unjustified. Those who insisted on them were "small-minded"; those who took legal action in the name of upholding laws and decrees were "sycophants."

ALCIBIADES AND THE LAWS

Gratified as he must have been by such outpourings on his behalf, Alcibiades did not assert any formal authority to defy the laws and decrees of Athens. Rather, he sought to channel popular support so that the laws and the decrees of Athens were identified with his own will. Over the months of summer, his chief concern was to bring the negotiations he had begun in the Aegean and the Hellespont to fulfillment in decrees of the Assembly. Fragments of inscribed decrees datable to the summer of 408, three of them bearing Alcibiades' name, attest to this activity. His prestige in foreign affairs was directly convertible into public policy.[47]

Laws, on the other hand, presented a more complicated issue when confronted with the influence of Alcibiades. Over decades of imperial administration, especially under Pericles and Cleon, the Athenians had enacted standing rules with no formal distinction between ad hoc guidelines and fixed, statutory laws. Testaments to the will of the sovereign *demos,* these rules and guidelines could not be entrusted to the memory of a hereditary elite, but had to be committed to writing and preserved by the officers of the people's business. The Athenian democracy thus spawned an unprecedented accumulation of written records that was growing rapidly by the middle decades of the fifth century. Many of these documents were publicly inscribed, but far more were preserved as papyrus documents in the custodies of the various officers of the state responsible for their implementation. In the last decade of the fifth century, the *nomothetai* were conducting the first extensive review of these records of the democracy. What they found, not surprisingly, was a tangle of sometimes conflicting enactments. Measures authorized at different times and for different purposes prescribed alternative and sometimes contradictory procedures. To resolve these contradictions and to determine which enactments had higher authority, the Athenians were attempting to give a systematic definition to the distinction between laws, *nomoi,* and decrees, *psephismata.* In asserting the priority of *nomoi* as statutory laws, the *nomothetai* were sure to encounter vexing and contested issues. Insistence by the *nomothetai* on their collective authority to decide these issues was the source of the complaints heard by Alcibiades about the "petty thinkers who were ruining the city."[48]

Alcibiades himself must have been vexed on more than one occasion, in 408, by assertions of this new form of public authority. We can recognize one such occasion behind an anecdote about Alcibiades told by Xenophon. When he was less than twenty years old, Alcibiades asked Pericles, who was his guardian, "What is 'the law'?" *(ti estin nomos;).* Pericles replied confidently that, "Laws are the written enactments approved by the majority in assembly, declaring what must, and what must not, be done." Alcibiades must have related this story in the course of some public debate in order to urge the Athenians, with the authority of Pericles, to believe that the assembled majority had the intrinsic ability to resolve on the spot what "the law" should be. The issue was clearly topical, for the argument reappears in public debate two years later.[49]

An anecdote recorded by Athenaeus attests to another confrontation between Alcibiades and the legal process, in this case regarding affairs abroad:

> At the time when the Athenians were in command of the seas, they used to refer lawsuits of the islanders to the courts of the city; someone indicted Hegemon [of Thasos, a comic poet,] and took his suit to Athens. He, upon his arrival there, gathered together the artists of Dionysus [the actors' guild] and went in their company to ask the assistance of Alcibiades. He urged them to have no fear, and telling them all to follow him he went to the Metroön, where records of lawsuits were kept; there he wet his finger in his mouth and rubbed out the record of the suit against Hegemon. The Secretary and the Magistrate were indignant, but held their peace on Alcibiades' account, especially since the plaintiff in the case had discreetly defaulted.[50]

Besides demonstrating Alcibiades' sympathy for actors and performers, the incident shows him momentarily arrogating due process. His act was probably not a serious challenge to the authority of law, however. The case involved overseas business, where Alcibiades was better qualified than anyone else to attest to extenuating circumstances, and to the interests of Athens. He must have known that he could win the case on behalf of Hegemon if it came to trial; and, as it turned out, his involvement assured that it did not.

Alcibiades, like Peisistratus in a bygone age, did not want to be seen as above the law. Rather, he wanted his interests to be identified with the due processes of law. As in other matters, to achieve this paramount goal Alcibiades evoked the faith and devotion of his followers by deploying powerful symbols of religion.

BELOVED OF THE MOTHER OF THE GODS

The passage quoted above is the earliest reference to the Metroön, or temple of the Mother of the Gods in the Agora, where, from around this time on, the state archives of the Athenians were kept. Other sources attest that the Metroön was also the Council-House, or Bouleuterion of the Athenians. As discussed in chapter 5, archaeological evidence reveals that early in the last decade of the fifth century a new Council-House was built beside its predecessor. The old Council-House, already a repository for public documents, became available for meetings of the 500 *nomothetai* and for the curation of state archives. At the same time, but for reasons that have never been convincingly explained, the old Council-House also became the temple of the Mother, or Metroön (map 4).[51]

The Mother of the Gods—sometimes identified as Rhea mother of Zeus, or Ge, Mother Earth, or Demeter, and closely associated with Artemis and Aphrodite—was the Asiatic deity, Cybele. Her cult was long known and widely observed among the Greeks, who nevertheless continued to regard Phrygia and Lydia to be her native lands. Her most famous temple was at Sardis, remembered especially for its destruction in the fire set by the Athenians and their Eretrian and Ionian allies in the Ionian revolt of 499. Herodotus draws attention to this act, above all else, as justification for the vengeance visited by the Persians on Miletus in 494, on Eretria in 490, and finally, on Athens in 480. To avert the awful vengeance of the goddess, the Athenians may have devoted a public shrine to her in the Agora after 494. A small, temple-like building beside the old Council-House in the Athenian Agora has been conjecturally identified as a shrine to the Mother of the Gods. It was destroyed in the Persian sack of 480 and not rebuilt when the Athenians returned. Athens herself had by then paid in kind for the destruction of Cybele's temple at Sardis, and after 480 the Athenians found more effective means of keeping the wrath of Asia at bay.[52]

It is probably significant, then, that the Mother of the Gods, Cybele, began to loom again in Athenian imagination in the years surrounding the next great Ionian revolt, the uprisings against Athenian dominion in 412. Allusions to her wrath occur among the extraordinary events following the mutilation of the Herms in 415; she is honored among the "new gods" of Peisetaerus' new city in Aristophanes' *Birds,* performed in 414; Euripides' choruses invoke her, once in a climactic prayer for the redemption of Helen, in the play of that name performed in 411, and a few years later, in the *Bacchae,* as the mistress of Lydian rites; Sophocles likewise invokes her in his *Philoctetes,* produced in 409 on the eve of Alcibiades' homecoming, depicting an outcast hero who must be accepted back by his fellow warriors, the Greeks at Troy, before the gods will grant them victory. It is certainly significant that the greatest victory won by the Athenians in these years, the battle of Cyzicus, was won under the watchful eye of Cybele.[53]

Among Asiatic Greeks, the cult of Cybele was best known at Cyzicus, where Mount Dindymus, towering above the town and the adjacent coastline, was her sacred mountain. Here, legend claimed, the Argonauts had established her altar and its customary sacrifices in thanks for delivering them from overpowering winds; for among the Mother's manifold powers over nature was command of storms and the deliverance or destruction of seafarers.[54]

Cybele was thus the patron goddess of the victory at Cyzicus, and the agent of divine favor for Alcibiades. Her providential storm clouds had given the Athenians the cover they needed to set the trap for Mindarus. She was also the mistress of Sardis, whose influence Alcibiades most fervently courted. Her cult was also closely identified with Artemis of Ephesus, a con-

FIGURE 5. The union of Athens and Asia: the Mother of the Gods, Cybele, enthroned, with libation dish, drum, and lion. Miniature marble replica, probably of the fourth century, after the fifth-century original by Agoracritus in the Metroön at Athens. Photo courtesy of the Allard Pierson Museum, Amsterdam, no. 3986.

nection maintained by several rulers of Sardis, among them Tissaphernes. As protectress of Ephesus, the goddess had inflicted the only significant setback experienced by the Athenians after 411, the defeat of Thrasyllus' force in 410. As of the winter of 409/8, with a treaty of peace and mutual dominion in hand from Pharnabazus and the same to be anticipated from Tissaphernes and King Darius, the favor of Cybele had become a fundamental symbol of harmony between the Athenians and the lords of Asia.[55]

She of many names, the progenitress of the gods, teacher of mysteries, famed as well for unleashing erotic passions, also embodied the paramount concept of the divinity to whom Alcibiades professed his allegiance. By embracing the Mother of the Gods, the Athenians were also accepting Alcibiades' account of the deeper piety of his own devotional acts. For all of the foregoing reasons and probably at the initiative of Alcibiades himself, the Athenians commissioned a monumental statue of Cybele enthroned, a work in marble by Agoracritus of Paros that became the most famous classical image of the goddess, and installed it in the old Council-House of Athens (see figure 5). Piety, law, democracy, victory, Athens, Asia, and Alcibiades were all united in this act.[56]

CHAPTER SEVEN

The Limits of Democratic Imperative, 408–405

The majority cried out that it was monstrous if anyone were to prevent the people from carrying out their will.

XENOPHON *HELLENICA* 1.7.12

By 408, the recent achievements of Alcibiades in war and diplomacy had significantly reduced his opportunities for continued success. The agreements Alcibiades had reached with Pharnabazus now obliged him to wait on the results of the promised intercession with King Darius. Meanwhile, the Athenians could not make war against the king's domains. This also limited Alcibiades' opportunities to use force against the Greeks of Asia who still sided with Sparta. The irresistible enthusiasm that Alcibiades had enjoyed upon his return to Athens could not be sustained without further tokens of victory. When these tokens appeared in the hands of the enemies of Athens instead, Alcibiades' aura of invincibility evaporated.

Politics at Athens in the interval between the fall of Alcibiades in 407 and the destruction of the Athenian navy in 405 were marked by such a welter of blame-laying that it became possible to ask if Athenians were more devoted to infighting than to war against Sparta. The trial of the generals after the battle of Arginusae, when all the victorious generals were condemned to death, was the epitome of this self-destructive madness. The most trenchant criticisms of the power of rhetoric to misguide a democracy were developed in these years, reflected in Plato's and Xenophon's Socratic writings, and in Aristophanes' *Frogs*. These were the years in which, as Thucydides observed, the Athenians brought defeat upon themselves.

LORDSHIP OF ASIA

Ambassadors from Sparta came to Athens in the summer of 408, and Alcibiades no doubt took a leading role in negotiations with them. Piety as well as practicality dictated that the Spartans offer terms of peace to the Athenians whenever divine favor seemed to lie more heavily on either side;

if the Athenians in their pride should reject the offer, as so often they did, then the Spartans had the gods as witnesses of their own humility in the face of Athenian arrogance. In this case, the ransoming of prisoners was the only substantive issue resolved. Any Spartan offer of peace would have been no more appealing to the Athenians now than in 410, especially since the Spartans probably felt no need to make any special concessions. The reason, as Alcibiades must already have known, was that the Spartans had concluded an alliance in their favor with King Darius.[1]

At the beginning of the previous spring, as the ambassadors sent by Alcibiades with Pharnabazus were on their way from Gordium to Susa, they met a returning Spartan embassy accompanied by Persian messengers who announced that the Spartans had won approval of their request for an alliance with Darius, and that his younger son, Cyrus, was coming as ruler of the coastlands (i.e., the Greek towns of Asia Minor) to join the Spartans in making war against the Athenians. Since Cyrus was to represent the royal authority of his father, the Athenians were instructed to await his arrival. The disappointing news must have been brought back to Athens by Euryptolemus son of Peisianax. Euryptolemus was among the kinsmen who greeted Alcibiades when he disembarked in Piraeus, so Alcibiades surely had word right away that there were difficulties in the way of his grand scheme for the recovery of Athens.[2]

Cyrus' appointment and the gratification of Spartan appeals had more to do with Persian court politics than with Aegean affairs. Cyrus' authority eclipsed the power of Tissaphernes, and the prince's commitment to Sparta was designed to give him strong allies where Tissaphernes, by his equivocal policies, had generated only frustration. The creation of a royal command in Asia Minor for young Cyrus, then no more than sixteen years old, was designed to strengthen the family of Darius against the constant threats of rebellion. It may also have been an element in the plan of Parysatis, the wife of the compliant Darius, to prepare their younger son, Cyrus, for the succession to the throne that was otherwise intended for their older son, the future Artaxerxes II. Parysatis' affection for her younger son is attested by Xenophon, who became personally involved in the struggle between the brothers following the death of Darius in 405. It is also attested by Ctesias of Cnidos, the Greek physician to Parysatis, who published his memoirs years after Artaxerxes had secured the succession.[3]

In 408, when the appointment of Cyrus was announced in Ionia, it was not immediately clear what its practical effect would be. The Athenian ambassadors with Pharnabazus in fact had a year to wait for the arrival of Cyrus to begin to find out. The young prince, embarking upon his first command, probably took the time between the announcement of his title and his arrival at Sardis to make state visits along the way. It was vital for Cyrus to forge bonds of loyalty to himself among the vassals and satraps of Asia Minor, especially since Tissaphernes, loyal brother-in-law to Artaxerxes, was bound to be jealous of his power and watchful for signs of his weakness. When, in the winter or spring of 407, Cyrus did reach Sardis, he was immediately approached by the Athenians, and by ambassadors from Sparta in the company of the Spartan naval commander in Ionia that year, Lysander son of Aristocritus. The Athenians expressed their dissatisfaction with this meeting by demanding to be escorted to Darius, something that Cyrus now forbade Pharnabazus to do. Meanwhile, Lysander had the good fortune of becoming a fast friend to a young man eager to use his influence and money to gain loyal allies.[4]

THE ECLIPSE OF ALCIBIADES

Even before the arrival of Cyrus and his open alignment with Sparta, Alcibiades was finding it difficult to satisfy the expectations he had inspired. In fall 408, Alcibiades set sail from Athens in command of a force practically the equal, in numbers of Athenian ships and men, of the force he had led to Sicily. Landing on Andros, Alcibiades led an assault on the pro-Spartan forces controlling the island's town. His force won a victor's trophy in the field, but failed to capture the town. Alcibiades established a fortified base at Gaurium to keep the enemy in check, but the overall result, by the time he led the bulk of his forces eastward across the Aegean, was that instead of booty to divide, he had continuing expenses to meet.[5]

Elsewhere, a spot of good news was provided by the surrender of Thasos to Thrasybulus, probably in the first half of 407. An inscription from Athens preserves a resolution proposed by Axiochus, Alcibiades' uncle, thanking allies who had made personal and financial sacrifices to support the siege. Another Athenian decree erected at Thasos invited grateful supporters of Athens among the Thasians to make voluntary contributions to Athens. Such funds could probably do no more than defray the costs of besieging Thasos. It is unlikely that there was any windfall of revenue to be had from this exhausted enemy.[6]

Alcibiades, meanwhile, operating out of Samos, had to support his forces by plundering the allies of Sparta among the islands, from Lesbos to Rhodes, while waiting for an opportunity to strike at the naval forces Lysander was assembling at Ephesus. Still hopeful that his embassy might yet incline Darius to favor Athens, Alcibiades had to restrain the Athenians from any affront to Persian dominion. Meanwhile, Lysander, having gained friendship and generous pay from Cyrus beginning in spring 407, could afford to wait as his forces grew in strength.[7]

In the summer of 407 a battle took place in the waters between Ephesus and Notium that had far greater consequences for the Athenians than indicated by their small material losses, for it marked the end of Alcibiades' career as an Athenian general. The Athenian fleet was drawn up at Notium, some fifteen miles from Ephesus, where it could block the exit of Lysander's fleet from Ephesus. Quiet for months, while ships were being built and crews prepared, Lysander was looking for an opportunity to strike. His opportunity came when word reached him that Alcibiades was away from his main force, on one of his many missions to support allies, reduce enemies, and secure funds.

The Athenians were probably in the habit of sending reconnaissance patrols close in to the harbor at Ephesus, and Lysander cut off one of these patrols in a surprise attack. Seeing the distress of their fellows, more Athenian ships were manned and put out. But Lysander's fleet had the initiative, and in the general engagement that followed his force drove the Athenian fleet off and disabled at least fifteen of its ships. The Athenians regrouped at Samos, where Alcibiades joined them a few days later and led them, still superior in numbers, to face the Spartans in front of the harbor of Ephesus. With no reason to attack a ready foe, Lysander once again kept his forces still and let his symbolic triumph play out its full effect.[8]

The mystique of invincibility that attended Alcibiades was shattered, and within a month or two it would collapse entirely. Lysander, encouraged by success at sea, had begun to encourage wider resistance to Athens among the Ionian Greeks. At Cyme, on the Asian coast south of Lesbos, Alcibiades attempted to use force to stem the development of a pro-Spartan movement. But Alcibiades' army suffered an unexpected defeat after plundering the territory of Cyme, and the Cymaeans sent an embassy to Athens to denounce Alcibiades' heavy-handed tactics. There they found an audience predisposed to listen to their complaints.[9]

The defeat at Notium had established a new mood at Athens, for it had shown that Alcibiades was no longer the favorite of the Great Goddess of Ephesus. The force that Alcibiades had led from Athens the previous year included among its officers men who were serving to advance the glory of Athens, but who had no particular desire to advance the glory of Alcibiades. Now that they had cause to criticize his leadership in public, every grievance, real or imagined, was given a hearing. If Alcibiades claimed (in dispatches, not in person) that the defeat at Notium could not be justly laid upon himself, his detractors could deride his choice of subordinate officers. If Alcibiades appealed for deference to his judgment as field commander, his enemies could claim that *too much* had been left to his personal discretion, and his word was not to be trusted. Vast sums of public money had been committed to his trust, with no return or accounting foreseeable. Force was used at his whim unjustly, as the Cymaeans could attest. As to Alcibiades' private meetings and negotiations with leading men in the towns of Ionia and the Hellespont, his detractors made them into occasions for "drunken indulgence and consorting with prostitutes." Above all, his tactful and formal relations with Pharnabazus, yielding no evident advantage for Athens, gave rise to allegations of his designs upon tyranny at Athens with Persian support. Athenians had ample cause from the events of 411 to fear treachery from officials unaccountable to the people. It was thus not difficult for skillful speakers to ignite old and new charges against Alcibiades. In such a mood, Cleophon persuaded the Assembly to impeach Alcibiades in the name of safeguarding the sovereignty of the *demos*. In all, the Athenians found reason to depose not only Alcibiades, but every other commanding general that had been recommended to the people as his friend.[10]

With all of the affairs under his personal direction now suspended, Alcibiades knew that only humiliation or worse could await him at Athens. When it was confirmed that he would be replaced at Samos by Conon son of Timotheus, Alcibiades set sail for the Thracian Chersonese, where he had earlier been given strongholds by Seuthes, king of the Odrysian Thracians. There he could safely ignore his ignominy at home and, using his friendship with powerful foreigners, he could wait for the pendulum of fortune to swing back in his direction.[11]

VICTORY AT ARGINUSAE

Toward the end of summer 407, the command of both Athenian and Spartan naval forces changed, and incoming commanders on both sides faced severe financial shortages. Conon, replacing Alcibiades, took over a force low in morale, with insufficient means to maintain it. He was compelled to reduce his fleet from over one hundred to seventy ships. Lysander, meanwhile, was obliged by law to yield his command in annual rotation to a successor, Callicratidas. Morale was high in the Spartan fleet, where Lysander boasted the title "master of the sea" *(thalattokrator)*. But the funds that sustained this claim were not to be forthcoming for Callicratidas as they had been for Lysander.[12]

The ambassadors sent by Alcibiades to Pharnabazus in the winter of 409/8, long delayed and ultimately frustrated by the appointment of Cyrus, finally returned home in the winter of 407/6 after Pharnabazus learned that these friends of Alcibiades could no longer give him a privileged channel of communication with the Athenians. Meanwhile, other Athenian ambassadors paid court to Tissaphernes, who served as an intermediary between them and Cyrus. For his own purposes, Tissaphernes shared the Athenians' desire to separate the Spartans from Cyrus' money. Xenophon reports that Tissaphernes advised Cyrus to follow the policy advocated by Alcibiades, namely, to allow neither of the opposing Greek forces to become too powerful. By such arguments, urged by Tissaphernes if not by Darius himself, over the winter of 407/6 Cyrus was persuaded to withhold pay from Callicratidas.[13]

Spurned by Cyrus, Callicratidas turned the lack of Persian funding into a virtue. Addressing a meeting of Sparta's allies from Chios, Rhodes, and Ionia, he challenged them to man and maintain an even larger fleet than Lysander's and to become masters of the sea without relying on Persia. In spring 406, Callicratidas led a force of 170 ships to a series of victories. He destroyed an Athenian siege camp on Chios, captured the town of Methymna on Lesbos, and, after a brief sea battle, blockaded the main Athenian fleet commanded by Conon in the harbor of Mytilene on Lesbos.[14]

Even before the confinement of Conon at Mytilene, the Athenians knew that their supremacy at sea was in peril. Probably over the winter of 407/6, in response to Conon's sober appraisal of the deterioration of their fleet, the Athenians began an urgent shipbuilding program. The board of generals, headed by Pericles, son of the famous Pericles, was authorized to divert public revenues directly to the shipbuilders. To raise the necessary funds, another *eisphora* was levied. Possibly in response to the legitimate complaints of the propertied class that their resources were not without limits, the Athenians instituted for the first time the practice of the joint-trierarchy, where the heads of two households could pool their resources in financing the operation of a warship. In this way, the honor of doing one's duty to the state was being converted from personal service to impersonal cash flow.[15]

News of the blockade of Conon at Mytilene drove the Athenians with an urgency beyond even that following the news from Sicily in 413 and Euboea in 411. With virtually all of their Ionian fleet lost or blockaded, the Athenians had to assemble a fresh fleet to match Callicratidas. Fortunately, new hulls were on hand in Athens and others could be found among subjects and allies around the Aegean. To expedite the gathering of ships and crews from among the allies, the Athenians converted a large sum of gold from dedications on the Acropolis into coinage. By these means, 80 ships were manned and brought to Samos, according to Diodorus, where ten more were added by the Samians. At Athens, 60 ships were manned by a call-up of all able-bodied citizens, including "many of the cavalrymen," according to Xenophon, who may have been one of them. Even these measures could not yield the roughly 12,000 men needed to fill out crews ready for battle, so citizenship was offered to any resident foreigners and slaves able to row. The fleet that assembled at Samos thirty days after the emergency was announced was thus a demographic anomaly, as far as the Athenians were concerned, for it represented an unparalleled elevation into the ranks of citizenship of the lowest classes from Athens, side-by-side with compulsory service for members of the highest echelons of Athenian society. Naval hegemony was never more a social leveler than at this moment (the Lenormant relief in figure 6 makes a demonstration of the social solidarity of Athenian forces at about this time).[16]

Within a few days of the assembly at Samos, before midsummer 406, Thrasyllus, Aristocrates, Pericles son of Pericles, and five other Athenian generals led their fleet of some 150 ships north to Lesbos, where Callicratidas had separated up to 140 ships from the blockading force to meet them. Between the southeastern tip of Lesbos and the Arginusae islands along the opposite coast of the mainland the two fleets came in sight of each other but were kept apart on the first day by strong winds. With calm weather at dawn the second day, the two sides took up formations and engaged in a hard-fought battle that resulted, by the early afternoon, in the death of Callicratidas, the loss of more than 70 of his ships, and the dispersal of the rest of his forces. The victorious Athenians had 25 of their ships put out of action. The crews from half of these ships were recovered as the Athenians regrouped, but before they could execute their next moves, a powerful storm arose and forced them to put ashore at the Arginusae islands. A great victory had been won, and the siege of Mytilene had been lifted, but the loss of life on the Athenian side was great. More than 2,000 crewmen of the disabled ships still at sea were lost overnight in the storm.[17]

The loss on this occasion was especially grievous to the Athenians because of the composition of the crews. The lost crews had belonged to the wing farthest from the mainland shore, where Callicratidas had engaged the ships commanded by Aristocrates, Pericles, Diomedon, and Erasinides. Most Athenian ships disabled in this part of the battle were therefore from among the 60 ships manned at Athens, where kinsmen, in larger numbers than usual for a force of this size, awaited news of the battle. Word of the victory and of the losses was immediately sent to Athens in an official dispatch. Sometime thereafter, two of the generals commanding at Arginusae, Diomedon and Erasinides, were replaced and summoned home to render accounts for their year of command.[18]

THE TRIAL OF THE GENERALS

The battle of Arginusae has been made famous by the trial of the generals who won the battle for Athens but were held accountable for the loss of life that occurred afterward. The trial took place more than three months after the battle, however, and came about not in a fit of grief and anger as a result of news of the battle, but as a result of maneuvers of political expediency that fell afoul of revelations of political chicanery before an angered public. Before then, the Athenians had commended the generals for the victory, had received and rejected another Spartan embassy offering to end the war, and had mourned their losses (the Lenormant relief, figure 6, may be a fragment of a memorial to the battle of Arginusae).[19]

The most memorable display of emotion following the battle of Arginusae was put on by Cleophon, when Spartan ambassadors presented the

FIGURE 6. Communal *arete* in battle: the Lenormant relief, a fragment with a rare depiction of rowers on an Athenian trireme, possibly from a memorial of the battle of Arginusae in 406. Athens, Acropolis Museum no. 1339. Photo courtesy of the Deutsches Archäologisches Institut, Athens, neg. no. 1860 AKR.

Athenians with an offer to evacuate Decelea and make peace under existing conditions. "But," Aristotle recounts:

> the masses paid no attention, being misled by Cleophon, who prevented peace from happening by coming into the Assembly drunk and wearing a breastplate, declaring that he would not allow it unless the Spartans surrendered all the cities.[20]

Like Cleon and Hyperbolus before him, Cleophon in this passage is the picture of the detested demagogue. We would do well to set aside the stereotype of the drunken madman, and to consider the method behind Cleophon's alleged madness. For his performance clearly made a great impression. The following winter, the comic poet Plato staged a played named *Cleophon.* Aristophanes, the prizewinning poet on that occasion, began a chorus in his *Frogs* with back-handed praise for Cleophon's well-known *philotimia,* love of honor, and closed the play, after prayers for an end to the sufferings of war, with a mock-heroic verse: "But let Cleophon, and whoever else wants, do battle in their ancestral fields."[21]

Cleophon, in his answer to the Spartans, had clearly made another powerful and persuasive appeal to the Athenians to carry on the fight until they had recovered all of their rightful dominion, for their empire was their "ancestral fields." Cleophon's appeal was evidently couched in archaic, probably poetic language, aided by his appearance, in armor, as a heroic warrior. Even men like Xenophon, who might not favor Cleophon as a model of heroic leadership, could not deny the appeal of his performance. Xenophon's *Memorabilia* depicts a conversation between Socrates and the younger Pericles that appropriates the themes that figured in Cleophon's performance:

> Pericles exclaimed, "How might we persuade [the Athenians] once again to devote themselves passionately to ancient virtue and fame and happiness?"
>
> "Well now," said Socrates, "if we wanted them to lay claim to money in the possession of others, the best way of inciting them to seize it would be to show them that it was theirs by ancestral right. Since we want them to strive for preeminence in virtue, we must show that this was theirs of old, and that by striving for it they will surpass all others."

It was Cleophon who was inciting the Athenians to fight on to recover their ancestral rights (measured in money), and to do so he encouraged all Athenians to think of themselves as the heroic warriors of yore. In Cleophon's rhetoric, the leveling effect of naval hegemony ennobled the majority.[22]

Mindful of the sacrifices they had made in pursuit of a noble purpose, the Athenians were in no mood to ignore evidence that individuals entrusted with the precious means of carrying out the people's will had profited personally from their trust. The generals who had fought at Arginusae had been given exceptional authority to dispose of money raised by unusual levies, including the gold coinage created by melting down statues of Victory, gifts of the Athenians to Athena. Audits of the accounts of the first two generals to return to Athens revealed actionable discrepancies in the case of one of them, Erasinides. Suit was brought against Erasinides by Archedemus, identified by Xenophon as the leader of the *demos* at that time and supervisor of the *diobelia*.[23]

The hearing of this case by a jury-court resulted in the imprisonment of Erasinides. Imprisonment was never imposed as a penalty, but only to enforce the exaction of a penalty; it was commonly employed to enforce the settlement of a monetary debt to the state. In this case, Erasinides' trial seems to have uncovered evidence of possible financial mismanagement by other generals as well. To carry out a thorough investigation, the remainder of the previous summer's board of generals was peremptorily recalled, with the exception of Conon. Accompanied by a large part of their Athenian crews, five of the seven generals of the summer still in office returned to Athens shortly before the beginning of winter 406. Their homecoming must have come close to the time of the festivals of the *Oschophoria* and the *Kybernesia,* both celebrations of the bittersweet homecoming of Theseus. The mood of triumph and loss recalled on those festivals certainly prevailed among the men of the fleet in the weeks that followed.[24]

The generals who fought at Arginusae were the men entrusted to save Athens after Alcibiades and his friends had been deposed in the previous year's scandal-driven hearings. Now sympathizers of Alcibiades had a chance for revenge. As in the case of Alcibiades, accusers came from within the ranks of the officer corps that served under the generals. Theramenes and Thrasybulus, both former colleagues of Alcibiades and both trierarchs at Arginusae, were central to the case being built against Erasinides and the other commanders at Arginusae, a case that, at this point, involved only allegations of financial improprieties.

A meeting of the Council was held to review the charges being made against the generals and to determine if judicial proceedings were justified. In an effort to escape the effects of a hostile audit, the six generals resorted to a legal tactic. They attempted to derail the action against them by filing a formal charge of murder against Theramenes and Thrasybulus, the chief witnesses against them, on the grounds that these men had failed in their assigned duty of recovering the shipwrecked sailors. For Theramenes and Thrasybulus had been placed in command of a rescue squadron whose work was called off because of the storm. The generals' stratagem had its desired effect, for their accusation was sufficiently serious that it forced the Council to refer the matter to the Assembly, where the people could exercise their sovereign authority to determine how to resolve the accusations made by the generals. But in the meantime the Council also exercised its authority to detain the rest of the generals pending the resolution of their audits.[25]

Nothing more is heard of accusations of financial impropriety. In all likelihood, except in the case of Erasinides, the evidence for such wrongdoing was still too insubstantial, or too complicated, to make a convincing case. But the emotional issue of the men lost at sea was bound to capture public attention, and the maneuverings of the generals had placed it first on the agenda of the Assembly. By standing together in their denunciation of Theramenes and Thrasybulus, the generals committed themselves as a group to the outcome of the rhetorical contest that followed.

In the first review of the case in the Assembly, Theramenes and Thrasybulus had to defend themselves against the charge of failing to pick up the shipwrecked sailors. This they were able to do, in the speech delivered by Theramenes, by reading from the official dispatch sent by the generals after the battle, in which the storm was said to be the sole cause of the failure to pick up the men. If, Theramenes argued, at the time the generals had agreed that human error was *not* a factor in this tragedy, but now they were offering sworn testimony to the contrary, then the blame must lie with the generals themselves for having attempted to cover up the incompetence of their own leadership when the storm was rising.

Confronted with the evidence of their own report and required by the Assembly to make brief individual statements on the matter, the generals dissembled and made no consistent response. Their charge had foundered. Many witnesses from among the officers and men in the fleet had come to the Assembly prepared to back up the generals' charge against Theramenes and Thrasybulus. But their testimony, confounded by Theramenes' counter-charge, likewise failed to clarify matters. Early nightfall put an end to the proceedings, and the Assembly assigned the case back to the Council, requiring the councilors to come up with a recommendation for how to proceed.[26]

Having initiated the investigation of the generals, the Council evidently had a majority who were inclined to prosecute them. The supporters of Theramenes were thus able to pass a resolution, put forward by one of the councilors, Callixeinus, recommending that, at its next meeting, the Assembly proceed immediately to a vote to determine if the Athenians thought that the generals, collectively, "were guilty of not recovering those who had won the naval battle ... or not," and if they were guilty, to have them put to death. The phrasing of the resolution pointed toward the expected result, for the mood of the majority, in the Assembly as well as the Council, was in Theramenes' favor.[27]

As the Assembly met to consider this proposal, Xenophon states that Theramenes and his supporters took advantage of the mood of mourning that prevailed. Many Athenians coming to the Assembly were then observing the kinship rites of the *Apatouria* and were dressed and shaved to display their bereavement of kin lost the previous summer. This was an opportunity for Theramenes, but it was not his contrivance; it was the generals who had attempted to pack the previous Assembly with seamen loyal to themselves, but they had been confounded when the hearing took an unexpected turn. The Assembly contained yet another constituency that may have endorsed Theramenes' portrayal of the irresponsibility of the generals. The newly enfranchised citizens, former slaves and metics who had fought in the battle, may have felt that they had a unique chance to exact retribution for the callousness with which aristocratic leaders had so long disposed of humanity by the shipload.[28]

Before such a crowd, Theramenes was a masterful choreographer. He produced the dramatic testimony of one survivor to the dying words of men around him who called out that, if he survived, he should "report to the *demos* that the generals did not recover men who had proved themselves *aristoi* on behalf of their fatherland." This was the language of the funeral oration, affirming the posthumous nobility of all who gave their lives in battle. Through a device as moving as any tragic messenger's speech, the Athenians heard voices from the grave calling for punishment, not so much for the loss of the living, but now, at a time of mourning, for the failure to honor the dead by recovering their bodies.[29]

Sentiment thus strongly favored proceeding with the vote proposed by Callixeinus. Struggling to hold off this step, the supporters of the generals, now led by Euryptolemus son of Peisianax, announced an indictment of Callixeinus on the grounds that his proposal was *paranomon,* in violation of the laws. Although some approved, Xenophon reports, "the majority cried out that it was monstrous if anyone were to prevent the people from carrying out their will." The people's will was then given focus in a countermeasure to the effect that the proposers of this indictment should be included in the vote on the guilt of the generals (its outcome already taken for granted), unless they withdrew their accusation. Intimidated by the angry outcries of the mob *(ho ochlos),* or because they could not obtain a hearing of the basis for their indictment, they withdrew the measure. The final step was to put the proposal of Callixeinus to a vote, which was the duty the *epistates* of the prytany, or chairman of the presiding board of the Council, who happened on that day to be Socrates son of Sophroniscus.

Desperate for any recourse, the friends of the generals must have appealed to Socrates to prevent the vote. Although the *demos* would not be restrained by Euryptolemus' arguments, Socrates could be persuaded. He refused to put Callixeinus' proposal to a vote and had in turn to endure the angry shouts of the Assembly. His reason, as Xenophon reports, was that "in no case would he act except in accordance with the law."[30]

Socrates' decision had no statutory basis; it was merely an endorsement of Euryptolemus' failed injunction. On strictly legal grounds, Euryptolemus' case was weak. In his lengthy speech in the final stage of the debate, as narrated by Xenophon, Euryptolemus offered precedents for trying the generals individually, either in the Assembly or in a law court, but he could refer to no statute that enjoined against the sort of one-verdict-for-all that Callixeinus proposed. In fact, one-verdict-for-all had been the procedure employed for the trial of Antiphon and his associates in 411. Furthermore, in the same year, in the posthumous trial of Phrynichus, provision had been made for including, under the same vote for condemnation, anyone who spoke in defense of the accused. Socrates' refusal, therefore, like Euryptolemus' argument, relied on the sense of *nomos* as custom, or the way things should rightly be done, rather than its more limited sense of written statute. But with leaders of the opposition insisting that the people's authority could not be curtailed by unwritten *nomoi,* there was no way to resist their demand. In this case, the people's will *was* the law.[31]

As important as this moment was, in retrospect, to his sense of uncompromising principle, Socrates' intransigence had no effect on the fate of his friend, Pericles son of Pericles, or any of Pericles' colleagues. Xenophon's account skips directly to the final sequence of speeches and proposals in the Assembly and omits to mention what is reported elsewhere, that they took place on the following day. Already long and tumultuous, Socrates' day as presiding officer in the Assembly was over. When the Assembly reconvened, a new *epistates* was chosen by lot, and, after discussion, Callixeinus' proposal was once again up for a vote. Euryptolemus delivered a carefully prepared speech, which Xenophon reports in its entirety, touching upon all aspects of the indictment of the generals and renewing the charges against Theramenes and Thrasybulus. Euryptolemus concluded with a counterproposal to give each man a separate trial, and when a vote was taken by show of hands between Euryptolemus' and Callixeinus' proposals, Xenophon states, Euryptolemus was declared the winner.[32]

But the vote was close, and in view of the strong feelings known to prevail even among the members of the prytany responsible for counting hands, a recount was demanded and obtained, and by the recount Callixeinus' proposal won. The vote by secret ballot for or against the guilt of the generals was carried out, the eight were found guilty, and the six of these in custody at Athens were taken away for execution.[33]

PLAYING ON REASON

The condemnation of the generals described the unfathomable paradox of justice under democracy at Athens. It was not the first time that military heroes had been condemned; both Miltiades and the great Pericles had been heavily fined when their leadership had failed to produce expected successes; Paches, the general who conquered the rebellious Mytileneans in 427, had committed suicide rather than bear the shame of a guilty verdict. It was not the first time that a board of officers was made to pay the ultimate penalty for the perceived mismanagement of their charge; sometime before 425 all but one of the imperial treasurers, the *Hellenotamiae,* were executed. But the condemnation of the generals of Arginusae was a more awful spectacle than any of these, and its quality as living theater was even more pronounced than usual. On trial were the lately triumphant heroes who had brilliantly rescued Athens from dark desperation. Their doom was played out in separate acts, over days, in front of the entire citizen Assembly; its justice was intoned by an impassioned messenger from the scene of battle, approved by a chorus of mourners, seemingly averted after the speech of a wise counselor, but then swiftly inflicted. Most terrible of all, the destruction of the generals was the outcome of accusations they themselves had initiated.[34]

Beyond the question of whether the generals deserved such a fate lay the question of how justice could be determined where the manipulation of emotions prevailed so completely over reasoned argument. Xenophon, probably eyewitness to these events, emphasizes precisely this in his narrative—so effectively, in fact, that the reason underlying the case against the generals almost disappears from view. In Xenophon's account, neither the reasoned arguments of Euryptolemus nor the principled stand of Socrates could avert the passion of the aroused Assembly. Yet the passion of the *demos* had long been acknowledged, in the rhetoric of Pericles and Alcibiades, as the force that would preserve the liberty of the *demos* and enable it to prevail over its enemies. Even Xenophon, in the conversation between Socrates and the younger Pericles quoted above (page 183), acknowledges the need to inspire the Athenians "to devote themselves passionately *[anerasthenai]* to ancient virtue" to better serve public policy. When guided by reason and inspired by a common vision of ancestral examples, all would agree that emotional appeals served a greater good. But now, those who saw their cause defeated by the passion of the *demos* could not acknowledge the presence of reason on the side of the victors. Unreasoning passion, it seemed, had been unleashed by theatrical rhetoric, with devastating results.[35]

Was it possible for reason to master passion in public debate? Pursuit of this question became a goal of another young witness to the occasion, Plato. The severe censorship of the performing arts that Plato later advocated was prompted by his distaste for the dramatic element in forensic and political rhetoric in these years. In the months immediately following the trial of the generals, Aristophanes shows that criticism of the irrational effects of the art of tragedy was well known among those who "sit quibbling with Socrates" (Xenophon and Plato among them). They sought to remove the musical, emotional element from tragedy, and, to judge from Plato's *Gorgias,* from rhetoric as well. Aristophanes called their exercises the fruitless work of deluded men.[36]

Attuned to the tastes of a wider public, Aristophanes' more popular recommendation was to restore noble purpose to the pathos of drama, and so to public discourse. Thus, by virtue of the ground shared by theatrical and political rhetoric, the deliberations of the Assembly would naturally be ennobled. This was, of course, what the most successful orators of the day, men like Theramenes and Cleophon, were striving to do. But if, in the critics' view, their achievements were misguided, then perhaps they were adopting an inferior model for their dramatic rhetoric. The soundest inspiration always came from emulating the proven achievements of past generations. And so, less than three months after the trial of the generals, Aristophanes won approval, in the *Frogs,* for his resurrection of Aeschylus as the way to salvation for Athens.[37]

In recommending Aeschylus to the Athenians, Aristophanes was responding to the undeniable popularity of the art of Euripides, and particularly to its impact on the political community. Recently deceased, Euripides himself was now part of a bygone age, and sorely missed by the Athenians. As Aristophanes tells it, Dionysus, god of the theater himself, set out for the Underworld with his slave, Xanthias, to satisfy the longing of one and all for their late great poet. But the adventure leads to a reappraisal of the merits of Euripides' poetry. Euripides, lately arrived in the Underworld, was fomenting unrest among the dead by his bid to take the seat of best tragic poet in the court of Hades away from Aeschylus:

> *Aeacus (gatekeeper of Hades):* Now when Euripides arrived, he was performing for the robbers and purse-snatchers and father-beaters and thieves—such are the masses *(to plethos)* in the kingdom of Hades—who, listening to his counter-arguments, his twists and turns, went mad for him and regarded him the wisest. . . . And so the *demos* shouted out for a judgment to be made.
>
> *Xanthias:* Which *demos*—the *demos* of scoundrels?
>
> *Aeacus:* Yes, piled up to heaven!
>
> *Xanthias:* Didn't Aeschylus have others on his side?
>
> *Aeacus:* The best are few, just like here [among the Athenians].[38]

In the course of the decisive contest, this time to be judged by Dionysus himself, Euripides boasts of his pupils, "Cleitophon and the clever Theramenes."

> *Dionysus:* Theramenes? A wise man, marvelous in all ways, who, as soon as he is in trouble has got out of it; "Achaean, not a Chian"—he's so quick!
>
> *Euripides:* Ah yes, that's the kind of thinking I've taught them, introducing calculation and judgment into art, so that they perceive everything right off, and figure out the rest, and understand where they are better than before, and look to the "how does this go" and the "where does this put me" and the "who got the benefit of that."[39]

Euripides is thus cast as the Muse of Theramenes at his recent celebrated performance, and Aeschylus, favored by the best and the few, is buffeted by Euripides' subtleties and their effects on the clamoring, degenerate masses. Although it needed no more explicit reference before an audience in the winter of 406/5, the trial of the generals is actually mentioned in a passing ironic remark. As the contest nears its climax, the two poets debate how opening lines should best set the tone for the story to follow. Aeschylus chastises Euripides for suggesting that Oedipus could *ever* have been a happy man, beginning life as a foundling with his feet pierced, and ending it with his eyes gouged out. Dionysus cannot resist interjecting: "He *would* have been happy, if he had been a general with Erasinides." Archedemus, who indicted Erasinides and set in motion the train of events leading to the trial, had evidently been exempted from the call-up for the Arginusae campaign because he was suffering from conjunctivitis at the time. Any affliction of the eyes, even Oedipus', according to Dionysus' joke, would have been more fortunate than to wind up in service among the truly ill-fated colleagues of Erasinides.[40]

In the *Frogs,* Aristophanes has opened a window into the frenetic pursuits of truth and justice that found expression in the poetry and rhetoric of the day. A poet himself, he cannot deny the power of the poetry of Euripides and its impact on those who have learned from it how to speak, how to listen, and how to be moved. Aristophanes does not approve, therefore, of the project of those around Socrates who think that the undesirable aspects of tragedy, the illogical, muse-inspired, emotional aspects, could be stripped away and leave anything worthy of the name tragedy. But Aristophanes is clearly sympathetic to the project of that circle to define the essence of truth and justice, qualities basic to the claim of some that only the "best" people are capable of the most commendable deeds. The example of Theramenes, however, was unsettling to this premise. This former leader of the Four Hundred was already famous for his knack for identifying the "best" people with those who happened to be enjoying success and power.

The inherent absurdity of it all could be expressed no better than in comedy. So the chorus of the *Frogs* praises the ridiculous machinations of the cowardly hero of the play, Dionysus, at a point where he seizes an opportunity to gain what he thinks to be his advantage:

These are the deeds of a man who sure knows
How to use his own wits, how to stay on his toes;
Worldly and ready to flow with the tide,
No icon, he, to be viewed from one side;
To change for the better, to seek out his ease,
He's clever by nature—a Theramenes![41]

The barbed praise shows how much Theramenes, like Cleophon, was in the public eye. His popularity was such that, not far from the time of the performance of the *Frogs,* he was elected general for the first time since he had come home with Alcibiades. But here the reputation of this one-time oligarch, sometime friend of Alcibiades, caught up with him, and he was rejected at his confirmation hearing. Others too were suffering the effects of orators urging the Athenians to be remorseless toward men who showed that they thought themselves better than the masses. Not long before, Cleophon had driven Critias, another friend of Alcibiades, into exile after delivering a speech that Aristotle later remembered for its effective use of the testimony of ancient poets, in this case Solon, to corruptible qualities in the ancestry of Critias.[42]

FINDING THE RIGHT PERSPECTIVE

With Alcibiades in exile, Thrasyllus and his fellows executed, Theramenes and others able to discredit their rivals but unable to assert their own leadership, the Athenians, according to some, were leaving too many of their best men strewn across rhetorical battlefields. So Xenophon, in his memoirs of Socrates, puts observations to this effect in the mouth of the younger Pericles on the eve of his fatal command:

> When will the Athenians show such harmony of purpose that they work together for the common good instead of being more envious and bitter against one another than against the rest of the world, instead of being the most quarrelsome of men in private and public gatherings, bringing more lawsuits against each other, and preferring to win thus over each other rather than to join together for any common benefit, treating public affairs as no concern of their own except as a place to do battle and to glory in having the power to do so?[43]

This describes the practice and the experience not only of the most prominent politicians, but of all men obliged by their standing and wealth to serve the state. Any of these could be stricken down in court by personal enemies, or by anyone claiming to act in the public interest—sycophants according to their victims.

Judgments involving exile or death were rare; most of those convicted of some misdeed suffered some form of *atimia,* literally "dishonor," technically a revocation or impairment of political rights. The heightened sense of urgency and danger in the year of Arginusae may well have intensified the recourse to litigation. Accompanying financial emergencies may have laid more men than usual open to accusations of failure to uphold the public interest. But, as the course of the generals' trial reveals, finances were but one of a range of issues that could erupt in such a volatile atmosphere of blame and recrimination.

One respect in which this process of litigation had intensified over the years, independent of the emergencies of 406, was in the competitive role of expertise, or *akribeia.* Legal *akribeia* had contributed much to Antiphon's reputation as an effective litigant. Historical *akribeia* had been influential in the expulsion of Alcibiades. Constitutional *akribeia,* combining history and law, had been the point of departure for the oligarchic reforms of the Four Hundred. However misguided their program seemed, in retrospect, the importance of constitutional *akribeia* lived on in the work of codifying traditional law being carried on by the commission of *nomothetai.* Even a form of literary *akribeia,* a fascination for nuanced allusions, in poetry and drama, to other literary works, was recognizable in the artistry of Euripides, especially in the last decade of the poet's life.

In every case, the foundation of *akribeia* was access to written texts, whether they were literary works or archival documents. So the *nomothetai,* by the nature of their task, were presiding over the formation of the first central state archive at Athens. So too, Euripides' subtle intensity derived from the poet's learned reading and large private library. Literary expertise was becoming something of a commercial commodity, available in books like those of Anaxagoras that, Socrates remarks, "sometimes can be had for a drachma at most in the Agora."[44]

Bought wisdom, and indeed the whole premise that more exacting precision would lead to truer results in whatever endeavor, prompted criticism and philosophical inquiry into the nature of *akribeia.* It is noteworthy that, with the events of 406/5, Aristophanes bears witness to the currency of discussions in the circle of Socrates on the nature of statesmanship, rhetoric, music, and the essence of virtue of the sort reflected in the later reminiscences of Xenophon and Plato. Plato's *Gorgias,* set in 405/4, exemplifies these discussions, and passages from a funeral oration pronounced by Gorgias over fallen Athenians, on an unknown but possibly proximate occasion, praises the dead for, among other estimable virtues, "preferring gentle fairness to inflexible justice, and truly-guided speech to exactness of law *(nomou akribeias).*" So Gorgias expressed the widespread feeling that true Athenians, at least, upheld standards hard to adhere to among the living, with conditions such as they were.[45]

But, complain as they might about current conditions, *akribeia* was essential to the competitive display of expertise. It impelled all Athenians who aspired to a role in their city's affairs to be conversant with documents and evidence, with precedents and with "facts" from the past. And although faulty logic might lead some astray, those who were convinced that they were right knew that *akribeia* was ultimately the servant of the truth. *Akribeia* was charting the Athenian political universe.

A case in point is the appendix to the trial of the generals. Both Xenophon and Diodorus state that a feeling of remorse later overtook the Athenians, and that Callixeinus and others responsible for the procedural motions that led to the condemnation of the generals were arrested on a charge of "deceiving the *demos.*" Although no further explanation of this charge is given, we can surmise that it reflects the progress of legal research, ongoing under the auspices of the *nomothetai,* by which the supporters of Euryptolemus were at last able to discover a technicality that would enable them to argue that the procedures of the trial had in fact been contrary to law.[46]

But, in this as in every case heard before a popular jury, the fine points of the law only confirmed what the public wanted confirmed. Remorse so moved the Athenians only when their outlook for the future had suffered a complete revolution. The arrest of Callixeinus took place after the generals replacing the condemned eight had suffered decisive defeat at Aegospotami in 405, and the Athenians once again had reason to consider who it was that had been fated to misguide them. By such measures the Athenian *demos* assigned blame elsewhere for its own misfortune.

TO HUMOR THE LION

The Athenians were fully aware that their politics of litigation were crippling the ranks of their political leadership. Not only Xenophon, reporting the sentiments of the younger Pericles, but also Aristophanes appealed to the Athenians to let "harmony of purpose" replace their vehement recriminations. Dicaearchus, a student of Aristotle, recorded that the *Frogs* won the singular honor of an encore performance precisely for this appeal. The appeal itself is contained in a song in which the chorus urges the Athenians to pardon those who had been condemned on account of some single error. By showing the same greatness of spirit by which they had granted citizenship to slaves who had served the city once in battle, the city would regain the services of men who, themselves or their ancestors, had fought often and well for the city.[47]

This appeal struck home not only because of a feeling that many men of quality had been dealt with harshly, but also for the feeling that the Athenians were depriving themselves of their very best. So the contest of Euripides and Aeschylus reaches its climax when Aristophanes has the poet/rhetors pronounce on the question that has been obsessing the Athenians for the past year:

> *Dionysus:* ... Now then, whichever of you two shall best advise the city, *he* shall come with me. So, first of all, about Alcibiades, let each of you say what he thinks, for the city labors painfully over this one.
>
> *Euripides:* But what is *her* opinion of the man?
>
> *Dionysus:* What? She *loves* him, and *hates* him, and *longs* to have him back. But tell me what *you* think about him.
>
> *Euripides:* I abhor the citizen whose nature it is to be slow to benefit his fatherland, quick to do it great harm, resourceful in his own interest, but powerless to help the city.
>
> *Dionysus:* Poseidon, that's well said! Now you, what's your opinion?
>
> *Aeschylus:* 'Twere best not to rear a lion in the city, but having reared him, 'tis best to humor his ways.
>
> *Dionysus:* Zeus the Savior, I've got a hard decision to make! One spoke so cleverly, the other so clearly. . . .[48]

A moment later, Dionysus states his preference for Aeschylus' archaic metaphors over Euripides' rhetorically clever antitheses. And so he summons Aeschylus to accompany him back from the Underworld, to "save our city by noble proclamations, and educate the ignorant (for they are many). . . ."

Aristophanes' judgment, that the Athenians might yet be saved by suppressing their reservations and embracing Alcibiades, seems to have been shared by Thucydides. The closest that the historian came to pronouncing, in his unfinished work, the reason for the eventual defeat of Athens is an opinion twice expressed pointing to the same conditions that animated Aristophanes in the *Frogs*. After reporting the death of the great Pericles, Thucydides remarks that Athens in due course fell, despite her remarkable resilience, when "those who came after were more on a par with each other, and each striving to be first yielded to the pleasures of the *demos* and surrendered control of affairs." Certainly not all of Pericles' successors were on a par with each other, least of all Alcibiades. When the Athenians turned away from Alcibiades, Thucydides comments later in his work, "they entrusted their affairs to other hands, and before long ruined the city." His account thus points to the period after Alcibiades' second exile, since, as he emphasizes, the Athenians were able to recover from their defeat in Sicily and from the revolts of their allies; even the funding provided to the Spartans by Cyrus was insufficient to bring Athens down. What the Athenians could not overcome, Thucydides plainly states, was their own private infighting. He refers specifically to conditions in the years 407–405.[49]

In the *Frogs*, Aristophanes was doing all he could through comic art to induce the Athenians to reinstate Alcibiades. By testing the worth of contemporary wit against olden wisdom, Aristophanes enthroned the poet of a bygone age who advocated reliance on the tried and true and advised the Athenians to accept the "lion reared in the city." This choice was affirmed by the king of the dead, Plouto, the giver of prosperity, and was enacted at the close of the play in a procession of the chorus of the blessed dead, initiates of the Eleusinian Mysteries. Not since Alcibiades had presided over the procession of initiates in 408 had the Eleusinian rites been so joyously celebrated. Now, after Arginusae, many of the initiates of 408 had arrived at their blessed destiny in the Underworld. From beyond the grave, dead Athenians again spoke to living Athenians, affirming that salvation lay in the wise counsel advocated by their poet.

CHAPTER EIGHT

Surrendering to Sparta, 405–404

"Grant good purposes for the greater good of the city, so that we may at last be done with grief and the toilsome onsets of war."

ARISTOPHANES *FROGS* 1530–32

In the space of just over a year, in 405 and 404, two great sovereigns passed away. The first was Darius II, ruler of the Persian empire; the second was the Athenian empire itself. Although Darius' death was natural and anticipated, while the destruction of Athenian sovereignty was violent and by no means inevitable, the two events were analogous in their consequences, and more closely intertwined in cause and effect than has generally been recognized.

The death of a king and the establishment of a new sovereign, in Persian history as in the history of all monarchies, was ever a period of uncertainty, often accompanied by sudden shifts of loyalty and fratricidal violence. So it was with the accession of Artaxerxes II and his rivalry with his younger brother, Cyrus, which played itself out in stages starting in 405, culminating in their confrontation in battle in 401.

The Athenian empire was laid on its deathbed in 405 by the destruction of its fleet at Aegospotami. As it lingered, for many months, deepening uncertainty overcame all of its devoted servants. The end of the Athenian empire, like the passing of a beloved king, was long the object of denial by those whose existence was defined by the life of their sovereign. In the case of Athens, their denial was not entirely irrational. Sudden reversals were transforming the relations of power within Persian dominions, and these might well have changed the balance of power in the Aegean as long as the roots of Athenian dominion were still in place.

This chapter describes the events that brought down the Athenian empire. Clear in broad terms, the causes, course, and chronology of these events have seemed increasingly obscure the more closely they have been examined. While aspects of these developments can be understood in terms of the internal dynamics of Athenian and Spartan politics, a comprehensive explanation must take account of the connections between Aegean events and the contest for dynastic succession in Persia.

THE FRIENDSHIP OF CYRUS

Callicratidas' death at Arginusae in 406 brought an end to the most vigorous Spartan offensive in Ionia since 412. The campaign had been financed by Sparta's Ionian allies, and its collapse left the future of Spartan operations in the Aegean in doubt. Chios was again put under a tight blockade by Conon and his colleagues. Over the winter of 406/5, the Athenian blockade nearly succeeded in forcing an insurrection among the hungry and underpaid troops of the Spartans on Chios. Meanwhile, the Ionians supporting Sparta found themselves even less able to contribute to the Spartan war effort than they had been to support Athens earlier. Many among the wealthy living on the Asiatic coast recalled fondly the close cooperation between Lysander and Cyrus nearly two years earlier that had enriched rather than impoverished them while building up a navy. A delegation of Ionians supported by Cyrus' emissaries requested that the Spartans send Lysander again as naval commander. Irregular though a second command was, the Spartans made it possible for Lysander to return to Ephesus. During the winter of 406/5, Lysander was once again assembling a navy and preparing to confront the Athenians at sea.[1]

Cyrus now could not be as openhanded now as he had been two years before, upon his arrival in Ionia. Either because of the constraints on his resources, or by reason of the king's policy, Cyrus could provide only the barest funding for Lysander's fleet. The advice of Alcibiades, to keep both sides in a state of neediness, may have gained a hearing at court, so that Darius did not wish to sponsor the Spartans generously. The most likely means by which Darius could maintain such a balance was to restrict Cyrus' resources while allowing Tissaphernes to provide limited support to the Athenians. Indeed, Cyrus at Sardis and Tissaphernes in Caria were territorial rivals with conflicting allegiances among the Greeks; such conditions could only persist if Darius wished them to. But the mortality of kings meant that these conditions could change. By uncanny fortune, in spring 405 Lysander found himself the beneficiary of a windfall, again the product of Persian dynastic intrigues.

Early in 405, Cyrus was summoned to the deathbed of his father, who wanted to resolve relations between his sons and to secure the succession for the eldest, Artaxerxes. Cyrus, however, was hopeful that his mother's influence would prevail in his favor. Wishing to leave no rival behind him, Cyrus invited Tissaphernes to accompany him, "on the pretense that he was his friend" (*hôs philon,* according to Xenophon). Tissaphernes, for his part, would not want to be overlooked in the dispositions to be made, and may also have been summoned as a true friend and ally of his brother-in-law, Artaxerxes.[2]

Not wanting to allow any Persian underling to turn against him in his absence, Cyrus apportioned a significant part of the affairs of his province to the most dependent of his personal friends, the Spartan, Lysander. Before his departure, Cyrus called Lysander to Sardis, explained the circumstances, and cautioned him not to move against the Athenians without gathering superior forces. He advised him that soon enough the king's resources would be at his disposal. In the meantime, he left Lysander in charge of the revenues of the cities of his province.[3]

Darius died and was succeeded by his eldest son, Artaxerxes II, sometime within the Babylonian year that began April 21, 405, and ended on April 10, 404. The death of Darius has been placed by some scholars late in that year, in early spring 404, but for insufficient reasons. A series of events transpiring in the summer of 405 indicate that a shift in Persian alignments had already taken place. It is most probable that Darius' death came early in Artaxerxes' accession year, in the spring of 405, and not a year after the brothers had been summoned to their father's bedside.[4]

Shortly after Artaxerxes became king, Tissaphernes denounced Cyrus for plotting against his brother. Cyrus was arrested and imprisoned, and may have been in danger of being put to death until his mother obtained his release. The eclipse of Cyrus was an event that must soon have become widely known. It marked a drastic reversal of fortune for Lysander. This explains why, early in the summer of 405, Lysander launched an aggressive campaign that both ignored Cyrus' caution and did violence to towns within Tissaphernes' satrapy in Caria. Already, in the summer of 405, Lysander knew that the windfall he had received from Cyrus would not last, and that Tissaphernes was the open enemy of his patron.[5]

Lysander's first move in spring 405 was to support a murderous conspiracy to establish a pro-Spartan oligarchy at Miletus. Lysander thus gained control of a town that had been in the hands of a *demos* that must have been backed by Tissaphernes. Miletus was probably claimed by Cyrus, and Lysander may have intervened there in the name of Cyrus. But Lysander's next moves were openly hostile to Tissaphernes. Lysander proceeded by sea into Tissaphernes' Carian satrapy, where he sacked towns allied to Athens along the coast of the Ceramic Gulf. Captives from these plundered towns were sold into slavery, possibly in the course of the stop Lysander made next at Rhodes.

"Unable," as Plutarch states, "to fight a naval battle because his force was no match [for the Athenians], but also unable to sit still with so many ships at his command," Lysander then made a bold move across the Aegean, probably early in summer. Raiding islands along the way, he landed plundering parties on Aegina, Salamis, and even on the coast of Attica, where he was joined briefly by the forces from Decelea under Agis. Pursued now by the assembled Athenian fleet, Lysander evaded it and sailed north into the Hellespont. Before the Athenians could catch up with him he captured Lampsacus, a stronghold on the Asiatic side of the Hellespont in Athenian hands since 410.[6]

THE BATTLE OF AEGOSPOTAMI

The Athenian fleet arrived too late to save Lampsacus, but in time to confront Lysander's fleet. No source reports the size of Lysander's fleet, but the Athenians, with 180 ships, had more in service now than at any time since the Sicilian expedition. Lysander's fleet must have been significantly smaller, and Lysander did not put out from Lampsacus to meet the enemy.

To maintain a close blockade the Athenians drew up their ships along the shore of the Chersonese facing Lampsacus, some three miles across the waters of the Hellespont. Their position on the beach at Aegospotami, "Goat-rivers," may have been known to the Athenians as a useful position for operations against Lampsacus. One of the Athenian generals, Menander, had served with Alcibiades five years earlier when Lampsacus was captured. Operations at that time had involved between 30 and 50 ships and were carried out, after Mindarus' fleet had been destroyed, without naval opposition. The tactical situation now was different, and, more importantly, the logistical situation was a challenge on a completely different order of magnitude.[7]

The beach at Aegospotami lay some twelve miles up the Hellespont from Sestos, the nearest town able to provide a market for the 36,000 men of the Athenian forces. The Athenians had taken on provisions at Sestos before arriving at Aegospotami, and so they had food sufficient for at least a few days on the beach. Besides foodstuffs, however, water and fuel for campfires had to be gathered daily. After putting out to sea in the Hellespont each day to offer battle, the crews had to send their foraging parties ever farther afield at the end of the day before evening meals could be prepared. Lysander, meanwhile, was well supplied from Lampsacus. He held his crews ready at their oars all day long each day, and did not allow his men to disembark until his scout ships reported that the Athenians were making camp for the evening.

The presence of these great fleets in the Hellespont drew the attention of Alcibiades, who had been maintaining himself as a warlord serving Seuthes, chieftain of the Odrysian Thracians. In the eyes of Seuthes and his Thracians, war among the neighboring Greeks brought opportunities to plunder rich targets. Such circumstances now also presented Alcibiades with a singular opportunity, in the words of Diodorus, "to achieve by his own efforts some great success for his country and through his benefactions to bring the people back to their old affection for him."

All accounts of Aegospotami report a conference between Alcibiades and the Athenian generals on the eve of the battle, most of them to the effect that Alcibiades foresaw the vulnerability of their position and advised them to move their camp to Sestos. According to Diodorus and Plutarch, the conference included an offer by Alcibiades to bring his Thracian allies into action in an assault on Lysander's camp by land if the generals would ferry them across the Hellespont and coordinate an attack by sea. Whatever the substance of the conference, the generals rejected the proposals of Alcibiades, allegedly on the grounds that success would be credited to him, while failure would be theirs.[8]

At the end of the fifth day of the stand-off, when the deficiencies of the Athenian arrangements were becoming noticeable, Lysander attacked. When his scout ships signaled that the Athenian crews were dispersing ashore, Lysander sent his men into action. The rowers of the Athenian fleet, meanwhile, were probably preoccupied with beating other crews in the race for fuel and water rather than concerned about the enemy. Their disarray can only have increased by the unexpected attack. Lysander relied on these factors to turns the odds for success in his favor.

As Lysander closed with the beached Athenians, Xenophon reports, "some of the ships had only two banks of oars manned, some only one, and some were not manned at all." Lysander had a landing force of infantry ready to attack the Athenians ashore while most of his ships took up the task of fixing grappling hooks on Athenian ships, dragging many away from the beach. The Athenians were utterly routed, and most of their men soon abandoned all efforts to fight and scattered ashore. No more than twelve ships, one of them commanded by Conon, were able to put out in sufficient order to avoid Lysander's attack. After raiding Lysander's camp on the opposite shore, Conon with the majority of the surviving ships set sail for the security of Athens' ally on Cyprus, Euagoras of Salamis. Two others, including the state trireme, *Paralus,* sailed directly to Athens with news of the disaster.[9]

Among the many captives taken by Lysander's men were 3,000 to 4,000 Athenians, including most of their generals. Anger among Lysander's allies against the Athenians prompted harsh measures. The Athenians had previously massacred some captured crews and had announced their intention of cutting off the right thumb (some sources say right hand) of every sailor who fought against them. For these outrages the Athenian captives were condemned en masse and were put to death, beginning with the general, Philocles, who had advocated the terror tactic. Only Adeimantus was spared, reportedly because he alone among the generals had opposed the measure.[10]

CONON, CYPRUS, AND THE NEW KING

The one general to emerge unscathed from catastrophe at Aegospotami was Conon son of Timotheus. His destination upon leaving the Hellespont was Cyprus, but no source explains why he should have looked immediately to the court of Euagoras for a warm welcome. Euagoras at the time was well-disposed toward Athens, and had even been awarded Athenian citizenship, but the reasons for this close bond have remained obscure.

We would have a clearer understanding of the relationship between Euagoras and Athens if an Athenian inscription honoring him had survived in a less fragmentary condition. Much of this inscription is formulaic and its purport can be made out, but gaps in the portions that refer to particular arrangements are frustrating. The greatest handicap is the absence of the archon's name which would date the transactions. Scholars have usually placed it between 411 and 407, but there are strong reasons to place it in 405, where it would be among the last public decrees before the disaster at Aegospotami overtook the Athenians.[11]

The most striking feature of this inscription is its reference to "the king," certainly the Persian king, in a context that apparently numbers him among the allies of the Athenians. Tissaphernes is also named in this context, and the natural inference is that the Athenians were announcing their gratitude to Euagoras for, among other things, facilitating an alliance with the king that involved the mediation of Tissaphernes. Obstacles to an alliance between Athens and the Persian king were cleared away by the denunciation of Cyrus by Tissaphernes, sometime in the spring of 405. In response to the allegations of treasonous collusion between Cyrus and the Spartans, a warm reception of Athenian overtures suddenly became appropriate, and the king receiving them was Artaxerxes II.

An alliance between Artaxerxes and the Athenians, in which Euagoras was involved, was appropriate for another reason of great moment in 405. In that year the long-threatened revolt of Egypt occurred, and Euagoras on Cyprus was probably a vital link in coordinating the Persian naval response. The Athenian decree honoring Euagoras contains a reference to what are probably ships involved in some mutual arrangement between the Athenians and Euagoras. In all likelihood, Euagoras was gathering forces both to safeguard himself in the tumultuous period of Persian dynastic succession, and to make himself serviceable to his new overlord, Artaxerxes. Under such conditions, after the disaster in the Hellespont Conon knew that he could find safe haven on Cyprus with Euagoras, who had a pressing need for ships and skillful commanders, and who might be induced to return the favor of support to Athens in her hour of need.[12]

THE SIEGE OF ATHENS

At Athens, the news from Aegospotami caused grief and consternation, but not complete desperation. Prospects for Persian aid were now more tantalizing than they had been since 411, and this hope sustained the Athenians as they prepared to endure a siege. There were still Athenian triremes at

Samos, and Conon's departure for Cyprus, announced to the Athenians by the crew of the *Paralus,* might lead to the formation of a new naval force to rescue Athens. But waiting for a rescuer was all they could do, for in this emergency the Athenians were utterly without the means to reassemble a fleet on their own.[13]

Grain supply was the chief concern of the Athenians, for as long as the people had food, they had the will to wait. To the north, Lysander was taking measures to close Athens' Black Sea grain route by capturing Byzantium and Chalcedon. But the Athenians looked to friends at Cyrene in north Africa and to Euagoras on Cyprus to make up for this loss, and as a measure of public confidence they instituted the distribution of grain at public expense to those who needed it. Lysander, meanwhile, detached part of his armada of 200 triremes to place Samos under siege, and set sail for Athens. With the approach of Lysander's fleet, probably two months or more after the defeat in the Hellespont, word reached the Athenians that Lysander had announced the death penalty for anyone importing grain to Athens.[14]

This decree was prelude to an awesome show of force. Salamis was ransacked and a fleet of 150 ships sat off Piraeus, while both Spartan kings, Agis and Pausanias, brought up the full levy of the Spartans and their Peloponnesian allies and encamped on the grounds of the sanctuary and gymnasium of the Academy, a mile outside the walls of Athens. Nothing of immediate consequence resulted from this massive deployment of forces around Athens. The Spartans were not prepared to assault the defenses of Athens or Piraeus, and so they reduced their forces by land and by sea to a level suitable for maintaining a blockade.[15]

During this, the longer period of the siege of Athens in the fall and winter of 405/4, the naval blockade was only loosely maintained. Individual triremes moved in and out of Piraeus, as evidently they also did past the Spartan besiegers of Samos. More remarkably, we learn that energetic Athenians were able to hijack grain ships bound for the Peloponnesians and divert them to Athens. Such windfalls could excite hopes, but they provided no long-term solution. Eventually, the exhaustion of public grain supplies by early winter confronted the Athenians with the futility of their optimism, and negotiations with the Spartans began in earnest.[16]

NEGOTIATING WITH SPARTA

The Spartans wanted peace with an Athens stripped of her tributary subjects and compliant to Spartan leadership. The destruction of their fleet had already deprived the Athenians of power and of tributary subjects. Willing at last to acknowledge these circumstances, Athenian ambassadors brought to King Agis an offer of peace with an alliance. Agis referred the ambassadors to the authorities at Sparta, and after they redirected their mission, they were rebuffed; the offer was inadequate. The Spartans required in addition that the Athenians tear down ten stades, or a mile and a quarter, of each of their long walls between Athens and Piraeus.[17]

The Long Walls, the "legs" of Athens, as they were called, bound the city to the sea, to maritime commerce, and to naval power. They were the stays of the democracy, and, like the fortification of Athens and Piraeus built by Themistocles, their construction in the early 450s had provoked an oligarchical conspiracy among those who resented the fact that the walls would shield the Athenians from Spartan influence. Perhaps because of the political implications of these walls, Pericles' speech proposing the construction of the third and newest wall, between the widely splaying original Long Walls, stood out in Socrates' memory as a stirring rhetorical display, according to Plato's *Gorgias.* These "legs" had been punningly transformed into the titanic stance of the demagogue, Cleon, in Aristophanes' *Knights,* and magnified, through the power they implied, into a stride spanning from the Assembly at Athens to the Athenian maritime fort at Pylos. Another power metaphor transformed Athens with its three Long Walls, under the sway of Alcibiades, into the omnipotent creature, Triphales, "He of the Three Phalluses," in Aristophanes' play of that name. The Spartans now wanted to sever these limbs, and the Athenian reaction may be described as visceral.[18]

Pragmatists and Spartan sympathizers recognized the need for such a concession before peace could be made. The Council, in reviewing the ambassadors' report, accordingly formulated a recommendation that the Athenians accept these terms. But pragmatism was not the prevailing mood among the *demos* as a whole. When the proposal came up for discussion in the Assembly, Cleophon made a vehement protest against peace on the terms proposed by Sparta. To sever Athens from Piraeus was to dismember the body politic; to entertain such a notion was to contemplate subversion of the democracy. By some such argument, Cleophon passed a resolution to have Archestratus, the councilor who had made the proposal, summarily imprisoned, probably to face trial on a charge of treason. Given the currency of cutting metaphors in the rhetoric of the moment, this was probably the occasion of Cleophon's threat, recalled by Aeschines two generations later, to slit the throat of anyone who proposed such a peace with Sparta.[19]

Neither was hunger yet pressing so hard, nor was hope of rescue from abroad so far gone that the Athenians could not be persuaded to wait. Help from abroad was a concern that must have had some weight in Spartan deliberations as well, for the arrest of Cyrus meant the ascendancy of Tissaphernes, and no Greek was yet sure what effect this would have on Aegean affairs. Samos as well as Athens was withstanding a Spartan siege, and a Persian naval build-up on Cyprus kept the specter of the Persian fleet lurking in everyone's calculations. There was even the possibility that Phoenician ships serving Artaxerxes might combine with a force from Carthage, which could work to the benefit of the Athenians. The previous year, the Athenians had hospitably received a delegation of Carthaginians who were gathering support for an offensive against the Syracusans in Sicily. By the summer of 405 the Carthaginians had achieved great success, and the Athenians could hope that, if all fell into place, their enemy's enemy might now become their friend and savior.

Closer at hand, King Archelaus of Macedon had been instrumental in the emergency naval build-up achieved by the Athenians in 406. No friend to the Spartans, it was not impossible that he would be an effective ally of Athens again, if Athenian gold could reach him. Above all, Alcibiades was still watching for his opportunity. With the Spartans ascendant from Byzantium to the Hellespont, he found it safer to move across the Bosporus and employ his Odrysian friends in plundering the Bithynian Thracians in Asia Minor. From this vantage he could also maintain close contact with Pharnabazus and the developments in Persian domains.[20]

THERAMENES' SECRET

The moment was ready for the initiative of someone familiar with all possibilities, and Theramenes stepped forward. The consummate public speaker, Theramenes was also a former partner of Alcibiades in the Hellespont, had dealt with Archelaus in Macedon, and had wide experience in the Ionian theater of war. He had also been in the forefront of the oligarchic conspiracy of 411, but having turned against those who were too eager to cooperate with Sparta, he could claim that his expertise was proven to be at the service of the Athenian *demos*. Cleophon could instruct the Athenians what *not* to do; Theramenes could claim to discern best what they *could* do.

But to exercise his ability required discretion, and the people had to trust him. For, as Theramenes admitted when publicly interrogated about his plans, he had secret information that would be useful for his purpose, but useless if it were divulged publicly. With the promise that he would preserve the *demos,* Theramenes was sent to the Spartans with full authority to negotiate on behalf of the Athenians. If, as all accounts indicate, Theramenes was the sole ambassador on this mission, this was a most exceptional act of public confidence in an individual.[21]

Theramenes went first to Lysander and spent more than three months abroad in his company. Since the fate of Athens depended so much on Persian inclinations and on the fortunes of Lysander, to be in attendance on Lysander at the head of Spartan naval forces in the Aegean would be the best place to pick up news that might be parlayed into an entente on behalf of the Athenians. Theramenes surely appreciated that time was an uncertain ally to Lysander as well, and so the most effective way to reach an acceptable settlement was to know the moment when Lysander was ready to close a deal and end the standoff with Athens.

A further consideration drew Theramenes into Lysander's orbit. Around Lysander was a circle of Athenian exiles offering advice and services with a view to their aggrandizement upon the surrender of Athens. These men included several of the pro-Spartan members of the Four Hundred who had survived in exile since 411, the most prominent among whom were Aristoteles son of Timocrates and Charicles son of Apollodorus. Among those who had later joined this group was Critias son of Callaeschrus, in exile since 406 and lately active in Spartan interests in Thessaly. These men were in contact with friends and *hetairoi* still in Athens, and these links had probably contributed to the vehemence of partisan prosecutions at Athens remarked on by various sources in the years just before the surrender of Athens. Theramenes therefore was well aware of their imminent ascendancy, and knew that he needed to inject himself into their midst and make it clear that he was the agent through whom all interests would find resolution.[22]

By waiting for an advantageous moment, Theramenes was using time in a way that could only cause anxiety among the Athenians in the city. For there, especially among the poor, starvation was now taking its toll. Later accusations against Theramenes claimed that this was his intention: to weaken the Athenians until they would accept any offer he brought. But Theramenes must have been waiting for a clear sign of the directions of Persian policy before sealing the fate of Athens.[23]

The decisive moment probably came with the news that Cyrus had been pardoned by Artaxerxes and would return to his seat at Sardis. The date of Cyrus' reinstatement is unknown, but if he had been arrested no later than midsummer 405, it seems improbable that his fate would have lingered unresolved for more than a year. His return to Ionia most likely was anticipated in the spring of 404, and this would have been a discouraging sign to those Athenians who had hoped that his eclipse would bring a more complete change of Persian policy in the Aegean.[24]

It was time to resolve the crisis at Athens. It was also time to bring into play the secret that Theramenes had promised the Athenians would be so useful. No source reveals what this was, and we are left to surmise from circumstances. If Theramenes had been in a position to apply pressure on Lysander in the event of favorable news coming from Persia, he probably was in touch with the network of Athenian sympathizers around the Aegean, in Asia Minor, and on Cyprus. If, as it seems, after three months there was no relief in sight for the Athenians, Theramenes may have been willing to sacrifice some of his contacts in order to cement an agreement with Lysander on terms that he could sell to the Athenians. In the coming months Lysander would show that he knew who his covert enemies were, most infamously in a purge of Athenian supporters on Thasos. Such treachery, if it was the result of information from Theramenes, would certainly have been an earnest token to Lysander of the loyalty of the man he would rely on to lead Athens in the right direction.

In support of this explanation of Theramenes' secret, we may note that his memory was execrated especially for his readiness to turn, with the winds of fortune, against his former friends. No condemnation of Theramenes on this score was more forceful than Critias' speech, late in 404, denouncing Theramenes before other oligarchs. Few would know better what Theramenes was capable of than Critias.[25]

THE SURRENDER OF ATHENS

When Theramenes returned to Athens at the end of the winter, he assured the Athenians that the Spartans were ready to make peace, would not massacre or sell them into slavery, and would respect the integrity of the Athenian *demos*. As to the integrity of their defenses, Theramenes was probably evasive; the details awaited the outcome of a formal embassy that Lysander instructed the Athenians to send to Sparta.[26]

Theramenes was immediately appointed as one of a mission of ten ambassadors sent to Sparta to conclude an agreement on terms for peace. Lysander had already instructed the authorities at Sparta what to expect from, and presumably how to respond to, the embassy accompanying Theramenes. Among those sent by Lysander to Sparta was Aristoteles, the senior statesman of the Athenian exiles. Aristoteles' role was surely to satisfy Spartan authorities about the dispositions for a new Athenian regime that had been worked out among Lysander, the exiles, and Theramenes.[27]

Formal agreement on terms for surrender required the approval of all warring parties, and for this purpose the Spartans had to seek the endorsement of their allies. So at the same time that the Athenians were instructed, through Theramenes, to treat with authorities in Sparta, Sparta's allies were also summoned to attend the proceedings. Custom also required the approval of Apollo's oracle at Delphi, consulted at the outset of the war and now at its conclusion. Even before the surrender of Athens, the proceeds of the booty taken at Aegospotami enabled Lysander to make a handsome dedication at Delphi in his name and the names of his chief officers and allied commanders. Probably at the same time, King Agis vowed to sponsor a dedication to Apollo from the booty of Attica. Spartan influence at Delphi was thus strong at this time, especially through the personal agency of these two commanders, and they could expect Apollo's word to affirm the arrangements they intended to impose upon the defeated Athenians.[28]

The conference at Sparta proceeded according to script. Just as in the conference attending the Peace of Nicias seventeen years earlier, only the Boeotians, the Corinthians, the Megarians, and the Eleans disapproved of the proposed settlement between Sparta and Athens. On this occasion, however, the Eleans were no longer allies of Sparta and therefore had no place at the conference; the Megarians shared the views of their Corinthian and Boeotian neighbors, but may have been intimidated by Lysander into holding their peace. Only the spokesmen for Corinth and for Thebes, representing Boeotia, went on record as opposing the terms of peace proposed by the Spartans. They demanded that Athens should be destroyed, the Athenians sold into slavery, and Attica made into grazing land dedicated to Apollo. To counter these demands the Spartans presented Apollo's own advice "not to destroy the common hearth of Greece." Another dictum attributed to the Spartans on this occasion has an oracular ring: they should not "put out one of the two eyes of Greece."[29]

Oracular rhetoric aside, the Spartan position was, in Xenophon's words, that "they would not enslave a Greek city which had done such great things for Greece at the time of her supreme danger." The allusion was to the united stand of Spartans and Athenians against the invasion by Xerxes, and it had contemporary implications. The former solidarity of Sparta and Athens against Xerxes had also entailed Spartan and Athenian solidarity against Thebes. Lysander was said to have seen an obedient Athens as a valuable bulwark against Theban aggrandizement on this occasion, and the Persian threat could also not be overlooked. The Lysandrian glove over the treacherous hand of Cyrus meant that Artaxerxes would not declare himself to be the friend of Sparta as readily as had his father.[30]

With the approval of the majority of their allies, the Spartans announced their terms for making peace with the Athenians: destroy the Long Walls and Piraeus walls; surrender all ships except for a number to be decided by ambassadors on the spot; evacuate all cities and keep to their own land; receive back their exiles; govern themselves according to their ancestral constitution; have the same friends and enemies and follow the Spartans by land or by sea, wherever they might lead.[31]

Theramenes and his fellow ambassadors brought these terms back to Athens, where a heated debate followed in the Assembly. The requirement that the Athenians tear down the walls joining them to the sea still aroused impassioned objections in the name of preserving the *demos*. But Theramenes, with more conviction now after some six months of siege, could claim that tearing down the walls now was the only way to save the *demos*. The proposed terms were accepted. The peace was solemnified on the 16th of the month Munychion, in April or May of 404, when the Athenians swore an oath of allegiance to the terms of the treaty and yielded control of their ships, harbor defenses, and Long Walls to the forces of Sparta.[32]

THE AGENTS OF OLIGARCHY

Through the turmoil of surrender the Athenian administration outwardly maintained its constitutional form. When the oath of surrender was sworn, the passage into oligarchy that would later be associated with the appointment of the infamous Thirty was still some four months in the future. But it was clear to all that the transition had begun even before Theramenes returned from Sparta and before the future leaders of the Thirty returned from exile. In anticipation of the change, the supporters of oligarchy and alliance with Sparta began to arrest, try, and execute the most outspoken of their opponents. Even before the surrender, Xenophon reports, Athens was in the grips of "a kind of *stasis*."[33]

The first victim of the movement into oligarchy was its most outspoken opponent, Cleophon. His demise was effected through the authority of the Council, and it was facilitated by the *nomothetai,* the standing commission for the revision of the laws. Cleophon was indicted by Satyrus, a member of the Council and future officer of the Thirty, for failure to report to night quarters for guard duty. Under siege conditions, this was tantamount to a charge of desertion in the face of the enemy, punishable by death. The case against Cleophon was heard before a jury-court, but the disposition of the jury was assured by a statute that Nicomachus, one of the *nomothetai,* was required to display. The statute probably required the Council to support the prosecution of anyone accused of endangering the *demos,* and probably empowered the Council to assess the penalty in the event of a guilty verdict. Tried in such a hostile setting, Cleophon was condemned and executed.[34]

At about the same time, rooting about among the legal instruments under the scrutiny of the *nomothetai* produced the basis for indicting Callixeinus and four of his associates, the councilors of the previous year most responsible for the measures leading to the condemnation of the generals of Arginusae. After bail was posted for them by their supporters, Xenophon reports, these men managed to flee Athens in the course of the *stasis* that beset the city. Thus the more fortunate among the victims of the oligarchic conspirators found refuge in exile even before the surrender was formalized.[35]

The democratic Council, and laws from the era of Pericles and Cleon intended to compel the prosecution of men who obstructed the business of the people, now became the tools of partisans working to undermine popular government. Selective use of specific laws was by now stock-in-trade for all active office-seekers, and on the eve of surrender to Sparta the balance of interests had tipped decisively in favor of men who looked forward to the changes to come. As in 411, the institutions of the democracy were proving serviceable for its undoing. But in 404 the process was underway with the full knowledge of hindsight, and with the added irony that the board of *nomothetai* had labored for years to recommend to the *demos* only laws consonant with the sovereignty of the people. In fact, the laws were no more than the instruments of sovereign authority, however it may be defined. To the extent that the Athenians entrusted executive and judicial initiative to the Council and its committees, as they often did in times of emergency, they were surrendering popular authority to bodies whose memberships could be controlled by interests other than those of the *demos* at large.[36]

Notionally representative of all Athenians, as a body the Council was always predisposed to identify itself with the aristocratic ideals embraced by the democracy. Through deliberate means, by 405/4 this inclination of ideals had been converted into a definite ideological bias.

Despite the role of the lot in determining membership, the Council was not a random demographic sample of citizenry. Candidates for allotment had to win, by formal or informal means, the approval of their fellow demesmen through a process that must have resembled the judgmental enrollment of the Five Thousand in 411. By peer pressure and collusion with deme officials, it was not difficult to influence the selection candidates. The exclusion of undesirables by an organized opposition may have been the most effective way of shaping the membership of the Council. Any allotted candidate could be challenged, and his candidacy would then become subject to judicial review before the Council. The business of attacking undesirables was the self-appointed task of members of the *hetaireiai,* the aristocratic groups who arranged to support friends and associates and to waylay their enemies along the avenues to office-holding. As noted in the previous chapter, the last few years before the defeat and surrender of Athens were notorious for the excesses of partisan prosecutions. By the time the Council of 405/4 was seated, as events confirm, the politics of elimination were having their effect on the balance of political sympathies among office-holders.[37]

With the surrender of Athens in the spring of 404 and the return of the pro-Spartan exiles, the process of controlling executive authority at Athens entered a new phase. When it came time for candidates for the Council of 404/3 to be preselected, the contemporary Lysias informs us that the conveners of the tribal assemblies, where nominees from the demes were put forward for allotment, were hand-picked by five "ephors," who were a sort of steering committee composed by the leadership of the pro-oligarchic *hetaireiai.* It would have been shocking if this group had actually adopted the Spartan title "ephors" while they were in operation. The title was probably given to them by their enemies after the effects of their doings had become apparent. Lysias' mention of Critias as one of the "ephors," soon to show himself as the most notorious Laconophile among the returned exiles, likewise cast a sinister light over the group from the viewpoint of those who knew what happened next. However they were perceived at the time, it is clear that the process of screening candidates for office in the summer of

404 was subject to scrutiny according to more openly and aggressively oligarchic criteria than was customarily the case. It was in this process that Lysias located the beginning of open *stasis* at Athens.[38]

AGAIN, THE ANCESTRAL CONSTITUTION

While the democracy was being forced by procrustean means into an oligarchic frame of mind, debate raged about the *patrios politeia,* the ancestral constitution of the Athenians that Theramenes had promised to preserve by the agreement negotiated with the Spartans. More than any other issue, the nature of this debate has been obscured by the retrospective accounts of orators and historians who sought to lay blame on certain individuals or groups for the cold-blooded violence that soon took hold of Athens in the name of the *patrios politeia.* Contradictions among the partial and tendentious accounts inspire little confidence in any one of them, and modern historians have often chosen to follow the collective judgment of antiquity and reduce the narrative of events to the story of the momentary sway of unscrupulous and bloodthirsty oligarchs followed by the resurgent triumph of democracy. This account best served to clear the conscience of the generation who lived through these events, which is why it quickly became the dominant narrative. Yet the failure of this story to explain adequately the role of the Spartans at certain stages, and especially the enduring problem of accounting for the ambiguous role of Theramenes, together betoken the inadequacy of the conventional story. As they were experienced, events were judged rather differently than they were even a year or two later.[39]

All hopes and fears for the fate of their city focused on the interpretation of the *patrios politeia* guaranteed to the Athenians by the terms of their surrender. Aristotle's *Constitution of the Athenians,* probably reflecting the *Atthis* of Androtion son of Andron, written a generation after the events of 404, describes the partisan divisions in interpretation that came to the surface over that summer:

> After they had made peace on the condition that they would govern themselves according to their ancestral constitution *(patrios politeia),* the champions of the people *(hoi demotikoi)* tried to preserve the democracy *(ho demos),* while among respectable Athenians *(hoi gnorimoi),* those who were members of the *hetaireiai* and those among the exiles who had returned after the peace was made wanted oligarchy, while those who had formed no *hetaireia,* but were otherwise regarded as inferior to no citizen, pursued the ancestral constitution. Among these were Archinus, Anytus, Cleitophon, Phormisius, and many others, foremost among whom was Theramenes.

Transparent here is a bias in favor of Theramenes and those "respectable Athenians" who were "otherwise regarded as inferior to no citizen," a bias that Androtion must have shared with his father, Andron, who had composed the indictment of Antiphon, a leader among *hetaireiai*, in 411. The "respectable" men who were at the center of no *hetaireia*, according to this passage, were those who truly aimed at what the Athenians had agreed upon with the Spartans, namely government according to their "ancestral constitution." Yet the passage offers no definition of this constitution, other than to associate it with a group of named individuals ("and many others") and to indicate the extremes that it avoided.[40]

In fact, *patrios politeia* was a polysemous slogan, and all parties, from *hoi demotikoi* to the openly oligarchic-minded among "respectable Athenians," must have identified *themselves* as champions of the particular form of constitution that they felt to be the true patrimony of the Athenians. Champions of the *demos* argued that complete democracy, the legacy of Themistocles and Pericles, *was* the "ancestral constitution" of the Athenians. Themistocles and Pericles, the chief architects of Athenian greatness, could be numbered among the lawgivers *(nomothetai)* of Athens, and the proof of their wisdom was evident to many. Oligarchs argued that the enactments of such men had perverted the more ancient laws and practices of the age of Solon and earlier, when office and authority was the exclusive reserve of "respectable Athenians." Among themselves, and in the straits to which Athens had been reduced, the folly of mob-pleasing imperialism was self-evident. Among the men who sought both truth and practicable policy in some middle ground was Cleitophon, singled out the year before by Aristophanes as the close associate of Theramenes. Cleitophon had already distinguished himself on the eve of the oligarchy of 411 by proposing that the "the ancestral laws established by Cleisthenes," chronologically intermediate between Solon and Themistocles, should be studied as a guide to what was both ancestral *and* democratic.[41]

Despite the elimination of Cleophon, a sizable element among the citizenry were still outraged by the terms of surrender imposed on Athens through Theramenes. The Athenians had long been taught, most eloquently by Pericles, that their walls were the basis of their freedom, without which they were liable to be enslaved by the Spartans; more to the point, they knew from their own practices what it meant to strip a defeated enemy of his walls. Plutarch preserves an exchange, from the debate in the Assembly on the terms of surrender, between an otherwise unknown demagogue, Cleomenes, and Theramenes. When asked by Cleomenes how he could dare to act and speak contrary to Themistocles by surrendering to the Spartans the walls that Themistocles had built against the wishes of the Spartans, Theramenes replied:

> In fact, young man, I am doing nothing contrary to Themistocles. For the very walls that he built for the preservation of our citizens we are taking down

> for their preservation. If walls brought prosperity to cities, then Sparta, which has no walls, would surely fare worst of all.

After the surrender, this issue continued to rankle. For once the walls were actually torn down there could be no second thoughts. Lysias claims, plausibly in this case, that many felt that better terms could be wrung from the Spartans. Better terms had been offered a few months earlier; Samos still held out against Lysander, and some still saw the prospect of help from friends of Athens abroad.[42]

Such defiant sentiments could only be aired in the Assembly, for by controlling the procedures for nomination and allotment of archons and councilors, by early summer the oligarchic conspirators had taken effective control of the Council and of all magistracies. The only offices beyond their grasp were the military commands, since these were elected directly by the Assembly. Having the authority to convene the Assembly, but lacking the ability to impose their will there, the oligarchs were deadlocked. The generals and divisional commanders, men who had been elected for their devotion to the visions articulated by Cleophon, were able to coordinate obstructive action in various ways against those who wished to move ahead in compliance with Sparta. Certainly, their authority in military matters gave them the legal standing, when backed by their popular standing, to prevent any movement to begin dismantling walls. As will be shown below, these men were evidently active by covert means as well, through intermediaries abroad, seeking a way to overturn the Theramenean settlement.[43]

BREAKING THE BACK OF THE DEMOCRACY

Enforcement of the terms of surrender, in particular, the requirement that the Athenians tear down their Long Walls and Piraeus walls, required the suppression of all politically effective democratic sentiment. In the summer of 404, the champions of this sentiment were the democratically elected generals and military officers. Among these men were Eucrates son on Niceratus, brother of the famous Nicias; Strombichides son of Diotimus, who had been a general with the democratic faction at Samos in 411; Dionysodorus, about whom more will be said below; and Calliades, who had been a general assigned elsewhere at the time of Arginusae. The deeds and fate of these and "many other good men," who, at the end of summer 404, were to become the first victims of the anti-democratic purge carried out by the Thirty, are known only through references made years later in the speeches of Lysias. In each case, Lysias raises their memory as martyrs for democracy, but says little about their deeds or the circumstances of their trial execution, with one exception.[44]

Some five years after the reign of the Thirty, Lysias composed a speech on behalf of a kinsman of Dionysodorus for the prosecution of one Agoratus, identified as the chief informant against the generals, officers, and their supporters. Amid the many circumstantial details mentioned in this speech it is remarkable, and no doubt significant, that the specific offense in which Agoratus and the generals were implicated is never discussed. Lysias only notes that Agoratus' testimony was sufficient to secure the arrest and execution of these men on a charge of "plotting against [the Athenian] populace." Lysias notes the irony of such a charge against men generally regarded as martyrs for the democracy, but he makes it clear that under the conditions then prevailing, this was the purport of the charge by which the Council was able to persuade the Athenian public to authorize the arrest of these men.[45]

Agoratus himself had been denounced by others and, implicated along with the generals in certain unmentioned actions, he was generally regarded as an unwilling informer (although it was important to Lysias' case to argue that Agoratus' claim of duress was a sham). Other men of standing among the Athenians, sympathetic to the cause in which he and the generals were involved, attempted to help Agoratus flee by ship from Athens before he could be forced to testify. It was thus evident to all concerned that the charge involved a widespread conspiracy to oppose the government as constituted by the Council and magistrates, and that the charge was based on such irrefutable evidence that even the Assembly, wherever its sympathies might lie, would not be able to overlook the matter.

Knowing that they would likely find only popular opposition to any other deliberative issue set before the Assembly, the oligarchic leaders of the Council of 404/3 did not convene the Athenian *demos* until it was instructed to meet to hear testimony on this matter. The Council may have offered a public pretext for the lack of meetings: the regular meeting place of the Assembly, on the Pnyx hill above the Agora, was closed for reconstruction. This project had probably been in planning since 408/7, but delayed because of financial stringencies by 407/6; now it became convenient to begin work. With the regular meeting place inaccessible, the Assembly was convened in the theater of Munychia, in Piraeus. Significantly, this new venue put it in the presence of the Spartan occupying force. Thus placed in unusual surroundings, and mindful of the presence of a new form of power at Athens, the Assembly heard the formal denunciation of the generals and officers, and it passed a resolution calling for their trial. The conspiracy of the generals had become the issue by which the oligarchic planners finally succeeded in bending the *demos* to their will.[46]

Agoratus' deposition to the Council, later repeated before the Assembly, was "the cause of all the evils that befell the city," according to Lysias' speech (13.33, 48). Supported by the testimony of other informers, it broke open a seam within the circle of supporters of the Periclean *politeia* that was even more divisive than their opposition to oligarchy. Yet we are given no clue to the substance of the charge against the generals. When, a few years later, scores came due for settlement, the villainy of the oligarchs was so overpowering that it was possible to leave the issues opened by Agoratus' testimony hidden in its shadow. What unmentionable circumstance could have so pitted democrat against democrat?

Only rival personal ambitions and allegiances, which, as Thucydides remarked, were the downfall of many an oligarchic conspiracy, could have had such a divisive effect among men otherwise united in their resistance to the friends of Sparta at Athens. Personal loyalties, absolutely compelling in the heat of action, were also a matter that could later be denied or recast in light of the outcome of events. In view of the radical swings in public policy brought about by rival ambitions in the previous decade, and under the circumstances of summer 404, it is most likely that the conspiracy of the generals and officers unraveled when Agoratus revealed undeniable links between them and Alcibiades.

Among the officers accused of conspiracy, Strombichides and Dionysodorus are known to have had links to the circle of Alcibiades' friends and kinsmen. The bond with Strombichides seems to have been particularly close: his father, Diotimus, who had once served on an embassy to the Persian court at Susa, was almost certainly the Diotimus who exchanged oaths with Pharnabazus on Alcibiades' behalf in 409. Other men implicated had connections with centers of Athenian support abroad. Among those executed as partners in the conspiracy, Lysias names Hippias of Thasos and Xenophon of Curium, both of whom may have had active ties to their native lands. The readiness of prominent Athenians to smuggle Agoratus out of Piraeus by ship before he could be forced to testify likewise suggests that the conspirators and their supporters had connections abroad. Finally, Agoratus was known to have devoted himself to the cause of Alcibiades. For Agoratus was among those who had taken part in the assassination in 411 of Phrynichus, a committed enemy of Alcibiades. In spring 409, when Alcibiades' reputation was being restored at Athens, Agoratus was among those given public honors for their role in the assassination of Phrynichus. Agoratus' one-time covert loyalties were thus a matter of public record.[47]

Altogether, these circumstances indicate that the conspiracy to which Agoratus was forced to testify, and for which the officers and their supporters were indicted, consisted of communications with Alcibiades and others working to oppose the Spartans abroad. Such communications were hostile to the interests of the Council and the magistracies it controlled, and hostile to the treaty that bound Athens to Sparta. Therefore, in the eyes of the Council and in the legal terms imposed by the treaty with Sparta, these men were guilty of "wrongdoings harmful to the interests of your *demos*" (Lysias 13.51).

In the eyes of the democracy restored after the fall of the Thirty, the intentions of Dionysodorus and his colleagues were honorable. But since all efforts to resist Sparta in the summer of 404 were crushed, and especially since Alcibiades ultimately failed to rescue Athens, it benefited Lysias' case to omit all mention of Alcibiades.

Hints of the frustrated conspiracy are found in the closing passages of Plutarch's biography of Alcibiades, where Plutarch attests the moods that prevailed at Athens over the summer of 404. As often, especially when describing a decisive turn of events, his account shifts between a sequential narrative and a description of regrets felt in retrospect, when the significance of events later became clear. Yet within this shifting perspective we can recognize the circumstances described above:

> The Athenians were greatly depressed at the loss of their supremacy. But when Lysander robbed them of their freedom too, and handed them over to thirty men, then, their cause being lost, their eyes were opened to the course they would not take when salvation was yet in their power.... [The expulsion of Alcibiades after the battle of Notium is remembered.] And yet, in spite of their present plight, a vague hope still prevailed that the cause of Athens was not wholly lost so long as Alcibiades was alive. He had not, in times past, been satisfied to live his exile's life in idleness and quiet; not now, if his means allowed, would he tolerate the insolence of the Lacedaemonians and the madness of the Thirty.
>
> It was not strange that the multitude indulged in such dreams, when even the Thirty were moved to anxious thought and inquiry, and made the greatest account of what Alcibiades was planning and doing. Finally, Critias tried to make it clear to Lysander that as long as Athens was a democracy the Lacedaemonians could not have safe rule over Hellas; and that Athens, even though she were very peacefully and well disposed towards oligarchy, would not be suffered, while Alcibiades was alive, to remain undisturbed in her present condition....[48]

The link between Alcibiades, empire, and democracy was never more directly expressed than in this passage. Such thoughts, as Plutarch describes them, haunted the Thirty for some time after they came to power at the end of summer 404. But, as Plutarch's wording reveals, Critias' advice to Lysander was first given *before* the decisive suppression of democracy at Athens that came with the election of the Thirty. As we will see in the final section of this chapter, it required the close collaboration of Critias and Lysander to bring this issue to a head and to achieve the results that both intended.

PULLING OUT THE ROOTS OF EMPIRE

Late in summer 404, Samos finally succumbed to the pressures of siege and surrendered to Lysander. The fall of this last remaining bastion of Athenian support in the Aegean marked the very end of the Athenian empire and set in motion the final demise of democracy at Athens as well. For immediately after settling the affairs of Samos, Lysander sailed to Athens, in September 404, and oversaw the establishment of an oligarchic government that came to be known, after its most powerful committee, as the Thirty. The establishment of the Thirty will be discussed in the next chapter. Here it remains to trace the connection between the fall of Samos and the end of democratic defiance of Sparta at Athens.[49]

The arrest of the generals and their supporters at Athens, as a result of the testimony of Agoratus, took place on the eve of Lysander's arrival at the end of summer. So Lysias describes events:

> For it was just when those persons had been arrested and imprisoned that Lysander sailed into your harbours, that your ships were surrendered to the Lacedaemonians, that the walls were demolished, that the Thirty were established, and that every conceivable misery befell the city.

Time, in such a partisan account, is often compressed to suggest a closer relationship between events than actually existed, and accounts of the various stages of surrender and suppression of democracy at Athens in 404 suffer notoriously in this respect. But in this case, Lysias' account has every likelihood of being accurate. The Assembly that met near the harbor in Munychia to hear the charges against the generals was probably no more than a few days prior to the more famous meeting of the Assembly in the same place, attended by Lysander, at which the Thirty were elected. Like the Assembly of the previous spring, where Theramenes persuaded the Athenians to accept the Spartan terms of surrender, this, too, was a meeting "concerning the peace." For Lysander had arrived to declare the Athenians in violation of their treaty, and to threaten them with the consequences of renewed war. This time the threat served an additional purpose: besides enforcing compliance with the treaty, it served to destroy popular resistance to the oligarchs.[50]

The fall of Samos had provided the tools Lysander needed to crush democratic opposition at Athens. Not only did it free the bulk of his armament to make an intimidating show of force, it also put into his hands men who had been trying to coordinate a larger campaign to oppose Sparta. The democratic Samian leaders were steadfast supporters of the Athenian *demos*. They and their associates were well known to Athenian leadership, certainly known to Theramenes. The identities and intrigues of key individuals among the Samians were probably part of information that Theramenes had used, earlier that spring, to barter his standing with Lysander and the Athenian oligarchs. Upon the surrender of Samos, Lysander probably had many of these men executed as soon as they were in his power. But one, at least, was more useful to Lysander alive. For one man connected to the fall of Samos proved to be the key to forcing Agoratus to testify, which in turn was the undoing of the most devoted supporters of democracy at Athens.[51]

The man who denounced Agoratus was, according to Lysias, "Theocritus, the man called 'the son of Elaphostictus,' ... a comrade and intimate of Agoratus." Elaphostictus is a nickname, meaning "bearing a deer-mark." A deer was one of the emblems of Artemis of Ephesus, and the "deer-mark" was almost certainly the brand of a slave or captive dedicated to the great goddess of Ephesus. Ephesus was the chief base for Lysander's operations against Samos, and the most likely occasion for such a branding was upon the surrender of Samos to Lysander.[52]

Xenophon informs us that, upon the surrender of Samos, Lysander allowed all free men *(eleutheroi)* to depart, while all else fell into his control. Spartans had a different concept than Athenians of who was truly *eleutheros* and who was a slave. Moreover, Lysander's vindictiveness in the disposal of Athenian captives was encouraged by, among other things, the practices of the Athenians themselves. When Samos had fallen to Athens after its revolt of 440/39, the branding of Samian captives with the owl of Athena had been a notorious act of the Athenians, so that when Lysander at length restored the fortunes of Samian oligarchs, the indignity of branding was probably generally inflicted upon Athenians captured at Samos. Among those who may have protested their segregation among those destined to be branded and sold as slaves, Theocritus was probably offered an opportunity to prove that he was, in truth, *eleutheros,* by freely doing a deed that would prove himself "worthy" *(chrestos)*. Theocritus' nickname, then, is probably a figurative allusion to the fact that he was a captive who had narrowly escaped being branded with the mark of Artemis of Ephesus.[53]

With Theocritus, Lysander had secured the man who could implicate Agoratus before the Council at Athens. Agoratus, because of his complicity and his standing as a hero of the democracy, was a valuable witness to turn. For through him the Council could acquire an authoritative deposition naming many men involved in a plot that reached from Athens to Samos and Thasos, probably to Cyprus, and certainly to Alcibiades. The value of this testimony was not the list of names itself, for Lysander and his Athenian allies already knew who their enemies were. Its value was as a legal instrument that would compel a democratically constituted court to pass judgment against these men, and thus, in effect, to condemn democracy itself. All of this was orchestrated, in communications between the Athenian oligarchs and Lysander, between the fall of Samos and Lysander's arrival in Athens.

With the ground so well prepared in advance, Lysander issued an ultimatum to the Athenians from his seat of command at Samos:

> ... he sent word to the people that he had caught the city violating the terms of its surrender; for its walls were still standing, although the days were past within which they should have been pulled down; he should therefore present their case anew for the decision of the authorities, since they had broken their agreements.[54]

Receipt of this ultimatum required a meeting of the Assembly in order to deliberate upon an appropriate response. This was perhaps the first Assembly convened by the Council of 404/3, for by virtue of Lysander's threat the Athenians were at last required to give ear to the advice presented by their Council. The carefully prepared indictments of the generals brought forth by the Council constituted their recommendation to the *demos:* the Athenians must absolve themselves of the guilt charged by Lysander by arresting and trying the men responsible for the violation of the terms of surrender.

All came to pass as the Athenian oligarchs desired because they, and Lysander, had known exactly whom to pressure into providing key testimony. The targets of that testimony, in addition to the generals and their supporters at Athens, were key individuals who were still at large outside of Attica and beyond the grasp of Lysander and the Spartans. Among these other "enemies of the people" condemned at the start of the regime of the Thirty were Thrasybulus, Anytus, and Alcibiades. The synchronism of their condemnation with the sentencing of the generals was not coincidental, for all had been named as conspirators against "the interests of your *demos.*" The condemnation of all of these men, in Athens and abroad, was an act of compliance with the obligation of the Athenians "to have the same friends and enemies" as the Spartans. Administered by Lysander and his Athenian partners, it was the *coup de grâce* for the democracy and for the empire of Athens.[55]

CHAPTER NINE

The Athenian Civil War, 404–403

Critias tried to make it clear to Lysander that as long as Athens was a democracy the Lacedaemonians could not have safe rule over Hellas.

PLUTARCH *ALCIBIADES* 38.3

Cut off from the roots of her empire and forced into compliance with the might of Sparta, Athens entered a strange period of transformation. It was marked throughout by violence: judicial violence at first; by the end, the violence of open civil war. Judicial violence had been a feature of democracy, so it was impossible to recognize this development, at the outset of the regime known as the Thirty, as the harbinger of more fundamental change. For months, in fact, no small number of Athenians viewed the regime as a corrective to the degenerate influence of men who for years had been the willing slaves of the *demos* rather than its rightful masters.

This inversion of the customary relations of power at Athens was made possible only by Spartan support of the rule of the Thirty. Some saw what this meant from the first, and still more came to realize, as events unfolded, the implications of the new roots of power for the administration of Athens. For, after years of private admiration of Spartan discipline, the Thirty were given the opportunity to put Spartan ideals into Athenian practice.

Herein lies the strangest feature of this episode: Athens became Spartan. But in the course of this radical transformation a struggle emerged over the rightful form of Spartan Athens. Although the civil war that eventually erupted in 403 was later viewed as the struggle of democracy against oligarchy, the issues perceived at the time were more complex. The conflict was shaped by factions seeking to accommodate Sparta in different ways. In the end, the civil war was won by the Athenian faction championed by the Spartan king, Pausanias, against the Athenian faction that had been created by Lysander.

FREEDOM AND SLAVERY

The arrival of Lysander at Piraeus near the end of summer 404 was a splendid, awful event. It stood out in the memory of the supporters of Sparta as the climax of a triumphal procession, starting from the capture of Samos and culminating with the humbling of the Athenians. Lysander arrived at Piraeus with a hundred ships, according to Diodorus. These comprised the portion of his allied contingents that, along with trophies, booty, and the remainder of the revenues granted by Cyrus, Lysander was conveying homeward after the surrender of Samos. At Athens, Xenophon notes, he acquired additional trophies in the form of triremes, or perhaps their severed rams, taken from the Athenians.[1]

For the Athenians, Lysander's arrival marked the beginning of their "enslavement" to Sparta, an event that Pericles had warned would come if ever Athens yielded to Spartan demands. As Aristotle succinctly notes, this was the occasion when "Lysander lent his weight to the oligarchic faction, and the frightened *demos* was compelled to elect the oligarchy." Accompanied by his staff officers, Lysander appeared before the Assembly meeting in Munychia, where, as described in the previous chapter, the agenda had been prepared well in advance by his supporters in the Athenian Council. Lysander's purpose was to compel the Assembly to accept the proposals put forward by their Council. He did so by threatening the Athenians with dire consequences if they did not comply with the terms of their surrender. The Athenians had not torn down their walls as the treaty required; therefore, if they did not immediately comply, Lysander promised to revive discussion among Sparta's allies of the option previously rejected, namely, the proposal of Erianthus of Thebes that the entire city be razed and the Athenians sold into slavery.[2]

Accounts vary concerning the Athenian response at this emotionally charged moment. Disagreement centers on the leadership of Theramenes, who once again stood forth as chief spokesman for the Athenians. Diodorus represents the tradition favorable to Theramenes, describing him as the defender of Athenian autonomy in the face of Lysander's threats. As a result of Theramenes' protests, the Athenians nominally retained the right to govern themselves, although in fact their choices were reduced to only those presented by the oligarchic faction and tolerated by Lysander. Lysias, writing for an audience unsympathetic to Theramenes' memory, depicts him as the arch-conspirator through whom all was brought to pass according to the wishes of Lysander and the opponents of democracy. Lysias explains the transaction in terms designed to save face for those Athenians still ill at ease about their participation in these events:

> Then all the good *(agathoi)* citizens in the Assembly, perceiving the plot that had been hatched for their compulsion, either remained there and kept quiet, or took themselves off, conscious at least of this—that they had voted nothing harmful to the city. But some few, of base nature *(poneroi)* and evil purpose, raised their hands in favor of the commands that had been given.[3]

The Assembly passed a proposal prepared by Dracontides to elect a commission of thirty, "who will compile the ancestral laws *(hoi tous patrious nomous syngrapsousi)* by which the Athenians are to govern themselves," as Xenophon reports. This commission was created, Lysias says, out of ten nominees identified by Theramenes (who was included among them), ten identified by the so-called "ephors," the oligarchic collaborators among the *hetaireiai* led by Critias (who was included among them), and ten "from among those present." The nominees thereby "elected" became the constitutional commission known to posterity as the Thirty.[4]

A triumph for Critias and the champions of oligarchy at Athens, the creation of the Thirty was seen by some to be a blending of interests, where Theramenes and his nominees were expected to be voices of moderation. In terms of public reputation, Theramenes was certainly the leading statesman among the Thirty. Theramenes might have had a successful career in his new role had the Thirty not been completely dependent upon Sparta. But that dependency, of which Theramenes had almost certainly been one of the chief architects, in due course was the undoing of the man who still claimed to speak to and for the people of Athens.

Lysander remained in Athens long enough to see the new regime begin to carry out his commands. The trial and execution of the Athenian officers most responsible for opposing the treaty with Sparta, as described in the previous chapter, was probably carried out during Lysander's stay. So too was the formal condemnation of Alcibiades and other Athenian enemies of Sparta still at large. Celebrations attended the destruction of Athenian ships and ship-sheds, and the Long Walls and Piraeus walls:

> Lysander sent for many flute-girls from the city, and assembled all those who were already in the camp, and then tore down the walls, and burned up the triremes, to the sound of the flute, while the allies crowned themselves with garlands and made merry together, counting this day as the beginning of their freedom.

This was the celebration of the independence of the Hellenes from Athens championed by Sparta at the outset of war in 431. The festivities were probably timed to coincide with an older celebration of freedom for Hellas, one especially dear to Athenian pride, the anniversary of the battle of Salamis on the twentieth of the month Boedromion. Only after this ceremony did Lysander disperse his allies and depart, trophies in hand, for Sparta.[5]

THE THIRTY "ESTABLISHERS OF THE LAWS"

Hindsight has encouraged a comparison of the Thirty to the oligarchies of ten, or decarchies, that Lysander established in order to promote loyalty to Sparta in other Greek towns. This comparison is surely valid, but it is well to keep in mind that the appointment of the Thirty also made sense in purely Athenian terms. A standing commission to define "ancestral laws" had long been in place at Athens before 404. Those who were so inclined could see the appointment of the Thirty as an act of self-determination in fulfillment of the strong desire of many to "set things right."

The election of ten elders as *probouloi* following the Sicilian disaster in 413 had been a major step toward seeking stability in a time of crisis by institutionalizing the advice of living exponents of ancestral custom. By adding twenty more men to their number in 411, the Athenians had created a commission of thirty who were to compile proposals *(syngrapsousi)* "for the preservation of the city." Although these thirty had served as little more than the vehicle for empowering the Four Hundred, they were specifically charged to seek guidance through the study of ancestral laws. After the fall of the Four Hundred the spirit of restorative reform was sustained by the election of *nomothetai,* "establishers of the laws," devoted to reviewing and rectifying the statutes by which the Athenians were to govern themselves. These *nomothetai* were probably constituted in the form of a drafting commission of thirty whose work was subject to a review board of 500 who, as the democratically appointed representatives of all Athenians, would ascertain that the rectified statutes conformed to traditional practices. The work of these *nomothetai* was still going on over the winter of 405/4, when one of the drafting commissioners, Nicomachus, was summoned by the Council to attest to the statutory basis for the procedures that led to the death sentence for Cleophon. The *stasis* of the summer of 404 suspended the democratic processes of lawgiving at the very time when circumstances demanded a fresh approach to restorative reform.[6]

Lysander's presence cut through the tangle of conflicting agendas, enabling a new commission of thirty *nomothetai* to take office. To this extent, Lysander merely upheld an established Athenian institution. From those of the Thirty who are otherwise known, we can conjecture that they were probably all men with previous experience as office-holders under the democracy. Some of them were lately returned exiles: Aristoteles, Onomacles, Charicles, Melobius, and Mnesilochus had all probably been fugitives since their involvement in the oligarchy of the Four Hundred; others, like Critias, had been driven into exile since 411. Still others, like Theramenes himself, had never been expelled. The selection of such a panel of *nomothetai* would have seemed to fulfill the reasoned plea of Aristophanes' chorus in the *Frogs* to forgive men of good Athenian ancestry for their single mistakes of the past, so that the city might again benefit from the services of worthy men. The Thirty were certainly not said, in any official capacity at least, to be an oligarchy. That they were so in fact resulted from the circumstances of their election, and from their ability to direct the authorization of their proposals by a Council of their own creation.[7]

The Thirty immediately oversaw the appointment of magistrates and the Council, the constitutional heart of the oligarchy. Firm control of the Council was essential from the start, since by invoking existing statutes that gave the Council exceptional judicial authority, the Thirty could rely in the Council rather than any jury-court to carry out the required condemnation of those who were deemed "enemies of the people."[8]

The most powerful and feared of the magistrates appointed by the Thirty were the Eleven. These men saw to the executions of all who were sentenced to death and had the authority to summarily execute confessed thieves, thugs, kidnappers, and temple-robbers. Ten men were appointed to oversee the same tasks in Piraeus, and among their number was Charmides, the nephew of Critias and uncle of Plato. Imposing law and order was a central feature in the appeal of the new regime to its supporters, and the elimination of undesirables could only be entrusted to men of judgment and discrimination.[9]

These developments were all to the good, according to those who felt that deference to the masses was the source of all error. With Theramenes associated in this venture, Athenians who held moderate views on the subject of constitutional revision could feel optimistic about the prospects before them. This was a view shared by, among others, Plato, who, then about twenty-four years old, later spoke of this era in his autobiographical *Seventh Letter:*

> Once upon a time in my youth I cherished like many another the hope of entering upon a political career as soon as I came of age. But it fell out that political events took the following course. There were many who heaped abuse on the form of government then prevailing, and a revolution occurred. In this revolution fifty-one men set themselves up as a government, eleven in the city, ten in the Piraeus—both of these groups were to administer the market and the usual civic affairs—and thirty came into power as supreme rulers of the whole state. Some of these happened to be relatives and acquaintances of mine, who accordingly invited me forthwith to join them, assuming my fitness for the task. No wonder that, young as I was, I cherished the belief that their administration would lead the city from an unjust life, as it were, to the habits of justice, and I was intensely interested to see what would come of it.[10]

SOCIAL ENGINEERING

Favored by conditions similar in some respects to those under which the Four Hundred came to power in 411, the Thirty and their minions met with general approval as they set to the tasks of "rectifying and removing ambiguities in the constitution," as Aristotle reports. The urban poor, once largely dependent upon the state and a vigorous commercial economy for livelihood, no longer constituted a dominant body within the citizenry. The war, and especially the losses suffered at Aegospotami combined with the unquantified effects of starvation in the siege of the previous winter, had depleted the numbers of the poorest Athenians at probably ten times or more the rate of attrition suffered by Athenians with measurable property. More significantly, with the executions of Cleophon and the democratically elected generals and military officers, all spokesmen for this sector of the populace had been removed. The balance of public sentiment, or, at least, the means for registering it, had been shifted strongly in favor of the aristocracy of Athens. After years in which, as Plato says, many privately "heaped abuse on the form of government then prevailing," those same were now glad to see authority vested in the hands of sensible men.[11]

The first concern of the Thirty in implementing their vision of the "ancestral constitution" was to remove those statutes by which the sovereignty of jury-courts had been affirmed. Laws dating to the ascendancy of Pericles were rescinded, but so too were laws as old as Solon that had been applied to assert the power of the people's courts over men of means and standing.

Aristotle singles out, as an example, the law enabling wills to be challenged on the grounds of "mental incompetence, age, or a woman's influence." This inroad of public jurisdiction into the most sensitive area of family relations and private property had been a matter of grievance and of comic quips since at least the 420s. An Aristophanic juror, in the *Wasps,* boasts of the jurors' indisputable power to bestow contested inheritances on whomever they like. Portending the program of the Thirty a decade in advance, Peisetaerus persuades Heracles to support his revolutionary new city of the *Birds* when he instructs him on how the gods, relying on a law of Solon, would deny him his inheritance. Something was wrong with the law, it was felt, when the possessors of great estates had to fear the attacks of opportunists threatening prosecutions that would embarrass them in their old age, or worse, malign their memory when they were dead. "The Thirty applied the same principle to other matters as well," Aristotle notes. They worked to eliminate assaults on the honor and authority of the best by the basest of Athenians, especially as these assaults had been launched in the jury-courts by their most despicable denizens, the sycophants.[12]

Opportunistic prosecution of men of standing had been a regular avenue to a public career for the young and upcoming. As noted in the previous two chapters, the number of such prosecutions had noticeably increased as political rivals sought to fill the leadership vacuum left by Alcibiades' voluntary exile in 407. From the point of view of the victims, a large part of the problem with politics at Athens was that there were too many sycophants. The groups allied in the Thirty had worked hard to come out on top in these rivalries, and now they were eager to channel public exasperation into policies that would close the door on attempts by others to embarrass them.

This context accounts for a remarkable innovation in the Thirty's legislative program, attributed by Xenophon to Critias and Charicles, namely, a prohibition on "teaching the art of speaking" *(logon techne)*. Xenophon, seeking to exonerate his teacher, Socrates, from calumnious association with Critias, claims that Critias aimed this prohibition specifically against Socrates. Although it is believable that Socrates would have felt that this was yet another sign that he and Critias had parted ways, it is not likely that Socrates was the special focus of Critias and Charicles' attention in this connection.

The ban can be understood as an element in a program of social engineering. Like the Spartans, the Thirty were prepared to honor the speech only of those who, in their eyes, deserved to be heard, not of anyone who might seek to advance a bad cause by ornamented speech. In effect, the measure was an encroachment on freedom of speech and association. For the broad application of such a prohibition would prevent groups of any size from convening for the purpose of preparing their rhetorical armaments for debate in any political or judicial forum. Again, the avenues to power used by Critias and his fellows were to be denied to others.[13]

Social engineering was the aim of the Thirty, under the leadership of Critias. The arrests, condemnations, and executions of "sycophants" and "criminals" were justified by the oligarchs' declared intention to "purge the city of unjust men and incline the rest of the citizens toward virtue and justice," as Lysias states. These goals were directly implemented, with little or no space for legislative or judicial debate. Such swift justice for the wicked, carried out on the authority of the Council, met with public approval, Xenophon notes, "at least among those who were conscious that they were not of the same sort themselves." But when the arrests began to include men whose criminality was more obviously a matter of partisan perspective, disaffection with the regime grew. As Plato put it:

> I saw in a short time that these men made the former government look in comparison like an age of gold. Among other things they sent an elderly man, Socrates, a friend of mine, who I should hardly be ashamed to say was the justest man of his time, in company with others, against one of the citizens to fetch him forcibly to be executed. Their purpose was to connect Socrates with their government, whether he wished or not. He refused and risked any consequences rather than become their partner in wicked deeds. When I observed all this—and some other similar matters of importance—I withdrew in disgust from the abuses of those days.[14]

Others with more established reputations withdrew in fear. Men with known personal ties to enemies of the oligarchs had been fleeing Athens since at least the time of the affair of Agoratus and the arrest of the generals. Within the first few months of their regime, the actions of the Thirty had confirmed the fears of their rivals, and began to trouble many of those who found no fault with their ideological program but saw its means as unduly harsh. Apprehension extended even into the ranks of the Thirty themselves, as Theramenes let his doubts about the wisdom of a severe policy be known. But the direction of the regime was affirmed by the dispatch of the senior statesman of the Thirty, Aristoteles, and a colleague to Sparta, to request the backing of a garrison in Athens, "until, through the elimination of all 'criminals,' they had established their government." The "criminals" targeted by the Thirty were not merely thugs and pick-pockets; they were men who had previously enjoyed an honorable standing in the Athenian community, a standing that the hard-liners among the Thirty now wanted to dispute. This was social engineering with a vengeance.[15]

MORE ANCIENT VIRTUES

The guise of legitimate Athenian tradition maintained at the beginning of the regime of the Thirty was rapidly revealing the radical idea at its core: order could be imposed on a disorderly society only by severe measures. According to a tradition repeated by Herodotus, Thucydides, Plato, and Xenophon, Sparta had long ago transformed itself from the worst to the best governed state under the visionary guidance of Lycurgus. Under the leadership of Critias, the Thirty would do the same at Athens, and they would do so by appealing to the ideals of a more ancient and therefore more pure Athenian past than that represented by the lawgivers of the democracy, Cleisthenes and Solon. Critias' vision looked to a past when even Sparta learned from Athens.[16]

At around the time that the Spartans granted the Athenian request and sent a garrison of 700 men to Athens, the Thirty announced their intention of limiting citizenship to 3,000 of the best qualified Athenians. Such a restricted number would exclude even a majority of those Athenians who might claim eligibility if the bearing of hoplite arms were made the criterion, as it had been in 411. The fluidity of that former definition had rendered it essentially worthless as an exclusionary device, however, and the Thirty must have wished to establish stricter controls over who was eligible to participate in government. The number 3,000 was probably suggested also because it was a close approximation of the number of Spartiates, the men who possessed full rights of citizenship at Sparta, just as the body of the Thirty echoed the Spartan *Gerousia,* their Council composed of twenty-eight elders and two kings. These were merely some of the more overt signs that the Thirty, under Critias' guidance, had a Spartan model in mind for Athens.[17]

Critias was known to be an admirer and student of Spartan customs, for among his writings preserved by later citations were a poem in elegiacs praising the moderation of Spartan drinking customs and a prose treatise on the *Constitution of the Lacedaemonians.* This work began with a discussion of procreation and child-rearing at Sparta, in terms closely echoed by Xenophon in the opening of his later work of the same title. The young Xenophon, a cavalryman obedient to the authority of the Thirty at this time, exemplifies the strong current of respect within the Athenian aristocracy for Spartan customs that Critias and his fellows relied upon in their ambitious undertaking.[18]

This current is revealed, among other places, in Xenophon's depiction of politics at Athens on the eve of the battle of Arginusae. The conversation between Socrates and the younger Pericles, quoted in part on page 183 above, opens with the observation that fear inclines men toward obedience, and that obedience is best employed to revive the "ancient virtue" *(archaia arete)* that formerly made Athens great. "How then," Pericles asks, "can they recover their ancient virtue?" Socrates goes on:

> There is no mystery about it, as I think. If they find out the ways of their ancestors and practice them as well as they did, they will be as good as they were; or failing that, if they imitate those who now have preeminence and practice their ways, and do so as carefully as they do, then they will be as good as they are or, if they are more attentive, even better.

There is no ambiguity about "those who now have pre-eminence," for Pericles goes on to exclaim:

> When will the Athenians show the Lacedaemonian reverence for age, seeing that they despise all their elders, beginning with their own fathers? When will they adopt the Lacedaemonian system of [physical] training, seeing that they not only neglect to make themselves fit, but mock those who take the trouble to do so? When will they reach that standard of obedience to their leaders, seeing that they make contempt for leaders a point of honor?[19]

Here was the conceptual link between the virtuous "ways" *(epitedeumata)* of the Spartans and the "ancestral constitution" *(patrios politeia)* of the Athenians. The ancient virtue inherent in both was a universal quality, so any model of excellence could serve as a guide to their restoration, and a working model would be the most practicable guide.

The logic of excellence was all the more compelling, however, when it could be seen that the model of virtue inspiring the Spartans was originally Athenian. To this end, the intellectual circles of the Athenian aristocracy had, over the preceding decade, come to recognize and make much of the fact that Tyrtaeus, the most ancient poet of Spartan virtues, was by birth an Athenian. Suffering in their war with the Messenians, so the story went, the Spartans were advised by Apollo's oracle to bring a "general" from Athens;

for their part, the Athenians were unwilling to give the Spartans anyone other than the lame poet, Tyrtaeus. As it turned out, his verses contained the inspiration needed to conquer, for he taught Sparta's warriors how to subordinate personal pride to the common good in order to achieve victory in battle. Thus the Athenian Tyrtaeus, two generations before Solon, assumed a place only slightly less distinguished than the legendary Lycurgus as a "lawgiver," or founder of Spartan customs.

Tyrtaeus, like Critias, is said to have written a *Constitution of the Lacedaemonians.* The title probably belongs rather to a collection of Tyrtaeus' poetry later recognized as comprising a literary heritage of ancient Spartan ways. Plato, from within the Socratic circle that also united Critias and Xenophon, attests the recognition of the poetry of Tyrtaeus as an original embodiment of the laws and ways of the Spartans and acknowledges its relevance in guiding legislative practices elsewhere among those who appreciate the qualities inherent in Spartan ways.[20]

Critias himself, according to another account by Xenophon, explicitly argued that Spartan custom should guide Athenian practice. "The best constitution," Critias says, using the term *politeia,* "is recognized to be that of the Lacedaemonians." The fact that the laws, or *nomoi,* comprising the constitution of the Spartans did not exist as a written code but consisted in the application of traditional wisdom by appropriate authorities had important consequences when the Thirty, as *nomothetai,* adopted a Spartan paradigm. As Aristotle attests, from the outset their legislative work consisted more in *eradicating* the written laws that had become the bases of illegitimate power than in promulgating new statutes.[21]

Part of the legislative work that had been carried out by the democratic *nomothetai* since 411/10 had involved the publication on stone of certain categories of statutes. Fragments of inscribed stelae bearing portions of these laws have been found in the Athenian Agora (see figure 7). Although the evidence is complicated and its interpretation is uncertain in some respects, the fragments attest a disruptive interlude in the inscription and display of laws that must have some connection with the regime of the Thirty. Stelae that had been inscribed in the Attic form of the Greek alphabet, the official script of Athenian inscriptions before 403, were erased, and sometime later reinscribed in the Ionic alphabet officially adopted at Athens in 403/2. It has been suggested that the erasure was the work of the Thirty in 404/3, undoing much of the work of earlier *nomothetai.* Whether or not the Thirty were responsible for the extensive erasures, the reinscription of a substantial body of public law in or soon after 403/2 provides physical evidence indicating that events around 404/3 were forcing a reappraisal of at least some categories of Athenian law.[22]

Written laws had been the tools by which the *demos* and its leaders had exercised power. The legislative authority of the Thirty was dedicated to up-

FIGURE 7. The written laws of Athens: fragment of the calendar of sacrifices inscribed on a recut surface for public display in the Agora, ca. 399. Athens, Agora no. I 727. Photo courtesy of the American School of Classical Studies: Agora Excavations.

rooting this democratic tradition. The primary creative effort of the Thirty thus lay in the notion that their own unwritten pronouncements were endowed with the force of statutory law by virtue of their reliance on universal truths, or "unwritten laws." This was by no means an alien concept to a generation of Athenians accustomed to identifying their values and ambitions with universal and divinely sanctioned truths. The process of enacting written laws had always relied on the notion that they were expressions of previously unwritten customs, *ta patria,* that had always existed.

The fact that in recent years things had gone astray for the Athenians confirmed a widespread feeling that some of these objective, written laws, were but poor approximations of these "ancient" truths. The Thirty were at liberty, in ways that their democratic predecessors had not been, to apply a more comprehensive vision of the extent of corrections needed to put the

Athenians back on the path "toward virtue and justice." Many of the Athenian aristocracy therefore supported the Thirty as they began to persuade, coerce, or eliminate those who "despised elders," those who "mocked self-discipline," and those who had "contempt for leaders." No one could quarrel with the endeavor to restore ancient virtues, until they began to realize what it meant.[23]

THOSE WHO ARE IN AND THOSE WHO ARE OUT

The problem of circumscribing virtue by a list of 3,000 names was almost as vexing for the Thirty as it had been for the oligarchs of 411, who had grappled unsuccessfully with the notion of naming 5,000 worthy Athenians. As in the previous oligarchy, publication of the list was repeatedly delayed.

Since inclusion for many meant exclusion for more, the public empowerment of the 3,000 required an opportunity to demonstrate their dominance over those deemed to be inferior. This was achieved by announcing a military muster, probably occasioned by the report of armed enemies gathering on Mount Parnes, toward the Boeotian frontier. Designated units of Athenians were ordered to assemble under arms at various points around the city, with a concentration of 3,000 hoplites assigned to the Agora, where the Council and the Thirty held their meetings. After an interval, a stand-down was announced, with the provision that arms should be left at the designated posts. An inspection carried out by trusted associates of the Thirty supported by troops of the Spartan garrison then saw to the collection of all arms except those of the 3,000 in the Agora. The unauthorized weapons were conveyed to the Acropolis, the stronghold guarded by the Spartan garrison.[24]

By this subterfuge the 3,000 were rendered the only legitimate, arms-bearing citizens. Soon thereafter, the Thirty advanced by decree their vision of a landowning, hoplite citizenry on the Spartiate model, expelling disenfranchised Athenians from the city and confiscating their properties for distribution among the men favored by the Thirty. Well-to-do metics, the resident aliens who generally made a living in commerce and industry, were also targeted in this movement. Their capital assets were confiscated, and many, if they did not flee, were put to death. Lysias and his brother, Polemarchus, are well-known victims in this purge (with fatal consequences in Polemarchus' case). They had inherited, but now lost, their father's profitable shield-making business. It is hard to imagine any trade that would have been more despised by the Thirty than one that enriched foreigners by producing hoplite arms, probably mostly at state expense, for "worthless" Athenians. Although the Thirty were often accused of wielding their power to enrich themselves illegally, venality was probably the least justified of the many charges against them. They carried out their confiscations in pursuit of an idealistic agenda. It was convenient, afterwards, to impute avaricious motives to them and thereby to obscure the fact that many other Athenians supported their goals.[25]

Blind idealism was never one of Theramenes' faults, and as these schemes were under discussion he urged a pragmatic consideration upon Critias and his colleagues. An Athenian government limited to 3,000 citizens was unduly restrictive; it would leave more capable men at odds with it than it had defenders. To Critias, such advice was an unwelcome form of opposition at a time when the authoritarian hand of the Thirty was becoming more widely feared and resented. Theramenes had been accepted among the Thirty because he commanded the respect of many Athenians. But now that he was challenging their agenda on behalf of a broader constituency, he was seen by Critias as a threat to the unity of the oligarchy, just as he had been in 411. In fact, Theramenes exemplified the sort of pandering to public opinion and contempt for meritorious leadership that Critias and his colleagues were determined to uproot.

Having prepared his followers to accept this line of reasoning, Critias denounced Theramenes before the Council. Theramenes, he said, was one who had proven that his first loyalty was always to himself, and one whose treachery had destroyed many a virtuous man, most notoriously the generals of Arginusae. Appealing to the wisdom of Spartan practice in dealing with those who defied the will of the ruling magistrates, Critias had him stricken from membership in the Thirty and then also from among the 3,000 eligible for office. Then, relying on their authority to summarily condemn any "non-citizen," Critias had the Thirty command Theramenes' execution. With armed supporters standing by to quell any resistance, Critias had Theramenes handed over to the Eleven, who carried out the sentence.[26]

With the execution of Theramenes, around the beginning of winter 404/3, events at Athens accelerated in the direction intended by the Thirty and warned against by Theramenes. The expulsion of the disenfranchised from the city swelled the population of Piraeus with men who no longer had a stake in the government of Athens. Those who foresaw danger in staying anywhere within reach of the Thirty sought refuge elsewhere, swelling the numbers of Athenians in exile. Behind them, men were being arrested and executed merely because they were deemed "most capable of resisting" the Thirty.[27]

How were these potential opponents identified? Attention was naturally drawn to men whose reputations had been advanced by public honors under the democracy, although, as Xenophon points out, Critias and Theramenes, and even others of the Thirty, were liable to be stigmatized if this were the sole criterion. The Thirty were discriminating men. They knew who their enemies were, and they knew that the friends and kinsmen of their enemies would naturally oppose them, given an opportunity. By such logic Niceratus son of Nicias and nephew of the recently executed general, Eucrates, was put to death. So too, we may infer, was the learned Euthydemus, who in his youth had been the object of Critias' unrestrained passions. Euthydemus had been prominent in high circles before 404, but was heard of no more following the execution of his brother, the general Dionysodorus. Euthydemus, in fact, was in jeopardy three times over. In addition to his brother's democratic politics, Euthydemus was a naturalized, not a native Athenian, and he had a reputation as a teacher of "the art of speaking."[28]

When an armed resistance organized by the exiles began to threaten the regime of the Thirty from the frontiers of Attica, the pace and scale of judicial murders increased. To secure Salamis and Eleusis against influence from exiles in Megara and Boeotia, the Thirty, accompanied by the Athenian cavalry, their most loyal native military arm, held a review and registration of residents eligible for cavalry service at Eleusis. The purpose of the registration, it was announced, was to determine what additional forces were needed to defend the Eleusinians. Xenophon, serving in the Athenian cavalry, describes what happened next:

> As each man registered, he had to leave through the small gate in the wall facing the sea. On the seashore they had posted the cavalrymen on either side, and, as each man came out, he was seized and bound by the servants in attendance on the cavalry. When they had all been seized, the Thirty ordered Lysimachus, the cavalry commander, to take them to Athens and hand them over to the Eleven.

By this ruse, three hundred of the most capable and ambitious men of military age from Eleusis and Salamis delivered themselves into the hands of the Thirty. Critias was taking yet another page out of the book of Spartan tricks for eliminating potential subversives. Following the delivery of the three hundred men from Eleusis to the Eleven at Athens, Critias convened the 3,000 and called for their condemnation, en masse, by an open vote of the 3,000 carried out in the presence of the armed Spartan garrison. The three hundred were put to death.[29]

Tradition is consistent about the magnitude of these atrocities: in all, the Thirty executed some fifteen hundred Athenians, many of whom were prominent citizens by virtue of wealth, birth, or reputation. Unless this figure is greatly exaggerated—and there is no reason to believe that it is—the casualties among Athenians of property and influence were thus higher in 404/3 than in any single campaign of the previous war, with the possible exception of the Sicilian disaster. Xenophon, reporting the speech of a contemporary, phrased the comparison thus: "The accursed Thirty... have, for the sake of their own personal gain, killed practically more Athenians in eight months than have all the Peloponnesians in ten years of war."[30]

BEATING OUT THE LION

The Spartans welcomed Critias' devotion to their ideals especially because Athens was essential as a bulwark against Boeotian influence. Unless they were rendered compliant in the face of a common enemy, the Boeotians were notoriously uncooperative with Sparta, and were capable of interfering with Spartan interests beyond the Isthmus. By autumn 404 reports were reaching Sparta to the effect that the Thebans were preparing to support Athenian exiles against the friends of Sparta at Athens. The Spartans must have regarded the Boeotian threat as a factor in their decision to send a garrison to Athens.

As attention turned to Athenian exiles, the Spartans and their friends had to be concerned about the most powerful of them, Alcibiades. Critias and Lysander knew that he posed the greatest threat to their common interests, not only for his connections among the Athenian exiles, but for his network of friends around the Aegean. Even more ominous, the Spartans knew, was his influence with Persian authorities.

In autumn 404 Alcibiades was in the satrapy of Hellespontine Phrygia, enjoying the hospitality of Pharnabazus. Alcibiades was able to support himself and benefit his host by carrying out raids against the hostile Bithynian Thracians on the northern fringe of Pharnabazus' satrapy. But Alcibiades probably also brought a more important gift to Pharnabazus, information about covert relations between Spartans and Ionian Greeks and the most dangerous foe of Pharnabazus and his king, the young prince, Cyrus.[31]

Restored to his position at Sardis, Cyrus was careful to make sure that Lysander and his fellow Spartans were mindful also of his interests as each sought to benefit from the reconfiguration of power around the Aegean. Among Spartans with wide experience in Ionia was Clearchus, a veteran of the battles of Cyzicus and Arginusae, and garrison commander at Byzantium until he was expelled by Alcibiades. Following the victory at Aegospotami, Clearchus had returned to his former haunts around Byzantium and was making war on the Odrysian Thracians and their chieftain, Seuthes. It was on his account that Alcibiades found it wise to leave the Odrysian lands and cross over into Asia.

At some point in his command, Clearchus entered into covert negotiations with Cyrus. The prince was quietly gathering allies against the day when he would attempt to overthrow his brother, King Artaxerxes. Thorax, Lysander's lieutenant at Ephesus and at Samos, was another Spartan commander whose dealings with his mercenaries and allies in Ionia were made easier by getting to know Cyrus. Through his network of friends, Alcibiades was in a position to know something of these covert relations, and knew that the information he could provide would be of value to Pharnabazus, who had to be wary of the intentions of Cyrus.[32]

According to Ephorus, Alcibiades was keen to gain the favor of Artaxerxes himself by bringing him word of these doings, and he appealed to Pharnabazus to convey him to the king. Pharnabazus surely found these reports useful, but, as he probably counseled Alcibiades, until Cyrus' arrangements resulted in some overt action, the reports could only be treated as hearsay. As credible as they were, Pharnabazus could not accuse the king's own brother on the say-so of an Athenian exile. Alcibiades was compelled to wait, much as his emissaries to Artaxerxes' father had had to wait several years earlier, until Pharnabazus deemed the moment was at hand.[33]

While waiting, however, Pharnabazus used this information to place the Spartans more firmly in his debt. The intelligence he received from Alcibiades he passed on to the authorities at Sparta, who wished to repair their reputation with King Artaxerxes now that Cyrus' star had dimmed. This communication resulted in a series of peremptory orders carried out over the winter of 404/3. Thorax was arrested and, when he was found to be in possession of unauthorized funds, he was executed. Clearchus was summoned from the Hellespont to a meeting at the Isthmus, but realizing what was afoot, he escaped arrest and sailed back to the Hellespont. After a sentence of death was pronounced on him and a Spartan force was sent against him in the Hellespont, Clearchus escaped to Sardis. From Cyrus he obtained a generous retaining fee and became a privateer leading a mercenary army in Thrace. Lysander himself, carrying out operations against towns on the Aegean coast of Thrace over this winter, was also summoned home.[34]

In this case, knowing that Pharnabazus was the source of the information against him, Lysander first approached Pharnabazus in an effort to reconcile their differences. At issue was money that Lysander had taken from Persian territory on the authority of Cyrus. Pharnabazus must have pressed Lysander on two points: Cyrus had no right to assign Lysander the tribute from domains that Pharnabazus now claimed; and Cyrus' intentions in doing so, and therefore Lysander's motives in accepting the money, were seditious. Pharnabazus allowed Lysander to believe that they had arrived at a resolution of their dispute, but the tale of the perfidy he practiced on Lysander, whatever its truth, indicates that the two ultimately failed to see eye to eye. In Lysander's presence, Pharnabazus prepared a letter to Spartan authorities explaining circumstances to Lysander's satisfaction. But after it was sealed, this letter was switched with another that conveyed an accusation of Lysander, delivered unknowingly by his own hand.

Pharnabazus' complaint seems not to have been so much a direct indictment of Lysander as an explanation, from a Persian point of view, of the implications of his having received money from the hand of Cyrus, now that Cyrus was viewed with suspicion by King Artaxerxes and those loyal to him. Such is the inference that can be drawn from a remark by Pausanias, in the context of an oracle warning the Spartans of the danger of coveting money and evidently referring to these circumstances: "I for my part follow the Persians, and judge by the Persian law, and decide that Lysander brought on the Lacedaemonians more harm than benefit." This affair indeed raised deep concerns among the Spartans over the influence of money on individual loyalty, and Lysander was granted the equivalent of a leave of absence while these matters were debated. The debate was surely complicated by, among other things, an abiding uncertainty about where the center of power among the Persians lay. For the moment, however, it was clearly wisest for the Spartans to follow Pharnabazus' advice and absolve themselves of any taint of collusion with Cyrus.[35]

Spartan authorities must have informed Pharnabazus that they would act upon his advice provided that he removed the appearance of divided loyalty implied by his hospitality for Alcibiades. For it was clearly Alcibiades' intent to use this taint of collusion to advance the cause of friendship between Artaxerxes and the Athenians, or the Athenians in exile.

To resolve this conflict of interest, Pharnabazus had to arrange for Alcibiades to leave the protection of his friendship. Perhaps he informed Alcibiades that the Spartans were demanding his head, and that it was time for him to be on his way to his meeting with the king. More likely, he displayed a growing coldness that let Alcibiades know that he would have to seek conveyance to the king elsewhere, for this accords with the account Diodorus attributes to Ephorus. Alcibiades, frustrated by the delay, "set out to the satrap of Paphlagonia in order to make the trip with his assistance."

Near the junction of his route with the Persian Royal Road from Sardis to Susa, Alcibiades stopped in the Phrygian village of Melissa. During the night, the house he was sleeping in was surrounded and set on fire by men sent to waylay him. As the flames became unbearable, Alcibiades heaped bedding on the fire, plunged through the flames, and charged with sword drawn at his assailants. They scattered, but shot him down with arrows and javelins.

The manner of Alcibiades' death, probably sometime early in 403, is not contested. The responsible party, however, is disputed. According to Ephorus, the men who killed Alcibiades were sent by Pharnabazus, who wanted Artaxerxes to learn of the intrigues of Cyrus from his own agents, not from Alcibiades. Others variously state that Pharnabazus did this at the bidding of Lysander and the Spartans or of Critias and the Thirty. In fact, there is probably truth in all of these statements: it took an exceptional alignment of powers to overwhelm Alcibiades.[36]

THE RETURN OF THE EXILES

The threat to Spartan interests posed by the Athenian exiles prompted the assertion of Spartan authority throughout Greece, in the form of a proclamation that refugees from the Thirty were the common enemies of all Hellenes. Following the denunciation of Alcibiades, Thrasybulus, and Anytus by the newly-empowered Thirty, the Spartans sent envoys to states known to be harboring Athenians to make public their demand. By this measure they opened the latent confrontations that would define the next generation of rivalry and warfare in Greece.

The strongest repudiation of this proclamation came from the Argives, who expelled the Spartan envoys. The most famous resistance came from the Thebans, who are said to have proclaimed penalties against anyone enforcing the Spartan demand. Our sources hint that the obstruction of Spartan demands and aid to Athenian exiles were initially more covert, however. The issue of supporting Athenian refugees seems to have become one of the divisive issues in a rapidly emerging factional rivalry among the Theban aristocracy. The Megarians, also harboring large numbers of refugees, made their non-compliance known to the Spartans.

Harsh words for both Megarians and Thebans attributed to Lysander may have been uttered during the weeks when Lysander was in Attica, presiding over the installation of the Thirty and the demolition of the walls of Piraeus. Pressure especially upon the Thebans and Megarians from that time on may even have forced the exiles into action in the winter of 404/3. The concerted Spartan agenda to root out opposition abroad certainly encouraged the severity of Critias' efforts to purge all opposition at Athens, for the Spartans were relying upon his regime to be a solid anvil under their hammer.[37]

Among Athenian exiles, Thrasybulus son of Lycus, at Thebes, was the man most capable of organizing armed resistance to the Thirty. Like Alcibiades, Thrasybulus was able to persuade his hosts that his personal enemies at Athens were the real enemy. He found sympathizers among Thebans who were anxious to demonstrate their independence from Sparta. One of these was Ismenias, whose career hereafter was to become identified especially with ties between Thebes and the leaders of democratic Athens.

The terms of this alignment were far from clear in the fall of 404, however. Sanctuary and support were provided covertly by Ismenias and his friends, and Plato gives a strong hint that Ismenias managed to enrich himself at the expense of some of the Athenian fugitives. By the beginning of winter 404/3, a combination of factors required action. Following in the footsteps of the Alcmaeonid opponents to the Peisistratid tyrants just over a century before, Thrasybulus and a core force of some sixty to seventy Athenians marched to Phyle on the Parnes frontier of Attica to challenge the authority of the Thirty.[38]

Posterity described the resultant contest in black and white terms: the Thirty represented oligarchy and sympathy for Sparta; opposition to the Thirty, which crystallized around the band led by Thrasybulus, represented democracy and the rejection of the Spartan yoke. But opposition to the Thirty did not rally around the standard of democracy. There was no *demos,* at the outset, to constitute a political or a military force. The Athenian poor were effectively dispersed and disempowered. They had no link to livelihoods that carried any public dignity in a state run by the Thirty, and survived only by obsequiousness before their masters.

Opposition grew rather among members of the Athenian aristocracy, that is, men of moderate or better means, who were united through common hatred of the Thirty and their exclusionist supporters. It was aided by well-placed friends abroad who shared not an affection for Athens' democratic past, but a common revulsion at the extremism of Critias and what it portended if the Spartans were to become the arbiters of wisdom and justice in other Greek states. The "ancestral constitution," among men of sense and moderation, meant something other than democracy as it had lately been practiced at Athens, but was surely not to be found in the radical practices of the Thirty.[39]

In the course of the fighting that followed, both factions represented themselves to the Spartans as proponents of the true ancestral constitution of the Athenians. The final outcome was determined when the opponents of the Thirty won not only decisive moments on the battlefield, but also the ideological contest. The Spartans embraced this outcome in part because, following the logic urged by Theramenes just before his condemnation, Spartan leadership itself began to take seriously the question of who among the Athenians would be the most valuable allies of Sparta, a rigidly orthodox but numerically enfeebled oligarchy, or a more robust moderate oligarchy.

This reassessment was encouraged by the fact that, in the critical interval of winter 404/3, other policies of Lysander had come under scrutiny, namely, his relations with Cyrus and the decarchies he had established in other states. The dissolution of Lysander's decarchies by the Spartan ephors, in the name of restoring "ancestral constitutions" to these states, signified that a new board of ephors was siding with those who felt that Lysander had gone too far.[40]

Thrasybulus and his followers had to survive and make headway against the Thirty in the face of what initially were staggering odds. Soon after their establishment at Phyle, Thrasybulus' men were challenged by the 3,000, probably not called out to their full number but still vastly outnumbering their foes. But holding a naturally strong defensive position in broken and difficult terrain, Thrasybulus had an advantage far better than the odds he was facing.

Imbued with the Spartan mystique of warlike *arete,* the heavily-armed hoplites of the 3,000 were the least capable of any infantry at dealing with the difficulties of mountain fighting. Two generations earlier, on Mount

Ithome in Messenia, Spartan hoplites had spent years demonstrating their inability to defeat a poorly armed enemy fighting a dogged guerrilla resistance. Critias' noble citizen-warriors were the last men likely to absorb any such lesson, however, despite the fact that the lesson had been administered even more severely to the Spartans on Sphacteria and to the Athenians themselves in Aetolia in the mid-420s. Heedless of these examples, the warriors of the 3,000 must have relished their first opportunity to prove by their daring in combat who the true Athenians were. So Xenophon accounts for the deeds of his peers by this terse summary:

> When they reached Phyle, some of the young men were so confident in themselves that they went straight in to attack the stronghold. But they achieved nothing and, after a number of them had been wounded, fell back again.[41]

With their finest thus beaten back, no doubt by stones and javelins, the Thirty made the sound but unappealing decision that blockade was the only way to root out this nuisance. But such ignoble duty was not a fit occupation for the 3,000 true Athenians, and so they withdrew a day or two later, in a heavy snow that had come upon them in the meantime. In the confusion of withdrawal in the snowstorm, they suffered the further indignity of hit-and-run raids that took a toll mostly on the slaves and followers of the 3,000 who, in Spartiate fashion, must have been present in numbers far greater than that of their noble warriors. The task of standing guard against depredations from Phyle was assigned to the Spartan-led garrison troops, of whom "all but a few," Xenophon says, were sent out to keep watch on the approaches to Phyle, supported, for mobility and reconnaissance, by two of the ten divisions of Athenian cavalry.

The initial victory at Phyle showed many that Thrasybulus and his co-captains knew how to fight the cocky 3,000, and the watch kept by the Spartan garrison could not keep men from coming to Thrasybulus' mountain fastness. Gradually, across the months of winter, the numbers under arms at Phyle grew to ten times the number that Thrasybulus had started with. By the approach of spring they were ready to take the offensive.

Under cover of night, Thrasybulus placed his miscellaneous force in ambush near the encampment of the enemy, and in a dawn attack routed them entirely. Of the hired hoplites, Xenophon reports, more than 120 were slain as the remainder took flight. Of the cavalry, three were slain, among whom Xenophon saw fit to record, with an almost audible sigh of regret, the passing of one "Nicostratus, called 'the beautiful.'"[42]

Between the blows struck by the men at Phyle, Critias saw the danger that opposition might grow far stronger and took measures accordingly. One such measure was the massacre of the Eleusinians. Xenophon says that the Thirty were motivated by the desire to create a safe refuge for themselves, should they be forced to retreat from Athens. This was a realistic precaution, and Eleusis, the Attic stronghold nearest to the Peloponnese, was the logical choice. Another measure of desperation was to sound out Thrasybulus, during parleys over prisoners held at Phyle, on the possibility that he and his leadership circle might put aside differences and share in the government of the Thirty. The idea of such an offer, whether or not it was actually made, illustrates how readily men seen from one side as the champions of democracy could be recognized from the other side as disgruntled aristocrats seeking redress for personal grievances. Considering the nature of the vacancy among the Thirty created by Theramenes' execution, this was an offer Thrasybulus was inclined to refuse.[43]

Thrasybulus' position in Mount Parnes was suited for a protracted resistance, but was not a position from which the Thirty could be defeated. The passage of time made Spartan intervention more likely, so Thrasybulus was impelled to bring the contest of Athenian factions to a head. On the night of the third day, by Xenophon's account, after the rout of the Spartan mercenaries below Parnes, Thrasybulus moved the largest part of his following, now numbering something over 1,000 armed men, down into the plain of Athens, past the city, and into Piraeus. There he found in abundance the resource most vital for bringing down the Thirty, a mass of manpower disaffected with the regime in Athens.

The administration of the Ten in Piraeus must have been at pains previously to disarm the populace in Piraeus as the Thirty had in Athens. But the commercial–manufacturing tradition was strong and resourceful in Piraeus, and make-shift arms must have been readily available in quantity. Moreover, access to the sea meant that arms could be shipped in. The arrival of Thrasybulus in Piraeus was probably the occasion when the industrialist arms-manufacturer, Lysias son of Cephalus, now in exile at Megara, provided money and some 200 shields to Thrasybulus' force.[44]

A major challenge had to be overcome before these resources could be mobilized, however. On the day of their arrival Thrasybulus' men had to face the attack of the Thirty and their followers, who still had a significant numeric advantage. Xenophon indicates that skirmishing along the approach to Piraeus went on for some time as Thrasybulus and his men assessed their defensive situation. Eventually they abandoned the perimeter of the urban area and concentrated their forces on the high hill of Munychia. The Thirty entered Piraeus and assembled in the central market square, the Hippodamian Agora. Massing their force into a compact formation fifty shields deep, Critias and the Thirty led them along the main road from the Agora up the slopes of the Munychia hill, heading toward the shrines of Bendis and of Artemis on the other side of the hill, by the Munychian harbor. On the high point of this road Thrasybulus massed his men, just ten shields deep, but supported by numerous skirmishers and javelin-throwers.

Thrasybulus held his men in place to await the attack. As the enemy approached, Thrasybulus harangued his troops to strike hard against the very men who were the authors of all evils that had lately befallen the Athenians, and encouraged them with the memory of their previous victories and the advantage of their present position on higher ground. As their foes drew near, Thrasybulus' seer, having foretold victory if their own blood were shed first, made the fateful sacrifice by throwing himself onto the spears of the Thirty's troops. As battle was joined, missiles, high ground, and resolve turned the tide in favor of Thrasybulus. The front ranks of the Thirty's men were cut down and their massed formation broke and ran, to be pursued as far as level ground. The dead included Critias himself and Hippomachus among the Thirty, Charmides among the Ten overseers of Piraeus, "and about seventy of the others," according to Xenophon.[45]

These unnamed seventy were among the best of their generation. It is a fair guess that among them was Glaucon son of Ariston, an older brother of Plato. Glaucon's valor in battle at Megara six years earlier seems to have caught the eye of Critias, and his ambition to rise in politics was noticed by Socrates and later recalled by Xenophon. Glaucon, at any rate, was no longer named in the company of his brothers a few years later, at the time of Socrates' trial.

Glaucon's memory is preserved, above all, in the conversation with Socrates that Plato composed in the *Republic,* which began with Socrates and Glaucon in Piraeus, walking back from the scene of a festal procession to the shrine of Bendis, certainly along the same road that soaked up the blood of the seventy devotees of Critias. The dialogue ranges, in the voice of Socrates conversing with Glaucon, across Plato's most intricate exposition of "the good" and its potential for political realization. It concludes in a mystic vision: a tale of the fate of souls in the afterlife facing the reckoning for their deeds in this one; a tale affirming salvation for those who "hold ever to the upward way and pursue righteousness with wisdom"; a tale told by a bold warrior slain in battle, whose unblemished corpse arose miraculously, days after its death, from out of the flames of the funeral pyre to tell its parable of the consequences for the immortal soul of the choices made in life and afterlife. Such was Plato's vision, inspired possibly by the memory of the last sight of the corpse of his beloved brother. The road to the shrines of Bendis and Artemis surely gave many eminent Athenians a place to ponder the nature of the path to "righteousness and wisdom."[46]

WAR BETWEEN ATHENS AND PIRAEUS

The victory at Munychia and the death of Critias meant the undoing of the Thirty. For in proving the futility of their *arete* on the battlefield, Thrasybulus had succeeded in driving a wedge between this clique and its disillusioned followers, not in the name of democracy over oligarchy, but in the name of justice and fair treatment among men of reason and men of property.

Xenophon describes Thrasybulus urging his followers at Munychia to avenge themselves on the Thirty, because they were men "who robbed us of our city when we were guilty of no wrong, and drove us from our homes, and proscribed those who were our closest friends." After the battle, as the two sides came together to allow the recovery of the dead, appeals for reconciliation were made by followers of Thrasybulus on the basis of the common bonds of kinship, marriage, fellowship, and communion in a range of social, civic, and religious institutions. Thrasybulus and his followers, in other words, identified themselves with the followers of the Thirty in Athens in all respects except one: as either victims or witnesses of the despotic terror of the Thirty, they could not tolerate their regime.[47]

After Munychia the majority of the followers of the Thirty were led to the same conclusion. Upon their return to Athens the men of the 3,000, in the various guardposts to which they had been assigned in the present state of emergency, fell to arguing among themselves about the wisdom of continuing to accept the orders of the Thirty. So debilitating was the crisis of command that, probably without the authority of the Thirty, word circulated that the full 3,000 should assemble the next day in a military muster to demonstrate where their allegiance lay. Thus, while the survivors of the Thirty met in fruitless council to review their options, the 3,000 gathered in the Agora, before the Council-House, and voiced their common opinion that the Thirty should step down. In their place a board of ten was elected to lead the 3,000, on the promise that they would put an end to the war between Athens and Piraeus.[48]

Yet even after most of the remaining members of the Thirty withdrew to their stronghold at Eleusis, Athens and Piraeus remained two opposed armed camps. Despite widespread sympathy for reconciliation with the Piraeus party among the 3,000, the new government of the Ten viewed a military solution as essential to the process. Reasonable terms, they felt, could not be negotiated with men full of the pride of victory, especially since, along with worthy opponents, that pride also swelled the self-esteem of a mass of worthless humanity. The men of Piraeus had to be humbled first. To assure that waverers among the 3,000 did not subvert the hard line of the Ten, guard-duty day and night was entrusted to the most loyal men of the cavalry corps, alongside the Spartan-led garrison troops still quartered in Athens. As a further measure, Aristotle notes, a conspicuous example was made of one Demaratus, a prominent Athenian, who was arrested and condemned to death by the Ten on grounds not reported, but almost certainly involving some manner of treasonous correspondence with men in Piraeus.[49]

A thankless war of skirmishes and reprisals over the countryside between Athens and Piraeus filled much of the spring and summer of 403, while both sides made preparations for more intense violence. Although their foragers were harassed by the strong cavalry force from the city, the more numerous partisans in Piraeus effectively cut Athens off from its regular sources of revenues and supplies, and threatened to bring siege engines up for an assault on the city.

To stem this crisis, emissaries from the Ten in Athens appealed to the Spartans for support against their common enemy, the *demos*. In fighting the friends of Sparta at Athens, they claimed, this populace had rebelled against the terms for peace between them and Sparta. As further evidence of anti-Spartan dealings, the emissaries pointed to the support the men in Piraeus had been receiving from Sparta's enemies in Boeotia. Emissaries from the Thirty at Eleusis joined the emissaries from Athens and no doubt made much of the fact that their stronghold at Eleusis was well placed to intercept any reinforcements the Boeotians might send to the men in Piraeus. As a result, these emissaries of the two oligarchic factions obtained a loan of one hundred talents from the Spartans, while Lysander himself was appointed harmost, or commander of foreign troops, for Attica and was given the support of a naval squadron under the command of his brother to effect a blockade of Piraeus.

Lysander's command at Eleusis, possibly to be explained by the presence there of his closest associates among the Athenians, more probably reflects the fact that, of all these claims, the Spartans were readiest to respond to the evidence that trouble in Attica was external in origin. In any event, the reinforcement brought by Lysander in effect equalized the balance of forces contending in the countryside around Athens and assured that time would no longer be an ally to the men of Piraeus. A more decisive resolution of the conflict awaited further action.[50]

THE SPARTAN SETTLEMENT

From the standpoint of Greeks outside of Attica, relations among the contending parties in the summer of 403 must have seemed ambiguous in the extreme. Ambiguity was surely heightened in the context of negotiations held at Sparta, where at some point, as we can infer from the eventual outcome, men from Piraeus made their views known as well. No source reports any embassy from the Piraeus party to the Spartans until much later, as the Spartans began to effect the reconciliation of the warring parties after the battles of the summer. But it is inconceivable that the Spartans would have begun this reconciliation with men with whom they had had no previous contact, save at the point of a spear.

Each party sought to make their own position comprehensible to the Spartans, and to place it in the best possible light with a view to the outcome that the Spartans were likely to support. From the Spartan perspective, this

Gordian knot would have to be cut by a sword seen by all to be in Spartan hands. Regardless of the details, it was essential that the settlement follow from the application of decisive military force. Accordingly, a second and more substantial expedition of the Spartans and their allies was given a mandate to intervene in Attica under the leadership of the Spartan king Pausanias.

According to our sources, the motive for this new directive was Pausanias' jealousy of Lysander. Whatever the personal dispositions of these two men, there must have been a more presentable pretext for the action that was taken after a vote by Spartan authorities and ratified by a convention of Sparta's allies. The objective of the expedition led by Pausanias was ostensibly the same as Lysander's: to support those loyal to Sparta against the foes of Sparta. But Pausanias and his fellow Spartans recognized that Lysander's friends were not the only Athenians worthy of friendship with Sparta. A more broadly-based and therefore stable Athenian oligarchy could still be a dependent ally of Sparta. This was the argument advanced by the late Theramenes, and it was now advanced privately by members of the city party not sympathetic to the hard line of the Ten, and, we may infer, by representatives from Thrasybulus and his fellows in Piraeus.[51]

The Peloponnesian army led into Attica by Pausanias was to be the tool for resolving a conflict among peers. Force was to be used only to the extent needed to assure that the final settlement was made in the name of the right principles. Initially, Pausanias' presence would demonstrate who Sparta's friends were by displaying those arrayed with and against him. Ultimately, Pausanias required all eligible parties to be arrayed with him. But one group, it was foreseen, could make the passage from one side to the other only after being winnowed on Peloponnesian spears and shields. Thrasybulus could not be allowed to embrace reconciliation until he had been humbled by defeat. Pausanias' arms would advance, then, for the cause not of the complete destruction of the men of Piraeus, but for the cause of displaying that their over-stuffed pride in their prowess at war was doomed, filled out as it was with the chaff of a worthless mob. It was the crowd of foreigners, slaves and ex-slaves, and honorless Athenian poor that made up the majority of Thrasybulus' force that had to be thrashed and scattered before the worthy Athenians among them could be welcomed back among their peers and kinsmen. If not the particular form of government, at least the higher principles for which Critias had fought and died had to be vindicated now by Spartan arms.

Bringing up the allied army and the mercenaries hired by Lysander to an encampment outside of Piraeus, Pausanias began operations by delivering an ultimatum to the men within to disperse. When it became clear that no such thing would happen, the forces of Pausanias and Lysander attacked the Athenians in Piraeus, with no particular effect. The latter, defending an urban area, even with walls dismantled, were able to withdraw to strong defensive positions, out of reach of the Peloponnesian phalanx. Skirmishing on a second day led to more significant action. Chasing off Athenian light-armed skirmishers, some of the Spartan hoplites let their enthusiasm draw them into a dangerously exposed position in the heart of Piraeus. They were repelled with losses, after which the two sides formed line and met head-on. Once again, the confines of the urban area and marshy ground on the outskirts initially favored the Athenians, at least to the extent that they could not be outflanked by the overwhelming numbers of the Peloponnesians. In the contest, however, the Athenians were forced to give ground at several points along their line, and Pausanias was able to erect a trophy over those of the enemy who had fallen. This demonstration of superiority was sufficient for Pausanias' purposes.[52]

At this point, emissaries from the Piraeus and private individuals from the city came to Pausanias, all at his covert prompting according to Xenophon, to propose a cessation of hostilities and a reconciliation of all Athenians willing to submit to Spartan authority. A speech composed by Lysias a few years later recalls a vivid scene of supplication.

Diognetus, the surviving brother of Nicias, approached Pausanias in the company of Nicias' nephews and grandson and placed the youngest of these, Nicias' grandson, on the lap of Pausanias. All of these young men had been orphaned by the remorseless purges of the Thirty, yet they, like King Pausanias himself, came of a line renowned for peace and friendship between Sparta and Athens. In 421 the elder Nicias had been the leading proponent of the treaties between Athens and Sparta that were championed, on the Spartan side, by Pausanias' father, King Pleistoanax. The ceremony of supplication invoked this past as a guide to present action. Pausanias, having presided over the requisite rituals of supremacy and supplication, now dispatched to Sparta representatives of the Athenians favoring reconciliation, with his endorsement of their proposals.[53]

The Ten at Athens meanwhile felt that democratic elements had not yet been sufficiently humbled, and they sent their own ambassadors to Sparta to demand that those in Piraeus be made to surrender their defensive positions to the Spartans before they treated for reconciliation. Their intransigence backfired. All had been so prepared beforehand by Pausanias that the Spartan authorities were content to appoint a commission of fifteen men to join the king and his leading counselors in Attica, to deliberate with him on the details of a final settlement. When it became clear that the most significant obstacle to reconciliation was the Ten themselves, they were deposed and replaced by a new Ten amenable to the goals of Pausanias and the majority of the Athenians both in Athens and in Piraeus.[54]

As a result of these transitions, near the end of summer 403, Pausanias and the Spartans gave their approval to terms of reconciliation worked out between the two major Athenian factions of the Piraeus and the city. Equity between these two factions was assured by the election of ten men from the partisans in Piraeus to join the Ten of the city in a new steering committee of twenty, "to superintend the city until the laws were established," that is, until the rules for deliberative and judicial procedures should be settled and regular officers appointed. Those at Athens who felt unable to abide the return of the exiles were allowed to remove themselves, within a stipulated period of time, to Eleusis. Eleusis thus became an enclave for the men most responsible for the judicial murders carried out over the previous year. These included most survivors of the Thirty, of the Eleven and of the Ten of Piraeus, and the hard-liners among the first board of Ten of the city, along with their staunchest supporters. All parties, the men from Piraeus, the men of the city, and those at Eleusis, were confirmed as "friends of Sparta."[55]

The treaty of 404 with its subordinate alliance to Sparta was reaffirmed in this process. Added to it was the obligation to repay Sparta the loan of one hundred talents advanced to the oligarchs to support the recent military activities directed by Lysander in Attica. As in 404, the Athenians undertook to establish "ancestral laws," with no prescription for what was to be included in, or excluded from, these laws. Having created the conditions for a constitutional debate at Athens among men who were regarded as likely to restrict political power to their own class, the policy of Pausanias, unlike that of Lysander, called for allowing the Athenians to resolve the issue among themselves.

The extreme oligarchy supported by Lysander had already proven a costly failure, so, ostensibly, a decision now had to be made about an appropriate form of moderate oligarchy. The way was indicated, to the satisfaction of Pausanias and his fifteen advisors, by a stipulation in the reconciliation agreement that judicial authority, in the case of the crimes of the Thirty and their colleagues in office, should be restricted to a court of peers defined by a property qualification. This provision was surely seen by the Twenty now administering the state, and by many of their supporters, as pointing the way toward an overall restriction of office-holding, jury service, and possibly even voting rights in the Assembly to a propertied class.[56]

The debate over the precise form of the *patrios politeia,* the "ancestral constitution," was about to resume. As on two previous occasions, in 411 and 404, the debate began from the assumption that some curtailment of the full democracy was required. That it did not, on this occasion, result in a pro-Spartan oligarchy was due in part to the profound revulsion at the recent deeds of the friends of Sparta, to deeply held feelings about the physical integrity of Athens and Attica, and to the tenacity of Thrasybulus and his followers, who showed that the many of lesser grace could no more easily be dismissed from politics than they could be from the field of battle.

PART THREE

Resurrecting Athens, 403–395

CHAPTER TEN

The Laws of Athens, 403–400

> *When the people assumed authority they established the constitution which is still in force, in the archonship of Pythodorus [404/3].... It was deemed just that the people should take part in the constitutional order because they had secured their return by their own efforts. This was the eleventh change of constitution.... The eleventh came after the return from Phyle and Piraeus; it has lasted until the present day with ever-increasing power being assumed by the majority.*
>
> ARISTOTLE *CONSTITUTION OF THE ATHENIANS* 41

A half-century after the end of the Athenian civil war of 404/3, Plato spoke of that period, when he was in his mid-to-late twenties, as the turning point of his life. He reflects on this episode in the continuation of the autobiographical remarks quoted previously from his *Seventh Letter.* It is a unique summation, at odds with the eulogy of restored democracy found in public orations (exemplified even in Plato's own *Menexenus*) and in the histories composed in the following generations.

Not that Plato's growing torment was unique, for many Athenians who shared his values likewise found themselves cut adrift and struggling, over the course of years, to redefine their direction in terms that would give political meaning to their lives. The biography of Plato's age-mate, Xenophon, is perhaps the most spectacular of these odysseys and homecomings. Their older contemporary, Isocrates, distinguished himself by steering a course in rhetoric, following the example of Theramenes, that strove to find the center of a broad and turbulent Athenian stream. Plato dived deep beneath the surface, and saw marvelous things. And though he, of all those of his generation, searched with the most imagination for a new outlet through which to direct his experience, his life's work remained immersed in Athens and driven by the currents that had impelled him through the treacherous narrows of 404/3.

Plato describes the beginning of his journey, after "the fall of the Thirty and of their whole system of government," as follows:

> Once more, less hastily this time, but surely, I was moved by the desire to take part in public life and in politics. To be sure, in those days too, full of disturbances as they were, there were many things occurring to cause offense, nor

> is it surprising that in time of revolution men in some cases took undue revenge on their enemies. Yet for all that the restored exiles displayed great moderation. As it chanced, however, some of those in power brought against this companion of mine, Socrates, whom I have mentioned, a most iniquitous charge, which he least of all men deserved. They put him on trial for impiety and the people condemned and put to death the man who had refused to take part in the iniquitous arrest of one of the friends of those in exile, at the very time when the people were suffering in exile themselves.
>
> Now as I considered these matters, as well as the sort of men who were active in politics, and the laws and the customs, the more I examined them and the more I advanced in years, the harder it appeared to me to administer political affairs correctly. For one thing, nothing could be done without friends and loyal companions, and such men were not easy to find ready at hand, since our city was no longer administered according to the standards and practices of our fathers. Neither could such men be created afresh with any facility. Furthermore the written laws and the customs were being corrupted at an astounding rate. The result was that I, who had at first been full of eagerness for a public career, as I gazed upon the whirlpool of public life saw the incessant movements of shifting currents, at last felt dizzy, and, while I did not cease to consider means of improving this particular situation and indeed of reforming the whole constitution, yet, in regard to action, I kept waiting for favorable moments, and finally saw clearly in regard to all states now existing that without exception their system of government is bad. The state of their laws is almost beyond redemption except through some miraculous plan accompanied by good luck. Hence I was compelled to say in praise of the correct philosophy that it affords a vantage point from which we can discern in all cases what is just for communities and for individuals, and that accordingly the human race will not see better days until either the stock of those who rightly and genuinely follow philosophy acquire political authority, or else the class of those who have political power be led by some dispensation of providence to become real philosophers.[1]

An exegesis of this nearly historical piece of writing by Plato provides an apt direction for the closing chapters of this work. The investigation will reveal something of "the sort of men who were active in politics" following the maelstrom of 404/3. It will also reveal what Plato had in mind when he spoke of the astounding corruption of written laws and customs transpiring in the early years of the restored democracy.

The attempt to penetrate the surface of eulogy and simplified history will involve us, as Plato warns, in a dizzying movement of viewpoints. Under these conditions, a unified narrative of events may be an elusive goal, or at least one that cannot be achieved without introducing new simplifications that are as problematic as any ancient narrative. From this point on, therefore, chronological narrative is no longer the most effective investigative mode for the issues presented in our sources, and it will be gradually subsumed by thematic analysis.

The goal of this final section is to appreciate the raw and seemingly contradictory forces at play in democratic Athens soon after the end of the Peloponnesian War and the oligarchy of the Thirty. For it is the thesis of this book that unique and significant conditions were generated out of the interplay of law, politics, piety, and personal agendas under the restored democracy at Athens, with the experiences of the final decades of empire and civil war still fresh in mind. These were conditions that both did away with Socrates and gave rise to a profound desire to express the truth, a desire that shines brightest in the pages of Plato and of Thucydides.

SOURCES

The speedy canonization of the heroes of Phyle as the restorers of democracy has obscured for us much of the sequence of events and arguments on which the constitutional debate of 403 turned. To recover a useful perspective on events lost in the deliberate foreshortening of public memory, we must first discard the habit of speaking of the reconciliation as an agreement between the men of the city and the "democrats" from Piraeus. In view of the constitutional questions that remained unresolved at the time of the settlement, and especially in view of the prejudice in favor of oligarchy that prevailed in the negotiations presided over by Pausanias and the Spartans, it is a mistake to treat the reconciliation as synonymous with the restoration of the democracy, even though within a few months the Athenians imposed this teleology on events.

Fortunately, despite the powerful urge to regard every act as a step toward the inevitable restoration of democracy, several contemporary sources preserve essential elements of a contentious debate. Xenophon's account in his *Hellenica* is of primary importance, for, though it was written years later, it is based on his participation as a cavalryman in the turmoil of 403 at Athens. He and others of his standing must have been anxious observers of events, concerned to assess their own prospects in the state that was being reformed. Lysias, the orator, was another individual anxious about his status in the rapidly shifting conditions of that day. Along with his numerous surviving speeches, we possess a portion of a speech arguing against a proposal to curtail the former democracy. Other speeches by Lysias, Isocrates, and Andocides composed within the first few years of the restored democracy show deference to the resurgent *demos,* yet manage also to reveal some of the tensions being mediated in this process.

These speeches come from a far richer array of contemporary works studied by following generations in a tradition that defined fourth-century rhetoric and historiography. The tradition included the study of contemporary decrees, some of which have come down to us in quotations or on stone in various states of preservation. These attest the pride with which the restoration was proclaimed and its supporters rewarded. Aristotle's *Constitution of the Athenians* is the single most important vestige of the Athenian tradition in fourth-century historiography, which is otherwise also represented in the much later historical compilation by Diodorus. Finally, as with everything Plato has written, his dialogues set within this period, in particular the *Meno, Euthyphro, Crito,* and *Apology,* repay attention. Through them and through Xenophon's Socratic writings we gain an uncommon perspective on the living moment.[2]

THE FEW AND THE MANY

How did the Spartan settlement of the Athenian civil war in 403 lead, quickly and despite strong sentiment to the contrary, to a restoration of democracy at Athens in 403? Our investigation may begin with Xenophon's account of the goals of the men in Piraeus.

Thrasybulus made no mention of the cause of democracy in his speech before the battle against the Thirty at Munychia. No constitutional issue was at stake here, only the revenge of peers. After battle had slaked anger, remorse over fallen fellow-Athenians prevailed and the appeal for rapprochement was strongly felt on both sides. But despite this profound awareness, and despite the change of government in Athens described in the last chapter, the men of the city continued to oppose Thrasybulus and his followers. The reason for this continued opposition was an underlying dissonance between the definitions of peerage accepted by the two sides. The men of Athens had been selected to uphold the most restrictive concept of worthiness for citizenship; the power of the men in Piraeus, on the other hand, lay in the inclusive potential of the *patrios politeia.*

According to Diodorus, Thrasybulus had announced his cause to be the return of "ancestral citizenship" (the most literal translation of *patrios politeia*) to the *demos* shortly before his march to Piraeus. Once in Piraeus, Thrasybulus had to increase his ranks quickly. In addition to rallying the many Athenians expelled from the city by the Thirty, he used a variety of appeals to attract a sufficient following to challenge the 3,000. Best attested is his promise of *isoteleia,* a form of tax-relief, to resident foreigners. All registered metics were subject to a poll tax *(metoikion),* and whenever *eisphorai* were imposed all metics were assessed. Citizens paid no poll tax and only contributed to *eisphorai* if they had a certain level of property. The promise of tax liabilities equal to those of citizens therefore appealed to tradesmen and businessmen of all social standings. As hostilities became drawn out over the summer and the stakes were raised by the men in the city, Thrasybulus let it be known that he would champion a grant of citizenship to all who fought with the Athenians in Piraeus. Such a measure had the precedent of the enfranchisement of slaves and metics who had fought three years earlier at Arginusae.[3]

Since the days of Cleisthenes, of Pericles, and most recently of Cleophon, the inclusive rhetoric of *arete* had become well developed, especially when proven in battle. But to the Thirty and their adherents, nothing could signal more clearly the debasement of the Athenian *politeia*. Laxity in enforcing the boundaries of citizenship, they felt, was directly responsible for the travesties committed and disasters suffered by the past democracy. Further, the ill effects of foreign influence were not to be measured solely in terms of the numbers who enjoyed the juridic status of citizenship. The great number of foreign immigrants who, especially under Pericles, took up residence in Athens in order to profit from the commerce of the imperial city were also a pernicious influence, according to the ideological allies of Critias. The wealth of these metics had enabled many of them to enter respectable society. But their sympathies could never coincide with those of the self-proclaimed true Athenians, according to the followers of Critias. These foreign residents were the men that the Thirty had tried most systematically to exterminate as a class. No wonder the Ten at Athens felt ill at ease at the prospect of embracing all the followers of Thrasybulus.[4]

As King Pausanias presided over negotiations on reconciliation, the Ten must have been at pains to explain to the Spartans that many of the men of Piraeus who sought to return to Athens under the cover of peace and unity had no legitimate claim to inclusion. But the Spartans had no patience for these quibbles. The oaths of subservience to Sparta embodied the only ideological issue of concern to the Spartans. They had obtained these oaths following the appropriate ceremonies of supplication, all in the shadow of their trophies of supremacy in battle. The Spartans dealt with honorable individuals, and, under the circumstances established by King Pausanias, they trusted such men to settle internal affairs according to custom.[5]

The Spartans had every reason to rely on such men, for they were well represented on both sides of the division being bridged by Pausanias. Not a few influential men among the Piraeus partisans were anxious that Thrasybulus' rhetoric of popular resistance should not lead to the renewal of popular government. Their sentiments matched exactly those of the men of the city: "There was a fear lest the populace might repeat their outrages on the affluent class through the recovery of their ancient liberties." So Dionysius of Halicarnassus introduces a proposal, surely one that circulated during negotiations with Pausanias, to limit citizenship to those who possessed a certain property qualification. The proposal came from Phormisius, one of those in Thrasybulus' company who shared the political perspective of the late Theramenes. It clearly embodied the principles that the Spartans expected the Athenians to put into practice.[6]

But with the disbanding of Pausanias' army, the constitutional debate became a domestic issue. The general who needed followers in the field now sought to secure that same following in the Assembly, and this could only be done by a full restoration of the democracy. Thrasybulus had to act quickly to stem the movement into oligarchy, and Xenophon's account of the ceremonial return of the men of Piraeus to Athens, immediately after the departure of Pausanias, shows how he did so.

The men from Piraeus and the men of the city party, with their respective leaders, made a procession under arms into Athens and up to the Acropolis to offer sacrifices to Athena. This was probably the occasion when oaths of reconciliation were taken by all members of the reconstituted Athenian community. The procession echoed that of the Panathenaic festival, when all Athenians, citizens and metics, and even slaves and visiting foreigners, joined together in offering devotions to Athena. On those occasions as on this, Athenian pride and strength was displayed in the armed procession of citizens, if not also of the metics who were regularly marshaled with citizens for military service. On this occasion, most Athenians in the ranks from Piraeus were men who had been armed by communal enterprise and through funds channeled in from supporters abroad. The elite hoplites from the city may have felt that many of the Piraeus men did not deserve their emblems of hoplite respectability, but before these exclusionary prejudices could be implemented politically, Thrasybulus seized the moment to make a point.[7]

Upon leaving the Acropolis, the assembled mass of Athenians was halted by the generals from Piraeus and was harangued by Thrasybulus. The speech is reproduced in part by Xenophon, who probably took part in the procession and now would have heard, for the first time since the trial of the generals after Arginusae, a public address by the man whose leadership had brought ruin on his own commanders.

Thrasybulus challenged the men of the city to justify their assertion of superiority over other Athenians. "I advise you, men of the city," Xenophon quotes Thrasybulus, "to 'know yourselves.' And you would best do so if you were to reckon the basis of your arrogance in striving to rule over us." In a series of rhetorical questions, Thrasybulus asked if they possessed a superior command of justice or of courage. He then goes on:

> Well now, would you say that you excelled in intelligence—you who had fortifications and weapons and money and Peloponnesian allies, and who have been outdone by men who had none of these? Or, perhaps, do you pride yourselves on your relationship to the Spartans? How could this be? *They* have handed you over, chained and muzzled like dogs that bite, to this outraged populace, and have gone off and left you![8]

For a speech at a ceremony of reconciliation, it had a remarkably belligerent tone. Thrasybulus' aim, through his rhetorical challenge, was to reduce to nonsense the former claims of the "best" Athenians to exclusive political power. Their sense of justice had led to supreme injustice; their courage had resulted in their defeat; their deliberative skills had left them outmaneuvered; and their choice of friends had left them surrounded and outnumbered by their former foes. Experience, in other words, had shown the ideological premises of their arrogance to be flawed.

Thrasybulus invited them not to reject the philosophy that underlay their past actions, but to seek a more perfect realization of its goals. His opening invitation to the men of the city, surely the most memorable phrase from this harangue, to "know yourselves," must have sounded a familiar invocation of the spirit of philosophic reflection among the elite of Athens. The Delphic maxim is quoted often in the works of Plato, usually put in the mouth of Socrates, and in one instance, significantly, as a capstone to a line of argument claiming that true philosophy and true philosophers reside at Sparta. In another instance the maxim is expressed, for the edification of Charmides, by Critias. In Thrasybulus' harangue, the maxim was prelude to wresting from the aristocracy the admission that their arrogation of the right to rule over other Athenians had no objective basis. Reflection would force the concession that truer justice, more unyielding courage, and greater intelligence, as well as more loyal friends, lay with the greater numbers of Athenians.[9]

In arguing across the dichotomy between the many who were poor and the self-acknowledged "best" of Athens, Thrasybulus adopted a remarkable rhetorical stance. Against the 3,000 of Athens who possessed "walls, arms, and money," Thrasybulus identified himself with "the poorer populace" *(penesteros demos)*. This was an inversion of the familiar demagoguery of the past decade. Cleophon had built his career by proclaiming that aristocratic attainments were the birthright of all Athenians, and to secure the means to them their supreme goal, in the Assembly and on the battlefield. Aristocratic disdain for the presumption of poor Athenians encouraged by Cleophon was eventually transformed, under the Thirty, into a violent display of the difference between the "best" and the "base." Now Thrasybulus seized upon this distinction to show how hollow and fragile the glistening ornament of Athenian aristocracy was when voided of the poorer and menial *demos* and its champions.

So Thrasybulus appropriated the distinctions lately championed by the Thirty and their successors, the Ten in Athens, but adopted the opposing stance in speaking as "we, the people," including "the poorer people," directly against "you, the men of the city," and "the wealthier men." Speaking so forcefully, and in the presence of the armed majority of his followers from Piraeus, he wanted to intimidate those who were contemplating the curtailment of democracy and to defeat beforehand any motion that would have been tantamount to voting oligarchy into existence, as had been done in assemblies convened to hear the motions of Peisander in 411 and of Dracontides in 404. If no specific proposal to limit citizenship were ever enacted, then, by default, the restoration of the ancient laws of Athens *(ar-*

chaioi nomoi) could only mean that citizenship again belonged to those who had possessed it under the late democracy.[10]

THE RESTORATION OF A DEMOCRACY

Not all of the men who marched into Athens with Thrasybulus applauded the message he delivered on that day. From Aristotle we learn that Archinus, Anytus, and Phormisius, all with Thrasybulus in 403, had, before the terror of the Thirty, been among the "many" advocates of an "ancestral constitution" that lay somewhere between democracy and oligarchy. It is unlikely that these men had experienced any fundamental change of convictions in the meantime. Archinus' record after the restoration shows him to be a dedicated champion of moderation. Anytus is somewhat ambiguous. He struggled, in whatever company he found himself, to maintain a reputation for good sense, decency, and modesty. Plato may have had his tongue pressed against his cheek when he attributed these qualities to Anytus, the man who became Socrates' most famous accuser, but his assessment reflects common opinion attested elsewhere. Phormisius, on the other hand, is on record as an orator of archaic stamp and, on the occasion of the return of the partisans from Piraeus, as the advocate of a distinctly exclusive form of Athenian *politeia*.[11]

Phormisius authored a proposal to limit Athenian citizenship to those who owned land, a proposal which would have disenfranchised about five thousand former citizens. How this round number was derived we are not told. Five thousand is close to the modern estimates of the number of Athenian *thetes* who survived the Peloponnesian War, and this traditional distinction may well have been the basis of the calculation underlying Phormisius' proposal. Athenians above thetic status in 403 were roughly double that number, so Phormisius might reasonably expect that his proposal would appeal to a decisive majority among Athenians. It was considerably more liberal than the former polity of the 3,000, yet it still conformed to the sort of constitutional settlement anticipated by Pausanias and the Spartans. But, as soon as the Spartans were gone, Thrasybulus identified himself as the champion of those who preferred to sanction no such exclusionary privileges. Either he or a close political ally must have been the speaker of a systematic denunciation of Phormisius' proposal composed by Lysias. It is important to consider the context in which Phormisius' proposal was debated and ultimately rejected.[12]

Lysias' arguments against Phormisius' proposal are directed to an audience made up of both men from the city and men from Piraeus. But these did not include all of the Athenians who came from Piraeus, for the speech was clearly directed to a propertied audience. In contrast to Thrasybulus' speech below the Acropolis, here the common people, the *demos,* are spoken of in the third person, while the audience, addressed in the second person, is said to possess the sort of property which is typically the target of unscrupulous oligarchs. The audience was thus almost certainly the body of "those possessing taxable property," the body qualified to sit in judgment on office-holders under the Thirty, according to the reconciliation, and in effect the same body to which Phormisius proposed to limit citizenship. Like the Assembly at Colonus in 411, this was a convention of interested Athenians who were expected to vote to empower themselves and to exclude the unworthies.[13]

We would like to know how such a group was convened. The Athenians who assembled to deliberate political measures, perhaps on this occasion for the first time after the reconciliation, must have had some provisional means at hand to discriminate between those who were in and those who were out. Although no source beyond the speech against Phormisius describes this stage of interim polity, there are clues that suggest the answer. Among the first undertakings of the Athenian *demos,* once it was constituted in what came to be described as the restored democracy, was to reappoint a board of 500 *nomothetai* to begin rectifying the confusion of statutes left after the collapse of the Thirty. This board was "elected by the demes," as we learn from a document cited by Andocides (and quoted below, at pp. 263–64). The local authorities of the demes, or townships of Attica, clearly had a means for determining eligible candidates for election to office, and this means is attested, elsewhere, as the *lexiarchikon grammateion,* the "office-selection register." The best evidence for the nature of this register, in an inscription from near the middle of the fifth century, indicates that it could be regarded as the comprehensive register of Athenian citizens above thetic status. Traditionally, those at or above hoplite status, or the Solonian zeugite census, had measurable property. A register of these Athenians was most likely the source of Phormisius' supposed group of Athenian land-owners, and deme officers were most likely the men responsible for granting admission to the provisional assembly of Athenians.[14]

One of the chief arguments composed by Lysias against Phormisius' proposal was that by limiting citizenship to property holders, the numbers of Athenians qualified for military service would be unduly diminished. Thrasybulus had made the difference in numbers plain to all in his harangue to the ceremonial gathering of reunited Athenians. Supporters of Phormisius might ask: were *all* the men of the procession into Athens legitimate Athenians? Were all the bearers of hoplite arms truly qualified to bear them? Did not the force from Piraeus include an indiscriminate mass of men, many of them foreigners and even slaves, whose arms were provided by others? Such querulous points, however, did little to turn the balance against the inherent logic and emotional appeal of the arguments of Thrasybulus and his supporters: a larger Athenian state would be a stronger one, would have a better chance at restoring former glories, and would be the surest safeguard against the excesses towards which oligarchy, even conceived in moderate terms, had twice turned in the last decade at Athens. The proposal to limit citizenship and curtail the democracy was thus defeated.

Despite the decision not to start again down the dangerous path of proscription, circumstances in the fall of 403/2 favored the allotment of councilors and others officers of state from within the pool of candidates that Phormisius had expected to embrace his proposal. Political disruption, expulsions, and confiscations of property on the one hand, and an enthusiastic mob of men returned from Piraeus on the other, all must have prompted caution while claims for the recovery of confiscated property were being adjudicated and while the limits of citizenship, in principle open to the lowliest of Athenians, still had to be defined. Juries to hear property suits and other matters of immediate urgency were most likely composed, like the 500 *nomothetai,* by nominees approved by deme officials, therefore *de facto* by men who were judged to be above thetic status.

Thus the government that came into being in the year of Eucleides, the first eponymous archon after the reconciliation, was composed of men who, by virtue of recent experience, could be persuaded to move away from any semblance of oligarchy, but who also felt that their collective project could at last make democracy something better than it had been. Although somewhat clouded and unpredictable, the climate seemed to encourage the cautious optimism expressed by Plato. It was characterized by a spirit of moderation, expressed by several sources in terms not unlike Thucydides' approval of the regime of the so-called Five Thousand eight years earlier.

Aristotle attributes the moderation to wise leadership on this occasion. But wise leadership, in an Athenian context, depended upon the sentiments prevailing within the voting public. Unlike conditions during the ephemeral government of the Five Thousand in 411/10, affairs abroad did not move rapidly to transform a mood of circumspection into the enthusiasm of popular aggrandizement. The battles that transformed Athens now were political, juridical, and internal. The high ground in these contests was held by those who could best articulate the prudence acquired, above all, from a keen sense of what they had lately regained but might lose again.[15]

THE HEROES OF PIRAEUS

Having triumphed in counsel in the cause for which he had fought in battle, Thrasybulus advanced a further proposal, one that would justify the support he had received for his cause under arms. Thrasybulus proposed the enfranchisement not only of all Athenians, but also of all foreigners who had joined him in Piraeus. In support of this proposal, Thrasybulus could appeal to the memory of another crisis of the Athenian democracy, the mobilization before the sea battle at Arginusae in 406. The metics and slaves who had served in the fleet on that occasion were rewarded with citizenship. Now, once again, metics and slaves had joined the ranks to fight for Athens, and, it could be argued, they deserved their reward even more than their comrades of three years past. After all, the rhetoric of Thrasybulus could claim, those men had merely preserved what already existed, but these had restored what was lost. As their leader in war and now their patron in politics, Thrasybulus would assure his own political ascendancy for some time to come if he could so swell the ranks of citizens in his debt.[16]

The groundswell of enthusiasm for the returned patriots that Thrasybulus hoped to ride into power was stemmed by his opponents before it could take effect. Archinus indicted Thrasybulus for having introduced the measure to the Assembly illegally, without first submitting it to the mandatory review of the Council. Thrasybulus had made his motion during the presidency of the Twenty appointed at the time of the reconciliation, before the regular Council had been constituted. Archinus' measure, a *graphe paranomon,* thus deftly suspended Thrasybulus' motion and submitted it to the judicial review of the Twenty, who were not likely to have been enthusiastic about the proposal.[17]

Archinus prevailed, and by his action the Twenty assigned the matter to a judicial hearing. Against the procedural charge Thrasybulus had no legal defense. Archinus had the established practices of Athenian law on his side, laws that Thrasybulus himself had vowed to uphold. Archinus may also have reminded the Athenians that, in the past, the admission of illegal proposals through the suspension of the *graphe paranomon* had been the vehicle by which the constitution had been subverted.

Even in defeat, Thrasybulus could not resist playing to the crowd. In the *timesis,* the hearing to set the penalty for his conviction, he is said to have quipped: "I deserve to be put to death, since I was the benefactor of such ungrateful Athenians." One would like to know how his jurors reacted to this wry allusion to the past severity of democratic justice. Their verdict in favor of the penalty proposed by the prosecution, however, displayed the prevailing spirit of restraint championed by Archinus: Thrasybulus was fined one drachma.[18]

There still remained the issue of how to reward partisans who had fought for the overthrow of the Thirty. According to Archinus, those who *initiated* the resistance by establishing themselves at Phyle deserved the highest honors, not those who joined the movement last of all. Therefore, probably early in the year of Eucleides, Archinus proposed the publication of a register of approximately sixty Athenians, "honored for their *arete* by the indigenous *demos* of the Athenians" and certified by the scrutiny of the Council, who first stood together at Phyle. Implicit in Archinus' measure, and highlighted by his recent suspension of Thrasybulus' proposal, was the priority accorded to native-born Athenians, among them Archinus and Thrasybulus themselves, in the honors of the day.[19]

The non-Athenians who joined the ranks in Phyle and Piraeus also deserved rewards, especially in view of the promises made in Piraeus in order to recruit them. Some of them did receive honors, but not until later, a matter of at least months, but more likely some two years after Thrasybulus' original proposal had been suspended. A partially preserved inscription records the award of citizenship to somewhat under a hundred foreigners who joined the fight at Phyle, and lesser honors (including *isoteleia*) to nearly nine hundred of those who joined the cause afterwards. The proposer of this decree, most likely, was again Thrasybulus. The belated passage of this measure and the comparatively small number of those honored (probably less than ten percent of the total numbers under arms by the time of the settlement of 403) reflect both pains taken to verify the participation of the individuals named and the reluctance of the reconciled factions to elevate to the status of Athenians men identified with the occupations listed on this monument. For the honorees named in this inscription are distinguished by the trades they practiced, among them, "onion-seller . . . cook . . . baker . . . wagon-maker . . . mule-driver . . . builder . . . contractor . . . shopkeeper . . . farmer."[20]

The men identified with these trades were not necessarily humble or poor. The orator Lysias, one of the financiers of the resistance, must have been named in one of the large missing portions of the list as a recipient of *isoteleia*. He was probably identified as "Lysias, shield-maker," despite the fact that he had been co-owner of a business that employed some 120 slaves, leased three well-appointed houses, and had more than once been a *choregos*. The list tacitly reflects the aristocratic bias against crafts and trades, a bias also reflected in the practice of the comic poets to pin trade-names on prominent demagogues, such as "tanner" (Cleon), "sheep-dealer" (Lysicles, who married Aspasia after Pericles' death), "lamp-maker" (Hyperbolus), and "lyre-maker" (Cleophon). It is likely that one of the criteria applied in drawing up this selective list of honorees was that they possessed some measurable fortune, or, at least (since many, like Lysias, suffered financial ruin as a result of the rule of the Thirty), that they had achieved some measure of social recognition among true Athenians.

That such men were honored at all attests to the persistence of Thrasybulus, whose military career had proven to him the utility of having such practical-minded men fighting for the recognition that others claimed by birth. It also bears witness to a gradually evolving mood of the restored *demos* (assuming as most likely the dating of this decree to 401/0) away from the high idealism of the leaders of the reconciliation toward a recognition, which could be traced back to Solon, of the value to Athens of men of crafts and trades.[21]

TRUE ATHENIANS

At issue, in the contests over citizenship between Archinus and Thrasybulus, and between Phormisius and his opponents, was the essence of being Athenian. Acknowledged innovation in this as in any practice of law and custom was absolutely inadmissible, so much so that the word for it, *neoterismos,* was also the pejorative term for "revolution." To this extent, Athenians and Spartans were in complete agreement: practice was to conform to ancestral tradition. But beyond sharing the ideal that ancestors, like parents, were the source of all sound instruction, Athenians and Spartans parted ways. More than two centuries of written tradition had endowed the Athenians with a far more complex system of access to their past than was available to the Spartans.

The Thirty, cleaving to their ideological and military masters, had rejected Athenian developments, superseding even the authority of Solon, whom they regarded as the introducer of unfortunate ambiguities into Athenian law, and had looked to the pre-Solonic poetry of Tyrtaeus as a sign that common ancestral ideals underlay the practices of both Spartan and Athenian aristocracy. This radical vision of ancestral essence, sought in a distant and ill-documented past, had endowed Critias and his fellows with the supreme authority, like that vested in the thirty revered Spartan elders of the *gerousia,* to interpret unwritten custom and to use its raw flame to burn away the dross and slag from the presumably pure Athenians.

The failure of the hyper-archaism of the Thirty left the Athenians seeking a more objective guide to ancestral tradition. Phormisius' proposal to link citizenship to land tenure had the virtue of utilizing a living tradition of peer affirmation, since ownership like citizenship ultimately rested on the testimony of kin and neighbors. The proposal was also rooted in the cherished notion that true Athenians were ultimately born of the soil of Attica itself. But, besides other objections, experience had shown that such an exclusionary definition would run into a certain awkwardness. There were Athenians who, because of some accident of circumstances, were technically not landowners but who, many would agree, ought nonetheless to be included among those who *could* be landowners. And there were those Athenians who happened to be owners of property but who, according to their enemies, had risen to that status only by some illegitimate means. Most importantly, however, since Solon had explicitly adjudicated on behalf of those Athenians who owned no property, written tradition ran counter to Phormisius' proposal to limit citizenship by a property qualification.

The issue was quickly resolved by reference to the only explicit criterion for citizenship to be found in the documentary evidence available to Athenians, namely, Pericles' citizenship law of 451/0. Reiterated in enactments of 403/2 attributed variously to one Nicomenes or to Aristophon, a politician whose long public career began with his service to the partisans in Piraeus, Pericles' law stipulated that citizenship belonged only to those who could show that they were the offspring of two Athenian parents. This qualification was also subject to the affirmation of peers and kinsmen, but it involved no material prerequisite. In fact, its application is best attested in instances of public distributions of grain, a concern of the poorest Athenians, which suggests that such a comprehensive definition of citizenship was only required when the affluence of democratic Athens was at its height and officers of the state required some guidelines for determining who among the otherwise indiscriminate masses deserved to receive its material benefits. Thus, in the fundamental matter of citizenship, ancestral tradition could provide no paradigm more ancient than Pericles' law that would restore legal conditions prevailing immediately before the oligarchy of the Thirty.[22]

Pericles' law, by affirming the nominal purity of Attic lineage, had affirmed the claim of even poor Athenians to ancestral Attic nobility by distinguishing them from the manifest newcomers attracted by the burgeoning wealth of Athens. The law implied the exclusion of newcomers from the upper echelons of Athenian society as well, but since this was most likely not its original intent, it did not immediately have this effect. Because of the number of known exceptions to Pericles' definition of citizenship within the era of the Peloponnesian War (most famously, his own youngest son by the Milesian Aspasia, the younger Pericles), it is commonly held that the attrition of war and plague had caused this law to be relaxed. It seems, however this may be, that the Athenians had always been inclined to accept as their own even individuals of completely foreign birth who sought kinship with Athenians, as long as they won the esteem of their peers.

Only such a flexible standard can account for the frequent allegations of foreign birth, even when demonstrably untrue, against prominent individuals both in comedy and in court speeches. Precisely because peer esteem was both malleable and decisive, accusations of alien parentage were productive stock for jokes on the comic stage, for attacks in the courtroom, and for the reforms of radical visionaries. Only a formal enactment of the Athenian *demos* could provide a bulwark against the inconstancy of opinion whenever an acknowledged foreigner sought integration into Athenian society. Although naturalized Athenians are attested across the fifth century, no public decree granting citizenship is known before the 420s, and it is perhaps significant that none inscribed on stone survives from before 410/9.[23]

The habit of limiting the rights of naturalization to those whose benefactions to the Athenian people could be attested before the Assembly seems only to have become a regular practice, though still rather infrequent, in the period of Cleophon's sway. By submitting such candidates to popular approval, in a procedure similar to the more common grants of proxeny status, demagogues had accustomed the *demos* to exert its authority over relations of friendship and kinship that had formerly been the domain of the aristocracy.

The Thirty had reacted against this development by destroying many of the inscriptions that recorded grants of citizenship and proxeny status. Perhaps they had targeted awards to individuals especially inimical to the pro-

Spartan ideology of the Thirty (although any friend of the *demos* satisfied this criterion). It is likely, however, that they were also seeking to destroy the influence of the democracy over social relations exerted through publicly enacted and recorded decrees.

The response of the Athenians in 403 was much the same as it had been after the overthrow of the Four Hundred in 411. Life, liberty, and property had all been imperiled by men who had acknowledged no limits to their powers and authority. Only by defining the political community in as explicit terms as possible could such arrogation of public authority be clearly repudiated and guarded against in the future.

All reform, restoration, and reconciliation movements at Athens, from 411 to 403, had advanced under the same slogan, namely, the establishment of the *patrios politeia.* But whereas the Thirty had eliminated citizens, overturned public enactments, and erased laws to achieve this end, the champions of reconciliation in 403 quickly recognized that their cause required the opposite course: the inclusion of all who had previously enjoyed citizenship, the restoration of public enactments (as long as they did not contradict the terms of reconciliation), and above all, the publication of the essential principles that defined what it meant to be Athenian, namely, the laws of Athens.

So in 403, as on the occasion of each revolution and counter-revolution of the preceding decade, the appointment of a commission to define the laws of the Athenian *politeia* was integral to the establishment of the new regime. The crucial difference between the work begun by democratic "establishers of the law," the *nomothetai,* in 410 and in 403, and the enactments of the Thirty was that, in the former cases, *publication* was an indispensable part of their mission. The process of producing texts that could support both the claim of traditional authority and the scrutiny of public approval was a fundamentally democratic process, and one that assured a high degree of continuity with the immediate, democratic past of Athens. Thus, to the degree that we can distinguish their activities, the work begun by the *nomothetai* of 403/2 seems by and large to resume the work of legislative collation left off in 405/4, almost as if nothing of consequence had intervened. What had intervened, however, had created by reaction a yet more profound reverence for law preserved by the written word.

ANDOCIDES AND THE LAWS

Andocides the son of Leogoras was among the many Athenian exiles who returned to Athens in the wake of the reconciliation of 403 to resume the rights of citizenship. His circumstances were unique, however, for he was the informant whose testimony, in 415, had allowed the Athenians to resolve the uproar caused by the mutilation of the Herms. By confessing his own involvement (something he later denied) in exchange for immunity, his testimony authorized the execution or exile of the men whom he named as participants in that conspiracy. Although released from arrest and exempt from prosecution for the affair of the Herms, he was despised by the friends of his victims and was soon compelled to go into voluntary exile when a decree was passed forbidding anyone who had confessed to a sacrilegious act from entering the Agora and the sanctuaries of Athens. On two previous occasions, in 411 and 405, when the state was in turmoil and the status of previous enactments was in question, Andocides had attempted to return to Athens, but withdrew again when he failed to secure the eradication of the embarrassing decree. Conditions in 403 favored another attempt at a homecoming. For then more than ever before, statesmen spoke of the importance of forgiveness and the need to restore the impaired nobility of Athens. Most importantly, this restoration included a new program to review the status of past laws and enactments.

Ambiguous but hopeful legal circumstances thus allowed Andocides to resume his participation in public life and his pursuit of the esteem of his fellow Athenians. His determination to live up to the accomplishments of his father and forebears reveals, incidentally, a jealous pride that accounts for his willful involvement in that earlier conspiracy to thwart Alcibiades. His determination itself is attested by his fulfillment of the liturgies of Gymnasiarch for the Hephaestia, a festival that in his youth began to be celebrated with lavish festivities, and as leader of the official embassies to the Isthmian and Olympic games, as well as by his election to the office of Treasurer of Sacred Funds on the Acropolis, all within three years of his return. Profits from commercial activities during his exile had made it possible for Andocides to enter these expensive games of status-seeking, and money and influence also made it possible for him, in his third year back at Athens, to secure financial backing and to outbid, at 36 talents, all rivals for the public contract to collect harbor taxes. One of his rivals attests to Andocides' ambition during the same period:

> Now he speaks before the people, makes accusations, is for disqualifying some of our magistrates; he attends meetings of the Council, and gives advice in debates on sacrifices, processions, prayers, and oracles.[24]

Above all, Andocides' determination is revealed in the artful preparation of his defense against the attack he surely foresaw. Through his involvement in public affairs and his business before the Council he must have endeavored to influence the course of legal reform. He certainly kept abreast of developments and knew full well what bearing the laws would have when, at last, he had made enough enemies that someone would revive the old charge against him, namely, that he had confessed to sacrilegious acts and was therefore forbidden to set foot in places where he wanted to make the finest show of himself.

Three years after his return, soon after his participation in the Mysteries of Eleusis, in the autumn of 400, Andocides defended his past actions against the charge of impiety that could carry a capital punishment. Callias son of Hipponicus, Torch-Bearer of the Eleusinian Mysteries, was the rival who brought suit against him, though Callias secured the cooperation of others to initiate the trial and to join in the accusations.

Andocides answered the charge against him with a tour de force, in a speech known by the title, *On the Mysteries*. Beginning with a review of the origins of the case in the denunciations of 415, it moves through a discussion of the legal conditions presently relevant to his case, paints a sordid picture of the motives of his opponents, and ends with an appeal to Athenians to embrace, through him, the former glories brought upon Athens by his forebears. Here the second section of his defense is our immediate concern. Its detailed, though not always candid, account of the laws affecting his case, provides our single most important, though by no means straightforward, guide to the legal reforms undertaken at Athens between 410 and 400.[25]

Describing the legal conditions under which his trial was being held, Andocides reminds his listeners that, with the appointment of the transitional administration of the Twenty, the Athenians had resolved that the "laws of Solon and the ordinances of Draco" would be in force, "until the laws were established." From the first, in other words, the Athenians recognized that, despite their ratification of the ancient laws of Solon and Draco, substantial legislative work was required before they could regard "the laws" as a whole to be set. The impending debate over political enfranchisement was but one of the issues still to be resolved. The experience of six years of legal research following the appointment of *nomothetai* in 411/10 had already revealed the sort of problems to be faced when collating archaic laws and more recent enactments, and the incisive treatment of this Gordian knot by the Thirty had only compounded the problem. Andocides is somewhat disingenuous, then, as he next identifies unacceptable legal liability as the sole reason for the systematic revision of the laws of Athens that followed. More was at stake than the issue that concerned him and his case.

It is worth quoting a portion of Andocides' account at length, since, through the document it quotes, it provides our clearest view of the process of legal review undertaken by the Athenians between 403 and 400.

> But after you selected by lot the members of the Council and elected *nomothetai*, they began to discover that there were not a few of the laws of Solon and Draco under which numbers of citizens were liable, owing to previous events. You therefore called a meeting of the Assembly to discuss the difficulty, and as

a result enacted that the whole of the laws should be examined and that such as were approved should be written up in the Stoa. Now read me the decree:

> Resolved by the *demos,* Teisamenus proposed: that the Athenians be governed in accordance with tradition, using the laws of Solon, his weights and measures, and using the ordinances of Draco, which we used in time past. Such further laws as may be necessary shall be written up on boards by the *nomothetai* elected by the Council, displayed facing the statues of the Eponymous Heroes for anyone who wishes to examine them, and handed over to the magistrates during the present month. The laws thus handed over, however, shall be submitted beforehand to examination by the Council and the 500 *nomothetai* elected by the Demes, when they have taken their oath. Further, any private citizen who so desires may come before the Council and suggest improvements in the laws. When the laws have been ratified, they shall be placed under the guardianship of the Council of the Areopagus, so that magistrates shall use only laws that are in effect. Those laws which are being authorized shall be written up on the wall, where they were written up previously, for anyone who wishes to examine them.

So, gentlemen, the laws were scrutinized in accordance with this decree, and those that were authorized they wrote up in the Stoa. When they were written up, we ratified a law which you all follow. Now read me the law:

> Law.—In no circumstance shall magistrates make use of an unwritten law *(agraphos nomos)*.[26]

Explicit as these texts are, their interpretation on several points has proven to be as difficult for modern scholars as, to compare small things with great, it evidently was among the Athenians. Fortunately, the principles guiding these enactments are fairly straightforward. Beginning with these, the following section moves gradually into details that have proven more controversial. Much discussion will focus on understanding procedures and physical arrangements, details that might at first seem essential only to specialists. These features, however, were part of the common knowledge of the jury addressed by Andocides, and will, by the end of this and in the following chapters, prove their relevance to our understanding of an important evolution in the concept of law at Athens.

THE WORK OF THE *NOMOTHETAI*

At the head of Teisamenus' proposal stands the statement that the Athenians are to constitute, or govern, themselves according to ancestral practices *(kata ta patria)*. The remainder of the proposal endeavors to remove the ambiguities from this problematic claim, beginning with the important declaration that ancestral authority is to be sought first of all in the oldest body of written legislation available to the Athenians, the *nomoi* of Solon and *thes-*

moi of Draco. Statutes of these lawgivers were still inscribed and publicly displayed on the venerable *axones* and *kyrbeis* and were thus acknowledged to be the living stock of ancient Athenian law; and although, as the decree makes explicit, they were subject to adaptation to render the laws suitable to current conditions, like the scarred but still living sacred olive trees of Attica they could still be regarded as ancient and ancestral.[27]

As conservative as this declaration was, it was an affirmation of democratic principles that was not entirely welcomed by those who still felt some sympathy for the legislative program of the Thirty. The reference to Solonic weights and measures in Teisamenus' proposal indicates how extensive the Thirty's revisionism had been, finding fault with even this seemingly neutral establishment of standards. Their objection probably had as its ideological motive the adoption of the Pheidonian–Aeginetan standard that prevailed in the heart of the Peloponnese, as opposed to the Attic-Euboic standard used in most maritime states. The Pheidonian standard was regarded as the older, and probably during the pre-404 phase of legislative research it had been discovered or recognized that Pheidon's weights and measures had been in use in Attica too, until Solon revised Attic usage, promoting commercial connections of the sort that, in the later words of Plato, "fills a city with wholesale traffic and retail huckstering, breeds shifty and distrustful habits of the soul." Even this restoration of Solonian practice, then, might have been seen by some as an element of the degenerative influence lamented by Plato when he notes that "our city was no longer administered according to the standards and practices of our fathers...."[28]

The standards guiding Teisamenus and his colleagues, however, were the attested laws, regulations, and practices in use "in time past," a term that could apply to any enactments of the *demos* before the oligarchy of the Thirty. In this respect, Teisamenus' proposal was a re-affirmation of the project to establish authoritative texts of the laws that had been underway between 411/10 and 405/4. During that period we know that an inscription displaying Draco's law of homicide had been set up, that Solon's laws were the object of an ongoing review, and that numerous statutes of diverse origin were inscribed for public display. This recent work was revalidated in another decree of 403/2, quoted by Demosthenes:

> Diocles proposed: that laws ratified under the democracy before the archonship of Eucleides [403/2] and those laws ratified during the archonship of Eucleides that have been written up shall have authority....[29]

Diocles' decree shows that the decree of Teisamenus was not, as Andocides suggests, merely a response to *newly discovered* legal ambiguities. Rather, the decree of Teisamenus was one of several steps taken to re-implement the processes of legislative reform that had been interrupted by *stasis* and the Thirty. As suggested in chapter 5, the dual boards of *nomo-*

thetai, those chosen by the Council to draft specific legislative proposals and a larger board to ratify the proposals, were probably similarly constituted during the period of legislative reform underway between 411/10 and 405/4. Andocides himself says that the *nomothetai* of 403/2 had already been elected by the time Teisamenus, probably himself one of their number, proposed his measure. Years of previous experience already indicated the magnitude of the work facing the *nomothetai* of 403/2.[30]

What appears to be new, and what certainly occupies the most space in Teisamenus' proposal, is the procedure for "writing up" new statutes that these *nomothetai* are to follow. Likewise in the decree of Diocles, public display of the laws ("those that have been written up") is essential to the validity of all measures passed as of the archonship of Eucleides.

The decree of Teisamenus specifies the temporary display of the texts under consideration for ratification in two stages. First, the texts as drafted by the *nomothetai* elected by the Council are to be written up on whitened boards and displayed, "facing the statues of the Eponymous Heroes," for a period of some days to allow "anyone who wishes to examine them" and to offer comments and suggestions when, afterward, the proposed laws come under consideration before the Council and the 500 *nomothetai* elected by the demes. Second, when these bodies have indicated their approval of the laws, and before they are "handed over to the magistrates" (i.e., to those archons responsible for the administration of specific statutes), the laws in the process of "being authorized" are again displayed, "written up on the wall, where they were written up previously, for anyone who wishes to examine them." This procedure is to be completed within "the present month," which is probably an awkward way of saying that each case, from drafting to final submission, is to be completed "within the space of a month."[31]

Interim display of measures under review by a special commission was nothing new, but such detailed instructions, especially involving a second stage of temporary display, show an unparalleled level of concern for public accountability. The concern probably arose from abuses of this process committed in 405/4. For during the period of growing factional conflict while the siege of Athens was underway, Cleophon had been condemned to death only after a law facilitating the designs of his opponents was opportunely "displayed." It is likely that the arrest of Callixeinus and others, probably his fellow *prytaneis,* on a charge of "deceiving the people," was arranged by just such a manipulation of statutes at that time, as perhaps was the intimidation of Agoratus and the arrest of the democratic generals in 404, actions that led directly to the appointment of the Thirty.[32]

The decree of Teisamenus was designed to prevent such abuses of the legislative process, and did not address the issue of how laws were to be preserved beyond stating that they were to be "placed under the guardianship of the Council of the Areopagus." At a moment when popularly allotted jury-courts were not being convened, this reference to the Council of the Areopagus may have been a hopeful remembrance of the broader jurisdiction that the venerable court of former archons had exercised until Ephialtes, in the late 460s, transferred to the popular courts nearly complete authority to enforce laws. Curation of the actual, authorized texts of the laws seems in fact to have been under the control of the allotted Council of 500.

The decree of Diocles, after the portion quoted above, goes on to instruct the Secretary of the Council to write the official effective date on the laws that were currently valid and to make such notations on future laws as they were enacted. From this it is clear that the authoritative repository of Athenian laws was under the jurisdiction of the Council and must in fact have consisted of the documents kept in the old Council-House. As described in chapter 6, by 408 the old Council-House, henceforth known as the Metroön after its tutelary deity, the Mother of the Gods, was devoted completely to the work of scrutiny and archival curation of public documents.[33]

Permanent display of laws and other public enactments on stone, on the other hand, was a selective matter. The decree of Teisamenus has often been interpreted to refer to such inscription, and the manner of Andocides' citation of it has encouraged the belief that the decree envisaged the inscription of all the valid laws of Athens. The process of reviewing the laws underway in 403/2 was wide ranging, and certainly had lasting effects on the concept and practice of law at Athens. But the inference that it also entailed the publication of a comprehensive law code on stone is not justified.

The decree of Teisamenus speaks of laws "written up on the wall, where they were written up previously." Andocides speaks of laws "written up in the Stoa" and seems to indicate that these were the same as the laws "written up on the wall." Modern commentators have accepted the implied connection and have taken it several steps further. "The wall" has been widely and without hesitation identified as a wall of the Stoa Basileios, where the old *axones* and *kyrbeis* of Draco and Solon are known to have been kept and where the archons traditionally took their oath to uphold the laws of Athens. As described in chapter 9, fragments of inscribed marble stelae bearing the texts of various regulations have been identified as vestiges of the laws "written up on the wall/in the Stoa" (see page 228). Taking their cue from Andocides, who states the intention of the Athenians to examine "the whole of the laws," many commentators have assumed that the surviving fragments preserve but a small sample of the laws originally inscribed, and that by the time Andocides spoke, something that could be described as "the Athenian law code" had been inscribed and was on display in the Stoa Basileios.[34]

Although much ingenuity has been devoted, over the years, to relating the physical evidence of stele-fragments and the remains of the Stoa Basileios to the hypothesis outlined above, a satisfactory arrangement has eluded description. Scholars have gradually recognized several factors that, taken together, compel a reassessment of the nature and extent of the display of inscribed laws: the decree of Teisamenus gives no clear instruction for inscriptions on stone, but it does provide for the temporary display of texts "written up on boards"; the small Stoa Basileios could not have accommodated anything like a comprehensive law code on stone; the absence of any mention by orators, after the speech of Andocides, of the "laws written up in the Stoa" raises strong doubts against the existence of anything like the hypothesized Athenian law code on stone.[35]

Recent reviews of these problems have begun to turn the balance of expert opinion toward the conclusion that most naturally emerges from the wording of Teisamenus' decree, namely, that his procedures make no reference to inscription on stone, but only describe a sequence of temporary displays, on painted boards, leading to a final, authorized text in an unspecified medium (but almost certainly papyrus). Some of these authorized texts were also published as inscriptions on stone, as actual fragments and other references to inscribed stelae attest. Andocides is probably referring to these when he mentions the laws "written up in the Stoa" (it is unfortunate that the verb "to write up," *anagraphein,* is also the usual verb for "to inscribe," so this word by itself can never distinguish temporary from permanent display). But Andocides is disingenuous to imply, as he does, that these displayed texts comprised the whole of valid Athenian law. He was skillfully playing on the sense of knowing the laws from having often seen them displayed in public that his audience of jurors had developed by the time of his trial late in 400.[36]

One consequence of the reconsideration of the display procedures described in the decree of Teisamenus has so far seemed difficult to accept in view of the long-held assumptions relating these procedures to the Stoa Basileios. According to the current reinterpretation, the second stage of temporary display, "on the wall, where they were written up previously," must refer to the same location as the original display, namely, "facing the statues of the Eponymous Heroes." These arrangements need have no relation to the later display of laws "in the Stoa" (be it the Stoa Basileios or any other stoa), which Andocides actually describes as a stage following the process of ratification. But in dissociating it from the Stoa Basileios "the wall . . . facing the statues of the Eponymous Heroes" has not yet been convincingly identified.[37]

Fortunately, it has recently become easier to visualize the physical settings and procedures for revising the laws of Athens in these years, thanks to a new identification by Ronald Stroud of an old monument in the Athenian Agora. Stroud has made a convincing case for recognizing the sixth-century structure by the southwest corner of the Agora, long conjecturally identified as the law court of the Heliaea, as the enclosure of Aeacus. This identification becomes relevant here in light of two further pieces of evidence. An entry preserved on a lexical papyrus discussing the Aeaceum at Athens states that "legal proceedings (*dik[ai]*) are written up on the Aeaceum." Standing on rising ground overlooking the Agora, the broad front wall of this enclosure would indeed have been a conspicuous and readily accessible surface for the display of public documents. The second point is that this enclosure lies immediately adjacent to the traces of a monument that is the most plausible candidate for the base of the statues of the Eponymous Heroes before they were moved to the north in the second half of the fourth century. Texts displayed on the wall of the Aeaceum could thus be well described as "facing the statues of the Eponymous Heroes"; the "Stoa" mentioned by Andocides would most likely be the prominent stoa adjacent to the Aeaceum, known archaeologically as South Stoa I (see figure 8 and map 4).[38]

A further circumstance favoring this identification is Aeacus' role as judge in the Underworld, according to Socrates in Plato's *Apology* and according to the "true story" told by Socrates at the end of Plato's *Gorgias*. Aeacus as judge of the dead is not attested elsewhere, but such a role suits the teleological mind of Plato, if not Socrates. Both Athenians would have been accustomed to seeing laws, decrees, and notices of suits posted on the face of Aeacus' shrine, and would have expected the practice to conform, however imperfectly, with the transcendent authority of the hero to pass final judgment.[39]

Amendments and additions to the laws of Athens thus moved month by month, before the view of all Athenians and under the gaze of their totemic tribal heroes, across the wall of Aeacus' shrine. We have no way of knowing if, as of the fall of 403, this occurred with any more frequency than it had earlier, during the work of the *nomothetai* of 411/10 to 405/4, but it must surely, in light of events just past, have transpired with an air of heightened solemnity. The process of authorizing the *nomoi* of Athens now had in view not only the prospective work of the Athenian *demos* and its officers, but it was also seen as the way of preserving the essential and time-tested practices of the Athenians against the possibility of future subversion. Since subversion of the *politeia* had twice been achieved by decrees, the time-tested *nomoi* of the past and their legitimate offspring of the present had to be accorded higher authority than decrees of the moment. Moreover, this higher authority had to be expressed in a publicly sanctioned manner, in writing. Such was the purpose of the series of succinct but highly significant statutes cited by Andocides shortly after his quotation of the decree of Teisamenus:

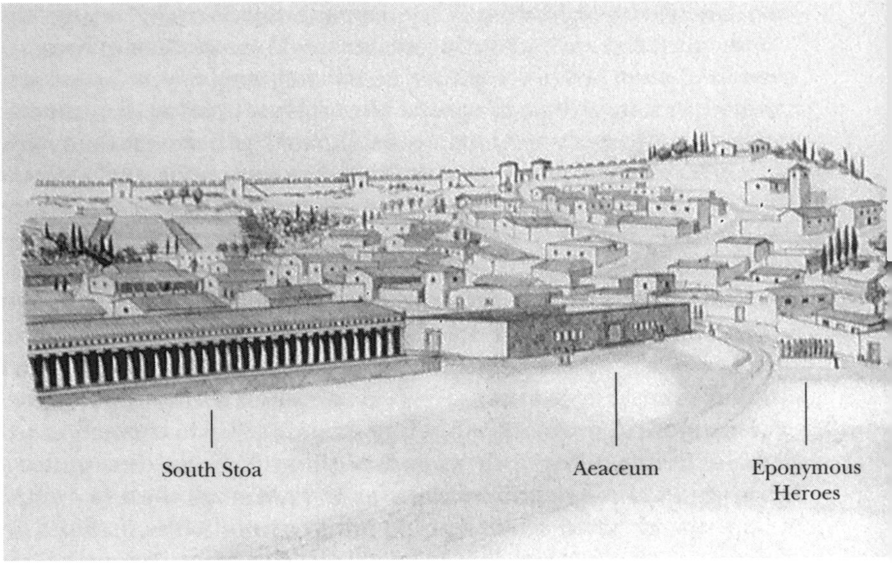

FIGURE 8. Reconstructed view of the southwest corner of the Athenian Agora, ca. 400.

> Laws.—In no circumstance shall magistrates make use of an unwritten law. No decree, whether of the Council or of the Assembly, shall have higher authority than a law. No law shall be directed against an individual without applying to all Athenians alike, unless an Assembly of six thousand so resolve by secret ballot.[40]

The Athenians had long recognized that enactments of the moment were inferior to their ancestral *nomoi,* the ways of the Athenians, but only in the sense that the part is lesser than the whole. For expressions of the will of the people were the living manifestations of the ways of the Athenians, and until the final decade of the fifth century the Athenians had felt no need to define explicitly what that whole consisted of. Circumstances, in 403/2, made such a definition urgent, and as a result the Athenians for the first time articulated a statutory distinction between laws and decrees.

THE LAWS OF ATHENS

The *thesmoi* of Draco and the *nomoi* of Solon, inscribed on venerable monuments, the *axones* and *kyrbeis,* were the Athenian prototypes of laws as codified words that deserved enduring reverence. But their very archaism, by the heyday of Pericles, made it possible to mix formulaic respect with jokes about their questionable utility. The rules governing the Athenian *politeia* were the living practices, adapted from precedent by experience, that en-

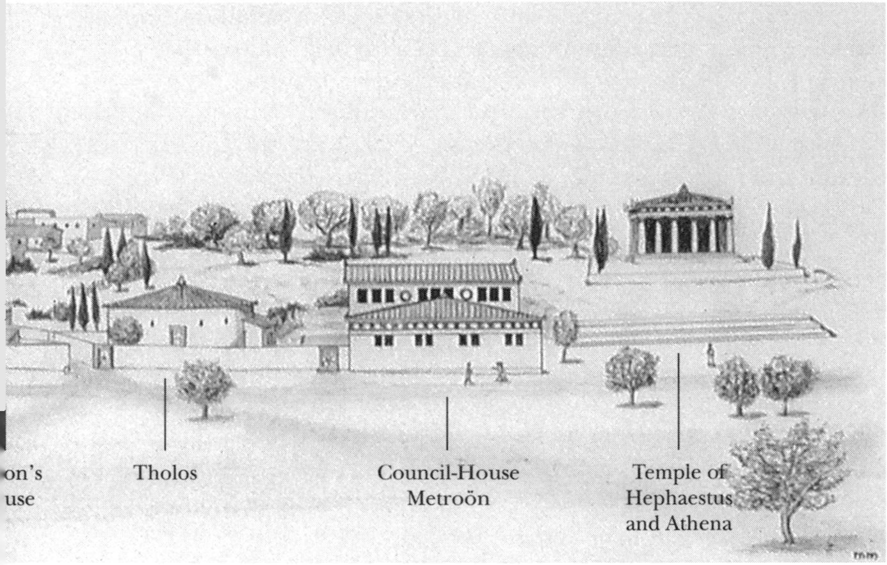

abled Athenians to deal most effectively with matters ranging from (most conservatively) family and property to (most innovatively) the affairs of state and empire. Pericles had endowed the whole of the Athenian *demos* with the faith that their collective wisdom was divinely favored. So long as the Athenian *demos* believed itself to be the living legacy of autochthonous ancestors, the ways and practices of the Athenians, their *nomoi,* were authentic. All rightfully enacted decisions of this democratic aristocracy were therefore manifestations of fundamental truths, and there was no need to discriminate between statutes that had enduring application and resolutions that addressed issues of the moment.

Manipulation of this engine of infallibility became both the focus of rhetorical contests, and the source of philosophical and pious disquiet. The effects of sophistic rhetoric in the practice of law reached a significant threshold when, through the forensic acumen of Antiphon in particular, it became apparent that power lay in the ability to cite and persuade a jury to apply whichever public enactments were most amenable to a litigant's suit or a defendant's case. Thus emerged, as the offspring of litigation, the contest of interpreting written statutes that became the process known as the *graphe paranomon.*

Only when it became necessary to decide which of several public enactments with conflicting implications should prevail in a particular case did it become apparent that some enactments had to be deemed inferior to others. In a contest of truths, this amounted to the determination that some enactments of the *demos* were flawed and therefore not authentic. The revolutionary implications of this realization were brought to the fore in the context of another refutation of democratic infallibility, the catastrophes that followed from the defeat in Sicily. So it was especially the circle of Antiphon that became the intellectual leaders of the oligarchy of the Four Hundred, a regime devoted to restoring the Athenian claim on truth by removing its most recent and flawed accretion, the sovereignty of the *demos.*

The failure of that regime and the reemergence of the full democracy required the condemnation and even execration of the intellectual leaders of the oligarchy, Antiphon and Phrynichus in particular. But the process they had begun, namely, to review past enactments of the Athenian *demos* to determine which ones were valid and which ones were flawed, was carried on after 411 in the democratically moderated work of the *nomothetai.* Some aspects of this review were completed by 404—most significantly, a review of the statutes of Draco and Solon. Their archaic statutes had little impact on the most sensitive business of the democracy, the administration of empire. The robust democracy had little interest in having its competence limited by the findings of legal scholars, and so in those years no precise definition of the relative authority of current and past enactments, or between laws and decrees, was formulated. This era gave us, in Xenophon's account of the trial of the generals after Arginusae, the most famous assertion of the sovereignty of the *demos* as it sat in session. When Euryptolemus attempted, by *graphe paranomon,* to halt Callixeinus' procedure for trying the generals, "the majority cried out that it was monstrous if the *demos* were to be prevented from doing whatever it wished." No wonder, then, that the work of the *nomothetai* was still in progress just over a year later, when it fell into the grip of *stasis.*

Following the regime of the Thirty, there no longer was an empire to defend. The restored but now conservative democracy of 403/2 thus had less concern for the wider activities of the former democracy and a greater concern for avoiding the violence and bloodshed that had erupted as a direct consequence of the radical definition of law applied by Critias and his fellows. As a result, this was the administration that pronounced, for the first time, the priority of laws over decrees.

The past would still inform and guide Athenians, but now the highest authority from the past was explicitly vested in the body of written statutes reviewed and authorized by the commissioned *nomothetai.* This was a blow to the aristocratic tradition that held that authoritative expertise was an expression of personal excellence, or *arete.* But since unconstrained *arete* had led to the butchery of the Thirty, the Athenians were finally willing to concede superior authority to publicly sanctioned documents. In this way the meaning of law, *nomos,* as written statute finally became definitive.[41]

CHAPTER ELEVEN

Eliminating Socrates, 401–399

In fact, as I have often heard my own father say, for he lived to be 95 years old and had shared in all the toils of the city, which he often described to me in his leisure hours—well, he said that in the early days of the reestablished democracy, if any indictment for an illegal motion came into court, the matter was no sooner said than done.... It frequently happened that they made the clerk stop and told him to read to them the laws and the motion a second time; and they convicted a man of making an illegal proposal not because he had overleaped the laws entirely, but if one syllable only was contravened.

AESCHINES 3, *AGAINST CTESIPHON* 191–92*

One of the hallmarks of forensic rhetoric of the fourth century is its extensive use of verbatim citations of statutes. The beginnings of this habit can be observed in Andocides' speech, *On the Mysteries,* delivered in 400. Although cases argued more than a decade earlier by Antiphon reveal an increasing sophistication in dealing with the technicalities of the laws, Andocides' speech represents this art brought to a new height, at a moment when the Athenian public had become fixated on determining the meaning of statutes according to their precise written expression.

The primacy of written statutes, as discussed in the previous chapter, was the outcome of a generation's experience of oscillations between the increasingly violent extremes of democracy and oligarchy. Only after 403 could civic concord and stability find substantial expression in authoritative texts. With no affairs of empire to distract them, the Athenians were at last ready to regard the business of the *nomothetai* as one of the highest priorities of the state.

Prior to the *stasis* of 404, despite the institutional investment in their work, the *nomothetai* had been unable to achieve finality in their tasks. This was largely due to the tension between the authority of law and the influence of charismatic leaders at a time when enterprising leadership held the promise of greater benefits than did the secure laws. After 403, the balance of opinion was turned decisively away from the free play of visionary leaders and toward the security of fixed laws. The tension between vision and a publicly sanctioned and textually fixed authority remained, but the vision-

*Modified translation of C. D. Adams.

aries were no longer so politically forceful. The few that we know of all seem to have experienced defeat in the Athenian courts.

The first of this varied group was Thrasybulus, a visionary in the model of the imperial democracy. Following the defeat of his motion to enfranchise his followers in Piraeus, discussed in the previous chapter, his career entered a period of quiescence. The second was the anonymous speaker of Lysias' *Against Nicomachus,* who challenged the authority of the *nomothetai* to regulate the religious affairs of the state. The third was Socrates, who also fell afoul of the state's newfound authority to regulate religion.

This chapter examines these last two cases. The object, in both cases, is to recognize how timeless issues of law and piety played out in the unique circumstances of democratic Athens soon after the civil war of 404/3. Among the relevant particulars, the amnesty of 403 and a significant set of movements abroad in 401 will come under consideration. Even without empire, the politics of Athens were sensitive to the affairs of a wider world.

THE CASE AGAINST NICOMACHUS

An important stage of the work of the *nomothetai* was completed by 399, as we know from a speech composed by Lysias for an attack against a member of the commission elected by the Council, Nicomachus. From the speech we deduce that Nicomachus' career had spanned nearly the entire period of legal review sponsored by the democracy, beginning in 410/09 and ending in 400/399, with a hiatus in exile during the regime of the Thirty. Before the establishment of the Thirty, according to Lysias' account, Nicomachus had held office for six years, "although he had been ordered to write up the laws of Solon within four months." Similarly, after the fall of the Thirty, "he spent four years composing official drafts, though he could have finished his business within thirty days."[1]

The speech misses no opportunity to heap contempt upon Nicomachus' achievements, and we must sift for the facts amidst the bulk of tendentious argument. The last remark evidently alludes to the period of one month prescribed by the decree of Teisamenus for the completion of a cycle of legislative proposals, not to any predetermined term of office. In a similarly derisive vein, Lysias' speech complains that, "though he was supposed to draw up statutes on specific subjects, he made himself the supreme authority over all," and accuses Nicomachus of "registering this and deleting that, reaching such a height of arrogance that you treat affairs of state as your personal affairs. . . ." To carry out their charge, the *nomothetai* naturally had to compare statutes and enactments from diverse sources and formulate recommendations on how to resolve contradictions among them. But no matter how thorough or judicious, ambiguities were bound to remain, and, as the speech by Lysias attests, interested parties would inevitably find fault with the results. As Aristotle later remarked, more sympathetically, "legislation requires lengthy consideration." Circumstances suggest that, before the suit brought against him in 399, Nicomachus' careful work had proceeded quietly and with respect from many quarters.[2]

In a speech composed by Isocrates possibly a year or two before the accusation composed by Lysias, Nicomachus (almost certainly the Nicomachus of Lysias' speech) is named as a longtime acquaintance of a certain wealthy Athenian who had been a member of the 3,000 and a friend of the Ten governing Athens when the reconciliation was achieved. Nicomachus had been chosen as an arbitrator in a dispute over confiscated property between this man and a certain Callimachus, a returnee at the time of the reconciliation. This testimony to Nicomachus' reputation as an impartial judge is consonant with his reelection as a *nomothetes* immediately after the reconciliation. It is noteworthy that despite the strenuous efforts of Lysias' speaker to impugn Nicomachus, his assertion that Nicomachus had abused his command of the law for personal gain is hardly more than perfunctory, and he never alleges the sort of blackmail that Lysias elsewhere alleges against other men who likely had been among the elected *nomothetai* in the period between 411/10 and 405/4.[3]

The accusations against Nicomachus were intended to prejudice the jury against him on account of the extraordinary nature of the office he held and to raise a general fear that laws had been abused in his hands. But the speaker has a difficult task, trying to impugn Nicomachus without attacking the sanctity of Athenian law, and as a result most of the grievances against Nicomachus remain vague and ill-defined. Eventually, however, the speaker arrives at the center of his dispute with Nicomachus, and this concerns the authority to ordain public sacrifices.

Nicomachus' more recent work involved a calendar of publicly sponsored sacrifices that, by the time of Lysias' speech, had only recently been displayed on stone stelae. To judge by the few surviving fragments of these stelae (see figure 7 on page 228), the calendar of festivals with a price-list for the publicly sponsored sacrificial victims may have been the most substantial body of laws to be inscribed on stone by the *nomothetai* elected in 403/2. It emerges that the speaker has previously raised objections to the omission of certain sacrifices from Nicomachus' calendar and has accused Nicomachus of introducing other sacrifices, involving greater expense, with insufficient authority.

This issue is sensitive, and the speaker introduces the subject by first defending himself against an anticipated counter-charge of impiety from Nicomachus. Rather than challenge specifically the sacrifices sanctioned by Nicomachus that he considers "excessive," the speaker claims that he demands only that Nicomachus defer to "common and established custom," and that he show respect for

> sacrifices ordained on the ancient pillars *(kyrbeis)* and on the stelae, in accordance with regulations *(syngraphai)*,... for these are things that you have decreed.... We must not, gentlemen of the jury, be instructed in piety by Nicomachus, but we must look to the past. Our ancestors, who performed the sacrifices ordained on the olden pillars, bequeathed to us the greatest and most prosperous city in Greece; it behooves us to perform the same sacrifices as did they, if for no other reason than the good fortune that resulted from those rites. How could a man show more piety than I when I demand, above all, that we sacrifice in accordance with ancestral custom *(kata ta patria)*...[4]

As in the allusive arguments elsewhere in this speech, the speaker never exactly equates the omitted but attested sacrifices with the customary rites he demands be restored. Presumably, the offerings sanctioned in the archaic documents that he refers to have fallen into abeyance for reasons that no one cares to challenge. But in a contest where written authority carries great weight, the speaker makes every effort to associate his view of past custom neglected by Nicomachus with documented offerings also neglected by Nicomachus.

In so doing, the speaker makes a subtle shift in the authority of his argument. The speaker asserts, and witnesses testify, that the sacrificial laws published by Nicomachus omit certain sacrifices that are attested on the archaic *kyrbeis.* The speaker also asserts, in a sequence of hypothetical propositions far more convoluted in the original language than is indicated in the translation offered here, that it is impious to overlook "sacrifices ordained on the olden pillars *(kyrbeis)* and on the stelae, in accordance with regulations *(syngraphai)*." Having linked *syngraphai* with the authority of older stelae, and still older *kyrbeis,* the speaker arrives at the heart of his case against Nicomachus in the following passage:

> Reflect, therefore, gentlemen of the jury, that when we proceed in accordance with the regulations *(syngraphai),* all the ancestral offerings *(ta patria)* are made; but when we are guided by the stelae that this man had written up, numerous rites are abolished.[5]

Syngraphai, translated above as "regulations," are the sole written authority available to our speaker, who would surely have approved of this translation. But a *syngraphe* is, more literally, a "composition," or "composed account," or "report." It can have the secondary meaning of "regulation" only in the context of a public decree that endorses a particular "report" drafted either by an individual expert or by a commission of men elected to compose a proposal.

Publicly commissioned *syngraphai* are attested in Athenian inscriptions at least as early as the mid-fifth century, and Nicomachus' jury will have been familiar with references to such *syngraphai* as the authority for some of the proposals drafted by Nicomachus and his fellow *nomothetai.* But *syn-*

graphai were also written on private initiative, and such texts first appear around the end of the fifth century, in precisely the period under examination here.

One such composition was *Peri teleton,* "On ritual initiations," by Stesimbrotus of Thasos. Another, better-known example was "the *Attike syngraphe* of Hellanicus," mentioned by Thucydides. Hellanicus' *syngraphe* connected contemporary Athenian institutions with the earliest reaches of Athenian and Hellenic legend, when kings and ancestral heroes were born of gods or from the earth herself. It is possible, perhaps even likely, that Nicomachus' accuser had such privately commissioned *syngraphai* in mind as he challenged the legitimacy of Nicomachus' work. For the years around 400, as illustrated in the previous chapter, mark a critical period when both public officers and informed private individuals participated in shaping the record of public authority. As Lysias wrote in another speech, a man like Andocides "attends meetings of the Council and gives advice in debates on sacrifices, processions, prayers, and oracles." Such advice was surely all the more cogent when it was based on a well-researched treatise.[6]

In the dispute with Nicomachus, we are never presented with detailed testimony or the citation of specific authorities. Given the delicacy of the case, rhetorical discretion allowed the speaker to go no farther than allusive references to *kyrbeis,* stelae, and *syngraphai.* Instead, the speaker turns the case into a contest of prestige and does all he can to denigrate Nicomachus personally. Confident of his own place in public esteem, the speaker calls Nicomachus the son of a public slave, a man who has performed no public benefactions, and a man unworthy to pose as an authority on a par with the likes of Solon, Themistocles, and Pericles, drafting laws for the Athenians.

By attacking the proposer of the calendar of public sacrifices rather than the proposal, the speaker avoids complaining about specific rites and sacrifices. To do so might draw against himself the anger of Athenians who had already approved of the calendar. Rather, the speaker seeks to persuade the jury that they have been misled by the whole project for which Nicomachus stands accountable. If, as the speaker suggests, the Athenians feel some difficulty at securing the funds for the sacrifices proposed by Nicomachus, this is only the first sign of the ruin that will befall them as they incur the wrath of the gods by perpetuating the neglect of *ta patria* that Nicomachus has, by his deceptive arguments, persuaded them to sanction.[7]

The case against Nicomachus was ultimately a contest for authority over *ta patria,* the ancestral practices of the Athenians. The contest was between, on the one hand, a representative of aristocratic tradition, a man who might well have been, as his denial indicates, a member of the Four Hundred, and, on the other hand, a man with no aristocratic lineage to boast of, possibly even of servile birth as his accuser asserts, but one who was obviously widely respected by other members of the aristocracy and generally favored by the *demos* as an impartial judge and as an expert in the legal archives of the Athenians. Although proof is lacking, the view of the majority of scholars who have studied the case is that Nicomachus was vindicated in this process. It does indeed seem that the moment favored the otherwise anonymous expert, the servant of the *demos,* against the spokesman for self-serving aristocratic authority.

In view of the fact that the litigant must have felt his personal influence threatened by the calendar of public sacrifices promulgated by Nicomachus, he must have been a man whose reputation was closely tied to religious observances, and who cared enough about his political prestige to make an issue of it. Callias son of Hipponicus, member of the clan of Ceryces, and Torch-Bearer for the Eleusinian Mysteries, was such a man. On several grounds, Callias is likely to be the one who commissioned Lysias to write the speech against Nicomachus.

Xenophon, introducing a later speech by Callias, describes him as "the sort of man who enjoyed being praised by himself no less than by others." Xenophon's speech of Callias dwells upon ancestral tradition in general, Eleusinian tradition in particular, and his family's central role in all such affairs. Callias' confident reference to what "is said" of his own ancestors in the original establishment of Eleusinian customs throughout Greece probably refers to the sanction given to these traditions in the writings of Hellanicus and other Atthidographers, as the writers who specialized in the history and customs of Attica came to be known.[8]

Callias' role in the denunciation of Andocides, a year before the trial of Nicomachus, likewise combined sacred law with personal prestige. The proceedings had begun after Callias, in his role as Eleusinian priest, had denounced Andocides for desecrating the Eleusinian sanctuary. In his defense, Andocides reminds the jury of Callias' embarrassment when he claimed to act as the exponent of ancestral law *(patrios nomos)*. Callias' right to expound ancestral law had been challenged in the presence of the Council, Andocides reports, and the terms of his indictment were confuted by reference to a nearby stele. Some of the style attributed to Callias by Andocides is reflected in another speech by Lysias for one of the prosecutors of Andocides. The speaker reminds the jury of the advice they had years before received from his grandfather, Diocles, the son of an Eleusinian Hierophant, or High Priest. The speaker also urges the Athenians to follow the advice of Pericles, and to rely, in cases of sacrilege, "not just on laws that have been written down, but on the unwritten laws *(agraphoi nomoi)* that the Eumolpidae (the clan of Eleusinian Hierophants) expound." Callias is almost certainly the speaker of this Lysian speech as well, and in this case we know that the prosecution of Andocides failed.[9]

These circumstances add irony to another reference to Callias in a speech delivered close to the time of the trial of Nicomachus. In the course of his defense against a charge of impiety, Socrates refutes the common opinion that he offered instruction for hire, as sophists did. As evidence, Socrates invokes the experience of Callias son of Hipponicus, "a man who has paid more in sophists' fees than all the rest put together." Although Lysias is not among the sophists that Socrates names, elsewhere Plato attests that Lysias had an unrivaled reputation as a versatile intellect and as a speech-writer. Lysias is even said to have composed a speech for Socrates' defense, which the latter declined to use, "because it did not suit him." Callias, on the other hand, is likely to have had no such qualms, and certainly had the means to employ Lysias' talents in representing himself before Athenian juries.[10]

AMNESTY AND REMEMBRANCE

Although neither the case of Andocides nor that of Nicomachus concerned events during the turmoil of 404/3, each of the three surviving speeches from these cases uses the powerful impression made by those events to place the opposing side in the shadow of the Thirty and their insufferable deeds. In this they are typical of many of the surviving speeches of Lysias and Isocrates composed at about this time. Arguments from probability often played a larger role than the presentation of evidence in Athenian forensic rhetoric, and no subject was more useful for character assassination than a comparison drawn between an opponent and the Thirty and their minions. Thus despite the fact that forgiveness was prominent in the rhetoric of reconciliation, Athenian juries were repeatedly subjected to emotional appeals to those recent events.

It is sometimes stated, as Andocides and many defendants alleged, that the amnesty clause in the reconciliation agreements of 403 made it illegal to prosecute individuals for public offenses committed before 403. In many respects, however, the terms of the amnesty were highly ambiguous and subject to dispute. The careful study by Thomas Loening has shown that the oath of the Athenians "to harbor no grievance" *(me mnesikakesai)* was taken as an injunction against prosecution for crimes against the Athenian state, but even this definition was challenged in several suits brought within the first year or two of the restored democracy. Many individuals involved in the regime of the Thirty were brought to trial in suits alleging not public crimes, but personal injuries, which were therefore not covered by the amnesty. The matter was so problematic that Archinus introduced a legal procedure, the *paragraphe,* enabling a defendant to argue for immunity by reason of the amnesty before hearing the case under indictment.[11]

Both the *paragraphe* procedure itself and contemporary speeches show that the amnesty agreement was continually pressed and stretched. Prosecutors claimed that it did not exempt wrongdoers from liability for personal injuries. Defendants claimed that the security of the state, and the sanctity of all oaths and agreements, required that the amnesty be extended to their individual case. In each case, it was up to the jury to resolve the matter.

Among the surviving speeches of Lysias, Isocrates, and Andocides, nearly twenty legal proceedings are attested within the first seven or eight years of the restored democracy. Few of them can be closely dated, although several make reference to circumstances that suggest that they are to be placed earlier or later in this period. At least half involve grievances allegedly affecting the welfare of the Athenian state, either in the form of behavior that rendered a candidate unsuited for office-holding, or for a crime committed in the course of conducting public business, or for an offense against the gods. The other half are suits for the recovery of property or the redress of a personal injury, and half of these introduce the experiences of Athens under the Thirty as instructive for the jury's deliberation on the issue at hand.[12]

The most incisive accusations of crimes committed by or in collusion with the Thirty are Lysias' speeches, 12 *Against Eratosthenes* and 13 *Against Agoratus*. Both of these were probably delivered in or soon after 401/0. The timing of these tests of the amnesty is probably significant. For in the summer of 401 a series of events made the Athenians mindful once again of the dangers of external influences on their internal order. Remembering the recent past, Athenian juries were probably becoming less tolerant of individuals with demonstrable sympathies for the oligarchy of the Thirty.

OMINOUS REMINDERS

With the approach of summer 401, the Athenians complied, probably for the second time, with a summons from Sparta to contribute troops for the war that Sparta had begun, the previous summer, against Elis. For two decades, the Eleans and Spartans had been at odds, and during that period the Eleans had become allies of Athens in war against Sparta. The latest chapter in this Peloponnesian rivalry was played out in 403, when Thrasydaeus, the democratic leader of the Eleans, had given substantial financial support to the Piraeus faction before the confrontation with Pausanias and the Spartan-led Peloponnesians. In the following year the Spartans made a show of their many grievances with Eleans. They declared that the Eleans had taken unlawful possession of certain communities between Elis and Messenia, and they demanded that these outlying communities *(perioikides poleis)* be left independent by the Eleans. When the Eleans refused to comply with these demands, the Spartans summoned their allies for war.[13]

According to Diodorus, the Spartans "gathered many soldiers from nearly all of their allies except the Boeotians and Corinthians." The campaign of 402 was inconclusive, but the campaign of 401, for which

Xenophon confirms Athenian participation, was far more destructive. Elean territory was widely plundered, the sanctuary at Olympia was occupied by the Spartans, and the town of Elis was assaulted. Under pressure of the Spartan attack, civil war broke out in Elis and Thrasydaeus narrowly escaped assassination. Early in the following year, facing the threat of renewed attack, Thrasydaeus and the Eleans made peace by ceding the territories demanded by the Spartans.

In the meantime, probably over the winter of 401/0, the Spartans employed their allied force to drive out other enemies. Messenian exiles were expelled from their settlements on the islands of Cephallenia and Zacynthus, and from the town of Naupactus in West Locris, on the Corinthian Gulf. The plight of the Messenians, longtime allies of Athens, must have been painful to behold, especially for the Athenians among the Spartan-led ranks. For two generations earlier, the Athenians had established the Messenians in these places after their expulsion from Messenia by the Spartans.[14]

The crushing of Sparta's longtime foes around the Peloponnese was more than a distant spectacle to the Athenians in 401. Scenes of civil strife, political dismemberment, and mass expulsions brought on by Spartan intervention were vivid reminders of Athenian suffering under the Thirty. And these events involved the Athenians as more than spectators, though by indirect means. For as elements of a larger movement underway throughout Greece, consequences of the collapse of the Athenian empire, these matters implicated the relationship between all of Greece and the Persian empire.

Circumspect as they had been in their dealings with Artaxerxes and his satraps, the Spartans had not been able to resolve the ambiguities of their overlapping spheres of interest in Asia Minor. The continuing rebellion of Egypt and the vulnerability of Artaxerxes that it signified were largely responsible for this condition, and probably contributed to the decision by Cyrus, over the winter of 402/1, to commit his forces to the overthrow of his older brother. To the Spartans, Cyrus' resolve to act and desire to cooperate were a welcome contrast to years of Persian vacillation, and the promises of abundant pay and substantial rewards brought to Sparta by Cyrus' emissaries were convincing inducements. The Spartans granted Cyrus the support of a fleet and a force of infantry, and probably assisted his emissaries in securing mercenaries from the Peloponnese.

In committing themselves to this course, the Spartans must have taken account of the opportunities that Cyrus' request presented to their offensive underway in the Peloponnese. Earnest money from Cyrus probably made the Elean campaign as effective as it was in the spring of 401, and a portion of the forces deployed in Elis was probably among those sent by sea, early in the summer, to meet Cyrus on the Cilician coast, when Cyrus' march toward Babylon was already nearly four months underway.[15]

Cyrus' designs touched Athens as well. For by uniting his interests with those of Sparta, Cyrus was reinforcing the latent threat to Athens posed by Spartan might, and was exerting unwelcome pressure on the friends of Athens who still enjoyed some measure of autonomy. Among the most important of these were the dynasts of Larisa and Pharsalus in Thessaly.

Sometime soon before the Lesser Mysteries at the end of winter 402/1, Meno of Pharsalus was in Athens as a guest of Anytus. Their relationship was one of hereditary *xenia*. Meno's namesake and possibly grandfather had been given Athenian citizenship in recognition of his substantial support of Cimon's expedition against the Persians at Eion on the Strymon river. His son, Thucydides of Pharsalus, had been in Athens in 411 at a time when his family had need of support in the face of the growing intervention of Sparta in Thessaly. Thessalian rivalries were at a boil a decade later when the visit to Athens of the young Meno son of Alexidemus (perhaps nephew of Thucydides of Pharsalus) was remembered in the dialogue with Socrates that bears his name.

Meno was acting as agent for Aristippus of Larisa, to whom Cyrus had granted money for mercenaries to be placed at his disposal when summoned. When the summons from Cyrus arrived, Aristippus and Meno may well have been reluctant to join a venture that, if successful, would guarantee the ascendancy of Sparta and of their various pro-Spartan rivals in Thessaly. Meno therefore must have been concerned to see if ancestral ties to the Athenians might afford some way out of their dilemma. Under the circumstances, they did not, and Meno fulfilled the obligation to serve Cyrus. At the beginning of spring, probably a few weeks after the conversations described in the *Meno,* Meno of Pharsalus was at the head of a mercenary force that met Cyrus in Phrygia.[16]

It is noteworthy that when Meno was captured by Tissaphernes along with the other Greek commanders after the death of Cyrus later that summer, he alone was spared. Xenophon, who detested the man, reports that he lived on in disgrace, soon to die the death of a base man. Ctesias states that Meno had formed ties of friendship with Tissaphernes, and was the means of delivering the other Greek commanders into Tissaphernes' hands. Diodorus merely notes that he was spared because "he alone was deemed ready to betray the Greeks on account of a quarrel with his allies." He had no wish, in the final analysis, to support a Spartan cause.[17]

Although Cyrus' intentions had been given a plausible explanation—he was warring with Tissaphernes over disputed towns—his ultimate goals were obscure to no one who had followed the recent course of Greek–Persian relations. Leading circles among the Athenians were thus mindful of the events moving around them early in 401. By their nature, the events eventually attracted public attention as well. This, in turn, required a public explanation and a public response.

No source describes a comprehensive Athenian perspective on these events, but revealing clues come from Xenophon's account of his personal involvement. At about the time of Meno's visit to Athens, Xenophon received a letter from his Boeotian friend, Proxenus, extending to him personally the same invitation to riches and favor that Cyrus' emissaries were presenting to the Spartan state. Xenophon describes the upshot thus:

> Xenophon having read the letter consulted Socrates the Athenian about the proposed expedition. Socrates, who had a suspicion that the Athenian state might look rather askance at any friendship with Cyrus, whose zealous cooperation with the Lacedaemonians against Athens in the war was not forgotten, advised Xenophon to go to Delphi to consult the god as to the desirability of such a journey. Xenophon went and put the question to Apollo: to which of the gods must he pray and sacrifice so that he might best and honorably accomplish his intended journey and return in safety, with good fortune? Then Apollo answered and told him to which gods he must sacrifice, and when he had returned home he reported to Socrates the oracle. But he, when he heard, blamed Xenophon that he had not, in the first instance, inquired of the god whether it were better for him to go or stay, but had taken on himself to settle that point affirmatively by inquiring how he might best make the journey. "Since, however," continued Socrates, "you did so put the question, you should do what the god instructed." And so Xenophon offered sacrifice to those whom the god named and set sail.[18]

Xenophon joined a force of 1,500 hoplites and 500 light-armed troops brought to Sardis by Proxenus the Boeotian. Officers must have been recruited from among friends, as in the case of Xenophon. Some officers must have brought men with them to form the bulk of Proxenus' following. Additional troops must have been attracted by word of mouth, as news of the expedition spread to places where men were likely to be ready for hire. One of these likely places was Eleusis, where less than two years earlier Lysander had assembled a mercenary force to protect his allies in Attica.

In the year of the archon Xenaenetus (401/0), as Aristotle informs us, the Athenians, as Xenophon elsewhere states,

> having heard that the men at Eleusis were hiring mercenaries, marched out in full force against them, and when the generals of the Eleusinians came out for a parley, they put them to death. Sending friends and relatives to the rest of the men at Eleusis, they persuaded them to be reconciled. And having sworn oaths that, in very truth, they would harbor no grievances, to this very day they live together as fellow-citizens, and the *demos* remains true to the oaths.

In this way, the remaining leadership of the Thirty was done away with, and the enclave at Eleusis was brought back within the Athenian state. It had never been entirely separated, but the rumors of a military build-up, and news of the Spartan campaign underway that summer in the Peloponnese, fomenting an anti-democratic revolution in Elis and forcing the Eleans to grant independence to outlying communities *(perioikides poleis)*, must have inflamed fears of the Athenians for what the Spartans, and their insidious friends in Attica, might yet do to them.[19]

The fall of Eleusis probably took place at the beginning of Xenaenetus' year. The following summer, in 400, saw the last recorded act of compliance of the Athenians to their treaty obligation to provide troops on request to the Spartans. The troops were sent to Asia Minor, where the Spartan commander, Thibron, was making war against the forces of Tissaphernes as a consequence of Cyrus' failure. Xenophon, who was shortly to find continued employment in that theater of war, reports that the Athenians willingly sent Thibron the 300 cavalrymen he had requested, "considering that it would be a benefit for the *demos* if they went abroad and died there." A cavalryman under the Thirty himself, Xenophon was well aware of the stigma that attached to all such past supporters of the oligarchy, regardless of the amnesty. This was probably why he had asked Apollo *how* to accomplish his sojourn abroad safely and honorably, not *whether* to do so. Socrates too knew that current circumstances would try the forgiveness of the *demos*.[20]

SOCRATES' OFFENSE

Andocides and Nicomachus were put on trial, in 400 and 399, because their actions were alleged to endanger all Athenians before the gods. The case against Andocides alleged that the Athenian state was imperiled by allowing a confessed offender against the gods to participate and even to officiate in civil and religious ceremonies. Nicomachus was on trial for allegedly misleading the Athenians into perverting their ancestral traditions, thereby arousing the anger of the gods. A few months after the trial of Andocides and before that of Nicomachus, at the beginning of spring 399, Socrates was put on trial for offenses that imperiled the Athenians before the gods.

The indictment of Socrates is well attested in several contemporary paraphrases, and is reliably quoted by Diogenes Laertius, at second hand, from a work by Favorinus of Arelate, a sophist of the early second century CE who consulted the text of the indictment still preserved in the official archives of the Metroön at Athens. It reads as follows:

> Meletus son of Meletus of Pitthus has written a sworn indictment against Socrates son of Sophroniscus of Alopece as follows: Socrates commits the offense of not acknowledging the gods acknowledged by the state and of introducing other new divinities. He commits the further offense of corrupting the young. Penalty proposed: capital punishment.[21]

As in the case of Nicomachus and Andocides, the commission of specific acts is not the focus of dispute. Rather, the case depends upon interpretation of actions or behaviors assumed to be a matter of common knowledge, but whose effect is revealed, through the expertise of the prosecution, to be harmful to the Athenian community. Socrates began his defense with the usual assertion of misrepresentations by the prosecution, but his demonstration of that argument paid no regard to the prevailing methods of rebuttal. The method of Socrates' argument is a significant, if indirect, indicator of the nature of the charges against him.

We know next to nothing about the case argued by the prosecution that does not come from the accounts of Socrates' defense by Plato and Xenophon. These two present a consistent picture of the line of argument used by Socrates, and show how Socrates responded to the accusations of Meletus. But we know that Meletus was joined in the prosecution by Anytus and Lycon, and, according to Socrates' remarks after the verdict was announced, these two, and Anytus in particular, developed the case against him significantly beyond the arguments of Meletus and were responsible, in Socrates' opinion, for securing the guilty verdict. What they may have said is a matter for conjecture; Plato and Xenophon have left only the faintest of hints. In response to Meletus, however, Socrates takes a position consistent with his views as expounded elsewhere by Xenophon and Plato. From this larger picture of Socrates we can recognize elements of his convictions that, in the hands of a skillful orator, could be offensive to the Athenian state, especially in terms of public reverence for the gods of the Athenians. For the indictment of Socrates, a *graphe asebias* enacted before the Archon Basileus, was, above all, an action for impious behavior.[22]

Much of Socrates' defense, as recounted by Plato, is stridently self-righteous. This strikes modern readers and it also struck those who heard him speak in court. Xenophon, who was not present but who later read what "others have written about his defense," was also struck by the way that "all have represented his self-righteous tone *(megalegoria)*." In writing about his beloved mentor, Xenophon felt it necessary not to dispute this feature of Socrates' defense, but to account for it in such a way that his "self-righteous tone" should not appear "ill-considered" *(aphronestera)*. Xenophon did so by stating that, to Socrates, "death had become preferable to life." Plato made the same point, in so many more words. The nature of Socrates' provocation and its motive are nowhere succinctly expressed, although they too are revealed in the words of his apologists.[23]

A prominent feature of Socrates' defense is his open contempt for public figures, statesmen, poets, and generally for "those who consider themselves wise *(sophoi)*, but are not." But arrogance and contempt for others is the hallmark of Attic forensic rhetoric, and would hardly attract the notice that Socrates' willful *megalegoria* did unless there was something peculiar about it. What distinguishes Socrates in this respect is that his contempt was not narrowly focused on his opponents in court. He distributed it over all who aspired to a role in public affairs, over all who fancied themselves poets, over all who possessed some technical expertise, and over all who considered themselves in any way *sophoi.* This amounted to open contempt for the Athenian public in general, as Plato has Socrates express more directly in private conversations. Socrates was not being cryptic in these remarks to the jury; he was reinforcing a reputation for contempt of the assembled public that had a long history. To drive the point home, he reminded the jury, to their vocal displeasure, that the oracle of Apollo at Delphi had pronounced no one to be wiser *(sophoteros)* than Socrates.[24]

Just six years earlier, in a choral ode of his *Frogs,* Aristophanes addressed the Athenians as "the great mass of folk, where wits *(sophiai)* by the ten-thousand sit, keener for honor than Cleophon. . . . " Love of honor is served by praise, and Aristophanes often so indulged his audience, hoping, not unlike a litigant in court, to win the victor's prize. Socrates, by contrast, was being openly provocative, and his remarks were several times interrupted by angry outbursts among the jurors, as both Plato and Xenophon attest. Aristophanes had already drawn the contrast between what Socrates took for wisdom and what won public approval. Near the end of the *Frogs,* when Aristophanes has provided a reincarnation of Aeschylus for his audience's pleasure, the poet's return is hailed by the chorus,

> as a blessing to the citizens, and a blessing to his kin and his friends, because he is intelligent *(sunetos)—not* the sort that graces the company of Socrates, sitting around quibbling . . . and making a study of being deranged.[25]

But was Socrates' derangement dangerous? Why, with such a long-standing reputation, was Socrates brought to trial for doing what he had been doing for years?

In response to Meletus' charge of impiety Socrates emphasized his obedience to a divine voice, his *daimonion.* This was a well-known feature of Socrates' personality, and, according to the seer Euthyphro, in Plato's dialogue in his name, Socrates' *daimonion* was instantly recognizable in the charge of impiety that Meletus had drawn up.

> I get it, Socrates! It is because you are always saying that your *daimonion* is with you! So he charges you in this indictment with introducing novelties in religion, and that is the reason why he comes to court with this slanderous complaint, well knowing how easily such matters can be misrepresented to the crowd. . . .[26]

Socrates nevertheless relies on his reverence for this form of divine guidance to refute the popular notion that sophists like himself were atheists, a prejudice that Meletus had tried to use to his advantage. But in declaring his unwavering allegiance to a personal *daimonion,* Socrates proves the most important feature of the case against him, namely, that "he introduced a new and different divinity" to which he paid higher regard than to anything else. This he affirms, according to Plato, by the examples he introduces to demonstrate that obedience to his *daimonion* never incited him, but always prevented him from committing "unjust and illegal acts" *(adika kai paranoma)*.

> I will offer you substantial proofs of what I have said—not words, but what you can appreciate better, deeds. Listen while I describe my actual experiences, so that you may know that I would never submit wrongly to anyone through fear of death, but would refuse even at the cost of my life. What I say will be vexatious to you, and controversial, but it is the truth.[27]

Socrates' first proof is his role in the trial of the generals after Arginusae, when he refused to put to a vote the motion that the generals be judged en masse, "illegally, as you all decided at a later time." He stood by his refusal "to do anything against the laws" *(para tous nomous)* despite the threats of legal injunctions made by the orators, and despite "your commands and shouts." His second example was his refusal to cooperate with the Thirty when they commanded him, among others, to arrest Leon of Salamis and deliver him to the Eleven for execution. By refusing to cooperate while others did the bidding of the Thirty, Socrates ran the risk of being summarily executed himself. "There are plenty of people here who will testify to these statements."[28]

By these examples Socrates made it explicit that he placed his own inspiration higher than *any* form of public authority, democratic or oligarchic. The most vexatious example was, of course, his confrontation with the assembled *demos* in 406, in the fullness of its fury and resolve to have its own way. The justness of Socrates' action—or refusal to act—on that occasion depends upon his assertion that he acted "in accordance with the laws" and that the proposal of Callixeinus was "unconstitutional" (as *para tous nomous* is often translated). This, as was shown in chapter 7, was an assertion that had no statutory basis. The later vindication claimed by Socrates was also a matter of contention, coming as it did from the maelstrom of legal conflict that marked the onset of *stasis* in 404. This instance, examples "vexatious to you, and controversial," as Socrates warns, proved that Socrates answered to a higher authority, in all issues of justice and law, than did the Athenians themselves.

The revolutionary reforms of the Thirty had likewise been justified through an appeal to a higher authority for law than those recognized by the democracy. Socrates did not side with the *demos* against the Thirty, but placed himself even beyond the Thirty on this intellectual continuum. Socrates' absolutism thus aroused in his audience the anger that anyone would defend such a departure from the publicly accepted standards, especially in light of recent experience. If Xenophon's account, relying on Hermogenes, who was present along with Plato at the trial, is accurate in detail, then Socrates indulged in even more inflammatory lessons in piety than Plato admits. "I have revealed to many of my friends the counsels that the god has given me, and in no instance has the event shown that I was mistaken" (noise of an angry jury ensues). Socrates likens the divinity *(daimonion)*, voice *(phone)*, or god *(theos)* that spoke to him to the oracular signs interpreted by others, and above all to the oracular "voice" by which the Pythia spoke for Apollo. And Apollo's response to the question posed by Chaerephon, "Is any man wiser than Socrates?" he paraphrases into the statement that he far excelled other men in this regard. To illustrate that Apollo's endorsement was an acceptable basis for expounding laws, Socrates cites the example of Lycurgus, founder of the (unwritten) laws and customs of the Spartans.[29]

No rational line of argument could be designed more deliberately to provoke an Athenian jury, at the time of Socrates' trial, than this. It defied all the standards by which the Athenians, at that very time, were seeking to fix the foundations of their system of law. It taunted them with the hateful example that they had twice already repudiated at the cost of much blood shed on Attic soil. More than this, it held up, as a model of authority, a man claiming personal access to divine guidance (and not from any one of "the gods acknowledged by the state"), whose claim was widely known to underlie the convictions and actions of his many friends. By his own examples Socrates gave Meletus and his colleagues considerable help in demonstrating to the jury that Socrates was effectively a *mystagogos*, a Guide of Initiates, of an illicit mystery cult.[30]

Only allegiance to an occult divinity could account for Socrates' utter indifference to the collective opinion of the Athenians around him. Yet this too was a well-known quirk of Socrates, and by and large it was a joking matter, not a serious concern. Aristophanes and others had long poked fun at the obscurantism of Socrates and his circle in these terms. So in the *Clouds* of 423, the protagonist, Strepsiades, barges into Socrates' "Thinkaterium" and upsets the thought process of one of Socrates' students:

> *Strepsiades:* 'Scuse me—I'm from way out in the country. But say, what's that thought of yours that miscarried?
>
> *Student:* It is forbidden *(ou themis)* to speak of it, except to the students.
>
> *Strepsiades:* Aw, c'mon, you can tell me. I'm here to become a student in the Thinkaterium.
>
> *Student:* All right, I'll tell you. But you have to treat these things as Mysteries *(nomisai de tauta chre mysteria)*. . . .[31]

As Plato's account shows, Socrates knew that the joke was now in earnest. He argued first that he had never actually taught anyone anything, and he answered the charge of atheism. But he failed to deal with the converse and more serious imputation that he was the dispenser of occult wisdom. How could this old joke become so serious a matter?

According to Plato's *Euthyphro,* set on the eve of his trial, Socrates knew that he was about to be held accountable as a teacher of religious doctrine. He suggests that he might escape the charge if he could claim that what he knew he learned, as a student, from someone else. In this case, the young seer, Euthyphro, an expert in sacred law and the expiation of *miasma,* pollution, is put forth as a possible authority for Socrates to name as a "corrupter of the old." But the fallibility of Euthyphro's expertise ultimately precludes this rejoinder to Meletus. In the meantime, however, we learn by implication that others had sought to escape blame or condemnation by claiming to be Socrates' students. Rightly or wrongly, they were probably encouraged to seek refuge in this claim precisely because Socrates had long been regarded as a harmless fool.[32]

Recent trials of various adherents of the late oligarchy must have produced admissions or assertions that a defendant had been motivated in his actions, in the name of a higher order of truth, by the teachings of Socrates. Critias himself was known to be a sometime companion of Socrates, and the pro-Spartan ideological links between them had probably been emphasized in front of other juries in efforts to condemn by association men who had shared Socrates' company. An accumulation of such assertions and admissions would have cast an increasingly sinister aspect on the society of Socrates. They had long been treated, by Aristophanes and others, as a definable group, "those who sit around Socrates" and "the students of Socrates." Some had already once been condemned, in the inquisitions of 415, for treasonous association under the guise of private cult, most notorious among whom was Alcibiades himself. By 401/0, the reputation of alleged or confessed members of this group will have focused increasingly hostile attention on their spiritual leader, the man who professed to have no interest in public affairs, yet whose one public office showed him to be a dedicated adversary of the people.[33]

Antiphon had had a similar reputation, according to Thucydides, as an enemy of the people and as the covert mastermind of the Four Hundred. But Antiphon had held office under the oligarchy of 411, and his actions as ambassador to the Spartans left him vulnerable to the more direct charge of treason by which he was condemned and executed. Socrates' offenses were committed through the agency of others, through those whom he had "corrupted." But it was not until 400/399, after a year or more of grievances and personal rivalries had been played out before democratic courts, that the name of Socrates had been invoked often enough in connection with the enemies of democracy to create an ill-defined yet pervasive aura of sinister power about the man.

Statesmen like Anytus, who identified themselves as champions of the public interest and who required victory over the enemies of democracy, found their effectiveness blunted in the presence of such evasiveness. Meletus had a more personal stake in bringing down Socrates. Previously an accuser of Andocides and probably involved in other litigation, he was fighting in the courts to salvage a reputation tarnished by association with the Thirty. For he had been one of the men who had arrested the democratic general, Leon of Salamis, at the command of the Thirty, and he must have been stung every time an opponent could say, "Not even *Socrates,* with the views we all know he holds, had the gall to commit the crime Meletus committed. . . . " Only by eliminating Socrates could this criticism be silenced. And then there was Lycon, a grieving father, desperate to make someone pay the price for the murder of his son. Lycon's son, Autolycus, celebrated athlete as a youth, was an age-mate of Plato and Xenophon, and like those two fine young men he had attracted the eye of Socrates. Among the favored ones of the Thirty, somehow Autolycus fell afoul of that regime and was put to death. Had Socrates in his arrogance misguided the young man's final fatal steps?[34]

Socrates, the officiant of an unknown *daimonion,* was made to bear this intolerable burden of blame. Nine years earlier, a similar scapegoat, Alcibiades, also given to *megalegoria,* had vindicated himself by repudiating the hurtful *daimonion,* Envy, that attended him, and by identifying his supernatural inspiration with Eros and the Mother of the Gods, forces who manifestly moved in the private and public affairs of all Athenians. In the end, however, Alcibiades' envious *daimonion* did him in. Socrates was an incorrigible elitist and would not miss the opportunity to show the Athenians why he held the views he held. He would not renounce his *daimonion,* because it embodied his quest for truth, and he would not identify it with any one of "the gods acknowledged by the state," because it justified his devotion to a higher cause than any that motivated the masses.

"Men of natural nobility *(agathoi)* willingly conform to divinely sanctioned law, but the masses must be compelled," according to an argument in Plato's *Symposium,* a text that comes as close as any to expressing the mystic faith of Socrates' society. If Socrates did not enunciate such a view outright, his accusers will have had no more difficulty associating Socrates with it than Plato did in his writings. As opposed to the inquisitors of 415, who looked to the distant past for signs by which to guide the *demos,* Anytus in 399 had the benefit of recent and painful memories among his listeners to induce them toward their decision.[35]

The fact that Socrates was condemned by no more than 281 out of his 501 jurors shows that the case was still not compelling to many Athenians, no matter how much support Socrates himself gave to the prosecution. He had had almost no personal role in public affairs, and he had long been accepted with a laugh as one of the exceptional features of an exceptional people. Was he really their insidious enemy? But one or another of the prosecutors' arguments persuaded a majority. He was condemned to death for the harm he had worked on blameless Autolycus, for the amoral guidance he had given to Critias, for the megalomania he had inspired in Alcibiades, and, above all, for the principles that still refused to acknowledge the sovereignty of the Athenian people.

CHAPTER TWELVE

Athenian Democracy and History, 399–395

Now Aristodemus could not remember what each speaker said verbatim, any more than I could repeat their speeches just as he told them to me. I shall simply recount those passages that were, in my judgment, the most memorable of each speech.

PLATO *SYMPOSIUM* 178A

Depictions of the conversations of Socrates, as in Plato's *Symposium* quoted above, present us with a remarkable feature of the passage from the generation of the Peloponnesian War to its successor: the following generation felt a pervasive need to revisit the spoken words of the bygone era. This need is represented, among other places, in the historical speeches reported by Thucydides and Xenophon. It is also found in the studied rhetoric of fourth-century orators, who occasionally reveal their debt to words spoken in the fifth. Among the orators we also find the evidence of the codification of earlier laws and decrees that began in the late fifth century. But the widest demand for words from the past generation was in the theater, where restaging tragedies of fifth-century poets became customary at Athens in the 380s, as did the restaging of old comedies in following years.

Tragedies and comedies were preserved in written texts, a medium vital to their original composition and performance. Writing was likewise essential to law and to rhetoric, especially to the forensic rhetoric of the later fifth century and afterward. The role of writing in the preservation of the words of Socrates and the political speeches of the later fifth century, however, is more problematic.

Socrates' single forensic speech was, he asserted, explicitly *not* the product of studied preparation. Although such a claim was, by the end of Socrates' life, well on the way to becoming an artifice of crafted rhetoric, there is no evidence that any of the abundant Socratic literature circulating in the fourth century ever came from the pen of Socrates. The essence of Socrates' dialectic method lay in the medium of spoken conversation, which makes the preservation of Socratic dialogues in writing something of a paradox. Modern scholars frequently yield to the urge to nullify that paradox by understanding the dialogues simply as Platonic texts. As Lesky has put it, "It should . . . be constantly borne in mind that a large part of our information [about Socrates] is derived not from work written for the purpose of historical truth but belonging to a literature which may be called Socratic fiction."[1]

There is no denying that the meaning of Plato's Socratic dialogues resides primarily in the thought of the man who composed them. But to ignore the presence of the historical Socrates is to overlook a vital dimension of the meaning of Plato's writings, however problematic its nature. Plato was the historian of Socrates. Even when we acknowledge that Plato's Socratic writings moved beyond the acceptable domain of history, his perspective was in many respects the same as that of other intellectuals of his generation looking back on the previous one. Xenophon wrote Socratic dialogues, and history, and much else that, from our post-Aristotelian disciplinary perspectives, defies classification. Xenophon's diverse methods of rendering meaning from the past reveal the breadth of the intellectual background shared by Plato and Thucydides.

Thucydides sought meaning in the context of political history, and expressed it most subtly by depicting spoken words. Like Plato, Thucydides is our sole authority for many speeches reported to us from the generation of the Peloponnesian War. Like Plato, Thucydides has been regarded as the artful creator of words that only distantly reflect, with uncertain fidelity, the spoken words of others. But such a view of Thucydides, as a historian, is even more problematic than such a view of Plato, the philosopher. Creative imagination has a wider, more legitimate domain within philosophy. In history, the literal truth about the past is supposed to limit the play of the imagination, and Thucydides himself is largely responsible for defining the historian's field of play. But where is the balance between literal truth and free imagination in the reporting of speeches, if decades intervened between the spoken and the written words? The definition of this balance is perhaps the central problem for all historians who have looked to Thucydides as a model for historical objectivity.

If we acknowledge that Thucydides' methods and interests had much in common with those of his contemporaries, then we may begin to unravel the problem of historical objectivity that underlies his use of speeches. We can move toward this goal by examining the relationship between spoken and written words in texts from around the end of the Peloponnesian War, and by considering the circumstances that may have prompted Thucydides to apply his expertise in this realm to the creation of what we now call a work of history.

All significant enactments of law, politics, philosophy, and poetry relied on living speech before their respective audiences. But from the late fifth century on, the drive to reify and preserve in writing the ephemeral enactments of speech was strong, particularly in the realms of law and forensic rhetoric. By the time of Socrates' trial, the pursuits of law and rhetoric had become highly literate and accessible chiefly to those who cultivated reading and writing. By virtue of the fact that legal disputes often dealt with the complexities of the recent, troubled Athenian past, the content of forensic rhetoric was often historical. But by virtue of its partisan nature, forensic rhetoric could never be completely objective. Socrates, for one, responded to this problem by adopting a deeply skeptical view of rhetoric in particular, and of the written word in general, a view that, as described in the previous chapter, brought him into fatal collision with the emerging definition of legal authority at Athens. Thucydides responded by probing as deeply into the problem of historical objectivity as his resources allowed. A new understanding of Thucydides' undertaking, outlined in the introduction to this book, requires a reappraisal of the resources at his disposal.

In common with the admirers of drama, with the practitioners of rhetoric, with the interpreters of law, and even, I suggest, with the devotees of Socrates, we should recognize that Thucydides had at his disposal written texts that preserved for him memorable speeches of the past. These texts were not perfect transcripts, but they were the memoranda that students of the spoken word had been collecting for a generation. The further implication of this hypothesis for our understanding of Thucydides is that his original motives must have been largely those of other students of the spoken word: the desire to master the rhetoric of law and politics in order to put it into practice. These were the motives that Plato admits to, prior to the death of Socrates, in his *Seventh Letter.* These must also have been the motives of Thucydides, even in exile.

In dealing with the biography of Thucydides, where so little is known, this hypothesis necessarily moves into a widening realm of speculation. None of what follows here, however, is more speculative than other hypotheses by which scholars heretofore have accounted for the life and literary output of Thucydides. I would venture to say, moreover, that what follows here is better grounded in terms of analogy with attested practices. We can only advance our understanding of Thucydides' achievement by seeing it in the context of contemporary influences. To do anything else is to accept Thucydides merely on faith.

A NEW PAST FOR A NEW BEGINNING

A few years after the trial of Socrates, when Athens was on the brink of renewed war against Sparta, an unnamed Athenian gentleman *(agathos)* was appointed by lot to a public office. He had been one of the 3,000 chosen by the Thirty, and his past left him vulnerable to attack by his enemies when his appointment came before a jury for confirmation. His speech, composed by Lysias, gives an instructive précis of the importance of knowing history.

> Now, first of all, you should reflect that no human being is naturally either an oligarch or a democrat: whatever constitution a man finds advantageous to himself, he is eager to see that one established; so it largely depends on you whether the present system finds an abundance of supporters. That this is the truth, you will have no difficulty in deducing from the events of the past. For consider, gentlemen of the jury, how many times the leaders of both governments changed sides. Did not Phrynichus, Peisander and their fellow-demagogues, when they had committed many offenses against you, proceed, in fear of the requital that they deserved, to establish the first oligarchy? And did not many of the Four Hundred, again, join in the return of the Piraeus party, while some, on the other hand, who had helped in the expulsion of the Four Hundred, actually appeared among the Thirty? Some, too, of those who had enlisted for Eleusis marched out with you to besiege their own comrades! There is thus no difficulty in concluding, gentlemen, that the questions dividing men are concerned, not with politics, but with their personal advantage. You should therefore apply this test in the probation of your citizens: examine their use of the citizenship under the democracy, and inquire whether they stood to benefit by a change in the government. In this way you will most justly form your decision upon them.[2]

Good men are found in both democracy and oligarchy, the argument goes, just as are bad. Deeds and motives must be examined in each case, and the recent past provides many examples to prove that simple equations are unreliable guides. Nothing was straightforward about the decade and a half from the profanation of the Mysteries to the fall of the Eleusinian oligarchy. The merits of every individual involved in those events had to be scrutinized in careful detail.

The past was ever put forth as a guide to present actions, and as these actions shaped the future, so, in subtle ways, did their justification shape the account of the past. After 403 there was something distinctively different about the construction of the recent Athenian past—its complexity. The Athenians were now two: those who had remained in the city during the reign of the Thirty, and those who had fought against them to return from exile. This division was the artifact of the Thirty's vision of Athenian aristocracy, and healing the rift required a denial of its legitimacy. The reunification proceeded from the recognition that there were "men of natural nobility" *(agathoi)* on both sides of the divide. Thrasybulus went even beyond this recognition of a community of peers. He argued that excellence was manifest in power, and reminded everyone that, by this standard, recent events placed the pride of the greater numbers of men from Piraeus above the arrogance of the 3,000. Henceforth, the division effected by the Thirty and defended by the 3,000 could no longer correspond to any publicly defensible notion of aristocracy; but the division had become an inescapable fact of circumstances.

No personal history was free of this complication. Anyone competing for public honors, seeking to persuade the Assembly or a jury, or even impersonally discussing public concerns was at some point obliged to situate himself historically within this community divided and reunited. Not even those who had removed themselves from the conflict, or who had by some circumstance been absent from the turmoil of 404/3, were immune. In fact, they had even more explaining to do to give a satisfactory account for themselves.[3]

Command of this complexity required a proficiency with the facts of the past and agility at casting them in the light most suitable to the purpose at hand. Because this was a competitive process and subject to challenge and to public approval, accuracy *(akribeia)* and command of detail were valuable. But only up to a point. As Socrates delighted in pointing out, the public was always more interested in its own gratification than in the truth. And as a practical matter, too much detail and subtlety would lose an argument, so there was also a powerful impetus to simplify. Proficiency with facts and the drive to simplify produced, over time, a "standard" account of the restoration of the democracy. Although this process began almost immediately, the fully simplified account of the triumph of the democrats did not become prevalent until just over a generation later, when the circumstances of 404/3 no longer applied to living individuals. After half a century it was even possible to conflate the events of 411 and 403 into a pastiche, historically garbled but publicly palatable.[4]

A PASSION FOR BOOKS

That we can even today discern popular distortions from historically nuanced accounts of Athens at the end of the fifth century is an indication of the intensity of the contemporary preoccupation to justify the present by articulating the past. Perils to empire and democracy were the source of this preoccupation. But because it was a *democracy* that experienced and ultimately survived these perils, they have left durable traces in written media. For the operations of an imperial democracy required the aid of written briefs and documents, and so did the private maneuverings of individuals competing for influence within a democratic system.

The convulsive changes afflicting Athens in the late fifth century thus befell a society uniquely primed to seek guidance in the meanings of articulate, durable words. Aristophanes, ever witness to the madnesses of the moment, attests to this in the months immediately following the condemnation of Alcibiades and other offenders against public piety in 415. A messenger comes to the new city of the *Birds* to bring a crown of honor to its founder for delivering the Athenians from their latest obsession, "up at dawn flitting about over laws, brooding over books, getting their fill of decrees. . . . " Every source—books of oracles, poetry, public decrees, the inscribed stones and *kyrbeis* of ancient laws—was scoured for guidance and authority in a troubled time.[5]

From this moment on we find the laws of Solon cited both in reverence and in ridicule. A research program underlying the oligarchy of 411 named the laws of Cleisthenes as a useful corrective to the embarrassments of Solon's legacy, and the Thirty applied more radical correctives. Democratic regimes affirmed the sanctity of the statutes of Draco and Solon (even while amending the latter), and an assessment of democratic legislation in 399 gave honorable mention to the lawgiving (drafting of decrees) of Themistocles and Pericles.[6]

The desire to own personal copies of valued texts, in the meantime, had become a commonplace. So Aristophanes, in 405, could depict a sailor musing over a copy of Euripides' *Andromeda* (staged in 411) during idle hours on campaign. At about the same time we find the earliest evidence that books had become a staple, commercial commodity. The comic poet Eupolis attests to a regular marketplace for books in Athens. Xenophon attests that books were a high-value cargo for overseas trade as well. Some of the Thracians in the domain of Seuthes, whom Xenophon was serving as a mercenary in 400, enriched themselves by gathering an unusual plunder from the ships wrecked on their coastal shoals: "Here was a rich treasure of many beds and boxes, with a mass of written books and all the various things that shipowners carry in their wooden chests."[7]

Book-owning seems to have become a matter of prestige, especially among those who aspired to public prominence (see frontispiece). Xenophon recounts the enchantment of Socrates for the young and handsome Euthydemus, "who had formed a large collection of the works of celebrated poets and sophists and therefore supposed himself to be a prodigy of wisdom for his age, confident of surpassing all his competitors in power of speech and action."[8]

The passion for books, as this passage indicates, was rooted in the practical desire to achieve "power of speech and action." Realizing this power on the comic stage, Peisetaerus, champion of Aristophanes' *Birds,* transcended the petty ambitions of oracle mongers, decree-sellers, and poets—all of them collectors and purveyors of books—and delivered his followers from the Athenian obsession for written texts. Peisetaerus' empire of the birds was founded on a vision of a new universal order, a radical reassessment of truths and beginnings. Through him, Aristophanes achieved in totalitarian fantasy what the Athenians, mired in confrontational democracy, could only dream of.

SOCRATES AND THE LAWS

Like Aristophanes, Socrates too was an observer and a critic of the Athenian obsession for collecting wisdom in writing. Socrates knew well how written words could be manipulated and given meanings that their author never intended. Words written in pen and ink, according to Plato's Socrates, do not deserve to be taken seriously, for they "can neither speak in their own defense nor present the truth adequately." Socrates' advocacy, by contrast, of the dialectic method of approaching the truth through the interchange of questions and answers allowed misdirections to be corrected in ways that a mute written text could never impart to a reader.[9]

Plato's *Phaedrus* expresses, through Socrates, a disdain for writers and their growing circles of readers:

> Anyone who leaves behind him a written manual, and likewise anyone who takes it over from him, on the supposition that such writing will provide something reliable and permanent, must be exceedingly simple-minded; he must really be ignorant... if he imagines that written words can do anything more than serve as a reminder, to one who knows, of the subject that the writing is concerned with.[10]

To those who do not know, by implication, written words provide no more than a semblance of knowledge. To those who *think* they know, but do not, words preserved in writing become a vehicle to deception.

The specific object of Socrates' criticism in the *Phaedrus* is the orator Lysias, whose power as a writer must have been felt by Socrates in his last years and was witnessed then and later by Plato. Lysias, in Plato's estimate at least, thus failed to achieve recognition by the master as a true "lover of wisdom," a philosopher. He was, on the contrary, one of those

> who has nothing to show of more value than the literary works on whose phrases he spends hours, twisting them this way and that, pasting them together and pulling them apart.... [He] will rightly, I suggest, be called a poet or a speech-writer *(logon syngrapheus)* or a law-writer *(nomographos)*.[11]

The criticism of written law is explicit in the *Phaedrus* and is implicit in several other passages in which Plato evoked his master at his most profound moments. The criticism reveals the priority that Socrates, in common here with Critias, placed on his *knowing* the laws of Athens, and not needing a written text of them unless to serve as a mere reminder. So Socrates would not allow himself to be diverted from what he *knew* was right, least of all by someone quoting a law to him. This he demonstrated in the Assembly deliberating the fate of the generals in 406, and again in his trial in 399.

In the days leading up to his execution, Socrates had another confrontation with the laws, depicted in the *Crito,* in which he justified his acceptance of his sentence as a demonstration of obedience to the laws of Athens. But his profession of loyalty, significantly, is made not to any attested statute, nor to anyone, living or dead, who had the authority to expound the laws. Rather, it comes in the form of an imaginary dialogue between himself and the Laws personified. Only in this deified form could Socrates envision the Laws exercising a naturally endowed authority, like that of parents who nurture their children. These Laws claim that the reverence due to them from their citizens exceeds even the reverence due to parents by their offspring. "Are you so wise," they ask Socrates,

> as to have forgotten that compared with your mother and father and all the rest of your ancestors your country is something far more precious, more venerable, more sacred, and held in greater honor both among gods and among all reasonable men?[12]

Socrates' allegiance to the laws of his native land was thus both profoundly patriotic and profoundly defiant of the legitimacy of laws expounded by orators and applied by popular juries. Laws were the embodiment of fundamental truths that most directly and explicitly guided human actions. The struggle to define the laws of the Athenian state brought, by 399, the underlying premises of law, truth, and justice into sharper focus. Yet, as precise as the public processes of legal definition might be, Socrates could claim the he was a lens of reason and piety that would yield a clearer image of truth.[13]

The most famous of Platonic/Socratic allegories for the pursuit of philosophy is constructed directly from this experience of law in the months leading up to Socrates' trial. In the seventh book of the *Republic,* Plato's Socrates likens the philosopher to one who has been freed from the bondage that constrains his fellow men to live in darkness, in a cave, prevented from seeing anything other than the shadows of puppets depicting men, beasts, and things cast on the wall of the cave in front of them by manipulators hidden behind them. The man who has risen from among these prisoners in the cave to see the world outside, in the light of the sun, would know the truth and would no longer be deceived by the illusions of the puppeteers. But he would be hard put to explain his new-found knowledge to his fellow men who knew only the shadows on the wall of the cave. Upon returning to the cave, he would, Plato says,

> cut a sorry figure and appear most ridiculous, if, while still blinking through the gloom... he is compelled in courtrooms or elsewhere to contend about the shadows of justice or the images that cast the shadows and to wrangle and debate about the notions of these things in the minds of those who have never seen justice itself.[14]

The wall of shadows, about which men contend and wrangle, was the wall of the shrine of Aeacus, on which the laws of the Athenians were being displayed as they were brought up for ratification. The unenlightened Athenians were transfixed by this display. Recognizing no more authentic guide to justice, they treated these shadow-laws with the highest seriousness, as the cases of Andocides and Nicomachus illustrate. Before this notion of law Socrates indeed appeared ridiculous. But always seeing a higher truth where the Athenians collectively were in darkness, Socrates knew that his actions in the end would be judged not according to these shadow-laws, but by the divinely sanctioned justice dispensed to the dead by Aeacus himself.

Although the Athenians did not have the wisdom to see the truth as Socrates did, in Plato's opinion, still they were near its presence and might yet be guided to the light. This hope was symbolized in the godlike tribal heroes of the Athenians, sanctioned by Delphi, whose statues stood before Aeacus' shrine (see figure 8 on page 270). These ancestral heroes, it seems, are called to mind at the close of Book 7, when Socrates concludes that living Athenians, endowed with hereditary excellence and educated in philosophy to serve as guardians and leaders of the Athenians, would be suitably honored, after their deaths, by monuments and public sacrifices sanctioned by Apollo's oracle. For this was the manner in which the ten tribal heroes had been honored at their institution. Standing before Aeacus' shrine, the statues of these virtuous ancestors symbolized the hope that the souls of their kinsmen might yet find enlightenment as they approached final judgment in Aeacus' court.[15]

REMEMBERING THE SPOKEN WORD

It is in one sense ironic that Socrates, with his disdain for the authority of writing, should be known to us only through the literate artistry of Plato and his other disciples. Yet the passion for capturing ephemeral utterances in durable form gripped the circle of Socrates as much as any intellectual circle. In fact, it is clear that the master as well as his disciples were enthusiasts of writing as a useful means of keeping reminders, *hypomnemata,* on hand. In this vein we find even Critias quoted as praising the Phoenician invention of letters as "the preserver of discourse." As long as they were not taken too seriously themselves, written texts were an acceptable means of prompting serious discussion.[16]

Plato's writings provide examples of how such *hypomnemata* came into existence and passed into circulation during Socrates' lifetime and later. The opening of the *Theaetetus* describes how one of Socrates' companions, Eucleides of Megara, reconstructed a conversation that Socrates had told him about in his last year:

> I made some notes at the time, as soon as I got home, and later on I wrote out what I could recall at my leisure. Then, every time I went to Athens, I ques-

> tioned Socrates upon any point where my memory had failed and made corrections on my return. In this way I have pretty well the whole conversation written down.... This is the book *(biblion),* Terpsion. You see how I wrote the conversation—not in narrative form, as I heard it from Socrates, but as a dialogue between him and the other persons he told me had taken part. These were Theodorus the geometer and Theaetetus. I wanted to avoid in the written account the tiresome effect of bits of narrative interrupting the dialogue, such as "and I said" or "and I remarked" wherever Socrates was speaking of himself, and "he assented" or "he did not agree," where he reported the answer. So I left out everything of that sort, and wrote it as a direct conversation between the actual speakers.... [To a slave] Now, boy, take the book and read....[17]

Plato's *Parmenides* is the narration of a conversation involving that eminent sophist, distinguished foreigners and Athenians, and Socrates. Some years later, the conversation was repeatedly narrated, by one of those who had been present, to the half-brother of Plato, Antiphon son of Pyrilampes, who "worked hard at getting that conversation by heart." Although no text is mentioned as the basis for Antiphon's later narration of the dialogue, the practice of memorizing lengthy prepared speeches from a written draft is the only way to construe such a feat of memorization. Similarly, Plato's *Phaedrus* opens with Phaedrus promising Socrates, with feigned modesty, that he will try to relate a speech he just heard Lysias declaim. It emerges, however, that Phaedrus has the text of the speech in hand and has been working hard at memorizing it. Socrates can think of nothing more inviting than to hear this speech of Lysias' and will follow Phaedrus wherever he likes to hear it. And, he tells Phaedrus, "if you offered me volumes of speeches *(logoi en bibliois)* you could lead me around all of Attica, or anywhere else you please."[18]

One might suppose that Plato has introduced these narrative touches for stylistic effect in dialogues that are more or less free invention. By the time he was composing the dialogues of his middle period this probably was the case. But fundamental to Plato's artistry was his ability to set his dialogues in a plausible context, and part of that context was often the framework of a written account originating with one of the witnesses to the conversation. Both tradition and contemporary evidence confirm that the practices of oral-textual transmission that Plato describes were familiarly employed in Socrates' lifetime. This was the way that spoken words of the late fifth century often passed directly into writing, sometimes as individual possessions, as Plato depicts them, and sometimes as written works that were more widely disseminated. "Volumes of speeches" were, in all probability, one of the largest classes of written works circulating in the final decades of the fifth century.

Plato's example from the *Theaetetus* is paralleled by Diogenes Laertius' account of Simon the cobbler, said to be among the first to compose Socratic dialogues: "When Socrates came into his workshop and began to converse, he used to make notes *(hyposemeioseis)* of all that he could remember." This practice of note-taking, familiar in sophistic circles, must have been just as common in political and forensic settings at least as early as the 420s. When Cleon, as reported by Thucydides, berated members of the Assembly for behaving "like spectators gathered around sophists," note-taking was surely one of the most obvious indicators of the habits he was condemning. For the contemporary practice of taking notes at speeches is directly attested by Aristophanes.[19]

In the *Wasps,* Aristophanes depicts the writing of notes *(mnemosyna)* on a speech *as it is being delivered* as a central device in the debate between the democratic juror, Philocleon, and his sophisticated son, Bdelycleon. Bdelycleon employs his written transcript as the means to twist phrases and pull apart the arguments of his opponent. In the *Knights,* when Aristophanes describes young enthusiasts of sophistic rhetoric gathered at a perfume-shop in the Agora to study the artistry of an admired orator, a written transcript must be assumed as the source of the phrases they admire. By the time of his *Frogs,* Aristophanes extends this image of skill at relating a spoken argument to a written text to the whole of his Athenian audience, "a battle-tried army, each one of whom, book in hand, grasps the subtle points."[20]

The earliest surviving examples of sophistic rhetoric, the works of Antiphon dating to the 420s or 410s, come from the period of active pursuit of rhetorical exemplars attested by Aristophanes. Like Lysias after him, Antiphon was in the business of preparing speeches for clients, but the circumstances under which his works entered a wider circulation are unknown. In the case of at least one of Antiphon's speeches, the dissemination of the text can be plausibly attributed to members of an interested audience.

Thucydides greatly admired Antiphon's famous final speech, delivered at his trial in 411. But Thucydides can have known it only from a text he read while in exile or years later in Athens. Like Socrates' defense, the circulation of this speech is less likely the product of Antiphon's industry during his final days than an achievement of a sympathetic minority among his listeners. No small number of Athenians had real reason to weigh the phrases by which the architect of the Four Hundred had defended himself in court. Scribblers in the audience quickly produced transcripts of a speech that was sure to find an immediate market.[21]

Other famous speeches before a packed jury-court, Assembly, or Councilhouse, were almost certainly likewise immediately committed to writing by those who craved the study of words in action. Euryptolemus' prepared speech on behalf of the generals after Arginusae was eagerly anticipated by those who hoped that reason would prevail over passion. Theramenes' speeches advocating a negotiated surrender to Sparta riveted the attention of his listeners. Likewise, the final debate of Critias and Theramenes in 404 was, for the intellectual circles frequented by Euthydemus, Xenophon, and Isocrates, a show not to miss. Theramenes' speech, as Xenophon narrates it, won the debate before the Council; Critias succeeded in destroying his foe only by arbitrary authority and brute force. To tell the truth by circulating transcripts of those speeches was a seditious act in the eyes of the Thirty, and was surely a consideration in the Thirty's ban on teaching "the art of speaking."[22]

But speeches did circulate and were studied as the legacy of Theramenes and his contemporaries became a matter of historical debate. It was no mere academic matter. Those who found themselves before a jury, in the years after 403, were facing much of the same, battle-tried, book-experienced army that Aristophanes addressed in 405. Those who won their contests were those speakers, like Lysias, who took this expertise seriously and employed it to their own ends. Just as the speaker quoted above on page 295 appealed to the events of this period, so other speakers must often have referred to the debate between Critias and Theramenes in jury trials after 403.

To some, Theramenes was a martyr to reason and fairness in the face of the extremism of Critias, and his name must have often been invoked by men attempting to justify their former association with Critias. Evidence of this is found in Lysias' famous attack on Eratosthenes, a surviving member of the Thirty. Lysias undermines any appeal to Theramenes' reputation by painting it in as sinister colors as possible. To buttress his case, he reminds the jury of the debate between Critias and Theramenes:

> For this you should rely, not on my word, but on that of Theramenes himself; since everything that I have mentioned was stated by him in his defense before the Council, when he reproached the [oligarchic] exiles with the fact that they owed their restoration to him, and not to any consideration shown by the Lacedaemonians, and reproached also his partners in the government....

By appealing to Theramenes' own words, Lysias' indictment gains credence from assuming his audience's prior familiarity with Theramenes' defense. In the process, incidentally, Lysias gives fine testimony to the subtle effects of rhetorical distortion; for the points he claims that Theramenes made in his own defense were, according to Xenophon's account, actually points made in Critias' speech of condemnation. The public was familiar with the debate, but a jury had no authoritative transcript to refer to. A speechwriter like Lysias, however, had the texts at home and could use them to shape popular opinion by playing with the public's sense of knowing the past that came from often hearing about it.[23]

THE ACCOUNT COMPILED BY THUCYDIDES

Across the same span of decades observed by Aristophanes and Socrates, Thucydides son of Olorus was acquiring the experience that would yield the most remarkable single piece of writing of this generation, his history of the war between Athens and Sparta. Elected general in 424, he commanded Athenian forces in the northern reaches of the empire, along the Thracian coast and on the island of Thasos, in the year that saw the arrival of a Spartan offensive in that region, led by Brasidas. The loss of Amphipolis on the Strymon river to Brasidas, in the winter of 424/3, was a catastrophe that ended Thucydides' career as a general. He remained in self-imposed exile for the rest of the war.

Aside from the obvious fact that he was an astute observer of war and diplomacy, little else is known about Thucydides. He informs us that he controlled gold mines in Thrace. This fact, his father's Thracian name, and the deduction drawn by later scholars that he was related to the family of Cimon, all serve to indicate that he was by birth a man of influence and substance, with prominent ancestral connections in Thrace. Such circumstances would account for his appointment to command in the region, and for his independence during exile. They also suggest that Thucydides, even in exile, was an important fixture in the politics of the region, a fact that would have encouraged his attention to the currents of diplomacy and war around him.[24]

By his own account, Thucydides maintained contact with men on both sides of the war during his exile. He was likely in contact with other Athenian exiles, and therefore aware of the divisions of Athenian politics that created two oligarchic regimes. His return to Athens in 404 was made possible by the peace treaty with Sparta. In Athens, Thucydides probably remained among the men of the city under the regime of Critias, although this is far from certain. Like Plato and Socrates, Thucydides was probably one who shifted from optimism to horror at the deeds of Critias' regime in 404/3.[25]

Thucydides was better able than most to recognize the complexity of the issues that had motivated Alcibiades, Theramenes, and Critias, and was therefore more sensitive than most to the distortions practiced on the public in the name of restoring the glory of Athens and the strength of her democracy. He knew, too, that leadership would win approval, and policy would be made, based on arguments from past experience. But what Thucydides knew could not be easily explained before a jury or an assembly. It required a lengthy exposition.

By the end of the fifth century a highly developed culture of reading had evolved at Athens, making such a lengthy treatise practicable. Demand for books among ambitious men, the likes of Callias, Lysias, Andocides, and the late Euthydemus, assured that all manner of treatises would find readership, especially treatises that promised to yield "power of speech and action." Thucydides' work provided more effective lessons in the "power of speech and action" than any treatise on rhetoric, leadership, or law.[26]

Thucydides appealed to this readership from the outset of his work by proclaiming the greatness of his subject and by declaring his own qualifications for writing its history: "Thucydides the Athenian compiled the account of the war between the Peloponnesians and the Athenians, beginning the moment that it broke out, and believing that it would be greater than any previous war. . . ." His was *the* great subject, greater than the Trojan War, the Persian Wars, or any other war affecting the Greeks. This claim, which he justifies in detail in the subsequent chapters of his first book, is intended to recommend his work as a suitable if not superior companion to the only comparable war-narratives in existence, the works of Homer and Herodotus. Likewise, his claim to have written his account of the war "beginning at the moment that it broke out" is another recommendation of the superiority of his work. Moreover, his relationship to the events he narrates was unique. Understanding this relationship is crucial to our assessment of his achievement.[27]

However we may understand his claim, Thucydides' involvement in writing contemporaneously with the events of the conflict is *the* essential condition that enabled him to compose his history. The dominant explanation in modern scholarship is that Thucydides began writing by taking notes on the course of events. Years later, after he had begun composing his notes into a coherent narrative, he fit in the speeches, reconstructed from memory and with some help from others, to give the work dramatic focus. There is nothing inherently implausible about this scenario, but neither is there any evidence that makes it particularly likely.[28]

When we consider the evidence of the nature of reading, writing, and rhetoric at Athens in Thucydides' generation, as examined in the course of this book, we find that it suggests a significantly different scenario for Thucydides' relationship to the writing of his subject. It is a scenario, moreover, that provides a new basis for understanding the much-discussed and controverted passage in Book 1, where Thucydides briefly defines his relationship to the process of writing.

Following his introductory survey of the rise of sea power in antiquity and his criticism of the inaccuracies of popular tradition, poetry, and rhetoric, in 1.22 Thucydides makes his famous methodological statement about subjectivity and accuracy in his presentation of historical speech and action. Significantly, he discusses the treatment of speeches first:

> As for the speeches that men on each side made, either when the war was about to begin or when it was already in progress, it was difficult for me to preserve exactly what was said in the speeches that I myself heard, and likewise for those who reported speeches to me from various sources. They are given as, in each case, I thought the speaker would have said what the particular situation required, keeping as close as possible, in overall intent, to what was actually said.[29]

The speeches in Thucydides' work are widely recognized as the most essential element of his genius as a historian. Thucydides used speeches in a more fundamental manner than Herodotus to frame the issues played out in the narrative of events, and in so doing he set a standard that clearly influenced later historians. Yet, by their very complexity, the speeches reported by Thucydides have confronted scholarship with a perplexing issue. If the speeches were the artifacts of unaided memory looking back over years and even decades, how accurate could they be? To what degree could Thucydides reproduce "what was actually said," as opposed to indulging in free invention, authorized by the admission that he wrote what "I thought the speaker would have said"? Given the assumption that Thucydides had no written notes on speeches, scholarly attention has inevitably become fixed on the paradox of an author obsessed with accuracy who has issued himself a license for free invention.[30]

A reassessment of Thucydides 1.22.1 dissolves this paradox. In chapter 4, we noted that the language of "hearing" can disguise the presence of written texts as the source of information "heard" *(akoei)*. So too can the language of "remembering" disguise the presence of written memoranda *(hypomnemata)*. In the phrase above, "it was difficult for me to preserve exactly what was said," the word translated "to preserve" is *diamnemoneusai*. It is often translated, "to remember" (so Warner), or even "to carry ... in one's memory" (Crawley). It *may* mean this, but it is also attested as meaning "to preserve a record [in writing] of," and this is how I believe it should be understood here. As in the opening of several Platonic dialogues (e.g., the quote from the *Symposium* at the head of this chapter), in 1.22.1 Thucydides is referring to the difficulty of achieving fidelity to words once spoken, relying, as one must, upon imperfect *written notes* gathered from various sources. The problem with accuracy is thus of a completely different order than what modern scholars have usually imagined.[31]

By the evidence considered here, we can now recognize Thucydides' speeches as artifacts of the widespread practice of taking notes as speeches were delivered, or immediately afterward, and of often cross-checking them among other listeners eager to learn the techniques and turns of argument that commanded the greatest respect at the moment. The parallel example of Socratic dialogues illustrates the various conditions under which the spoken word could be committed to writing, transmitted, and collected by interested parties. For us, the receivers of a polished collection of such transcripts, the assessment of the accuracy versus the creativity of any rendition is still problematic. We can see that it was so for Thucydides too, just as it was for Plato. But now the problem can be seen, as Thucydides' original readership understood it, to be truly a question of *degree* of fidelity within speeches where at least the more memorable phrases and expressions can be accepted as authentic.[32]

It was particularly with reference to the speeches, then, that Thucydides could claim—and could expect to be believed—that he had begun writing even as the war began. In 431, Thucydides was a privileged member of the young and ambitious crowd of aristocratic intellectuals eager to secure their share of the benefits of empire. Under Pericles, Thucydides beheld the power of rhetoric to set great forces in motion. Along with the most engaged of his competitive peers, Thucydides must have assembled a collection of notes on actual debates before the Assembly and in the jury courts, all for the practical purpose of advancing his career. For Thucydides was well placed to rise to prominence, and was on his way up when he had the misfortune to preside over the most notorious loss of imperial territory before the Ionian revolts of 412, namely, the fall of Amphipolis to Brasidas in the winter of 424/3.[33]

THUCYDIDES IN EXILE

In exile, as Thucydides informs his readers, he had the benefit of learning firsthand from participants on both sides of the conflict. Yet even before exile Thucydides' interests were not parochial or purely Atheno-centric. To rule an empire, he and his fellow Athenian aristocrats had to see Athens as others saw her. In the process, he and his fellows were building intellectual links to aristocrats abroad. The "we/you" stance of Pseudo-Xenophon's treatise on the *Constitution of the Athenians* suggests that a literary interchange was going on between Athenians and Peloponnesians at least by the early years of the Peloponnesian War. A year after Thucydides went into exile, Aristophanes referred to seditious sympathies for Brasidas among Athenian intellectuals, suggesting that Brasidas' articulate views (as Thucydides notes, "he was not a bad speaker, for a Lacedaemonian") and not just his warlike deeds were known to them. Exile placed Thucydides in an even better position to examine this perspective than most of his Athenian contemporaries.[34]

Modern readers have tended to view Thucydides in exile as resigned to his condition and ready to embrace historical composition as a suitable way of occupying his keen mind while waiting for "the war" to end. But this is to confuse the eventual outcome with the foreseeable future for Thucydides in exile. Bygone generations, including among them Thucydides' own Philaid kinsmen, were replete with careers punctuated by long sojourns away from Athens, where political enemies held sway, until a turn of events brought a triumphant homecoming. In his own generation, not a few men of influence endured years of expatriation before returning to political activity at Athens. Thucydides had every reason to expect his political fortunes to change sooner or later.[35]

For reasons such as these, Thucydides very likely remained engaged in events, attuned to the words and deeds of powerful men around him. To seize the moment, as Brasidas had, meant among other things that one had to speak persuasively, as Brasidas did. It was not enough to know how to use ships, men, and money; a successful career was built on speaking persuasively about them in deliberative assemblies. A key element of persuasion was command of the facts, both present conditions and precedents. Thucydides was certainly attuned to the importance of a clear exposition of the facts "for those who want to understand the past as a useful guide to the probable future course of events."[36]

Thucydides probably looked forward to a leading role in affairs of the north Aegean whenever the Athenians and Spartans finally became committed to peace. Peace in 421 had foundered in part because of the failure of the two sides to implement their agreements regarding Amphipolis and other key sites in the north Aegean. When rapprochement with Sparta was once again seriously under discussion at Athens, in 411, Thucydides must again have been looking to his opportunities. Again, however, affairs in the heart of his domain of influence complicated Athenian interests.[37]

In 411 Thasos revolted, and a newly formed aristocratic government soon accepted a Spartan garrison to safeguard their freedom from Athens. Thucydides describes this revolt to illustrate the misguided policies into which Peisander had led the Four Hundred. Thasos, however, was equally problematic for the Spartans. Probably late in 409, another revolution resulted in the expulsion of the Spartan garrison from Thasos. Pasippidas, the Spartan naval commander for 410/9, was accused by Spartan authorities of complicity with Tissaphernes in arranging this revolution, and was forced into exile.[38]

The circumstances of this second Thasian revolution reveal a link to Alcibiades' vision for a general peace and an imperial alliance between Athens and Persia (chapter 6). Late in 409, Pasippidas and a group of Spartan envoys, along with Hermocrates the Syracusan and his brother, had joined Argive and Athenian envoys on the mission to King Darius arranged in the treaty of Chalcedon by Pharnabazus and Alcibiades. Hermocrates, now an exile, had earlier been an influential spokesman for compromise and peace, and we must assume that all of the principal ambassadors to be conducted by Pharnabazus were sympathetic to this cause. One of their objectives was probably a widening of the scope of the autonomy, or independent self-government, that had been accorded to a limited number of subject-states of the Athenian empire under the terms of the Peace of Nicias. Thasos, a vital link among Greek towns in western Thrace, was clearly striving to achieve such a status. The envoys may well have intended Thasos to be the showpiece for moderation and reconciliation in the polarized politics of the Aegean, through which the initiative begun by Pharnabazus and Alcibiades could attract more adherents.[39]

In due course it became clear that compromise was not to be the order of the day and that this diplomatic initiative would fail. The Athenians then strengthened their efforts to force the Thasians to a negotiated surrender. Despite the resort to a "military solution," the political settlement worked out in 407 as a consequence of the surrender of Thasos was characterized, as inscriptions attest, by a conciliatory attitude among the former warring parties. Of all the states rent by *stasis* in the course of the war, Thasos showed the greatest hope of reaching a durable peace through reason and reconciliation. Following the surrender of Athens to Sparta in 404, Lysander took notorious advantage of this trusting attitude to exterminate Athenian supporters there.[40]

There is some probability that Thucydides was involved, or at least in contact with the principal actors, in all of these affairs, before his return to Athens on the eve of Lysander's purge. Historically, Thasos had a dominant influence over the gold mines of the opposite coast that were now a personal concern of Thucydides. Thasos had been Thucydides' base of operations when Amphipolis fell to Brasidas in 424/3. In the course of his narrative in Book 8, Thucydides' choice of the Thasian revolt to illustrate the errant policies of the Four Hundred is arbitrary, but it reveals his close familiarity with internal affairs of that island state. Like Thucydides himself, the relationship of Thasos to the contending powers of the Aegean was ambiguous, changeable, and not inconsequential.[41]

Explicit testimony establishes another link between Thucydides and Athenian interests in the area of Thasos, most likely in the period of the Thasian revolt. Pausanias, the second-century CE travel writer, in his tour of the Acropolis at Athens, mentions a monument of one Oenobius and adds that he had secured a resolution recalling Thucydides to Athens. This Oenobius was probably the general of that name who, in 410/9, commanded along the Thracian coast opposite Thasos, where he may have encountered Thucydides. The decree of Oenobius was probably passed in recognition of Thucydides' services to Athens in the interval between the second revolution on Thasos in 409 and the negotiated surrender of Thasos in 407. Whatever its exact date, the decree is proof that Thucydides was recognized during his exile for services to democratic Athens and therefore that he was actively engaged in the affairs of empire.[42]

Thucydides was probably serving Athenian interests in more than just a diplomatic capacity. Accounts of the Treasurers of Athena at Athens, probably from the year 409/8, record the presence of a number of "ingots of Scaptesylican gold." Scapte Hyle, "Woodland Diggings," was the locale of Thucydides' gold mines. The ingots from Scapte Hyle were among payments to Athena that included Cyzicene and Lampsacene staters and "coined silver from miscellaneous sources," probably representing the booty from the campaigns of Alcibiades and his colleagues in 410/9. It seems likely that the ingots from Scapte Hyle became part of this revenue flow as a result of the joint efforts, in the interval 411–407, of Thucydides and Athenian commanders along the Thracian coast, among whom we can name Thrasybulus and Theramenes in addition to Oenobius.[43]

By all indications, Thucydides' career, both before and during his exile, was that of an Athenian aristocrat devoted to the empire. Although personal experience was responsible for a certain pessimism about Athenian leadership, as readers of his work often remark, in all probability Thucydides pursued what he perceived to be the best interests of the empire, and of himself, during his twenty years of exile. But with the catastrophe of 405/4, the object of his devotion ceased to exist. Lysander's interventions in Thrace and on Thasos deprived him of his land holdings and shattered his network of influence in the region.

When Thucydides finally did return to Athens, under the general recall of exiles following the surrender to Sparta, his expertise was marginalized. His contacts may have made Thucydides useful to some, but assured him no official role in the machinations of the Thirty. Somehow surviving the turmoil of 404/3, Thucydides found himself with time to reflect. His abiding interests lay with those who cherished the notion that the Athenian empire might yet be rebuilt. But for several years there was little opportunity for a man like Thucydides to pursue the career for which he had so long prepared himself.[44]

THUCYDIDES IN ATHENS

Thucydides was a rare survivor among the elite of his generation. He was uniquely equipped, moreover, with a personal collection of notes and transcripts of speeches that set the legacy of the last decades of the Athenian empire in a perspective reaching back to Pericles. Pericles was represented, to those not old enough to remember him after 403, through the texts of his decrees, through comic satires, and through the contesting traditions that viewed him either as a great democratic legislator or as one of a long line of demagogues who had set Athens on the path to corruption and decline. Thucydides could add subtlety and forgotten substance to these stereotypes. Moreover, because of his long absence from the eye of the storm, Thucydides was able to give a more dispassionate appraisal of the leading figures of previous decades than could his countrymen still immersed in Athenian politics.[45]

In view of the vigorous industry of manufacturing heroes and villains from hindsight after 403, Thucydides' work embodies some remarkable perspectives. His high regard for Antiphon, "an Athenian second to none in his day in *arete,* who proved himself a most able intellect and articulate speaker," and his respect for the judgment of Phrynichus, are unparalleled. If he were partisan rather than personal in his perspective, these judgments would align him with the foes of Alcibiades. But they did not cloud his high estimate of Alcibiades, whom he calls "the most capable at leading the state in war." Among the few statements he makes with a view toward the eventual outcome of the war, Thucydides makes it clear that he blames no public conduct by Alcibiades, but rather the rivalries of his enemies that played upon public fears of Alcibiades' greatness, as the cause of the eventual defeat of Athens. Alcibiades' leadership may have been the best embodiment of Pericles' vision of empire, in the view of Thucydides and, while Alcibiades still lived, of not a few Athenians.[46]

The appraisal of Alcibiades remained a vexed question as the Athenians looked back on the collapse of their empire. If Alcibiades had once seemed Athens' last, best hope, then perspectives had shifted in hindsight. The empire was gone, Pericles' vision had failed, and so had Alcibiades'. Living Athenians, with a future to build, were all too ready to blame their misfortunes on Alcibiades, dead and gone. The almost gratuitous nature of this trend is nowhere better illustrated than in a Lysian speech delivered sometime close to 400.

The speech was composed for a spectacularly wealthy young Athenian, an age-mate of Plato, who had to defend himself against a charge of mishandling public money. To deflect the allegation of his opponents that he had made free use of the people's money, he dwells upon his own generosity on the people's behalf. It was a delicate task, to boast of benefiting the Athenian people while also glorifying oneself. In support of his own reputation for lavish expenditure in public service, he reports that, during Alcibiades' final year of service as an Athenian general,

> my vessel was the best found in the whole armament. And I will tell you the surest evidence of that fact: at first Alcibiades—I would have given a great deal to prevent his sailing with me, as he was neither my friend nor my relative nor a member of my tribe—was aboard my ship. Now I am sure you must be aware that, being a commander who was free to do as he pleased, he would never have gone aboard any but the best found vessel, when he was himself to have his part in the danger.[47]

Here we see the irony of someone aspiring to the magnificence of Alcibiades—for which only the man himself could provide the measure—yet having to avert the animus that attached to his name.

The animus was serious, for in the minds of many Athenians Alcibiades had become linked not only with the ruin of empire, but also with the brutal excesses of tyranny. Contemporary sources attest that the regime of the Thirty was dubbed a "tyranny" as soon as it was gone. Contemporary sources also attest that Alcibiades was associated, for what his enemies claimed he *might* have done, with Critias and his fellows, for what they *did* do. This conjunction was rendered plausible through the attack on their most demonstrable link, Socrates.[48]

FIGURE 9. Celebrating the tyrant-slayers, again: Panathenaic prize amphora, ca. 400, with Athena displaying the statues of Harmodius and Aristogeiton on her shield. Photo © The British Museum, inv. no. B. 605, neg. no. PS 160378.

Tracts condemning Socrates, the most influential of them by a certain Polycrates, were composed and circulated in the decade after his execution. Interest in the subject was sustained by the fascination with the private knowledge and personal power associated with Socrates' circle and identified with the power of tyranny. In such a context, it was easy to elide the historical tyranny of the Peisistratids, the metaphorical tyranny of the Thirty, and the apprehended, would-be tyranny of Alcibiades, all as hated subverters of democracy. Democracy required its defenders, and consequently the tyrant-slayers, Harmodius and Aristogeiton, were in the forefront of popular imagination close to the time of Socrates' trial.[49]

FIGURE 10. Celebrating the tyrant-slayers, again: fragment of an oinochoe, ca. 400, showing the garlanded statues of Harmodius and Aristogeiton, from the grave of Dexileos. Photo courtesy of the Museum of Fine Arts, Boston, Henry Lillie Pierce Fund, no. 98.936.

In 402 and again in 398, the quadrennial celebrations of the Great Panathenaea took place. A revival of the heroic reputation of the Athenian tyrant-slayers was possible on either of these occasions, but more appropriate to the latter following the extermination of the Thirty at Eleusis in 401. A unique series of Panathenaic prize amphoras produced most likely for the Panathenaea of 398 bear the image of the tyrant-slayers on the shield of Athena (see figure 9). The popularity of the tyrant-slayers in the early 390s is further attested by their depiction, crowned with celebratory garlands, on a vase found in the grave of Dexileos, a cavalryman who died in battle against the Spartans in 394, at the age of twenty (figure 10, see also figure 11). Perhaps, four years before his death, Dexileos had joined his age-mates in honoring the statues of Harmodius and Aristogeiton, overlooking the orchestra of the Agora, in dance and choral song. Such songs and dances were the means by which the Athenians reforged the links that bound them

FIGURE 11. Heroic *arete* in battle, again: the grave relief of Dexileos (mounted), Athenian cavalryman killed near Corinth in 394. Athens, Kerameikos Museum. Photo courtesy of the Deutsches Archäologisches Institut, Athens, neg. no. KER 5976.

to their image of democratic heritage and political equality. By these means, a difficult past was being made simple.[50]

Thucydides wrote as a witness to this process of celebration. More than once he expresses a desire to counteract popular misconceptions among Athenians specifically on the subject of tyranny. But Thucydides was swimming against a current of popular sentiment at Athens in the 390s when he criticized the views of the majority of Athenians about their own history. "Most people," Thucydides declares, "will not take trouble in finding out the truth, but are much more inclined to accept the first story they hear." By contrast, Thucydides tells us, he has devoted great effort to accuracy. But why did he feel the need go to such trouble?[51]

WHY THUCYDIDES WROTE

At the end of his concise preface, in 1.22.4, Thucydides states that his careful account of the words and deeds of the men involved in this war

> will be useful for those who will want a clear understanding of the past as well as of the future which at some time or other, as far as human nature is concerned, will occur in much the same way. These things are compiled not for a contest of the moment, but as a possession for all time.[52]

The "contest of the moment" *(agonisma es to parachrema akouein)* has generally been construed as a reference to Herodotus and his reading of his *Histories,* which was richly rewarded by the Athenian Council. Aside from this passage from Thucydides, however, there is no indication that Herodotus' reading was in any sense a contest. By the evidence examined in chapter 4, Herodotus' reading was a contribution to deliberative testimony being gathered, in 415, by the Athenian Council. By his own account, and by the evidence to be considered below, testimony for deliberation is precisely what Thucydides envisioned his *syngraphe* to be.

Works written "for the contest of the moment" were the compositions of *logographoi,* the "speech-writers," like Lysias, whose works were "composed with more attention to persuading their listeners than to telling the truth," as Thucydides states in 1.21.1. Unlike those works, which were designed solely to be persuasive "upon first hearing" *(es to parachrema akouein),* Thucydides intended his work to be a storehouse of information, that could be revisited with profit at any time.[53]

This understanding of 1.22.4 entails a significant shift in our general assessment of why Thucydides wrote history, and when. Misguided both by the interpretation of *logographoi* as a reference to writers, like Hellanicus and Herodotus, of the earliest historical treatises, and *agonisma,* "contest-piece," as referring to some form of literary competition, the common view has been that Thucydides wrote to be recognized as the "best" historian by later generations of readers and writers of history. That he directed his work to a readership beyond his own time has also been inferred from the pessimistic judgments that punctuate his work. These have encouraged the view that Thucydides despaired of the wisdom of his contemporaries and admitted hope only if future generations would learn from his testimony. The common view, therefore, is that Thucydides wrote solely for posterity.[54]

While this assessment of Thucydides' intentions is not completely without merit, it does, in my view, confuse inception with posterity, and therefore distorts our understanding of what prompted Thucydides to write. Thucydides moved in an intensely competitive world of political writers, thinkers, and speakers; historians were not yet distinct from these. He wrote for the politically inquisitive mind, and for politically active men. Only after his work, and largely under its influence, did political inquiry expand to give permanent place to the historian's perspective.[55]

Thucydides, like Herodotus, clearly intended his work to endure, like a monument in stone. But all monuments are established for an immediate purpose. As the occasion passes, their significance changes into meanings that come only from the passage of time. Thucydides and Herodotus both, in my view, wrote to influence their contemporaries, with current circumstances in mind. The lasting value that both foretold at the beginning of their histories was a feature designed in each case to call attention to their works as more worthy of contemplation than the works of poets, or the words of skillful orators.[56]

Herodotus wrote to illuminate the pitfalls of sovereignty, as has been considered in chapters 1 and 4. Thucydides was the historian of Athens at war with Sparta, fighting to maintain sovereignty over her empire. As discussed above, when Thucydides returned to Athens in 404 he possessed a wealth of relevant texts, and in Athens he will have gained access to still more documents that would enable him to construct an account of the late war. It is hard to discover a public or a private concern during the civil war of 403 or in the next year or two that would justify Thucydides' undertaking. But we do not have to look far beyond that time to find evidence of the renewed interest in war and empire.

Between 401 and 399, as described in the previous chapter, the Athenians achieved political stability and began to look again to their place in the world beyond Attica. These years should therefore mark an approximate upper limit for the period within which Thucydides wrote. That Thucydides may have been writing after 399 has long been recognized on the basis of a passage (2.100.2) where Thucydides summarizes the achievements of King Archelaus of Macedon; such a notice would be most appropriate if it had been written after Archelaus' death in 399. This passage and the general tenor of Thucydides' discussion of tyranny and the tyrant-slayers, as discussed above, are suggestive, but do not prove that Thucydides wrote his whole account after 399. But these indications are all confirmed, and the evidence leads to a more specific date, when we consider the circumstances of the following years from an Athenian perspective.[57]

Following the death of Cyrus in 401, the Spartans found themselves at odds with King Artaxerxes and soon were at war with his forces in Asia Minor. Athenian hopes for an alliance with Persia, meanwhile, were quickly reawakened. By 398, Conon's relations with Euagoras of Cyprus, with Pharnabazus, and, through them, with King Artaxerxes, had raised the possibility that Persian interests could facilitate the reestablishment of the Athenian empire. By 397, Conon was in command of Artaxerxes' fleet along the southern coast of Asia Minor, and fascination with his cause among Athenians was growing. By 396, diplomatic missions were testing the prospects for the revival of Athenian power, and there was widespread popular support at Athens for opposition to Sparta. By the summer of 395, Athens was again at war with Sparta, and Athenian aspirations to recover their former empire were a matter of open discussion.[58]

The outbreak of what came to be known as the Corinthian War (395–386) was, by all indications, the event that Thucydides, along with his contemporaries, clearly foresaw when he advocated the value of his *syngraphe* of the Peloponnesian War "for those who will want a clear understanding of the past as well as of the future." In the events and circumstances of 396 and the following year, when war broke out, we find the clearest indications that both major and minor themes occurring in Thucydides' account of the previous war were at the center of public attention.

In his so-called "Archaeology," the survey of ancient history with which Thucydides opens his first book (1.1–19), Thucydides dwells at length upon the evidence indicating that Agamemnon had been the most powerful king of his day and that the greatest force previously assembled by Greeks was the army that sailed with Agamemnon against Troy (1.9–11). Regarding the former greatness of the king of Mycenae, Thucydides makes his famous observation that the slight remains of Mycenae in his own day should not deceive observers conjecturing about its former greatness:

> Suppose, for example, that the city of Sparta were to become deserted and that only the temples and foundations of buildings remained; I think that future generations would, as time passed, find it very difficult to believe that the place had really been as powerful as it was represented to be. Yet the Spartans occupy two-fifths of the Peloponnese and stand at the head not only of the whole Peloponnese itself but also of numerous allies beyond its frontiers. Since, however, the city is not densely settled and contains no temples or monuments of great magnificence, but is simply a collection of villages, in the ancient Hellenic way, its appearance would not come up to expectation. If, on the other hand, the same thing were to happen to Athens, one would conjecture from what met the eye that the city had been twice as powerful as in fact it is.

It has been noticed that this comparison of the power of Sparta and Athens as they "in fact are" corresponds better with their relative status on the eve of the Corinthian War, when Sparta was far more powerful than Athens, than at any time during or preceding the Peloponnesian War. Prior to their alliance with Boeotia, Argos, and Corinth in 395, the Athenians were formally subservient to Sparta (though they possessed monuments of an imperial city). Sparta, after the subjugation of Elis in 400 and before the outbreak of war in 395, was the leader of more allies than at any time in its previous history.[59]

The glorious stature of Sparta at this time, moreover, was proclaimed with great ceremony in 396 by King Agesilaus of Sparta. In the spring of that year he assembled an army of Sparta's allies for an expedition to Asia against the Persians, and he celebrated the launching of the expedition by a sacrifice at Aulis, whence Agamemnon had launched his expedition to Asia against the Trojans. Although his army of some eight thousand men was a token force, not a full levy (and not all of Sparta's allies contributed men), Agesilaus made the most of the occasion to announce his claim to be carrying on the leadership of Greece that had been the right of Agamemnon. The comparison of the power of Sparta to that of Mycenae, just as examined by Thucydides, was made explicit on this occasion, according to Pausanias: "Agesilaus, then, claimed to be king of a more prosperous city than was Agamemnon, and to be like him overlord of all Greece."[60]

Such a claim, publicly broadcast, would require close examination by all parties who might have occasion to debate its implications. Accordingly, Thucydides subjects the power of Agamemnon to close scrutiny. Although, in the passage quoted above, he gives only passing reference to the conditions of Spartan power in 396, his history itself provides the primary material for discussing what Agesilaus' claim amounted to in "real" terms. Agesilaus' pronouncement at Aulis, and its impact in the politically charged atmosphere of Athens, and Greece generally, in the spring of 396, provided, in my view, the immediate impetus for Thucydides to compose the account for which he was so expertly prepared. Agesilaus, issuing a manifesto of Spartan supremacy, relied upon the simplified concepts of a distant past. The Athenian response had to take account of the complicated concepts of a recent past. To justify the juxtaposition of both ancient and recent precedents, Thucydides commenced his analysis by demonstrating that the distant past was comprehensible by the same standards of judgment that had to be applied to contemporary events.[61]

Thucydides notes that Agamemnon's expedition made an impressive showing but lacked the revenues needed to sustain it as an effective fighting force (1.11–12.1). Such revenues came from the commerce that could flourish only with the suppression of piracy. Piracy could be put down, Thucydides notes, only through naval power and the protection of coastal settlements by fortifications (1.7–8, 13–15). Athens, in 396, lacked both the navy and the coastal fortifications that had been the twin sources of its former power. This subject certainly played a significant part in any discussions of the relative might of Sparta and Athens, and its implications are reflected throughout Thucydides' first book. The evolution of naval power and the revenue that it yields is the guiding theme of the "Archaeology" (1.1–19) and of the "Pentecontaetia" (1.89–117), and it is a turning point in all the debates that led to the decision for war in 431.

Thucydides' expansive discussion of the manner in which Themistocles achieved the fortification of Athens and Piraeus (1.89–93) in 478 was particularly topical in 396. The walls had been built against the wishes of the

Spartans through the cleverness of Themistocles. Upon their completion, Themistocles delivered a speech to the Spartans, summarized by Thucydides (1.91.4–7), that amounted to a "declaration of independence" of the Athenians from the supremacy that Sparta had exercised during the invasion of Xerxes. The desire of the Athenians to recover their "walls and ships" at the commencement of the Corinthian War is well attested in contemporary rhetoric. Themistocles' precedent was surely prominent in their minds and was the object of discussion as the Council met in closed session in 396, debating various means by which the Athenians might again contest the Spartan claim to supremacy.[62]

Thucydides' excursus on this subject, moreover, contains another reference to circumstances appropriate to the eve of the Corinthian War. While describing the manner of construction of both the walls of Athens and Piraeus, he gives details of the width and inner construction of the Piraeus walls, "just as one can see it today around Piraeus" (1.93.5). This describes conditions that existed only after the destruction of the mudbrick superstructure in 404 and before the reconstruction of the walls that commenced in 394. The reference would best suit the awareness and concerns of an audience engaged in the intense debate over the state of preparedness of Athens on the brink of war with Sparta.[63]

Following Agesilaus' departure for Asia Minor at the head of a Hellenic army, another controversy became the subject of public debate. Timocrates of Rhodes came as a representative of Pharnabazus on an embassy to the potential foes of Sparta in Greece, and the Spartans let it be known that he was corrupting leading politicians at Athens and elsewhere with Persian gold. The Spartan effort to turn public sympathy away from the proponents of war in Greece paralleled their campaign, in 432/31, to have Pericles expelled from Athens because he was tainted by the ancient "curse" of the Alcmaeonidae. Thucydides' account of this propaganda war in 432/1 is the occasion of another long digression (1.126–38) with further details relevant to the events of 396.[64]

After describing the Spartan demand and the Athenian counter-demand on the eve of the Peloponnesian War, Thucydides enters into an excursus on the later careers of Pausanias, the Spartan regent and victor at the battle of Plataea in 479, and Themistocles. The detailed narrative describes and documents—with quotations of letters from Pausanias, Xerxes, and Themistocles—the scandalous end of the career of Pausanias, and how his fall brought about the flight of Themistocles. Both men, in the end, were accused of being corrupted by Persian influence, though the greater fault, by this account, was Pausanias'.

The excursus, Gomme notes, is "long, and for his purposes quite unnecessary," yet it is "the best example of Thucydides' interest in biography and personality, which he elsewhere kept in check." It is so exceptional, by comparison with his usual narrative style, that many commentators have regarded it as a youthful essay, grafted onto his mature work by the mere pretext of a passing reference to Pausanias. A more probable explanation of the stylistic singularity of this excursus is that Thucydides was following closely the account of another written source. Why there should be such interest in this story, on the part of Thucydides and one or more other authors, has not been explained. But the reason emerges when the history of Pausanias and Themistocles is considered from the perspective of 396.[65]

The Spartans were engaged in a war of propaganda against their detractors at Athens and elsewhere. At issue was the Hellenic cause and its betrayal to Persia. The fall of both Pausanias and Themistocles was an interpretive battleground in which, no doubt, parallels were drawn to the more recent histories of Lysander and Alcibiades, both of whom had dallied with the Persians and had become involved in scandal. Denunciation of the mission of Timocrates and his Persian gold in 396 represented the latest and most intense phase of this controversy. Thucydides, using every documentary source at his disposal, put the background of this dispute in order from an Athenian perspective. For his purposes, the excursus was highly relevant.[66]

The chief lessons of 432–431 for Athenians in 396 and 395 were the lessons of the ability, and the limits, of reason to foresee and guide events. So reasoned preparedness, *paraskeue* ("resources" or "preparations"), figures prominently in Thucydides' first book and is repeatedly reassessed in light of events as the narrative of the war proceeds. So too the faculty of reason, *gnome* or *synesis,* and the impact of chance, *tyche,* are illustrated throughout the war that followed. These salient characteristics of Thucydides' work as a whole are entirely comprehensible from the perspective of Athens on the brink of renewed war. There are, however, some more singular features that have been the focus of attention of scholars who have thought that Thucydides composed his work over the course of decades, as events unfolded. Yet these features too are accountable when we recognize that Thucydides began writing in 396 and stopped, probably, in 395.[67]

Before Agesilaus set out for Asia Minor in 396 to fight the forces of Artaxerxes, the Spartans requested an Athenian contribution to his army. Obliged by their oaths of allegiance sworn in 404 and confirmed in 403, the Athenians had honored a similar request in 400. This time, however, the Athenians declined to support the Spartans. They did so, Pausanias, the second-century CE author, informs us, "on the ground that their city was returning to its former state of prosperity after the Peloponnesian war and the epidemic of plague." The reference to the plague, which afflicted Athens chiefly between 430 and 426, demonstrates that, when this claim was made, the entire period during which losses were incurred, from 431 until the surrender of Athens in 404, was conceived as an era of continuous war between Athens and Sparta.[68]

This observation unites a significant feature of Thucydides' history with the outlook of many Athenians in 396. For at the outset of his account of the great war between the Peloponnesians and Athenians, Thucydides implies, and later states, that the entire period from the first invasion of Archidamus (431) until the surrender of Athens (404) was a single war. But in Book 5, where he recounts the formalization of the Peace of Nicias in 421, he digresses from his narrative, in what is called Thucydides' "second preface" (5.25–26), to explain why, despite the formal end to ten years of war, he has continued his account, year by year, through the interval of some seven years before open war between Sparta and Athens resumed. The reason, Thucydides states, is that the Peace of Nicias of 421 was no true peace, since it was filled with ill-will, broken promises, and incidents of open hostility. These arguments were profoundly relevant to public attitudes at Athens in 396 and 395. All the same reasons were being alleged by those who were denouncing the forcible settlements and policies of the Spartans between 404 and 395 in order to prepare the Athenians, Argives, Corinthians, and others for renewed war with Sparta. When war did come in 395, it was begun, from the Athenian perspective, by a Spartan act of aggression, an invasion of Boeotia. To the Athenians in 395, Thucydides' account was a reminder that "the war" had begun likewise in 431 with a Spartan act of aggression, the invasion of Attica. Thucydides' account was thus testimony to the fact that "the [same] war" was once again alive, this time, as in 431, as a result of Spartan aggression.[69]

Only a few years later, when the Athenians were contemplating a proposal for peace with Sparta in 392/1, the orator Andocides summarized the previous century of Spartan–Athenian relations in order to demonstrate the benefits of peace. In his speech, Andocides clearly separates the war ending in the Peace of Nicias from the later, more disastrous war against Sparta, begun "then as now at the instigation of Argos." Andocides implicitly contradicts Thucydides' interpretation of the interval between 421 and 414. He does so in order to advance an argument for peace, whereas Thucydides' account rendered the past meaningful to a world on the brink of war. No example better illustrates how immediate circumstances could color perceptions of the recent past, and how Thucydides' narrative and interpretive choices reflect the perspective of 396/5. The example of Andocides' speech shows how deadly serious these interpretive choices were.[70]

The fluid relationship between Athens and other potential or actual foes of Sparta in 396–395 corresponds in significant ways with several other features of Book 5 that have troubled modern commentators. So Hornblower has remarked: "Book V is, from the point of view of the modern historian, a very unsatisfactory book indeed because of what it puts in and what it leaves out." What it puts in, to no self-evident benefit, are the "intricate and ultimately futile" starts and stops of Peloponnesian diplomacy; what it leaves out, to the greatest distress of modern historians, is any indication of the influential shift in Athenian–Persian relations that must have been developing after 424 and before 412, when Thucydides begins to notice it, in Book 8.[71]

During both intervals preceding the outbreak of war with Sparta, 421–414 and 404–395, Athenian alignments with Argos and other states opposed to Sparta were crucial but ultimately problematic. To instruct the Athenians on the pitfalls encountered in the past, Thucydides traces these themes in careful, even documentary detail. Athenian relations with Persia, on the other hand, were inscrutable. The hopes and expectations that inflamed popular aspirations in 396 could not be balanced by any clear assessment from the Persian perspective—the sources that Thucydides relied upon for his account of Greek affairs did not exist for the royal and satrapal courts of the Persian empire. It seemed best, therefore, to remain silent until the events themselves proved where Persian commitments lay.[72]

Perhaps most telling of all, in the interval between 397 and 395, the younger Alcibiades was twice brought to trial, as speeches by Isocrates and Lysias attest. The disparate charges against him were clearly designed to make a public issue of the career and reputation of his father, the senior Alcibiades. In speeches written both against and in defense of the younger Alcibiades we find all issues laid out, in rhetorical hyperbole, in praise and in blame of the senior Alcibiades. At a time when Thrasybulus was orchestrating diplomatic relations in Greece with a view to a grand alliance against Sparta, and when Conon was commanding the fleet of Pharnabazus and inspiring hopes for the revival of the Athenian maritime empire, the man who had done or promised all of these things before was again at the center of public debate.[73]

Alcibiades enters Thucydides' narrative in his fifth book as the chief mover behind the momentous and fitful alliance between Athens and Argos in 420. Historians attentive to the evidence from Aristophanes and other sources have recognized that Alcibiades was active in the affairs of Athens and her empire for at least half a decade before he is mentioned by Thucydides. Those who take their lead from Thucydides, on the other hand, date Alcibiades' "entry on the political stage" to 420 (so Bloedow 1991b). This discrepancy is another consequence of the assumption that Thucydides' interest in the subject of his narrative was as remote as ours. Alcibiades' introduction at this point of Thucydides' narrative, as the spoiler of the Peace of Nicias, is another narrative choice colored by the events of 396–395, when the Athenians were again contemplating an alliance with Argos and rupturing relations with Sparta.[74]

In sum, all of the major themes developed by Thucydides—the relationship between sea-power and empire, the remote origins and proximate causes of war between Athens and Sparta, the effects of war on Athenian democracy, the relations between Persia and the Greeks—were relevant to the political debates and diplomatic exchanges of 396 that led to the outbreak of war between Athens and Sparta in 395. Thucydides' book prepared the Council and the officers of the Athenian state to deal with these issues. In the months leading up to the outbreak of the Corinthian War, prospective allies would rehearse old grievances with the Athenians and with each other; within the Athenian Assembly, voices of opposition would raise the fearsome specter of defeat as a caution against renewed war. Such fears and differences of opinion are well attested. Yet, as Xenophon reports and as several scholars have remarked, when, in 395, the issue of alliance with Boeotia was presented for a vote that meant war, the Athenian decision for war was unanimous. The way to the decision had clearly been well prepared in advance.[75]

By the line of reasoning developed in this book, we may now understand what prompted Thucydides to write, and when. The whole of Thucydides' account, written in 396–395, served as a resource for comprehending a difficult past in order to make the most informed decisions about a daunting future. At that time, just as in 432–431, events were foreseeably leading to war between Athens and Sparta. As the Athenians prepared to renew their struggle for empire, they hoped to avoid the pitfalls of their recent past. To illuminate the turnings of Athenian policy in the past, for better and for worse, is precisely the purpose Thucydides announces in 1.22.4.

THE UNFINISHED CONDITION

Thucydides' work may be recognized, then, as a deliberative brief composed to instruct officers and members of the Athenian Council as they devised policy to present to the Athenian *demos* and its allies facing war again with Sparta in 396–395. It has been described above as a *syngraphe,* the usual term for such a document, on the basis of the verb *syngraphein,* by which Thucydides describes his authorship in his opening sentence and throughout his work. As such, it is part of a tradition of expertise, committed to writing, placed at the service of the Athenian democracy. This tradition developed with a special intensity in the generation of the Peloponnesian War.[76]

If this explanation is difficult to accept, because Thucydides' treatise is so long, because it is so "literary" in style, or because it contains no overt statement of its relation to the events of 396–395, it may be that the difficulty lies in our preconceptions about the nature of a deliberative *syngraphe* and a historical treatise at the beginning of the fourth century. The absence of any explicit reference to the historical conditions under which, by this account, Thucydides wrote is problematic only for posterity. To the limited and specific audience for which the work was written, no such statement would be needed. Moreover, the very value of such a treatise for immediate concerns is predicated on the notion that it reflects timeless truths, equally valuable for similar purposes at some later date. To declare that the present work was written at such-and-such a date, to satisfy such-and-such needs, would undermine its immediate authority and trivialize its enduring worth. Thucydides, I have argued above, was devoted to the service of Athens and her empire. Just so, Thucydides' *syngraphe* is an artifact of democratic Athens gripped by the vision of its own destiny. It does not question its own premise—that Athens is eternal and its destiny manifest—it acts upon it.[77]

Does the present thesis, that Thucydides' work was composed as a deliberative brief on the eve of the Corinthian War, afford any insight into the work's abrupt ending? Most ancient and modern explanations, which are no more than guesses, involve some form of sudden death stilling the hand of the author. All such speculations emanate from the nature of the text, which halts in the midst of events late in 411. The present study justifies at least one more conjecture on this subject, even if this matter must in truth remain a mystery.[78]

Before his history halts abruptly in the eighth book, Thucydides had entered a form of narrative in which he had given up the use of speeches in direct discourse, had offered more frequent authorial opinions, in which covert events played a growing role, and in which fruitless initiatives were recorded to a level of detail that includes verbatim quotes of diplomatic documents. In all of these respects, Book 8 closely resembles Book 5, and both books have accordingly been described as the least polished of Thucydides' work. Book 8 is distinguished from Book 5, however, by the growing prominence of Persian affairs, and herein lies a clue to its relationship to circumstances at the outbreak of the Corinthian War.

Book 5, it is suggested above, is accounted for by the twists and turns of Greek diplomacy on the brink of war with Sparta in 396–395. From the official Athenian perspective, the Corinthian War began for purely local, purely Greek reasons: Spartan intervention in the frontier disputes of Phocis and Locris. Persia had no official relation with these events, although everyone knew that Persian influence was covertly at work.[79]

In his eighth book, Thucydides was beginning to explore the ambiguities of the relationship between Athens and Persia in ways that correspond also to the ambiguities of Athenian–Persian relations on the brink of the Corinthian War. Unlike the autonomous might of Periclean Athens, the affairs of this decisive axis were not determined by the debates of democratic assemblies. They were the outcome of covert negotiations and of promises made but long left unfulfilled. They were dependent on personalities, veiled loyalties, and private affections. In public rhetoric, such relations could only be described in the allusive language of destiny and mythic symbolism that played more on emotions than intellect. To a pragmatist of the Periclean empire, such language obscured more than it revealed of the logic of events. It did not advance the purposes for which Thucydides was writing.[80]

Likewise, Athenian ambitions to empire in 395, where they became intertwined with Persian interests, depended upon the wisdom, foresight, and subtlety of individuals working in secret. This was not a deliberative matter, and so Thucydides' treatise had no purpose in it. For this the Athenians needed a savior, and they knew this well enough without requiring Thucydides to retail the bitter yearning of Athenian experience from the spring of 410 until the fall of 404.[81]

It is possible to suppose, therefore, that Thucydides deliberately left off writing at a point where, in the winter of 411/10, Athenian fortunes were on the rise, when good advice from Alcibiades began to yield sound resolutions on the part of both the Athenians at Athens, recovering from the effects of the Four Hundred, and the Athenians of the fleet at Samos, beginning to beat back the Spartan navy. Soon afterward, Alcibiades experienced the duplicity of Tissaphernes, but recovered to win his great victory at Cyzicus and, in the following year, reached his hopeful entente with Pharnabazus. Through all these latter events, divine favor, private initiative, and the intentions of the lords of Asia had a far greater effect upon the fate of Athens than did purposeful resolutions of the Athenian *demos.* Whether or not Thucydides was still writing when war broke out in 395, he had reached a point in the course of events that suited his purposes, and he stopped.[82]

But he stopped most abruptly, in the midst of describing Tissaphernes' response to his deteriorating relations with the Spartans: "Tissaphernes... fearing further injury... went first to Ephesus and made sacrifice to Artemis."[83]

If Thucydides chose the circumstances appropriate for ending his narrative, then he must have also chosen the specific end point—unless, for this purpose, we wish to revive again the notion of an accidental ending. On the assumption that all was purposeful, I suggest that Thucydides made of his ending an invocation of divine favor. Having written, thus far, to instruct the Athenians in the ways of the past and the future, "as far as human nature is concerned" (*kata to anthropinon,* 1.22.4), he had reached the point that the Athenians would soon enough reach where they had to trust to fortune and the gods to secure the outcome. Thucydides therefore devoted his *syngraphe,* by his final words, *tei Artemidi,* "to Artemis." The first words of his work, "Thucydides the Athenian," name the maker of this dedication.[84]

The question, "why Artemis?" has been asked recently in another context that elucidates this one. Robert Parker, in his study of Athenian religion, raises the question in connection with Themistocles' dedication of a shrine to Artemis Aristoboule ("She of the Best Counsel"). Without following Parker's invitation to speculate about Themistocles' purposes, we may conclude that we have found the example that Thucydides followed.

Themistocles, as noted above, was very much on the minds of Athenians in 396–395, and was the example that Thucydides clearly wished to evoke in the hour of Athens' need:

> Indeed, Themistocles was a man who showed an unmistakable natural genius; in this respect he was quite exceptional and beyond all others deserves our admiration.... He was particularly remarkable for looking into the future and seeing what was hidden there for better or for worse. To sum him up in a few words, it may be said that through force of genius and by rapidity of action this man was supreme at doing precisely the right thing at precisely the right moment.[85]

Artemis Aristoboule was the divine patron to whom Themistocles attributed his paramount sagacity in securing the victory at Salamis. Artemis Agrotera, "The Huntress," was also the goddess of sacrifice before battle. Among Athenians, she was especially associated with the victory over the Persians at Marathon, and her cult was officially maintained by the Polemarch. Themistocles had acknowledged a debt to this goddess for the gift of strategic cunning. Her cult can be connected only conjecturally with the deliberations of the Athenian Council in Thucydides' lifetime, but it is noteworthy that a cult of Artemis Boulaia is attested in the Athenian Council in Hellenistic times. The personification, Euboule, "Good-Counsel," had been invoked sarcastically by Aristophanes in 410, in connection with both the deliberative failures of the Athenian Council in 411 and, as is argued in chapter 4, in reference to the time, in 415, when the Council had honored Herodotus' deliberative advice.[86]

Other associations illustrate the propriety of a dedication to Artemis in this context. Artemis, in Euripides' *Hippolytus,* is shown to be the patron of truth that reveals the deceptions practiced, under the influence of Eros, through writing. Artemis was also the patron of the philosopher Heraclitus of Ephesus, who wrote on subjects difficult for most people to comprehend. In an act that signified, simultaneously, his personal accomplishment as an author and his acknowledgment of a debt to the goddess, Heraclitus dedicated his treatise to Artemis in her temple at Ephesus. His example was probably known to Thucydides, as it reportedly was known to Euripides and Socrates. Ephesian Artemis, moreover, provides the specific link to the scene Thucydides describes in 8.109.[87]

Tissaphernes later invoked the same goddess, Xenophon notes, to give victory to his forces against the Athenians led by Thrasyllus; the anger of this goddess was surely not soon forgotten by the Athenians when their thoughts turned to empire in Asia. She was the goddess whose anger, at Aulis, demanded such a high price before Agamemnon could lead his army to Asia. Ephesian Artemis was also the divine patron invoked by Xenophon during his sojourn with Cyrus and propitiated by the offering of a sacred grove on his estate in the Peloponnese after his safe homecoming. Artemis was invoked by Agesilaus at Aulis, and surely again upon his arrival at Ephesus in 396. The anger of the goddess, it would seem, was displayed to Tissaphernes himself in 395; after Agesilaus plundered the territory of Sardis that summer, Tissaphernes was summarily arrested and beheaded at the command of Artaxerxes. This event may have made the conjunction of Tissaphernes and Artemis in the narrative of winter 411/10 seem a propitious point for Thucydides to cut off his account.[88]

Artemis of Ephesus was also closely linked with Cybele of Sardis, and so was identified with the Mother of the Gods. This goddess was the object of Themistocles' devotion in his final years at Magnesia, in Asia Minor, where Thucydides knew of Themistocles' memorial. The Mother of the Gods was also the divine patron of the Athenian archives. She was probably therefore the curator of the *syngraphe* of Thucydides, which most likely was placed in the Metroön at Athens.[89]

THE BEGINNINGS OF POSTERITY

Composed for a special purpose, long and circumstantial in its details, and eschewing pleasure in its pursuit of meaning, Thucydides' work is not likely to have entered wide circulation very soon after its composition. It has been suggested that the influence of Thucydides is detectable in the latest speech of Andocides, in 392/1. As discussed above, Andocides was certainly aware of the historical arguments that Thucydides supported. Given Andocides' devotion to the advancement of his career through the mastery of documents collected in the Athenian archives, as noted in chapter 10, it is quite possible that he did consult Thucydides' work. Likewise, Thucydides' influence has been seen in the *Panegyricus* of Isocrates, written a decade later. Neither of these writers demonstrate indisputable awareness of Thucydides' work, however. All that can be said is that, for three or four decades, there is no indication that the work was read by any but those who might have consulted its original copy, probably in the Metroön.[90]

The first unmistakable notice of Thucydides' work came not until a full generation later, when his narrative was continued beyond 411 by others. The task was undertaken by several historians, probably first by Xenophon, whose work alone survives intact. It is perhaps significant that this was also a generation in which Athenian statesmen and scholars like Androtion and Cleidemus began to mine the resources of official archives to propagate the type of historical treatise, the local chronicle, or *Atthis,* pioneered earlier by Hellanicus. A wider dissemination of Thucydides' work may have been a consequence of this research.[91]

In view of his concern to correct mistaken beliefs about the past, it is perhaps ironic that Thucydides' work had no perceptible effect in the arena of popular opinion. The intensely focused, topical relevance of his work undermined its wider impact. To influence the general public, Thucydides' work required a motivated few to seek out the "clear understanding" it conveyed and then to apply their insights to the immediate concerns of a politically engaged public. Thucydides' purpose, like his unfinished narrative, relied on others to bring it to fruition. In the meantime, the undistinguished but patriotic resonances of poetry and the flourishes of rhetoric continued to satisfy the needs of most Athenians to know about their past.[92]

The study of history, as Thucydides conceived it and as it was pursued in the next generation, was primarily a matter of personal interest for those engaged in politics, who sought by its vicarious means to enlarge their base of instructive experience. This is precisely how Aristotle perceived the subject, when he remarked in his treatise on rhetoric that "the investigations (*historiai*) of those writing about past deeds are useful for political deliberation." Aristotle's passing references to history here and elsewhere thus give it only a supporting role among various intellectual endeavors that deal with the past and with truth.[93]

It has often been remarked how Aristotle, with his interest in defining fields of knowledge, lavished attention on the study of laws and constitutions, on rhetoric, and on poetry, but had next to no regard for history. It was too circumstantial, he claimed:

> Poetry is more philosophical and more weighty than history, for poetry speaks rather of the universal, history of the particular. By the universal I mean that such or such a kind of man will say or do such or such things from probability or necessity; that is the aim of poetry, adding proper names to the characters. By the particular I mean what Alcibiades did and what happened to him.[94]

The proper study of universal truths and meanings lay elsewhere than history, according to Aristotle. It lay in contemplating the poetics of drama, or in philosophy itself.

It is noteworthy, however, that among the traditions of philosophy in which Aristotle was educated, the Socratic tradition represented by Plato was profoundly historical and circumstantial in nature. Its point of departure was actual experience, its means lay in the transformative link between spoken and written words that characterized Socrates' generation, and its consummation was in Plato's poetic gift. Through these, and with the passage of time, the particular life of Socrates was transformed into one of universal meaning.[95]

Much the same can be said about the historical particulars encompassed by the genius of Thucydides. That his feat could not be replicated by his successors was perhaps not so much a measure of their deficiencies when compared to his sagacity as it was a matter of the subject that the times presented to Thucydides. This was Athens, at the peak of its struggle to realize its destiny. This was the cause to which Alcibiades had devoted his life, and the subject that Socrates, Plato, Euripides, Aristophanes, and Thucydides all had in common. Aristotle, too, may have acknowledged the elusive quintessence of that generation when he chose to juxtapose the universal meanings expressible through poetry to the particular, historical experience of Alcibiades. But by Aristotle's day, not enough time had yet passed to place the lessons of his story, and that of Athens, in perspective.

APPENDIX A

Epigraphic Chronology

A major advance in the study of Greek history in the course of the past century and a half has come from the study of inscriptions. While documents from Athens have always been more plentiful than from any other classical Greek city, this balance was shifted even further in the favor of Athens by the discoveries of the American excavations in the Athenian Agora between the 1930s and the 1960s.

This enrichment of our access to original documents, particularly from the era of the fifth-century Athenian empire, was accompanied by a hardening of scholarly orthodoxy in the crucial field of chronology. The growing number of inscriptions seemed to verify notions of a measurable rate of change in Attic letter-forms over the fifth century, so that, in the absence of direct textual evidence of date, the presence of certain old-fashioned letters was taken to indicate the early date of an inscription. Belief that the three-barred sigma in particular was no longer used in Attic inscriptions after 445 led to the reassignment before that date of the Athenian decree on coins, weights, and measures (*IG* I3 1453 = ML 45, Fornara 97) after a new fragment of that decree was discovered with a three-barred sigma. The seemingly decisive redating of this text in turn reinforced arguments for mid fifth-century dating of other inscriptions that previously had been placed in the 420s or later. The historical implications of these conclusions were considerable, and the interpretations of this orthodoxy were advanced by such authorities as the four-volume study of *The Athenian Tribute Lists* by Meritt, Wade-Gery, and McGregor (Princeton 1939–1953), the standard *Selection of Greek Historical Inscriptions* edited by Meiggs and Lewis (Oxford 1969), the historical survey of *The Athenian Empire* by Russell Meiggs (Oxford 1972), and the third edition of *Inscriptiones Graecae* volume 1, edited by David Lewis (Berlin and New York 1981).

In 1961, Harold B. Mattingly challenged the heart of the orthodox chronology in a paper arguing for a date in the 420s for the coinage decree and related texts (Mattingly 1961a/1996). Mattingly adduced strong circumstantial evidence then and in later papers, but in the absence of proof Mattingly gained few adherents to his views. Confidence of most specialists in the orthodox chronology was not substantially undermined until 1990, when Mortimer Chambers, Ralph Gallucci, and Pantelis Spanos published the results of their examination, by laser-aided photography, of key letter traces in another contested document, the treaty of alliance between Athens and Segesta (*IG* I3 11 = ML 37, Fornara 81). This document uses three-barred sigmas and preserves part of an archon's name, which would yield a date if the name could be read with confidence. Their results established, to the satisfaction of a growing number of scholars, that the archon's name is Antiphon, and that the document, with its old-fashioned letters, was inscribed in 418/17 (doubts by A. S. Henry 1992 are unconvincing; see Chambers 1993; Fornara and Samons 1991, 179–81; Pritchett 1996, 2–3; Mattingly 1996, with the Foreword by Chambers). The dating of the Segesta treaty to 418/17 has removed the basis for a mid fifth-century date for the coinage decree, and Mattingly (1993) has since found further evidence to place that document no earlier than the 420s.

Although Mattingly's patient arguments have at last won out, it will be some time before the affected documents are thoroughly reassessed and the changes are generally reflected in scholarly literature. For this reason, wherever reference is made in this book to the contested documents, their previously assigned early dates are acknowledged along with their probable later dates. No argument here depends upon this redating, but several points made in the first four chapters are reinforced by this accumulation in the 420s and 410s of inscriptions formerly dated from the 450s to the 430s. As noted in the introduction and first chapter, and again in chapter 12, the urge to make an enduring record of ephemeral resolutions was one of the most distinctive characteristics of democratic Athens defining and defending its empire in the years after 430.

APPENDIX B

Euripides' *Helen* and Aristophanes' *Thesmophoriazusae*

Although the dates of the prize-winning productions of Attic playwrights were among the earliest subjects of ancient chronological scholarship, this information has been imperfectly preserved. As a result, the dates of many classical plays are matters of estimation. The commonly accepted dates of Euripides' *Helen* (412) and Aristophanes' *Thesmophoriazusae* (411) are often cited as if they were among the certainties of dramatic chronology, but in fact they are in a problematic intermediate category where the evidence is liable to differing interpretations. The interval of a year between the two plays is one of the few certainties (*Thesmophoriazusae* 850ff. parodies the opening of the *Helen,* and at 1060 refers to a scene from the *Andromeda,* known to have been produced with the *Helen,* as having been acted "last year"). I have accepted the views of a minority among contemporary scholars who date these plays to 411 and 410 respectively.

The evidence has been thoroughly reviewed by Alan Sommerstein (1977), who demonstrates that the decision ultimately rests upon our interpretation of the political circumstances alluded to, particularly in *Thesmophoriazusae.* Following, therefore, an analysis that rests on many a priori assumptions, Sommerstein decides in favor of the majority view, placing *Thesmophoriazusae* in 411 and *Helen* therefore in 412. Andrewes, in Gomme et al. 1981, 184–93, reviews much of the same evidence and, following an interpretation that differs at points from Sommerstein's (see addenda to p. 193, 455), arrives at the same conclusion about dates. To answer their arguments point by point would be more involved than is appropriate here; in fact, this book constitutes a thorough reappraisal of the issues (popular opinion of Alcibiades, perceptions of democracy on the brink of oligarchy, and views of alliance with Persia) on which Sommerstein's and Andrewes' arguments turn. Suffice it here to note that, at the beginning of this century, B.B. Rogers' influential commentary (1904) argued that the *Thesmophoriazusae* should be placed in 410; Peter Rhodes (1972a, 185, 190) has seen fit to caution about confidence in its common placement in 411; and Michael Vickers (1989a), whose perceptions of Alcibiades are a useful antidote to the critical trend of past decades, understands the political background and dates of *Thesmophoriazusae* and *Helen* much as do I.

The compelling point, in my judgment, is the reference in *Thesmophoriazusae* 808–809 to the shameful contrast between *Euboule,* Good-Counsel personified, and "any one of last year's councilors," each of whom "handed over counsel to another." This certainly describes the surrender of authority by the democratic Council to the oligarchic Council of the Four Hundred early in the summer of 411 (Thucydides 8.69.4–70.1; Aristotle *Constitution* 32.1). Sommerstein (116–17), understanding *tôn perusin tis bouleutes* as "a *certain* one of last year's councilors," insists that this refers to an unnamed individual whom the chorus nonetheless directly indicate and the audience recognize, and he leaves unresolved the question of how this individual's action was ill-counseled. But in the company of the other political figures named in this chorus (Charminos, Cleophon, Hyperbolus, Lamachus, and, as argued in chapter 4 note 52, Anytus), such an oblique reference seems highly improbable. Andrewes (188) sees the passage as a reference to "last year's councilors" as a body, as do I, but prefers to see their ill-counseled action as "the surrender of some functions to the *probouloi* late in 413." Andrewes offers no further explanation of the nature of this surrender, nor of its supposed impropriety as seen at a time when, in 411, the Athenians were preparing to make even greater concessions to the advice of a small body of experts (see chapter 5, with note 20). The date of 410, in the aftermath of the manifest failure of the Four Hundred, resolves all such ambiguities. As is argued in chapter 5 (with notes 10–12), the resulting date for Euripides' *Helen,* on the eve of the oligarchy of 411, when both the recall of Alcibiades and the possibility of peace with Sparta were being mooted (in vain, as it turned out), makes eminent sense of the peculiar themes of recognition and reconciliation of that play, and of the retrospective parody of it the following year in *Thesmophoriazusae.*

APPENDIX C

Chronology of the Events of 410–406

The most conspicuous shortcoming of Xenophon's *Hellenica* as a continuation of Thucydides' history of the Peloponnesian War is its lack of a clear chronology of events. This is not the place to discuss such indicators of dates as are found in the first two books of Xenophon's *Hellenica* (see Henry 1966, 39–45; Krentz 1989b, 11–14). We need only note that, based on Xenophon's account, scholars have offered various chronologies for the events between the two relatively secure points, the battle of Cyzicus (early spring 410: Diodorus 13.49.2) and the trial of the generals after the battle of Arginusae (fall 406, time of the *Apatouria:* Xenophon *Hellenica* 1.7.8). The central dispute involves the date of Alcibiades' return to Athens (Xenophon *Hellenica* 1.4.8–21). Scholars following a "high" chronology place it in 408 (Meyer 1901, vol. 4, 616–19; Busolt 1904, vol. 3.2, 1529–32); but the prevailing opinion of the past century of scholarship has followed a "low" chronology, placing it in 407 (Beloch 1914, vol. 2.1, 394–402, 413–21, 1916, vol. 2.2, 242–54, and Ferguson 1927 have been influential; Underhill 1900, xxxvi-xlii, reviews the controversy in the previous century).

Misgivings over aspects of this "low" chronology have been quietly noted by its staunch defenders (Andrewes 1953, 2 n. 1; Lewis 1977, 126 n. 112; Kagan 1987, 297–98 n. 21), and more recently elements of it have been reappraised (Robertson 1980c; Krentz 1988–1989). The date of Thrasyllus' departure for Ionia (Xenophon *Hellenica* 1.2.1), placed in 409 by most proponents of the "low" chronology, has increasingly been placed in 410 (Robertson, Krentz, Ostwald 1987, 388), as it is here (see chapter 6, with evidence discussed in notes 23 and 26). Movement of Thrasyllus' campaign up or down by a year has the effect of moving all of the events in the Hellespont that follow, at least until the surrender of Chalcedon and Byzantium.

The "high" chronology, placing Thrasyllus' departure in 410 and the fall of Calchedon and Byzantium in 409 instead of 408, has the advantage of accounting for a flow of revenue by mid-409 that enabled work on the Erechtheum to continue (chapter 6, with note 37). But either sequence must allow for a year of inactivity by Athenians on the Ionian front, if Alcibiades' homecoming was not until 407.

Robertson 1980c, followed by Krentz 1988–1989, has ingeniously suggested that Alcibiades spent most of 408 on campaign in Caria before coming to Athens in 407. But chapter 6, with note 35, offers reasons for viewing, with most commentators, the Carian campaign as a short excursion in the spring of the year of Alcibiades' homecoming. With Thrasyllus' Ionian campaign underway in 410 and the major events of the following year well enough attested, no sequence of events justifies the insertion of a year of inactivity before Alcibiades' homecoming. I have therefore been drawn to the conclusion that Alcibiades returned as his popularity, based on recent achievements, was reaching a peak in the spring of 408 (time of the *Plynteria,* Thargelion 25, Plutarch *Alcibiades* 34.1).

Apparent inactivity on Alcibiades' part is easier to account for between his departure from Athens in early autumn 408 (following the Mysteries, in Boedromion) and his flight into exile roughly a year later. For this was the period in which the Athenians began to feel that Alcibiades was "resourceful in his own interest" but "slow to benefit his fatherland" (Aristophanes *Frogs* 1428–29). Slow as Alcibiades' progress may have been, there are events enough to fill the interval between autumn 408 and the battle of Arginusae, sometime in the summer of 406.

The "low" chronology places the battle of Notium, in which Alcibiades' fleet was humbled by Lysander, and the battle of Arginusae, in which Callicratidas' military successes were brought to an end, both in 406; the former in March and the latter in August (Beloch 1916, vol. 2.2, 392–93; Ferguson 1927; there is no direct evidence for the specific month of either of these events, it should be noted). By such a scheme, 406 becomes an impossibly crowded year. After Lysander's victory at Notium, Alcibiades still had misfortunes to encounter at Cyme, where he was pitted against forces probably backed by Lysander (chapter 7, with note 9). After both of these commanders left office, their replacements each faced grave difficulties in rebuilding forces to fighting strength (chapter 7, with notes 12 and 13). Callicratidas' career is most instructive: he had to assemble crews from allied states; face disaffection among his officers; assemble a conference of commanders; pay court to Cyrus at Sardis, in vain; request funds from Sparta; assemble a conference of Ionian allies; commence, from his base at Miletus, a series of military operations that included destruction of the Athenian base on Chios, the capture of Teos; and operations on Lesbos that included the capture of Methymna and the blockade of Conon's squadron at Mytilene; thereafter, it took the Athenians a month to assemble the forces needed to confront Callicratidas at Arginusae (chapter 7, with notes 13–17). I cannot believe that all of this took place in the same campaigning season as the battle of Notium.

The utter impossibility of the "low" chronology becomes undeniable when it is recognized that the battle of Arginusae took place in the archonship of Antigenes (407/6), therefore *before* midsummer 406. Diodorus 13.76–79 places it in the archonship of Antigenes. The value of this evidence might be questioned, but for the testimony of Hellanicus (*FGrHist* 323a F 25, scholion to Aristophanes *Frogs* 694 = Fornara 164A), who places in the archonship of Antigenes the liberation of the slaves who fought at Arginusae and their enrollment as citizens. Aristotle *Constitution* 34.1 has been cited as evidence that the battle took place in the archonship of Callias (406/5), but the passage provides no such evidence: "in the archonship of Callias of the deme Angele, after the naval battle of the Arginusae, it happened that the ten generals who had won the victory in the battle were all condemned" (translated by von Fritz and Kapp).

The archon date is given to the trial of the generals, not to the battle, which is mentioned (in an aorist participle in a genitive absolute construction) as a past event that specifies the occasion of the trial. Athenaeus 5.218a, on the other hand, *does* place the battle in the archonship of Callias, though here too, the only reason for mentioning it is the trial of the generals, and the error could derive from a misunderstanding of the reference in Aristotle. On balance, the evidence of Hellanicus, confirmed by Diodorus, carries greatest authority. Further confirmation is noted below.

Callicratidas' preparations therefore spanned the winter and spring of 407/6 before his military operations got underway. Similarly, his predecessor, Lysander, faced a long period of preparation after taking over command from Cratesippidas before his brief but brilliant offensive. Xenophon *Hellenica* 1.5.1–10 reports that first Lysander went to Rhodes, Cos, Miletus, and Ephesus assembling allied ships; at Ephesus he waited (an unspecified period) "until Cyrus arrived at Sardis" (1.5.1); he then paid court to Cyrus, gained his request, and thereafter bolstered the morale of his crews by distributing back and advance pay; then, "after Lysander had reorganized the fleet, he dragged ashore the ninety ships which were at Ephesus and remained inactive while they were being dried out and refitted" (1.5.10, translated by R. Warner); after an unspecified period, Lysander seized his opportunity to attack. Lysander's activities are thus best understood as spanning the winter of 408/7 before engaging the Athenian fleet at Notium sometime in the spring or summer of 407.

This reconstruction of events harmonizes well with the attested sequence of annual Spartan naval commanders (Mindarus 411/10, Pasippidas 410/9, Cratesippidas 409/8, Lysander 408/7, Callicratidas 407/6; see

Meyer 1901, vol. 4, 619; Beloch 1916, vol. 2.2, 273–75). The "low" chronology, making both Lysander and Callicratidas active in 406, must do violence to this sequence. This reconstruction also harmonizes with a factor that Ferguson has claimed as "a decisive objection to dating Notium in 407." On the mistaken assumption that the battle of Arginusae was fought in the archonship of Callias, Ferguson observes that "the ten generals elected after Notium (Xenophon, *Hell.* I, 5. 16; Diod. XIII, 74. I), to serve for the calendar year next following, actually served in the archonship of Callias (406–5 B.C.); for they commanded the fleet at Arginusae and this battle was admittedly fought in Callias' year" (Ferguson 1927, 484). This observation in fact confirms the dating of the battle of Arginusae in the archonship of Antigenes, as argued above, for the generals elected *after* Notium, in 407 (late in the archonship of Euctemon, 408/7), were elected for the year of Antigenes (407/6). Furthermore, this circumstance accounts for the inquiry into the financial practices of the generals after Arginusae, since the end of their term of office was the normal time for them to undergo a formal audit (*euthyna;* on the events leading to the trial of the generals, see chapter 7, with notes 18 and 23–25).

This reconstruction places Lysander's meeting with Cyrus early in 407, in the winter or beginning of spring, which is where proponents of the "low" chronology generally place it. The occasion was Cyrus' arrival at Sardis, which most commentators assume followed shortly after the Athenian embassy conducted by Pharnabazus encountered the Spartan embassy under Boeotius (Xenophon *Hellenica* 1.4.2). The latter event took place, according to the "high" chronology that I follow, in the spring of 408. For reasons given in chapter 7, with note 4, I follow the suggestion of Robertson 1980c, 290–93, and believe it most likely that a year transpired between the announcement of Cyrus' appointment and his arrival at Sardis. Xenophon *Hellenica* 1.4.4 clearly indicates that some interval passed between the time the Athenian ambassadors received the news of Cyrus' appointment and the time when they actually met with him; it is representative of the imprecisions that abound in his narrative that this interval could be as much as a year (note that, at 1.4.7, Xenophon did indicate that this embassy was detained until its third year, so that, by any reckoning, the period that the ambassadors waited for the arrival of Cyrus was part of a longer period of waiting).

A final point regarding the date of Alcibiades' homecoming requires comment. Beloch 1916, vol. 2.2, 252, and others following his chronology, have referred to the scholion on Aristophanes *Frogs* 1422 as evidence placing Alcibiades' return to Athens in 407. In fact, the scholion supports the "high" chronology advocated here, as the following analysis of Fornara's translation (159) of it shows (Fornara's additions are in parentheses; square brackets indicate my notes). Referring to Dionysus' lines on the dilemma of Alcibiades (*Frogs* 1422–23), the scholion notes:

> He is speaking about his [Alcibiades'] second withdrawal, into voluntary exile. He had returned [*katelthon*] in the archonship of Antigenes (407/6), one year before the production of the *Frogs,* (and he fled) because he had entrusted the fleet to Antiochus his steersman and, being defeated by Lysandros, he became hated by the Athenians. Androtion differed from Xenophon about (the date of) the return [*kathodou*].

The subject of the scholion is Alcibiades' return *to exile,* which is where he was when the *Frogs* was produced. Antigenes' archonship, presumably cited from Androtion (*FGrHist* 324 F 45), thus refers to the date of Alcibiades' second flight into exile, after the battle of Notium, not his return to Athens. This becomes clear when we translate the second sentence literally ("He returned in the archonship of Antigenes... because he had entrusted the fleet to Antiochus..."), and remove Fornara's "(and he fled)." The verb *katelthon,* literally "he went down," and the noun *kathodos,* "the way down," often refer to the "the way back" or "the return" home. In this case both certainly refer to Alcibiades' "return" to exile, as is demonstrated in the next sentence, which Fornara did not include in his excerpt: "But Callistratus says that this was the occasion on which Alcibiades was exiled (*ekpeson*) and went to Sparta...." The scholion *never* refers to a homecoming, but is *always* discussing Alcibiades' departure to exile.

APPENDIX D

The Surrender of Athens and the Installation of the Thirty

Xenophon's narrative of the surrender of Athens and the installation of the Thirty in the year 404 (*Hellenica* 2.2.23–2.3.11) obscures the chronology of a sequence of events troublesome both in their significance for Athenians and for the understanding of historians (not unrelated problems). Plutarch's description of the same events, *Lysander* 15, repeats some of Xenophon's account and supplements it. Although there are inconsistencies within each of these two narratives, they are not immediately obvious. Chronological difficulties become apparent, however, when we attempt to reconcile Xenophon and Plutarch with the additional information we have about these events from other sources, most significantly from the forensic speeches composed a few year later by Lysias, 12, *Against Eratosthenes* and especially 13, *Against Agoratus*. The problems have been analyzed recently by Krentz 1982 and Green 1991, who refer to the previous efforts of scholars to resolve these apparent difficulties. Here I will focus on the testimony of our sources and indicate the interpretation that I believe renders a satisfactory account.

In 2.2.23, after describing the Athenian acceptance of the terms of surrender brought by Theramenes, Xenophon states:

> After this Lysander sailed into Piraeus, the exiles returned, and the walls were pulled down among scenes of great enthusiasm and to the music of flute girls. It was thought that this day was the beginning of freedom for Greece. (Translated by R. Warner)

In 2.3.11, he states: "At Athens the Thirty were elected directly after the demolition of the Long Walls and the walls of Piraeus." The impression given is that all of these events, from the surrender to the installation of the

Thirty, took place in immediate sequence over a few days, or no more than a few weeks. A similar impression comes from the first reading of Plutarch's account, which adds that Lysander's arrival at the time of the surrender took place "on the sixteenth day of the month Munychion, the same on which they conquered the Barbarian in the sea-fight at Salamis" (15.1, translated by B. Perrin). The date of Munychion 16, roughly in April (hereafter described simply as "April"), corresponds with Thucydides' observation (5.26.1–3) that the war lasted twenty-seven years "and not many days more," presumably from the attack on Plataea in early spring 431 (2.1–2), until the Spartans and their allies "took control of the Long Walls and Piraeus" (on the relationship between the surrender and the death of Darius II, as reported by Diodorus 13.108.1, see chapter 8 note 4).

Difficulties begin to appear when we test some of the details of this composite account against further information. At the time of Critias' death, at the battle of Munychia in 403, Xenophon quotes a speech in which the Eleusinian Herald, Cleocritus, states that "the accursed Thirty... have killed practically more Athenians in eight months than have all the Peloponnesians in ten years of war" (2.4.21). Within a matter of days, the Thirty were deposed and replaced by the Ten (2.4.23–24). If the Thirty had come to power in April, then their eight months would have ended in December. In light of other information, this seems too early for the fall of the Thirty (Krentz 1982, 150; Green 1991, 3–4). A more decisive objection to the simple interpretation of Xenophon and Plutarch is found in the statement of Aristotle *Constitution* 35.1 that the Thirty were established in the archonship of Pythodorus (404/3), which means that they came to power sometime after June or July of 404.

A surprising but revealing problem emerges from Plutarch's notice of the date of Munychion 16 itself. He identifies this as the date of the defeat of the Persians at Salamis, but this is an error. The battle of Salamis took place at the end of summer 480, and Plutarch elsewhere gives its correct date in the month of Boedromion, roughly September (*Camillus* 19.3; see Badian and Buckler 1975). If the Thirty were installed in September, their fall should be placed in May 403, which is plausible (see Krentz and Green). It seems that Xenophon and Plutarch have compressed events several months apart, and we see that Plutarch gives us two dates: April for the surrender of Athens (confirmed by Thucydides), and September for the installation of the Thirty (consistent with Aristotle's notice). Two questions follow: is this observation consistent with other evidence, and which other events of 404 should be associated with the spring and the fall dates?

Plutarch indicates that after the initial surrender, the Athenians were uncooperative and unruly, so that Lysander

> sent a letter to the *demos* saying that he held the city in violation of the treaty; for the walls were still standing, though the period of days within which they were to be destroyed had passed; therefore he would have to present their case anew for decision, since they had broken their agreements (*Lysander* 15.2).

These circumstances indicate a passage of some significant period of time after surrender but before the destruction of the walls. Diodorus 14.3.4–7 similarly reports an interval of non-compliance after the acceptance of the terms of surrender, and gives a similar account of the ultimatum delivered to the Athenians by Lysander. Diodorus adds the revealing detail that Lysander's intervention came at the request of Athenian oligarchs, and that the resolution of this crisis came with the appointment of the Thirty. Diodorus also reports that, in the interval between surrender and ultimatum, Lysander was chiefly occupied with the siege of Samos, which Xenophon also reports between his two notices of the installation of the Thirty (2.3.2, 6–7). Xenophon *Hellenica* 2.2.23 is thus clearly shown to be deceptively compressed, although 2.3.11, placing the election of the Thirty "directly after the demolition of the Long Walls and the walls of Piraeus," appears reasonably accurate; these latter events all took place several months after the surrender in April.

Lysias is our only source for a significant sequence of events that took place at some time in this episode. In *Against Agoratus* 13.13–48 and in *On the Confiscation of the Property of Nicias' Brother* 18.5 Lysias reports the resistance of Athenian officers, Strombichides, Dionysodorus, and others, to the terms of surrender negotiated by Theramenes. This resistance was overcome, Lysias 13.17 reports, only when Theramenes' supporters arranged, "before the assembly concerning the peace," to arrest and condemn these officers as enemies of the state. Several scholars have identified the occasion as the surrender of Athens in April, when war at last gave way to peace (so Krentz 1982, 43 n. 35; Ostwald 1986, 459 n. 171; Kagan 1987, 411; Green 1991, 10). Such an interpretation seems to reinforce the compressed account of Xenophon. For at 13.34, Lysias states,

> it was just when those persons had been arrested and imprisoned that Lysander sailed into your harbors, that your ships were surrendered to the Lacedaemonians, that the walls were demolished, that the Thirty were established.

But this interpretation also requires us to understand that a complex series of covert and official actions, described in Lysias 13.17–34, took place in the space of only a day or two. This "very crowded account of events," as Kagan 1987, 411 n. 137, terms it, is not satisfactory (see Rhodes 1981, 428). For reasons already noted, the demolition of walls and establishment of the Thirty must be placed after midsummer 404. This is also where we must place the arrest of the officers.

The correct interpretation, as described in chapter 8, with notes 44–50, recognizes that objections to Theramenes' terms voiced already in the spring led to non-compliance over the summer, and that these difficulties were only overcome by the arrest of the officers on the eve of Lysander's arrival, probably at the end of summer, after the surrender of Samos and when Lysander was about to present his demands for compliance to the Athenians in person. As Beloch recognized (1914, vol. 2.1, 430–31 and n. 1), Lysias' "assembly concerning the peace" (13.17) was an assembly met in order to preserve the peace in accordance with Lysander's ultimatum, and is identical with—or more likely, separated by no more than a few days from—"the assembly concerning the constitution" (Lysias 12.71–72) presided over by Lysander upon his arrival from Samos.

From the foregoing it emerges that Lysander's most memorable arrival in Athens was after the surrender of Samos, when he threatened the Athenians with the consequences of their violation of the treaty made the previous spring. Only after this event were the Long Walls and Piraeus walls torn down and the Thirty elected. It is doubtful if Lysander came to Athens on the occasion of the surrender in April. Only the misleading passage at *Hellenica* 2.2.23 and a confused notice of Lysander's departure for Samos in 2.3.3 seem to indicate that he did so. But 2.3.3 says that Lysander went to Samos *after* the election of the Thirty, which makes no sense. This passage of the *Hellenica* (2.2.23–2.3.11) is widely acknowledged as the point of a clumsy juncture between the earlier portion of the *Hellenica,* completing the account of the war that Thucydides had promised, and Xenophon's own continuation (MacLaren 1934; Dillery 1995, 12–15). Numerous interpolations have been suspected here and in the preceding portion of the *Hellenica;* it would not be surprising if 2.3.3 were an interpolator's errant effort to make a logical bridge between events left in suspense by Xenophon's compressed and misleading account (Green 1991, 3, also indicates this problem, but resolves it by suggesting, 11–15, that Lysander made another round-trip to and from Samos after the installation of the Thirty).

Yet Xenophon's account provides the proof that Lysander's celebrated entry into Athens came near the end of summer 404 and may well have coincided with the time of the observance of the Hellenic victory at Salamis, as Plutarch reports. The evidence is found in Xenophon's summation of the years of the war, which, he states, lasted "twenty-eight years and six months" (2.3.9). This seems another shocking error, in view of Thucydides' careful chronology and authoritative statement that the war lasted twenty-seven years "and not many days more" (5.26.1–3). The explanation for the discrepancy is easy to find, and it reveals the reason why Thucydides is so insistent on his method of measuring the passage of years (5.20).

Xenophon *Hellenica* 2.3.9–10 lists all the Spartan ephors who held annual office since Aenesias, "in whose ephorate the war began," until Endius, "in whose term of office Lysander sailed home after the accomplishments described above." We know that the ephors changed office sometime after April and before September or October (see Thucydides 5.36.1; Gomme et al. 1970, 38). We know that the war began in spring or early summer, depending on where one commenced counting (Thucydides 2.2.1 or 2.19.1), some months before the end of Aenesias' term. Xenophon's reckoning of the end of the war "at the end of summer" (2.3.9) must come not long after the beginning of Endius' term. From Aenesias to Endius, counting inclusively, Xenophon names twenty-nine ephors. Xenophon commits the common fallacy of regarding a list of twenty-nine annual magistrates as equivalent to twenty-nine years; if one were to count from the same point in the year at the beginning and at the end of a list of twenty-nine annual magistrates, one would count the passage of twenty-eight years. Mistakenly regarding his twenty-nine names as equal to twenty-nine years, but knowing that the ending was six months earlier in Endius' term than the beginning of hostilities in Aenesias' term, Xenophon subtracted six months to come up with his count of "twenty-eight years and six months."

Correcting Xenophon's fallacious count yields a war lasting twenty-seven years and six months. This harmonizes with Thucydides' count, since Thucydides reports the end of the war from the Athenian perspective, coinciding with the surrender in April, when the Spartans "took control of the Long Walls and Piraeus" (5.26.1; cf. Lysias 12.71). Xenophon reports the end of the war from the Spartan perspective, "at the end of summer" (2.3.9), after the surrender of Samos, when Lysander came to take his prizes from Athens (*Hellenica* 2.3.8), to burn the remaining ships and shipsheds (Plutarch *Lysander* 15.4; Lysias 13.34, 46), to get the destruction of the Long Walls and Piraeus walls finally underway, and to celebrate "the beginning of freedom for the Greeks" (I cannot accept Green's scenario that has Lysander holding two such celebrations in 404, one in spring and one in fall). Xenophon's reckoning of the length of the war, corrected for the fallacy of counting by annual magistrates (see Thucydides 5.20; the identical fallacy is responsible for the count of "six years" for the time Hyperbolus spent in exile before his murder, see chapter 5 note 25), shows clearly when the Spartans and their allies regarded the war ended and freedom at hand. This was the occasion of Lysander's visit to Athens and the election of the Thirty, and it took place in September (approximately), not long after the surrender of Samos and six months after the surrender of Athens in April (approximately) 404.

ABBREVIATIONS

Colonna	Colonna, A., ed. *Himerii, Declamationes et Orationes*. Rome, 1951.
Dindorf	Dindorf, W., ed. *Aristides*. 3 vols. Leipzig, 1829.
DK	Diels, H., and W. Kranz, eds. *Die Fragmente der Vorsokratiker*. 6th ed., 3 vols. Berlin, 1951. Reprint 1961.
Edmonds	Edmonds, J. M., ed. *The Fragments of Attic Comedy*. 3 vols. Leiden, 1957–1961.
Edmonds *Elegy*	Edmonds, J. M., ed. *Greek Elegy and Iambus*. 2 vols. Loeb Classical Library. Cambridge, Mass., 1931.
Edmonds *LG*	Edmonds, J. M., ed. *Lyra Graeca*. 3 vols. Loeb Classical Library. Cambridge, Mass., 1922–1927.
FGrHist	Jacoby, F., ed. *Die Fragmente der griechischen Historiker*. Berlin and Leiden, 1923-.
Fornara	Fornara, C. W., ed. *Translated Documents of Greece & Rome*. 1, *Archaic Times to the End of the Peloponnesian War*. 2nd ed. Cambridge, 1983.
Harding	Harding, P., ed. *Translated Documents of Greece & Rome*. 2, *From the End of the Peloponnesian War to the Battle of Ipsus*. Cambridge, 1985.
IG	*Inscriptiones Graecae*. Berlin, 1873-.

Kock	Kock, T., ed. *Comicorum Atticorum Fragmenta.* 3 vols. Leipzig, 1880–1888.
ML	Meiggs, R., and D. M. Lewis, eds. *A Selection of Greek Historical Inscriptions to the End of the Fifth Century B.C.* Oxford, 1969.
Nauck	Nauck, A., ed. *Tragicorum Graecorum Fragmenta.* 2nd ed. Leipzig, 1889.
PCG	Kassel, R., and C. Austin, eds. *Poetae Comici Graeci.* Berlin and New York, 1983-.
POxy	Grenfell, B. P., and A. S. Hunt, eds. *The Oxyrhynchus Papyri.* London, 1898-.
Radt	Radt, S. L., ed. *Tragicorum Graecorum Fragmenta.* Vol. 3, *Aeschylus.* Göttingen, 1985.
Sandys	Sandys, J., ed. *The Odes of Pindar.* 2nd ed. Loeb Classical Library. Cambridge, Mass., 1919.
Thalheim	Thalheim, T., ed. *Antiphontis orationes et fragmenta.* Leipzig, 1914.
Tod	Tod, M. N., ed. *A Selection of Greek Historical Inscriptions.* 2 vols. Oxford, 1946 and 1962.
Wendel	Wendel, C., ed. *Scholia in Apollonium Rhodium Vetera.* Berlin, 1958.

The titles of periodicals are abbreviated according to the conventions employed by *L'Année Philologique.*

NOTES

INTRODUCTION

1. On the literate revolution of the late fifth century, see Havelock 1963, esp. 38–41; Goody and Watt 1968, esp. 49–55; Havelock 1982, 261–92; Lenz 1989; Thomas 1989, esp. 15–94, and 1992, 123–57; the subject is taken up again in chapter 12. Aristotle's reading in historical, constitutional, and rhetorical sources: Jacoby 1949, 204–14; Hignett 1952, 28; Weil 1960, 311–25; Day and Chambers 1962, 12–23; Rhodes 1981, 15–38; Cole 1991, 115–38.

2. "School of Hellas": Thucydides 2.41.1; cf. Euripides *Medea* 824–43, *Children of Heracles* 379–80; Plato *Protagoras* 337d, *Gorgias* 461e. From a critical rather than eulogistic standpoint, much the same is said of the unique influence of Athens by Pseudo-Xenophon *Constitution* 1.4–5, 10–13, 2.7–12. Roberts 1994 provides a stimulating review of controversies in the ancient and modern traditions critical of Athens and its democracy; she also reviews, 298–301, the positive assessments of Athenian democracy characteristic of scholarship of the 1980s and early 1990s (which has been less interested in the Athenian empire than was scholarship of the 1950s-1970s).

3. The quotations from Thucydides are translated by R. Warner. Hornblower 1987, 155–90, surveys such statements of opinion by Thucydides. I cannot agree with Hornblower, 147, that Thucydides' use of such superlatives even of events after 415 might at times be merely a "strengthening device," and need not require a perspective from after the surrender of Athens.

4. On Xenophon's *Hellenica,* its selectivity and its narrative strategies, see Gray 1989, esp. 14–28, 81–106, 137–40, and Dillery 1995, esp. 241–54. Although the *Hellenica* as a whole was not completed until after 362, the date of composition of its earliest part, before 2.3.10, is a vexed question; see the references cited in chapter 12, note 89.

5. On signs thought to indicate the incompleteness of Book 8, see Andrewes, in Gomme et al. 1981, 369–75: according to Andrewes' interpretation of Thucydidean composition, "Book viii as a whole represents an earlier stage in Thucydi-

des' process of composition than any other part of the *History*" (382); see also Dover, in Gomme et al. 1981, 384–444. Hornblower 1987, 136–44, 155, follows their analysis. Regarding the changing conditions of the war and Thucydides' changing style, Westlake 1968, 308–19, notes that in Books 5.25–8 Thucydides devotes more attention to characterizing individuals according to personal motives, as opposed to individuals who exemplify general principles in the earlier books. Sealey 1967 illustrates the extreme complexities of tracing the influence of personal motives in events in Book 8. Connor 1984, 210–30, does not see signs of lack of polish in Book 8, but does recognize that "the political dimension of the war, now more fully developed than in any preceding portion of the *Histories,* transforms the book from a relatively simple story of Athenian endurance and recovery into a much more complex narrative" (214).

6. Quote: Thucydides 3.82.2–4, translated by R. Warner. The implications of this passage and other aspects of Books 3 and 4 for Thucydides' conceptualization of events in Book 8 and beyond are thoughtfully explored by Rawlings 1981.

7. Thucydides on Alcibiades: 5.43.2, 6.15.3–4, 8.86.5–7, discussed further below in chapter 12, with note 46. Alcibiades has been the subject of a romanticizing tradition in art, biography, and drama from the Renaissance until the early twentieth century, and scholarship from the mid-nineteenth century on has been careful to distance itself from that tradition (see note 8 below). Hatzfeld 1940 (with a brief overview of earlier works, xi-xii) provides what remains the best scholarly biography of Alcibiades (although my account differs from Hatzfeld on numerous points of assessment). Bloedow 1973 offers a strongly negative, revisionist portrait, critical also of Thucydides' judgment. The trend is reflected by Kagan 1987, 420: "Alcibiades was no military genius but a talented soldier of the second rank whose confidence and ambitions went far beyond his ability." Rhodes 1985, Cartledge 1987b, and Ellis 1989 are less dismissive in their efforts to reappraise Alcibiades (against Ellis 1989, Bloedow 1990, 1991a and b, and 1992 has reasserted his views). Forde 1989 and 1992 devotes attention to the problem specifically of Thucydides' assessment of Alcibiades. Vickers 1987, 1989a and b, 1993, and 1997 is often right in detecting allusions to Alcibiades on the contemporary Attic stage. De Romilly 1995 has written a popularizing account of Alcibiades, emphasizing his profound influence on his generation.

8. Xenophon notes the significance of the association of Socrates with Alcibiades in *Memorabilia* 1.2.12. Plato's *Alcibiades* 1 is listed among dialogues of questionable authenticity by Lesky 1963/1966, 512, and Kraut 1992, 35 n. 18. The judgment in this case may be because the portrayal of the intimacy of Socrates and Alcibiades is deemed a lesser use of "Platonic property" (Lesky). Stylistic analysis has found no basis for excluding the *Alcibiades* 1 from the genuine works of Plato; see Brandwood 1992, 112. Vickers 1994 offers a speculative and ultimately unconvincing analysis of the significance of Alcibiades particularly in the *Gorgias.* Brickhouse and Smith 1989, 71–73, collect references to the associations that were later cited in reproach of Socrates.

9. Plato's Alcibiades is compared to Thucydides' by Forde 1992. Quote: Aeschines 1.173.

10. In *Athènes devant la défait de 404* (1976), Edmond Lévy is the only scholar, to my knowledge, to devote a book to the intellectual issues discussed in the present

work with a similar recognition of the need to span the divide of 404–403. Lévy's analysis falls short of its potential chiefly through its predominant focus on ideological themes without penetrating sufficiently into the events that shaped them. David Lewis' *Sparta and Persia* (1977) *is* a circumstantially detailed study that spans practically the identical period as this book. Although Athens is not his focus, the insights that emerge from Lewis' novel scope have been exceptionally influential in giving my work its direction. Scholarship on Thucydides has generally viewed his work from the perspective of the earlier side of the 404–403 divide. Jacqueline de Romilly and especially John Finley have recognized the importance of widening our inquiry to include the post-404 retrospective, but the bolder speculations of Hunter R. Rawlings, III, in *The Structure of Thucydides' History* (1981), deserve credit for revealing what a profound effect this retrospective has in our assessment of Thucydides' goals.

CHAPTER ONE. THE PAST OF DEMOCRATIC ATHENS

1. Quote: Homer *Odyssey* 19.203, a line echoed by Hesiod in the prologue to his *Theogony* 27. Recent scholarship has become fascinated by the interplay between truth and falsity, or fiction and lies, in archaic poetry; see Bowie 1993 and Pratt 1993. On the developing concept of truth in Greek thought, see note 2 below.

2. Quote: Hecataeus *FGrHist* 1 F 1. On the etymological relation of *aletheia,* "truth," to *lethe,* "forgetfulness," with the privative prefix *a-*, see Chantraine 1974, 618. Detienne 1973, 9–50, examines the semantic field of *aletheia* and its relationship, in archaic Greek poetry, to *mnemosyne,* "memory," and its opposite, *lethe;* see also Nagy 1990, 58–60. Adkins 1972 and Pratt 1993, 17–22, demonstrate that *lethe* and *aletheia* describe a wider field of consciousness than memory or its absence, but their challenge to Detienne's formulation does not alter its terms as it relates specifically to the past. Cole 1983 affirms the subjective quality of *aletheia* in archaic usage and demonstrates that, by the mid-fifth century, *aletheia* has acquired an increasingly objective sense. Similarly, Nagy 1990, 66–67, and 1996, 122–28, discusses the concurrence, in Homeric diction, of the terms *mythos* and *aletheia* as markers of significant speech, and their later divergence, as *aletheia* came to denote a privileged category within a wider field that includes mistaken *mythoi;* in the fifth-century usage of Pindar, this distinction begins to resemble our more familiar opposition between "myth" (meaning something like fiction) and "truth." It has been customary to emphasize the boundary between "myth" and a new concept of objectively verifiable "truth" as essential to Greek historical thought (so, e.g., Collingwood 1946, 17–20), although every commentator who has insisted on the distinction immediately faces the troublesome task of explaining the amazing permeability of this boundary (so, briefly, Collingwood 1946, 20–21; inconclusively, Wardman 1960; incisively, M.I. Finley 1965/1975; and at length but with less cogency, Gomme 1954 and Veyne 1988). Woodman 1988, 5–45, inverts the usual premise and seeks the thematic continuities between Homer and Thucydides.

3. On the widening circles of public authority and venues of poetic performance in archaic Greece, see Detienne 1973, 98–103; Nagy 1990, 52–115. The *Homeric Hymn to Dionysus* 1–8 provides a clear case of locally competing claims to truth. On novelty and entertainment in the competitive process of conveying poetic truths, see M. Griffith 1990, 188–89.

4. Seven Sages: Snell 1938/1971 and Lesky 1963/1966, 156–57, argue for a sixth-century formation of a canon of Seven; Fehling 1985 insists on its origin with Plato, when the Seven are first so called; Martin 1993 makes the case for a pre-Platonic canon of the Seven, as poets, politicians, and performers. Hecataeus: Herodotus 5.36, 125; Pearson 1939, 25–28. Solon, "the first Greek politician who still speaks to us," as Ehrenberg notes (1973, 1), wrote poetry describing his laws and their effects.

5. Herodotus' claims "to know" the truth are scattered throughout his work, as are his disclaimers of the truth of what others tell. 1.6.2, on Croesus, "the first whom we know" to compel Ionian Greeks to pay tribute, is programmatic to his work (cf. 3.122.2 on Polycrates); see Evans 1991, 100–101, 105–107. Lateiner 1989, 104–108 lists instances where Herodotus disputes or affirms other sources of information. Nagy 1990, 231–36, 273, links Herodotus' claims "to know" to his reliance on *semata,* "signs," or on features or circumstances that "indicate" *(semainein).* Immerwahr 1960 similarly links Herodotus' historical thought to his reliance on monuments; Steiner 1994, 10–60, demonstrates the connections between signs, tokens, and texts. Thucydides is more sparing in making direct claims "to know" than Herodotus, and, like Herodotus, he usually makes the claim of remote events, e.g. 1.4.1, 13.4, 18.1, 6.2.1–2 (contrast 3.113.6). Thucydides asserts knowledge by periphrasis, in terms like "judging by the evidence," and asserts that "the truth" can only be ascertained by laborious effort (1.1, 9.1, especially 1.20–22); see Hornblower 1987, 77–109. On the authorial stance adopted by Herodotus and Thucydides, see Dewald 1985 and 1987 on Herodotus.

6. Pausanias 1.3.3.

7. On monuments to *Demokratia* in fourth-century Athens, see Raubitschek 1962/1991; Lawton 1993; Tzachou-Alexandri 1993. On Theseus in Athenian cults, institutions, and literature, see Robertson 1992, 3–137; Walker 1995. On the connections of Theseus specifically with the ancestral democracy in fourth-century rhetoric and historiography, see Ruschenbusch 1958. On the "truly astonishing ignorance of most of the Attic orators and the little use they made of the history of their city," see Jacoby *FGrHist* IIIb Suppl. Bd. I, 95.

8. The earliest attested uses of the term *demokratia,* ca. 420s: Herodotus 6.131.1; Pseudo-Xenophon *Constitution* 1.4–5, 2.20, 3.1; Thucydides 2.37.1; Aristophanes *Acharnians* 618. Quote: "...when Cleisthenes introduced *demokratia,*" Aristotle *Constitution* 29.3, quoting a document of 411. Those who have conjectured an early, Cleisthenic use of the term *demokratia* include Ehrenberg 1950; Kinzl 1978; and Hansen 1986 and 1991, 69–71. Those who have argued for a date not long after the middle of the fifth century include Debrunner 1947/1995; Ostwald 1969, 120 n. 2, 153–54; Meier 1970, 48–49; Sealey 1973 and 1987, 91–106. Raaflaub 1995, 46–48 cites evidence (the personal name *Demokrates,* Davies 1971, 142, 359–60, also considered by Hansen) for a date in the 460s. For a sacrifice to *Demokratia,* attested in the fourth century, see Raubitschek 1962/1991, 224–25. For recent scholarship on Cleisthenes' reforms, see Ostwald 1986, 15–28, and 1988; Fornara and Samons 1991, 38–58; Raaflaub 1995; Ober 1996, 32–52.

9. Taylor 1991 reviews literary and artistic evidence for the institutions honoring Harmodius and Aristogeiton as tyrant-slayers. Day 1985 convincingly identifies the epigram on the base of the second statue group, erected in 477 to replace the

original statues removed by the Persians in 480, with an inscribed epigram from Chios. Regular offerings to Harmodius and Aristogeiton are attested by Aristotle *Constitution* 58.1; their grave is identified by Pausanias 1.29.15; Fornara 1970 and Taylor 1991, 5–7, consider it likely that offerings were made at their grave already in the sixth century; Clairmont 1983, 14–15, sees their cult as an antecedent to public honors for Athenian war dead. *Sitesis*, or honorary dining at the Prytaneum, is affirmed for the closest living relatives of Harmodius and Aristogeiton in *IG* I^3 131.5–7. Further testimonia and scholarship on the controversies surrounding especially the original institution of Harmodius and Aristogeiton are cited below, notes 11–12.

10. The assassination of Hipparchus and subsequent expulsion of Hippias are described by Herodotus 5.55–57, 62–65, 6.123; Thucydides 1.20.2, 6.53.3–59; Aristotle *Constitution* 18–19. Jacoby 1949, 152–68, examines the nature of the learned tradition about the Peisistratids and their fall, although many of his arguments have not won wide acceptance; see note 11 below. Fornara 1968 reviews the controversies associated with the assassination of Hipparchus; his conclusions, however, need to be modified in light of the discussion in chapter 4 below, pages 114–16.

11. The remarkable elevation of the tyrant-slayers to heroic status has led to elaborate speculations about its circumstances. Jacoby 1949, 160 and 339 n. 53, suggested that it was the product of anti-Cleisthenic partisanship; his view was disputed by Ehrenberg 1950, 531–32. Podlecki, 1966a, elaborated Jacoby's argument by placing the rivalry and heroization of the tyrant-slayers after 480. The Jacoby/Podlecki partisan theory has been rejected by Ostwald 1969, 130–34, and Fornara 1970, 158–61, but revived by Garland 1992, 94–96, and modified by Lavelle 1993, 27–58, who argues that an anti-Peisistratid movement of the 490s or 480s was the impetus for the heroization of the tyrant-slayers. This explanation slights the strong evidence indicating that the original statues of the tyrant-slayers, by Antenor, were made in the 500s (see below, note 12), and the indications that before the battle of Marathon, in 490, Harmodius and Aristogeiton were already widely if not unanimously celebrated as heroes by the Athenians, see especially Herodotus 6.109 and the so-called Harmodius skolia. On the skolia, see Ostwald 1969, 121–30, and Taylor 1991, 22–32; translation in Fornara 39.

12. Original statues of Harmodius and Aristogeiton dedicated in 509: Pliny *Natural History* 34.17; attributed to Antenor by Pausanias 1.8.5. The fame of the tyrant-slayers as the first men to be honored by statues in the Agora is noted by Aristotle *Rhetoric* 1368a; cf. Demosthenes 20.70. On their location, see also Pausanias 1.8.5; Timaeus *Lexicon Platonicum* s.v. *orchestra;* Photius s.v. *orchestra;* recently discussed by Ajootian 1998. Dismissing the testimony of Pliny, Raubitschek 1940/1991, 211 n. 24, suggested that the first statues honoring the tyrant-slayers were not erected until after the battle of Marathon in 490. Among art historians, Raubitschek's argument has not convinced Deyhle 1969, 39–46; Brunnsåker 1971, 97; Kleine 1973, 67–76, 132; these accept a date of 509 or soon after for the original statues of the tyrant-slayers, as do Ostwald 1969, 132–33; Fornara 1970, 158 n. 22; Taylor 1991, 13–15. Raubitschek's argument for a later date has recently been taken up by Landwehr 1985, 47, and Shapiro 1994, 124; I find their arguments to be inconclusive; Mattusch 1994, 76 and 79, favors the traditional dating. For the later history of the statues, replaced in 477/6 after the originals were removed by the Persians, see

Frazer 1898, vol. 2, 92–99; Brunnsåker 1971, 33–42; Taylor 1991, 15–19. On dithyrambic competition at the Dionysia, see below, note 13.

13. Dithyrambic competition at the Dionysia began with the victory of Hypodicus of Chalcis in the archonship of Lysagoras, according to the *Parian Marble, FGrHist* 239 F A46; on the identification of this archonship with the year 509/8, see Cadoux 1948, 113; for assessments of the social/political context of tragedy and dithyrambs at the Athenian Dionysia in the late sixth century, see Pickard-Cambridge 1962, 63–89; Lesky 1963/1966, 226–30; Knox 1978; Herington 1985, 93–94; Zimmermann 1992, 32–35, and 1993, 42–43. Departing from conventional opinion, Connor 1989, 7–16, proposes to date the inauguration of the City Dionysia to ca. 501, but he does not dispute that the first contest in choral dithyrambs was held "between 510 and 508," 13 n. 21. On the orchestra in the Agora as the location of the tyrant-slayers, see note 12 above. *Parian Marble, FGrHist* 239 F A54, records a choral victory by Simonides at Athens in 477, when "the statues of Harmodius and Aristogeiton were erected" (i.e., the statues replacing those removed by Xerxes). Dithyrambs in the manner of Simonides: Aristophanes *Birds* 904–21.

14. The testimony to the victory of Hypodicus of Chalcis is cited in note 13 above. The migrations of the Gephyraei are described by Herodotus 5.57, 61; on their origin and ancestral cults, see Toepffer 1889, 293–300.

15. Dispute between Athenians and Boeotians over the Asopus frontier: Herodotus 6.108. Thucydides 3.68.5 dates the dispute to 519; Buck 1979, 112–28, accepts Thucydides' date; Badian 1993, 218–19 n. 18 and 222–23 nn. 33 and 34, doubts it, and regards the expulsion of the Peisistratids as a more likely occasion for Athenian–Boeotian hostilities to emerge. The victory of 506 and the praise of recently-won liberty is described by Herodotus 5.74–78; 79–81 and 89–91 refer to continued Boeotian-Athenian hostilities as the background to wider conflicts between the Athenians and their neighbors. On poetic reckoning of the balance due for glorious deeds, see Kurke 1991, 97–103, 106–107, 157, 228–38, and Kurke 1993.

16. On Phrynichus, see Lesky 1963/1966, 230–32. His first recorded victory in a dramatic competition was in the 67th Olympiad, 511–508, which should indicate his appeal to the sensibilities of the nascent democracy. *Sack of Miletus* might not have been the title of the play but a description of its subject; see Pickard-Cambridge 1962, 63 n. 3. On the reasons for the reaction to Phrynichus' play, Rosenbloom 1993 is to be preferred over Roisman 1988; on its dates, see below, note 17.

17. Although Herodotus 6.21 gives no indication of the date of Phrynichus' play, Wade-Gery 1940/1958, 177, has reinforced the belief that the *Sack of Miletus* was performed in 493, close to the election of Themistocles as archon in 493/2. Fear of Persia was probably the motive behind Themistocles' fortification of Piraeus, which many commentators assume that Themistocles commenced during his archonship. But the office held "from year to year," when the walls were begun (Thucydides 1.93.3), was more likely an office held for the duration of Themistocles' shipbuilding program, beginning in 483/2 (Herodotus 7.144.1; Aristotle *Constitution* 22.7); see Gomme 1945, 261–62; Fornara 1971c; Mosshammer 1975; Sealey 1976, 184–85; Chambers 1984, where dissenting opinions are cited.

18. Themistocles as *choregos* for Phrynichus in 476: Plutarch, *Themistocles* 5.4, citing the evidence of an inscription. On *Phoenician Women,* see the hypothesis to Aeschylus' *Persians;* Lesky 1963/1966, 230–30. Evidence of Themistocles' self-

promotion is found in his dedication of a shrine to Artemis Aristoboule, "Of the Best Counsel"; see Plutarch *Themistocles* 22; Threpsiades and Vanderpool 1964; Travlos 1971, 121–23.

19. Singers at the halls of great men: *Odyssey* 1.150–55, 325–72, 4.15–19, 8.43–100, 17.385, 22.330–53. Quote: *Odyssey* 1.351–52. Rösler 1990 discusses the role of poetry in the transmission of *mnemosyne,* memory, in the social setting of the archaic symposium.

20. On the poetries of praise and their social circles in archaic and early classical Greece, see Gentili 1988; Kurke 1991, 1–12, 257–60; Cole 1992; Thomas 1995. On the agonistic nature of archaic and classical poetry, see Griffith 1990; Nagy 1990, 136–45; Shapiro 1992.

21. Themistocles and Simonides: Plutarch *Themistocles* 1.3, 5.4–5, 15.2; cf. Simonides fr. 91 Edmonds *LG;* Suda s.v. *Simonides.* Rutherford 1996, 169–88, reviews themes from the Persian Wars sung by Simonides. Bowie 1986 discusses the range of occasions, from private to public, for which Simonidean elegy would be suited. Themistocles "all the talk" *(eboesthe)* at Isthmia, honored at Sparta, and admired at Olympia: Herodotus 8.124; Plutarch *Themistocles* 17.

22. Themistocles' hospitality at Isthmia, grudgingly attested by Timocreon of Rhodes: Plutarch *Themistocles* 21.3 = Timocreon fr. 1.10–12 Edmonds *LG;* at Olympia: Plutarch *Themistocles* 5.3. His shrine of Artemis Aristoboule: see above, note 18. Simonides attests his rebuilding the shrine of the Lycomidae: Plutarch *Themistocles* 1.3, cf. 15.2.

23. Quotes: Herodotus 8.59, 8.26.3, translated by A. de Sélincourt, with modification. The vote for *aristeia:* Herodotus 8.123–24, cf. 8.11, 93, 9.81; cf. Pindar *Isthmian* 5.46–50; awards of *aristeia* are discussed by Pritchett 1974, 276–90. For other acknowledgments of prowess, see below, note 24.

24. Sophanes of Decelea: Herodotus 6.92, 9.73–75; Plutarch *Comparison of Aristides with Marcus Cato* 2.2; his grave at Athens was noticed by Pausanias 1.29.5. Athletes in battle noticed by Herodotus: Philippus of Croton (honored by his foes after death), 5.47; Cylon of Athens, 5.71; Eualcidas of Eretria, 5.102; Eurybates of Argos, 6.92, 9.75; Phayllus of Croton, 8.47 (his statue at Delphi is mentioned by Pausanias 10.9.2, and his memory was later honored by Alexander III of Macedon, Plutarch *Alexander* 34.2); Teisamenus of Elis, 9.33–35 (cf. Pausanias 3.11.6–8 and 6.14.13). Other examples of individual prowess: Archias and Lycopas of Sparta, 3.55; Pytheas of Aigina, 7.181, 8.92; Leonidas, Dieneces, Alpheus, Maron, and Eurytus among the three hundred Spartans at Thermopylae "whose names I have learned as those of men who deserve to be remembered" (Herodotus 7.224), along with Dithyrambus of Thespiae and the Acarnanian seer, Megistias, some of whom were remembered in monuments on the spot, 7.220–33; Lycomides of Athens, 8.11 (cf. Plutarch *Themistocles* 15.2); Cleinias of Athens, 8.17 (cf. Plutarch *Alcibiades* 1.1); Polycritus of Aegina and Eumenes and Ameinias of Athens, 8.93 (cf. Plutarch *Themistocles* 14.3); Arimnestus of Sparta, 9.64 (cf. Plutarch *Aristides* 19.1); Aristodemus, Poseidonius, Philocyon, and Amompharetus of Sparta, 9.71; Ameinias, Aristides, Callimachus, and Cynaegeirus of Athens: Plutarch *Comparison of Aristides with Marcus Cato* 2.2. See Kurke 1993, 133–37.

25. On *kudos* in epinician poetry, see Kurke 1993; Carter 1986, 1–7. Nagy 1990, 199–214, examines the relationship of praise poetry to the *kleos* (also "glory") of victors.

26. Themistocles honored for *sophia* (at Sparta) and *deinotes kai gnome* (by Simonides), see above, note 21. These honors are reflected in the terms of praise later given to Themistocles by Thucydides, 1.138.3, cf. 1.74.1; cf. also Plato *Gorgias* 455e, 503c, 516d. The dedication of Pausanias at Delphi: Thucydides 1.132.2–3.

27. Themistocles demands respect: Herodotus 8.61–62, 125; Thucydides 1.91.4–7; Plutarch *Themistocles* 2.3, 11.3–5, 18.3–4, 22.1, 23.3–4. Timocreon of Rhodes: Plutarch *Themistocles* 20 = Timocreon fr. 1–3 Edmonds *LG;* Suda s.v. *Timokreon;* Lesky 1966, 185. Meiggs 1972, 414–15, and Robertson 1980a examine the historical circumstances of Timocreon's relation to Themistocles. Aristides, "the choicest man *(lostos)* from Athens": Timocreon fr. 1.2–4 Edmonds *LG.* On Aristides as a symbol of Athenian equity in the 420s, see below, chapter 3, with note 30.

28. Aeschines 3.181–82 affirms that no monument at Athens recorded the distinction of a crown awarded to Themistocles or any of his contemporaries. Likewise, Themistocles is not mentioned by name in Aescylus' *Persians,* produced probably in the year of his ostracism; see below, with note 36. On *isonomia* and *isegoria* in early democratic Athens, see Ostwald 1969, 96–136; Meier 1980/1990, 30, 162–63; Raaflaub 1995, 49–51, and 1996, esp. 139–50.

29. Themistocles' arrogance: Herodotus 8.111–12; Plutarch *Themistocles* 2.3, 5.3, 7.5, 18.5, 20.1–2, 22.1–3; stolen foresight: Herodotus 8.57–58, 108–10; cf. Plutarch *Themistocles* 2.4, 16, *Moralia* 870f-871a (= Simonides fr. 125 Edmonds *LG*); worn-out fame: Plutarch *Themistocles* 2.6, 22.1; *Cimon* 5.4. Themistocles and Pausanias in disgrace: Thucydides 1.135–38; Plutarch *Themistocles* 22.3–23; see further below, notes 36 and 47.

30. Altar of Boreas: Herodotus 7.189; Simonides fr. 12–16 Edmonds *LG;* Plato *Phaedrus* 229c; Travlos 1971, 112; new fragments of Simonides may belong to this occasion, see West 1992, fr. 1–4; Rutherford 1996, 171–72. It is likely that Themistocles, as general and therefore chief executive officer for the Athenians at Artemisium, himself negotiated the commission of Simonides to accompany the public observations in honor of Boreas; Plutarch *Themistocles* 5.4 describes negotiations between Simonides and Themistocles in a public capacity; see Podlecki 1975, 50–51.

31. Pindar's dithyramb on Artemisium: fr. 77 Sandys (= Plutarch *Themistocles* 8.2, *Moralia* 867c); on Salamis: fr. 76 Sandys; in *Pythian* 1.75–77, Pindar boasts that he will win the favor of the Athenians by singing of Salamis. Aristophanes' parody: *Acharnians* 636–40, cf. *Knights* 1329. Isocrates 15.166 cites public honors and a monetary reward given to Pindar in exchange for the phrase, "pillar of Greece." A statue of Pindar was set up, at an unknown date, beside the tyrannicides, Pausanias 1.8.4; Richter 1984, 176–80.

32. Cimon's capture of Eion: Herodotus 7.107; Thucydides 1.98.1; Plutarch *Cimon* 7; scholion Aeschines 2.31. Bones of Theseus: Plutarch *Theseus* 36; *Cimon* 8.3--6. The events and their symbolism are discussed by Connor 1970, 157–66; Podlecki 1971; Meiggs 1972, 68–69; Tyrrell and Brown 1991, 167–70; Castriota 1992, 33–133; Walker 1995, 54–61.

33. On Theseus and the Amazons, and the Persian wars, see Boardman 1982; Tyrrell 1984, 10–19; Castriota 1992, 33–89.

34. The Painted Stoa was erected probably no earlier than the mid-460s, and possibly as late as the 450s, see L.S. Meritt 1970; Shear 1984, 13–18; Camp 1986, 66. Plutarch *Cimon* 4.5 indicates a loose connection between Cimon and the

Peisianactian Stoa; Meiggs 1972, 276–77, suggests that the stoa was built before Cimon's ostracism in 461; Hölscher 1973, 74–78, recognizes multiple influences in the stoa and accepts the possibility that it was built during Cimon's exile; Connor 1970, 162, suggests that it was erected after Cimon's recall in the 450s. Theseus in the Painted Stoa: Pausanias 1.15; Plutarch *Cimon* 4.5–6; for discussions, see Frazer 1898, vol. 2, 134–37; Hölscher 1973, 50–73; Castriota 1992, 76–89 (Amazonomachy only); Walker 1995, 59–60. Plutarch *Theseus* 35.5 attributes the cult of Theseus at Athens especially to the popular belief that his ghost had fought at Marathon; cf. Pausanias 1.17.6. Miltiades accused of tyranny and other offenses: Herodotus 4.137, 6.39, 104, 136; Plato *Gorgias* 516d; Plutarch *Cimon* 8.4. On the depiction of the battle of Oenoe, see below, note 70.

35. Mythical and recent exploits as the moral framework for Athenian destiny, as expressed in literature, rhetoric, art, and drama of the mid-fifth century and later, see Kierdorf 1966, 89–100; Loraux 1981/1986, 57–76; Thomas 1989, 196–237; Castriota 1992; Rosenbloom 1995, 100–101. On the rapid transformations in Athenian political culture and economy underway in this period, see Raaflaub 1998. Spartan anxiety about affairs across the sea is illustrated in several episodes: Cleomenes' meeting with Aristagoras of Miletus, Herodotus 5.49–51; the debate over the fate of Ionia, Herodotus 9.106.3; Sparta's inability to manage Pausanias' successes in the Hellespont, Thucydides 1.75.2, 95, 128–33, cf. 1.70.

36. The hypothesis to Aeschylus' *Persians* reports its similarity to Phrynichus' *Phoenician Women* and gives the date (Menon's archonship, 473/2). *IG* II^2 2318.9 reports that Aeschylus was awarded the prize for tragedy in that year and that Pericles was his *choregos*. On the ostracism of Themistocles, see Cawkwell 1970, 47; Rhodes 1970, 396–98; Badian 1993, 88–89; sources in Fornara 65.

37. On the theme of Aeschylus' *Persians*, the failure of *hybris* is examined by Meier 1988/1993, 63–78; Raaflaub 1988, 284–86; Castriota 1992, 19–23; Rosenbloom 1995, 91–98. Others mine the work for evidence of political context at the time of production and historical fact at the time of the battle: Podlecki 1966, 8–26; Lazenby 1988; Pelling 1997, 1–19.

38. The *Persians* is not usually so interpreted (see above, note 37). Rosenbloom 1995, 93–98 and 117, especially emphasizes the implicit warning against the exercise of naval hegemony, but in doing so he neglects the distinction between a naval hegemony misused by a monarch's ambition and the natural autonomy of a fleet of free Greeks, who are the agents of divine retribution against Xerxes. "Someone else's" disaster is not directly transferable into "one's own" in this case, for the Athenians regularly depict themselves as bearers of a unique standing in the realms of gods, heroes, and men, as Rosenbloom elsewhere recognizes, 99–102. The tension of witnessing the failure of a monarch who was also beyond reproach was also a topical theme, in light of the allegations of tyrannical pretensions against Pausanias and Themistocles at about the time of the play.

39. This message is affirmed by Herodotus in terms that almost echo Aeschylus: "It was the Athenians who—after the gods—drove back the Persian king" (7.139.5, translated by A. de Sélincourt); the same message, without reference to gods, is found in Thucydides 1.73.4–74.

40. On the foundation of the Delian League, see Meiggs 1972, esp. 42–49; Robertson 1980b. On Phrynichus' *Sack of Miletus*, see above, notes 16 and 17. Per-

sian *Yauna* = Ionia = Greece: Olmstead 1948, 44, 225; Seager and Tuplin 1980, 148; cf. Aristophanes *Acharnians* 104, 106. Quote: Thucydides 1.96.1.

41. The titles of plays accompanying Aeschylus' *Persians* are reported in the hypothesis. Few modern scholars comment on the relation of the *Persians* to the two tragedies accompanying it, and those who do so usually deny any thematic connection; so Lesky 1963/1966, 244–45; Pickard-Cambridge 1968, 81; Sommerstein 1996; Bowie 1997, 43 n. 43. I have noted only Donaldson 1860, 105–106, who recognized the connections between the plays along the lines suggested here.

42. There are many variants to the story of Phineus; see Apollonius *Argonautica* 2.178–489; Diodorus 4.43.3–44.7; Apollodorus 1.9.21, 3.15.3; Aeschylus fr. 260 (Radt) attests the role of the Boreads as saviors in Aeschylus' version rather than avengers. Scenes from Aeschylus' *Phineus* represented on Attic and Lucanian vases: Trendall and Webster 1971, 58–61. Boreads in Simonides fr. 12 Edmonds *LG*, invoked for the Panathenaea, fr. 15 Edmonds *LG* (= Himerius *Orations* 12.32, 47.14, Colonna); see now West 1993, 3–4.

43. Boreads born at the Sarpedonian rock: Simonides fr. 12 Edmonds *LG;* Apollonius *Argonautica* 1.216–18; dwelling at Mount Pangaeum: Pindar *Pythian* 4.179–83; cf. scholion to Apollonius 1.211c (Wendel); Ovid *Metamorphoses* 6.708–21. Athenian settlers at Eion and Ennea Hodoi on the Strymon and gold mines disputed with Thasos: Herodotus 9.75; Thucydides 1.98.1, 100.2–3, 101.3, 4.102, 105.1; Plutarch *Cimon* 7–8.2; Aeschines 2.31 and scholion.

44. Glaucus and his horses: Hyginus *Fabulae* 250, 273; Vergil, *Georgics* 3.267–68; Strabo 8.2.24 (409); Pausanias 6.20.19. The foundation of the Olympic games is associated with these events in Diodorus 4.53.4–6, cf. Pausanias 5.8.2–4; the games of Pelias were depicted on the chest of Cypselus at Olympia (Pausanias 5.17.9–11), on the throne of Apollo at Amyclae (Pausanias 3.18.16), and in the painting by Micon in the sanctuary of the Dioscuri at Athens (Pausanias 1.18.1), painted probably after the performance of Aeschylus' play; see Frazer 1898, vol. 2, 166–67. The *Glaucus at Potniae* was sufficiently famous in the fifth century to merit a quotation in Aristophanes' *Frogs* 1403.

45. The Greek oath before Plataea: Diodorus 11.29.2–3; Lycurgus *Against Leocrates* 80–81; it is found in a fourth-century Athenian inscription, Tod 204 (= Fornara 57). The oath was declared a fabrication of the Athenians by Theopompus *FGrHist* 115 F 153. Herodotus 7.132.2 attests an oath among Greek allies sworn early in Xerxes' campaign. Meiggs 1972, 504–507, and Siewert 1972 accept the oath as genuine; Pritchett 1985, 116–17, doubts its authenticity. The Persian camp described by Herodotus 9.15 straddled the road to Thebes via Potniae, where Pausanias, 9.8.1–3, describes the horse-maddening spring and uneatable grasses; cf. also Strabo 8.2.24 (409). On Masistius see Herodotus 9.20–25.

46. The alleged cowardice of the Corinthians: Herodotus 9.69; protested by Plutarch *Moralia* 872c-e. The Corinthians, "countrymen of Glaucus," were praised for bravery at Plataea by Simonides (fr. 92 Edmonds), quoted by Plutarch. This passage is now connected with the newly discovered fragments of the Simonidean elegy on Plataea, see West 1993; Boedeker 1995 and 1996. "The great hatred": Thucydides 1.103.4; the nature of this enmity is examined by de Ste. Croix, 1972, 211–20, who rightly looks to territorial disputes as the most likely cause.

47. On Pausanias see Herodotus 5.32, 8.3, 9.64; Thucydides 1.94–95, 128–34. Lang 1967 points out the strongly tendentious nature of Thucydides' account; see also Rhodes 1970, 387–92, 395–99; Meiggs 1972, 72–73, and 465–68; Badian 1993, 86–87; sources in Fornara 61.

48. Victories of the Boreads at the games of Pelias: Hyginus *Fabulae* 273. Aeschylus' play was evidently part of an Athenian polemic against the Corinthians who were praised for bravery by Simonides (fr. 92 Edmonds *LG*). Plutarch *Moralia* 872d-e turns the polemic against Herodotus by quoting from this elegiac poem by Simonides.

49. The popularity of this tragic trilogy has perplexed scholars adhering to the more limited interpretation of the *Persians* and its companion plays; see McCall 1986, e.g. Beginnings of empire: Thucydides 1.97.2–98; by 472 Eion and Scyros had been taken, and (probably) Carystus forced into submission; see Meritt, Wade-Gery, and McGregor 1950, 158–60, 175; Meiggs 1972, 68–70. Athenian daring: Thucydides 1.70 and 2.41. By 415 this has become self-avowed *polypragmosyne,* "interventionism"; see Thucydides 6.87; Ehrenberg 1947.

50. These characteristics in fifth-century Athenian drama are well described by Knox 1979; for another assessment, see Vernant 1972/1988.

51. The process described here is the ongoing "functional revaluation" of categories of historical meaning discussed by Sahlins 1985; on this process in archaic Greece, see Dougherty and Kurke 1993, 3–5. On the subjective construction of an ethically meaningful "truth," see above, note 2. On Harmodius and Aristogeiton, see above, notes 9–13, and see especially McGlew 1993, 152–53. The strength of popular sentiment in the events following the overthrow of Hippias is emphasized by Ober 1996, 34–52, who makes no mention, however, of the powerful symbolism of Harmodius and Aristogeiton.

52. Eponymous archon assigns poets and *choregoi:* Aristotle *Constitution* 56.3–5; Pickard-Cambridge 1968, 75–78, 86–93. The antiquity of the archon's responsibility for festivals probably explains the association of Hippocleides as archon (566/5) with the introduction of competitions to the Great Panathenaea; see Cadoux 1948, 104; Hignett 1952, 113. Note that the Peisistratids, known as superintendents of the sacrifices of the city (Thucydides 6.54.5), marshals of festal processions (Thucydides 1.20.2, 6.56–57; Aristotle *Constitution* 18.2–3), and patrons of poets (especially Hipparchus; see Herodotus 7.6.3; Aristotle *Constitution* 18.1; [Plato] *Hipparchus* 228b-29d; Knox 1978), were always concerned to have partisans in the archonships (Thucydides 6.54.6).

53. Phrynichus: see above, with note 16. *Proagon:* Pickard-Cambridge 1968, 67–68. Note the customs or laws restraining comic slander of the *demos:* Pseudo-Xenophon *Constitution* 2.18; discussed by Halliwell 1991; Atkinson 1992.

54. On the venue of the Dionysia, and other dramatic contests, see Pickard-Cambridge 1968, 57–101; Meier 1988/1993, 51–61. Connor's proposal (1989) to date the establishment of the City Dionysia as late as 501 is not impossible (see, e.g., Rosenbloom 1995, 120 n. 48), but in view of the manifest concern of the Peisistratids for such powerful features of communal identity as poetry and festivals (above, note 52), I consider it highly improbable; see also Herington 1985, 84–93. For appreciations of its significance to civic identity see Winkler 1985; Goldhill

1987/1990. On the competitive aspect of Attic drama, see R. Osborne 1993. On the display of tribute and of war-orphans, see Meiggs 1972, 290, 294, 433–34; Meier 1988/1993, 56–58.

55. For the relation of Aeschylus' *Eumenides,* 287–98, performed in 458, and the events leading up the battle of Tanagra, see Thucydides 1.102.4–108; cf. *Eumenides* 762–74, where Orestes appropriately curses any army that marches against Attica from the Peloponnese. On chronology, see Meritt, Wade-Gery, and McGregor 1950, 164–68, 171–73, 177. Although these authors discuss the *Eumenides* passage at 321, with n. 88, they do not associate it with these events, apparently because they are misled by *Phlegraian plaka,* line 295, into looking to Pellene in the Chalcidice (cf. Herodotus 7.123.1). But Pellene is not a *plax,* and the next line, ... *tagouchos hos aner episkopei,* makes clear that this plain was the domain of a *Tagos* (i.e., Thessaly; for the *Tagos* of Thessaly, see Xenophon *Hellenica* 6.1.8; for Orestes, "king" of Thessaly and Athenian ally at this time, see Thucydides 1.111.1); *Phlegrai* is thus an acceptable alternative to *Phleguai,* the people of *Phleguas,* a native Thessalian (cf. Pindar *Pythian* 3.8). Spartan ambassadors are attested at the Dionysia in 423, 421, and later: Thucydides 4.118.12, 5.20.1, 23.4.

56. Ion of Chios on Cimon: Plutarch *Pericles* 5.3–4, *Cimon* 9. Pericles' rhetorical style: Plutarch *Pericles* 8, 15; cf. Thucydides 2.65.9; Plato *Phaedrus* 269e-270a, *Symposium* 221c; Eupolis *Demes* fr. 102 *PCG* (94 Kock); other sources in Fornara 74. Aeschylus' style: Aristophanes *Frogs* 1058–60. Sophocles as general: Androtion *FGrHist* 324 F 38; Plutarch *Pericles* 8.5; as *hellenotamias: IG* I^3 269.36; on Sophocles' public career, see Jameson 1971.

57. Justin 4.4.1–2, translated by J.C. Yardley. The Catanian embassy followed the return of the Athenian expeditionary force after the Peace of Gela in 424, Thucydides 4.65. The Euripidean device of depicting suffering in beggar's rags is parodied at this time in Aristophanes *Acharnians* 393–490.

58. Plutarch *Nicias* 29.2–3, translated by B. Perrin.

59. Plutarch *Lysander* 15.2–3, translated by B. Perrin. On these circumstances, see below, chapter 8, with note 29.

60. The epitaph of Euripides attributed to Thucydides similarly expresses the Panhellenic appeal of this poet of Athens: "Though his bones lie in Macedon where his life was ended, the whole of Greece is the monument of Euripides; but his birthplace was Athens, the Greece of Greece *(patris d' Hellados Hellas, Athenai)* and giving much joy by his Muses, he hath the thanks for it of many men" (*Life of Euripides* 135W, translated by J.M. Edmonds *Elegy* II, 27; cf. *Palatine Anthology* 7.45; Athenaeus 5.187d). The growing taste for Attic drama in Sicily and southern Italy is evident in the frequent depiction of scenes from tragedy and comedy in vase-painting of the region beginning in the late fifth century following Attic prototypes; see Trendall and Webster 1971, 11–12; Trendall 1991; Taplin 1993.

61. The inception of state funerals at Athens is variously dated: after the battle of Plataea by Diodorus 11.33.3 (anachronistically, cf. Herodotus 9.85); upon the return of the slain from Drabescus in Thrace, ca. 464, by Pausanias 1.29.4 (favored by Jacoby 1944, 52); after the battle of Tanagra, in 458, by Plato *Menexenus* 242b-c. Gomme 1956, 94–100, is troubled by Jacoby's placement of the inception of a *patrios nomos* so late; Pritchett 1985, 112–24, supports Jacoby's conclusions; Clairmont 1983, 10–15, favors a date in the late 470s; other commentators avoid commitment

to a date: so Ostwald 1969, 175–76; Loraux 1981/1986, 28–31; Thomas 1989, 207–208; the problem is discussed further below, with note 66. On alternative burial practices, see Pritchett 1985, 249–51.

62. Thucydides 2.34 is the fundamental text describing the customary practices at state funerals. Clairmont 1983, 48–53, lists the headings attested on public casualty lists. Raubitschek 1943, 48 n. 102, has suggested that thetes were not named on the casualty lists; Bradeen 1964, 25 n. 15, opposed his suggestion, and Loraux 1981/1986, 34 n. 128, has concurred with Bradeen; Mattingly 1966/1996, 145, has concurred with Raubitschek; Raaflaub 1996, 156, expresses cautious support for the inclusive tendency evident in fifth-century democracy. While in no case is the question of the inclusion of thetes in casualty lists proven, the principle of inclusion is generally observable in a variety of indicators. Thucydides 2.34.4 notes the presence of citizens (*astoi*) and foreigners (*xenoi*) among those observing the funeral rites; so too Plato *Menexenus*, quoted below at note 64. Pausanias 1.29.7 reports the commemoration of slaves "who demonstrated their noble nature (*agathous... genesthai*), on behalf of their masters, in war," (possibly on the occasion of the battle of Arginusae). Lysias 2.66 records the inclusion of foreigners (*xenoi*) among those accorded public rites in 403. Finally, Pausanias 1.29 lists the graves of many allied and foreign troops along the same road as the graves of the Athenian war-dead; although they were formally honored in separate monuments, their juxtaposition suggests a form of inclusion in "Athenian" glory.

63. Philostratus *Sophists* 1.9.5 states that Gorgias delivered his epitaphios at Athens; see 1.9.2–4 and Diodorus 12.53.2–5, Plato *Greater Hippias* 282b-c, on his popularity at Athens. Fragments of Gorgias' speech survive, DK 82 B 5–6, translated by Kennedy in Sprague 1972, 48–49, and by Cole 1991, 71–72, who comments on its oddness to the modern ear. Loraux 1981/1986, 9, simply states that "Gorgias the Sophist and Lysias the metic were by definition excluded from the tribune of the Kerameikos," but she offers no evidence for this statement; again, modern notions of national pride seem to intrude. The funeral oration attributed to Lysias (the authenticity of which is doubted by some, e.g. Loraux, chiefly for this reason) is further evidence that distinguished foreigners, in this case a metic and honored supporter of democracy in the recent civil war, *could* deliver the oration (Plato *Phaedrus* grudgingly attests the high repute of Lysias; see below, chapter 12, page 298).

64. Quote: Plato *Menexenus* 235a-c, translated by Benjamin Jowett; "praise of Athenians to Athenians:" 235d, cf. Aristotle *Rhetoric* 1367b, 1415b; inferior orators: 235e-236a, where Antiphon is named.

65. Surviving funeral orations are listed by Loraux 1986, 8–9. Thomas 1989, 196–237, regards them as the chief repository for what may loosely be termed an "official version" of Athenian history. Kierdorf 1966, 97–100, 105, 109, studying the list of Athenian deeds represented in the funeral orations, suggests that they were conventional themes in rhetoric not limited to the funeral oration. Day 1980 describes the same body of traditions, and traces its transmission to Aelius Aristides in the second century CE (see below, note 72).

66. *Patrios nomos:* Thucydides 2.34.1. For scholarship, see note 61 above. *Hellenikos nomos:* Lysias 2.9; cf. *Panhellenon nomos* in Euripides *Suppliant Women* 671, and *agrapta k'asphale nomima theon* in Sophocles *Antigone* 454–55. The Athenians recovered the legendary Argive dead after negotiating with the Thebans, according to

Aeschylus' *Eleusinians,* or after defeating the Thebans in battle according to Euripides' *Suppliant Women;* see Plutarch *Theseus* 29.4–5. Euripides' *Suppliant Women* is widely recognized as a reflection of the problematic recovery of Athenian dead from the battle of Delium in 424 (cf. Thucydides 4.97); see Delebecque 1951, 203–24; J. H. Finley 1938/1967, 37; Collard 1972; Boegehold 1982, 151–53 and n. 8; Raaflaub 1992, 10; Bowie 1997, 45–56.

67. Recent proofs of ancient virtues: Marathon, in the speeches reported by Herodotus 9.27 and Thucydides 1.73; cf. Aristophanes *Acharnians* 692–701, *Thesmophoriazousae* 806; Salamis, in Thucydides 1.73–74, implicitly in 2.36, 6.83; cf. Aristophanes *Knights* 810–12 (where Paphlagon/Cleon likens his recent success at Pylos to the deeds of Themistocles), and *Wasps* 1075–90 (where deeds of Marathon meld with those of Salamis); overthrow of tyranny, in Herodotus 5.78, cf. 1.59, Aristophanes *Lysistrata* 614–35. All three proofs are mentioned seriatim in Aristophanes *Knights* 781–87. By the early fourth century, Lysias 2, *Funeral Oration* 18–53, shows the influence of historiography on this recitation of past and recent triumphs. Note that formal observances of the overthrow of tyranny, the victory at Marathon, and commemoration of war-dead were routine duties of a single official, the Polemarch, who was responsible for sacrifices to Artemis Agrotera vowed at Marathon, and funeral games for Athenian war dead and offerings to Harmodius and Aristogeiton: Aristotle *Constitution* 58.1–2.

68. Menestheus epigram: Aeschines 3.185; Plutarch *Cimon* 7. The fame of Athenians among warriors at Troy is noted in speeches reported by Herodotus 9.27 and, implicitly, by Thucydides 2.41, where the rejection of Homeric praise invites comparison.

69. The revolts of Boeotia, Megara, and Euboea were the occasion, in 446/5, of a campaign to Euboea led by Pericles, resulting in the expulsion of the Chalcidian *Hippobotai,* according to Plutarch *Pericles* 23.2. Herodotus 5.77 describes the events of 506 in much the same terms. Aelian *Miscellany* 6.1 refers to similar events and to the consequent distributions of Euboean land recorded in inscriptions in the Agora; the inscriptions in this instance were probably set up no earlier than 424/3; see Raubitschek 1943, 28–33, and see below, chapter 3 note 30. The year 424/3 saw the Athenian defeat at Delium on the Euripus (Thucydides 4.89–101) and a campaign on Euboea (Philochorus *FGrHist* 328 F 130); the funerals from these campaigns surely evoked memorials of past Athenian conquests and sacrifices; see above, note 66. Mattingly 1961b/1996, 64–66, notes the relationship among these events; see chapter 6 note 12 on the symbolic importance of Euboea to the Athenians. Epigram and spoils from Boeotians and Chalcidians: Herodotus 5.77; Pausanias 1.28.2; *IG* I^3 501 (= ML 15, Fornara 42); Raubitschek 1949, 168, 173. On Herodotus' tendency to recognize past deeds through visible monuments, see Immerwahr 1960.

70. Epigram for Eion, on a herm-base in the Agora: Aeschines 3.184; Plutarch *Cimon* 7; epigrams referring to Eurymedon and Cyprus: Diodorus 11.62.3 = Aristides *On the Four* 156 (260) = [Simonides] fr. 171 Edmonds *LG;* also [Simonides] fr. 131 and 132 Edmonds *LG;* Wade-Gery 1933, 71–95. Battle of Oenoe: Pausanias 1.15.1, cf. 10.10.4. Interpreting this otherwise unattested battle is a vexed issue; I favor the effort of Meiggs 1972, 469–72, to situate it early in the Argive-Athenian alliance (see above, note 55). The suggestion of Jeffery 1968 that it was a mythical

event has not won favor (see Hölscher 1973, 68–70), nor has the argument by Andrewes 1975 that Pausanias was "somehow wrongly informed" (see Pritchett 1980, 49–50). Francis and Vickers 1985 have offered an ingenious account of it as a preliminary to the battle of Marathon, pictured elsewhere in the stoa, a view that has found some approval (e.g., Castriota 1992, 78–79), and disapproval (e.g., Badian 1993, 98; I also find it unconvincing). Pritchett 1994, 1–25 offers the intriguing hypothesis that Pausanias' *Oinoe* is a copyist's error for *Orneai,* and relates the event to the capture of Orneae in 416/15 (Thucydides 6.7.2). Note Thucydides' criticism of the chronological imprecision of Hellanicus' Attic history, 1.97.2, and his own vague chronology for the half-century before the Peloponnesian War, 1.98–118, most recently discussed by Badian 1993, 73–107, and Pritchett 1995 and 1996, 40–91. Cimon is remembered in the contemporary elegaics of Archelaus, and, after his death, in the works of Melanthius, Ion, Cratinus, Eupolis, Stesimbrotus, and Critias: Plutarch *Cimon* 4, 9, 10, 15, 16. Wade-Gery 1933, 75, draws attention to *Palatine Anthology* 7.255, an epigram attributed to Aeschylus commemorating the anonymous dead of another otherwise unknown battle.

71. Where such terms occur (as *arche* and *hypekoos* in Thucydides 2.36.2 and 41.3), I would argue that they are indicative of an emerging shift in the rhetoric of empire, discernable by the 420s. In the absence of more than a phrase from an attested oration before 431 (Plutarch *Pericles* 8.6, from ca. 439), this is not directly demonstrable, although H. B. Mattingly's redating of several Athenian documents to this period (rather than earlier), based in part on the terminology of empire found in them, points to the same conclusion; see Appendix A. Loraux 1981/1986, 79–88, reviews these issues in the case of funeral orations under the heading, "The Terrain of a Strategy: From De Facto Hegemony to the Hegemonic Speech." Her discussion, ranging eventually into the retrospective views of empire from the fourth century, gives more place to the rhetoric of empire and hegemony than does the present discussion, which endeavors to characterize the antecedents to Pericles' funeral oration in Thucydides. Her summary remarks are consonant with the view advanced here: "Indeed, for the orator, the empire is merely the *sign* of a deeper, more durable reality, namely, the greatness of Athens" (85); "Was the funeral oration an imperialistic speech, then? There is no simple answer to this question" (87).

72. Quotes: Herodotus 1.1; Thucydides 1.1.3. It must be stressed that "the essentially oral traditions of public history" were preserved in epigraphic and literary forms, chiefly as poetry and eventually as rhetoric (see above, note 65, and below, note 80). Day 1980 has demonstrated that many traditional accounts originating in fifth-century Athens were still accessible to Aelius Aristides seven centuries later. We should not follow Day, however, and suppose that the absence, to us, of written evidence for these traditions prior to Aristides' day means that they were "transmitted from the fifth century B.C. to the second A.D. through oral or other non-literary media" (173). The studies of Thomas 1989 reveal how improbable this would be. In Herodotus' day written accounts of these sources were being compiled (see below, notes 73–74), and were the basis of Thucydides' account of events prior to the Peloponnesian War (see Westlake 1977/1989 and Lenardon 1981).

73. On the date of Herodotus' work, see below, with note 78. Hellanicus of Lesbos: Pearson 1939, 153–233; 1942, 1–26; Jacoby 1949, 68–69, 88–90; see further

below, chapter 3, with note 67. Archon-list: see below, chapter 3, with note 65. Hippias of Elis: Jacoby 1949, 58–59; Guthrie 1969/1971, 280–85. Antiochus of Syracuse: Pearson 1987, 11–18. Glaucus of Rhegium: Lesky 1963/1966, 231, 331. Ion of Chios: Lesky 1963/1966, 409–11; Dover 1986/1988. Stesimbrotus of Thasos: Lesky 1963/1966, 329; Tsakmakis 1995. Damastes of Sigeum: Lesky 1963/1966, 331. Charon of Lampsacus: Jacoby 1949, 100–101; Westlake 1977/1989, 12–13. Dionysius of Halicarnassus *On Thucydides* 5 provides important but not entirely reliable testimony to the relationship among many of these early historiographical writers; see Pritchett 1975, 50–57; Fornara 1983, 16–23.

74. See Jacoby 1949, 59: "in the last decades of the fifth century authors began to publish lists particularly of musical contests in order to write with the assistance of these lists the history of Greek music and poetry. If these writings are to be described by a general term, this must be History of Culture.... [Their authors were] foreign 'sophists' and historians, partly the same to whom we owe the first local chronicles (or local histories)." Flory 1980 notes the exceptional *size* of Herodotus' work (and Thucydides') in the company of the many other contemporary treatises. Fowler 1996 notes Herodotus' conversance with the works of many contemporary writers; Fehling 1971/1989 has observed the same phenomenon, but his radical explanation—that Herodotus made up his sources—is rightly rejected by Fowler and by Pritchett 1993. On Hecataeus, see above, with note 4; on Pherecydes, see now Toye 1997.

75. The influence of monuments and eulogy on Herodotus is discussed by Immerwahr 1960, 263–75. On the elusive significance of objects in Herodotus' narrative, see Dewald 1993. The influence of tragedy on Herodotus is discussed by Ostwald 1991, 143–48, who discusses the close relationship in expression between Sophocles and Herodotus; see also Jacoby 1913/1956, cols. 232–37; Morrison 1941, 11–14; Vidal-Naquet 1973/1988, 308–10. Although he does not explore the relationship to Herodotean narrative, Vernant 1969/1988 and 1970/1988 provides a relevant discussion of the role of semantic ambiguities in creating dramatic tension in tragedy, especially Sophoclean tragedy.

76. Phrynichus: Herodotus 6.21; see above, note 16. Rosenbloom 1993, 163–65, describes the shift from Phrynichus' depiction of "one's own" suffering to Aeschylus' and later poets' subtle use of the sufferings of "others" to comment on one's own condition. "The beginning of evils for Greeks and barbarians" (Herodotus 5.97.3) is a phrase with epic resonances (see Woodman 1988, 63 n. 186), and is of great importance to Herodotus' account of the origin of conflict from the Athenian perspective. The passage is noticed, e.g. by Lateiner 1989, 35, and Evans 1991, 30–33, but its significance is muted by the presence of several other levels of causal explanation in Herodotus' complex account. The degree of closure at the end of Herodotus' *Histories* is a matter of some debate; see Boedeker 1988; Lateiner 1989, 44–50.

77. Herodotus' use of beginnings and endings, and the thematic resonance of the story of Croesus and Solon's advice to him, is brought out by Lateiner 1989, 35–50. Lateiner also examines the important theme of boundaries and transgressions in Herodotus, 1985 and 1989, 127–44. Moles 1996 points out the relevance of Herodotus' narrative devices to the Athenians of the 420s. Quote: Thucydides 1.1.2, translated by R. Warner, with modification. The anecdote about Thucydides'

tears is told in Marcellinus 54. Hornblower 1987, 29, remarks that "we do not know whether the [anecdotal] tears were because he thought it was very good or very bad." Marcellinus' further remarks, however, clearly show that this story was taken as a compliment to the power of Herodotus' work, and as a motivation for Thucydides to turn *pros mathemata,* "to studies," presumably to penetrate more deeply into the tensions implicit in Herodotus' work.

78. The debate about the date of Herodotus' "publication" and his purposes in writing his *Histories* touches on virtually all aspects of his composition. Meyer 1899, 196–98, argued that Herodotus wrote as a champion of Athens and her policies under Pericles on the eve of the Peloponnesian War. Jacoby 1913/1956, 352–72, rightly pointed to problems with this view, but his own view, that Herodotus' main phase of writing belongs nearly two decades earlier, has entailed other difficulties. Fornara 1971a, 43–58, emphasized the improbability that a work shaped by the Athenian experience in the 440s would have been revised and published for an audience of the 420s; in 1971a, 1971b, and 1981 (responding to the critique of Cobet 1977), Fornara has provided the most forceful arguments for the appearance of Herodotus' work sometime between 425 and 415. I find Fornara's arguments largely convincing, and add further evidence in their favor in chapter 4. Jacoby's views remain influential (see, e.g., Sansone 1985a; Hornblower 1987, 18 n. 11; Brown 1988; Ostwald 1991), and Herodotus' *Histories* are still popularly accepted as a work of the middle of the fifth century (e.g., Bernal 1987, 98). But Fornara's arguments have increasingly encouraged scholars to look for Herodotus' motives for writing in light of Athens of the 420s; see Evans 1982, 15–18; Konstan 1987; Raaflaub 1987; Evans 1991, 9–40; Scanlon 1994, 144; Moles 1996.

79. Quotes: Thucydides 4.65.4, translated by R. Warner; Herodotus 1.33, translated by A. de Sélincourt. Those who shared the sentiments of wariness and weariness of war after 424, detected by Boegehold 1982, would have been those who listened sympathetically to Herodotus. See Scanlon 1994 for further discussion of Herodotean resonances in Thucydides.

80. Quotes: Thucydides 1.20.1, 21.1. Flory 1990, 194, perceptively identifies Thucydides' renunciation, in 1.22.4, of the pleasurable aspects of story-telling as a refusal to tell "stories which exaggerate and celebrate the glories of war. Such stories, if Thucydides had included them, would have given pleasure to listeners by encouraging them to feel flattered by praise of their own, their ancestors', or their cities' achievements and ideals." Thucydides was distancing himself, therefore, from rhetorical accounts like that which Plato describes in the *Menexenus,* quoted above, on page 37. For this and other reasons, I am opposed to the general preference for interpreting *logographoi* in Thucydides 1.21.1 as a (unique) reference to Ionian prose-writers like Hecataeus, Hellanicus, and Herodotus (e.g., Jacoby 1949, 81; Hornblower 1991, 58–59), and favor the translation, "speech-writers," well attested in Attic literature (e.g., Plato *Phaedrus* 257c; Aeschines 1.94; and especially Demosthenes 19.246, a passage that combines the same imputations of untrustworthiness to poets and *logographoi* that Thucydides makes). The point will be discussed further in chapter 12. On the relationship between Herodotus and Thucydides in the development of historiographical thought, see Momigliano 1966, 130–34, 214–16, and 1961/1990; Hornblower 1987, 13–33, and 1992. Collingwood 1946, 28–31, finds, in comparison to Herodotus, Thucydides' interpretive assumptions to be deeply

troubling, especially in the matter of his treatment of speeches. The question of speeches in Thucydides remains a central point of debate, and Collingwood's views are still influential (see Robinson 1985). One purpose of this book is to shake some of the assumptions that have underlain Collingwood's criticism of Thucydides.

CHAPTER TWO. THE ARISTOCRACY OF DEMOCRATIC ATHENS

1. Nixon and Price 1990 provide an illuminating quantitative survey of the revenues of empire. Kallet-Marx 1993, esp. 37–108, examines Thucydides' expression of the importance of the imperial revenue, and (1994) the place of revenues in Athenian rhetoric. See, in general, Meiggs 1972, 255–72; M.I. Finley 1978/1982; Kallet 1998.

2. The funeral oration of Pericles reported by Thucydides, esp. 2.36–41, is the *locus classicus* for the link between democracy and empire in fifth-century Athens. Pseudo-Xenophon *Constitution,* from a critical viewpoint, explains the same link. Plato *Gorgias* 515e, 518e-519a decries the acquisitive habits encouraged among the majority of citizens specifically by Pericles; cf. *Laws* 704e-705b. On the transformative effect of the Athenian democracy and empire specifically on less affluent Athenians, see Meier 1980/1990, 140–54; Sinclair 1988, 9–20; Raaflaub 1996 and 1998; Kallet 1998, 52–54. On the Solonic foundations of, and Peisistratid and Cleisthenic contributions to, the concept of Athenian citizenship, see Ostwald 1986, 5–28, and 1995; Frost 1990 and 1994.

3. For reasons briefly stated by Davies, in Lewis et al. 1992, 287–88, 302–303, the study of the private economy of fifth-century Athens is not as well developed as it is for the fourth century. French 1964, 107–62, describes the effects of empire on the Athenian economy, but places undue emphasis on the relationship between economy and imperial policy; for correctives, see M.I. Finley 1978/1982, 51–57. Hopper 1979, 47–189, and Davies 1981, 38–37 survey a variety of sources of income and wealth available in fifth- and fourth-century Athens. Casson 1984, 23–34, Millett 1991, and Cohen 1992 and 1993 examine banking, borrowing, and investment practices best known from fourth-century sources. R. Osborne 1991 and Hodkinson 1992 discuss agriculture and pastoralism as sources of cash. The following means of income are attested specifically for the fifth century. Land-holdings abroad, the purchase of agricultural futures *(epikarpia),* and probably grazing rights: Pritchett 1956, 310–11; Andocides 1.92; Lysias 32.6, 15; Plutarch *Pericles* 16.3–5. Control of mines abroad: Thucydides 1.100.2, 101.3, 4.105.1. Large-scale investments in mine slaves: Plutarch *Nicias* 4.2. Large-scale investments in skilled slaves: Pseudo-Xenophon *Constitution* 1.11, Thucydides 7.27.5, and Lysias 12.8, 19. Investment in tax-farming: *IG* I^3 52.7 (= ML 58, Fornara 119), *IG* I^3 133.24–25, Aristophanes *Frogs* 363, Andocides 1.133–35, and Plutarch *Alcibiades* 5.2–3. Mercantile loans, on a scale far above the average amounts attested for the fourth century: Lysias 32.6–7, 25. Pseudo-Xenophon *Constitution* 1.16–19, 3.1–3, attests the pervasive benefits for Athenians of their of imperial administration.

4. The debate over the funding of the Parthenon is reported by Plutarch *Pericles* 12.1–4, 14; see the recent discussions by Kallet-Marx 1989, and Kallet 1998, 7–12; Giovannini 1990 and 1997. On the symbolism of the Parthenon, see Meiggs 1963/1974; Pollitt 1972, 78–95; Castriota 1992, 134–38. On Thucydides son of

Melesias and his rivalry with Pericles, see Wade-Gery 1932/1958; more recent discussions have seen the ideological divide of the 450s and 440s described by Plutarch *Pericles* 11 as an anachronistic retrojection of the divide beginning to appear in the 430s, fully evident in the 420s: Frost 1964; Andrewes 1978, 1–5; Krentz 1984a; Fornara and Samons 1991, 29–35.

5. Ostwald 1986, 199–290, emphasizing different features, identifies many of the same characteristics of the ideological split that developed at Athens in what he characterizes as "the polarization of the 420s." Elements of the polarization of the 420s have also been examined by Connor 1971; Carter 1986; Strauss 1993; Bourriot 1995.

6. It is noteworthy that *aristokratia,* like *demokratia,* is a term whose attested usage goes back no further than the 420s (on *demokratia,* see chapter 1, note 8). See Graham and Forsythe 1984 for an excellent discussion of the occurrence of the term *aristokratia* in Thucydides 3.82.8. Like *demokratia,* the term had an earlier history attested in the bestowal of personal names at Athens: Aristocrates son of Scellias, born probably in the 470s (the evidence cited by Davies 1971, 56, for a homonymous grandfather is not persuasive). Aristophanes *Birds* 126 puns on the political implications of his name.

7. Plato's family connections and property are traced by Davies 1971, 329–35; see also Diogenes Laertius 3.1–3. The opening of the poem for Glaucon and Adeimantus, possibly by Critias, is quoted in *Republic* 368a; the distinctions of Critias and Pyrilampes are mentioned in *Charmides* 157e-158a; for Critias see also *Timaeus* 20e; for Pyrilampes and Demus, see also Plutarch *Pericles* 13.10, and Lysias 19.25; for Antiphon son of Pyrilampes, see Plato *Parmenides* 126b-c. For a definition of nobility as ancestral reputation and wealth, see Aristotle *Politics* 1294a21–22, 1301b2–3.

8. The testimonia on Charmides are sorted out by Davies 1971, 330–31; see Plato *Charmides,* where the elusive definition of *sophrosyne* is the object of the dialogue; see Xenophon *Memorabilia* 3.7 on Charmides as a man of high repute; on *sophrosyne* see also North 1966; Donlan 1980, 90–91, 105, 138, 148–50.

9. The nature of *eugeneia* in aristocratic perceptions of fifth-century Athens is discussed by Donlan 1973a. On *arete* in general, see Donlan 1980. The concern of the sophists with these issues is discussed below, in chapter 3. The relationship of these issues to Plato's early Socratic dialogues is surveyed by Irwin 1992, esp. 58–69, 73–78, and Penner 1992.

10. Poetic fragments by Critias: DK 88 B 1–29, translated by D.N. Levin in Sprague 1972, 249–61; see also Edmonds *Elegy* I, 484–93; Plutarch *Cimon* 10.5, *Alcibiades* 33.1; Athenaeus 184d. Testimonia and poetic fragments attributed to Plato: Edmonds *Elegy* II, 2–11. The reciprocal benefit of well-aimed praise is described by Plato *Lysis* 205a-e; Pindar praises praise: *Olympian* 7.7–12, *Pythian* 1.42–45, *Isthmian* 4.37–45.

11. Xenophon son of Gryllus was born ca. 430–425: Delebecque 1957, 24; Anderson 1974, 9–10. Plato and Socrates: Aelian *Miscellany* 2.30; Diogenes Laertius 3.5.

12. Bourriot 1995 surveys *kalokagathia* in detail, affirming the appearance of the term in the 420s; see also Donlan 1973b. Aristocratic ideology and terminology among the Athenian elite in the fifth century are more generally discussed by Donlan 1973a and 1980, 113–74; Carter 1986, 1–25.

13. Morris 1992, 128–49, discusses the "end of restraint" in burial practices. The renewed production of funerary reliefs after 430 is noticed as an unexplained phenomenon by Ridgway 1981, 129; examples are discussed and illustrated by Ridgway, 144–48; catalogued by Vedder 1985.

14. "Homeric" burial: Morris 1992, 132–34.

15. Potidaea campaign: Thucydides 1.56–65, 2.58, 70; "best" hoplites chosen: Isocrates 16.29. Adeimantus and Athenian animosity against Corinth: Herodotus 8.94; see chapter 1, with note 46; on Aristeus, see also Thucydides 2.67. Rate of pay of soldiers at Potidaea: Thucydides 3.17; the authenticity of this passage has been questioned by Steup, Smith, Busolt, and others, but is defended by, among others, Gomme 1956, 272–77; Pritchett 1971, 14–16; Hornblower 1991, 400–402; Kallet-Marx 1993, 130–34; it is accepted here. Comparison of attested rates of military: Pritchett 1971, 14–28. Expense of Potidaea campaign: Thucydides 2.13.3, 31.2, 70.2, 6.31.2. The overall cost, 2000 talents (2.70.2), is coupled with the cost of the Periclean building program, specifically the Propylaea (2.13.3); Diodorus 12.40.2 reports a total figure of 4000 talents spent for both projects; Kallet 1998, 48, regards 2000 as a plausible figure for the entire Periclean building program. The nine-month siege of Samos in 440/39, costing over 1400 talents (references in Kallet-Marx 1993, 122) may have involved a similarly high rate of pay, although the expense was also due to the greater number of ships engaged and lost in that campaign.

16. Although reference to news from Potidaea is made in the *Charmides,* Alcibiades' exploits are described elsewhere: Plato *Symposium* 220d-e; Isocrates 16.29; Plutarch *Alcibiades* 7.2–3.

17. Dueling instructors: Plato *Laches* 178a-184c; *Euthydemus* 271a-273e. On winners of *aristeia* from the Persian wars and earlier, remembered by Herodotus in the 420s, see chapter 1, with notes 23 and 24. Quote: Xenophon *Symposium* 3.5. Nicias, father of Niceratus, is one of the chief interlocutors in the *Laches.*

18. On the standard hoplite of the Peloponnesian War era, see Anderson 1970, 13–42. Aristophanes on arms-dealers and martial poetry: *Peace* 1208–1304.

19. Quote: Thucydides 6.31.1, 3–4, translated by R. Warner, with modifications.

20. The death of Lamachus: Thucydides 6.101.6; Plutarch *Nicias* 18.2–3, translated by Ian Scott-Kilvert. Philistus: Plutarch *Nicias* 19.5; Pearson 1987, 28; as a young man in Syracuse at the time, Philistus' account was probably influenced chiefly by how the story of the encounter was told among the youthful aristocrats of Syracuse. While Lamachus was alive, Aristophanes made jest of his striking appearance and heroic demeanor: *Acharnians* 566–98, 1071–1142, 1174–1227; after he was dead, his Homer-inspired heroism was recalled with approval: *Frogs* 1039.

21. Lamachus' character: Plutarch *Alcibiades* 18.1; see also note 20 above. Tydeus son of Lamachus (*PA* 13884) was general in 404: Xenophon *Hellenica* 2.1.16, 26. It is noteworthy that the spokesman for the boys' chorus with its martial fixation, depicted by Aristophanes *Peace* 1289–94, is identified as the son of Lamachus. Tydeus was probably also the name of the son of the foremost Homerist of this era, Ion of Chios; see Thucydides 8.38.3 and Dover 1986/1988, 11.

22. Sophanes of Decelea: Herodotus 6.92, 9.73–75; his grave: Pausanias 1.29.5. Pythion of Megara: *IG* I^2 1085 (= ML 51, Fornara 101). Tellus: Herodotus 1.30; the state burial *(demosiei)* given to Tellus, according to Herodotus, was probably an

anachronistic projection of fifth-century Athenian customs back to a seventh- or sixth-century event, rather than the earliest instance of state burial, as Clairmont 1983, 8, 11, suggests.

23. On liturgies, their costs, and the evidence for Athenian wealth, see Davies 1967, 1971, and 1981; Gabrielsen 1994; see also Pseudo-Xenophon *Constitution* 1.13, 2.9. *Dynatoi, chrestoi, plousioi,* and other such terms of social approbation are well represented in Pseudo-Xenophon, discussed further below, in chapter 3.

24. Quote: Isocrates 15, *Antidosis* 159–60. Thucydides 2.67.4 and 3.32.1 attests the increased hazards of war for maritime trade; 7.27–28 comments on the great increase in financial hardship at Athens after 413. Aristophanes *Clouds* depicts a property-owner of the 420s who has let his commitments to the trappings of aristocracy exceed his means. On the financial economy of fifth-century Athens, see above, note 3. Davies 1981, 114–22, discusses the changing composition of the "political class" based on the fluidity of wealth. *Euporoi* is used by Demosthenes 1.28 and by Aristotle *Politics* 1291a as a synonym for the liturgical class; earlier, the cognate *aporos,* "without means," is more commonly attested as a plea of the moderately well-to-do (e.g., by the son of Alcibiades) when appealing to the mercies of a jury, Isocrates 16.47; cf. Lysias 31.12. On the practices of obscuring personal income, see Gabrielsen 1986.

25. Examples of Plato's acknowledgment of, and cynicism about, success in money-making: *Apology* 19e-20c, *Gorgias* 452b-e, *Protagoras* 310d-311e, *Hippias* 1 282b-283d, *Lysis* 211e, *Meno* 90a, *Republic* 330a-c; cf. Xenophon *Oeconomicus* 1.13–14. Plato's critique of money-making is much sharper farther along in the *Republic,* 562b, 589d-590a (e.g., and in his later works [e.g., *Laws* 704d-705b, 743d]), perhaps reflecting the transition from Socratic to Platonic thought.

26. On trierarchies see Gabrielsen 1994 and further references below, note 32.

27. Pride in festival liturgies: Antiphon 6.11–14; [Andocides] 4.42; Isocrates 16.35; Lysias 21.1–5; Demosthenes 21. R. Osborne 1993 discusses the competitive aspect especially of dramatic festivals; further scholarship on festival liturgies is cited below, note 33.

28. On Nicias: Plutarch *Nicias* 3–4.1; Plato *Gorgias* 472a. Nicias' *theoria* to Delos was presumably on the occasion of the purification of Delos in 426/5: Thucydides 3.104; Diodorus 12.58.6–7. On Thucydides' judgment of Nicias, 7.86.5, Dover, in Gomme et al. 1970, 461–64, argues for a different translation of *dia ten pasan es areten nenomismenen epitedeusin* from that offered here. His suggested rendering, "'through his practice all observed into goodness,' i.e. 'because he had ordered his whole life by high moral standards,'" unnecessarily avoids the usual meaning of *nenomismenen,* "commonly regarded," which I take in agreement with *areten* and render, "earning a reputation for *arete.*" *Nenomismenen,* as Dover recognizes, "suggests the practice of a whole society rather than of an individual." This has important implications for Thucydides' moral standpoint, which, I believe, is to approve of the intent of Nicias' piety while recognizing that its form was dictated (too unimaginatively, as it turned out) by customary practice.

29. Quote: Thucydides 6.16.1–4, translated by R. Crawley.

30. Alcibiades and Taureas: [Andocides] 4.20–21; Demosthenes 21.147; cf. Aeschines 1, *Against Timarchus.* Alcibiades was in the habit of administering such blows, according to Plutarch *Alcibiades* 8.1. Such behavior was evidently tolerated at

the time; cf. Pseudo-Xenophon *Constitution* 1.10 on the arrogance, typical to Spartans, of striking inferiors. Later such behavior became a hallmark of outrage: so Isocrates 20.2–11; cf. Plato *Gorgias* 486c, 508d, 527a. Kinship of Taureas: Andocides 1.47.

31. Praise of Alcibiades by his son: Isocrates 16.33. Alcibiades' triumph at Olympia is praised in a poem attributed to Euripides, quoted by Plutarch *Alcibiades* 11 and *Demosthenes* 1.1; see also Thucydides 6.16.2, quoted above, on page 59; Isocrates 16.32–34; [Andocides] 4.26–31; Diodorus 13.74.3–4; Plutarch *Alcibiades* 12. On the dispute with Teisias over the team of horses, see further below, chapter 4 with note 61 and chapter 7, note 10. Public hospitality was due to Alcibiades as a Panhellenic victor by the terms stipulated in *IG* I^3 131, 11–17; cf. [Andocides] 4.31. Antisthenes, quoted by Athenaeus 534d-e, says that Alcibiades dedicated a painting depicting himself seated in the lap of the personification of Nemea and another of himself crowned by the personifications Pythias and Olympias; it is perhaps most likely that these dedications were made during the period of Alcibiades' triumphal return in 408 (below, chapter 6). Both Plutarch *Alcibiades* 16.5 and Pausanias 1.22.7 mention only the painting commemorating Alcibiades at Nemea (had Teisias' suit challenging the Olympic victory eventually prevailed?), and Pausanias locates it in what is now known as the *pinakotheke* of the Propylaea. On the *pinakotheke* as a dining room, see Travlos 1971, 482 and 491.

32. Gabrielsen 1994, 74 and 176–77, following Kalinka, plausibly suggests that the 400 trierarchs appointed annually, according to Pseudo-Xenophon *Constitution* 3.4, was the number appointed before adjudication of exemptions reduced the number actually available for service each year to close to 300. Thucydides 3.17.2 gives 250 as the number of ships in service in 428 (on this passage, see note 15 above). Exemptions from trierarchic service and the introduction of the syntrierarchy are discussed by Gabrielsen 1994, 85–102, 173–82. Gabrielsen's estimate of the size of the trierarchic class is given on pages 178–80; Davies 1981, 15–17, argues for a minimalist figure of 400. Exemptions waived in the last decade of the Peloponnesian War: Xenophon *Hellenica* 1.6.24; Lysias 21.1–5; Isaeus 5.41, 7.38. The maximum number of Athenian ships in service at one time after 412 is 180 at Aegospotami in 405: Xenophon *Hellenica* 2.1.20; Diodorus 13.105.1; it is probable that some of these ships were provided by allies, cf. Xenophon *Hellenica* 1.6.24–25; Gabrielsen 1994, 126–27.

33. On festival liturgies, see Pickard-Cambridge 1968; Davies 1967, 1971, xx-xxiv, xxix-xxx, and 1981, 15–28; Rhodes 1982, 1–5; Gabrielsen 1994, 85; Kallet 1998, 54–58. Pseudo-Xenophon *Constitution* 1.13, 3.4; Aristotle *Constitution* 56.3–5; see also note 27 above.

34. Inheritance: Strauss 1993, 66–74. Inheritability of liturgical status, and its largely voluntary nature: Gabrielsen 1994, esp. 43–67. Liturgical estates vulnerable to fragmentation: Davies 1981, 73–87. Eponymous archon concerned with estates: Aristotle *Constitution* 56.6–7. Calculation of the proportion of liturgists over the age of 50: M.H. Hansen 1985, table p. 12.

35. Athenian cavalry service: Bugh 1988, 39–119. Spence 1993, 180–210, discusses social attitudes associated with cavalry service. Worley 1994, 68–74, estimates that the number of Athenians included from the wealthiest through the cavalry class may have amounted to 4000.

36. Property qualifications for office: Pseudo-Xenophon *Constitution* 1.3; Aristotle *Constitution* 7.3–4, 26.2, 55.3; Sinclair 1988, 106–107. Davies 1981, 122–31, discusses the correlation between wealth and office-holding. Two speeches by Lysias, 16 and 31, argue the suitability of candidates for membership on the Council, and both claim, on slight evidence, that the candidates could, if they chose, qualify as either liturgists or cavalrymen; see Davies 1981, 24–27, on the competitive incentive, specifically to perform festival liturgies, and Gabrielsen 1994, 43–102, 220–21, on ambition and peer-pressure as a factor in trierarchic service. The parody of Aristophanes' *Clouds* is based on the tension between aspirations and tenuous means.

37. Estimates of the number of adult male citizens in 431 between 40,000 and 50,000: Gomme 1933, esp. chart p. 26; Patterson 1981, 68–71; Strauss 1986, 70–81; Sinclair 1988, 9–10, 223; about 50,000: Thompson 1964; as much as 50,000–60,000: M.H. Hansen 1982 and 1988, 14–28. Morris 1992, 135, suggests that, "at a guess... around 10% of the population" were able to display monuments on their family tombs by the time the trend beginning in the 420s reached its peak in the fourth century. On the unparalleled size of the Athenian navy: Herodotus 7.161; Thucydides 1.33.1, 2.62.2, 3.17.1–2. On the exceptional number of festivals at Athens: Pseudo-Xenophon *Constitution* 3.2, 4; Thucydides 2.38.1; Isocrates 4.43–46; cf. Athenian piety measured in exceptional numbers of shrines and altars: Pausanias 1.17.1, 24.3; *Acts of the Apostles* 17.16–23; see also Mikalson 1975. Comparisons of Athenian cavalry numbers to other states: Xenophon *Cavalry Commander* 7.1; Spence 1993, 1–33; Worley 1994, 59–122, esp. 81. Cf. also the praise of various aristocratic qualities at Athens: Plato *Protagoras* 337c-e; Xenophon *Memorabilia* 3.3.12–13, 5.3. *En Athenais panta kala:* Plutarch *Moralia* 236b-c.

CHAPTER THREE. SERVANTS OF THE ATHENIAN DEMOCRACY

1. On the fifth-century population of Athens, see chapter 2 note 37. On the economic benefits of empire to poorer Athenians, see chapter 2 note 2. Markle 1985 discusses the economic and political effects of Athenian jury pay. Laborers, craftsmen, or tradesmen included all *thetes* and many *zeugitai,* including those with some agricultural land but not earning their sole livelihood as farmers. Quantifying the sources of livelihood especially for the poorer majority of the populace is notoriously difficult (see, e.g., Jameson 1977–1978). Justification for the distinction made here comes from Xenophon *Oeconomicus* 6.6–7 (cf. 4.3, 5.7, 6.10), where a hypothetical division of "farmers" from "craftsmen" is said to correspond to the votes of those who would defend the countryside and those who would be content to see it overrun; since the latter describes the course taken by the Athenians under Pericles in 431 and thereafter, Xenophon's model presumably derives from the experience that the majority of voters in late-fifth century Athens identified themselves more with the "craftsmen." Public pay augmented by war: Aristotle *Constitution* 24.3; Aristophanes *Acharnians* 600–603, *Wasps* 698–724. On the blurring of the distinction between *thetes* and *zeugitai,* see Aristotle *Constitution* 7.3–4, 26.2; Pseudo-Xenophon *Constitution* 1.2–4; *IG* I^3 46.43–46 (= ML 49.39–42, Fornara 100); Jones 1957, 7, 79–81, 166; Rhodes 1981, 142–46; Meier 1980/1990, 142–54.

2. Thucydides 2.37.1, a highly polemic passage in the Periclean funeral oration that includes a conspicuous definition of *demokratia,* commends Athenian equality

before law *(metesti de kata tous nomous... pasi to ison)*, and repudiates those who would "admire the laws of neighboring states." The avoidance of the term *isonomia* itself, remarked by Ostwald 1969, 114 and n. 3, does not mean that Pericles does not here advocate democratic *isonomia.* Rather, as the consummate politician, he prefers circumlocutions that allow both the enthusiasts of *isonomia* and the aristocratic advocates of *protimia ap' aretes* to find something to embrace in the ideal of democracy. *Isonomia* as a catchword for democracy in the 420s: Thucydides 3.82.8; Herodotus 3.80.6; cf. Euripides *Suppliant Women* 430–41. The singular nature of Athenian citizenship, by comparison with Greek and Carthaginian oligarchies, is clear from the discussion of Aristotle *Politics* 1269a-78a, esp. 1274a, 1275b-76a, 1277b-78a; see also Frost 1994; Raaflaub 1994 and 1998. Athenian economy and the working class: Pseudo-Xenophon *Constitution* 1.17, 19–20; Aristotle *Constitution* 24; Plutarch *Pericles* 12; see also Jones 1957, 3–20; M.I. Finley 1978/1982; Sinclair 1988, 117–18, 226–27.

3. Quote: Pseudo-Xenophon (commonly referred to as the "Old Oligarch") *Constitution* 1.2. The date of this treatise is much discussed; I side with the majority who place it in the 420s: see Ostwald 1969, 82; Connor 1971, 207–209; de Ste. Croix 1972, 307–10. Lévy 1976, 273–75 places it no earlier than 431. Fornara and Samons 1991, 64–65 n. 86, prefer a date in the 440s, and cite further scholarship for both early and late dates.

4. Illegitimacy is implicit in the phrase "to have more," *pleon echein* (Pseudo-Xenophon *Constitution* 1.2), which is cognate with the term *pleonexia,* usually translated "greediness," or "seeking undue advantage." See Ehrenberg 1947, 49–50, on the relationship between Athenian *pleonexia* and *polypragmosyne. Poneroi* is used throughout Pseudo-Xenophon; *ochlos* 2.10; *cheirous* 1.4, 3.10; *mainomenos anthropos* 1.9; *apaideusia* 1.5; *amathia* 1.5, 7. Access to offices and exercise of power by the poor and the *demos* is noted at 1.2–9, 13–16, 19–20, 2.17, 3.1–7, 13.

5. Quote: Pseudo-Xenophon *Constitution* 1.10–12, translated by G.W. Bowersock, with modifications. "Acknowledged folly": Thucydides 6.89.6.

6. Quote: Pseudo-Xenophon *Constitution* 1.8, translated by G.W. Bowersock, with modifications; cf. Cleon's critique of those Athenians who consider themselves "wiser *(sophoteroi)* than the laws," Thucydides 3.37.3–4. On the use of *eunomia* and *kakonomia* by Pseudo-Xenophon, see Ostwald 1969, 82–85. Both terms are evocative of Spartan experience (cf. Herodotus 1.65.2; Thucydides 1.18.1) and as such they refer more to "good/bad customs" than to "good/bad statutes." With this implicit comparison in mind, I am not fully persuaded by Ostwald's insistence that this passage refers "unambiguously" to the statutory basis of a partisan "constitutional programme." Pseudo-Xenophon avoids reference to specific statutes, and describes rather the various manifestations of a "badly-ordered," though effectively self-serving, society.

7. Quote: Pseudo-Xenophon *Constitution* 1.5.

8. On *xenia,* guest-friendship, see Herman 1987. On *xenia* as an instrument of Spartan policy, see Cartledge 1987a, 139–59, 242–66.

9. On *proxenia* in fifth-century Athens, see Schuller 1974, 99–100; Walbank 1978. Most of the inscriptions studied by Walbank date after 431, and some of those regarded by him as earlier than 431 are plausibly dated to the 420s by Mattingly 1963/1996, 94–97, and 1992, 137–38. *Xenia,* as state-sponsored hospitality to visit-

ing foreign dignitaries, is not certainly attested before 431 when Mattingly's dates are accepted (see Appendix A); for a review of decrees inviting foreigners to *xenia,* see A.S. Henry 1983.

10. Pericles and Archidamus: Thucydides 2.13.1. Nicias and Pleistoanax: Thucydides 5.16.1; Plutarch *Nicias* 9.3–10.3; Lysias 18.10. Alcibiades and the Argives: Thucydides 5.43–47, 53, 55.4–56.3, 61.2, 76.3, 6.61.3; Plutarch *Alcibiades* 14.3, 15.1, 23.1.

11. On tribute assessments, see below, notes 28–30. Athenian assistance to foreign representatives: cf. attested speeches by Antiphon, *On the Tribute of Lindos* and *On the Tribute of Samothrace;* Pseudo-Xenophon *Constitution* 1.14. Thucydides son of Melesias lost popular support in his rivalry with Pericles (chapter 2 note 4) in large part because he identified himself too closely with the interests of tribute-paying allies, while Pericles spoke for the Athenian *demos.*

12. Thucydides 3.2.3; Aristotle *Politics* 1304a.

13. Quote: Thucydides 3.36.5, translated by R. Warner (emphasis added).

14. Fate of Paches: Plutarch *Nicias* 6.1–2; *Aristides* 26.3; cf. Aristophanes *Knights* 832–35, *Wasps* 522–23. Rape of Hellanis and Lamaxis: Agathias, in Palatine Anthology 7.614. Most commentators (e.g., Grote 1862, 4.366–67; Beloch 1884, 33 n. 1; Busolt 1904, 3:2.1034; Adcock 1927, 218 n. 3; Gomme 1956, 332; Connor 1971, 139–40; Kagan 1974, 167) accept the account of Paches' suicide, but, Grote and Gomme excepted, hesitate to accept the story of Hellanis and Lamaxis. Westlake 1975/1989, unconvincingly, considers the whole account of Paches' suicide to be spurious. Division of Mytilenean land: Thucydides 3.50; Antiphon 5, *On the Murder of Herodes,* 76–77. Some measure of official Athenian goodwill toward the Mytileneans spared in 427 is indicated by *IG* I^3 66 (= Tod 63); see Meiggs 1972, 317. Beloch 1884, 33, makes the plausible suggestion that Cleon was involved in the prosecution of Paches.

15. Surveys of Athenian imperial administration (e.g., Meiggs 1972, 220–33; Schuller 1974, 48–54; M.I. Finley 1978/1982) focus on the impact of legal sanctions on subject-allies, but nearly overlook their more direct impact on Athenian officials, on which, see the regulations for Miletus: *IG* I^3 21 (= Fornara 92), formerly dated to 450/49 but more probably to be placed in 426/5; the decree of Cleonymus of 426: *IG* I^3 68 (= ML 68, Fornara 133); the second Methone decree of 426: *IG* I^3 61.51–56 (= ML 65, Fornara 128); the decree of Thudippus of 425/4: *IG* I^3 71 (= ML 69, Fornara 136); the decree of Cleinias: *IG* I^3 34 (= ML 46, Fornara 98), formerly dated to 447 but more probably to be placed in 425/4 or later; the coinage decree: *IG* I^3 1453 (= ML 45, Fornara 97), formerly placed in the 440s but more probably to be placed in 425/4 or later. On the redating of these decrees by H.B. Mattingly and others, see Appendix A. Although he did not accept Mattingly's dates, Lewis 1974 drew attention to the language of "entrenchment clauses" that first appears in them. Pseudo-Xenophon *Constitution* 3.1–6 explains why it is difficult for interested parties to get a hearing before the Athenian *demos.* Carter 1986, 26–51, 99–130, discusses resentment of the invasive influence of the *demos* on members of the aristocracy in the government of the empire, with examples drawn chiefly from the 420s and later.

16. Because sycophants and their activities are noticed only to disapprove of them, the nature of their vexatious litigation is difficult to assess objectively; see the

contrasting views of R. Osborne 1990 and Harvey 1990. Sycophants are frequently reviled, especially for preying upon the wealthy or the oligarchically inclined among Athenian subject-allies: Pseudo-Xenophon *Constitution* 1.14; Aristophanes, *Wasps* 1094–97, *Birds* 1422–35. The comic scenes of sycophants preying on Nicias (below, note 17) suggest a certain level of social familiarity existed between sycophants and their prey. On sycophants and *ho boulomenos,* see MacDowell 1978, 62–66; Ostwald 1986, 209–11; note the concentration of testimonia in the 420s and later (the inscriptions cited by Ostwald are plausibly placed in the 420s, see Appendix A).

17. Nicias and the sycophants: Plutarch *Nicias* 4.3–4, quoting from a comedy by Telecleides; Plutarch 4.5–6 quotes passages of comedies by Eupolis, Aristophanes, and Phrynichus (the comic poet) to the effect that Nicias was easily intimidated by the threats of demagogues like Cleon and Hyperbolus. Nicias fears the examples of Paches, among others: Plutarch *Nicias* 6.1–2.

18. Execution of the Hellenotamiae: Antiphon 5.69–71, translated by K.J. Maidment, with modifications; see Meiggs 1972, 246.

19. Quote: Pseudo-Xenophon *Constitution* 2.19–20, translated by G.W. Bowersock, with modifications.

20. Pericles as "Olympian" and "Thunderer": Plutarch *Pericles* 8.2–3; as "Lord": Eupolis *Demes* fr. 104 *PCG* (= 100 Kock), cf. fr. 384 *PCG* (= 117 Kock); on Pericles as an effective orator, see above, chapter 1 note 56. Quote: Thucydides 2.65.9, translated by R. Warner; cf. Plutarch *Pericles* 9; Plato *Gorgias* 515c-519b. Pericles had "given the people what was theirs": Aristotle *Constitution* 27.4; cf. Aristophanes *Wasps* 682–85; Andocides 2.17; Plutarch *Pericles* 9, 12–14. *Demagogos* is first attested, in the form *demagogia,* in Aristophanes *Knights* 191, quoted on page 73 at note 23; Thucydides 4.21.3 calls Cleon *aner demagogos* in the context of the events of 425. On the terminology and politics associated with demagogues beginning in the 420s, see Connor 1971, 87–136.

21. Cleon's family and wealth are discussed by Davies 1971, 318–20; see also Connor 1971, 91–198, on his social standing. Cleon was responsible for the capture of the Spartans on Sphacteria in 425, and for negotiations with Sparta: Thucydides 4.21–22, 27–41; Plutarch *Nicias* 7–8; cf. Theopompus *FGrHist* 115 F 92, where Cleon represents the public interest in *xenia.* Cleon died in battle at Amphipolis: Thucydides 5.2–10. Aristophanes *Wasps* 1220–64 jests at Cleon in refined company, but with the clear implication that he was not out of place there.

22. Cleon described unflatteringly: Thucydides 3.36.6, cf. 4.21.2; Aristophanes *Wasps* 596, cf. *Knights* 136–37. Quote: Aristotle *Constitution* 28.3, translated by von Fritz and Kapp, with modifications; cf. Plutarch *Nicias* 8.3.

23. Quote: Aristophanes *Knights* 191–93.

24. Quote: Aristophanes, *Knights* 773–76. Cleon's concern to wring public money out of private individuals renders his demagoguery at times indistinguishable from sycophancy, as in Aristophanes *Knights* 435–43.

25. On the "first" *eisphora* in 428, see Thucydides 3.19.1. Thomsen 1964, esp. 147–93, is the fundamental study of this institution. Most commentators agree that the natural meaning of this passage is that this was the first *eisphora* ever levied by the Athenians (as argued by Mattingly 1968/1996, 216–17; Sealey 1984, 77–80; Kallet-Marx 1993, 134–36; accepted without comment by Gabrielsen 1994, 116; Ostwald 1995, 368). Others have argued that this was merely the first *eisphora* of the

Peloponnesian War (so, e.g., Gomme 1956, 278–79; Thomsen 1964, 139–46; Meiggs 1972, 519–20, with citations of earlier scholarship), or the first time as much as 200 talents was levied by an *eisphora* (J. G. Griffith 1977). The reason for adding unattested qualifications to Thucydides' statement has been the assumption that the *eisphora* was already an established practice, since it is attested in the second of the two Callias decrees, *IG* I^3 52, A & B (= ML 58, Fornara 119), long believed by most scholars to date to 434/3. Mattingly 1964, 1968/1996, 215–25, and 1975/1996, 353–60, and Fornara 1970b have argued for later dates of 422/1 and 418/7 respectively. The question has been closely examined by Kallet-Marx 1989, who finds little basis for the 434/3 date, and plausibly argues that the two decrees were passed on different occasions, and that the second decree could well be as late as 418/7 (see esp. 112–13 n. 84). A different form of taxation existed in the 6th century, probably connected to the Solonian census classes and administered by the *prytaneis* of the *naukraroi;* see Thomsen 1964, 14–23, 119–46, and more recently Gabrielsen 1994, 19–24; Ostwald 1995.

26. Quote: Aristophanes *Knights* 923–26. On the voluntary nature of liturgical service, and on property qualifications for office-holding, see the references in chapter 2 note 36 above. Although the *lêxiarchika grammateia* have been regarded as registers of all citizens (such is implied in the problematic "Themistocles decree," ML 23.29–30, Fornara 55), the earliest secure attestation, in *IG* I^3 138.6 of the third quarter of the fifth century, indicates that members of the lowest census class of *thetes* were not included. Suda, s.v., indicates that these were lists only of those eligible to hold office; since they were kept by demes, they would seem to be lists based on locally recorded property holdings. Other interpretations are possible, however, and scholarship on this debate is inconclusive; see Habicht 1961, 5–6; Jameson 1963, 399–400; Whitehead 1986, 35 n. 130; Ostwald 1995, 377–78, with further references.

27. Aristophanes *Knights* 923–26 and Lysias 20.23 demonstrate that liability to pay *eisphorai* could be dodged or contested; Antiphon *First Tetralogy* 2.12, 3.8 exemplifies a wealthy Athenian who has paid "many *eisphorai*" not later than the 410s. *Adeia* for proposals of *eisphorai* and access to other funds: *IG* I^3 52 B15–19 (= ML 58, Fornara 119, see above, note 25); *IG* I^3 370.15, 28, 30, 33, 63 (= ML 77, Fornara 144); cf. Thucydides 2.24.2; Ferguson 1932, 17 n. 2, 156; Lewis 1974, 83–84.

28. The reassessment decree: *IG* I^3 71 (= ML 69, Fornara 136). On Cleon's connection with the reassessment, see Meritt and Wade-Gery 1936. Actual assessment figures are not well preserved, and restorations have been much discussed, see Meiggs 1972, 324–39; Meritt 1981; Kallet-Marx 1993, 164–70. The "effective doubling" of the assessed tribute total (not, it should be noted, the doubling of individual quotas) is alleged by [Andocides] 4.11 and by the figures cited by Plutarch *Aristides* 24.3.

29. Thudippus and his family: Davies 1971, 228–30. Alcibiades is said, in [Andocides] 4.11, to have been among the ten Assessors who "practically doubled" the tribute. This is surely a reference to the assessment of 425/4, although some commentators have doubted that Alcibiades, at about 25 years of age, was old enough to serve in such a capacity; Develin 1985, 153 and 159, and 1989, 131, argues that there is no difficulty in accepting the year 425/4 for Alcibiades' service as Assessor.

Axiochus, with young Alcibiades at Abydos: Lysias, cited by Athenaeus 574e, cf. 534f-535a; Antiphon fr. C1 (Maidment in Loeb = Athenaeus 525b, Sprague 1971, n. 158, p. 235); his dealings on behalf of the Neopolitans in Thrace: *IG* I³ 101.48 (= ML 89, Fornara 156).

30. [Andocides] 4.11–12 complains that the assessment by Alcibiades and his colleagues violated the fairness embodied by Aristides; like the complaints against Pericles' use of revenues a generation earlier, this was a partisan perspective. "The tribute fixed by Aristides" in 421: Thucydides 5.18.5. The notion, prevailing at the time, that the reassessment merely restored the tribute to its rightful level, city by city, explains the "astonishing" omission of any mention of a "radical re-assessment" by Thucydides, remarked by M. I. Finley 1972, 24, among others. Grant of Euboean land to Lysimachus son of Aristides: Demosthenes 20.115; Plutarch *Aristides* 27.1. Mattingly 1961b/1996, 53–67, and 1992, 135–36, offers persuasive reasons for dating the Athenian treaties with Eretria and Chalcis, *IG* I³ 39 and 40 (= Fornara 102 and 103, ML 52 Chalcis only), to ca. 424/3; *IG* I³ 418, probably dating to about this time, gives fragmentary details of an apportionment of agricultural lands on Euboea, described as *temene;* Aristophanes *Clouds* 202–13 and *Wasps* 715–18 attest a sharing of interests in Euboean land among the Athenian *demos* at this time; see further below, chapter 5, with note 42.

31. Athens as *tyrannis/tyrannos:* Thucydides 1.122.3, 124.3, 2.63.2, 3.37.2, 6.85.1; Aristophanes *Knights* 1111–14. The tyranny of Athens alluded to in these passages is exercised over subject-states, although the image of *Demos* in the *Knights* also implies tyranny over domestic subjects. On Athens as a *tyrannis polis,* see Lévy 1976, 137–42; Connor 1977; Raaflaub 1979; Tuplin 1985; Scanlon 1987; Kallet 1998, 52–54. Moles 1996, 260–62, discusses the significance of the contemporary discussion of tyranny in Herodotus' *Histories.*

32. Pericles' policy, and the *orge* especially of the young: Thucydides 2.21.2–22.1, and see further below, note 54. Quote: Pseudo-Xenophon *Constitution* 2.1.; cf. Plato *Laws* 706b-c.

33. On the cavalry as the defenders of Attica, see Thucydides 2.22.2, 3.1.2; see the discussions of Ober 1985; Spence 1990. Testimony to Cleon's attacks on the cavalry are gathered by Fornara 131, and interpreted by Fornara 1973.

34. On the state-sponsored subvention *(katastasis)* for the cavalry, see Bugh 1988, 56–58. On the probable nature of Cleon's charges against the cavalry, see Fornara 1973, and Bugh 112–14. Diodorus 13.72.7–9 provides a vivid account of a cavalry battle below the walls of Athens (in 408/7) as a spectator sport. On Spartan hostages from Sphacteria, see Thucydides 4.41.1. Quote: Aristophanes *Knights* 222–29; see also line 580 on the cavalrymen's airs of refinement.

35. Cleon "coughed up five talents": Aristophanes *Acharnians* 5–8. A scholion to this passage offers a confused explanation, derived from Theopompus' excursus on Athenian demagogues in his *Philippica;* on the confusion, see Connor 1968, 48–59; on the probable explanation, see Fornara 1973.

36. Debate over the teachability of *arete:* Guthrie 1969/1971, 250–60; Plato *Protagoras, Laches,* and *Meno.* Advantages of the wealthy in education: Plato *Protagoras* 326c. Socrates expresses disdain for the judgment of *hoi polloi* in, for example, Plato *Crito* 44c-d, *Laches* 184d-e, cf. *Gorgias* 483b, 488b-90a; for nuanced contrasting views of the subject of public opinion in drama, cf. Euripides *Hippolytus* 986–89 and *Sup-*

pliant Women 410–43. Compare also the speech by Cleon in Thucydides 3.37.3–4, discussed below, and Euripides *Andromache* 481–82. Links between Thucydidean rhetoric and Euripidean drama are traced by J.H. Finley 1938/1967.

37. Plato, *Protagoras* 316c-326c, provides, in the voice of Protagoras, an account of the kinds of expertise deployed by sophists. Guthrie 1969/1971, 27–34, discusses the range of skills embraced by *sophia,* and the evolution of the meaning of *sophistes,* from a more general "sage," or "teacher," which could describe Solon or Pindar, to a clever contriver like Prometheus, to, by the fourth century, a term of opprobrium implying the ability to deceive. On the poetry of the Presocratics, see Havelock 1966/1982, 220–60. Quote: Plato *Protagoras* 339a, translated by W.K.C. Guthrie. The emerging interest in the late fifth century in persuasive, non-poetic speech (i.e., rhetoric) is studied by Cole 1991, esp. 71–112.

38. The ideas of Protagoras are chiefly known to us through the filter of Plato (esp. *Protagoras* 320c-328c), whose anti-democratic orientation provides serious challenges to our assessment of Protagoras. For reconstructions of Protagoras' philosophy, see Havelock 1957, 155–254; Guthrie 1969/1971, 181–92, 262–69; Ostwald 1986, 238–43; Farrar 1988, 44–98; testimonia and fragments of Protagoras are translated by O'Brien in Sprague 1972, 3–28. On Pericles and Protagoras, see Plutarch *Pericles* 36.3.

39. On Protagoras as the first to demand payment as a teacher of *arete:* Plato *Protagoras* 349a, cf. *Hippias* 1 282d; Diogenes Laertius 9.52. The claim made here, that interest in the study of rhetoric increased significantly at Athens after ca. 431, is supported chiefly by the accumulation of rhetorical tracts, including the speeches of Thucydides and the dialogues of Plato, beginning at about that time, contrasted with their dearth from any earlier period; see Cole 1991, 71–94. The transformation is also represented in the shift from the broader scope envisioned by Protagoras in his teaching of "the art of politics" *(politike techne),* through which Protagoras claimed to be able to "make men good citizens" (Plato *Protagoras* 318e-319a), to the more specific focus claimed by Gorgias for his teaching of rhetoric, an art that gives one "dominion over others" (Plato *Gorgias* 452d), while denying that he taught virtue per se (*Meno* 95b-c).

40. Sophistry defined as "the art of making clever speakers": Plato *Protagoras* 312d, *Meno* 95b-c. Gorgias' arrival: Diodorus 12.53.2; Plato *Hippias* 1 282b. Gorgias as a teacher: Plato *Gorgias* 447a-462b, *Meno* 70b-71d, *Apology* 19e, *Hippias* 1 282b-e; Xenophon *Anabasis* 2.6.16; Philostratus *Lives of the Sophists* 1.9.1; these and other testimonia are translated by G. Kennedy in Sprague 1972, 30–42; see also Guthrie 1969/1971, 192–200, 269–74.

41. Aristophanes *Banqueters* fr. 205 *PCG* (= 198 Kock, Edmonds).

42. Quote: Thucydides 3.38.2–7, translated by R. Warner, with modifications.

43. Woodman 1988, 16–23, in the context of Thucydides' own claims of autopsy, documents the inability of men involved especially in the confusion of war to assess the overall significance of events they have experienced without the benefit of analyses composed at some remove of time from the events themselves. Diodotus defends the need for public debate informed by such analyses in Thucydides 3.42–43, 48.

44. The assimilation of audience and orator is foreshadowed in Pericles' speech in Thucydides 2.40.2–3; cf. Aristophanes *Knights* 228, *Frogs* 1113–14.

45. On Protagoras' *politike techne* see above, notes 37 and 38, and below, with notes 53 and 62. On style in sophistic rhetoric, see Cole 1991, 12–19. Note the frequent citations by later authors of unique words and phrases, especially from the works of Antiphon and Critias (e.g., in Sprague 1972, 200–40, 262–70). On Gorgias' style, Cole 1991, 71–74, remarks on its extreme oddity, to modern sensibilities; Van Hook's translation of Gorgias' *Helen,* in the introduction to his Loeb edition of Isocrates' *Helen,* successfully conveys a sense of Gorgias' style that evokes the cadences found both in the rhetoric of some American evangelical preachers and in contemporary rap poetry. Alcibiades' lisp is noted by Plutarch *Alcibiades* 1.2 and parodied in Aristophanes *Wasps* 44–46; this hallmark of his speech is exploited by Vickers 1987, 1989a and b, and 1993, to discover allusions to Alcibiades elsewhere in Aristophanes' plays. Other speech mannerisms of Alcibiades are described by Theophrastus, reported by Plutarch *Alcibiades* 10.3. Alcibiades is mentioned as a glib young speaker by Aristophanes in the *Banqueters* fr. 205 *PCG* (= 198 Kock, Edmonds) and in the *Acharnians* 716.

46. Cleon locates the fascination for sophistic rhetoric specifically with those interested in *andragathizesthai,* "proving their manly excellence" (i.e., pursuing aristocratic *arete*) at the expense of the public good, according to Thucydides 3.40.4. Parodies of sophistry are both explicit and implicit in Aristophanes *Knights* 1375–83, *Clouds* 1353–1446, *Wasps,* 538, 559, 576–77, cf. 1122–1264; cf. also *Banqueters,* cited above, note 41. McGlew 1996 recognizes these themes as a distinctive feature of this generation.

47. The relationship between rhetoric and history, specifically Thucydides' history, is taken up in chapter 12 below. On taking notes and using them to reconstruct a speech, see Plato *Theaetetus* 143a, in addition to the passages from the *Wasps* cited above, note 46. On the rhetorical demonstration-texts of the sophists, see Cole 1991, 74–94. On the interplay of literacy and orality, its democratic qualities and its unsettling effects on conservative sensibilities, see Steiner 1994, 216–20, 239–41.

48. On the great press of judicial business of empire at Athens, see Thucydides 1.77.1–5; Pseudo-Xenophon *Constitution* 1.16–18, 3.1–9; Aristophanes *Wasps* 548–631, 1104–13; see also note 15 above. On audits *(euthynai)* of public officers, and the role of *synegoroi* and *syndikoi,* "(co-)advocates," as officially appointed prosecutors, see Rhodes 1972, 111–12; MacDowell 1978, 61, 170–72; Roberts 1982, 17–26; see also note 49 below.

49. Prosecutions by *synegoroi* or *syndikoi* are attested by Lysias 16.7; [Plutarch] *Ten Orators* 833f; Aristophanes *Acharnians* 679–718, *Knights* 1358–62, *Wasps* 686–94; cf. Plutarch *Pericles* 10.5. The reputation of demagogues like Cleon and Hyperbolus as prosecutors in the courts is clear in Aristophanes *Acharnians* 846–47, *Knights* 255–65, *Clouds* 873–75, *Wasps* 197, 240–44. The theme of honest but unsophisticated men (some identified as wealthy) victimized by sophistic prosecutors is parodied by Aristophanes *Acharnians* 679–718. Polus' claim for the power of rhetoric: Plato *Gorgias* 466b-c.

50. *Logographoi,* speech-writers: Cole 1991, 116–17; see above, chapter 1 note 80, and below, chapter 12, with notes 52–53. [Plutarch] *Moralia* 832c-e notes that neither Pericles nor any of his predecessors preserved their speeches in writing, but that this practice, and the composition of speeches for the use of others, began with Antiphon (below, chapter 4, with note 16). Note also the "bought" rhetoric of the

420s (below, note 52), and the contrast between the elderly Thucydides son of Melesias, tongue-tied in court when confronted with glib young *rhetores* and *synegoroi:* Aristophanes *Acharnians* 679–718, esp. 703–18; see Wade-Gery 1932/1958, 244, 270, who dates this trial to 426. On *synegoroi* and *syndikoi* as advocates for the defense, see Andocides 1.150; Demosthenes 21.127, 23.206; cf. Aeschylus *Suppliants* 726, *Eumenides* 576–79; the fourth-century conditions described by M.H. Hansen 1991, 194–95, generally apply to the late fifth century as well.

51. Debate over the control of money: Aristophanes *Wasps* 548–759. Kallet-Marx 1994 emphasizes the importance of arguing finance in simple terms in the rhetoric of the later fifth century. The conviction of Pericles in 430: Thucydides 2.65.2–4; Plato *Gorgias* 515e; Plutarch *Pericles* 35.4; Diodorus 12.45.4; see Kagan 1974, 90 n. 60, on the distinction between this trial and earlier trials involving misappropriation of funds. The advice of Alcibiades: Plutarch *Alcibiades* 7.2.

52. Quotes: Plato *Gorgias* 452d; Aristophanes *Clouds* 98–99; see also, for Aristophanes' parody of the "bought" rhetoric of sophists, *Clouds* 110–18, 433–75, 873–75, and *Wasps* 481–84; cf. the fragments of his *Banqueters,* cited above, note 41 Cf. Socrates' critique of rhetoric: Plato *Gorgias* 452d-72b, 501d-17a, *Menexenus* 234b-36b, *Phaedrus* 260a-62d, 266c-72d; *Republic* 365d; cf. his skepticism about the teachability of virtue, *Protagoras* 319b-20b, *Meno* 71e-94d. Sophists and sophistry were parodied by Cratinus' *Archilochi,* Ameipsias' *Connus,* and Eupolis' *Flatterers.*

53. Cf. Cleon's complaint, quoted above, on page 80. Protagoras' "political *arete*": Plato *Protagoras* 323a-29d. Infallibility of the Athenian *demos:* Thucydides 1.70, esp. 70.2 and 7; 2.40.2–3; 4.65.4; Aristophanes *Knights* 565–94. Celebration of victory in debate: Plutarch *Alcibiades* 16.4.

54. Pericles' prestige suffers: Thucydides 2.21.2–22.1, 59–65.3; Plutarch *Pericles* 29.5–35; cf. Plato *Gorgias* 515e-16c. Nicias' circumspection: Plutarch *Nicias* 6.1–2; cf. Thucydides 4.28, 6.8.4, 6.47, 7.42, 48–50. Cleon's boldness is exemplified, despite Thucydides' animosity toward him, by his initiative at Pylos (Thucydides 4.27–39) and at Amphipolis (Thucydides 5.2–10). Alcibiades' boldness: Plutarch *Alcibiades* 8.1, 13.1 (e.g., cf. Thucydides 6.15, 6.47). The occasion for the creation of the victory frieze on the parapet of the temple of Athena Nike on the Acropolis (from which figure 3 is a fragment) is uncertain. Stylistically it is usually dated to ca. 415, although a date of ca. 410, following the victory of Cyzicus, is possible; on the frieze, see Jameson 1994.

55. Both Pericles and Alcibiades were noted for quick retorts and the ability to put setbacks in a good light: Plutarch *Pericles* 8.4; *Alcibiades* 2.2; cf. Thucydides 6.16.6, where the defeat at Mantinea becomes a reason to boast.

56. Quote: Thucydides 2.62.3, translated by R. Warner.

57. On the oracles of Paphlagon/Cleon, see Aristophanes *Knights* 61, 109–220 960–1099, 1085. On the familiar advice of seers and consultation of oracles, especially written collections of oracles, see Plato *Republic* 364b-e, *Euthyphro* 3c, 4b-e; Aristophanes *Birds* 521, 959–90, *Peace* 1047; other references are given below in notes 58–61; see the discussions of Parke and Wormell, 1956, 180–202; Fontenrose 1978, 145–65; and cf. Pritchett 1971, 109–15; Jameson 1991 on seers and divination before battle.

58. Marinatos 1981a and Dover 1987/1988 review the evidence for Thucydides' acceptance of oracles. Dover, agreeing here with Marinatos, opens with the admission,

"I cannot any longer sustain my earlier view that Thucydides was a lifelong sceptic..." (p. 65). Quotes: Thucydides 5.103.2; Thucydides 2.17.2, translated by K.J. Dover, 67; Thucydides 5.26.3–4, modified from translations of Dover and Warner.

59. Diopeithes and Lampon: Aristophanes *Birds* 988. Diopeithes, who had a long and illustrious career, is also lampooned in *Knights* 1085, *Wasps* 380; Diopeithes is named by Plutarch *Pericles* 32.1 as the proposer of a decree by which it was possible to impeach "those who do not accept what has to do with the gods." Diopeithes' decree is said to be the basis for legal action against Anaxagoras, although Plutarch's testimony to this is not altogether credible; see Dover 1976/1988 146–47. Lampon was also associated with Anaxagoras and Pericles, Plutarch *Pericles* 6.2, and was one of the founders of Thurii, Diodorus 12.10.3–4. The names Diopeithes and Lampon turn up as proposers of decrees in the 420s, the former quite possibly and the later almost certainly the same as the famous seers: see *IG* I^3 61.4–5 and Mattingly 1996, 525–27, with further references to Diopeithes, and *IG* I^3 78.47 and Mattingly 1976/1996, 393 n. 13, for further references to Lampon.

60. Quote: Thucydides 8.1.1, translated by R. Crawley. On divination and oracles before the departure for Sicily, see below, chapter 4, with note 23.

61. Marinatos 1981b, 43, likens Thucydides to Herodotus, among others, in his acceptance of oracles. On Herodotus' views of the role of divinity in causation, see Immerwahr 1966, 311–14; Lateiner 1989, 196–210.

62. Quote: Plato *Protagoras* 319b-d, translated by W.K.C. Guthrie. On this theme, cf. Plato *Gorgias* 455b, and see the discussion of Penner 1992, 125–27; Brickhouse and Smith 1994, 5–10, 163–66.

63. Various forms of *syngraphai,* the work of *syngrapheis,* are attested in fifth-century texts. Architects' reports: *IG* I^3 35.7–8, 13, 17 (= ML 44.6–7, 12, 16, Fornara 93); *IG* I^3 45.6–7; *IG* I^3 79.16–17; cf. *IG* I^3 132. Treaty terms and diplomatic memoranda: *IG* I^3 21.3 (= Fornara 92); *IG* I^3 46.19 (= ML 49.15; Fornara 100); *IG* I^3 71.40 (= ML 69, Fornara 136); Thucydides 5.35.3, 41.3; possibly *IG* I^3 14.2; cf. Meritt, Wade-Gery, and McGregor 1950, 146–47. Memoranda on leasing sacred land: *IG* I^3 402.19 (= ML 62, Fornara 121); *IG* I^3 84.4–7, 12–13, 31. Religious regulations: *IG* I^3 78.3–4, 47 (= ML 73, Fornara 140); *IG* I^3 238; *IG* I^3 250.11. A proposal concerning sacred funds: *IG* I^3 99.8. A legislative proposal: Thucydides 8.67.1–2; Aristotle *Constitution* 29.2, 30.1. A law and oath: Andocides 1.96. Cf. *IG* I^3 135. Although a few of these inscriptions have been dated as early as the 450s, it is possible that none of them are earlier than the 430s; see Appendix A. *Syngraphai* concerning public works in the fifth and fourth centuries are reviewed by Rhodes 1972a, 122–27, 220.

64. Consultation of documents is explicitly attested in *IG* I^3 46.19; *IG* I^3 78.3–4; Aristotle *Constitution* 29.2–3; consultation is implicit in Andocides 1.96–97; see Hignett 1952, 167; Ostwald 1955.

65. Archon-list: ML 6 = Fornara 23; Cadoux 1948; Jacoby 1949, 169–77; Bradeen 1963. Davies (1971) collects the testimonia for the descendants of the archons, Cypselus (298), Onetorides (421), Cleisthenes (375), Miltiades (301), Phaenippus (with some uncertainty, 269), and Aristides (48); the filiation of Calliades is uncertain, although his name is attested in at least one distinguished lineage (Davies 360) and two more obscure families (Davies 253, 474), any one of which might have had him for an ancestor. Stroud 1978, 33 and n. 57, properly cautions

that the date of the inscription, ca. 425, is subjective, and that it could easily date a decade or more later. Note that not until 421 does the use of an archon's name become a nearly regular feature of the heading of Athenian decrees: Mattingly 1974/1996, 326–27. While perhaps not a hard and fast "rule," Mattingly's observations are largely confirmed in the critical review of A. S. Henry 1979; see Pritchett 1996, 3–4; Appendix A.

66. The sources of the archon-list are controversial. Plommer (1969) believes that it was drawn up for the first time in the 420s; Stroud (1978, 32–35) believes that an authoritative list existed from its beginning in 683/2; Thomas (1989, 287–88) points out that the mnemonic function of annual archons does not require a written list, but believes that "the archon list as it appears in the 420s must have been based partly on some form of written record, not necessarily inscribed, which was being kept by the Peisistratid period" (288). According to Thomas' view, which I find reasonable, the list of the 420s was "the product of a new scholarly attention to lists and other written records" (288).

67. On Hippias of Elis and the list of Olympic victors, see Plutarch *Numa* 16; cf. Plato *Greater Hippias* 285d. On Hellanicus' *Carneonicae, Priestesses of Hera at Argos,* and *Attike syngraphe* (Thucydides 1.97.2), see Pearson 1939, 209–32; on the last, see further below, chapter 12 note 90. Athenaeus 635e-f refers to two versions of Hellanicus' *Carneonicae,* one *emmetrois* (a poetic version) and one *katalogaden* (a mere list). *Syngrammata katalogaden,* along with *meta metrou poiemata,* "rhythmic poetry," are examples of written sources of education, according to Isocrates 2.7, cf. 42. *Katalogaden,* often translated "prose," specifically conveys the sense of systematic compilation, even a list, which only incidentally is not poetry. The same sense of systematic works (and therefore tedious to listen to), contrasted with poetic works, is expressed in Plato *Lysis* 204d and *Symposium* 177b. On expert treatises as the work of *syngrapheis,* see Plato *Phaedrus* 235c, 272b, 278e, also discussed below, chapter 12, on page 298.

68. Quotes: Thucydides 8.54.4, translated by R. Warner; Plato *Apology* 36b, translated by H. Tredennick. On *hetairos* used in a social sense, see, for example, Herodotus 5.95; Antiphon 1.18; Thucydides 7.75.4; Plato *Gorgias* 482a; Xenophon *Memorabilia* 2.8.1. On *hetaireiai* and *hetairoi* in a political context, see Herodotus 5.71; Thucydides 3.82.5, 7.73.3, 8.48.4, 65.2; Plato *Seventh Letter* 325d-e; Calhoun 1913; Aurenche 1974, 15–32. Although the terms are not used, confrontations of such politically-motivated groups in the courts are illustrated by the circumstances narrated in Antiphon 6.35–50, and by Antiphon's role in Thucydides 8.68.1. On *synomosiai,* see also: Aristophanes *Knights* 475–79; Thucydides 6.27.3, 60.1, 8.48.2. *Hetairoi* and *synomotai* are synonymous in [Andocides] 4.4, cf. Lysias 12.43; Aurenche 1974, 32–41.

69. Quote: Aristophanes *Knights* 475–79. *Synomotai* are associated with alleged plots to establish tyranny in Aristophanes *Wasps* 463–508 and Thucydides 6.60.1.

CHAPTER FOUR. THE EXPULSION OF ALCIBIADES, 415–413

1. Quote: Thucydides 2.43.1, translated by R. Warner, with modifications.

2. On Alcibiades' early career, see Hatzfeld 1940, 66–141, with the observations, sometimes at variance with Hatzfeld, above, chapter 2, with notes 16, 29–31,

and chapter 3 notes 10, 29–30. Alcibiades' dealings in the Peloponnese: Thucydides 5.43, 45, 46.5, 52.2–56, 61, 76.3, 84.1; cf. Plutarch *Alcibiades* 14–15; Diodorus 12.78–81.3. Ostracism of Hyperbolus: Plutarch *Nicias* 11; *Aristides* 7.2–4; *Alcibiades* 13.3–5, where it is noted that Phaeax rather than Nicias may have been a candidate; cf. [Andocides] 4, *Against Alcibiades*. The ostracism of Hyperbolus is placed by some in 416 (see Andrewes in Gomme et al. 1981, 258–64; 417 is excluded on the evidence of *IG* I³ 85); the date of 415, accepted here, is favored by Raubitschek 1948/1991 and 1954; Rhodes 1994; Cawkwell 1997, 137 n. 9; see further in chapter 5 note 25.

3. Popular opinion favorable to Alcibiades is reported in Xenophon *Hellenica* 1.4.13–16 (discussed in chapter 6, with notes 41–42) and later in Aristophanes *Frogs* 1422–25, and Plutarch *Alcibiades* 38.2–4 (discussed in chapter 7, with note 48, and chapter 8, with note 48). Thucydides' view of Alcibiades is expressed at 6.15.3–4 and implied at 2.65.11. The consistency of Thucydides' judgment has been challenged, e.g., by Brunt 1952; Bloedow 1973; Dover 1981/1988, 80–81; Hornblower 1987, 149–51; Cawkwell 1997, 75–91; see also introduction, note 7.

4. Alcibiades as chameleon: Plutarch *Alcibiades* 23.3–5; cf. Athenaeus 534b-c; Nepos 7.11.2–6. Alcibiades and the wife of Agis: Plutarch *Alcibiades* 23.7–8; *Lysander* 22.3; *Agesilaus* 3.1–2. On the sources and nature of the biographic tradition for Alcibiades, see below, with note 38. Aristotle's *politikon zoön* and *apolis: Politics* 1253a, 1–5, 27–29.

5. Athenian alliances in Italy and Sicily: Rhegium and Leontini in 433/2, *IG* I³ 53 and 54 (= ML 63 and 64, Fornara 124 and 125), renewed in 427, Thucydides 3.86, 6.6.2; Segesta in 418/7, *IG* I³ 11 (= ML 37, Fornara 81; on the date see Chambers, Gallucci, and Spanos 1990, and Appendix A here). Campaigns in Sicily: Thucydides 3.86, 88, 90, 99, 103, 115, 4.1, 24–25, 65, 5.4–5; cf. Justin 4.3.4–7; see above, chapter 1, with notes 57 and 79. Intentions in Sicily: Thucydides 1.44.3, 3.86.4, 115.5, 4.60.2, 61.5, 65.3; Diodorus 12.54.1–3; Plutarch *Alcibiades* 17; Justin 4.3.5; Aristophanes *Wasps* 700. Hyperbolus: Aristophanes *Knights* 1300–15, cf. 174. Trials of Athenian generals: Thucydides 4.65.3; Justin 4.4.2; see also note 6 below.

6. Laches targeted for prosecution: Aristophanes *Wasps* 240, 836–38, 896–97. Laches linked with Nicias as an opponent of Alcibiades: Thucydides 5.43.2. Alcibiades as *synegoros* in court: Aristophanes *Acharnians* 716; the context is recalled in *Wasps* 944–48. Phaeax, commanding in Sicily in 422 (Thucydides 5.4–5), is depicted as an often-tried, often-acquitted, bitter opponent of Alcibiades at the time of the ostracism of 415: [Andocides] 4.8; Plutarch *Alcibiades* 13.4; cf. Aristophanes *Knights* 1377.

7. Ostracism normally took place in the eighth prytany (Philochorus *FGrHist* 328 F 30), which was also normally the prytany in which the Great Dionysia took place. It is likely that the assembly "at the beginning of spring" at which the Segestans appeared with the sixty talents promised to the Athenians (Thucydides 6.8.1–2) was the assembly following the Dionysia, when tribute from allies was also publicly displayed; see chapter 1, with notes 54 and 55. On the date of Hyperbolus' ostracism, see note 2 above.

8. Ehrenberg 1947, 64–65, discusses comments that *eros* has attracted in this passage. Compare the desirability of victory displayed in the figures of Nike on the Acropolis at this time (represented in figure 3). According to Plutarch *Alcibiades*

17.2, Alcibiades is the agent of *eros* on this occasion. *Eros* is mentioned elsewhere in Thucydides only in Diodotus' speech, 3.45.5, as one of the motives that will always lead men to bold or rash action. In Pericles' funeral oration, 2.43.1, quoted above on page 96, Pericles urges Athenians to become inspired *erastai,* lovers, of Athens, a phrase echoed to comic effect by Aristophanes *Knights* 732–40, 1163, and *Birds* 1279 (where *eros* also figures prominently, as discussed later in this chapter); see the discussion of Forde 1989, 31–50. Appointment of generals: Thucydides 6.8; largest force: 6.1.1. Kagan 1981, 170–91, suggests that the conquest of Sicily was not seriously envisioned until after Nicias' caution incited the Athenians to increase the fleet from 60 to at least 100 triremes; his suggestion is contradicted by Thucydides, Diodorus, and Plutarch, who state that conquest was on everyone's mind from the first, cf. note 5 above.

9. Socrates and Meton: Plutarch *Alcibiades* 17.4–5; other ill-omens are listed in *Nicias* 13.

10. Quote: Thucydides 6.24.3, translated by R. Warner.

11. Athenian operations, 417–415, are attested in Thucydides 5.80–116, 6.7; *IG* I^3 370 (= ML 77, Fornara 144); discussed in Kagan 1981, 139–58.

12. Decrees concerning the Sicilian expedition: *IG* I^3 93 (= ML 78, Fornara 146). The dating of these fragmentary texts is inferred from their contents; they were passed on more than one occasion, probably beginning in the several (unnumbered) assemblies (Thucydides 6.6.3) during the winter of 416/15 when the Athenians first decided to sail to Sicily (6.1.1). Meiggs, Lewis, Dover, and other commentators place all of these decrees in 415; Thomsen 1964, 174–75, followed by Mattingly 1968/1996, 219–20, argues that the provision for the *eisphora* in fragment c is reason to date this fragment to the relief expedition of 413, led by Demosthenes (Thucydides 7.20.2, 26). But the decree in fragment c speaks of the *eisphora* as a contingency, not an enactment (*[ea]n te apo to timematos dokei*... line 11 = ML 78 c2, and...*-ei espheren hotan dee*[-...] line 14 = ML 78 c5), and refers to generals in the plural in connection with meetings of the Assembly prior to the sailing of the ships, none of which suits the circumstances of Demosthenes' departure, but conforms with preparations for the original departure of the fleet under Alcibiades, Lamachus, and Nicias.

13. Arming *thetes* in 415: Thucydides 6.43. On the blurred distinction between hoplites and *thetes,* see chapter 3 note 1. Quote: Pseudo-Xenophon *Constitution* 1.2; see above, chapter 3, with note 3.

14. "To make all the *thetes* hoplites," Antiphon Fr. B 6 Maidment (= Thalheim 61, Morrison B 48 in Sprague, 1972, 208), attributed to *Against Philinus.* Philinus, it should be noted, was probably the brother of Cleophon, the most prominent demagogue between 410 and 405; see Raubitschek 1954; Mattingly 1991, 21–24. "Arming men of military age," [Plutarch] *Moralia* 832f.

15. Liturgies and trierarchies in 415: Plutarch *Nicias* 12.2; cf. Diodorus 13.2.2.

16. Quote: Thucydides 8.68.1, translated by R. Warner, with modifications. The biography of Antiphon in [Plutarch] *Moralia* 832c-34b openly confuses Antiphon son of Sophilus with two other contemporary Athenians of the same name. Morrison 1961 argues persuasively for identifying the surviving works attributed to Antiphon as the product of the same man, the son of Sophilus; so also Gagarin 1997, 5–6; see the collection of fragments and testimonia by Morrison in Sprague 1972, 106–240.

Plato's snub: *Menexenus* 236a; cf. the snub of Plato the comic poet, in his *Peisander,* cited by [Plutarch] *Moralia* 833c; cf. also Philostratus *Lives of the Sophists* 1.15.2.

17. Wolff 1970, 21–22, and M.H. Hansen 1974, 59–61, and 1991, 205–12, regard the *graphe paranomon* as a device developed to oppose the excesses of the "radical democracy" of the Peloponnesian War era; see also Ostwald 1986, 135–36. Leogoras, father of Andocides, brought the first datable *graphe paranomon* to trial in 415 (Andocides 1.17); Antiphon himself brought one to trial at about the same time: [Plutarch] *Moralia* 833d; Hansen 1974, 28. It is probably significant that Antiphon is named, by a chorus of jurors in Aristophanes *Wasps* 1270, as a hungry diner at the table of the affluent Leogoras.

18. Praise of Draco's laws on homicide (though not by name): Antiphon 5 *On the Murder of Herodes* 14, and 6 *On the Choreutes* 2, translated by K.J. Maidment. Fragment from *On Truth: POxy* XI, no. 1364, col. I, lines 6–11 = Morrison B 90 in Sprague 1972, 218; fragment from an unknown work: Thalheim 78 = Morrison B 167, in Sprague 1972, 236.

19. Draconic and Solonic law regarding *thetes:* Aristotle *Constitution* 4.2, 7.3–4; on the longevity of this archaic census class, see M.H. Hansen 1980 and Ryan 1994. Fuks 1953, affirming the judgment of earlier scholarship, identifies the research undertaken in 411 as the origin of the debate about the Athenian "ancestral constitution" and its alleged form under the so-called "constitution of Draco," described by Aristotle *Constitution* 4; see also Rhodes 1981, 53–56, 84–87.

20. Discovery of the mutilation of the Herms is described by Thucydides 6.27; cf. Plutarch *Nicias* 13.2; *Alcibiades* 18.3–19.1, 20.2–5; Diodorus 13.2.3–4; Nepos 7.3.2. Aristophanes *Lysistrata* 1094 demonstrates that exposed phalluses were the target of the *Hermokopidai.* Alcibiades' birth in the archonship of Phallenius is attested in a fragment of Aristophanes' *Banqueters,* fr. 244 *PCG* (= 554 Kock, Edmonds, as formerly attributed to *Triphales*); Alcibiades remains associated with *Triphales* through fr. 556 *PCG* (= 543 Kock, Edmonds = Athenaeus 525a).

21. On the interpretation of *tomia,* see Burkert 1983, 36 n. 8, and 1985, 251–53; Karavites 1986, 118–19; cf. Antiphon 5.88; Demosthenes 23.67–68; on *tomia* on the oath-stone *(lithos),* see Aristotle *Constitution* 55.5, and for the identification of the *lithos* in front of the Stoa Basileios, see Shear 1994, 242–44; cf. Camp 1986, 101–102, and 74–75 on the Herms concentrated there. The self-castration on the nearby altar of the Twelve Gods associated with the episode by Plutarch *Nicias* 13.2 conforms to the same symbolism.

22. Quote: Antiphon 5 *On the Murder of Herodes* 81–82, translated by K.J. Maidment, with modifications; similar attitudes underlie Andocides 1.137–39. The sea and its divinities were long seen as powerful arbiters truth and justice; see Detienne 1973, 29–50.

23. Soothsayers: Plutarch *Nicias* 13.1; Thucydides 8.1.1; cf. the parody of the oracle monger in Aristophanes *Birds* 958–90, performed in 414; see also above, chapter 3, with notes 57–61. Nicias reputed to be fortunate: Thucydides 5.16.1, 6.17.1, 23.3, 7.77.2; cf. Plutarch *Nicias* 2.4, 6.2–4. Allegations of the Alcmaeonid curse: Aristophanes *Knights* 445–46; Herodotus 5.70–72; Thucydides 1.126–27.

24. The profanations of the Mysteries: Thucydides 6.28.1–2; Andocides 1.11–24; Isocrates 16.6–7; Lysias 6.50–51, 14.42; Plutarch *Alcibiades* 19.1–2, 20.3, 22.3; Nepos 7.3.6; Pausanias 1.2.5. Discussing a scene of mock-initiation in Aris-

tophanes' *Clouds*, Burkert 1983, 268–69, points out the degree of mimicry of initiatory ritual that might be publicly tolerated at Athens, although he feels that "Aristophanes would presumably not have dared to write such a scene" following the scandals of 415. The line crossed by Alcibiades' alleged act has previously not been adequately explained; De Vries' criticism (1973) of Adcock illustrates the wide divergence of opinion on this subject.

25. Thucydides 6.27–29, 53, 60–61, provides the chief narrative of the inquisition; Andocides 1.11–68 gives a detailed account of the denunciations made before the Commissioners, and their consequences; cf. Plutarch *Alcibiades* 20.3–22.

26. *Apomimesis* or *hubrisma*, or cognate terms, are found in the accounts of Thucydides, Lysias, Isocrates, and Plutarch cited in note 24 above; in addition, Alcibiades or others are said to have "transgressed/violated" *([ex]amartanein)*, or "impiously treated/profaned" *(asebein)* the Mysteries. Most often, however, as Burkert 1983, 287, and Murray 1990, 155–56, note, the perpetrators are simply said to have "performed" *(poiein* or *dran)* the Mysteries.

27. Quotes: Lysias 6 *Against Andocides* 51, translated by W.R.M. Lamb (on the identity of the speaker, see below, chapter 11 note 9); the younger Alcibiades, Isocrates 16.6, translated by L. van Hook, with modification.

28. Andocides 1 *On the Mysteries* 11–24 provides the chief testimony to the various occasions on which the Mysteries were privately performed; see the commentary of MacDowell 1962. Andocides is the subject of Lysias 6.51, quoted above, with note 27. Aurenche 1974 examines the prosopography of these groups; Murray 1990, 153–60, assesses the implications of their acts through comparisons to aristocratic scandals of other times.

29. On oaths, and rituals of solidarity and initiation, see Burkert 1985, 250–64. Lycomidae: Plutarch *Themistocles* 1.3; Pausanias 1.22.7, 4.1.5, 9.27.2; Toepfer 1889, 208–25. Gephyraei: Herodotus 5.57, 61; Toepfer 1889, 293–300.

30. For the date of the ostracism of Hyperbolus, see note 2 above. Plato comicus, quoted by Plutarch *Nicias* 11.6 and *Alcibiades* 13.5. Thucydides on Hyperbolus: 8.73.3, translated by R. Warner. Plutarch on Hyperbolus: *Nicias* 11.3 and *Alcibiades* 13.3, translated by B. Perrin.

31. Connor 1971, 79–84, provides a thorough account of Hyperbolus' influence. His ability to wield the power of the *demos* is attested by *IG* I^3 85, of 418/17, which seems to record measures he proposed for holding an inquiry into the conduct of one of the prytanies of the Council of that year. Hyperbolus and the west: see note 5 above. Plutarch *Aristides* 7.2 describes the customary aim of ostracism.

32. Quote: Plutarch *Nicias* 11.4; cf. *Alcibiades* 13.4, where more than two factions are involved. On aristocratic groups, see above, chapter 3, with note 68, and the excellent discussion of Strauss 1986, 11–41.

33. Quote: Plutarch *Aristides* 7.4, translated by B. Perrin. Connor 1971, 83, likewise suggests that Plutarch's account of the ostracism of Hyperbolus "must be viewed more critically and in some measure amended" (cf. 135–36). The present account helps to explain the why the democracy never again resorted to ostracism, even though its use long remained a legal possibility: Aristotle *Constitution* 43.5; see Christ 1992.

34. Blessings of Demeter, and fear of her anger, are expressed in the *Homeric Hymn to Demeter;* on the sanctity of secrecy, see Burkert 1983, 248–56.

35. Aristophanes *Clouds* 250–74 mimics elements of mystic initiation, see note 24 above. Eros: Hesiod *Theogony* 120–22, cited in Plato *Symposium* 178a-b, where the ensuing conversation, set in 416, is devoted to the praise of Eros; cf. the (mock) hymn to Eros in Aristophanes *Birds* 693–702, staged in 414. On Eros in Orphic literature, see West 1983, 68–115. On Eros in Athenian rhetoric, see above, note 8. Note also the concentration of erotic references in the Thucydides' digression on the tyrannicides, 6.54–59. Eros also appears in Xenophon's *Symposium* 1.8–10 and 8.1–9.7. Eros and the Mysteries are linked by the concepts and vocabulary of seeing, remembering, becoming initiated, the soul, and afterlife in Plato *Phaedrus,* esp. 246b-57a; see Riedweg 1987, 30–69. A convergence of other themes of divine eroticism at this time cannot be merely coincidental. Aristophanes recalls the ritual laments for Adonis, dying beloved of Aphrodite, at the same time as preparations for the departure for Sicily: Aristophanes *Lysistrata* 387–98; Plutarch *Alcibiades* 18.3; *Nicias* 13.7. The death by self-castration of Attis, beloved of the Great Mother, Cybele, was enacted at this time over the altar of the Twelve Gods in the Agora by an unnamed individual, according to Plutarch *Nicias* 13.2.

36. Alcibiades' seductive charm: Plutarch *Alcibiades* 1.3–6.2, 23.7, 24.5; Athenaeus 534c-35e, 574d-e; cf. Plato *Protagoras* 309a-c. Alcibiades hunted by women: Xenophon *Memorabilia* 1.2.24. Alcibiades' erotic jealousy: Plato *Symposium* 213c-d. Alcibiades' shield: Plutarch *Alcibiades* 16.2; Athenaeus 534e.

37. Thucydides 6.28.2, cf. 61.1. "All of his other exotic and perverse habits" is a translation of *ten allen autou es ta epitedeumata ou demotiken paranomian.*

38. Quote: [Andocides] 4, *Against Alcibiades* 10, translated by K.J. Maidment. Fragments from Antiphon's invective *Against Alcibiades* are quoted in Plutarch *Alcibiades* 3 and Athenaeus 525b (= Morrison in Sprague 1972, 234–33). On the scurrilous character of Alcibiades, see Aristophanes *Acharnians* 716; Lysias 14.41–42; [Andocides] 4, *Against Alcibiades* 13–32, 39; Plutarch *Alcibiades* 2–10, 16, 23, 36.1–2, 39.5; Antisthenes in Athenaeus 220c, cf. 534e-35c, 574d-e.

39. Quote: [Andocides] 4, *Against Alcibiades* 15, translated by K.J. Maidment; cf. Plutarch *Alcibiades* 8.2. On the date of [Andocides] 4, see chapter 12 note 73. On Callias, and the priestly curses on Alcibiades, see Plutarch *Alcibiades* 8.2, 22.4, 33.3; Nepos 7.6.5. On the marriage of Alcibiades to Hipparete, see Isocrates 16.31; [Andocides] 4, *Against Alcibiades* 13; Plutarch *Alcibiades* 8. On the stereotype of the tyrant, see below, note 47.

40. Antiphon's invective *Against Alcibiades* (note 38 above) is usually associated, like the spurious [Andocides] 4, *Against Alcibiades,* with the ostracism of Hyperbolus. Such accusatory speeches accompanying ostracisms are unknown (Rhodes 1994, 89), and Antiphon's tract, probably a prime source for [Andocides] 4, better suits the mood of the summer of 415. For another example of a speech full of personal invective that was published but never delivered, see Demosthenes 21, *Against Meidias,* with Aeschines 3.52; Plutarch *Demosthenes* 12.

41. Quote: Lysias 14, *Against Alcibiades* 41–42, translated by W. R. M. Lamb, with modifications. On scrutinies before confirmation in office, and audit hearings following office, see Roberts 1982; Lysias 16, 21, 25, 26, 31 are illustrative examples of speeches of condemnation or defense.

42. Thucydides 6.53.3, cf. 60.1.

43. Thucydides' digression on Harmodius and Aristogeiton in Book 6 much discussed; see, e.g., Jacoby 1949, 158–68; Fornara 1968; Dover in Gomme et al. 1970, 317–29; Taylor 1981, 161–75. All assume that *akoei* in 6.53.3 means "oral tradition" rather than aural reception of an authoritative account, and as a result none see the relevance of the digression to the surrounding narrative as it is understood here (although Dover, 329, comes closest). For *akoei* as the source of reliable knowledge, compare the confidence of *akoei epistamai* in Thucydides 4.126.3, and the force of the verb *epistamai* in 2.35.2, 4.10.5, e.g.; contrast the uncertainty of *oiomai,* to "suppose," in 4.73.1 (cf. 1.20.2, 3, 6.54.2).

44. On traditions of the tyrannicides, see above, chapter 1, with notes 9–13.

45. Quote: Thucydides 1.22.4, discussed further in chapter 12, page 315ff. On hearing authoritative history, cf. Aristotle *Constitution* 29.3, the text of an amendment to a decree of 411, the so-called rider of Cleitophon, prescribing the preparation of a report by a panel of *syngrapheis* on the laws that Cleisthenes enacted, "so that by also hearing about them *(akousantes kai touton)* they will take the best counsel." On the codification of expertise in *syngraphai,* see above, chapter 3, with notes 63–67.

46. Fornara 1971b finds other evidence to indicate that Herodotus' text was becoming known to a wide audience at Athens in 415; on the date of Herodotus' "publication," see above, chapter 1 note 78. On the Athenian mood following the end of the Sicilian expedition of 424, see Thucydides 4.65.4, quoted in chapter 1 on page 44; on fears of tyranny, see above, chapter 3, with note 69. On the "wise advisor" in Herodotus, see Lattimore 1939; Dewald 1985; Raaflaub 1987. The pervasive theme of transgression in Herodotus, discussed by Lateiner 1989, 126–44, often entails the failure to recognize wise advice. *Akribeia* as an aristocratic quality: Pseudo-Xenophon *Constitution* 1.5; as essential to decision-making: Antiphon 4.3.1. The power of reason to comprehend fate in Euripides' *Trojan Women,* in 415, is well summarized by Gregory 1986, 9: "[Euripides] makes his Trojan women demonstrate the ability of human beings to use language and reason to survive and impose order on a universe that may or may not be intelligible.... Whatever his conclusions about divine justice, in *Troades* Euripides celebrates the uniquely human ability to endow past and present with an order mirrored and created through language."

47. Stereotypes of the tyrant: see Herodotus 1.6–71 (Candaules, Gyges, and Croesus), 1.59–64 (Peisistratus), 1.96–100 (Deioces), 3.14–38 (Cambyses), 3.39–45, 122–25, 142–43 (Polycrates and Maeandrius), 3.48–53 (Periander), 3.80 (Otanes' speech), 5.55–65 (Hippias), 5.67–68, 6.126–31 (Cleisthenes), 5.92 (Sosicles' speech); cf. Xenophon *Hiero* 1.26–28. Argives and other foreign supporters of Athenian tyrants: Herodotus 1.61, 5.63, 91, 93, 6.103, 107, 121; cf. Thucydides 6.29.3, 61.3–5; Diodorus 13.5.1; Plutarch *Alcibiades* 23.1.

48. Rewards given to informers: Thucydides 6.27.2; Andocides 1.27–28. The decision of Andocides to become an informer: Thucydides 6.60.2–5; Andocides 2, *On His Return* 7–8; Andocides 1, *On the Mysteries* 47–68; Lysias 6.21–24; cf. Plutarch *Alcibiades* 21.1–5. On the chronology of events, and the fates of those convicted, see MacDowell 1962, 173–89; Pritchett 1953, 230–32; Dover in Gomme et al. 1970, 264–88; Aurenche 1974, 155–228.

49. The decree of Thessalus: Plutarch *Alcibiades* 22.3.

50. The recall and flight of Alcibiades: Thucydides 6.53, 60–61, 88.9–10; Diodorus 13.5; Plutarch *Alcibiades* 21.5–23.1; Justin 5.1.1–3; Nepos 7.4.

51. The Eusebian date of 445/4 for Herodotus' reading to the Council (1572, or in the 84th Olympiad, according to the Armenian chronicle, Schoene 1866, v. 2, 106) is surely a conjecture based either on an Apollodoran estimate of his *floruit* at age 40, or on his connection to the colony at Thurii in Italy, which was founded in 444/3; on the arbitrariness of many Eusebian/Apollodoran dates for fifth-century literary figures, see Mosshammer 1976 and 1979, 305–19. The award given to Herodotus on the motion of Anytus is reported by Plutarch *Moralia* 862b on the authority of Diyllus (whose father, the Atthidographer Phanodemus, was likewise honored by the Council for his excellent advice in 343/2: *IG* II^2 223). The amount of the award reported by Plutarch, ten talents, is unbelievable; ten minae is a credible award, and even ten times that amount is within reason, see Andocides 1.27–28. Aristophanes *Birds* 1074–75 facetiously refers to the reward of one talent "to anyone who slays one of the long-dead tyrants," suggesting that rewards and dead tyrants were both under discussion before that play was staged, in the spring of 414.

52. The interpretation of Aristophanes *Thesmophoriazusae* 809 presented here depends upon Maas' emendation of *AYTOS* to *ANYTOS,* and Küster's emendation of the second person *PHESEIS* to the third person *PHESEI* (see Coulon's text in the Budé edition). Elsewhere, an emendation of *AYTOY* to *ANYTOY* is a certainty, required to correct a mistake in the papyrus of Aristotle *Constitution* 27.5, see Rhodes 1981, 343–44; a similar error in *Thesmophoriazusae* 809 would explain the corruption of the verb. On the contested interpretation of this passage, and the date of the *Thesmophoriazusae,* see Appendix B.

53. On Athens as "tyrant," see above, chapter 3 note 31. The range of seemingly contradictory values associated with this image attests both to its complexity and to its adaptability, as exemplified in the discussion above, to changing circumstances. Pericles on not yielding to slavery: Thucydides 2.63.1; cf. 1.140–41, 144.2–3, 2.61–65 (see also the references in note 54, below).

54. Quote: Thucydides 6.85.1. On the imperatives of power: Thucydides 2.62.2 (Pericles); 4.61.5 (Hermocrates); 6.18.2–3 (Alcibiades); see the discussions of Raaflaub 1994 and Orwin 1994.

55. Quote: Thucydides 5.89.

56. Quote: Thucydides 6.16.3–4, translated by R. Crawley, quoted also in chapter 2 on page 59. Athenians turn against Alcibiades: Thucydides 6.15.4. *Paranomia,* "lawlessness," can be translated "perversion," as it is in passages referring to Alcibiades above, at notes 37 and 41. *Paranomia* is semantically opposed to *isonomia* (cf. Thucydides 6.28.2, *ou demotiken paranomian*).

57. See chapter 3, pages 85–87, on oracles and public piety. Yunis 1988 provides a thoughtful analysis of Athenian beliefs in the late fifth century. Parker 1996 surveys the forms of Athenian religion, esp. 122–217 on the fifth century.

58. Quote: Euripides *Trojan Women* 884–88. On the intellectual focus of the play, see the remarks of Gregory quoted above, note 46.

59. On Euripides *Alexander,* see Lesky 1963/1966, 382; on the unity of the trilogy as a whole, with *Palamedes* as the middle play, see Scodel 1980.

60. Quote: Thucydides 5.105.1–2, translated by R. Warner, with modifications. The capture and execution of the Melians is noted in Thucydides 5.116; the event

was remembered: Xenophon *Hellenica* 2.2.3; Isocrates 4.100–102; 12.62–66; [Andocides] 4.22–23; cf. Plutarch *Alcibiades* 16.5; Strabo 10.5.1.

61. Teisias: Thucydides 5.84.3; Isocrates 16, *On the Team of Horses* 1–3, 45, 50. Davies 1971, 501–503, explains the confusion in the accounts of the dispute over the "horses of Diomedes" reflected in [Andocides] 4.26–29, Diodorus 13.74.3–4, and Plutarch *Alcibiades* 12.2–3. Teisias' suit became an issue again when Alcibiades was deposed from command in 407; see below, chapter 7, with note 10. Charicles: Isocrates 16.42–43; Andocides 1.36, 101; Lysias 12.55; Xenophon *Hellenica* 2.3.2; *Memorabilia* 1.2.31–37; Thucydides 7.20, 27; Diodorus 13.9.2.

62. Spartan activities in the Peloponnese: Thucydides 5.33, 57–60, 64–74, 76–81, 83.1–2, 116.1, 6.7.1, 105.1. Athenian hostilities: 5.115, 6.7.2, 105, 7.18. On personal connections in Spartan diplomatic practice, see chapter 3, with note 8.

63. Alcibiades' speech at Sparta: Thucydides 6.89–92; his Spartan name: Thucydides 8.6.3.

64. This pro-Spartan idealism is reflected throughout Xenophon's *Hellenica* and in other works (see Proietti 1987), and in Herodes *On the Constitution,* a work that reflects the pro-Spartan interest of Critias (see Morrison 1942, 63–76, and Wade-Gery 1945/1958 on the political perspective of Herodes; Albini 1968 on authorship). See chapter 3 note 8.

65. Alcibiades in central Greece: Nepos 7.11.3–4; cf. Plutarch *Alcibiades* 23.5; Athenaeus 534b; see Westlake 1938; doubts are expressed, with insufficient reason, by Hatzfeld 1940, 207 n. 2.

66. Fear of the courts: Aristophanes *Birds* 37–41, 114–24, 1694–1705. Pun on birds in flight and allegations of impiety: 34 *(ou sobountos oudenos* for *asebountos oudenos).* Pun on *epops* as initiate: 57–59. Hymn to Eros: 693–704. The Cuckoo of Argive Hera: Pausanias 2.17.4; cf. 2.36.1–2, and Zimmerman Munn 1986 on the shrine of Zeus and Hera atop Mount *Kokkygion* in the southern Argolid. Hymn to Peisetaerus as winged *tyrannos,* "supreme of all daimones": 1706–65. Pliny *Natural History* 36.28 attests a statue of Alcibiades as Eros wielding a thunderbolt in the Curia of the Roman Senate. Dunbar 1995 and MacDowell 1995, 221–28, see no close allusions to Alcibiades and contemporary events in the *Birds.* By contrast, Vickers 1989b and 1997, 154–89, sees much of Alcibiades here, but overburdens his interpretation with a load of *bomolochia.* Hubbard 1991, 159–82, recognizes some of the associations with the profanation of the Mysteries noted here, but does not recognize how thoroughly they evoke Alcibiades. Craik 1987 comes closest to recognizing the fun made of Alcibiades and his alleged impiety.

CHAPTER FIVE. RATIONALIZING OLIGARCHY, 413–411

1. Colophon: *IG* I^3 37 (= ML 47, Fornara 99); cf. Thucydides 3.34; see Amit 1975 on the ambiguous status of Athenian–Persian relations; Balcer 1979 on social conflict in Ionia; Seager and Tuplin 1980 on the developing identity of the Greeks of Asia; Nakamura-Moroo 1988 on Ionian–Persian relations. Accession of Darius II: Ctesias 44–49; Thucydides 4.50.3; Parker and Dubberstein 1956, 18, 33; Lewis 1977, 70–76; Andrewes in Gomme et al. 1981, 13. Revolt of Pissouthnes: Ctesias 52; Lewis 1977, 59–62, 80–81; Keen 1993, 156–57. "Sworn dealings with the Medes and the king": Aristophanes *Knights* 478. Epilycus: Andocides 3.29; Lewis 1977, 76–77.

2. Tissaphernes and Amorges: Thucydides 8.5.5, 19.2, 28, 54.3; Lewis 1977, 83–91.

3. Invasive effects of Athenian imperial administration are noted by Pseudo-Xenophon *Constitution* 1.14–16, 3.5–11; cf. Thucydides 8.48.5–6; see also Meritt et al. 1950, 142–48; de Ste. Croix 1954/1955, 6–9; Meiggs 1972, 205–54; M.I. Finley 1978/1982; and see above, chapter 3 notes 11, 15, 28, 31, and 48. 5% tax *(eikoste)*: Thucydides 7.28.4; on the date see Dover in Gomme et al. 1970, 402.

4. Embassies at Sparta and the advice of Alcibiades: Thucydides 8.5–7, 12; Plutarch *Alcibiades* 24.1; Justin 5.1.5–8; Diodorus 13.34.1–2.

5. With the revolts of Chios and Miletus, Thucydides begins a detailed narrative of the war in Ionia (8.14–48), after which its effects on Athenian politics begin to enter the account. First and second Spartan treaties with Persia: Thucydides 8.17.4–18, 36–37; Lewis 1977, 90–95.

6. Alcibiades and Tissaphernes: Thucydides 8.45–46, 52; cf. Plutarch *Alcibiades* 24–25; Justin 5.2. Andrewes, in Gomme et al. 1981, 95–105, and Kagan 1987, 70–77, assuming that the Athenian empire was always inimical to Persian interests in Ionia, are more skeptical than I am about the soundness of Alcibiades' advice. But Alcibiades' advice was put into effect, for a short time, in the settlement he achieved with Pharnabazus in 409/8 (discussed in chapter 6). Seager and Tuplin 1980 demonstrate that the idea of "freedom for the Greeks of Asia" is first attested at this time; consonant with Alcibiades' advice, this was a theme promoted by Spartans. Note that Diodorus 13.37.2–5, 38.5, conflates Pharnabazus with Tissaphernes in 412, probably because Alcibiades' later connection with Pharnabazus was more prominent and a matter of public record.

7. Pay from Tissaphernes: Thucydides 8.5.1, 29, 36.1, 45.2–3, 46.5, 53.2, 57–58, 87.1–3 (to the Peloponnesians); 48.3, 81.3 (hoped for by the Athenians); cf. Aristotle *Constitution* 29.1. Athenian financial straits are indicated by the release of the 1,000 talent reserve fund (8.15.1, cf. 2.24.1) following the revolt of Chios in the summer of 412, and by statements of financial exhaustion by the spring of 411: Thucydides 8.53.2, 63.4; cf. 8.1.2–3, 8.4, 8.65.3. Examples of "how rapidly enormous sums were being swallowed up by naval operations" are cited by Gabrielsen 1994, 114–16.

8. Athenian officers consider Alcibiades' plan: Thucydides: 8.47.2–49, 54.4. Popular knowledge of Alcibiades' plan: Thucydides 8.47.2, 48.2–3, 53–54.3.

9. Displeasure of priests at the proposal to recall Alcibiades: Thucydides 8.53.2. Phrynichus: Thucydides 8.48.4–54.2; Plutarch *Alcibiades* 25.5–10. Popular anger against seers: Thucydides 8.1.1

10. Quote: Euripides *Helen* 1353–68, following the text of A.S. Way in the Loeb edition; cf. Dale 1967, 153; Austin 1994, 178–82. On the various legends of Helen, see Austin 1994. On Euripides' *Helen,* see Delebecque 1951, 338–46; Lesky 1963/1966, 386–87; Dale 1967; Germaine 1972; Sansone 1985b; Segal 1986, 222–67; Vickers 1989a, 49–50, 52–64; Austin 1994, 137–203. On the date, see Appendix B. On the Mother of the Gods in Attic drama, see Roller 1996; Roller 1994 suggests that Greek custom of approximately this period influenced the later tradition of Cybele's grief for Attis.

11. The allusion to Alcibiades in *Helen* has been considered by Delebecque, Germaine, and Vickers among those cited in note 10 above. "The same woman as ever":

Plutarch *Alcibiades* 23.6, quoting Euripides *Orestes* 129. Eupolis *Baptae:* scholion to Aristides 3.8 (Dindorf vol. 3, 444 = *PCG* vol. 5, 332; Kock p. 273; Edmonds p. 331). Pherecrates: Athenaeus 535b (fr. 164 *PCG* = 155 Kock, Edmonds). On the bisexuality of Alcibiades, see also Eupolis *Flatterers* fr. 171 *PCG* (158 Kock, Edmonds = Athenaeus 535a-b); Diogenes Laertius 4.59; Plutarch *Alcibiades* 2.2, 16.1. Aristophanes *Thesmophoriazusae* and Alcibiades: Vickers 1989a.

12. Theano: Plutarch *Alcibiades* 22.4; and Theonoë: Germaine 1972; Vickers 1989a. Theonoë, virgin prophetess, also evokes Athena: Plato *Cratylus* 407b; Sansone 1985b; Austin 1994, 172–73.

13. Previous efforts to find, in Aristophanes' *Lysistrata,* any "serious advice [to the Athenians] about the war in which they were engaged" (Westlake 1980, 44; see also Henderson 1987) have dwelt upon details and have failed to recognize the overarching allusions to the features of Alcibiades. Eupolis seems to have parodied Alcibiades under the name Amphiptolemopedesistratus, translated by Edmonds as "Jumping-Jack-o'-both-sides-istratus," Edmonds 1957, 365 (fr. 424 *PCG* = 393 Kock); Edmonds suggests the name may have been used in Eupolis *Demes,* possibly produced in 412 (see below, note 15).

14. *Probouloi:* Thucydides 8.1.3; Aristotle *Constitution* 29.2; for evidence that such a special commission could be conducive to rapprochement with Sparta, see Diodorus 12.75.4, and Andrewes and Lewis 1957. Council of the Areopagus: Aristotle *Constitution* 23.1–2, 41.2; cf. Andocides 1.77; Wallace 1985, 77–83. Hagnon: Lysias 12.65; see Davies 1971, 227–28 for the testimonia on his career. Sophocles: Aristotle *Rhetoric* 1419a; Jameson 1971.

15. Eupolis *Demes:* fr. 99–146 *PCG* (= 90–135 Kock, Edmonds); an interpretive reconstruction of this play is offered by Edmonds, vol. 1, 978–94, who advocates a date of 411; cf. Lesky 1963/1966, 424–25, who advocates 412; Schwarze 1971, 125–35, advocates a date of 413, on the occasion of the Sicilian disaster (134), and discusses attested personae of the play (125 n. 57). On Myronides, see Thucydides 1.105.4, 108.2, 4.95.3; Lysias 2.52; Plutarch *Aristides* 10.8, 20.1; *Moralia* 185f; Diodorus 11.79.3, 81.4–82. Quote: Thucydides 8.1.4.

16. Quote from Thrasymachus: DK 85 B 1 (= Dionysius of Halicarnassus *Demosthenes* 3), translated by F. E. Sparshott, in Sprague 1972, 90–91. On the stereotype of the radical young, sometimes referred to as the "Athenian generation gap," see chapter 3, with note 46, and the discussions of Forrest 1975; Ostwald 1986, 229–50; Carter 1986, 52–75; Strauss 1993, 100–78.

17. Quote, see note 16 above.

18. The nebulous quality of the *patrios politeia* before the late fifth century has rendered its interpretation as subjective in modern scholarship as it was in ancient; see M. I. Finley 1971/1975. Aristotle's *Constitution of the Athenians* was a landmark in ancient scholarship on the subject (see chapter 10, with the quote from Aristotle *Constitution* 41 at its head), relying on more than a generation of study by the Atthidographers; see Pearson 1942; Jacoby 1949; Ruschenbusch 1958; Walters 1976; Rhodes 1981. Fuks 1953 is a fundamental study on the relationship of this concept to late fifth-century political ideology; see also Hignett 1952; Ostwald 1986, 337–480.

19. Quote of Theramenes reported by Xenophon *Hellenica* 2.3.48.

20. The decree commissioning the thirty *syngrapheis:* Aristotle *Constitution* 29.2–4; cf. Thucydides 8.67.1–2; Androtion *FGrHist* 324 F 43 (= Fornara 148); see

Andrewes, in Gomme et al. 1981, 164–65; Rhodes 1981, 372–81. Quote (addendum of Cleitophon): Aristotle *Constitution* 29.3.

21. Quote: Thucydides 8.67.2–3; see also Aristotle *Constitution* 29.4–5.

22. Property qualifications were the basis for political participation in contemporary Boeotia (*Hellenica Oxyrhynchia* 16.2–4; cf. Aristotle *Politics* 1278a; Thucydides 5.38.2), which may have been the source of inspiration for some of the specific constitutional ideas developed at the establishment of the oligarchy of the Four Hundred; see Rhodes 1981, 393. Herodes *On the Constitution* 30–31 attests the widespread limitation of political rights among the allies of Sparta to those who possessed a certain level of wealth (on Herodes, see chapter 4 note 64).

23. The creation of the Four Hundred: Thucydides 8.67.3–70.1; Aristotle *Constitution* 30–32; cf. [Lysias] 20.13–14; Diodorus 13.38.1–2; Justin 5.3.4–6; Plutarch *Alcibiades* 26.2. Andrewes in Gomme et al. 1981, 164–256, Rhodes 1981, 362–410, Ostwald 1986, 358–87, and Harris 1990 provide detailed commentary and references to scholarship on these events; see also notes 27, 28, and 40 below.

24. Strauss 1986, 179–81 calculates approximate Athenian losses in Sicily as 2,520 men of hoplite or higher status, and 6,600 men of thetic status. Losses to plague a decade earlier were high; Thucydides 3.87.3 counts 4,700 Athenians of hoplite or cavalry rank as plague casualties, and comments, "among the masses, no one ever discovered the number of deaths." On the Athenian population, see chapter 2 note 37 and chapter 3 notes 1 and 2.

25. Quotes: Thucydides 8.65.2–66.5, 73.2–3. Theopompus is quoted as saying that Hyperbolus had been ostracized "for six years" when he was murdered on Samos (scholion to Aristophanes *Wasps* 1007; *FGrHist* 115 F 96b = Fornara 145b), which has been the chief reason some have dated his ostracism to 417. If, however, he was ostracized shortly before the end of the archon year of 416/15, as is argued in chapter 4 (see note 2), and he was murdered shortly after the beginning of the archon year of 411/10, then his murder occurred in the sixth archonship of his ostracism, counting inclusively. See the end of Appendix D on the common fallacy of reckoning years by inclusive lists of annual officers.

26. Peisander as demagogue: Thucydides 8.53–54.3, 68.1; Aristophanes *Peace* 395; *Birds* 1556–58; *Lysistrata* 490; Andocides 1.27, 36, 43; Xenophon *Symposium* 2.14; Lysias 25.9; Plato Comicus composed a play called *Peisander,* no doubt satirizing him as a demagogue. Peisander as oligarchic ringleader: Thucydides 8.49.1, 53–54, 67–68.1, 90.1, 98.1; Andocides 2.14; Lysias 12.66, 25.9, cf. 7.4; Aristotle *Constitution* 32.2. On Peisander, see Woodhead 1954, McCoy 1973. Revolution to save Athens: Thucydides 8.54.1, 86.3.

27. Assembly at Colonus: Thucydides 8.67.2–68.1, 69.1; cf. Aristotle *Constitution* 29.4. On the constitutional measures voted, see note 23 above. On the symbolic importance of Colonus and Poseidon's shrine, see Siewert 1979 and Andrewes in Gomme et al, 1981, 165–67.

28. On the creation of the Five Thousand, see note 23 above. In a careful review of apparent contradictions in the testimonia to these events, Harris 1990, 259–67, argues, against the view of most scholars, that the Five Thousand were formally selected prior to the creation of the Four Hundred. The view advanced here resolves these contradictions otherwise, by recognizing the difference between the "notional" Five Thousand, assembled at Colonus, and the failure of the Four Hundred

to formalize that ad hoc group for the future by an official registration, which never was completed. For the testimonia, see below, note 40.

29. Athenian negotiations with Tissaphernes: Thucydides 8.56. Third Persian–Spartan treaty: Thucydides 8.57–59. See Lewis 1977, 100–107.

30. Judgment of Phrynichus: Thucydides 8.48.4–7. Peisander and Aegean oligarchies: Thucydides 8.63.3–65.1.

31. Samian revolution of 412: Thucydides 8.21; Diodorus 13.34.2; *IG* I^3 96. Ostwald 1993, 51–53, sees the revolution as a democratic uprising against an established oligarchy; Legon 1972, 154–56, argues against this view; Shipley 1987, 120–28, views the question as irresolvable in simple terms. On the meaning of Samian autonomy, see Ostwald 1982 and 1993; Shipley 1987, 129–31; Whitehead 1993. On the favored status of Chios prior to the rebellion of 412, see Aristophanes *Birds* 879–80; Thucydides 3.10.5, 7.57.4, cf. 8.15.

32. Samian coup of 411: Thucydides 8.73. Response to news from Athens and election of Thrasybulus and Thrasyllus: Thucydides 8.74–76; Diodorus 13.38.3. On Thrasybulus and Thrasyllus, see McCoy 1977 and 1991, 302–17.

33. Athenians on Samos hopeful of Persian aid through Alcibiades: 8.76.7, 81.1; cf. Plutarch *Alcibiades* 26.1–3; Diodorus 13.37.3–5. Strained relations of Tissaphernes with the Spartans: Thucydides 8.78, 80.1, 83–85, 87; Lewis 1977, 108–17.

34. Recall of Alcibiades to Samos: Thucydides 8.81–82; Plutarch *Alcibiades* 26.3–7; Justin 5.3.6–9; Diodorus 13.40.4–42.1 (placing the event out of chronological order).

35. Egyptian conspiracy: Diodorus 13.46.6. Lewis 1958 has gathered further evidence for Darius' concerns in Egypt and Phoenicia in 411; see also Olmstead 1948, 363–67; Lewis 1977, 133. Abdemon and Euagoras: Diodorus 14.98.1. Spyridakis 1935, 49–50, suggests that Alcibiades was involved in negotiations between Euagoras and Tissaphernes in 411; see also Costa 1974, 40–47. The early chronology of Euagoras' reign has few foundations, and the best evidence of his friendship with Athens, *IG* I^3 113, is probably to be dated to 405; see chapter 8, with notes 11–12. Alcibiades and the Phoenician fleet: Thucydides 8.87–88; Diodorus 13.37.5, 38.5; Hatzfeld 1940, 251–53. Lateiner 1976 doubts that the Phoenician fleet was concerned with Egypt, but his explanation, that Tissaphernes did not use his fleet because he knew it would be too weak to use against the Athenians, is unconvincing.

36. On the eve of revolution, negotiations with Sparta are viewed favorably in Aristophanes' *Lysistrata.* The Four Hundred negotiate with Sparta: Thucydides 8.70.2, 71.3, 86.9, 90.1–2, 92.2. Thucydides attests territorial demands in the case of Panakton a decade earlier (5.3.5, 42.1), and in 411 in the case of Oropos (8.60.1), Oenoe (8.98), and Euboea (8.5.1, see further below, with note 42).

37. Athenians at Samos repudiate the Four Hundred: Thucydides 8.72.2, 74–77, 81–82, 86. Alcibiades' reply: Thucydides 8.86.6–7, 89.1; and the ephebic oath: Plutarch *Alcibiades* 15.4; on the oath, see Siewert 1977.

38. The fort on Eetionia: Thucydides 8.90–93.

39. Theramenes and Aristocrates, and opposition to the Four Hundred: Thucydides 8.89–93; Aristotle *Constitution* 33.2.

40. Original description of the Five Thousand: Thucydides 8.65.3, cf. 63.4. Registrars *(katalogeis)* of the Five Thousand: [Lysias] 20, *For Polystratus,* one of the elected Registrars, an old man (3) who compiled the list liberally (13). Thucydides

8.66.5, 72.1, 86.3, and especially 89.2–3 and 92.1, and 93.2, make it clear that publication of the list of the Five Thousand was often promised but never achieved; so also Aristotle *Constitution* 32.3, 33.2. For scholarship, see notes 23 and 28 above.

41. Assassination of Phrynichus: Thucydides 8.92.2; Lysias 13.70–76; *IG* I^3 102 (= ML 85, Fornara 155). Theramenes rallies the hoplites and the *peripoloi* in the name of the Five Thousand: Thucydides 92.5–11.

42. Importance of Euboea: Thucydides 2.14.1, 26.1, 32, 3.17.2, 93.1, 7.28.1, 8.1.3, 74.2, 86.9, 95.2, 96 (96.2: "worth more than Attica"); Lysias 34.3; Isocrates 4.108; Aristophanes *Clouds* 210–13; *IG* I^3 40.76–79 (= ML 52, Fornara 103). Euboean land controlled by Athenians: Herodotus 5.77, 6.100; Thucydides 1.114.3, 7.57.2, 8.95.7; Andocides 3.9; Demosthenes 20.115; Plutarch *Pericles* 7.6, 23.2; *IG* I^3 418; *IG* I^3 422.90, 218, 376–78; *IG* I^3 426.162; Meiggs 1972, 121–23, 262; see also chapter 3 note 30. Euboean dole: Aristophanes *Wasps* 715–18. Symbolic connections between Athens and Euboea, especially Eretria, are noted below, chapter 6 note 12. Spartan support for rebellion of Euboea: Thucydides 8.5.1–2, 60.1–2, 92.3; see also note 43 below.

43. Battle in the straits, rebellion of Euboea, and alarm at Athens: Thucydides 8.95–96; [Lysias] 20.14; Aristotle *Constitution* 33.1; Diodorus 13.47.3.

44. The end of the Four Hundred: Thucydides 8.97, 98.4; Aristotle *Constitution* 33. We are not told how the new council (presumably of 500, see Thucydides 8.86.6) and officers were chosen, although it is most likely that they were elected, not allotted, from a pool of candidates deemed to be qualified; see Aristotle *Constitution* 30.2. For recent scholarship, see notes 45 and 50 below.

45. The meaning of Thucydides 8.97.2 has been the focus of considerable scholarship. The most significant question concerns the phrases that I translate "political conduct" and "spirit of moderate compromise." While I, with some scholars (de Ste. Croix 1956; Sealey 1967, 122–30; Andrewes in Gomme et al. 1981, 331–39) see these phrases as describing attitudes affecting conduct, others (Rhodes 1972b; Ostwald 1986, 395–96 n. 199; Harris 1990) take these as references to specific constitutional forms that governed procedures, and speculate about what, beyond the few items mentioned in our sources, these forms and procedures were. See the discussions of de Ste Croix 1956; Sealey 1967, 120–32; Jameson 1971; Rhodes 1972b; Andrewes in Gomme et al. 1981, 323–40; Ostwald 1986, 395–411; Harris 1990, 273–76.

46. *Nomothetai* of 411/10: Thucydides 8.97.2; see Andrewes in Gomme et al. 1981, 330. The relation of these *nomothetai* to earlier and later legal commissions is controversial. While some, like Rhodes 1991, 88–89, see important distinctions between the various legal commissions attested between 411 and 399, I follow Ostwald 1986, 407, in interpreting Thucydides 8.97.2 "as meaning that the *ad hoc* work the commissions he calls *nomothetai* undertook before and under the Four Hundred was transformed by the intermediate regime into a long-term enterprise that lasted until the end of the Peloponnesian War and ended only after the Thirty were overthrown." See also: Hignett 1952, 300; Sealey 1987, 45–46; further discussion below, with notes 48 and 50; chapter 9, with notes 4 and 6; chapters 10 and 11.

47. On the thirty *syngrapheis* of 412/11, see above, with note 20.

48. *Nomothetai* in 403/2: Andocides 1.83–84, discussed below in chapter 10, with note 26. Authority of the Four Hundred to ratify laws: Aristotle *Constitution* 31.2.

49. Camp 1986, 90, dates construction of the new Council-House "in the years around 415–406": Shear 1995, 184, places it "well into the last decade of the 5th century." Boegehold 1972 discusses the establishment of the state archives; see now J. P. Sickinger, *Public Records and Archives in Classical Athens,* which has appeared too recently to be utilized here; see also discussion below, chapter 6, with notes 48 and 51.

50. "The *demos* soon took over": Aristotle *Constitution* 34.1; list of constitutional changes: 41.2. Thucydides 8.68.2 refers to the government that tried Antiphon as "the democracy." Various interpretations of this transition are offered by Hignett 1952, 375–78; de Ste. Croix 1956; Rhodes 1972b; Sealey 1975a; Ostwald 1986, 395–400; Harris 1990. After 411 a few features of the "constitution drafted for the future," described by Aristotle *Constitution* 30.2–31.1, were actually instituted (see most recently, Harris 1990, 257), but the evanescence of the Five Thousand as a discrete "constitutional" phase militates against the idea, argued by Harris 1990, that the constitution described by Aristotle (30.2–6) was implemented in its entirety after the fall of the Four Hundred.

51. The Four Hundred regarded government by the Five Thousand as "tantamount to outright democracy" according to Thucydides 8.92.11. "All Athenians under arms" in 413: Thucydides 7.28.2, 8.69.1. Arming of *thetes* in 415: Thucydides 6.43; see chapter 4, with notes 13 and 14.

52. Indictment of Antiphon: [Plutarch] *Moralia* 833e-34b; Thucydides 8.68.2; Lysias 12.67. Flight of Peisander and others: Thucydides 8.98; cf. Lysias 7.4, Xenophon *Hellenica* 1.7.28. On treasonous dealing with Sparta, and the betrayal of Attic territory to the enemy, see above, note 36.

CHAPTER SIX. A PROCESSION OF VICTORIES, 411–408

1. Battles of Cynossema and Abydos in the Hellespont: Thucydides 8.99–109; Xenophon *Hellenica* 1.1.1–8; Diodorus 13.38.3–42.4, 45.1–46.5.

2. Proposal to recall Alcibiades: Thucydides 8.97.3; Diodorus 13.38.2, 42.2. Thrasyllus: Xenophon *Hellenica* 1.1.8.

3. Theramenes: Xenophon *Hellenica* 1.1.12, who reports his arrival at Sestos with twenty ships; Diodorus 13.47.6–8, who reports thirty ships under Theramenes' command (possibly a confusion with the thirty ships he later commanded on the Bosporus, Xenophon *Hellenica* 1.1.22), and 49.1. Thucydides 8.64 describes the oligarchic rebellion at Thasos and among other Aegean allies earlier in 411.

4. Battle of Cyzicus: Xenophon *Hellenica* 1.1.11–23; Diodorus 13.49.2–51.8; Plutarch *Alcibiades* 28; Frontinus 2.5.44; Polyaenus 1.40.9. For recent discussions of the events and accounts of the battle, see Andrewes 1982, 19–23; Kagan 1987, 236–46. Xenophon reports the size of Mindarus' fleet as 60 ships; Diodorus and Justin 5.4.2 follow a source that gives its size as 80, the number accepted by most commentators.

5. Chrysopolis, "Golden-city," and plunder in the Propontis: Xenophon *Hellenica* 1.1.20–22, 35; Diodorus 13.64.2–4, 66.1–6; Justin 5.4.6.

6. Quote: Diodorus 13.52.4–6, translated by C.H. Oldfather. Celebration at Athens, and the Spartan embassy are also attested by Justin 5.4.4 and Nepos 7.5.5–7.1.

7. Pharnabazus supports the Spartans: Xenophon *Hellenica* 1.1.24–26. Meyer 1901, 4.616, places the departure of a Spartan embassy to the king in 410; on the

return of this embassy, led by Boeotius, see chapter 7, with note 2. Median revolt: Xenophon *Hellenica* 1.2.19; Lewis 1977, 133–34.

8. Cleophon, and the enthusiasm for Alcibiades: Diodorus 13.53.2–4, quote translated by C. H. Oldfather. Cleophon first comes to our notice in literary sources in spring 410 in Aristophanes *Thesmophoriazusae* 805; his name on ostraca (below, note 15) indicates political prominence before 415; for further references see below, note 10, and Rhodes 1981, 354–58.

9. Evidence for the tribute assessment of 410 has been discussed by Meritt 1936, 386–89, who cites the evidence of renewed tribute payments in Xenophon *Hellenica* 1.3.9; see also Meritt, Wade-Gery, and McGregor 1950, 91–92, 363; Meiggs 1972, 438–39. Evidence for the continued 5% harbor tax *(eikoste):* Aristophanes *Frogs* 363.

10. *Diobelia:* Aristotle *Constitution* 28.3, cf. *Politics* 1267b; Xenophon *Hellenica* 1.7.2; the common explanation of the *diobelia* as poor relief is expressed by Ferguson in Bury et al. 1927, 344; Rhodes 1981, 355–56; Andrewes in Lewis et al. 1992, 485. Denigration of Cleophon's memory: Aeschines 2.76; Aristotle *Constitution* 28.3, 34.1.

11. "Give the people what is theirs": Aristotle *Constitution* 27.4 (Pericles); Andocides 2.17 (ca. 410–405). Procedures for screening non-eligible persons from sessions of the Assembly are described by Hansen 1987, 88–89. Markle 1985, 280, calculates that "1.65 obols would provide a family of four with the most essential part of their [daily] diet."

12. Euboean dole: Aristophanes *Wasps* 715–18; scholia to the passage attest a military expedition to Euboea in 424/3 as the occasion; see Philochorus *FGrHist* 328 F. 130; see also chapter 3, with note 30. Conquest of Chalcis: Herodotus 5.77–78; on this passage, see chapter 1, with notes 15 and 69. Athens and Eretria: Herodotus 1.61, 5.57, 99, 6.43, 100; Plato *Menexenus* 240a-c. Theseus and the pedimental sculpture of the temple of Apollo Daphnephoros, possibly related to Antenor's sculpture of the tyrannicides: Deyhle 1969, 44–46; Kleine 1973, 96; considered with caution by Ridgway 1977, 299. Francis 1990, 8–16, recognizes the Athenian connection of the Eretria temple, but radically redates it. Elephenor and Theseus: Plutarch *Theseus* 35.5; Pausanias 1.17.6; cf. the haircut of Abantid warriors, *Iliad* 2.540–43, shared by Theseus, Plutarch *Theseus* 5.1. Pindar's *Paean* 5, to Delian Apollo on behalf of the Athenians, refers to Ionians from Athens taking possession of Euboea. On the sanctity of Athenian interests in Euboea, note the reference to "sacrifices required by the oracles concerning Euboea" in the decree publishing Athenian treaty relations with Chalcis, probably in 424/3: *IG* I^3 40.64–65 (= ML 52, Fornara 103); see Mattingly 1961b/1996.

13. On the revolt of Euboea in 411, see chapter 5, with notes 42–43. General "from Eretria": *IG* I^3 375.17 (= ML 84, Fornara 154); for the fort, see Thucydides 8.95.6.

14. Theseus and the *diobelia:* Aristophanes *Frogs* 140–42.

15. The foreign parentage of demagogues was a stock accusation of the comic stage: MacDowell 1993 reviews some examples; Aeschines 2.76 has taken the comic slander as fact. Cleophon's father, Cleippides (identified from ostraca, ML 21), was a general in the 420s (Thucydides 3.3.2); his mother, vulnerable perhaps because she had no public reputation in her own right, was said to be a foreigner, see Aristophanes *Frogs* 678–85; Plato Comicus *Cleophon, PCG* 61 (= 60 Kock, Edmonds).

16. *IG* I[3] 105, discussed most recently by Ryan 1994, who regards the source of the text to be Solonian; see also Ostwald 1986, 31–36, and 419, who regards it as early fifth-century; on epigraphic details see Lewis 1967. Philochorus *FGrHist* 328 F 140 attests another measure introduced in 410/09, mandatory random seating assignments, evidently designed to prevent the Council from being controlled by factional cliques as it had been in 411.

17. The oath against tyranny in the decree of Demophantus is quoted by Andocides 1.96–97; Demophantus, a *syngrapheus* promulgating a *nomos,* was probably a member of the commission of *nomothetai;* see chapter 5, with notes 46–49; see Ostwald 1955, 1986, 414–18.

18. Andrewes 1953 discusses the independence of the generals in the Hellespont from financial authority at Athens. Kagan 1987, 265–70, disputes Andrewes' emphasis on a political rift. Financial independence was a fact, however, and, as recognized by Hatzfeld 1940, 290–95, Alcibiades' formal recall and caution upon his homecoming are sufficient to indicate that, despite movements to bridge the rift, there were significant suspicions and political differences between the leadership at Athens and the commanders in the Hellespont. Krause 1914, 13, shows that at least twelve men acted as generals in the course of 410/9, further indicating that Athens and the Hellespontine fleet were not fully coordinated at that time. Note that the present account follows a different chronology for the events of 410–407 from that accepted by Hatzfeld, Andrewes, and Kagan; see Appendix C.

19. Aristocrates: *IG* I[3] 375.35 (= ML 84, Fornara 154); see chapter 5 note 39, chapter 7, with notes 10, 17; cf. Aristophanes *Birds* 124–26; Plato *Gorgias* 472a. Anytus, see above, chapter 4, with note 51. Thrasyllus: Xenophon *Hellenica* 1.1.33–34; see also above, note 2, and McCoy 1977.

20. Xenophon *Hellenica* 1.1.34 reports that Thrasyllus was authorized to command fifty triremes, while Diodorus 13.64.1, confusing him with Thrasybulus, says he was sent out by the Athenians with thirty ships (cf. 13.52.1). I believe both are correct, in that Thrasyllus was authorized to assemble fifty ships after his arrival in Samos (Xenophon *Hellenica* 1.2.1–2); his 5000 armed sailors (*nautai,* the usual term for rowers) would be the rowers specifically of the thirty ships he brought from Athens ($30 \times 170 = 5100$; on rowers/ship, see Morrison and Williams 1968, 254–59). Chios is not explicitly mentioned as an objective of Thrasyllus, but hopes for its recovery were high two years later (Plutarch *Alcibiades* 35.2), and there is no reason to think that it was not an objective in 410, as it had been in 412/11; see below, notes 32 and 36.

21. Peltasts: see Best 1969. Arming sailors and unarmed troops: Thucydides 6.43 (in 415, discussed above, chapter 4, with notes 13–14); see also 6.100.1, 7.1.5 (414); 8.17.1, 23.4, 25.1 (412); Xenophon *Hellenica* 1.1.24, 2.8 (410).

22. Thrasyllus' campaign: Xenophon *Hellenica* 1.2.1–13, 15–17, 3.1–8; Lysias 32.5–7; Diodorus 13.64.1–3, where Thrasyllus is confused with Thrasybulus; cf. the papyrus fragment published by Koenen 1976.

23. Accounts at Samos: *IG* I[3] 375.20–21 (= ML 84, Fornara 154), in the 6th prytany, records a transfer of 57 talents, 1000 drachmas handled at Samos. The amount would pay a force of 6000 men, roughly the number brought by Thrasyllus from Athens, at three obols per day, for nearly four months; on the rate of pay, see Thucydides 8.45.2, and Pritchett 1971, 14–24. Andrewes 1953, 5–6, also connects these

expenditures with Thrasyllus' Ionian campaign, but he provides no convincing explanation of the gap of at least six months between the date of the payment and the beginning, by his chronology, of Thrasyllus' campaign. Ferguson 1932, 39–40, recognized this possibility, but preferred to avoid the chronological embarrassment by supposing that it went to fund unspecified Athenian interests on Samos; Ferguson was at a loss to suggest where such a large amount came from (35–36). See Appendix C on the need to revise the chronology followed by Andrewes and Ferguson.

24. The fall of Pylos: Diodorus 13.64.6–7; Xenophon *Hellenica* 1.2.18.

25. Trial of Anytus: Aristotle *Constitution* 27.5; Diodorus 13.64.6. The wealth of Anytus (e.g., attested by Plato *Meno* 90a, Plutarch *Alcibiades* 4.4–5) gave him high social standing, but not necessarily the ability to buy a jury (as supposed by Davies 1971, 41, among others). Lipsius 1908, 401–403, examines usages of *dekazein* and *syndekazein* and argues that they describe something other than *dorodokia,* the usual term for bribery.

26. *IG* I^3 375 (= ML 84, Fornara 154) records disbursals of the *diobelia* in the 3rd–5th prytanies of 410/9 (i.e., from late summer through fall) but none in the 6th prytany, when accounts for operations in Ionia and Euboea were cleared, with no profits to be shared at home (above, note 23); two payments of *diobelia* in the 7th prytany in the winter may be the result of Anytus' dealings, but no such payments were made in the 8th–10th prytanies of spring 409. Lysias 21.3 refers to two *eisphorai* between 411/10 and 404/3; Thomsen 1964, 176, accepts the evidence of Diodorus 13.64.4 for the date of the first *eisphora* in 409 and places the second in 406.

27. Lampsacus: Xenophon *Hellenica* 1.2.13, 15; Diodorus 13.66.1.

28. Alcibiades and Tissaphernes: Plutarch *Alcibiades* 26.4–27.1; Xenophon *Hellenica* 1.1.9–10.

29. Troops of Thrasyllus and of Alcibiades: Xenophon *Hellenica* 1.2.13–17; Diodorus 13.64.3–4, 66.1 (confusing Thrasybulus for Thrasyllus); Plutarch *Alcibiades* 29.1–2. Chalcedon and Byzantium: Xenophon *Hellenica* 1.3.2–7, 10; Diodorus 13.64.2–3; below, notes 30–31.

30. Siege and treaty of Chalcedon: Xenophon *Hellenica* 1.3.8–12; Diodorus 13.66.1–2; Plutarch *Alcibiades* 29.3–30.1, 31.1–2; see also note 31 below. Selymbria: Xenophon *Hellenica* 1.1.21, 3.10; Diodorus 13.66.4; Plutarch *Alcibiades* 30.2–5; *IG* I^3 118 (= ML 87, Fornara 162). Byzantium: see below, note 34.

31. Autonomy in Peace of Nicias: Thucydides 5.18.5; see Ostwald 1982, 44–46, who notes the growing Athenian interest in granting defined autonomy to their allies after the defeat in Sicily (Ostwald does not extend his analysis beyond the period covered by Thucydides, however). The fact that Cyzicus, recently taken from Pharnabazus by force, was the meeting place for Pharnabazus and the Athenian ambassadors suggests that the entente established at Chalcedon had wider application. Amit 1973, 449, points out that the treaty entails Athenian recognition of Pharnabazus' domain, with potential wider application to the king's dominion in Asia. Lewis 1977, 122–25, has recognized the existence of a new form of autonomy among the Greek towns of Ionia by the time of Cyrus the Younger's arrival (below, note 33 with references), and attributes it to the agreement negotiated by the Spartan embassy led by Boeotius. That embassy was undertaken at roughly the same time as the Athenian negotiations through Pharnabazus; the concept of Greek autonomy

was probably similarly represented in both initiatives. Note the probable grant of autonomy by Athens to Selymbria in the treaty negotiated by Alcibiades and ratified at Athens in 408, *IG* I[3] 118.10–12 (= ML 87, Fornara 162). An Athenian perspective on this emergent entente is found in the opening of Euripides' *Bacchae,* 13–172, describing the sacral bonds between Asia and Greece, where Phrygia (the satrapy of Pharnabazus) and "gold-abounding" Lydia (the satrapy of Tissaphernes, before the arrival of Cyrus) are prominently mentioned. The coin shown in figure 4a–b is usually identified as an issue of Tissaphernes, ca. 412–411, to pay the Peloponnesian fleet (so, e.g., Kraay 1976, 74), but the conjunction of Persian and Athenian symbols better suits the circumstances of the treaty of Chalcedon, when Pharnabazus and the Athenians officially acknowledged the co-tributary status of Greek cities in the King's territory.

32. Embassy sent with Pharnabazus: Xenophon *Hellenica* 1.3.8–9, 13–14, 4.1; Plutarch *Alcibiades* 31.1. Accompanying the Athenians, Xenophon names "the Argives, Cleostratus and Pyrrolochus; Pasippidas and other ambassadors of the Lacedaemonians; and with them Hermocrates, who was already an exile from Syracuse, and his brother, Proxenus." Scholars are uncertain about the role of these Spartans and Hermocrates. Because Xenophon previously reported that Pasippidas was forced into exile as the result of a revolt on Thasos and intrigues with Tissaphernes (*Hellenica* 1.1.32), Amit 1973, 454–55, and Kagan 1987, 284 n. 33, suggest that these men accompanied the Athenians in a private capacity and treat their presence as of no great consequence. Xenophon clearly describes them as official representatives of Sparta, however, a fact that Amit seeks to remedy by textual emendation. The apparent contradictions are resolved if we understand that, unlike Hermocrates, Pasippidas was *not yet* an exile. This is how Meyer 1901, 4.622, understood Pasippidas' status (although, 625, he suggests that the purpose of Pasippidas' official mission was to oppose the Athenians; I believe that representing the Spartan side of an initiative of interest to all parties is a more accurate characterization). Pasippidas was the successor to Mindarus as Spartan naval commander for the year 410/9; the embassy to Darius was assembled late in 409, when Pasippidas' term of command was just completed and he was replaced by Cratesippidas; the embassy would have been an occasion for negotiations with Tissaphernes; the peace initiative in progress may have encouraged the Thasians to expel their foreign garrison, just as it evidently encouraged the Chians to exile pro-Spartan hard-liners at this time; over the winter of 409/8, Cratesippidas became aligned with the pro-Spartan Chian exiles (Diodorus 13.65.3–4) and eventually overturned arrangements that Pasippidas had overseen on Chios (cf. Xenophon *Hellenica* 1.1.32); meanwhile, the success of a separate Spartan initiative in the spring of 408 (Xenophon *Hellenica* 1.4.2, see chapter 7, with notes 1–2) encouraged Spartan authorities to repudiate Pasippidas' diplomatic venture, and to make of him a scapegoat and an exile. The connections between Thasos, Pasippidas, and peace are discussed further in chapter 12, with notes 37–39.

33. Xenophon *Hellenica* 1.4.6 states that the ambassadors were detained by Pharnabazus for three years. This has seemed improbable to most commentators, who have favored the suggestion by Amit 1973, 252 n. 16, to emend Xenophon's text to read "three months." There is no justification for this; the delay is accountable by the combination of Cyrus' dilatory progress, the ambiguities of satrapal pol-

itics in the prince's presence, and the mutual advantages that Pharnabazus and the Athenians sought to preserve, until Alcibiades' final expulsion brought the venture to nothing. See chapter 7, with notes 2–4, 10, 13.

34. Byzantium: Xenophon *Hellenica* 1.3.14–22; Diodorus 13.66.3–67; Plutarch *Alcibiades* 31.2–6; Polyaenus 1.47.2. Siege of Thasos: Xenophon *Hellenica* 1.4.9 gives a compressed account; *IG* I³ 101 (= ML 89, Fornara 156) attests a siege underway in early 409; Xenophon *Hellenica* 1.1.12 attests operations early in 410; see also Andrewes 1953, 6–8, and further discussion in chapter 7, with note 6, and chapter 12, with notes 39 and 40. Alcibiades at Samos and Caria: Xenophon *Hellenica* 1.4.8, 11. Thrasyllus sails to Athens: Xenophon *Hellenica* 1.4.10.

35. Robertson 1980c, 287, recognizing the question, has sought to explain Alcibiades' fundraising in Caria as the result of a military campaign lasting a year. But the Ceramic Gulf is an unlikely location for a year-long campaign, and offensive operations against territory controlled by Tissaphernes are unlikely in any event, at a time when Alcibiades was seeking a diplomatic settlement with Persia. Ransom of prisoners sent to Athens: Androtion *FGrHist* 324 F 44 (= Fornara 157). Note the issue made over the sale of Athenian prisoners by the Spartans in 406, and of Athenian allies in the Ceramic Gulf in 405: Xenophon *Hellenica* 1.6.14–15, 2.1.15; Diodorus 13.104.7.

36. Alcibiades' route: Xenophon *Hellenica* 1.4.9–11. Alcibiades, Chios, and Chian anti-Spartan movement: Diodorus 13.65.3–4; Plutarch *Alcibiades* 35.2; see above, note 32. Importance of Paros: Diodorus 13.47.8 refers to Parian "oligarchs" submitting to Athens in 411/10; *IG* XII 5, 109, discussed by Graham 1983, 76–79, and Grandjean and Salviat 1988, 272–76, attests the political and symbolic ties between Paros and Thasos, its colony, at this time. Andros: see below, chapter 7, with note 5.

37. Work on the Erechtheum: *IG* I³ 474–479; the resumption of this project, proposed by Epigenes in the first prytany of 409/8, must be directly related to the revenues sent to Athens by Alcibiades in 409: Diodorus 13.64.4. The "low" chronology favored by Ferguson and others has hitherto prevented scholars from recognizing Alcibiades' connection to the continuation of work on the Erechtheum. The connection is confirmed by the link between Epigenes and Alcibiades in a decree of 408, the former as president of the Assembly and the latter as proposer of the resolution: *IG* I³ 119.2 (= ML 88, Fornara 163). On the chronology followed here, see Appendix C. Critias on Alcibiades: Critias fr. 3–4 Edmonds *Elegy* (= DK 88 B 4–5); Plutarch *Alcibiades* 33.1. Alcibiades elected general: Xenophon *Hellenica* 1.4.10, 12.

38. Booty and trophies: Diodorus 13.68.2–3; Plutarch *Alcibiades* 32.1; Athenaeus 535c-d; Justin 5.4.8; Nepos 7.5.5–7. Thrasyllus: above, note 34; Diodorus 13.68.1–3 speaks of "the generals" coming to Athens with booty before mentioning Alcibiades himself; Plutarch *Alcibiades* 32.1, similarly enumerates booty before describing the arrival of Alcibiades. Prisoners sent previously: Xenophon *Hellenica* 1.2.13, 3.22; Diodorus 13.67.7; Plutarch *Alcibiades* 31.4.

39. Diodorus on the arrival of Alcibiades: 13.68.3. Duris of Samos on the arrival of Alcibiades: Plutarch *Alcibiades* 32.2–3; Athenaeus 535d; other dramatic entrances: Athenaeus 534c; cf. Plutarch *Alcibiades* 9, 10.1, 16.1. In defense of Duris' account, and on the methodological divide between Duris and Plutarch, and Plutarch's sources, see Gentili and Cerri 1988, 14–24. Sounds of the harbor: Aristophanes *Acharnians* 544–54.

40. Anxieties about Alcibiades' arrival, and the *Plynteria:* Xenophon *Hellenica* 1.4.12, 17; Plutarch *Alcibiades* 32.3, 34.1–2. The *Plynteria* "appears to have been a festival that few Athenians knew very much about," according to B. Nagy 1994, 276, who argues that "the evidence suggests... that the crowd at the Piraeus, along with Alcibiades and his supporters, had all been unaware that this was the day of the Plynteria" (285).

41. Quote from Justin 5.4.10, 15, translated by J. C. Yardley. Popular adulation of Alcibiades: Xenophon *Hellenica* 1.4.13–16, 20; Diodorus 13.68.2–69.1; Plutarch *Alcibiades* 32.4–5; Justin 5.4.9–18; Nepos 7.6. "Land and sea": Plutarch *Alcibiades* 32.5; Justin 5.4.7; Nepos 7.5.5, 6.3; Diodorus 13.69.3; in the accounts of the Treasurers of Athena: *IG* I^3 376.39 and 63, with the restorations proposed by Ferguson.

42. Xenophon *Hellenica* 1.4.13–16 summarizes arguments in defense of Alcibiades as they were alleged by "the crowd" *(ochlos),* and reports his own speeches more briefly, 1.4.20; cf. Plutarch *Alcibiades* 32.4–5, 33.2; Diodorus 13.69.1; Justin 5.4.11–12; Nepos 7.6.4. Isocrates 16, *On the Team of Horses,* is an extant defense of Alcibiades, delivered by his son on a later occasion; 16.5–11 bears comparison to the issues discussed in 408. Testimony against Alcibiades in 415 had come from Andromachus, a slave, and Agariste wife of Alcmaeonides and kinswoman of Alcibiades: Andocides 1.11–12, 16; cf. Plutarch *Alcibiades* 22.3. Adeimantus and Axiochus: Andocides 1.16; ML 79 B 53, 116, 118 (= Fornara 147 d); Xenophon *Hellenica* 1.4.21; Diodorus 13.69.3; *IG* I^3 101.48 (= ML 89, Fornara 156).

43. Alcibiades' *phthoneros daimon,* and conciliatory effect: Plutarch *Alcibiades* 33.2; Diodorus 13.69.1; Justin 5.4.13–18; Nepos 7.6.4.

44. Honors voted to Alcibiades: Xenophon *Hellenica* 1.4.20; Plutarch *Alcibiades* 33.2–3, 35.1; Diodorus 13.69.2–3; Justin 5.4.13–16; Nepos 7.6.5. Generalship as *autokrator:* cf. Thucydides 6.8.2, and see the comments by Dover in Gomme et al. 1970, 228.

45. Renunciation of curses: Plutarch *Alcibiades* 33.3; Diodorus 13.69.2; Justin 5.4.16; Nepos 7.6.5.

46. Celebration of the Mysteries: Xenophon *Hellenica* 1.4.20; Plutarch *Alcibiades* 34.3–6 (quote 34.5–6, translated by B. Perrin, with modifications).

47. Three decrees containing treaties negotiated by Alcibiades survive from the summer of 408 (the date, in all cases, depends upon the date of Alcibiades' return to Athens, see Appendix C): *IG* I^3 118, a treaty with Selymbria; *IG* I^3 119, a treaty with Clazomenian exiles (= ML 87 and 88, Fornara 162 and 163); probably *IG* I^3 120, subject uncertain. *IG* I^3 117 (= ML 91, Fornara 161), a decree datable to 407/6, should not have Alcibiades' name restored in it; so also Ostwald 1986, 433 n. 88.

48. On the growth of archival documents at Athens, see Boegehold 1972 and 1990; Stroud 1978; Thomas 1989; see now Sickinger, *Public Records.* On the complex but essential relationship between literacy and democracy, see Goody and Watt 1968; Hedrick 1994; Steiner 1994, 227–41. On the development, late in the fifth century, of the concept of writing as fundamental to the definition of *nomoi,* "laws," see Ostwald 1969, esp. 45–51, 57–61, and 1986, 89–93. The distinction drawn between *nomoi,* "laws," and *psephismata,* "decrees," by the end of the period under consideration here is discussed below, chapter 10, with note 41.

49. Conversation between Alcibiades and Pericles: Xenophon *Memorabilia* 1.2.40–42; the continuation of this conversation in the form of Socratic dialectic

probably represents the examination, in private circles, of the initial premise coming from public remarks of Alcibiades. Later assertion of sovereignty of the *demos:* Xenophon *Hellenica* 1.7.12, discussed in chapter 7, with note 30.

50. Athenaeus 407b-c, quoting Chamaeleon of Pontus, translated by C.B. Gulick, with modifications.

51. On the construction of the new Council-House and the creation of the state archives, see chapter 5, with note 49. On the Metroön and its cult: Vermaseren 1977, 32–35; Shear 1995, 171–78; Parker 1996, 188–94.

52. On the cult of Cybele and its associations, see Vermaseren 1977, 24–37; Burkert 1985, 177–79, and 1987, 33–36. Temple of Cybele/Kybebe at Sardis: Herodotus 5.102.1; punishment of Miletus, 6.18–19, which caused the Athenians to show "their profound distress in a number of ways," 6.21.2; punishment of Eretria, 6.101.3; punishment of Athens 5.105, 7.8.b, 8.53; cf. 6.96, 8.33. Note the close association between Themistocles and the cult of the Mother of the Gods during his exile in Asia Minor, Plutarch *Themistocles* 30–31. The early fifth-century building next to the old Council-House was identified as a temple of the Mother of the Gods by Thompson 1937, 135–40; the identification has been challenged (Boersma 1971, 31–34; Francis 1990, 112–20; Miller 1995, 135–37 n. 6; Shear 1995, 171–72, 176–77), but no alternative has won favor.

53. Plutarch *Nicias* 13.2 reports the self-castration—attested elsewhere as an act of devotion, or madness, inspired by Cybele—of an unknown individual over the altar of the Twelve Gods in the Agora at the time of the scandal over the mutilation of the Herms. Aristophanes *Birds* 873–76; Euripides *Helen* 1301–68, see chapter 4, with notes 9–11; *Bacchae* 64–87; Sophocles *Philoctetes* 391–402; Jameson 1956 draws plausible connections to Alcibiades and contemporary events; Vickers 1987, 172–87, presses specific identities rather too closely. Roller 1996 reviews the evidence for Cybele/Mother of the Gods in Attic tragedy.

54. Cybele/Mother Dindymene on Mount Dindymus, also called Arctonesus, at Cyzicus: Herodotus 4.76; Apollonius *Argonautica* 1.936–1152; Strabo 1.2.38, 12.8.11; Pausanias 8.46.4, cf. 7.17.9–12; see Vermaseren 1977, 28–29; Robertson 1996, 267–69, 272, 287–92. Cybele/Mother of the Gods as protector of seafarers: Pindar *Pythian* 3.68–79; Timotheus *Persians* 115–50; Diodorus 3.55.8; Apollonius (above).

55. Cybele and Artemis of Ephesus: Timotheus *Persians* 127–73; cf. the Lydian element in the foundation legend of the cult of Artemis of Ephesus as discussed by Pausanias 7.2.6–8. Although the two goddesses are sometimes distinguished, they are also closely associated, especially in their cults at Sardis and Ephesus: Hanfmann and Waldbaum 1969; Vermaseren 1977, 27; Lou Bengisu 1996, 10–11; cf. Smith 1996. The association sometimes becomes identification: see the Kula relief, cited by Vermaseren 1977, 30 and figure 16; note also the probable identity of the cult-place of the Mother and Artemis at Magnesia on the Meander: Bean 1966, 248–50; cf. Plutarch *Themistocles* 30–31; the same may be true of the cult-places of Cybele/Kybebe and Artemis at Sardis: Bean 1966, 266. Artemis of Ephesus and Tissaphernes: Thucydides 8.109.1; Xenophon *Hellenica* 1.2.6; cf. Croesus and Artemis of Ephesus: Herodotus 1.92.1.

56. The statue of the Mother of the Gods was attributed to Pheidias by Pausanias 1.3.5 and Arrian *Periplous* 9, but the attribution to Pheidias' pupil Agoracritus of Paros by Pliny *Natural History* 36.17 is chronologically more probable.

CHAPTER SEVEN. THE LIMITS OF DEMOCRATIC IMPERATIVE, 408–405

1. Spartan embassy to Athens: Androtion *FGrHist* 324 F 44 (= Fornara 157).

2. Spartan embassy from Persia (embassy of Boeotius): Xenophon *Hellenica* 1.4.2–4; see Meyer 1901, 4.616, 627–28; Lewis 1977, 124–25; Seager and Tuplin 1980, 144 n. 36; chapter 6, above, with notes 7 and 33. Euryptolemus: Xenophon *Hellenica* 1.3.13, 4.19.

3. Cyrus favored by Parysatis: Xenophon *Anabasis* 1.1.1–5; Ctesias *Persica* epitome 57; cf. Plutarch *Artaxerxes* 2; Olmstead 1948, 369; Lewis 1977, 134–35. Cyrus was born after the accession of Darius in 424: Plutarch *Artaxerxes* 2.3; for the date of Darius' accession see Lewis 1977, 72.

4. Arrival of Cyrus: Xenophon *Hellenica* 1.4.4–7, 5.1–7; Diodorus 13.70.3; Lewis 1977, 134–36. Character and motives of Cyrus: *Anabasis* 1.1.5. The interval of a year between the announcement and the arrival of Cyrus, suggested by Robertson 1980c, 290–93, has not otherwise been generally recognized; see Appendix C.

5. Alcibiades at Andros: Xenophon *Hellenica* 1.4.22–23; Diodorus 13.69.4–5, cf. 72.3; Plutarch *Alcibiades* 35.1–3.

6. Surrender of Thasos: Xenophon *Hellenica* 1.4.9; Diodorus 13.72.1–2; Axiochus proposed the second decree in *IG* I^3 101.48–68 (= ML 89, Fornara 156); from Thasos, *IG* XII 8, 262, supplemented by a new fragment discussed by Grandjean and Salviat 1988, is an Athenian decree approving the restored democracy on Thasos, passed probably in the archonship of Antigenes (after midsummer 407). For further discussion, see chapter 12, with notes 39 and 40.

7. Lysander at Ephesus: Plutarch *Lysander* 3.2; Diodorus 13.70.2–4.

8. The battle of Notium: Xenophon *Hellenica* 1.5.10–15; *Hellenica Oxyrhynchia* 4 (Florence); Diodorus 13.71; Plutarch *Alcibiades* 35.4–6, *Lysander* 4.5–6.2. Russell 1994 suggests a plausible modification of the usual explanation of the opening of this battle (see Andrewes 1982, 15–19). On the approximate date, see Appendix C.

9. Alcibiades at Cyme: Diodorus 13.73.3–6; Nepos 7.7.1–2. Spartan presence in a defeat of Alcibiades on land, certainly at Cyme, is reported by Justin 5.5.2–3; Plutarch *Lysander* 5.3 reports Lysander's efforts to gather political allies, supporters of oligarchy, in Ionia as an immediate result of the victory at Notium.

10. Impeachment of Alcibiades: Xenophon *Hellenica* 1.5.16; Lysias 14.37–38; 21.7; Diodorus 13.73.3–74.1; Plutarch *Alcibiades* 36.1–3; Justin 5.5.4–7; Nepos 7.7.2–4. It is possible that the impeachment resulted from the annual audit of Alcibiades' tenure of office, held at the beginning of the archonship of Antigenes (407/6); see Appendix C. Cleophon is identified as leading the indictment by Himerius 36.18 (= Photius *Library* 377). Diodorus 13.74.3–4 notices the suit at this time of Diomedes (= Teisias, see chapter 4 note 61) against Alcibiades over the chariot team that won at Olympia in 416; like the allegations that Themistocles' wisdom was stolen (see chapter 1, with note 29), it was essential to strip the fallen champion of his claims to fame. Thrasybulus and Adeimantus were impeached with Alcibiades, but Xenophon, *Hellenica* 1.4.10, 21, 5.18, attests that Aristocrates and Conon were generals both with Alcibiades and after his impeachment.

11. Alcibiades in the Chersonese: Xenophon *Hellenica* 1.3.8, 10, 5.17; Lysias 14.38; Diodorus 13.66.3, 74.2, 105.3; Plutarch *Alcibiades* 30.2, 4, 36.2–37.2; Nepos

7.7.4. Seuthes: Thucydides 2.97.3, 4.101.5; Xenophon *Anabasis* 7.2.31–38, 3.19. In addition to the strategic importance of the Chersonese for maritime trade with the Black Sea, Athenians of means had money invested in land there: Lysias 32.6, 15; Andocides 3.9, 15.

12. Conon reduces number of ships: Xenophon *Hellenica* 1.5.20; Diodorus 13.76.1, 77.1; cf. Justin 5.6.1–2. Lysander and Callicratidas: Xenophon *Hellenica* 1.6.1–3.

13. Athenian ambassadors return from Pharnabazus: Xenophon *Hellenica* 1.4.6–7. Athenian ambassadors negotiate through Tissaphernes: Xenophon *Hellenica* 1.5.8–9. Cyrus withholds pay: Xenophon *Hellenica* 1.6.6–11.

14. Callicratidas, and the blockade of Conon at Mytilene: Xenophon *Hellenica* 1.6.1–23; Diodorus 13.76.2–79.7.

15. Urgent measures for shipbuilding: *IG* I^3 117 (= ML 91, Fornara 161), dated to 407/6 by Meritt 1936, almost certainly correctly, since the name P[ericles] in lines 5–6 is the only name of a known general after Pythodorus in 415/4 that could fit in the space (see Krause 1914, 11–14; Develin 1989, 153–81); Meritt's restoration of Alcibiades as the proposer of the decree, however, relies on the "low" chronology for his return to Athens and is certainly not correct; see Appendix C. *Eisphora:* see Thomsen 1964, 176. Joint-trierarchy: Lysias 32.24, 26; Gabrielsen 1994, 174, places this innovation "in the immediate vicinity of 408/7."

16. Manning the fleet: Xenophon *Hellenica* 1.6.24–25; Diodorus 13.97.1–2; Hellanicus *FGrHist* 323a F 25 (= Fornara 164A); cf. Aristophanes *Frogs* 190–91, 693–94, 718–20. Gold coinage: Hellanicus *FGrHist* 323a F 26; Philochorus *FGrHist* 328 F 141 (= Fornara 164B). That Xenophon fought at Arginusae has been plausibly suggested by Delebecque 1957, 24, 44, 58–61. The Lenormant relief, figure 6, is usually dated to the period of Arginusae; for a different interpretation, see Beschi 1969–1970, 117–32.

17. Battle of Arginusae: Xenophon *Hellenica* 1.6.26–38, 7.29–32; Diodorus 13.97.2–100.6. On the date of the battle, before the end of the archonship of Antigenes (407/6), see Appendix C.

18. The mention of "the generals with P[ericles]" as responsible for the shipbuilding program at Athens (*IG* I^3 117 = I^2 105, ML 91, Fornara 161, cited above, note 15) identifies Pericles as the senior partner among the generals at Athens before Arginusae, a role in keeping with his experience as a financial officer (*IG* I^3 375.8, 11, 13, 18, = ML 84, Fornara 154); Xenophon *Hellenica* 1.6.29 locates Pericles on the wing engaged by Callicratidas, while Diodorus' highly dramatic narrative, although inconsistent in other details, describes the ships of these two opposing commanders as locked together at the climax of the battle (13.99.4). Official dispatch: Xenophon *Hellenica* 1.7.4. The return of Diomedon and Erasinides prior to the recall of the other generals involved in the battle is inferred from their absence from the list of recalled generals in Diodorus 13.101.5 and from the fact that Xenophon, *Hellenica* 1.7.1, reports that the Athenians initially appointed two replacement generals, Adeimantus and Philocles. These replacements probably represent changes in the elected board of generals for the archonship of Callias (406/5) prior to the recall and trial of the rest of the generals except Conon; see Appendix C.

19. The trial of the generals after Arginusae looms large in any evaluation of Athenian democracy in the late fifth century. I have gained useful insight from An-

drewes 1974, and Ostwald 1986, 434–45, where earlier scholarship is cited (the more recent essays by Lang, 1990 and 1992, tend to render any understanding problematic). The present interpretation differs significantly from previous accounts on details of motives and of legal means involved in the trial. On the Lenormant relief, see note 16 above.

20. Quote: Aristotle *Constitution* 34.1.

21. Quote: Aristophanes *Frogs* 1532–33.

22. Cleophon's performance echoes the feigned poetic frenzy by which Solon was said to have inspired the Athenians to fight for Salamis: Plutarch *Solon* 8.1–2; it is noteworthy that Cleophon was known to have been well versed in Solon's poetry: Aristotle *Rhetoric* 1375b. Quote: Xenophon *Memorabilia* 3.5.7–8.

23. Erasinides and Archedemus: Xenophon *Hellenica* 1.7.2; cf. Aristophanes *Frogs* 416–21, and 588, where the double-edged joke at Archedemus probably refers to his control of the *diobelia,* as does the apparent reference to his control of the fee to be paid on arrival in Hades by Eupolis *Goats* fr. 9 *PCG,* Kock (= Edmonds fr. 71). Xenophon *Memorabilia* 2.9 singles out Archedemus for his scrupulous honesty.

24. Trial and imprisonment of Erasinides: Xenophon *Hellenica* 1.7.2. Recall of other generals: Diodorus 13.101.5; see also above, note 18. The *Oschophoria* and *Kybernesia* took place at Phaleron within the three weeks preceding of the climax of the trial of the generals around the time of the *Apatouria* (Xenophon *Hellenica* 1.7.8); on the former festivals, see Plutarch *Theseus* 17.6, 22–23; Deubner 1932, 142–47, 225; Mikalson 1975, 68–71.

25. The generals accuse Theramenes and Thrasybulus in the Council: Xenophon *Hellenica* 1.7.3–4, cf. 2.3.35. The Council detains the generals: Xenophon *Hellenica* 1.7.3. An exactly analogous example of diverting prosecution by bringing against the accuser an unrelated charge specifically of murder, a *dike phonou* by *apographe,* is described by Antiphon 6.35–37; were the generals reading their Antiphon? This form of *apographe,* not otherwise attested, is noticed only in passing by Lipsius 1908, 300–302, with n. 11.

26. Speech of Theramenes in the first Assembly: Xenophon *Hellenica* 1.7.4–7, 2.3.35. Diodorus 13.101.2–6 provides an account that confuses the dispatch (*epistole,* cf. Xenophon *Hellenica* 1.7.4) sent by generals to Athens after the battle with the written accusation (the *graphe* or *apographe,* above, note 25) filed by the generals in the Council as the instrument of their indictment of Theramenes and Thrasybulus; as a result he also confuses the sequence of Assembly meetings. Xenophon's account, although elliptical on certain points, is consistent with the account reconstructed here.

27. Callixeinus' resolution: Xenophon *Hellenica* 1.7.9–10.

28. *Apatouria:* Xenophon *Hellenica* 1.7.8. Men from the fleet on hand to support the generals: Diodorus 13.101.5. Unusual influence of the poor and newly enfranchised citizens: Aristophanes *Frogs* 273–76, 686–705, 718–37, 771–83.

29. Dramatic performance by Theramenes: Xenophon *Hellenica* 1.7.9–11; Diodorus 13.101.6, and see 97.6, where Thrasybulus (again a mistake for Thrasyllus, see chapter 6 note 22) dreamed before the battle that he and his fellow generals were actors in Euripides' *Phoenician Women* while their opponents were competing with the *Suppliant Women,* both plays dealing with the recovery of the dead after battle; see chapter 1, with note 66.

30. Euryptolemus' motion, popular outcry, and the intransigence of Socrates: Xenophon *Hellenica* 1.7.12–15; Plato *Apology* 32b-c.

31. Gray 1989, 87–91, rightly notes that Euryptolemus' speech relies on an appeal to *philanthropia*. Trial en bloc of Antiphon and associates in 411: [Plutarch] *Moralia* 833e-34a. Trial en bloc of Phrynichus and his defenders: Lycurgus *Against Leocrates* 113–14. Euryptolemus seems aware of these precedents when he urges the example of the trial of another oligarch of 411, Aristarchus, who was given "one day in which to defend himself as he pleased" (1.7.28); but Aristarchus had fled in 411 (Thucydides 8.98) and was apprehended and tried sometime later, when he had no more colleagues in crime. Note that Aristophanes *Lysistrata* 269–70 refers, hypothetically, to the execution of malefactors after "one vote for all," *(pasas hypo psephou mias)*. Although their behavior is no measure of standard practice, it is worth noting that the Thirty later used trial en bloc as a means to condemn large numbers of political foes: Xenophon *Hellenica* 2.4.9.

32. Resolution of the trial on the day following Socrates' prytany: [Plato] *Axiochus* 368d-e, recognized by Cawkwell 1979, note to *Hellenica* 1.7.15. Speech of Euryptolemus: Xenophon *Hellenica* 1.7.12–33. Reasons for the disproportionate space given to this speech are considered by Gray 1989, 83–91. On the personal interest of Xenophon in this speech, see note 16 above and chapter 12, below, with note 22.

33. The most probable explanation of the *hypomosia* of Menecles, Xenophon *Hellenica* 1.7.34, is that it was a demand for a recount of the *diacheirotoneia*, as observed by Hansen, 1977/1983, 113–14. The vote for condemnation was by secret ballot as prescribed by Callixeinus: Xenophon *Hellenica* 1.7.9–10; cf. Aristotle *Constitution* 69.1.

34. Condemnations of Miltiades: Herodotus 6.136; Plato *Gorgias* 516d; Plutarch *Aristides* 26.3; of Pericles: Thucydides 2.65.3; Plato *Gorgias* 515e-16a; Plutarch *Pericles* 35.4; *Aristides* 26.3; Diodorus 12.45.4; of Paches: Plutarch *Nicias* 6.1–2; *Aristides* 26.3; see chapter 3, with note 14; of the *Hellenotamiae:* Antiphon 5.69–70, see chapter 3, with note 18.

35. On passion, or *eros,* in the rhetoric of Pericles and Alcibiades, see chapter 4, with notes 8 and 35, and chapter 6, with notes 46

36. Plato's critique of poetry is expressed widely in his works, most famously in the *Republic* Books 2–3 and 10; on the relation between poetry and rhetoric see *Gorgias* 500–502. Amidst the vast modern commentary on this subject, Havelock 1963 is still incisive; Asmis 1992 provides a more recent survey. Those who "sit quibbling with Socrates": Aristophanes *Frogs* 1491–99.

37. The restoration of Aeschylus, at the end of Aristophanes' *Frogs,* is not only for the salvation of the city, but also for the salvation of the poetry of the theater (lines 1418–19).

38. Quote: *Frogs* 771–83.

39. Quote: *Frogs* 967–79; the pun, here loosely translated "Achaean, not a Chian," exemplifying Theramenes' verbal dexterity, is a play on the homonyms *Chios,* "man from Chios," and *Keios,* "man from Keos." Keos was the home of the sophist and orator, Prodicus, famous for his studies of synonyms and homonyms, and reputedly a teacher of Theramenes (DK 84 A 4b, 6, 7 = Sprague 1972, 73–74).

40. Quote: *Frogs* 1195–96. Archedemus, dubbed the "bleary-eyed" in *Frogs* 588, seems to have been excused from service in 406 for that reason; see *Frogs* 192.

41. Quote: *Frogs* 533–41.

42. Theramenes elected and rejected: Lysias 13.10; Theramenes' past collaboration with Alcibiades was probably the chief reason for his ambiguous reputation in 405; see Andrewes 1953, 2–3; Ostwald 1986, 392–93, 443, 447. Cleophon and Critias: Aristotle *Rhetoric* 1375b; cf. Xenophon *Hellenica* 2.3.35–36, *Memorabilia* 1.2.24.

43. Quote: Xenophon *Memorabilia* 3.5.16.

44. On Euripides' library and bookishness, see Aristophanes *Frogs* 943, 1409; Athenaeus 1.3a; implications of Euripides' bookishness, especially in the *Frogs,* are examined by Steiner 1994, 209–12. Plato *Apology* 26d reports the books of Anaxagoras on sale "in the orchestra," a central area of the Agora (see chapter 1 note 12). See further discussion in chapter 12, below, pages 296–98.

45. Date of Plato's *Gorgias* is established by the reference, in 473e, to Socrates' service as prytanis "last year," and is confirmed by, among other topical allusions, the references to Euripides' *Antiope* (performed after 411), and to Archelaus, king of Macedon, much on the mind of Athenians in the younger Pericles' last year: *IG* I^3 117 (= ML 91, Fornara 161), discussed above, note 15. Funeral oration of Gorgias: DK 82 B 6, translated by Kennedy in Sprague 1972, 48–49.

46. Remorse of the Athenians, and indictment of Callixeinus: Xenophon *Hellenica* 1.7.35; Diodorus 13.103.1–2; cf. Plato *Apology* 32b; see below, chapter 8, with note 35.

47. Forms of *atimia:* Andocides 1.73–79; see MacDowell 1962, 106–19, and 1978, 74–75; Boegehold 1990. The encore performance of the *Frogs* recorded by Dicaearchus is noted in the ancient *hypothesis* to the play; when it took place is uncertain. The favorite passage was the *parabasis,* 635–737.

48. Quote: *Frogs* 1420–34.

49. Gomme 1956, 198, and Dover, in Gomme et al. 1970, 242–45, likewise assign the fatal dissention described by Thucydides 2.65.10–12 and 6.15.4 to 407–405.

CHAPTER EIGHT. SURRENDERING TO SPARTA, 405–404

1. Chios: Xenophon *Hellenica* 1.6.38, 2.1.1–5, 16. Reinstatement of Lysander and first meeting with Cyrus: Xenophon *Hellenica* 2.1.6–7, 10–11; Diodorus 13.104.3; Plutarch *Lysander* 7, 9.1.

2. Cyrus' expectations: Xenophon *Hellenica* 2.1.8–9; Plutarch *Artaxerxes* 2.2. Cyrus summoned: Xenophon *Hellenica* 2.1.9, 13–14, *Anabasis* 1.1.1–2; Diodorus 13.104.3–4; Plutarch *Lysander* 9.1–2.

3. Cyrus' second meeting with Lysander: Xenophon *Hellenica* 2.1.13–15; Diodorus 13.104.4; Plutarch *Lysander* 9.2.

4. Artaxerxes' accession year (which precedes his Year 1), and therefore the year that Darius' death was announced, is identified by Mesopotamian documents cited by Parker and Dubberstein 1956, 18, cf. 33. Diodorus 13.108.1 reports that Darius died and Artaxerxes began his reign "a little after the peace" (between Sparta and Athens in spring 404). Hamilton 1979, 66; Krentz 1982, 32 n. 8; Kagan 1987, 409, are among those who accept this as evidence that Darius died in March 404. Lewis 1977, 120 and n. 81, is skeptical of the accuracy of Diodorus' synchro-

nism and places the accession in 405. It seems probable that Diodorus' statement, which enumerates the years of both Darius' and Artaxerxes' reigns, was based on an accurate report of the beginning of Artaxerxes Year 1 in Babylon (April 10, 404), with which Darius' death was connected by inference.

5. Tissaphernes denounces Cyrus: Xenophon *Anabasis* 1.1.3–4; Ctesias *Persica* epitome 57; cf. Plutarch *Artaxerxes* 3; Justin 5.11.1–5.

6. Lysander at Miletus, in Caria, and across the Aegean: Xenophon *Hellenica* 2.1.15–19; cf. *Anabasis* 1.9.9; Diodorus 13.104.5–8; Plutarch *Lysander* 8.1–3, 9.2–4; quote: 9.2. The raid on Attica, joined by Agis' full army, probably took place close to the grain harvest at the beginning of summer. Note that the Athenian attack on "the king's land" at this time, Xenophon *Hellenica* 2.1.16, must refer specifically to Cyrus' dominion.

7. Battle of Aegospotami: Xenophon *Hellenica* 2.1.20–32; Plutarch *Lysander* 9.4–11.7, *Alcibiades* 36.4–37.3; Polyaenus 1.45.2. The account of Diodorus 13.105.2–106.7 differs in certain details from Xenophon and Plutarch, and is probably less reliable in this instance; Ehrhardt 1970, and Kagan 1987, 386–95, argue otherwise; see also Strauss 1983; Wylie 1986.

8. Alcibiades at Aegospotami: Xenophon *Hellenica* 2.1.25–26; Diodorus 13.105.3–4; Plutarch *Alcibiades* 36.5–37.2; Nepos 7.8.2–6; Lysias 14.38.

9. Athenian disarray: Xenophon *Hellenica* 2.1.28. Xenophon *Hellenica* 2.1.28–29 reports that Conon took eight ships to Cyprus, while one, the *Paralus,* went to Athens; Lysias 21.10–11 reports the twelve ships escaped, including two that sailed to Athens; Isocrates 18.59–60 indicates that more than one trireme returned to Athens; Diodorus 13.106.6 reports a total of ten surviving ships; Ehrhardt 1970 worries these discrepancies.

10. Execution of prisoners: Xenophon *Hellenica* 2.1.30–32; Plutarch *Lysander* 11.6, 13.1–2; Pausanias 9.32.9. Diodorus 13.106.7 reports only the execution of Philocles.

11. Decree for Euagoras: *IG* I^3 113; conventional passages restored by M.J. Osborne 1981, D3, 31–33. The decree is dated in 411 by Spyridakis 1935, 49–50; "between 411 and 407" by Lewis 1977, 129; tentatively in "the early part of 407" by M.J. Osborne 1982, 21–24; Costa 1974, 45–46 and n. 30, is indecisive.

12. Euagoras, see chapter 5 note 35. Revolt of Egypt in 405: Olmstead 1948, 373. *IG* I^3 113.47: [...]*as Chias*[...] is probably a reference to Chian ships, more likely allies of the Athenians and of Euagoras than foes. These may have been ships manned by pro-Athenian Chian exiles based at Atarneus, a stronghold on the mainland north of Chios (Diodorus 13.65.4; Xenophon *Hellenica* 3.2.11). Possibly some of the ships captured by the Athenians at Arginusae were provided to these Chians exiles, who would have supported the efforts of Conon and his colleagues to reduce the island of Chios (above, note 1), and may have continued to serve under the command of Conon.

13. Lysander's strategy: Xenophon *Hellenica* 2.2.1–2, 5–9; Plutarch *Lysander* 13.2–14.3; Diodorus 13.106.8. Athenians' reactions: Xenophon *Hellenica* 2.2.3–4; Isocrates 18.59–60; Diodorus 13.107.1; Justin 5.7.4–12. Athenian triremes at Samos: *IG* I^3 127.25–32 (= ML 94, Fornara 166), lines 25–32.

14. A grain dole seems to have replaced the *diobelia* at this time: *IG* I^3 379.86–87, 90–91, see Ferguson 1932, 82–84; Woodward 1956, 116–17. The honors recorded

in *IG* I^3 125, for Epicerdes of Cyrene (see also Demosthenes 20.41–43), and in *IG* I^3 126, for Polybus of Calydnos (= Calymnos; the names are conjectural restorations, the ethnic suggested here for the first time), both in the year 405/4, may be connected with the grain imports mentioned by Lysias 6.49 and Isocrates 18.61, where Lysander's decree is reported. Andocides 2, *On His Return* 20–21 refers to the imminent arrival of grain ships from Cyprus. Customarily dated ca. 411–408 (see Maidment in the Loeb, *Minor Attic Orators,* vol. 1, 1941, 454–58), in fact the speech belongs in 405, after Aegospotami; cf. Andocides 2.18, 20–21, and Isocrates 18.61, and especially Lysias 6.47–49, where Andocides is explicitly said to have failed to import grain into Athens, following the defeat in the Hellespont (i.e., Aegospotami), while others succeeded in doing so; Andocides 2.23 seems to refer to awards to the murderers of Phrynichus (in 409) and to grants of citizenship after Arginusae (406). The circumstances indicated by placing *IG* I^3 113 in 405 conform well to this redating of Andocides 2, *On His Return.*

15. Spartan show of force: Xenophon *Hellenica* 2.2.7–10; Lysias 13.5; Plutarch *Lysander* 14.1; Diodorus 13.107.2.

16. Loose blockade of Piraeus: Diodorus 13.107.3; Lysias 6.47–49; Isocrates 18.60–61; cf. the travel of Samian envoys to Athens during this period: *IG* I^3 127.7–8, 24–25, 33 (= *IG* II^2 1, ML 94, Fornara 166).

17. Xenophon *Hellenica* 2.2.11–15; Lysias 13.8.

18. Political significance of Themistoclean fortifications and the Long Walls: Thucydides 1.91.4–7, 93.7, 107.1, 4; Plato *Gorgias* 455e, 518e-19b; Aristophanes *Knights* 74–79; *Triphales* fr. 556–69 *PCG* (= 542–57 Kock, Edmonds). On Alcibiades and other long walls, see Plutarch *Alcibiades* 15.2–3; Thucydides 5.52.2, 82.5–6.

19. Proposal of Archestratus and response by Cleophon: Xenophon *Hellenica* 2.2.15; Lysias 13.5–8, 30.10; Aeschines 2.76.

20. Fleet at Cyprus: in addition to whatever forces Euagoras had at his disposal (see above, note 12). Carthaginian embassy: *IG* I^3 123 (= ML 92, Fornara 165); cf. Diodorus 13.80–96, 108–14. Archelaus: *IG* I^3 117 (= ML 91, Fornara 161). Alcibiades: Plutarch *Alcibiades* 37.3–4; cf. Xenophon *Hellenica* 3.2.2–5.

21. Theramenes' mission: Xenophon *Hellenica* 2.2.16; Lysias 12.68–70, 13.9–10; see also the "Theramenes Papyrus," Merkelbach and Youtie 1968; Krentz 1982, 34–35 n. 17. Secret information was common currency among those who claimed to be able to benefit the Athenians at this time; see Andocides 2.19–22 (see above, note 14, on the date).

22. Aristoteles: Xenophon *Hellenica* 2.2.17, 3.13, 46; Plato *Parmenides* 127d; Avery 1959, 95–100. Charicles: Isocrates 16.42; Avery 1959, 108–17. Critias: Xenophon *Hellenica* 2.3.36, where Critias' alleged "democratic" activities in Thessaly were probably akin to the pro-Spartan opposition to dynastic power portrayed in the pseudo-Critian, Herodes *On the Constitution* (see the references in chapter 4, note 64); on Critias see also Avery 1963; Krentz 1982, 45–46; Ostwald 1986, 460–66. Aristotle *Constitution* 34.3 refers to these men and their colleagues collectively as those "among the notables who were in the *hetaireiai,* and those among the exiles who returned after peace was made, [who] were bent on oligarchy."

23. Starvation in Athens: Xenophon *Hellenica* 2.2.10–11, 14, 21 reports "many dying in the city from starvation"; Lysias 13.11 reports "bad conditions for the majority in need of sustenance." Derivative from these and possibly other contempo-

rary accounts, Plutarch *Lysander* 14.3 reports that "those in the city were in a bad way"; Diodorus 13.107.4 reports that "the city was filled with corpses"; Justin 5.8.3 reports "starvation and constant deaths." Although Xenophon's word should command respect on this occasion, the emphasis on deaths may be somewhat exaggerated; see Garnsey 1988, 35.

24. Return of Cyrus and Tissaphernes to Ionia: Ctesias *Persica* epitome 57; Justin 5.11.5; cf. Xenophon *Anabasis* 1.1.5–8; Lewis 1977, 120.

25. Theramenes' treachery: Lysias 12.66–67, cf. 77, his "many pledges of faith by deed" to the oligarchs. Lysander on Thasos in 404: Polyaenus 1.45.4; Nepos 6.2.2–3; Grandjean and Salviat 1988, 276–78, argue that Lysander intervened on Thasos in 405, immediately after Aegospotami, before his arrival at Athens; the improbability of this has already been seen by Andrewes 1971, 217; Bommelaer 1981, 157–58. Critias' speech: Xenophon *Hellenica* 2.3.29–33.

26. Theramenes' first return to Athens: Xenophon *Hellenica* 2.2.17.

27. Theramenes' embassy to Sparta: Xenophon *Hellenica* 2.2.17–19. This mission is conflated with Theramenes' previous sojourn with Lysander in the accounts of Lysias 12.68–70 and 13.10–16.

28. Convention of Spartan allies: Xenophon *Hellenica* 2.2.19 and see below, note 29. Apollo consulted in 432: Thucydides 1.118.3; note also the prominence of relations with Delphi in the terms of the Peace of Nicias, Thucydides 5.18.2. Dedications to Apollo: Plutarch *Lysander* 18.1–2; Diodorus 14.13.3; Parke 1932.

29. Conference negotiating the Peace of Nicias: Thucydides 5.17.2. Status of Eleans: Xenophon *Hellenica* 3.2.21–23. Lysander threatens Megarians: Plutarch *Lysander* 22.1. Demand by Thebans and Corinthians to destroy Athens, denied by Spartans: Xenophon *Hellenica* 2.2.19–20, 3.5.8, 6.5.36; Andocides 3.21; cf. Isocrates 14.31; Demosthenes 19.65; Diodorus 15.63.1; Plutarch *Lysander* 15.2; Justin 5.8.3–4. Oracle of Apollo: scholion to Aristides *Panathenaicus* 196.18, Dindorf vol. 3, p. 341; Aelian *Miscellaneous Histories* 4.6; cf. Athenaeus 187d. Zeilhofer 1959, 77–80, plausibly points out that the Spartans may have referred to their obligations as members of Delphic Amphictyony not to destroy a fellow-member of that league. The statement by Pausanias 3.8.6 that Lysander and Agis proposed, at their own initiative, that the allies resolve to destroy Athens most likely reflects their agency in inquiring at Delphi (knowing the answer they would receive) whether this proposal deserved the approval of the allies. "Eyes of Greece": Justin 5.8.4. The phrase recalls Cimon's appeal to the Athenians to support Sparta, on the occasion of the helot revolt of the 460s, so that "Hellas not be crippled nor a yoke-mate city lost." Cimon's example of Spartan–Athenian solidarity was recalled, significantly, by Critias: Plutarch *Cimon* 16.8.

30. Lysander and Thebes: Polyaenus 1.45.5; cf. Plutarch *Lysander* 27.2. Spartan sentiment favoring common cause against Persia: Xenophon *Hellenica* 1.6.7; Plutarch *Lysander* 6.7.

31. The terms of surrender given here are an amalgamation of the terms reported by Xenophon *Hellenica* 2.2.20; Plutarch *Lysander* 14.4–5; Diodorus 13.107.4, 14.3.2 and 6; Aristotle *Constitution* 34.3. The present account of the treaty largely accords with those of McCoy 1975; Krentz 1982, 42; Ostwald 1986, 458, where earlier literature is cited.

32. Theramenes' return: Xenophon *Hellenica* 2.2.21–22; Lysias 13.13–16; Plutarch *Lysander* 14.5–6. Oath and stele: Andocides 3.22; cf. Diodorus 14.3.6. The date of Munychion 16, given by Plutarch *Lysander* 15.1, is probably the date of the oath-taking, upon which the Spartans formally "took possession of all their ships except twelve, and of their walls"; cf. Thucydides 5.26.1, and see Appendix D.

33. "Stasis" (factional strife): Xenophon *Hellenica* 1.7.35.

34. Condemnation of Cleophon: Lysias 13.12, 30.10–13. The statutory basis of his trial must have resembled the terms for trial of malefactors specified in the Cleinias decree, *IG* I³ 34.31–41 (= ML 46, Fornara 98; on the date, see chapter 3, note 15): the Council is required to receive any written indictment, to make a preliminary judgment, and, in case of a guilty judgment, to refer the matter to trial by jury-court; in the event of a guilty verdict in court, the penalty is to be assigned by the *prytaneis* of the Council; Lysias 30.11 states that in Cleophon's case the Council exercised its statutory duty to support the prosecution *(syndikazein)* in court as well.

35. Indictment of Callixeinus: Xenophon *Hellenica* 1.7.35; see also chapter 7 note 46. Cf. also the indictment of Agoratus, Lysias 13.18–34.

36. The Council empowered to initiate judicial proceedings (e.g., *IG* I³ 34 (= ML 46, Fornara 98), 31–41; *IG* I³ 68 (= ML 68, Fornara 133), 39–50; *IG* I³ 71 (= ML 69, Fornara 136), 38–40, 48–50, 53–54; cf. Aristophanes *Thesmophoriazusae* 78–79). Handling of the trial of the generals by the Council in 406/5 may have especially strengthened a reactionary movement to control the Council in 405/4.

37. Judicial review of candidates by the Council: Lysias 16, 31, cf. 26.10; 26.6 demonstrates that by 382 rejections by the Council were subject to review in a *dikasterion,* but Aristotle *Constitution* 45.3 and 55.2 states that "formerly" (i.e., probably before 403, cf. 41.2) decisions by the Council were final. Allegations of illicit appointment to the Council: Aeschines 1.106, 3.62; Aristotle *Constitution* 62.1 indicates that "formerly" deme officials sold appointments (see Whitehead 1986, 279–90, for a review of opinions on the meaning of this passage). Council of 405/4 said to have oligarchic leanings: Lysias 13.20. On the enrollment of the Five Thousand, see [Lysias] 20.13–14, and see above, chapter 5 note 40. On the aristocratic tendencies innate in the methods of selecting members of the Council, see Rhodes 1972, 1–8; Sinclair 1988, 106–14. It is possible, perhaps even likely in view of the manifest bias of the Council at this time, that the law limiting citizens to no more than two (possibly non-consecutive) years of service on the Council was a democratic safeguard introduced after 403. Aristotle *Constitution* 62.3 states the rule as it applied in the late fourth century; Sinclair 1988, 66 n. 82, points out that evidence for this rule is no earlier than mid-fourth century.

38. The "ephors": Lysias 12.43–44. Tribal allotment of councilors: Whitehead 1986, 268–70.

39. The ambiguous roles of Theramenes and of the Spartans have been recently discussed by Harding, 1974, 1978, and 1988, Buck 1995, and Ehrhardt 1995, whose conclusions differ in some respects from those that follow here. Scholars have sought to identify a consistent "moderate" constitutional ideology with Theramenes and with the catch-phrase of the *patrios politeia;* see Fuks 1953; Ruschenbusch 1958; McCoy 1970 and 1975; Walters 1976; Ostwald 1986, 364–67, 469–72. These were ancient debates (see, e.g., Thucydides 8.68.4, 97.2, and Aristo-

tle *Constitution* 28.5 on Theramenes and his politics; Xenophon 6.5.36 and Isocrates 8.105 on Sparta).

40. On the sources of and influences on Aristotle's *Constitution of the Athenians*, see Rhodes 1981, 15–30, where earlier literature is cited. Quote: Aristotle *Constitution* 34.3. On the *Atthis* of Androtion, see, most recently, Harding 1994. Andron and Antiphon: [Plutarch] *Moralia* 833e. The identification of this Andron as the father of Androtion and as a member of the Four Hundred is almost certain, despite doubts expressed by Harding 1994, 14–15; see Avery 1959, 22–28; Pesely 1995. The statement repeated by Demosthenes (22.33–4, 56, 68; 24.125, 168) that Andron father of Androtion was a state-debtor who was imprisoned and later escaped, is best understood in the context of the partisan prosecutions leading up to the oligarchy of 404 (cf. the escape of Callixeinus and colleagues, above, with note 35).

41. Fuks 1953, 52–83, distinguishes especially the perspective attributed to Theramenes and Cleitophon; see the further discussion cited above in note 39. On Cleitophon: see above, chapter 5, with note 20, and chapter 7, with note 39. Themistocles and Pericles as *nomothetai:* Lysias 30.28.

42. Quote: Plutarch *Lysander* 14.5–6. Sentiment for better terms: Lysias 13.14–16, cf. 12.70; Isocrates 7.64.

43. Election of military commanders: Aristotle *Constitution* 44.4, 61.1. Suspension of Assemblies: Lysias 12.71. Opposition to Theramenes by the generals and officers is described by Lysias 13, esp. 13–17.

44. Generals and taxiarchs of 404 named: Lysias 13.13, 18.4, 30.14. Calliades was probably elected in 406 to replace Archestratus, who was killed during in the blockade of Mytilene: Lysias 21.8; Diodorus 13.101.5. Dionysodorus and Strombichides are discussed below, note 47. On chronology, see Appendix D.

45. The charge against the generals given in Lysias 13.48 is "plotting against your *plethos* [majority]," paraphrased in 51 as "performing criminal acts against the interest of your *demos.*"

46. The remodeling of the Pnyx is attributed by Plutarch *Themistocles* 19.4 to the oligarchy of the Thirty; this makes little sense, given that the Thirty had no interest in democratic assemblies (see chapter 9, and the first point in Moysey 1981, 32–33; also Krentz 1984b). The project becomes more intelligible if the work is seen as a delayed project of the democracy, of the sort sponsored by Alcibiades. On the nature of the changes, see Kourouniotis and Thompson 1932; Hansen 1987, 12–19; the probable reason for the change was to improve audibility in an era of increasingly sophistic rhetoric (above, chapter 7); see Johnstone 1996. Assembly in Munychia: Lysias 13.31. Spartan force bivouacked "in town" *(epedemese to ton polemion stratopedon):* Lysias 12.71. Lysias 12.71 reports that no Assembly was held until Lysander had been summoned from Samos.

47. Dionysodorus was probably the brother of Euthydemus, known from Plato's *Euthydemus* to have associated with Alcibiades' uncle and cousin, Axiochus and Cleinias. Although the identification of the Socratic Dionysodorus and the general executed in 404 appears not to have been previously considered, it can be inferred from the Socratic's fame as a teacher of generalship and practitioner of rhetoric, and from the evidence that he and Euthydemus were naturalized Athenians: *Euthydemus* 271b-72b; cf. Xenophon *Memorabilia* 3.1.1. Although not explicitly stated, the naturalized status of the executed general was evidently an issue in Lysias' speech.

Dionysodorus' family history or record of public service is never mentioned in the speech, but sympathy is aroused for him by allusions to other worthy Athenians victimized by the Thirty, among whom, besides Strombichides, only naturalized Athenians or resident aliens are named; see Lysias 13.1–2, 39–48, 53–54, 58–63, 92–97. For other naturalized Athenians serving as generals, see Plato *Ion* 541c-d; Osborne 1983, 30–33. Xenophon *Memorabilia* 4.2.3–5 attests Euthydemus' aspiration to a public career at Athens; for his fate, see below, chapter 9 note 28. Strombichides in 411: Thucydides 8.15–17, 30, 62–63.1, 79. Strombichides' father, the senior Diotimus, general in 433/2 and ambassador at an unknown date: *IG* I³ 364.9 (= ML 61, Fornara 126); Strabo 1.3.1. Diotimus and Pharnabazus in 409: Xenophon *Hellenica* 1.3.12. Hippias of Thasos and Xenophon of Curium: Lysias 13.54. Agoratus and the murder of Phrynichus: *IG* I³ 102 (= ML 85, Fornara 155) 26–27; cf. Lysias 13.70–76; Thucydides 8.92.2; cf. the murder of Androcles, Thucydides 8.65.2.

48. Quote: Plutarch *Alcibiades* 38.1–4, translated by B. Perrin; cf. Isocrates 16.40; Justin 5.8.12.

49. Surrender of Samos: Xenophon *Hellenica* 2.3.6–7; Diodorus 14.3.5. On chronology see Appendix D.

50. Quote: Lysias 13.34, translated by W. R. M. Lamb. Although he does not mention the indictment of the generals, Diodorus 14.3.4–7 likewise coordinates the end of democratic resistance at Athens with the fall of Samos; see further discussion in Appendix D.

51. *IG* I³ 127 (= ML 94, Fornara 166) testifies to the devotion of Samian democrats to Athens at the time of the sieges of 405/4, and the republication of this decree by the Athenians in 403/2 attests the steadfastness of this devotion; see Shipley 1987, 130–31.

52. Theocritus, so-called son of "Elaphostictus": Lysias 13.19. The forequarters of a deer (usually a stag) appears as a device on Ephesian coins: Kraay 1976, nos. 903–904. Lysander and Ephesus: Xenophon *Hellenica* 2.1.6, 10; Diodorus 13.104.3–4. Andrewes 1971, 214, concludes, on the basis of *IG* II² 1.48–49, that Ephesus, which received pro-Athenian Samian refugees, was already controlled in 404 by Tissaphernes and not by pro-Lysandrians loyal to Cyrus; but Pausanias 6.3.15 describes dedications of both Samians and Ephesians in honor of Lysander and his officers, best understood as products of an interval soon after the surrender of Samos, while the fall of the pro-Lysandrians at Ephesus is most probably an event connected with the curtailment of Lysander's influence over the winter of 404/3; see below, chapter 9, with note 40.

53. *Eleutheroi* expelled from Samos: Xenophon *Hellenica* 2.3.6. Spartan notion of slaves: Pseudo-Xenophon *Constitution* 1.10–12, quoted in chapter 3, page 66; cf. the sale of Athenian captives at Methymna in 406: Xenophon *Hellenica* 1.6.14–15. Branding of Samians: Plutarch *Pericles* 26.3–4; Aelian *Miscellaneous Histories* 2.9; cf. Diphilus 67.7–8 *PCG* (= 66 Kock, Edmonds); cf. also Athenian captives branded at Syracuse: Plutarch *Nicias* 29.1. It is possible that Lysias 13.19 means that Theocritus' father was a branded captive whose fate was in Lysander's hands; but the unusual expression ("Theocritus, the man called 'son of Elaphostictus'") suggests to me rather that Theocritus himself was all but branded, and Lysias wanted to make sure that the shame of the name was attached to him even if the brand was not.

54. Quote: Plutarch *Lysander* 15.2, translated by B. Perrin.

55. Condemnation of the generals: Lysias 13.37–38, 30.14; see Appendix D on chronology. Condemnation of Alcibiades, Thrasybulus, and Anytus: Xenophon *Hellenica* 2.3.42; Isocrates 16.37, 40; Justin 5.8.12.

CHAPTER NINE. THE ATHENIAN CIVIL WAR, 404–403

1. Lysander's arrival: Lysias 12.71; 13.34; Diodorus 14.3.5; Xenophon *Hellenica* 2.2.23, 3.8. On the chronology of events, see Appendix D.

2. Enslavement: Thucydides 1.141.1, 2.63.1, 3; cf. Lysias 12.73. Quote: Aristotle *Constitution* 34.3. Lysander's threats: Lysias 12.72–74; Diodorus 14.3.5–7; Plutarch *Lysander* 15.2–3; see above, chapter 8, notes 28 and 29.

3. Quote: Lysias 12.75, translated by W.R.M. Lamb. Theramenes' response: Lysias 12.73–76; Diodorus 14.3.6.

4. Decree of Dracontides and election of the Thirty: Aristotle *Constitution* 34.3; Xenophon *Hellenica* 2.3.2; Lysias 12.73–77; Diodorus 14.3.7–4.1. On the membership of the Thirty, see below, with note 7.

5. Quote: Plutarch *Lysander* 15.4, translated by B. Perrin; cf. Xenophon *Hellenica* 2.2.23, 3.1–10; Lysias 13.34–35. Independence for Hellenes: Thucydides 1.139.3. Plutarch *Lysander* 15.1 notices the synchronism of Lysander's visit with the anniversary of the battle of Salamis; see further discussion in Appendix D.

6. Probouloi: see chapter 5, with note 14. Nomothetai: see chapter 5, with notes 46–48. Nicomachus: Lysias 30.11–12, discussed below, chapter 11.

7. Membership of the Thirty: Whitehead 1980; Krentz 1982, 45–56; Ostwald 1986, 460–68. On the Thirty as *nomothetai,* see Xenophon *Memorabilia* 1.2.31; Dio Chrysostom 21.3 (= Levin in Sprague 1972, 266 no. 48); Ruschenbusch 1956.

8. Appointment of magistrates and Council: Xenophon *Hellenica* 2.3.11; Lysias 13.20; Aristotle *Constitution* 35.1; Diodorus 14.4.1–2. Condemnation of "enemies of the people," see Lysias 18.6, and chapter 8, note 55, and below, with note 14.

9. Jurisdiction of the Eleven: Aristotle *Constitution* 52.1; cf. Xenophon *Memorabilia* 1.2.62; *Hellenica* 2.3.54. Appointment of the Eleven and the Ten in Piraeus: Aristotle *Constitution* 35.1; Plato *Seventh Letter* 324c (below).

10. Quote: Plato *Seventh Letter* 324b-d, translated by L.A. Post, with modifications. On the authenticity of the *Seventh Letter,* see below, chapter 10 note 1.

11. Quote: Aristotle *Constitution* 35.2. The relative effects of wartime losses on thetes compared to men of hoplite status are calculated by Strauss 1986, 176–82 (losses due to starvation are not reckoned).

12. Solon's law on inheritance: Aristotle *Constitution* 35.2–3, cf. 9.2; Aristophanes *Wasps* 578–87; *Birds* 1655–73; cf. *Clouds* 1187.

13. "Teaching the art of speaking," Xenophon *Memorabilia* 1.2.31; on *logon techne,* see Cole 1991. The Spartan disdain for articulate or ornamented speech is anecdotal, and exemplified, for example, by Sthenelaidas in Thucydides 1.86; the Spartans, their magistrates, and King Cleomenes, in Herodotus 1.152, 3.46, 5.49–50 and 97; the ephors in Plutarch *Lysander* 14.4; cf. Plato *Protagoras* 342a-e.

14. Quotes: Lysias 12.5; Xenophon *Hellenica* 2.3.12; Plato *Seventh Letter* 324d-325a, translated by L.A. Post. On the goals of the Thirty, cf. Aristotle *Constitution* 35.3–4; Diodorus 14.4.2.

15. Garrison requested from Sparta: Xenophon *Hellenica* 2.3.13–14; Diodorus 14.4.3–4; Justin 5.8.11. From this point, Krentz 1982, follows a significantly different order of events by placing the invitation of the Spartan garrison much later in the regime of the Thirty, on the basis of Aristotle *Constitution* 37.2. I am not convinced by his arguments, which attribute the chronology suggested by Aristotle's account to a hypothetical, more reliable account in the *Hellenica Oxyrhynchia,* Krentz 1982, 131–47. Although the *Hellenica Oxyrhynchia* may have been a superior authority in some portions of its narrative, the account of Xenophon, an eyewitness to the events at Athens, deserves credence here, especially as his account is supported in this respect by Diodorus and Justin. Plutarch *Lysander* 15.5 has the garrison established by Lysander before his departure. Rhodes 1981, 416–22 and 455, reviews chronological conflicts between Aristotle and other sources at this time and regards Aristotle's account as less reliable in this and other contested points.

16. Lycurgus, and Spartan *eunomia:* Herodotus 1.65; Thucydides 1.18.1; Plato *Phaedrus* 258b-c; *Laws* 624a, 632d; cf. *Protagoras* 342e; Xenophon *Constitution of the Lacedaemonians* 1.2.

17. The "laconizing" of the Thirty is discussed by Krentz 1982, 64–68; Whitehead 1982–1983; Brock 1989, 163. See also Isocrates 4.110; 15.318–19.

18. The fragments of Critias' treatises on Sparta are collected in DK 88 B 6–9, 32–37, and translated by D.N. Levin in Sprague 1972, 251–52, 261–63. The treatment of *nomoi,* "laws," and *politeia,* "constitution," as consisting in unwritten "customs" attributed to a distant, semi-divine, or even divine lawgiver is echoed not only in Xenophon's *Constitution of the Lacedaemonians,* but also in Plato's *Laws* (esp. 624a-25a, 630c-31a, 793a-d, 858e) and in his *Crito* (esp. 50a-e). See further, below, note 23.

19. Quote: Xenophon *Memorabilia* 3.5.14–16, translated by E. C. Marchant, with modifications.

20. Tyrtaeus as the Athenian teacher of Spartan virtues: Plato *Laws* 629a-30c, 667a, 858e; cf. Lycurgus *Against Leocrates* 105–108; Diodorus 8.27, 15.66.3; Pausanias 4.15.6; Athenaeus 630e; further testimonia are collected by Edmonds *Elegy* I, 50–59; cf. Fornara 12. Other ancient debts of Sparta to Athens: Isocrates 4.61–65.

21. Xenophon *Hellenica* 2.3.34 quotes Critias in his condemnation of Theramenes. Eradication of statutes: Aristotle *Constitution* 35.2; Dio Chrysostom 21.3 (= Levin in Sprague 1972, 266 no. 48).

22. Fragments of inscribed laws, with newer discoveries: Oliver 1935; Dow 1941, 1960, 1961. Erasure is attributed to the Thirty by Fingarette 1971, acknowledged as a possibility by Clinton 1982, 32, and Rhodes 1991, 95, although both prefer to see most of the erasure as work of the *nomothetai* after the Thirty, a view also advanced by Robertson 1990, 66, 73, 75. See further below, in chapter 10, with note 34, and chapter 11, with notes 1, 4. Adoption of Ionic alphabet in 403/2: Theopompus *FGrHist* 115 F 155 (Harding 6).

23. "Unwritten" or "universal laws": Sophocles *Antigone* 454–55; Thucydides 2.37.3; Euripides *Suppliant Women* 311, 526, 563; see the discussion of the evolving concept of *nomos,* "law," in Ostwald 1969, esp. 57–61. Critias' speech: Xenophon *Hellenica* 2.3.34. *Epitedeumata* are equated with the "laws," *nomoi,* of Lycurgus in Xenophon's *Memorabilia* 4.4.15 and *Constitution of the Lacedaemonians* 1.1–2, 5.1, 8.1–5, and, in 10.8, with "the most ancient laws," *palaiotatoi nomoi;* cf. the universal

applicability of "unwritten laws," *Memorabilia* 4.4.19. Isocrates, another young Athenian imbued with the ideas of this time, later expressed the commensurability of Spartan and ancestral Athenian excellence in his *Areopagiticus* 60–61, where, in praising "well-ordered" democracies, he states that the Lacedaemonians have the best government because it is the most democratic! Cf. the praise of Spartan *epitedeumata* by Aristotle *Nicomachean Ethics* 1180a.

24. Naming the 3,000: Xenophon *Hellenica* 2.3.18–20; Aristotle *Constitution* 36.2, 37.2; Isocrates 18.16; cf. Lysias 12.94–95; Diodorus 14.4.2, 32.4; Justin 5.8.10.

25. Expulsions and confiscations: Xenophon *Hellenica* 2.3.21–22, 4.1; Lysias 12.21–22, 40, 13.47; Aristotle *Constitution* 35.4; Diodorus 14.4.4, 5.5–6; Justin 5.8.12, 9.1–3; see Krentz 1982, 80–82. Lysias and Polemarchus: Lysias 12.5–40.

26. Condemnation of Theramenes: Xenophon *Hellenica* 2.3.18–56, who provides a vivid account, possibly firsthand, remarkable for the length of the reported speeches of Critias and especially Theramenes (see Delebecque 1957, 36, 70–72; Gray 1989, 94–99); see also Lysias 12.77–78 (discussed below, chapter 12, with note 23); Aristotle *Constitution* 37.1; Diodorus 14.4.5–5.4; Justin 5.9.2.

27. "Most capable of resisting": Xenophon *Hellenica* 2.3.16; see also above, note 14, on the motives of the Thirty. Number of exiles: Isocrates 7.67 says more than 5,000 fled; Diodorus 14.5.7 says that more than half of all Athenians fled; Justin 5.8.10 says that the 3,000 were practically the only Athenians left.

28. Athenians "honored by the *demos*": Xenophon *Hellenica* 2.3.15. Niceratus: Xenophon *Hellenica* 2.3.39; Lysias 18.6–7. Euthydemus: Plato *Euthydemus* passim; Xenophon *Memorabilia* 4.2, 3, 5, 6; and Critias, Xenophon *Memorabilia* 1.2.29–30; on the identification of his brother, Dionysodorus, see above, chapter 8 note 47.

29. Eleusinian review: Xenophon *Hellenica* 2.4.8–10; Lysias 12.52, 13.44; Diodorus 14.32.4. A similar Spartan ruse used to eliminate potentially dangerous helots is described by Thucydides 4.80. Critias' familiarity with such Spartan practices is attested by Libanius *Orations* 25.63–64 (Sprague 1972, 263).

30. Numbers of Athenians killed by the Thirty: Xenophon *Hellenica* 2.4.21; cf. Aristotle *Constitution* 35.4; Isocrates 4.113, 7.67, 20.11; Aeschines 2.77, 3.235; the scholion to Aeschines 1.39 attributes the number of 2,500 slain to Lysias. For comparative casualty figures, see Strauss 1986, 179.

31. Alcibiades and Pharnabazus: Plutarch *Alcibiades* 37.3–4; Diodorus 14.11.1–2; Nepos 7.9.3–10.1.

32. Cyrus at Sardis: see chapter 8, with note 24. Clearchus: Diodorus 13.40.6, 51.1–4, 66.5–6; 98.1; Xenophon *Hellenica* 1.1.35–36, 3.15–19; *Anabasis* 2.6.2; Polyaenus 2.2.5–10. Thorax: Diodorus 14.3.5. See also below, note 34.

33. Ephorus on Alcibiades: Diodorus 14.11.1–4.

34. Thorax: Plutarch *Lysander* 19.4. Clearchus: Xenophon *Anabasis* 1.1.9, 2.6.2–5; Diodorus 14.12.2–9. Lysander in Thrace: Plutarch *Lysander* 16.1, 20.5; Pausanias 3.18.3; see Andrewes 1971, 217–26, where it is plausibly suggested that Lysander had established ties in Thessaly at this time as well.

35. Plutarch *Lysander* 19.4 states that Pharnabazus complained that Lysander was plundering his land, which could describe monetary exactions that Lysander made still relying on the assignments made by Cyrus; see chapter 7, with note 4. For simultaneous encroachments on Cyrus' former domain by Tissaphernes, see Xenophon *Anabasis* 1.1.7–8; Andrewes 1971, 214–15. Pharnabazus' trick: Plutarch *Lysander* 20.1–4;

Polyaenus 7.19. Pausanias' remark: 9.32.10, cf. 3.9.1. Controversy over private vs. public money at Sparta is noted by Plutarch *Lysander* 16–17; Athenaeus 6.233f-34a.

36. Ephorus' account of the death of Alcibiades: Diodorus 14.11.1–5, paralleled in many details by Plutarch *Alcibiades* 39.1–4, with the variant in 39.5. Spartans and Lysander: Isocrates 16.40; cf. Plutarch *Alcibiades* 38.4–39.1. Critias and the Thirty: Justin 5.8.12–14; cf. Plutarch *Alcibiades* 38.3; Nepos 7.10.1. Melissa: Athenaeus 574e-f.

37. Proclamation of banishment: Isocrates 16.40; Lysias 12.95. Argives: Demosthenes 15.22; Diodorus 14.6.2; Justin 5.9.4. Thebans: Xenophon *Hellenica* 2.4.1; Plutarch *Lysander* 22.1, 27.2–4; *Pelopidas* 6.4; Deinarchus 1.25; Diodorus 14.6.3; Justin 5.9.4, 8; *Hellenica Oxyrhynchia* 7.2, 17. Megarians: Xenophon *Hellenica* 2.4.1; Plutarch *Lysander* 22.1.

38. Anti-Spartan faction at Thebes and the role of Ismenias: *Hellenica Oxyrhynchia* 7.2, 16.1, 17; Plutarch *Lysander* 27.2–4; Diodorus 14.6.3; Justin 5.9.8; cf. Thucydides 5.17.2, 31.6. Ismenias profits from the exiles: Plato *Meno* 90a; *Republic* 336a; see Morrison 1942, 76–78. On the force at Phyle, see below, note 42.

39. Opposition to the Thirty arose among the *kaloi k'agathoi* according to Xenophon's account of a speech by Theramenes, *Hellenica* 2.3.38; among "those with the greatest reputation for *arete*," according to Isocrates 8.123, probably also a witness to this speech (see [Plutarch] *Moralia* 836f and correct "Socrates" to "Isocrates" in Diodorus 14.5.2–3; see Pesely 1988); among *gnorimoi*, "notables," and "those who excelled in wealth, birth, and esteem," according to Aristotle *Constitution* 34.3, 35.4, probably following the account of another young contemporary, Androtion; see chapter 8, note 40.

40. Repudiation of Lysander's policies: Xenophon *Hellenica* 3.4.2; Diodorus 14.33.6; Plutarch *Lysander* 19, 21.1; Nepos 6.2–3.1. Andrewes 1971, 206–16, reviewing scholarship on the eclipse of Lysander and favoring a date late in 403 or in 402, makes his decision based on conditions that, as discussed in the present study, belong to the winter of 404/3.

41. Quote: Xenophon *Hellenica* 2.4.2, translated by R. Warner, with modification. The defensive position of the Athenians at Phyle is not certain; it was probably atop Megalo Vouno tis Filis, and not at the site of the fortress built decades later at Phyle; see Skias 1900. Ithome: Thucydides 1.102; Aetolia: Thucydides 3.94–98; Sphacteria: Thucydides 4.31–40.

42. The chief account of the fighting around Phyle comes from Xenophon *Hellenica* 2.4.2–7, who was a cavalryman under command of the Thirty; see also Diodorus 14.32; Aristotle *Constitution* 37.1; Lysias 12.52, 13.77–79; and Nepos 8.2.1–4, who emphasizes the ineffective watch kept, over a long period of time, by the forces of the Thirty. On the original size of the force at Phyle, see also Pausanias 1.29.3, and Raubitschek 1941/1991 (Harding 7). Some accounts, like Justin 5.9.6–15 and [Plutarch] *Moralia* 835f, do not clearly distinguish aid and reinforcements received by Thrasybulus at Phyle from support gathered later in Piraeus; it was in the interests of many late supporters to obscure this distinction, and in the interest of others to specify it: see *IG* II^2 10 + *addenda* (M.J. Osborne 1981 and 1982, D6), Aeschines 3.187, and Lysias 28.12.

43. Offer to Thrasybulus: Diodorus 14.32.5–6; Justin 5.9.13; cf. Xenophon *Hellenica* 2.3.34.

44. March to Piraeus: Xenophon *Hellenica* 2.4.10; Diodorus 14.33.2. The working-class character of the forces assembled in Piraeus is revealed in *IG* II^2 10 + *addenda* (M.J. Osborne 1981 and 1982, D6, partially represented by Tod 100 = Harding 3, each with various restorations; I follow Osborne 1982, 26–43); see the discussion of this text below, chapter 10, with note 20. Lysias supports Thrasybulus: [Plutarch] *Moralia* 835f; see Osborne 1982, 30 n. 77.

45. Fighting in Piraeus and the battle of Munychia: Xenophon *Hellenica* 2.4.11–22; Diodorus 14.33.2–3 notes a second engagement after the death of Critias; Nepos 8.2.5–7, perhaps confirming Xenophon's notice of preliminary skirmishing outside Piraeus, says Critias fell in the second engagement. Thrasybulus' harangue: Xenophon *Hellenica* 2.4.13–17.

46. Glaucon son of Ariston: Plato *Republic* passim; *Parmenides* 126a; *Symposium* 172–73b; Xenophon *Memorabilia* 3.6; note his absence at Plato *Apology* 34a. Tale of the dead warrior (Er): Plato *Republic* 10.614b-21d, quoting the translation of P. Shorey. It is worth remarking, of the blood shed on this road, that Critias had pronounced that blood was the soul *(psyche),* according to Aristotle *On the Soul* 405b.

47. Address to the followers of the Thirty: Xenophon *Hellenica* 2.4.20–22; Lysias 12.53; cf. Justin 5.10.1–3; Nepos 8.2.6. Lysias 12.92 and Plato *Menexenus* 244a-b likewise emphasize the consanguinity of the parties pitted against each other by the Thirty.

48. Fall of the Thirty: Xenophon *Hellenica* 2.4.23; Aristotle *Constitution* 38.1; Lysias 12.53–55; Justin 5.10.4.

49. Hard line of the Ten: Aristotle *Constitution* 38.1–2; Lysias 12.55–56; Justin 5.10.5. Demaratus, named by Aristotle, was possibly the general who, in 414, shared command with Laispodias and Pythodorus: Thucydides 6.105.2. The latter two became members of the Four Hundred, and Pythodorus was probably the eponymous archon during the regime of the Thirty, see Dover in Gomme et al. 1970, 378, and Avery 1959, 199–206, 270–74.

50. Fighting between Piraeus and Athens: Xenophon *Hellenica* 2.4.24–28, 37; *Memorabilia* 2.7; Lysias 12.54–60; 14.33; 25.21–22; 31.17–18; Isocrates 18.45, 49. Embassies to Sparta and Lysander's mission: Xenophon *Hellenica* 2.4.28; Lysias 12.58–60; Aristotle *Constitution* 38.1–2; Diodorus 14.33.5; Plutarch *Lysander* 21.2.

51. Mission and motives of Pausanias: Xenophon *Hellenica* 2.4.29–30; Plutarch *Lysander* 21.3; Diodorus 14.33.6; cf. Lysias 18.10–12. For modern assessments, see: de Ste. Croix 1972, 144–46; Hamilton 1979, 79–81; Funke 1980, 27–36; Krentz 1982, 98–101; Cartledge 1987a, 94, 283–86, 351–52; Harding 1988. Advice of Theramenes: Xenophon *Hellenica* 2.3.17–19, 38–42. Sympathy for the Piraeus party among the oligarchs in Athens: Xenophon *Hellenica* 2.4.23–24, 35; Lysias 12.53–55; 25.22; Aristotle *Constitution* 38.3–4.

52. Battles with Pausanias: Xenophon *Hellenica* 2.4.30–35, a circumstantially detailed and probably firsthand account; cf. Isocrates 18.49; Diodorus 14.33.6.

53. Pausanias' intentions: Xenophon *Hellenica* 2.4.31, 35–36. Diognetus and the kinsmen of Nicias: Lysias 18.10–11. Pleistoanax and Nicias: Thucydides 5.16.

54. The appointment of a new board of Ten: Aristotle *Constitution* 38.3–4. The present account reconciles a variety of sources that scholars have considered problematic. Cloché 1915, 170–85, and more recently Rhodes 1981, 459–60, and Harding 1988, 187, are among those who regard a new board of Ten as a fiction of later propagandists; Krentz 1982, 97, Ostwald 1986, 482–83, 492–93, and Loening

1987, 14, accept Aristotle's account, but place the election of the new Ten shortly before the arrival of Pausanias. Aristotle reports that Rhinon and Phayllus were the most prominent members of the new Ten, and that these men "even before Pausanias' arrival" had entered into negotiations with the men in Piraeus. The present account, advanced previously by Beloch 1922, vol. 3.1, 12, accepts Aristotle but identifies the preliminary contacts by Rhinon and Phayllus (like the embassy of Cephisophon and Meletus, Xenophon *Hellenica* 2.4.36) as the initiatives of "private individuals," since they were alike at odds with the hard line being maintained by "the government in the city," according to Xenophon 2.4.37, still *after* the battles fought by Pausanias. Xenophon 2.4.35 reports that Pausanias "divided the men in the city," which must refer to his efforts to demonstrate that, contrary to the government of the Ten, the majority *(hos pleistous)* of men in Athens favored the impending settlement; cf. Lysias 25.21–22.

55. The reconciliation: Xenophon *Hellenica* 2.4.38; Aristotle *Constitution* 39; Diodorus 14.33.6; Plutarch *Lysander* 21.3; Nepos 8.3; cf. also Lysias 18.10–12; Isocrates 18.17. Election of the Twenty: Andocides 1.81; that the Twenty consisted of ten from the city and ten from the Piraeus party is a plausible inference made by Ostwald 1986, 500. Date of the reconciliation: Plutarch *Moralia* 349f. On the reconciliation see Rhodes 1981, 462–72; Loening 1987.

56. Confirmation of treaty with Sparta: Lysias 18.15. Reparations: Aristotle *Constitution* 39.6, 40.3; Lysias 30.22; cf. Isocrates 7.68; Demosthenes 20.11–12. "Ancient laws": Xenophon *Hellenica* 2.4.42; Lysias 34; Diodorus 14.32.6. Property qualification for jurors: Aristotle *Constitution* 39.6; cf. Dionysius of Halicarnassus *Lysias* 32; Lysias 34; for further discussion, see chapter 10, with notes 6, 12–14.

CHAPTER TEN. THE LAWS OF ATHENS, 403–400

1. Plato *Seventh Letter* 325a-26b, translated by L. A. Post, with modifications. Although contemporary scholarship regards most of the letters attributed to Plato as spurious, the balance of opinion supports the authenticity of Plato's *Seventh Letter.* For opinions favoring authenticity, see Lesky 1963/1966, 507; Guthrie 1975, 16 and n. 2; Brandwood 1992, 112–13; Penner 1992, 130. Guarded or negative judgments are expressed by Kraut 1992, 21–24, 28; Irwin 1992, 78–79 n. 4. For present purposes, the nuances of this debate are insignificant, since even those who regard the *Seventh Letter* as spurious treat it as a work of someone intimately familiar with Plato's thought and the details of his biography, post-dating his life by no more than a century. I prefer to regard it as a genuine work of Plato.

2. For reviews of scholarship and ancient sources treating the restoration of democracy at Athens, see Cloché 1915; Ostwald 1986, 497–524. Delebecque 1957, 29–75, discusses the many indications that Xenophon's account was shaped by personal experience of these events (although his conclusion that *Hellenica* 1–2.4.42 was written in 402–401 is not persuasive; see W. P. Henry 1966, 54–88; Dover in Gomme et al. 1981, 437–44; Krenz 1989a; Dillery 1995). The grouping of Plato's dialogues named here is according to dramatic date and presumes nothing about date of composition.

3. Thrasybulus' speech before the battle of Munychia: Xenophon *Hellenica* 2.4.13–17. Thrasybulus' championship of the *demos:* Diodorus 14.32.6. *Isoteleia* of-

fered to metics: Xenophon *Hellenica* 2.4.25; citizenship offered: Aristotle *Constitution* 40.2; see further below, note 16. The numerous tradesmen listed in *IG* II^2 10 illustrate the interests of the many metics who joined Thrasybulus (see below, note 20 for the bibliography on this text). On the tax liabilities of metics, see Andreades 1933, 277–81; Thomsen 1964, 96–104, 187–92.

4. The inclusive politics of Cleisthenes: Herodotus 5.69, 78; Aristotle *Constitution* 20–21.2. Pericles, responsible for a restrictive definition of citizenship (see below, notes 22–23), was also known for encouraging capable metics to share in many of the rites and duties of Athenians: Thucydides 2.13.7, 34.4, 39–41; Pseudo-Xenophon *Constitution* 1.1–2, 10–12; Lysias 12.4; see Whitehead 1977, 151–53. Cleophon: see above, chapters 6, with notes 8, 10, 15, and 7, with notes 20–22, 37, 42.

5. Oath of allegiance and Spartan hegemony: de Ste. Croix 1972, 108, 114–15; on Spartan policy toward allies, see chapters 3, with note 8, and 4, with notes 62–64. Spartan championship of *autonomia* (autonomy, or self-rule) and *patrioi politeiai* (traditional/ancestral governments): Thucydides 5.18.2, 77.5, 79.1; Xenophon *Hellenica* 3.4.2, 5; Ostwald 1982, 3–9; Cartledge 1987a, 10.

6. Phormisius' proposal for limiting citizenship: Dionysius of Halicarnassus *Lysias* 32; see further below, note 12. Phormisius: Aristotle *Constitution* 34.3; Aristophanes *Frogs* 965.

7. Procession to Acropolis: Xenophon *Hellenica* 2.4.39; cf. Lysias 13.80–81. Lysias 31.15–16 attests the practice of well-to-do Athenians providing their fellow demesmen with arms for the benefit of the Piraeus party; Demosthenes 20.139 and [Plutarch] *Moralia* 835f attest substantial gifts and loans obtained from abroad for this purpose; on the presence of "all sorts of people" among the fighting men from Piraeus, see Xenophon *Hellenica* 2.4.25; Aristotle *Constitution* 40.2. Metics in the Panathenaic procession: Parke 1977, 44, with references. Although it is generally held that they did not march in procession under arms, metics regularly served as hoplites: Thucydides 2.13.7; Xenophon *Ways and Means* 2.2–5; *Cavalry Commander* 9.3–7. On the military reviews of the Thirty, see above, chapter 9, with notes 24, 29.

8. Speech of Thrasybulus: Xenophon *Hellenica* 2.4.40–41. As with all reported speeches, the historicity of this speech has been questioned, most forcefully by Strauss 1986, 92, who dismisses it, along with Thrasybulus' earlier speech at Munychia, as "rather conventional..., what Xenophon would have said had *he* been Thrasybulus." By contrast, Cloché 1915, 248–50, Anderson 1974, 59, and Gray 1989, 103–106, recognize the strong characterization and vivid tone evident in the speech and its singular relevance to the events at hand; Ostwald 1986, 502, quotes the speech, but leaves the issue of historicity undecided.

9. "Know yourself": Plato *Charmides* 164d; *Protagoras* 343b; *Phaedrus* 230a; *Philebus* 48c-49b; *Laws* 923a; cf. *Seventh Letter* 341b; *Alcibiades* 1 124a, 129a, 132c; Xenophon *Memorabilia* 4.2.24.

10. The motion of Peisander: Thucydides 8.68.1; the motion of Dracontides: Lysias 12.73; Aristotle *Constitution* 34.3. *Archaioi nomoi:* Xenophon *Hellenica* 2.4.42.

11. Archinus, Anytus, and Phormisius: Aristotle *Constitution* 34.3, cf. 40.1–2; Aristophanes *Frogs* 965; Plato *Meno* 90a-b; *Hellenica Oxyrhynchia* 6.2–3; cf. also Lysias 13.82; Isocrates 18.2, 23; Demosthenes 24.135; Aeschines 2.176; 3.187; Strauss 1986, 90–101; see also note 12 below.

12. Phormisius' proposal: Dionysius of Halicarnassus *Lysias* 32; see the discussions of Krentz 1982, 109–10, and Ostwald 1986, 504–505. Lysias' response: Lysias 34. The number of adult male Athenians at the end of the Peloponnesian War is estimated by Strauss 1986, 78–81 and 179–82, at 14,000–16,250, of whom probably no more than 5,000–7,000 were *thetes.*

13. The audience of Lysias 34, addressed as "Athenians," is distinct from a *demos* whose numbers include many fighting men who have restored "your homeland to you" (i.e., to exiled men of means, 34.4–5). Within the audience is a smaller group of men who "seek to deceive us...with the selfsame decrees with which they have tricked us twice before" (34.1, i.e., the decrees of 411 and 404); these men might be the Twenty of Andocides 1.81. "Those possessing taxable property" (*hoi ta timemata parechomenoi*): Aristotle *Constitution* 39.6, as interpreted by most scholars; see the commentary of Rhodes 470–71, and cf. *timemata* as property qualification for office-holding in Aristotle *Politics* 1318b, 30–32.

14. The *lexiarchikon grammateion: IG* I[3] 138.6; ML 23.29–30 (Fornara 55); Suda, s.v. The nature of this register has been much debated: Jameson 1963, 399; Whitehead 1986, 35 n. 130. In 411, participation in the government of the Five Thousand was likewise supposed to have been authorized by a list drawn up by men registering eligible fellow deme-members: [Lysias] 20.13; cf. chapter 5 note 40. Solonian census classes: Aristotle *Constitution* 6.3–4.

15. Moderation of democratic leadership: Plato *Seventh Letter* 325b, quoted above, with note 1; *Menexenus* 244b; Aristotle *Constitution* 40.2–3; cf. Demosthenes 24.135. Thucydides on the Five Thousand: 8.97.2.

16. Thrasybulus' proposal to enfranchise metics and slaves in 403: Aristotle *Constitution* 40.2; scholion to Aeschines 3.195; [Plutarch] *Moralia* 835f-36a; see the discussions of Rhodes 1981, 476, and M.J. Osborne 1982, 29–30, and n. 77. Enfranchisement after Arginusae: Hellanicus *FGrHist* 323a F 25 (Harding 164A); Aristophanes *Frogs* 190–91, 693–94; Diodorus 13.97.1; see Osborne 1983, 33–37, T10.

17. The proposal is said to have been approved before it was indicted by Archinus on a *graphe paranomon* because it was *aprobouleuton,* at a time when the Council had not yet been constituted: [Plutarch] *Moralia* 835f-36a; *POxy* XV, no. 1800 frs. 6 & 7; scholion to Aischines 3.195; Ostwald 1986, 503–504.

18. Condemnation of Thrasybulus: see the references cited above in note 17. Previous suspension of the *graphe paranomon:* Thucydides 8.67.2; Aristotle *Constitution* 29.4; Aeschines 3.191. Archinus' reputation: Aristotle *Constitution* 40.1–3; Isocrates 18.2; Demosthenes 24.135; Aeschines 2.176, 3.187; Deinarchos *Against Demosthenes* 76; cf. Plato *Menexenus* 234b.

19. Archinus' decree in honor of the Athenians at Phyle: Aischines 3.187, 190; Raubitschek 1941/1991; Harding 7.

20. Citizenship and *isotelia* awarded to non-Athenians: *IG* II[2] 10 (Tod 100); additional fragments are associated with this inscription by Hereward 1952; for a full text see Krentz 1980 and M.J. Osborne 1981, D6; for a partial translation see Harding 3; see also Whitehead 1984 and Krentz 1986 for discussion (Krentz now accepts the dating to the archonship of Xenaenetus, 401/0, as argued by Osborne 1982, 29–32).

21. *Isoteleia* awarded to Lysias: [Plutarch] *Moralia* 836a; Loening 1981; M.J. Osborne 1982, 30 n. 77. Sneers against the livelihoods of politicians in comedy: Connor 1971, 152–53, 171–75; Davies 1981, 43–44. Solon and craftsmen: Plutarch *Solon* 2.3–4, 22, 24.2. Events influencing a change in mood at Athens by 401/0 are discussed below in chapter 11.

22. Citizenship law proposed in 403/2 by Aristophon: Demosthenes 57.30–32; Athenaeus 577b; by Nicomenes: scholion to Aeschines 1.39. Pericles' citizenship law: Aristotle *Constitution* 26.3; Plutarch *Pericles* 37.3. Qualification for grain dole: see above, chapter 6, with note 12. For various views on the purpose of Pericles' citizenship law, see Patterson 1981; Rhodes 1981, 331–34; Walters 1983; Sinclair 1988, 24–27; Boegehold 1994.

23. Differing views on the nature of exceptions to Pericles' citizenship law in the late fifth century are discussed by Rhodes 1981, 331–32. Allegations of alien parentage, see above, chapter 6 note 15; cf. Aristophanes *Birds* 1649–52. Evidence for formal naturalization is collected by M.J. Osborne 1981–1983.

24. Quote: Lysias 6, *Against Andocides* 33. Career of Andocides: Andocides 1.132–34, 144–47; 2.11–16, 20–21; cf. above, chapter 4, with notes 28, 48, chapter 8, note 14. On the distortions in Andocides' account of his family history, see Thomas 1989, 139–44.

25. Chief evidence for the trial of Andocides is Andocides 1, *On the Mysteries;* cf. Lysias 6, *Against Andocides.* Commentary on the legal issues is provided by MacDowell 1962.

26. Decree of Teisamenus, quoted by Andocides 1, *On the Mysteries* 82–85. In the phrase translated here "facing the statues of the Eponymous Heroes" (*pros tous eponymous*), others have variously construed the preposition *pros:* "*before* the Tribal Statues" (Maidment, in the Loeb); "*near* the statues of the Eponymous Heroes" (Ostwald 1986, 515); "*at* the Eponymi" (Robertson 1990, 46); or, more commonly, "*in front* of the tribal heroes" (e.g., MacDowell 1962, 121; Rhodes 1991, 96). This last translation is least appropriate grammatically, and is influenced by the conflation of this passage with other references to the *eponymoi,* as Robertson shows, 50–51. The physical setting is discussed further below, with notes 37 and 38. Commentary on the decree of Teisamenus is provided by MacDowell 1962, 121–26 and 194–99, and more recently by Clinton 1982, 30–35; Ostwald 1986, 511–520; Sealey 1987, 35–37; M.H. Hansen 1990; Robertson 1990, 46–52, 60–65; Rhodes 1991, 95–100.

27. On the survival of inscribed laws of Draco and Solon, see Stroud 1978 and 1979; on the republication of Draco's law on homicide, see Stroud 1968.

28. Solon departs from Pheidonian standards: Aristotle *Constitution* 10.2; on the Pheidonian–Aeginetan standard in use in the Peloponnese, see Thucydides 5.47.6; on its history, see the commentary of Rhodes 1981, 164–68. Quotes: Plato *Laws* 705a, translated by A.E. Taylor; *Seventh Letter* 325d, translated by L.A. Post.

29. Law of Diocles: Demosthenes 24.42; see M.H. Hansen 1990. Draco's law on homicide: *IG* I^3 104 (= ML 86, Fornara 15); Stroud 1968. Solon's laws re-edited: Lysias 30.2. For other, older laws adapted and republished by the *nomothetai* between 410 and 405, see above, chapter 6 notes 16 and 17 and chapter 9 note 22.

30. The relationship of the boards of *nomothetai* in the decree of Teisamenus to other officials responsible for drafting, approving, and curating the laws has been

variously understood by the scholars cited in note 26 above. For the interpretation adopted here, see chapter 5, with notes 46–48; cf. chapter 6, with notes 46 and 48, and chapter 9, with note 6.

31. The procedures for provisional display of laws under consideration are discussed in detail by Robertson 1990, 46–52; see also Rhodes 1991, 98–99. On points of translation, see above, note 26. Precedents are attested in regulations of the 430s and 420s dealing with tribute collection, *IG* I³ 60.28–33 and 68.18–21 (= ML 68.17–20, Fornara 133), and in *IG* I³ 84.23–28, publicizing contractors to sacred property. "Within the present month" (*en tode to meni*) in Andocides 1.83 is paralleled by the stipulation for judicial action "within the month" (*emmena*) in *IG* I³ 68.48 (= ML 68.47, Fornara 133); fourth-century procedures for *nomothesia* stipulate that "the *demos* will vote on the time allowed for the *nomothetai* in proportion to the number of laws to be ratified," Demosthenes 24.23.

32. Condemnation of Cleophon: Lysias 30.10–13. Arrest of Callixeinus and others: Xenophon *Hellenica* 1.7.35. Agoratus and the generals: Lysias 13.7–38; cf. 30.14. On these events, see above, chapter 8, with notes 34, 35, and 44.

33. Curation of public enactments in the Council-House by the Secretary of the Council is attested at least as early as the mid-fifth century: *IG* I³ 27, 7–10; see Shear 1995, 185–87. On the conversion of the old Council-House to the Metroön and archives, see chapter 6, with note 51. On the venerable reputation of the Council of the Areopagus, see Aristotle *Constitution* 23.1, 25.1 (cf. Andocides 1.77); in general, see Wallace 1985.

34. The hypothetical placement of the stelae inscribed with laws (see chapter 9 note 22) in the Stoa Basileios (the Royal Stoa) has long been widely accepted; see, e.g., Oliver 1935, 8–9; Ferguson 1936, 146; Hignett 1952, 302–303; Dow 1960, 277–78; MacDowell 1978, 47–48; Wycherley 1978, 31–32; Camp 1986, 104; Rhodes 1991, 90–91.

35. The careful discussion of the evidence adduced for the display of an inscribed law code in the Stoa Basileios by H. Hansen 1990, xii-xiv, reveals the difficulties; see also Fingarette 1971, 335 n. 22; Thompson, in Rhodes 1981, 134–35; Ostwald 1986, 519. Problems with the standard interpretation are more directly discussed by Clinton 1982, 33; Kuhn 1985, 204–18; M.H. Hansen 1990; Robertson 1990; Rhodes 1991.

36. Teisamenus' decree prescribes temporary display only: Thompson, in Rhodes 1981, 134–35, and in Ostwald 1986, 519; Kuhn 1985, 216–18; Robertson 1990, 47–49; Rhodes 1991, 99. "Stelae" inscribed by authority of the *nomothetai* of 403–399: Lysias 30.21, discussed in chapter 11, with notes 4–5.

37. Robertson 1990, 46–52, has advocated the identification of the display "facing the statues of the Eponymous Heroes" (or "at the Eponymi," as he translates the phrase; see above, note 26) with the display on "the wall." In this regard, his conclusions have been cautiously accepted by Rhodes 1991, 99. But Robertson's suggestion, 51–52, for the location of "the wall" and the monument of the Eponymous Heroes outside of the Agora, in the vicinity of the Prytaneum, has yet to win supporters.

38. Aeaceum: Herodotus 5.89; Stroud 1993, 1994a, and 1996, who cites among his evidence *POxy* XVII, no. 2087, lines 16–18. The probable location of the earlier base of the Eponymous Heroes, as shown here in figure 8, is identified by Shear

1970, 205–22, and indicated in fig. 66, Camp 1986, 89, as adjacent to the "Heliaia" = Aeaceum. In light of the present discussion, *prosthe[n to Aiakeio]* must be considered as a more probable restoration in line 21 of *IG* I^3 68 (= ML 68, line 20; Fornara 133).

39. Aeacus as judge of the dead: Plato *Apology* 41a; *Gorgias* 523e-24a, 526c; cf. Isocrates 9.15. Aeacus as gatekeeper to Hades in Aristophanes' *Frogs* 465–813 serves an analogous function. It is noteworthy that the house of Simon the cobbler, known to have been frequented by Socrates (Diogenes Laertius 2.122), lies immediately adjacent to the foundations associated with the monument of the Eponymous Heroes and the Aeaceum, see Camp 1986, 145–46; figure 9 and map 4 here.

40. Quote: Andocides 1.87. This text provides the point of departure for Ostwald's two great studies of law and Athenian democracy (1969, 1, and 1986, 523). I am indebted to Martin Ostwald for pointing out that *agraphos nomos,* "unwritten law," here means specifically "a law that is not part of the written code" (i.e., a law that is not *anagegrammenos*). In view of the passionate assertions of the validity, and even priority, of "unwritten laws" in the rhetoric and poetry of the generation just passed (Sophocles *Antigone* 450–61, e.g.), it seems significant that the more philosophic, even poetic term, *agraphos* (or *agraptos*), is used in this text instead of a more juridically precise definition such as *ouk anagegrammenos.* By using the broadest term to designate a law or custom that has not yet been submitted to the formal procedures of democratic enactment, the new law asserts its authority most comprehensively.

41. On the *graphe paranomon,* see chapter 4 note 17. On the origin of the commission of *nomothetai,* see chapter 5, with note 46, and chapter 6, with notes 16 and 17. On law vs. decree in fourth-century Athens, see Harrison 1955, 26–27; Sealey 1982 and 1987, 32–35; M.H. Hansen 1983, 161–77. On the emergence, from the experiences of 411–399, of the fourth-century Athenian legislative procedures, *nomothesia,* see MacDowell 1978, 41–52; Sealey 1982 and 1987, 35–52; M.H. Hansen 1991, 161–77. See Thomas 1994 on the consequent manipulations of the image of the ancient lawgivers in fourth-century Athenian rhetoric.

CHAPTER ELEVEN. ELIMINATING SOCRATES, 401–399

1. The speech, Lysias 30, *Against Nicomachus,* along with Andocides 1, *On the Mysteries,* is essential to our understanding of the work of the *nomothetai;* see chapter 5 note 46; chapter 9 note 22; chapter 10 note 30. On the identification of Nicomachus as a *nomothetes,* see M.H. Hansen 1990, 68–69. Quotes: Lysias 30.2, 4.

2. Quotes: Lysias 30.5; Aristotle *Rhetoric* 1354b; cf. Demosthenes 24.23, quoted on page 265.

3. Nicomachus as arbitrator: Isocrates 18.10, 13–14; date: Loening 1987, 124. The identification of Nicomachus in Isocrates 18 with the Nicomachus of Lysias 30 has not been generally recognized; it is circumstantially probable but cannot be proven. Nicomachus' alleged misdeeds: Lysias 30.2–5, 9–12, 19–21, 24–25. Blackmailers: Lysias 25.25–27, where Demophanes, Cleisthenes, and Epigenes are named; Schwartz 1889, 121 n. 1 suggested that the first two names should be corrected to Demophantus and Cleigenes, the proposer and secretary of a law of 410, a work of the *nomothetai,* cited in Andocides 1.96; see MacDowell 1962, 135;

Cleigenes is denounced by Aristophanes *Frogs* 709; Epigenes is an officer of the Council in 408: *IG* I[3] 119 (ML 88, Fornara 163); on the date, see chapter 6 note 47. Callixeinus, who had proposed the resolution of the Council that the generals at Arginusae be judged en masse, may also have been a *nomothetes,* or at least had legal advice from colleagues who were; Xenophon *Hellenica* 1.7.35 reports that Callixeinus was one of several men placed under arrest, in the shift toward oligarchy in 404, for misdeeds described in terms like those of Lysias 25.25–27.

4. Quote: Lysias 30.17–19. On *kyrbeis,* distinctive, upright pillars on which, most famously, the archaic laws of Draco and Solon were inscribed, see Stroud 1978, esp. 42–60; H. Hansen 1990, 127–99. The sacrificial calendar is discussed in Lysias 30.17–22, 25; on its surviving remains, see references above in chapter 9 note 22. The largest fragment is translated in Harding 9 and illustrated here in figure 7, p. 228. For recent scholarship, see Clinton 1982, 34–35; H. Hansen 1990; Robertson 1990, 67–71; Rhodes 1991, 93–95.

5. Quote: Lysias 30.21, translated by W. R. M. Lamb.

6. Quote: Lysias 6.33, also cited above, chapter 10, at note 24. On public and private *syngraphai,* see chapter 3, with notes 63–67, and cf. chapter 5, with note 20. "The *Attike syngraphe* of Hellanicus": Thucydides 1.97.2. On the contents of Hellanicus' *Attike syngraphe,* see: Pearson 1942, 1–26; Jacoby 1949, 88–89, 106, 215–17, 223–25; *FGrHist* 323a; on his other attested works see also Pearson 1939, 152–235; Lesky 1963/1966, 330–31. On Stesimbrotus, see: *FGrHist* 107; Lesky 1963/1966, 329; Richardson 1974b, 71–72; Burkert 1986.

7. Allegation (possibly true, though see chapter 6 note 15) of Nicomachus' servile ancestry: Lysias 30.2, 27, 30. The charge of financial embarrassment caused by Nicomachus, Lysias 30.19–22, is seen by Robertson 1990, 58, 71–75, as the heart of the case against Nicomachus; it should rather be seen as an accessory charge, like servile birth, to prejudice the jury against Nicomachus.

8. Pride of Callias: Xenophon *Hellenica* 6.3.3–6; cf. *Symposium* 8.40. Beginning a tradition followed by practically all Atthidographers, Hellanicus wrote on the priestly clan of Hierophants, as well as about the clan of Ceryces (where, perhaps significantly, Andocides' lineage was noticed): *FGrHist* 323a F 8, 24; see Jacoby 1949, 124–25.

9. Callias as accuser of Andocides: Andocides 1.112–32; Callias embarrassed by the citation from a stele: Andocides 1.116, where it is stated that Callias' paternal descent in the clan of Ceryces does not give him the authority to expound "ancestral law" in Eleusinian matters. Because the speaker of Lysias 6, *Against Andocides* clearly claimed the right to speak on behalf of Eleusinian tradition, scholars have generally excluded Callias from consideration as the speaker (e.g., MacDowell 1962, 14–15). But Andocides 1.116 makes it clear that Callias *did* assert this right, even though it could be challenged. The speaker of Lysias 6.54, in citing the advice of his grandfather, Diocles, on the subject of piety, notes that Diocles was the son of the Eleusinian Hierophant, Zacorus; it is surely significant that the speaker can claim no more proximate relationship to a Hierophant than his great-grandfather. If the speaker was Callias, then the Hierophant was his mother's grandfather, and Callias' otherwise unknown mother, formerly the wife of Pericles, was the daughter of the Eumolpid Diocles; for the testimonia see Davies 1971, 262–63. Reference to "what many of us heard the Hierophant say" (Lysias 6.2) and "the unwritten laws

that the Eumolpidae expound" (Lysias 6.10) demonstrates that the speaker is ready to invoke Eumolpid authority without claiming that it is his right to expound it. This corresponds precisely to Callias' status and disposition.

10. Callias and the sophists: Plato *Apology* 20a; *Protagoras* 311a, 314b-17e; Xenophon *Symposium* 1.5, 4.1–2, 62. Lysias' reputation: Plato *Phaedrus* 228a, 278c. Lysias and Socrates: Diogenes Laertius 2.40–41.

11. The terms of the amnesty are reviewed by Cloché 1915, 251–308, and more recently by Loening 1987, 39–58; cf. Rhodes 1981, 468–69, on Aristotle *Constitution* 39.6. Suits frustrated by the amnesty: against Epichares: Andocides 1.95–102; against Philon: Isocrates 18.22; see Loening 1987, 121–23. Creation of the *paragraphe* by Archinus: Isocrates 18.1–4; Wolff 1966; MacDowell 1978, 214–17. Aristotle *Constitution* 40.2 praises Archinus' statesmanship in other respects; his account bears signs of an idealization of Archinus, as enforcer of the amnesty, also evident in Demosthenes 24.135, Aeschines 2.176, and probably in Plato *Menexenus* 234b.

12. On the chronology of the early speeches of Lysias and Isocrates see: MacDowell 1971; Loening 1981 and 1987, 59–146.

13. Spartan dispute with Elis over *perioikides poleis:* Xenophon *Hellenica* 3.2.21–23; Diodorus 14.17.4–7; cf. Thucydides 5.31. On the chronology of these events, see Funke 1980, 32 n. 16, and Cartledge 1987a, 248–49.

14. Elean campaigns: Diodorus 14.17.7–12, 34.1; Xenophon *Hellenica* 3.2.25–29. Cephallenia, Zacynthus, and Naupactus: Diodorus 14.34.2–3, 78.5.

15. Cyrus and Sparta: Xenophon *Hellenica* 3.1.1; *Anabasis* 1.4.2–3; Diodorus 14.19.4–5; Plutarch *Artaxerxes* 6.2–3. Although mercenary commanders were summoned to Cyrus under false pretenses, in his negotiations with Sparta Cyrus' ultimate goal must have been made clear; a campaign against the Pisidians, the ostensible goal of his land force, had no use for a fleet along the Cilician coast.

16. Meno in Athens: Morrison 1942; Plato *Meno* 70a-71a, 76e, 78d; Meno and Anytus: Plato *Meno* 90b, 92e. Testimonia for Meno the elder are gathered and discussed by M.J. Osborne 1983, 20–23. Thucydides (son of Meno) of Pharsalus: Thucydides 8.92.8; Marcellinus *Life of Thucydides* 28.

17. Aristippus and Meno: Xenophon *Anabasis* 1.1.10, 2.6; Plato *Meno* 70. Meno spared by Artaxerxes: Xenophon *Anabasis* 2.6.29; Ctesias *Persica* epitome 60; Diodorus 14.27.2; Plutarch *Artaxerxes* 18.3. It is possible that Proxenus, the Boeotian, was also spared, for reasons similar to Meno's; Xenophon *Anabasis* 2.5.38 indicates that he was not immediately executed, and it may have been hard for Xenophon to admit that his friend had saved himself in the same way that Meno had.

18. Quote: Xenophon *Anabasis* 3.1.5–8, translated by H.G. Dakyns, with modifications.

19. End of the enclave at Eleusis: Aristotle *Constitution* 40.4; quote: Xenophon *Hellenica* 2.4.43; Justin 5.10.8–11.

20. Quote: Xenophon *Hellenica* 3.1.4.

21. Indictment of Socrates: Diogenes Laertius 2.40; cf. Plato *Euthyphro* 2c, 3b; *Apology* 24b, 26b; Xenophon *Memorabilia* 1.1.1; *Apology* 10. On the indictment and trial see also: Chroust 1957; Stone 1988; Brickhouse and Smith 1989; Connor 1991; and Hansen 1995, who argues convincingly for the reliability of the many common features in Plato's and Xenophon's accounts of Socrates' defense.

22. Influence of Anytus and Lycon: Plato *Apology* 36a; cf. Xenophon *Apology* 24, 29. Arguments of "the accuser" reported by Xenophon *Memorabilia* 1.2.9–61 may reflect the arguments of Anytus, although they probably derive more immediately from Polycrates' *Indictment of Socrates,* published a decade or so after the trial; see Diogenes Laertius 2.38; Chroust 1957, 76–77; M.H. Hansen 1995, 8–15.

23. Socrates' "self-righteous tone" and readiness to die: Xenophon *Apology* 1, 5–9; cf. Plato *Apology* 28b-29b, 30b-31a, 32a, 38e, 40b-42; *Crito; Phaedo; Gorgias* 521b-27e.

24. Quotes: Plato *Apology* 33c; Plato *Apology* 21a; Xenophon *Apology* 14. On Socrates' contempt, cf. his reference to "these so-called jurors," Plato *Apology* 41a, and his sarcastic remarks to the hypothetical "children of the jury," Plato *Gorgias* 521e.

25. Quotes: Aristophanes *Frogs* 676–77, 1487–99.

26. Quote: Plato *Euthyphro* 3b, translated by Lane Cooper, with modifications. On Socrates' *daimonion* and his trial, see Plato *Apology* 27b-e; Xenophon *Apology* 12–13; *Memorabilia* 1.1.2–4. Against the reductionism of Vlastos, McPherran 1996, 185–208, accounts for the irrational cognition provided by Socrates' *daimonion* within a coherent epistemological system, much as does Xenophon, *Memorabilia* 1.1.6–9.

27. Preventative *daimonion:* Plato *Apology* 31d; Xenophon *Memorabilia* 1.1.2–9. Quote: Plato *Apology* 32a.

28. Socrates, the trial of the generals, and the Thirty: Plato *Apology* 32b-e; *Seventh Letter* 324e-25a; Xenophon *Memorabilia* 1.1.18, 32. See above, chapter 7, with note 30, and chapter 9, with note 14.

29. Socrates' *daimonion,* Apollo's oracle, and the authority of Lycurgus: Xenophon *Apology* 12–16. On Lycurgan laws and Delphi, see also Xenophon *Constitution of the Lacedaemonians* 8.5. On the relationship between Apollo's oracle and Socrates' mission, see McPherran 1996, 208–32.

30. From his review of the case against Socrates, M.H. Hansen 1995, 26, arrives at a similar conclusion: "Sokrates was not charged with being an atheist, but with being a missionary." As Hansen also notes (p. 19), a generation later Hyperides could report that "our ancestors punished Socrates for what he said" (*epi logois,* fr. 14.1, Burtt). It is likely that Socrates' pervasive concern for the fate of one's soul *(psyche)* placed his eschatological lessons (e.g., Plato *Gorgias* 523a-27e, *Phaedrus* 245c-56b, *Apology* 39c-42, *Phaedo*) in competition with the mystic doctrines of Eleusis. If so, Socrates was prosecuted on grounds not too dissimilar from the charges of profaning the Mysteries brought against Alcibiades in 415 (see above, chapter 4).

31. Quote: Aristophanes *Clouds* 138–43. Aristophanes *Birds* 1553–64 describes Socrates as *Psychagogos,* conjuror of souls from the Underworld, and depicts Peisander as a patron of his arts of divination.

32. Socrates as devotee of Euthyphro: Plato *Euthyphro* 3c-5c.

33. Xenophon *Memorabilia* 1.2.9–47 dwells at length on the argument that Socrates had taught his associates to "despise the established laws" and that, in particular, he was an impetus behind the public deeds of Alcibiades and Critias; so also Isocrates 11.5 and Aeschines 1.173; Plato was more discreet, although *Gorgias* 481d-86c and 519a-b is suggestive. Aristophanes *Birds* 1280–83 describes Socrates as the center of a group of Athenian devotees of Spartan ways; cf. Plato *Gorgias* 515e.

34. Annoyance of Anytus: Plato *Meno* 90b-95a; cf. Xenophon *Apology* 29–30. The identity of Meletus, Socrates' accuser, with Meletus, accuser of Andocides, and the Meletus summoned by the Thirty to arrest Leon (Andocides 1.94) has been doubted by (e.g., MacDowell 1962, 208–10); the unity of their motivation, however, suggests that they are the same; see Blumenthal 1973. The identity of Lycon, accuser of Socrates, with Lycon, father of Autolycus, has also been doubted (e.g., by M. H. Hansen 1995, 33–34); but their amicable relations with Socrates, as depicted in Xenophon *Symposium* 9.1, pose no difficulty to a different relationship after the turmoil of 404/3; see Chroust 1957, 36. On Autolycus, see Plutarch *Lysander* 15.5; Diodorus 14.5.7; Pausanias 9.32.8.

35. Quote: Plato *Symposium* 181e. In this context Plato's *Phaedrus* also deserves special mention; both texts expound the cosmic power of Eros.

CHAPTER TWELVE. ATHENIAN DEMOCRACY AND HISTORY, 399–395

1. Lesky 1963/1966, 496. Opinions about the historicity of Plato's Socrates range widely. Brickhouse and Smith 1989, 2–10, and 1994 represent a less skeptical perspective than Lesky; Montuori 1992 surveys the long history of scholarship on this question.

2. Lysias 25.8–10, translated by W. R. M. Lamb. For a different use of the same evidence, namely, that men given to offensive behavior are just the sort who fomented oligarchy in 411 and 404, see Isocrates 20, *Against Lochites.*

3. Lysias 26, *On the Scrutiny of Euandros* demonstrates how powerful this division still was more than twenty years after the fall of the Thirty. On those who took no active role in events of 404/3: Lysias 31, *Against Philon* and Isocrates 18, *Against Callimachus* 49 are accusatory; Isocrates 21, *Against Euthynus* defends withdrawal. The "Solonian" law against neutrality during *stasis,* or civil war (Aristotle *Constitution* 8.5; Plutarch *Solon* 20.1), clearly did not yet exist (see Lysias 31.27; Hignett 1952, 26–27), but must have become part of the legal tradition by virtue of the issue being raised, in an accusatory manner, in numerous cases heard at a time when "ancestral" statutes were being (re)codified. Lipsius 1908, 407–408, and Rhodes 1981, 157, believe the law was genuinely Solonian, but was forgotten or overlooked through long disuse, only later to be discovered. But the intensity of research into documents and laws from the past at precisely this time makes it most improbable that any such archaic statute was extant but somehow forgotten or overlooked by those involved in litigation in the years ca. 400.

4. A pastiche of democratic heroics of 411 and 403 was created, ca. 341, by a kinsman of Aristocrates (one of the generals executed after Arginusae, a fact discreetly hidden by the distortion): [Demosthenes] 58.66–68; see the discussion of Thomas 1989, 132–38.

5. Quote: Aristophanes *Birds* 1286–89.

6. *Kyrbeis* of Solon and Draco treated with humor and respect: Cratinus fr. 300 *PCG* (= 274 Kock), in Plutarch *Solon* 25.1; Aristophanes *Clouds* 447–48; *Birds* 1353–57. Research into laws of Solon and Cleisthenes: Aristotle *Constitution* 29.3; see above, chapter 5, with note 20. Sanctity of Draco and Solon: Andocides 1.82–83, 95, 111; Lysias 30.2, 26, and of Themistocles and Pericles, 28; Xenophon *Symposium* 8.39; cf. the hagiography of Isocrates 15.231–35.

7. Aristophanes *Frogs* 52–54. Eupolis fr. 327 *PCG* (= 304 Kock). Quote: Xenophon *Anabasis* 7.5.14. Turner 1952, 20–23, offers insightful comments on the informal nature of "publishing" in the late fifth century and recognizes that "by the first thirty years of the fourth century books have established themselves." On the commerce in books, see also above, chapter 7, with note 44.

8. Quote: Xenophon *Memorabilia* 4.2.1, translated by E. C. Marchant, with modifications. On Euthydemus, see above, chapter 9, with note 28.

9. Quote: Plato *Phaedrus* 276c.

10. Quote: Plato *Phaedrus* 275c, translated by R. Hackforth, with modifications.

11. Quote: Plato *Phaedrus* 278d-e, translated by R. Hackforth.

12. Quote: Plato *Crito* 51a-b, translated by H. Tredennick.

13. Vlastos is wrong, therefore, to conclude from the *Crito* that "Socrates' preference for Athenian law is *a preference for Athens' democratic constitution*" (1983/1994, 92, emphasis his own). Vlastos goes on to make this interpretation a basis for concluding that Xenophon's portrayal of Socrates' critique of democracy is at odds with, and less credible than, Plato's account. But Socrates does *not* identify the legitimate laws of Athens with democracy; I see no incompatibility between Plato and Xenophon on this point.

14. Quote: Plato *Republic* 517d, translated by P. Shorey. On the theme of the wise man appearing the fool in his hour of trial, cf. *Gorgias* 485d-86c, 519a-22e; *Meno* 94e-95a.

15. Vlastos is therefore right to assert that "for Plato's Socrates... everyone is called upon to make perfection of soul the supreme concern of his or her personal existence" (1983/1994, 103). Though imbued with the social biases of his day, Socrates embraced Panathenian ideology on the theological level; see Plato *Apology* 39e-42a. McPherran 1996, 252–71, examines Socratic eschatology and defends a view that Socrates is rationally agnostic on the subject of the afterlife; I would accept McPherran's conclusion with the proviso that rationality was but half of Socrates' attitude, and that Socrates was piously committed to faith in the immortality of the soul. On the shrine of Aeacus, see chapter 10 notes 38 and 39. On the education of the guardians, and their commemoration as divinely sanctioned heroes, see Plato *Republic* 519c-41b, esp. 540b-c. On the sanctioning of the ten tribal heroes by the Delphic oracle, see Aristotle *Constitution* 21.6; cf. Herodotus 5.66.2; Pausanias 1.5.1–4; Kearns 1989, 80–92.

16. Critias on *grammata alexiloga:* Athenaeus 28b (DK 88 B 2.10 = Sprague 1972, 250). Plato on *hypomnemata* and the essential lack of seriousness in writing: *Seventh Letter* 341b-45a, esp. 344c; Steiner 1994, 103–105, 233–39.

17. Quote: Plato *Theaetetus* 143a-c, translated by F. M. Cornford.

18. Quotes: Plato *Parmenides* 126c; Plato *Phaedrus* 227c-28c, 230d. Steiner 1994, 212–16, suggests that the depiction of Socrates led outside of Athens by his passion for written texts is another comment on their seductive power.

19. Simon: Diogenes Laertius 2.122, translated by R. D. Hicks; see also chapter 10 note 39 on Simon's workshop near the Agora. Several followers of Socrates are credited with "genuine" dialogues, or are said to have "borrowed" them from others; see Athenaeus 11.508c-d; Diogenes Laertius 2.60, 61–62. For Cleon's critique of his over-sophisticated audience, see Thucydides 3.38.7, quoted above in chapter 3, page 80.

20. Transcribing a speech: Aristophanes *Wasps* 530–31, 538–39, 559, 576–77. Discussing a speech: Aristophanes *Knights* 1373–81. "Book in hand...": Aristophanes *Frogs* 1113–14.

21. On Antiphon's literate legacy, see: [Plutarch] *Moralia* 832c-d; Thucydides 8.68.1–2; further discussion above, chapter 4, with note 16. On Antiphon's trial, see chapter 5, with note 52.

22. On Xenophon at the trial of the generals, see above, chapter 7 note 32. One or more transcripts of Theramenes' speech proposing negotiations for surrender may account for the verbal echoes between Lysias 12.69 and the historical fragment preserved in the "Theramenes papyrus" better than supposing a common oral source (as argued by Sealey 1975b, 281), or than supposing that the papyrus author consulted Lysias' speech (as argued by Henrichs 1968, accepted by Andrewes 1970). On Xenophon and Isocrates among the witnesses to the debate of Theramenes and Critias, see chapter 9 notes 26 and 39. On Euthydemus, see chapter 8 note 47 and chapter 9, with note 28. On the Thirty's prohibition of the teaching "the art of speaking," see chapter 9, with note 13.

23. Quote: Lysias 12.77, translated by W.R.M. Lamb. Critias refers to Theramenes: Xenophon *Hellenica* 2.3.28. Unraveling a similar rhetorical misdirection, Socrates accuses Meletus of relying on his audiences' familiarity with the writings of Anaxagoras to make his accusations of Socrates seem more plausible, according to Plato *Apology* 26d.

24. Secure knowledge of Thucydides' biography comes from his few statements: 1.1, 22, 2.1, 4.104.4–107.2, 5.26. Thucydides provides incidental information that probably come from personal experience abroad: 2.97 on Thrace and Thracians; 2.99–100.2 on Macedonia; 4.81.2 on the esteem for Brasidas among Athenian allies; 4.109.2–4 on ethnic groups in the Chalcidice; 1.100.2–101.3 and 8.64.2–5 on the politics of Thasos (discussed further below). Plutarch *Cimon* 4.1–2 and Pausanias 1.23.9 add a few details; less reliable information comes from two biographies compiled in the later Roman era; see J.H. Finley 1942, 9–16; Hornblower 1987, 1–4. Stroud 1994b makes a convincing case for Thucydides' intimacy with, and occasional presence in, Corinth and the Peloponnese; Stroud's evidence, however, does not require an "extended residency in Corinth after 424 B.C.," as he argues.

25. Date of Thucydides' return to Athens: Thucydides 5.26.4–5; see Andrewes in Gomme et al. 1970, 13.

26. On the late fifth-century culture of reading, see above, with notes 5–8, and the introduction, with note 1, chapter 1, with notes 73–74, and chapter 3, with notes 66–67. Weil 1975 draws attention to the extensive use Thucydides makes of written evidence (so too Westlake 1977/1989 and Lenardon 1981) and regards the passage of the year 403 to mark the beginning of "the century of prose." Gentili and Cerri 1988, 11–13, likewise see in Thucydides' work the completion of a technological transformation of historiography from the oral culture of poetry, logographers (i.e., orators, in my understanding), and even of Herodotus, into the culture of written communication. Edmunds 1993 examines the evidence for this transformation in the presence Thucydides establishes as the *writer* of his work.

27. Quote: Thucydides 1.1.1. See Woodman 1988, 1–7, on the relationship envisioned by Thucydides between his work and those of Homer and Herodotus.

28. See M.I. Finley 1972 (introduction to Penguin edition) for a strong statement of the dominant view of composition, namely that, writing between 431 and 404, Thucydides "wrestled constantly with the techniques of his historical composition" (12) and that the speeches were "worked up by Thucydides not contemporaneously but nearly thirty years later" (13). For similar views of the late insertion of the speeches, see Hornblower 1987, 45–72, and Yunis 1996, 61–63. Scholarship analyzing the evidence for the progressive composition of Thucydides' work begins with Ullrich 1846, who identified the so-called "second preface," Thucydides 5.25–26, as evidence that Thucydides originally wrote a history of the war down to the Peace of Nicias in 421 and only later realized that the renewal of war justified continuing his work toward the goal of surrender in 404. De Romilly 1963, 3–10, summarizes the diverse opinions generated in the first century of "analyst" scholarship, which has been pursued by, among others, Gomme, Andrewes, Dover, Westlake, and Hornblower; see Hornblower 1987, 136–54, for a recent overview. A tenet of the "analyst" interpretation has been that Thucydides' judgment changed sufficiently over the period of composition that he felt impelled to revise sections of his earlier writing. Since the result was a more unified work, the "analysts" have, understandably, been unable to reach consensus, beyond Ullrich's original hypothesis, on what portions were revised when. The "analyst" approach is opposed by the "unitarian" interpretation, which seeks to define an aboriginal conceptual consistency to the whole of Thucydides' work. The "unitarian" position has been most forcefully argued by J.H. Finley 1940/1967, who also argues for a comparatively brief period of composition after 404, and by de Romilly 1963, who nevertheless accepts the concept of progressive composition beginning in 431. More recent "unitarians," with varying views of the time of composition, include Edmunds, Hunter, Rawlings, Connor, Salviat and Pouilloux, and Orwin.

29. This translation of Thucydides 1.22.1 is discussed below, with note 31.

30. Gomme 1937, 156–89, and 1945, 140–41, exemplifies those who defend the accuracy of Thucydidean speeches, despite uncertainty about the means available to Thucydides for preserving authentic words. Yunis 1996, 61–86, represents a recent formulation of the argument that the speeches are essentially Thucydidean creations. On the essential nature of the speeches in the work of Thucydides, see, for example, the essays edited by Stadter 1973, especially the introductory comments by G. Kennedy, ix-xii; Dover 1973, 21–27; Pouncey 1980, 13–15; Cogan 1981; Hornblower 1987, 45–72; Develin 1990. On this aspect of Thucydides' contribution to Graeco–Roman historiography, see Fornara 1983, 142–68.

31. On "hearing" *(akoei)* as a reference to written texts, see chapter 4, with notes 43 and 45. In Diodorus 12.13.2, *diamnemoneusai* means "to preserve a record [in writing] of." Similarly, *mnemosynon,* means "[written] memorandum," as it does in Aristophanes *Wasps* 538, 559; *epimnesasthai,* "to remember" or "mention," can also mean "to mention [in writing]," as it does in Thucydides 1.97.2 and 3.104.5. The act of writing is frequently used, in fifth-century poetry, as a metaphor for memory; see Steiner 1994, 100–105.

32. The distinctive syntactic patterns and variations that characterize different speakers in Thucydides' work, examined by Tompkins 1972 and 1993, must represent the authentic idiosyncrasies of speakers heard by or reported to Thucydides.

Tompkins' studies answer the objection of those who claim that all Thucydidean speeches sound like Thucydides and therefore have no claim to authenticity.

33. Distinctive qualities of the rhetoric of empire under Pericles have been recognized in both the speeches and narrative of Thucydides. Allison 1989 has drawn attention to Thucydides' focus on material resources and preparation, *paraskeue.* Kallet-Marx 1993 and 1994 has examined the connection specifically of naval power to financial resources in Thucydides. All of these elements are essential to the analysis of empire that de Romilly 1963 demonstrates to be the consistent and unifying theme of Thucydides' work; so also Orwin 1994. On Thucydides' reflection of the rhetorical styles of the late 430s and 420s, see J. H. Finley 1942, 48–50, 250–88, and 1939/1967, 55–117. Note the yearning for the old rhetoric of ships and wealth attributed to Aeschylus, but echoing Pericles, in Aristophanes *Frogs* 1463–65.

34. On the outlook of Pseudo-Xenophon, *Constitution of the Athenians,* and Laconophiles among the Athenian aristocracy, see chapter 3, with notes 3 and 5. Brasidas: Aristophanes *Wasps* 475; quote: Thucydides 4.84.2; cf. 81.2. Stroud's demonstration (1994b) of Thucydides' intimate familiarity with the affairs of Corinth reveals one of the key crossroads of Athenian–Peloponnesian intelligentsia.

35. Prominent exiles of the past included the Peisistratids, the Alcmaeonids, and the Philaids, including Miltiades and Cimon. Ostracism, which Cimon experienced, institutionalized an "honorable" form of exile for many other prominent Athenians, but none, except Hyperbolus (see above, chapter 4, with notes 2 and 33), are known from the era of the Peloponnesian War, when judicial banishment seems to have become the norm. Several members of the Thirty in 404 had gone into exile with the fall of the Four Hundred in 411 (Krentz 1982, 54–56; see chapter 8, with note 22). One of the Thirty was Sophocles, probably the son of Sostratides, formerly a general condemned to exile in 423 and, like Thucydides, a returnee to Athens in 404 (Thucydides 4.65.3 and Krentz 1982, 54). Attic tragedy frequently addressed the theme of the returning exile in these years, and Aristophanes broached the subject directly in the *Frogs* 686–737.

36. The quote paraphrases Thucydides' programmatic statement in 1.22.4 (discussed further below, with note 52); cf. Diodotus in Thucydides 3.42.2. On the Periclean rhetoric of resources and empire, see above, note 33. The importance of commanding material facts in political rhetoric is also stressed by Xenophon *Memorabilia* 3.6.1–18.

37. Obstacles to the settlement of north Aegean affairs according to the Peace of Nicias of 421 are described by Thucydides 5.21, 35, 38, 46.2, cf. 83.4. Rapprochement with Sparta in 411: see chapter 5, with notes 13, 14, and 36. For other exiles as peacemakers, note Pasippidas of Sparta and Hermocrates of Syracuse (chapter 6 note 32 and below, note 39) and the earlier example of Cimon: Plutarch *Cimon* 17.6–18.1.

38. Revolt of Thasos from Athens: Thucydides 8.64.3–4; *Hellenica Oxyrhynchia* 7.4; see also chapter 6, with notes 3, 34, and chapter 7, with note 6. Pasippidas, Tissaphernes, and Thasos: Xenophon *Hellenica* 1.1.32; see chapter 6 note 32.

39. Embassy to Darius: Xenophon *Hellenica* 1.3.13; see above, chapter 6, with notes 30–33. Hermocrates had been the architect of peace in Sicily in 424: Thucydides 4.58–65; Thucydides' opinion of Hermocrates, 6.72.2–3, places him in the

company of Pericles and Alcibiades (cf. 2.65.8–9, 6.15.4). On the ties of Thasos to its founder, Paros, and to its own colonial foundations in Thrace, and the importance of these relations in reconciliation agreements, see Graham 1983, 71–91, 96–97; Grandjean and Salviat 1988, 272–76. Chios was probably part of the design for Aegean reconciliation in 409; see chapter 6 notes 32 and 36. In 412, the Athenians had granted autonomy to the Samians; see chapter 5 note 31.

40. Failure of the mission of Alcibiades and Pharnabazus: see chapter 6 note 33 and chapter 7, with note 2. Thasian surrender and settlement: see chapter 7, with note 6. In several respects the Thasian settlement of 407 anticipates the Athenian reconciliation agreements of 403; see Grandjean and Salviat 1988, esp. 271, 275–76. Lysander at Thasos and in Thrace: see above, chapter 8, with note 25, and chapter 9, with note 34.

41. Thasos, Thucydides, and mines: Thucydides 1.100.2–101.3, 4.104.4–105.1; see also Graham 1983 (above, note 39).

42. Oenobius' decree: Pausanias 1.23.9; Pliny *Natural History* 7.111 confirms the existence of a decree recalling Thucydides, but offers an anachronistic explanation. Oenobius' generalship: *IG* I[3] 101.47 (= ML 89, Fornara 156). Oenobius may have been the proposer of the decree supporting the restoration of democracy at Thasos in 407; see Grandjean and Salviat 1988, 256. Although some commentators have associated Oenobius' decree of recall with Thucydides' return in 404/3, it is unclear why a personal recall would have been needed or desired when a universal recall of exiles was in effect (chapter 8, with note 31). A recall on some appropriate occasion before the surrender of Athens seems more probable, and therefore Andrewes in Gomme et al. 1970, 14–15, follows Jacoby in favoring a date of 410/9 for Oenobius' decree.

43. Ingots of Scaptesylican gold: *IG* I[3] 376.105–106, 118–19. Thucydides and Scapte Hyle: Plutarch *Cimon* 4.2; Marcellinus *Life of Thucydides* 14, 19, 25, 47. Theramenes and Thrasybulus: Xenophon *Hellenica* 1.1.12; Diodorus; 13.49.1–3, 72.1; see chapter 6, with notes 3 and 34. Brunt 1952 and Westlake 1985/1989 explore the likelihood that Thucydides was in contact with Alcibiades in this period (though for different reasons from those proposed here).

44. Davies 1971, 308, considers the possibility that a certain Miltiades, envoy in the company of Lysander in 404 (Lysias 12.72), was a Philaid, hence a kinsman of Thucydides; against this view, see Krentz 1982, 48 n. 20. The meager evidence for Thucydides' age at the time of his return is reconsidered by Fornara 1993.

45. Views of Pericles ca. 400: Plato *Gorgias* 503b-19b is highly critical; brief, favorable mention is found Lysias 6.10, 12.4, and 30.28. Stesimbrotus of Thasos may have published his *On Themistocles, Thucydides [son of Melesias], and Pericles* at this time, but not enough survives to reveal its tenor (but see Plato *Meno* 93a-94e on the failure of each of these three statesmen to produce worthy offspring); see Tsakmakis 1995 who, however, places Stesimbrotus' work in the 420s.

46. Thucydides on Phrynichus: 8.48.4–7, and Antiphon: 8.68.1–3. Thucydides on Alcibiades: 6.15.3–4, cf. 2.65.11–12, 5.43.2, 8.86.5–7; cf. Alcibiades' own words, 6.16, 89. On Alcibiades and Pericles, see chapter 4 at note 1. Rawlings 1981 considers Thucydides' presentation of Pericles and Alcibiades to be influenced by the close parallels Thucydides saw between them (see further below, with note 74). Forde 1989 and Orwin 1994 (esp. 15–29, 123–26) likewise regard Alcibiades, by

Thucydides' account, as devoted to the Periclean vision of Athens. For the debate over Thucydides' assessment of Alcibiades and Alcibiades' role in the fate of Athens see introduction, note 7. On popular assessments of Alcibiades in 405/4, see chapter 7 at notes 48–49 and chapter 8 at note 48; assessments of Alcibiades in the 390s are discussed below, with note 73.

47. Quote: Lysias 21.6–7, translated by W. R. M. Lamb. See below, note 73, on execration of the memory of Alcibiades in the mid-390s.

48. On the "tyranny" of the Thirty, see Lysias 12.35; Xenophon *Hellenica* 2.3.16, 4.1; Lysias 12.35; Polycrates in Aristotle *Rhetoric* 1401a; cf. Aristotle *Constitution* 41.2. On the link between Alcibiades and Critias, see sources in note 49 below. Contemporary and topically relevant, Isocrates 20, *Against Lochites,* is an impassioned defense of democratic equality against those who suppose that social superiority might permit personal injury.

49. Polycrates' indictment of Socrates: Isocrates 11.4–6; Chroust 1957, 69–100; Hansen 1995, 8–15. Xenophon's defense of Socrates: *Memorabilia* 1.2.12–47. Note that contemporary sources give no support to the later tradition (Diodorus 14.37.7; Diogenes Laertius 2.43) that the Athenians soon felt remorse for the execution of Socrates; see Aeschines 1.173.

50. Harmodius and Aristogeiton on Panathenaic prize vases, ca. 400: Peters 1942, 143; Brunnsåker 1971, 104–105. Shield-devices on Panathenaic amphoras of this period seem to have been officially selected, perhaps to identify the year in which the prize was awarded: Boardman 1974, 168–69. *Chous* from the grave of Dexileos (Boston, Museum of Fine Arts 98.936): Vermeule 1970, 103–107; Burn 1987, 7–8, 87–88; Ajootian 1998, 8. The epigram on the monument of Dexileos is translated in Harding 19C.

51. Thucydides 1.20.2 and 6.53.3–60.1 discusses popular misconceptions concerning the tyrant-slayers. On the early veneration of Harmodius and Aristogeiton, see above, chapter 1, with notes 9 and 12. On the tyrant-slayers in 415, see chapter 4, with notes 42–44. Quote: Thucydides 1.20.3.

52. Thucydides 1.22.4. "These things *(auta),*" in the final clause, refers to the "things that will be useful," in the previous clause. Warner offers "these words of mine" and Crawley "my history" for *auta,* and both make "my work" the subject of the predicate "possession for all time." Although the translation offered here is less elegant than either Warner's or Crawley's, it preserves a sense that other translations lose. *Auta* in 1.22.4 refers to "the speeches that men delivered" (*hosa men logôi eipon hekastoi,* 1.22.1) and "the deeds that were done during the war" (*ta d' erga tôn prachthentôn en tôi polemôi,* 1.22.2); so Gomme 1945, 140 n. 1, although others (e.g., Edmunds 1975, 150) assert that only "the deeds" *(erga)* are meant to be the subject. By understanding the sources of the speeches as I have argued here, I believe that both 1.22 and Thucydides' work as a whole make it clear that he means that, to the extent of his ability, *actual* speeches and *actual* deeds are the "things that are compiled as a possession for all time." Likewise, in 1.1.1 Thucydides announces that he "composed *the war*" *(synegrapse ton polemon),* not "*an account* of the war," or, like Herodotus, "an investigation" *(historia)* of past deeds. Thucydides thus claims for his entire account, speeches and deeds alike, an immediacy with the past that surpasses that of Herodotus; it is an immediacy between words and reality that orators of his day repeatedly struggled to achieve (so Pericles, 2.35.2) and repeatedly condemned

each other's failure to achieve (so Cleon, 3.38.4). Edmunds 1993 examines this immediacy of Thucydides as an author.

53. *Agonisma* is employed by Thucydides' contemporaries specifically to mean a rhetorical argument designed to win a case before a jury; see Antiphon 5.36; Lysias 13.77; cf. Plato *Phaedrus* 269d.

54. This misconception of Thucydides' historical stance is typified in Gomme's comment on 1.22.4 (1945, 149): "It should not be necessary, but it is, to explain that τῶν μελλόντων... ἔσεσθαι is future to Thucydides, not to his readers: the latter will not find his work useful in order to divine what will happen in the future, as though it were a sort of horoscope, but for the understanding of other events besides the Peloponnesian war, future to Thucydides, but past or contemporary to the reader." Influenced by his own viewpoint on recent events (as his following comments emphasize), Gomme's preoccupation with Thucydides' prescience about human nature, *es aiei*, is understandable; but we should not accept his verdict on Thucydides' meaning; Classen and Steup 1897, 66, contradict Gomme's interpretation of 1.22.4 on this point. Thucydides did not write for a readership of historians; he wrote for a readership engaged in events and, like many a speaker in his history (e.g., 2.40.2, 3.42.2, 4.126.4, 5.111.2–5), struggling to discern their outcome; see de Romilly 1958; Hunter 1977, 282; note that Aristotle *Rhetoric* 1360a-b regards historical works as useful for those who must deliberate for the future *(ton melonta sumbouleuein)*.

55. The distortions of a posterity that admired Thucydides but nevertheless found fault with him began with Cratippus' criticism of Thucydides' overuse of speeches (*FGrHist* IIA 64 F 1) and are typified by Dionysius of Halicarnassus' ludicrous critique of Thucydides' choice of subject (*Letter to Pompeius* 3), beginning and ending (*On Thucydides* 10–12), and choice and placement of speeches (*On Thucydides* 17–18). These criticisms are sensible according to the priorities of Cratippus and Dionysius, but they are utterly insensitive to Thucydides' concerns.

56. Woodman 1988, 1–10, 28–32, recognizes various forms of rhetorical magnification (*auxesis/amplificatio*) in the openings of Herodotus and especially Thucydides.

57. The implication of Thucydides' summation of Archelaus of Macedon, 2.100.2, was recognized by Ullrich 1846, 145–48, who cited it as evidence of a "late insertion" by Thucydides into a text that he had composed earlier; the passage has since been widely recognized, though regarded as inconclusive (e.g., J.H. Finley 1942, 15–16; Gomme 1956, 247–48; Hornblower 1987, 143). Thucydides' discreet reference to the confession and alleged guilt of Andocides in the affair of the Herms (6.60.2: "whether true or false... no one, either then or later, could say for certain...") would be most poignant if written after Andocides' trial late in 400 (above, chapter 10), though by itself this too is inconclusive; see Pouilloux and Salviat 1983, 400–401. The identification of Lichas son of Arcesilaus in an archon-list of 398/7 from Thasos as the Spartan of that name, whose death Thucydides mentions in 8.84.5, has been cited by Pouilloux and Salviat 1983 and 1985 as proof that Thucydides was alive and writing after 397. The identification is probably correct, although, as Robert and Robert 1984 and Cartledge 1984 point out, here too the case is not conclusively proven.

58. Conon's relations with Euagoras, Pharnabazus, and Artaxerxes: Harding 12; Diodorus 14.39, 79.5–6; for chronology, see Hamilton 1979, 115–16, 187–89;

March 1997. Enthusiasm for Conon's cause at Athens: *Hellenica Oxyrhynchia* 6 (= Harding 11A). Athenian ambitions to reestablish their empire: Xenophon *Hellenica* 3.5.2, 10; see Funke 1980; Strauss 1986, 104–14. On these developments, Lewis 1977, 141, remarks: "All Alcibiades' predictions to Tissaphernes were now coming true." The events of 396–395 mentioned here are discussed in detail by Hamilton 1979, 156–60, 177–84; Cartledge 1987a, 290–93, 356–59.

59. Quote: Thucydides 1.10.2, translated by R. Warner, with modification. The chronological implications of this passage have been pointed out most recently by Pouilloux and Salviat 1985, 16–18. Previous commentators have been divided about whether the power of Athens must be understood as at its height, sometime before 413, or humbled, after 404. Those, like J.H. Finley, 1940/1967, 166–67, and Gomme 1945, 112–13, who assume the former are troubled by the present tense, "as it in fact is," and resort to rationalizations like Gomme's: "there is no need to press for strict logic here" (113). Strict logic favors 400–395.

60. Quote: Pausanias 3.9.4, translated by W.H.S. Jones; cf. Plutarch *Agesilaus* 6.4; Xenophon *Hellenica* 3.4.2–4. Note also Andocides 3.17: "When the Spartans began the war with you and your allies, they controlled both land and sea." On Pausanias' sources see below, note 68. On Sparta's claim to the Atreid legacy, see de Ste. Croix 1972, 96–97.

61. An argument *against* a date as late as 396 must be countered here. Thucydides 3.116 describes an eruption of Mt. Etna in 425, and goes on: "It is said that this was the first eruption for fifty years, and that, since Sicily was colonized, there have been three eruptions in all" (Warner translation). Hornblower, 1987, 143–44, following Gomme 1956, 431–32, cites this as evidence that Thucydides had "no knowledge of an eruption in 396 [Diodorus 14.59.3]. Therefore, Thucydides was dead by 396." On the contrary, since Thucydides states that common knowledge holds that there were no more than three eruptions since the arrival of the Greeks in Sicily, and since he identifies only two of them, it would be reasonable to assume that the third eruption in 396 was so recent and, given Athenian attention to the career of Dionysius of Syracuse (Hornblower 1983/1991, 187–90), so much the talk that Thucydides did not need to identify it. Despite his judgment about Thucydides' death, Hornblower 1987, 151–54, makes several observations that adumbrate the conclusions argued here, as does Hunter 1977, 292–93. Only Pouilloux and Salviat to my knowledge have argued with conviction that Thucydides was writing as late as 396.

62. Xenophon *Hellenica* 3.5.16 demonstrates that the ruinous condition of the Piraeus walls was a rhetorical topic in 395. The recovery of "walls and ships" is repeatedly mentioned by Andocides 3, *On the Peace With Sparta* (12, 14, 23, 36–39; cf. 5, 7, 31) as the chief objective of the Athenians in the war that began in 395. *Hellenica Oxyrhynchia* 6.1 (= Harding 11A), describing the Demaenetus affair, attests closed meetings of the Council while discussing potential hostilities with Sparta in 396.

63. On the implications of observing the construction of the Piraeus walls, see Pouilloux and Salviat 1985, 16. Other scholars have made the same observation, but Gomme 1945, 264–66, voices skepticism about the soundness of the inference. His doubts are misguided, for he is unaware that the dismantling of the walls in 404 generally involved no more than the destruction of the mudbrick superstructure

(see Lawrence 1979, 115–16), and he fails to notice that description of the rubble and clay fill of the walls and the iron clamps on the outer blocks (1.92.5) could *only* be made when the superstructure was gone.

64. Timocrates and his Persian gold: *Hellenica Oxyrhynchia* 7 (Harding 11A); Xenophon *Hellenica* 3.5.1, 4.2.1, 5.2.35; Plutarch *Artaxerxes* 20.3–4; Pausanias 3.9.8; Polyaenus 1.48.3. Effects of the controversy over Timocrates' mission are found in Xenophon's singular denial (3.5.2) that any Athenian actually received his money.

65. Quotes: Gomme 1945, 27, 431. Excursus as "a product of youth": Adcock and Rhodes, cited by Westlake 1977/1989, 14 n. 10, and Hornblower 1987, 24. Westlake argues that the excursus is derived from the work of another author, possibly Charon of Lampsacus.

66. On Timocrates see above, note 64. Note that Thucydides, while introducing his discussion of the power of Agamemnon, makes the point that, according to "those who recount the most authentic traditions of the Peloponnesians," Agamemnon was heir to the legacy of Pelops, who was a "newcomer" (*epelyn*) who had arrived from Asia with "a lot of money" (*plethei chrematon*) and so gained influence (1.9.2). Rawlings 1981, 90–117, has recognized the parallel between Pausanias and Lysander, and between Themistocles and Alcibiades, implicit in Thucydides' account.

67. On the theme of *paraskeue,* see above, note 33. Edmunds 1975 examines the theme of chance, *tyche,* and reason or intelligence, *gnome* or *synesis.* Other noteworthy studies of the "unitarian" themes found in Thucydides include Hunter 1973, Pouncey 1980, Rawlings 1981, Cogan 1982, Forde 1989, and Orwin 1994. On the division of scholarship over the "composition problem" into "analysts" and "unitarians," see note 28 above.

68. Quote: Pausanias 3.9.2, translated by W.H.S. Jones. Pausanias' sources for this period are generally good and include, directly or indirectly, information from the *Hellenica Oxyrhynchia;* see Bruce 1967, 21; Cartledge 1987a, 134.

69. The "second preface" (5.25–26) has been otherwise understood as evidence that Thucydides changed his idea about the length of the war sometime after he had written its history to the Peace of Nicias, and has been, as J.H. Finley puts it (1940/1967, 162–63): "without a doubt the principle cause of the whole controversy on when he wrote his work and, from the time of Ullrich on, has afforded the chief argument to those who doubted its unity." On Ullrich's thesis and its followers, see note 28 above. Thucydides 7.18.3 notes the significance of Spartan defeats suffered as a consequence of their own aggression in 431, contrasted with Spartan victory as the outcome of war provoked by Athenian aggression in 414.

70. Peace of Nicias as true peace, upset by Argives: Andocides 3, *On the Peace With Sparta* 8–9.

71. Quote: Hornblower 1987, 139. Critique of Book 5: Hornblower 1987, 138–41. Regarding Peloponnesian diplomacy, Westlake 1971/1989, 84, has observed: "the accounts of negotiations and intrigues, mostly in the Peloponnese, which occupy much of the fifth book, have tended to be ignored, being thought to be obscure, confusing, and tedious. Scholars interested in the history of the period have experienced difficulty in tracing a coherent pattern in its catalogue of diplomatic manoeuvres and in establishing the motives which prompted them. Scholars interested in the historical techniques of Thucydides have been disappointed, even

repelled, because his facility for mastering his material seems to have to a large extent deserted him." Regarding Persia, see Lewis 1977, 82: "It is clear that there is a real gap in Thucydides' treatment [of Persian affairs], to be explained by the unfinished nature of his history; at a minimum, it cannot be denied that he gives us insufficient background to the events he describes in Book VIII." On what little is known of Persian affairs between 424 and 412, see chapter 5, with notes 1–2.

72. Westlake 1971/1989, 92, concludes that Thucydides' purpose in much of Book 5 was "to focus attention upon the utter bankruptcy of Greek statesmanship at this time, especially in the Peloponnese." The contrast between the Theban forecasts of 395 and the arrangements achieved by 394 (Xenophon *Hellenica* 3.5.10–15, 4.2.10–18) point to much the same quality in statesmanship in 395/94. Regarding Persian affairs during the period covered by Thucydides Book 5, Lewis 1977, 82, notes: "Darius' attention will have been wholly fixed on his struggle to secure his throne and reestablish control of his empire." The need felt to assess the Persian perspective probably accounts for the appearance of Ctesias' *Persica* sometime after 394. Like Thucydides' work, Ctesias' account of Persian history and court intrigues was based upon both personal experience and documentary sources (Diodorus 2.32.4; Plutarch *Artaxerxes* 21.3), but the remarkably different nature of Ctesias' history reveals the intractability of the subject according to the methods and interests of Thucydides.

73. Isocrates 16 *On the Team of Horses* (discussed above, chapter 2, with note 31 and chapter 4, with note 61) is dated to 397 or soon after by the legal maturity of the younger Alcibiades at about that time; see Jebb 1876 vol. 2, 228. Lysias 14 and 15, *Against Alcibiades* 1 and 2 (discussed above, chapter 4, with note 41), belong to a suit against the younger Alcibiades following the battle of Haliartus in 395. Plutarch *Alcibiades* 1.4 draws attention to the comic poet Archippus' satire of the younger Alcibiades' imitation of his father. Heftner 1995, noting the resonance with Isocrates 20, *Against Lochites,* argues that [Andocides] 4, *Against Alcibiades* was composed at about this time. See Strauss 1986, 108, for the memory of Alcibiades in the rivalry between Conon and Thrasybulus in the later 390s.

74. The case of Alcibiades in particular demonstrates that the arguments of Rawlings 1981, that Thucydides' narrative was influenced by an overarching sense of the paradigmatic significance of events, deserve more attention than they have received; see above, note 46.

75. Unanimous vote: Xenophon *Hellenica* 3.5.16. The remarkable unity of purpose (which, of course, can disguise the presence of a dissenting minority) among Athenians in the summer of 395, despite abundant evidence for factional and ideological differences, is the thematic focus of Funke 1980 (p. 102) and Strauss 1986 (p. 113); cf. Lévy 1976, 209–22, on the currency of the theme of *homonoia,* "like-mindedness" or "concord." Funerary monuments from the opening campaigns of the Corinthian War reflect the close allegiance between personal ideals and public purposes and echo themes introduced in the 420s; see the Dexileos relief, figure 11, and cf. figure 2.

76. On *syngraphe, syngraphein,* and *syngrapheis,* see above, chapter 3, with notes 63–67, chapter 4, with note 45, and chapter 5, with note 20. Note also the relationship of the work of *syngrapheis* to the research into documents carried out by the *nomothetai* of 410–399: chapter 5, with notes 46–49, chapter 6, with notes 16–17,

48, 51, chapter 7, with notes 44–46, chapter 8, with note 41, chapter 9, with notes 6, 21–22, and chapters 10 and 11.

77. Thucydides can, of course, imagine a time when Athens, like Mycenae, has passed away and only its ruins remain to testify to its past greatness. But the Greek vision of destiny, like Sparta's claim on Mycenae, was constantly revitalizing ruins of the past, and constantly seeking to immortalize what was manifestly ephemeral. The intensity of Thucydides' historical vision comes from such a conviction. Even accepting that, sooner or later, Athens would be an abandoned ruin, Thucydides worked to perpetuate and augment her greatness. After all, his father and grandfather's generation had seen Athens abandoned and in ruins, and their devotion to such a vision had raised Athens to the pinnacle of her power.

78. For a recent review of scholarship, and a reconsideration of the reason for the abrupt end of Thucydides' history, see Flory 1993. Flory begins with a premise not unlike my own: "I believe that something like... despair caused Thucydides to abandon his work" (116–17).

79. The incident of Demaenetus, probably early in 396, and the alleged mission of Timocrates of Rhodes to corrupt Greek leaders with Persian gold illustrate the "public secret" of Persian involvement in the alignments of Greece; see *Hellenica Oxyrhynchia* 6–7 (Harding 11A), Aischines 2.78, and other sources cited above in note 64.

80. A parallel thematic shift in the plays of Euripides after 415 has been noticed; see Gould 1996, 573; Lesky 1963/1966, 402–404. The rhetoric of Cleophon relied heavily upon heroic and mythic themes and theatrical presentation; see chapter 6, with notes 12–15, chapter 7, with notes 20–22, 37, 42, and chapter 8, with note 19. According to Dionysius *On Thucydides* 16 (= *FGrHist* IIA 64 F 1), Cratippus states that Thucydides came to recognize that speeches were an unnecessary distraction from the narrative of events and so deliberately omitted speeches from the final portions of his work.

81. The incompatibility of the Greek mode of decision-making by debate and the Persian mode by royal edict is represented, from the Persian perspective, in Herodotus' famous quote of Cyrus the elder, 1.153: "I have never yet found occasion to fear the kind of men who set aside a space in the middle of their town where they can meet and make false promises to one another. If I remain healthy, their tongues will be occupied with events at home rather than those in Ionia" (translated by R. Waterfield). The incompatibility of the historical standards of Thucydides and Ctesias (above, note 72) are explicable by the same circumstances. Note that Conon's naval victories of 394 and 393, at the head of Pharnabazus' fleet, were both celebrated as the restoration of Athenian naval supremacy (Isocrates 7.12, 65; 5.64; Demosthenes 20.68–70; 22.72; 24.180; Xenophon *Hellenica* 4.8.1–2, 8–10; Diodorus 14.84.3–85.3; cf. Tod 106, 109) and demeaned or reviled as evidence of barbarian imperialism (Lysias 2.59–60; Isocrates 4.119, 154; Plato *Menexenus* 245a; cf. Andocides 3.15). On the development of Spartan relations to Persia at this time, see Lewis 1977, 144–47; Hamilton 1979, 301–25. Athenian ambivalence to the "King's Peace" that ended the Corinthian War in 386 is illustrated, for example, by the reference to the king later erased in *IG* II^2 43, 13–15 (= Tod 123, Harding 35), the so-called "Charter of the Second Athenian Confederacy." The history of the "King's Peace" in relation to later Athenian policy is examined by Cargill 1981 and, in relation to Greek politics in general, by Ryder 1965.

82. Thucydides 2.54.3 might indicate that war had not begun when this was written, although the possibility of "Doric war" might refer specifically to a Dorian invasion of Attica (which did not occur until 378). The conditions surrounding the historical end-point of Thucydides' narrative are discussed at the end of chapter 5 and in the first half of chapter 6.

83. The quote paraphrases the twelve lines (in the Oxford text) of Thucydides 8.109; in fact, the final phrase is a separate sentence, but not a satisfactory one. As Andrewes remarks (Gomme et al. 1981, 358): "Phrases of this form... cry out for completion."

84. For the numerous parallels to a votive inscription in the form, *Thoukydides Athenaios... tei Artemidi,* see Rouse 1902, 323, 326–27. On Thucydides' piety, see chapter 3, with note 58, and Marinatos 1981b, 56–65.

85. Quote: Thucydides 1.138.3, translated by R. Warner, with modifications. Parker 1996, 155, with references in n. 10.

86. On Themistocles and Artemis Aristoboule, see chapter 1, with notes 18 and 22. On Artemis Agrotera, see Xenophon *Anabasis* 3.2.12; Aristotle *Constitution* 58.1; cf. Xenophon *Hellenica* 4.2.20. On Artemis Boulaia, see Rhodes 1972a, 132. On *Euboule* and Herodotus, see chapter 4, with notes 51 and 52.

87. Artemis and the revelation of *pseudeis graphai:* Euripides *Hippolytus* 1311; see Steiner 1994, 38–40. Heraclitus and his book (*biblion,* also *syngramma*) dedicated in the temple of Artemis: Diogenes Laertius 9.6; copy of it read by Euripides and Socrates: Diogenes Laertius 2.22. On Heraclitus' book, see Steiner 1994, 20–24, 202–203; on the significance of books dedicated as first-fruits of wisdom, see Steiner 86–91; Rouse 1902, 64–65.

88. Tissaphernes invokes Artemis in 410: Xenophon *Hellenica* 1.2.6; on the occasion, see chapter 6, with note 22. Xenophon and Artemis of Ephesus: Xenophon *Anabasis* 5.3.4–13, cf. 3.1.5–8. Agamemnon at Aulis: Aeschylus *Agamemnon* 104–257. On Agesilaus and Artemis at Aulis, see above, with note 60; at Ephesus: Xenophon *Agesilaus* 1.27. Execution of Tissaphernes: Diodorus 14.80.6–8; Xenophon *Hellenica* 3.4.25; Plutarch *Artaxerxes* 23.1; see Westlake 1981/1989.

89. On Cybele/Mother of the Gods as patron of the Athenian archives, and her syncretism with Artemis of Ephesus, see above, chapter 6, with notes 52–55; note especially Timotheus *Persians* 127–73, composed probably between 400 and 395. On Themistocles and the Mother of the Gods, and his monument at Magnesia, see Plutarch *Themistocles* 30–32 (note that Plutarch, 32.3, cites a reference to this monument by Andocides); Thucydides 1.138.5. At Magnesia as at Sardis, the earlier cult of Cybele/Mother of the Gods was later supplanted by the cult of Artemis; see Pausanias 1.26.4.

90. Andocides 3, *On the Peace with Sparta* 2–9, in both language and content, bears striking resemblance to parts of Thucydides Book 1. Raubitschek 1981/1991 argues that this is because Andocides knew Thucydides' work; Lenardon 1981 argues that much of the similarity comes from their common reliance on Hellanicus; see also Thomas 1989, 119–23. Thucydides and Isocrates: Isocrates 4, *Panegyricus* 99–109; Buchner 1958, 108–23.

91. Thucydides and posterity: Diogenes Laertius 2.57 says that Xenophon, who carried on the history of events after 411 in his *Hellenica,* also made Thucydides' work public. This is probably only a guess, given the close relationship between their

works. Xenophon's continuation of Thucydides is imperfect in several puzzling ways, see W.P. Henry 1966; Andrewes in Gomme et al. 1981, 437–44; Gray 1989, 1–6, 193–96; Krentz 1989a; Dillery 1995, 9–14. Theopompus, Cratippus, and the unknown author of the *Hellenica Oxyrhynchia* (possibly Cratippus) all wrote histories continuing that of Thucydides; see Bloch 1940, 308–16; Bruce 1967, 3–9 and 22–27; Hornblower 1995. Writing ca. 350, Aeneas Tacticus, 2.3–6, seems to have read Thucydides, or an excerpt from his work; see Whitehead 1990, 38 n. 114. [Plutarch] *Moralia* 844b reports that Demosthenes was an admirer of Thucydides and Plato. On the *Atthides,* see Pearson 1942 and Jacoby 1949; on Androtion, see Harding 1994.

92. On the relationship between popular tradition and critical history, see M.I. Finley 1965/1975, esp. 11–12, and 1971/1975, esp. 57–58.

93. Quote: Aristotle *Rhetoric* 1360a. On Aristotle's use of the term, *historia,* "investigation," see Weil 1960, 87–95. Aristotle evidently had in mind the same assortment of undistinguished (to his mind) historical treatises that Xenophon sets in contrast to his own historical writing when he refers to "all *syngrapheis* [who] record the fine accomplishments of great cities" (*Hellenica* 7.2.1).

94. Quote: Aristotle *Poetics* 1451b.

95. In this connection, see L. Strauss 1964, esp. p. 143.

BIBLIOGRAPHY

Adcock, F.E. 1927. "The Archidamian War, 431–421 B.C." In Bury et al. 1927, 193–253.

Adkins, A.W.H. 1972. "Truth, ΚΟΣΜΟΣ, and ΑΡΕΤΗ in the Homeric Poems." *CQ* 22, 5–18.

Ajootian, A. 1998. "A Day at the Races: The Tyrannicides in the Fifth-Century Agora." In *ΣΤΕΦΑΝΟΣ: Studies in Honor of Brunilde Sismondo Ridgway,* K.J. Hartswick and M.C. Sturgeon, eds., 1–13. Philadelphia.

Albini, U. 1968. *[erode attico] ΠΕΡΙ ΠΟΛΙΤΕΙΑΣ.* Florence.

Allison, J.W. 1989. *Power and Preparedness in Thucydides.* Baltimore and London.

Amit, M. 1973. "Le traité de Chalcédoine entre Pharnabaze et les stratèges athéniens." *AC* 42, 436–57.

———. 1975. "The Disintegration of the Athenian Empire in Asia Minor (412–405 B.C.E.)." *SCI* 2, 38–72.

Anderson, J.K. 1974. *Xenophon.* New York.

Andreades, A.M. 1933. *A History of Greek Public Finance.* Vol. 1. Revised ed. trans. C.N. Brown, Harvard. Reprint New York, 1979.

Andrewes, A. 1953. "The Generals in the Hellespont, 410–407 B.C." *JHS* 73, 2–9.

———. 1970. "Lysias and the Theramenes Papyrus." *ZPE* 6, 35–38.

———. 1971. "Two Notes on Lysander." *Phoenix* 25, 206–26.

———. 1974. "The Arginousai Trial." *Phoenix* 28, 112–22.

———. 1975. "Could there have been a battle at Oenoe?" In *The Ancient Historian and his Materials: Essays in Honour of C.E. Stevens on his Seventieth Birthday,* B. Levick, ed., 9–16. Farnborough.

———. 1978. "The Opposition to Perikles." *JHS* 98, 1–8.

———. 1982. "Notion and Kyzikos: The Sources Compared." *JHS* 102, 15–25.

Andrewes, A., and D.M. Lewis. 1957. "Note on the Peace of Nicias." *JHS* 77, 177–80.

Asmis, E. 1992. "Plato on Poetic Creativity." In Kraut 1992, 338–64.

Atkinson, J.E. 1992. "Curbing the Comedians: Cleon Versus Aristophanes and Syracosius' Decree." *CQ* 42, 56–64.

Aurenche, O. 1974. *Les groupes d'Alcibiade, de Léogoras et de Teucros: Remarques sur la vie politique athénienne en 415 avant J.C.* Paris.

Austin, N. 1994. *Helen of Troy and her Shameless Phantom.* Ithaca and London.

Avery, H.C. 1959. "Prosopographical Studies of the Oligarchy of the Four Hundred." Princeton dissertation. Ann Arbor.

———. 1963. "Critias and the Four Hundred." *CPh* 58, 165–67.

Badian, E. 1993. *From Plataea to Potidaea: Studies in the History and Historiography of the Pentecontaetia.* Baltimore and London.

Badian, E., and J. Buckler. 1975. "The Wrong Salamis?" *RhM* 118, 226–39.

Balcer, J.M. 1979. "Imperialism and Stasis in Fifth Century B.C. Ionia: A Frontier Redefined." In Bowersock et al. 1979, 261–68.

Bean, G.E. 1966. *Aegean Turkey: An Archaeological Guide.* London.

Beloch, J. 1884. *Die Attische Politik seit Perikles.* Leipzig. Reprint Stuttgart, 1967.

———. 1912–1927. *Griechische Geschichte.* 2nd ed. 4 vols. Strassburg, Berlin, and Leipzig.

Bernal, M. 1987. *Black Athena: The Afro-Asiatic Roots of Classical Civilization.* Vol. 1, *The Fabrication of Ancient Greece 1785–1985.* Rutgers.

Beschi, L. 1969–1970. "Rilievi votivi attici ricomposti." *ASAA* 47–48, 85–132.

Bloch, H. 1940. "Studies in Historical Literature of the Fourth Century B.C." In *Athenian Studies Presented to William Scott Ferguson, HSPh* supplement 1, 303–76. Cambridge, Mass., and London. Reprint New York, 1973.

Bloedow, E.F. 1973. *Alcibiades Reexamined. Historia* Einzelschrift 21. Wiesbaden.

———. 1990. "'Not the Son of Achilles, but Achilles Himself': Alcibiades' Entry on the Political Stage at Athens II." *Historia* 39, 1–19.

———. 1991a. "*Alcibiades:* A Review Article." *AHB* 5, 17–29.

———. 1991b. "On 'Nurturing Lions in the State': Alcibiades' Entry on the Political Stage in Athens." *Klio* 73, 49–65.

———. 1992. "Alcibiades 'Brilliant' or 'Intelligent'?" *Historia* 41, 139–57.

Blumenthal, H. 1973. "Meletus the Accuser of Andocides and Meletus the Accuser of Socrates: One Man or Two?" *Philologus* 117, 169–78.

Boardman, J. 1974. *Athenian Black Figure Vases.* New York.

———. 1982. "Herakles, Theseus, and Amazons." In *The Eye of Greece: Studies in the Art of Athens,* D. Kurz and B. Sparkes, eds., 1–28. Cambridge.

Boedeker, D. 1988. "Protesilaos and the End of Herodotus' *Histories.*" *ClAnt* 7, 30–48.

———. 1995. "Simonides on Plataea: Narrative Elegy, Mythodic History." *ZPE* 107, 217–29.

———. 1996. "Heroic Historiography: Simonides and Herodotus on Plataea." *Arethusa* 29.2, 223–93.

Boegehold, A.L. 1972. "The Establishment of a Central Archive at Athens." *AJA* 76, 23–30.

———. 1982. "A Dissent at Athens ca. 424–421 B.C." *GRBS* 23, 147–56.

———. 1990. "Andokides and the Decree of Patrokleides." *Historia* 39, 149–62.

———. 1994. "Perikles' Citizenship Law of 451/0 B.C." In Boegehold and Scafuro 1994, 57–66.

Boegehold, A.L., and A.C. Scafuro, eds. 1994. *Athenian Identity and Civic Ideology.* Baltimore and London.

Boersma, J.S. 1970. *Athenian Building Policy from 561/0 to 405/4 B.C.* Scripta Archaeologica Groningana, 4. Groningen.

Bommelaer, J.-F. 1981. *Lysandre de Sparte. Histoire et traditions.* Paris.

Bourriot, F. 1995. *Kalos Kagathos—Kalokagathia.* 2 vols. Spudasmata 58/1 & 2. Zurich and New York.

Bowersock, G.W., W. Burkert, and M.C.J. Putnam, eds. 1979. *Arktouros: Hellenic Studies presented to Bernard M. W. Knox on the occasion of his 65th birthday.* Berlin and New York.

Bowie, A.M. 1997. "Tragic Filters for History: Euripides' *Supplices* and Sophocles' *Philoctetes.*" In Pelling 1997, 39–62.

Bowie, E.L. 1986. "Early Greek Elegy, Symposium and Public Festival." *JHS* 106, 13–35.

———. 1993. "Lies, Fiction and Slander in Early Greek Poetry." In *Lies and Fiction in the Ancient World,* C. Gill and T.P. Wiseman, eds., 1–37. Exeter.

Bradeen, D.W. 1963. "The Fifth-Century Archon List." *Hesperia* 32, 187–208.

———. 1964. "Athenian Casualty Lists." *Hesperia* 33, 16–62.

Bradeen, D.W., and M.F. McGregor. 1974. *Phoros: Tribute to Benjamin Dean Meritt.* Locust Valley, N.Y.

Brandwood, L. 1992. "Stylometry and Chronology." In Kraut 1992, 90–120.

Brickhouse, T.C., and N.D. Smith. 1989. *Socrates on Trial.* Princeton.

———. 1994. *Plato's Socrates.* Oxford.

Brock, R. 1989. "Athenian Oligarchs: The Numbers Game." *JHS* 99, 160–64.

Brown, T.S. 1988. "The Greek Exiles: Herodotus' Contemporaries." *AncW* 17, 17–28.

Bruce, I.A.F. 1967. *An Historical Commentary on the Hellenica Oxyrhynchia.* Cambridge.

Brunnsåker, S. 1971. *The Tyrant-Slayers of Kritios and Nesiotes: A Critical Study of the Sources and Restorations.* Skrifter utgivna av Svenska Institutet i Athen 17. Stockholm.

Brunt, P.A. 1952. "Thucydides and Alcibiades." *REG* 65, 59–96.

Buchner, E. 1957 *Der Panegyrikos des Isokrates: Eine historisch-philologische Untersuchung, Historia* Einzelschrift 2. Wiesbaden.

Buck, R.J. 1979. *A History of Boeotia.* Edmonton, Alberta.

———. 1995. "The Character of Theramenes." *AHB* 9, 14–23.

Bugh, G. 1988. *The Horsemen of Athens.* Princeton.

Burkert, W. 1983. *Homo Necans: The Anthropology of Ancient Greek Sacrificial Ritual and Myth.* Trans. P. Bing from the German edition of 1972. Berkeley.

———. 1985. *Greek Religion.* Trans. J. Raffan from the German edition of 1977. Cambridge, Mass.

———. 1986. "Der Autor von Derveni: Stesimbrotos ΠΕΡΙΤΕΛΕΤΩΝ?" *ZPE* 62, 1–5.

———. 1987. *Ancient Mystery Cults.* Cambridge, Mass., and London.

Burn, L. 1987. *The Meidias Painter.* Oxford.

Bury, J.B., S.A. Cook, and F.E. Adcock, eds. 1927. *The Cambridge Ancient History.* Vol. 5, *Athens 478–401 B.C.* Cambridge.

Busolt, G. 1893–1904. *Griechische Geschichte, bis zur Schlacht bei Chaeroneia.* 3 vols. (incomplete). Gotha.

Cadoux, T.J. 1948. "The Athenian Archons from Kreon to Hypsichides." *JHS* 68, 70–119.

Calhoun, G.M. 1913. *Athenian Clubs in Politics and Litigation.* Bulletin of the University of Texas no. 262. Austin.

Camp, J.M. 1986. *The Athenian Agora: Excavation in the Heart of Classical Athens.* New York.

Cargill, J. 1981. *The Second Athenian League: Empire or Free Alliance?* Berkeley.

Carter, L.B. 1986. *The Quiet Athenian.* Oxford.

Cartledge, P. 1984. "A New Lease on Life for Lichas Son of Arkesilas?" *LCM* 9, 98–102.

———. 1987a. *Agesilaos and the Crisis of Sparta.* Baltimore.

———. 1987b. "A Patriot for Whom? Alcibiades of Athens." *History Today,* October 1987, 15–21.

Cartledge, P., and P. Millett, eds. 1990. *Nomos: Essays in Athenian Law, Politics, and Society.* Cambridge.

Casson, L. 1984. *Ancient Trade and Society.* Detroit.

Castriota, D. 1992. *Myth, Ethos, and Actuality: Official Art in Fifth-Century B.C. Athens.* Madison.

Cawkwell, G. 1970. "The Fall of Themistocles." In *Auckland Classical Essays, presented to E.M. Blaiklock,* B.F. Harris, ed., 39–58. Auckland.

———. 1979. Introduction and notes to *Xenophon: A History of My Times.* Trans. R. Warner, Penguin Books. London.

———. 1997. *Thucydides and the Peloponnesian War.* London and New York.

Chambers, M. 1984. "Themistocles and the Piraeus." In *Studies Presented to Sterling Dow on his Eightieth Birthday,* 43–50. Durham, N.C.

———. 1993. "The Archon's Name in the Athens–Egesta Alliance (*IG* I³ 11)." *ZPE* 98, 171–74.

Chambers, M., R. Gallucci, and P. Spanos. 1990. "Athens' Alliance with Egesta in the Year of Antiphon." *ZPE* 83, 38–63.

Chantraine, P. 1974. *Dictionnaire étymologique de la langue grecque: Histoire des mots.* Vol. 3, Λ–Π. Paris.

Christ, M.R. 1992. "Ostracism, Sycophancy, and Deception of the Demos: [Arist.] *Ath.Pol.* 43.5." *CQ* 42, 336–46.

Chroust, A.-H. 1957. *Socrates Man and Myth: The Two Socratic Apologies of Xenophon.* London.

Clairmont, C. 1983. *Patrios Nomos: Public Burial in Athens During the Fifth and Fourth Centuries B.C.* 2 vols. *British Archaeological Reports* 161. Oxford.

Classen, J., and J. Steup, eds., 1897. *Thukydides.* Vol. 1. 4th ed. Berlin.

Clinton, K. 1982. "The Nature of the Late Fifth-Century Revision of the Athenian Law Code." In *Studies in Attic Epigraphy and Topography Presented to Eugene Vanderpool. Hesperia* Supplement 19, 27–37. Princeton.

Cloché, P. 1915. *La restauration démocratique à Athènes en 403 avant J.-C.* Paris. Reprint Rome, 1968.

Cobet, J. 1977. "Wann wurde Herodots Darstellung der Perserkriege publiziert?" *Hermes* 105, 2–27.

Cogan, M. 1981. *The Human Thing: The Speeches and Principles of Thucydides' History.* Chicago and London.

Cohen, E.E. 1992. *Athenian Economy and Society: A Banking Perspective.* Princeton.

———. 1993. "The Athenian Economy." In Rosen and Farrell 1993, 197–206.

Cole, T. 1983. "Archaic Truth." *QUCC* n.s. 13, 7–28.
———. 1991. *The Origins of Rhetoric in Ancient Greece.* Baltimore and London.
———. 1992. *Pindar's Feasts, or the Music of Power.* Rome.
Collard, C. 1972. "The Funeral Oration in Euripides' *Supplices.*" *BICS* 19, 39–53.
Collingwood, R. G. 1946. *The Idea of History.* Oxford.
Connor, W. R. 1968. *Theopompus and Fifth-Century Athens.* Harvard.
———. 1970. "Theseus in Classical Athens." In *The Quest for Theseus,* A. G. Ward, ed., 143–74. New York.
———. 1971. *The New Politicians of Fifth-Century Athens.* Princeton.
———. 1977. "Tyrannis Polis." In *Ancient and Modern: Essays in Honor of Gerald F. Else,* J. d'Arms and J. Eadie, eds., 95–109. Ann Arbor.
———. 1984. *Thucydides.* Princeton.
———. 1989. "City Dionysia and Athenian Democracy." *C&M* 40, 7–32.
———. 1991. "The Other 399: Religion and the Trial of Socrates." In *Georgiaca: Greek Studies in Honour of George Cawkwell. BICS* supplement 58, 49–56. London.
Costa, E. A., Jr. 1974. "Evagoras I and the Persians, ca. 411 to 391 B.C." *Historia* 23, 40–56.
Coulson, W. D. E., O. Palagia, T. L. Shear, Jr., H. A. Shapiro, and F. J. Frost, eds. 1994. *The Archaeology of Athens and Attica Under the Democracy.* Proceedings of an International Conference celebrating 2500 years since the birth of democracy in Greece, held at the American School of Classical Studies at Athens, December 4–6, 1992. Oxbow Monograph 37. Oxford.
Craik, E. M. 1987. "'One for the Pot': Aristophanes' *Birds* and the Anthesteria." *Eranos* 85, 25–34.
Dale, A. M., ed. 1967 *Euripides: Helen.* Oxford.
Davies, J. K. 1967. "Demosthenes on Liturgies: A Note." *JHS* 87, 33–40.
———. 1971. *Athenian Propertied Families, 630–300 B.C.* Oxford.
———. 1981. *Wealth and the Power of Wealth in Classical Athens.* Salem, N.H.
Day, J. W. 1980. *The Glory of Athens: The Popular Tradition as Reflected in the Panathenaicus of Aelius Aristides.* Chicago.
———. 1985. "Epigrams and History: The Athenian Tyrannicides, a Case in Point." In Jameson 1985, 25–46.
Debrunner, A. 1947/1995. "ΔΗΜΟΚΡΑΤΙΑ." In *Festschrift für Edouard Tièche,* 11–24. Bern. Reprinted in Kinzl and Raaflaub 1995, 55–69.
Delebecque, É. 1951. *Euripide et la Guerre du Peloponnèse.* Paris.
———. 1957. *Essai sur la vie de Xénophon.* Paris.
Detienne, M. 1973. *Les maîtres de vérité dans la grèce archaïque.* 2nd ed. Paris.
Deubner, L. 1932. *Attische Feste.* Reprint Berlin, 1966.
Develin, R. 1985. "Age Qualification for Athenian Magistrates." *ZPE* 61, 149–59.
———. 1989. *Athenian Officials, 683–321 B.C.* Cambridge.
———. 1990. "Thucydides on Speeches." *AHB* 4, 58–60.
Dewald, C. 1985. "Practical Knowledge and the Historian's Role in Herodotus and Thucydides." In Jameson 1985, 47–63.
———. 1987. "Narrative Surface and Authorial Voice in Herodotus' *Histories.*" *Aresthusa* 20, 147–70.
———. 1993. "Reading the World: The Interpretation of Objects in Herodotus' *Histories.*" In Rosen and Farrell 1993, 55–70.

Deyhle, W. 1969. "Meisterfragen der archaischen Plastik Attikas." *MDAI(A)* 84, 1–64.

Dillery, J. 1995. *Xenophon and the History of His Times.* London and New York.

Donaldson, J. W. 1860. *The Theatre of the Greeks.* 7th ed. London.

Donlan, W. 1973a. "The Role of *Eugeneia* in the Aristocratic Self-Image during the Fifth Century B.C." In *Classics and the Classical Tradition: Essays Presented to Robert E. Dengler on the Occasion of His Eightieth Birthday,* E. N. Borza and R. W. Carrubba, eds., 63–78. University Park, Pa.

———. 1973b. "The Origin of καλὸς κἀγαθός." *AJPh* 94, 365–74.

———. 1980. *The Aristocratic Ideal in Ancient Greece: Attitudes of Superiority from Homer to the End of the Fifth Century B.C.* Lawrence, Kansas.

Dougherty, C., and L. Kurke, eds. 1993. *Cultural Poetics and Archaic Greece.* Cambridge.

Dover, K. J. 1968. *Lysias and the Corpus Lysiacum.* Berkeley.

———. 1973. *Thucydides. G&R* New Surveys in the Classics no. 7. Oxford.

———. 1976/1988. "The Freedom of the Intellectual in Greek Society." *Talanta* 7, 24–54. Reprinted in Dover 1988, 135–58.

———. 1981/1988. "Thucydides' Historical Judgement: Athens and Sicily." *Proceedings of the Royal Irish Academy* 81. Reprinted in Dover 1988, 74–82.

———. 1986/1988. "Ion of Chios: His Place in the History of Greek Literature." *Chios: A Conference at the Homereion in Chios 1984,* 1–12. Oxford. Reprinted in Dover 1988.

———. 1987/1988. "Thucydides on Oracles." Originally published in Italian in *Miscellenea di studi di filologica classica in Onore di Giusto Monaco.* Palermo. Translated in Dover 1988, 65–73.

———. 1988. *The Greeks and Their Legacy: Collected Papers.* Vol. 2, *Prose Literature, History, Society, Transmission, Influence.* Oxford.

Dow, S. 1941. "Greek Inscriptions: the Athenian Law Code of 411–401 B.C." *Hesperia* 10, 31–37.

———. 1959. "The Law Codes of Athens." *Proceedings, Massachusetts Historical Society* 71, 3–36.

———. 1960. "The Athenian Calendar of Sacrifices: The Chronology of Nikomakhos' Second Term." *Historia* 9, 270–93.

———. 1961. "The Walls Inscribed with Nikomakhos' Law Code." *Hesperia* 30, 270–93.

Dunbar, N. 1995. *Aristophanes Birds.* Oxford.

Edmunds, L. 1975. *Chance and Intelligence in Thucydides.* Cambridge, Mass.

———. 1993. "Thucydides in the Act of Writing." *Tradizione e innovazione nella cultura Greca da Omero all'età ellenistica. Scriti in onore di Bruno Gentili,* R. Pretagostini, ed., 831–52. Rome.

Ehrenberg, V. 1947. "Polypragmosyne: A Study in Greek Politics." *JHS* 67, 46–67.

———. 1950. "Origins of Democracy." *Historia* 1, 515–48. Reprinted in part in Kinzl and Raaflaub 1995, 70–86.

———. 1973. *From Solon to Socrates: Greek History and Civilization During the 6th and 5th Centuries BC.* 2nd ed. London.

Ehrhardt, C. 1970. "Xenophon and Diodorus on Aegospotami." *Phoenix* 24, 225–28.

———. 1995. "Lysias on Theramenes." *AHB* 9, 125–26.

Ellis, W. M. 1989. *Alcibiades*. New York.

Evans, J. A. S. 1982. *Herodotus*. Boston.

———. 1991. *Herodotus, Explorer of the Past: Three Essays*. Princeton.

Farrar, C. 1988. *The Origins of Democratic Thinking: The Invention of Politics in Classical Athens*. Cambridge.

Fehling, D. 1971/1989. *Herodotus and his 'Sources': Citation, Invention and Narrative Art*. Trans. J. G. Howie from the German. Leeds.

———. 1985. *Die Sieben Weisen und die frügriechische Chronologie: Eine traditionsgeschichtliche Studie*. Bern, Frankfurt, New York.

Ferguson, W. S. 1927. "The Chronology of the Period 410–406 B.C." In Bury et al. 1927, 483–85.

———. 1932. *The Treasurers of Athena*. Harvard.

———. 1936. "The Athenian Law Code and the Old Attic Trittyes." In *Classical Studies Presented to E. Capps*, 144–58. Princeton.

Fingarette, A. 1971. "A New Look at the Wall of Nikomakhos." *Hesperia* 40, 330–35.

Finley, J. H., Jr. 1938/1967. "Euripides and Thucydides." *HSPh* 49, 23–68. Reprinted in Finley 1967, 1–54.

———. 1939/1967. "The Origins of Thucydides' Style." *HSPh* 50, 35–84. Reprinted in Finley 1967, 55–117.

———. 1940/1967. "The Unity of Thucydides' History." In *Athenian Studies Presented to William Scott Ferguson*. Harvard Studies in Classical Philology, Supplement 1, 255–97. Cambridge, Mass., and London. Reprint New York, 1973. Also reprinted in Finley 1967, 118–69.

———. 1942. *Thucydides*. Cambridge, Mass. Reprinted 1963, Ann Arbor.

———. 1967. *Three Essays on Thucydides*. Cambridge, Mass.

Finley, M. I. 1953/1982. "Land, Debt, and the Man of Property in Athens." *Political Science Quarterly* 68, 249–68. Reprinted with a bibliographical note in Finley, with Shaw and Saller, 1982, 62–76 and 258–61.

———. 1962. "The Athenian Demagogues." *P&P* 21, 3–24.

———. 1965/1975. "Myth, Memory, and History." *H&T* 4, 281–302. Reprinted with additions in Finley 1975, 11–33.

———. 1971/1975. "The Ancestral Constitution." Inaugural Lecture, Cambridge. Reprinted in Finley 1975, 34–59.

———. 1972. Introduction to *Thucydides: History of the Peloponnesian War*, trans. R. Warner. Penguin Books. London.

———. 1975. *The Use and Abuse of History*. New York.

———. 1978/1982. "The Athenian Empire: A Balance Sheet." In *Imperialism in the Ancient World*, P. D. A. Garnsey and C. R. Whittaker, eds. Reprinted in Finley, with Shaw and Saller, 1982, 41–62.

———. 1982. *Economy and Society in Ancient Greece*, B. D. Shaw and R. P. Saller, eds. New York.

Flory, S. 1980. "Who Read Herodotus' *Histories*?" *AJPh* 101, 12–28.

———. 1990. "The Meaning of τὸ μὴ μυθῶδες (1.22.4) and the Usefulness of Thucydides' *History*." *CJ* 85, 193–208.

———. 1993. "The Death of Thucydides and the Motif of 'Land on Sea.'" In Rosen and Farrell 1993, 113–23.

Fontenrose, J. 1978. *The Delphic Oracle: Its Responses and Operations, with a Catalogue of Responses.* Berkeley.

Forde, S. 1989. *The Ambition to Rule: Alcibiades and the Politics of Imperialism in Thucydides.* Ithaca and London.

———. 1992. "Political Ambition in Thucydides and Plato: the Case of Alcibiades." In *Politikos II: Educating the Ambitious. Leadership and Political Rule in Greek Political Thought,* L. G. Rubin, ed., 9–30. Pittsburgh.

Fornara, C.W. 1968. "The 'Tradition' About the Murder of Hipparchus." *Historia* 17, 400–24.

———. 1970a. "The Cult of Harmodius and Aristogeiton." *Philologus* 114, 155–80.

———. 1970b. "The Date of the Callias Decrees." *GRBS* 11, 185–96.

———. 1971a. *Herodotus: An Interpretative Essay.* Oxford.

———. 1971b. "Evidence for the Date of Herodotus' Publication." *JHS* 91, 25–34.

———. 1971c. "Themistocles' Archonship." *Historia* 20, 534–40.

———. 1973. "Cleon's Attack Against the Cavalry." *CQ* 23, 24.

———. 1981. "Herodotus' Knowledge of the Archidamian War." *Hermes* 109, 149–56.

———. 1983. *The Nature of History in Ancient Greece and Rome.* Berkeley.

———. 1993. "Thucydides' Birth Date." In Rosen and Farrell 1993, 71–80.

Fornara, C. W., and L. J. Samons II. 1991. *Athens from Cleisthenes to Pericles.* Berkeley.

Forrest, W. G. 1975. "An Athenian Generation Gap." *YClS* 24, 37–52.

Fowler, R. 1996. "Herodotus and his Contemporaries." *JHS* 116, 62–87.

Francis, E. D. 1990. *Image and Idea in Fifth-Century Greece.* London.

Francis, E. D., and M. Vickers. 1985. "The Oenoe Painting in the Stoa Poikile, and Herodotus' Account of Marathon." *ABSA* 80, 99–113.

Frazer, J. G. 1898. *Pausanias's Description of Greece.* 6 vols. London.

French, A. 1964. *The Growth of the Athenian Economy.* London.

Frost, F. J. 1964. "Pericles, Thucydides, son of Melesias, and Athenian Politics before the War." *Historia* 13, 385–99.

———. 1990. "Peisistratos, Cults, and the Unification of Attica." *AncW* 21, 3–9.

———. 1994. "Aspects of Early Athenian Citizenship." In Boegehold and Scafuro 1994, 45–56.

Fuks, A. 1953. *The Ancestral Constitution: four studies in Athenian party politics at the end of the fifth century B.C.* London. Reprint 1971, Westport, Conn.

Funke, P. 1980. *Homonoia und Arche, Athen und die griechische Staatenwelt vom Ende des peloponnesischen Krieges bis zum Königsfrieden. Historia* Einzelschrift 37. Wiesbaden.

Gabrielsen, V. 1986. "Φανερά and Ἀφανὴς Οὐσία in Classical Athens." *C&M* 37, 99–114.

———. 1994. *Financing the Athenian Fleet: Public Taxation and Social Relations.* Baltimore and London.

Gagarin, M. 1997. *Antiphon: The Speeches.* Cambridge.

Garland, R. 1992. *Introducing New Gods: The Politics of Athenian Religion.* Ithaca.

Garnsey, P. 1988. *Famine and Food Supply in the Graeco-Roman World: Responses to Risk and Crisis.* Cambridge.

Gentili, B. 1988. *Poetry and Its Public in Ancient Greece: From Homer to the Fifth Century.* Trans. A. T. Cole from the Italian edition of 1985. Baltimore and London.

Gentili, B., and G. Cerri. 1988. *History and Biography in Ancient Thought.* Amsterdam.

Germaine, G. 1972. "Théano: Théonoè—sur un personnage d'Euripide." In *Studi classici in honore di Quintino Cataudella,* vol. 1, 259–73. Catania.

Giovannini, A. 1990. "Le Parthénon, le trésor d'Athéna et le tribut des alliés." *Historia* 39, 129–48.

———. 1997. "La participation des alliés au financement du Parthénon: *aparchè* ou tribut?" *Historia* 46, 129–48.

Goff, B., ed. 1995. *History, Tragedy, Theory: Dialogues in Athenian Drama.* Austin.

Goldhill, S. 1987/1990. "The Great Dionysia and Civic Ideology." *JHS* 107, 58–76. Reprinted in Winkler and Zeitlin 1990, 97–129.

Gomme, A.W. 1933. *The Population of Athens in the Fifth and Fourth Centuries B.C.* Oxford. Reprinted Chicago, 1967.

———. 1937. *Essays in Greek History and Literature.* Oxford.

———. 1945–1981, with A. Andrewes and K.J. Dover in 1970 and 1981. *A Historical Commentary on Thucydides.* 5 vols. Oxford.

———. 1954. *The Greek Attitude to Poetry and History.* Berkeley.

Goody, J., and I. Watt. 1968. "The Consequences of Literacy." In *Literacy in Traditional Societies,* J. Goody, ed., 27–68. Cambridge.

Gould, J. 1989. *Herodotus.* New York.

———. 1996. "Euripides." In *The Oxford Classical Dictionary.* 3rd ed., S. Hornblower and A. Spawforth, eds., 571–74. Oxford.

Graham, A.J. 1983. *Colony and Mother City in Ancient Greece.* 2nd ed. Chicago.

Graham, A.J., and G. Forsythe. 1984. "A New Slogan for Oligarchy in Thucydides III.82.8." *HSPh* 88, 25–45.

Grandjean, Y.G., and F. Salviat. 1988. "Décret d'Athènes, restaurant la démocratie à Thasos en 407 av. J.-C.: *IG* XII 8, 262 complété." *BCH* 112, 249–78.

Gray, V. 1989. *The Character of Xenophon's Hellenica.* Baltimore.

Green, P. 1991. "Rebooking the Flute-Girls: A Fresh Look at the Chronological Evidence for the Fall of Athens and the ὀκτάμηνος ἀρχή of the Thirty." *AHB* 5, 1–16.

Gregory, J. 1986. "The Power of Language in Euripides' *Troades.*" *Eranos* 84, 1–9.

Griffith, J.G. 1977. "A Note on the First Eisphora at Athens." *AJAH* 2, 3–7.

Griffith, M. 1990. "Contest and Contradiction in Early Greek Poetry." In *Cabinet of the Muses: Essays on Classical and Comparative Literature in Honor of Thomas G. Rosenmeyer,* M. Griffith and D.J. Mastronarde, eds., 185–207. Atlanta.

Grote, G. 1862. *A History of Greece.* 8 vols. 2nd ed. London.

Guthrie, W.K.C. 1969/1971. *A History of Greek Philosophy.* Vol. 3, part 1, reprinted as *The Sophists.* Cambridge.

———. 1975. *A History of Greek Philosophy.* Vol. 4, *Plato, the Man and His Dialogues: The Earlier Period.* Cambridge.

Habicht, C. 1961. "Falsche Urkunden zur Geschichte Athens im Zeitalter der Perserkriege." *Hermes* 89, 1–35.

Halliwell, S. 1991. "Comic Satire and Freedom of Speech in Classical Athens." *JHS* 111, 48–70.

Hamilton, C.D. 1979. *Sparta's Bitter Victories: Politics and Diplomacy in the Corinthian War.* Ithaca.

Hanfmann, G.M.A., and J.C. Waldbaum. 1969. "Kybele and Artemis: Two Anatolian Goddesses at Sardis." *Archaeology* 22, 264–69.

Hansen, H. 1990. *Aspects of the Athenian Law Code of 410/09—400/399 B.C.* New York and London.

Hansen, M.H. 1974. *The Sovereignty of the People's Court in Athens in the Fourth Century B.C. and the Public Action against Unconstitutional Proposals.* Odense University Classical Studies vol. 4. Odense.
———. 1977/1983. "How did the Athenian *Ecclesia* Vote?" *GRBS* 18, 123–37. Reprinted in Hansen 1983, 103–17.
———. 1980. "Prerequisites for Magistrates in Fourth-Century Athens." *C&M* 32, 105–25.
———. 1982. "Demographic Reflections on the Number of Athenian Citizens 451–309 BC." *AJAH* 7, 172–89.
———. 1983. *The Athenian Ekklesia: A Collection of Articles, 1976–83.* Copenhagen.
———. 1985. *Demography and Democracy: The Number of Athenian Citizens in the Fourth Century B.C.* Herning.
———. 1986. "The Origin of the Term *demokratia.*" *LCM* 11.3, 35–36.
———. 1987. *The Athenian Assembly in the Age of Demosthenes.* Oxford.
———. 1988. "Three Studies in Athenian Demography." *Historisk-filosofiskes Meddelelser* 56, Royal Danish Academy of Sciences and Letters. Copenhagen.
———. 1990. "Diokles' Law (Dem. 24.42) and the Revision of the Athenian Corpus of Laws in the Archonship of Eukleides." *C&M* 41, 63–71.
———. 1991. *The Athenian Democracy in the Age of Demosthenes.* Oxford.
———. 1995. "The Trial of Sokrates—From the Athenian Point of View." *Historisk-filosofiskes Meddelelser* 71, Royal Danish Academy of Sciences and Letters. Copenhagen.
Harding, P.E. 1974. "The Theramenes Myth." *Phoenix* 28, 101–11.
———. 1978. "O Androtion, You Fool!" *AJAH* 3, 179–83.
———. 1988. "King Pausanias and the Restoration of Democracy at Athens." *Hermes* 116, 186–93.
———. 1994. *Androtion and His Atthis.* Oxford.
Harris, E.M. 1990. "The Constitution of the Five Thousand." *HSPh* 93, 243–80.
Harrison, A.R.W. 1955. "Law-Making at Athens at the End of the Fifth Century B.C." *JHS* 75, 26–35.
Harvey, D. 1990. "The Sykophant and Sykophancy: Vexatious Redefinition?" In Cartledge and Millett 1990, 103–21.
Hatzfeld, J. 1940. *Alcibiade. Étude sur l'histoire d'Athènes à la fin du Ve siècle.* Paris.
Havelock, E.A. 1957. *The Liberal Temper in Greek Politics.* London.
———. 1963. *Preface to Plato.* Oxford.
———. 1966/1982. "Preliteracy and the Presocratics." *BICS* 13, 44–67. Reprinted in Havelock 1982, 220–60.
———. 1982. *The Literate Revolution in Greece and Its Cultural Consequences.* Princeton.
Hedrick, C.W. 1994. "Writing, Reading, and Democracy." In Osborne and Hornblower 1994, 157–74.
Heftner, H. 1995. "Ps.-Andokides' Rede gegen Alkibiade ([And.] 4) und die politische Diskussion nach dem Sturz der 'Dreißig' in Athen." *Klio* 77, 75–104.
Henderson, J. 1987. *Aristophanes Lysistrata.* Oxford.
Henrichs, A. 1968. "Zur Interpretation der Michigan-Papyrus über Theramenes." *ZPE* 101–108.
Henry, A.S. 1979. "Archon-Dating in Fifth Century Attic Decrees: the 421 Rule." *Chiron* 9, 23–40.

———. 1983. "The Spelling χσένια/ξένια in Fifth-Century Invitations to the Prytaneion." *Chiron* 13, 61–67.

———. 1992. "Through a Laser Beam Darkly: Space-Age Technology and the Egesta Decree (*IG* I³ 11)." *ZPE* 91, 137–46.

Henry, W.P. 1966. *Greek Historical Writing: A Historiographical Essay Based on Xenophon's Hellenica.* Chicago.

Hereward, D. 1952. "New Fragments of *IG* II² 10." *ABSA* 47, 102–17.

Herman, G. 1987. *Ritualised Friendship and the Ancient Greek City.* Cambridge.

Herington, J. 1985. *Poetry into Drama: Early Tragedy and the Greek Poetic Tradition.* Berkeley.

Hignett, C. 1952. *A History of the Athenian Constitution to the end of the Fifth Century B.C.* Oxford.

Hodkinson, S. 1992. "Imperial Democracy and Market-Oriented Pastoral Production in Classical Athens." *Anthropozoologica* 16, 53–61.

Hölscher, W. 1973. *Griechische Historienbilder des 5. und 4. Jahrhunderts vor Chr.* Beiträge zur Archäologie 6. Würzburg.

Hopper, R.J. 1979. *Trade and Industry in Classical Greece.* London.

Hornblower, S. 1983/1991. *The Greek World, 479–323 B.C.* Revised ed. 1991. London and New York.

———. 1987. *Thucydides.* London.

———. 1991. *A Commentary on Thucydides.* Vol. 1, Books I–III. Oxford.

———. 1992. "Thucydides' Use of Herodotus." In ΦΙΛΟΛΑΚΩΝ*: Studies in Honor of Hector Catling,* J.M. Sandars, ed., 141–54. London.

———. 1995. "The Fourth-Century and Hellenistic Reception of Thucydides." *JHS* 115, 47–68.

Hubbard, T.K. 1991. *The Mask of Comedy: Aristophanes and the Intertextual Parabasis.* Ithaca and London.

Hunter, V. 1973. *Thucydides, the Artful Reporter.* Toronto.

———. 1977. "The Composition of Thucydides' *History:* A New Answer to the Problem." *Historia* 26, 269–94.

Immerwahr, H.R. 1960. "*Ergon:* History as Monument in Herodotus and Thucydides." *AJPh* 81, 261–90.

———. 1966. *Form and Thought in Herodotus,* American Philological Association Monograph 23, Cleveland. Reprint Chapel Hill, 1986.

Irwin, T.H. 1992. "Plato: The Intellectual Background." In Kraut 1992, 51–89.

Jacoby, F. 1913/1956. "Herodotos." In Pauly-Wissowa, *Realencyclopädie der classischen Altertumswissenschaft,* Supplement vol. 2, cols. 205–520. Stuttgart. Reprinted in *Griechische Historiker.* Stuttgart.

———. 1944. "*Patrios Nomos:* State Burial in Athens and the Public Cemetery in the Kerameikos." *JHS* 64, 37–66.

———. 1949. *Atthis: The Local Chronicles of Ancient Athens.* Oxford.

Jameson, M.H. 1956. "Politics and the Philoctetes." *CPh* 51, 217–27.

———. 1963. "The Provisions for Mobilization in the Decree of Themistokles." *Historia* 12, 395–404.

———. 1971. "Sophocles and the 400." *Historia* 20, 541–68.

———. 1977–1978. "Agriculture and Slavery in Classical Athens." *CJ* 73, 122–45.

———, ed. 1985. *The Greek Historians, Literature and History: Papers Presented to A. E. Raubitschek.* Saratoga, Calif.

———. 1991. "Sacrifice Before Battle." In *Hoplites: The Classical Greek Battle Experience,* V. D. Hanson, ed., 197–227. London.

———. 1994. "The Ritual of the Athena Nike Parapet." In Osborne and Hornblower 1994, 307–24.

Jebb, R. C. 1876. *The Attic Orators from Antiphon to Isaeos.* 2 vols. London.

Jeffery, L. H. 1968. "The *Battle of Oinoe* in the Stoa Poikile." *ABSA* 60, 41–57.

Johnstone, C. L. 1996. "Greek Oratorical Settings and the Problem of the Pnyx: Rethinking the Athenian Political Process." In *Theory, Text, Context,* C. L. Johnstone, ed., 97–128. Albany, N.Y.

Jones, A. H. M. 1957. *Athenian Democracy.* Oxford.

Kagan, D. 1974. *The Archidamian War.* Ithaca and London.

———. 1981. *The Peace of Nicias and the Sicilian Expedition.* Ithaca and London.

———. 1987. *The Fall of the Athenian Empire.* Ithaca and London.

Kallet, L. 1998. "Accounting for Culture in Fifth-Century Athens." In *Democracy, Empire, and the Arts in Fifth-Century Athens,* D. Boedeker and K. Raaflaub, eds., 43–58. Cambridge, Mass.

Kallet-Marx, L. 1989. "The Kallias Decree, Thucydides, and the Outbreak of the Peloponnesian War." *CQ* 39, 94–113.

———. 1993. *Money, Expense, and Naval Power in Thucydides' History 1–5.24.* Berkeley.

———. 1994. "Money Talks: Rhetor, Demos, and the Resources of the Athenian Empire." In Osborne and Hornblower 1994, 227–51.

Karavites, P. 1986. "Homer: Horkia, Horkos." *AncW* 14, 115–28.

Kearns, E. 1989. *The Heroes of Attica. BICS* supplement 57. London.

Keen, A. G. 1993. "Athenian Campaigns in Karia and Lykia during the Peloponnesian War." *JHS* 113, 152–57.

Kienitz, F. K. 1953. *Die politische Geschichte Ägyptens vom 7. bis zum 4. Jahrhundert vor der Zeitwende.* Berlin.

Kierdorf, W. 1966. *Erlebnis und Darstellungen der Perserkriege. Hypomnemata* 16. Göttingen.

Kinzl, K. H. 1978. "*Demokratia:* Studien zur Frühgeschichte des Begriffs." *Gymnasium* 85, 117–27, 312–26.

Kinzl, K. H., and K. A. Raaflaub, eds. 1995. *Demokratia: Der Weg zur Demokratie bei den Griechen.* Wege der Forschung 657. Darmstadt.

Kleine, J. 1973. *Untersuchungen zur Chronologie der attischen Kunst von Peisistratos bis Themistokles. MDAI(I),* Beiheft 8. Tübingen.

Knox, B. M. W. 1968. "Silent Reading in Antiquity." *GRBS* 9, 421–35.

———. 1978. "Literature." In *Athens Comes of Age: From Solon to Salamis. Papers of a Symposium Sponsored by the Archaeological Institute of America, Princeton Society, and the Department of Art and Archaeology, Princeton University,* 43–52. Princeton.

———. 1979. *Word and Action: Essays on the Ancient Theater.* Baltimore and London.

Koenen, L. 1976. "A New Fragment of the Oxyrhynchia Historian." *StudPap* 15, 55–76.

Konstan, D. 1987. "Persians, Greeks, and Empire." *Aresthusa* 20, 59–73.

Kourouniotis, K., and H.A. Thompson. 1932. "The Pnyx in Athens." *Hesperia* 1, 90–217.
Kraay, C.M. 1976. *Archaic and Classical Greek Coins.* Berkeley.
Krause, A. 1914. *Attische Strategenlisten bis 146 v. Chr.* Jena dissertation. Weimar.
Kraut, R., ed. 1992. *The Cambridge Companion to Plato.* Cambridge.
Krentz, P. 1980. "Foreigners against the Thirty: *IG* II^2 10 Again." *Phoenix* 34, 298–306.
———. 1982. *The Thirty at Athens.* Ithaca.
———. 1984a. "The Ostracism of Thoukidydes Son of Melesias." *Historia* 33, 499–504.
———. 1984b. "The Pnyx in 404/3 B.C." *AJA* 88, 230–31.
———. 1986. "The Rewards for Thrasyboulos' Supporters." *ZPE* 62, 201–204.
———. 1988–1989. "Athenian Politics and the Strategy after Kyzikos." *CQ* 84, 206–15.
———. 1989a. "Had Xenophon Read Thucydides VIII Before He Wrote the 'Continuation' (*Hell.* I-II.3.10)?" *AncW* 19, 15–18.
———, ed. 1989b. *Xenophon Hellenica I-II.3.10.* Warminster.
Kuhn, G. 1985. "Untersuchungen zur Funktion der Säulenhalle III. Die Stoa Basileios in Athen." *JDAI* 100, 200–26.
Kurke, L. 1991. *The Traffic in Praise: Pindar and the Poetics of Social Economy.* Ithaca and London.
———. 1993. "The Economy of *Kudos.*" In Dougherty and Kurke 1993, 131–63.
Landwehr, C. 1985. *Die antiken Gipsabgüsse aus Baiae.* Berlin.
Lane, E.N., ed. 1996. *Cybele, Attis, and Related Cults: Essays in Memory of M.J. Vermaseren.* Leiden and New York.
Lang, M. 1967. "Scapegoat Pausanias." *CJ* 63, 79–85.
———. 1990. "Illegal Execution in Ancient Athens." *PAPhS* 134, 24–29.
———. 1992. "Theramenes and Arginousai." *Hermes* 120, 267–79.
Lateiner, D. 1976. "Tissaphernes and the Phoenician Fleet (Thucydides 8.87)." *TAPhA* 106, 267–90.
———. 1985. "Limit, Propriety, and Transgression in the *Histories* of Herodotus." In Jameson 1985, 87–100.
———. 1989. *The Historical Method of Herodotus.* Toronto.
Lattimore, R. 1939. "The Wise Advisor in Herodotus." *CPh* 34, 24–35.
Lawrence, A.W. 1979. *Greek Aims in Fortification.* Oxford.
Lawton, C. 1993. "Representations of Athenian Democracy in Attic Document Reliefs." In Ober and Hedrick 1993, 12–16.
Lavelle, B.M. 1993. *The Sorrow and the Pity: a Prolegomenon to a History of Athens Under the Peisistratids, c. 560–510 B.C. Historia* Einzelschrift 80. Stuttgart.
Lazenby, J.F. 1988. "Aischylos and Salamis." *Hermes* 116, 168–85.
Legon, R.P. 1972. "Samos and the Delian League." *Historia* 21, 145–58.
Lenardon, R.J. 1981. "Thucydides and Hellanikos." In Shrimpton and McCarger 1981, 59–70.
Lenz, T.M. 1989. *Orality and Literacy in Hellenic Greece.* Carbondale and Edwardsville, Ill.
Lesky, A. 1963/1966. *A History of Greek Literature.* Trans. J. Willis and C. de Heer from the second German edition. New York.

Lévy, E. 1976. *Athènes devant la défaite de 404: Histoire d'une crise idéologique.* Bibliotèque des Écoles Françaises d'Athènes et de Rome 225. Paris.

Lewis, D. M. 1958. "The Phoenician Fleet in 411." *Historia* 7, 392–97.

———. 1967. "A Note on *IG* I^2 114." *JHS* 87, 132.

———. 1974. "Entrenchment-Clauses in Attic Decrees." In Bradeen and McGregor 1974, 81–89.

———. 1977. *Sparta and Persia.* Lectures delivered at the University of Cincinnati, Autumn 1976, in Memory of Donald W. Bradeen. Leiden.

———. 1993. "Oligarchic Thinking in the Late Fifth Century." In Rosen and Farrell 1993, 207–11.

Lewis, D. M., J. Boardman, J. K. Davies, and M. Ostwald, eds. 1992. *The Cambridge Ancient History.* Vol. 5. 2nd ed. Cambridge.

Lipsius, J. H. 1905–1915. *Das attische Recht und Rechtsverfahren.* 3 vols. Leipzig.

Loening, T. C. 1981. "The Autobiographical Speeches of Lysias and the Biographical Tradition." *Hermes* 109, 280–94.

———. 1987. *The Reconciliation Agreement of 403/402 B.C. in Athens: Its Content and Application. Hermes* Einzelschrift 53. Stuttgart.

Loraux, N. 1981/1986. *The Invention of Athens: The Funeral Oration in the Classical City.* Trans. A. Sheridan from the French edition of 1981. Cambridge, Mass.

Lou Bengisu, R. 1996. "Lydian Mount Karios." In Lane 1996, 1–36.

MacDowell, D. M. 1962. *Andocides: On the Mysteries.* Oxford.

———. 1971. "The Chronology of Athenian Speeches and the Legal Innovations in 401–398 B.C." *RIDA* 18, 267–73.

———. 1978. *The Law in Classical Athens.* Ithaca and New York.

———. 1993. "Foreign birth and Athenian citizenship in Aristophanes." In Sommerstein et al. 1993, 359–71.

———. 1995. *Aristophanes and Athens: An Introduction to the Plays.* Oxford.

MacLaren, M., Jr. 1934. "On the Composition of Xenophon's Hellenica." *AJPh* 55, 121–39 and 249–62.

March, D.A. 1997. "Konon and the Great King's Fleet, 396–94." *Historia* 46, 257–69.

Marinatos, N. 1981a. "Thucydides and Oracles." *JHS* 101, 138–40.

———. 1981b. *Thucydides and Religion.* Beiträge zur klassischen Philologie, no. 129. Königstein.

Markle, M. M. 1985. "Jury Pay and Assembly Pay at Athens." In *Crux. Essays Presented to G. E. M. de Ste Croix on his 75th Birthday,* P. A. Cartledge and F. D. Harvey, eds., 265–97. Exeter and London.

Martin, R. P. 1993. "The Seven Sages as Performers of Wisdom." In Dougherty and Kurke 1993, 108–28.

Mattingly, H. B. 1961a/1996. "The Athenian Coinage Decree." *Historia* 10, 148–88. Reprinted in Mattingly 1996, 5–52.

———. 1961b/1996. "Athens and Euboea." *JHS* 81, 124–32. Reprinted in Mattingly 1996, 53–67.

———. 1963/1996. "The Growth of Athenian Imperialism." *Historia* 12, 257–73. Reprinted in Mattingly 1996, 87–106.

———. 1964. "The Financial Decrees of Kallias (*IG* I^2 91/2)." *PACA* 7, 35–55.

———. 1966/1996. "Athenian Imperialism and the Foundation of Brea." *CQ* 16, 172–92. Reprinted in Mattingly 1996, 117–46.
———. 1967/1996. "Two Notes on Athenian Financial Documents." *ABSA* 62, 13–17. Reprinted in Mattingly 1996, 205–13.
———. 1968/1996. "Athenian Finance in the Peloponnesian War." *BCH* 92, 450–85. Reprinted in Mattingly 1996, 215–57.
———. 1974/1996. "Athens and Eleusis: Some new ideas." In Bradeen and McGregor 1974, 90–103. Reprinted in Mattingly 1996, 325–45.
———. 1975/1996. "The Mysterious 3000 Talents of the first Kallias Decree." *GRBS* 16, 15–22. Reprinted in Mattingly 1996, 353–360.
———. 1976/1996. "Three Attic Decrees." *Historia* 25, 38–44. Reprinted in Mattingly 1996, 391–98.
———. 1979/1996. "Periclean Imperialism." In *Perikles und sein Zeit,* G. Wirth, ed., 312–49. Reprinted in Mattingly 1996, 147–79.
———. 1991. "The Practice of Ostracism at Athens." *Antichthon* 25, 1–26.
———. 1992. "Epigraphy and the Athenian Empire." *Historia* 41, 129–38.
———. 1993. "New Light on the Athenian Standards Decree (ATL II, D 14)." *Klio* 75, 99–102.
———. 1996. *The Athenian Empire Restored: Epigraphic and Historical Studies.* Ann Arbor.
Mattusch, C. C. 1994. "The Eponymous Heroes: The Idea of Sculptural Groups." In Coulson et al. 1994, 73–81.
McCall, M. 1986. "Aeschylus in the *Persae:* A Bold Stratagem Succeeds." In *Greek Tragedy and its Legacy. Essays Presented to D. J. Conacher,* M. Cropp, E. Fantham, S. E. Scully, eds., 43–49. Calgary.
McCoy, W. J. 1970. "Theramenes, Thrasybulus and the Athenian Moderates." Yale dissertation. Ann Arbor.
———. 1973. "The 'Non-Speeches' of Pisander in Thucydides, Book Eight." In *The Speeches in Thucydides: A Collection of Original Studies with a Bibliography,* P. A. Stadter, ed. Chapel Hill, 78–89.
———. 1975. "Aristotle's *Athenaion Politeia* and the Establishment of the Thirty Tyrants." *YClS* 23, 131–45.
———. 1977. "Thrasyllus." *AJPh* 98, 264–89.
———. 1991. "Thrasybulus and his Trierarchies." *AJPh* 112, 303–23.
McGlew, J. F. 1993. *Tyranny and Political Culture in Ancient Greece.* Ithaca and London.
———. 1996. "Everybody Wants to Make a Speech: Cleon and Aristophanes on Politics and Fantasy." *Arethusa* 29, 339–61.
McPherran, M. L. 1996. *The Religion of Socrates.* University Park, Pa.
Meier, C. 1970. *Entstehung des Begriffs 'Demokratie': Vier Prolegomena zu einer historischen Theorie.* Frankfurt.
———. 1980/1990. *The Greek Discovery of Politics.* Trans. D. McClintock from the German edition of 1980. Cambridge, Mass., and London.
———. 1988/1993. *The Political Art of Greek Tragedy.* Trans. A. Webber from the German. Baltimore.
Meiggs, R. 1963/1974. "The Political Implications of the Parthenon." In *Parthenos and Parthenon. G&R* supplement to vol. 10, G. T. W. Hooker, ed., 36–45. Reprinted in *The Parthenon,* V. J. Bruno, ed., 101–11. New York.
———. 1972. *The Athenian Empire.* Oxford.

Meritt, B. D. 1936. "Greek Inscriptions: The Tribute Assessment of 410 B.C." *Hesperia* 5, 386–89.

———. 1981. "Kleon's Assessment of Tribute to Athens." In Shrimpton and McCarger 1981, 89–93.

Meritt, B. D., and H. T. Wade-Gery. 1936. "Pylos and the Assessment of Tribute." *AJPh* 57, 377–94.

Meritt, B. D., H. T. Wade-Gery, and M. F. McGregor. 1950. *The Athenian Tribute Lists.* Vol. 3. Princeton.

Meritt, L. S. 1970. "The Stoa Poikile." *Hesperia* 39, 233–64.

Merkelbach, R., and H. C. Youtie. 1968. "Ein Michigan-Papyrus über Theramenes." *ZPE* 2, 161–69.

Meyer, E. 1884–1902. *Geschichte des Altertums.* 5 vols. Stuttgart and Berlin.

———. 1899. *Forschungen zur alten Geschichte.* Vol. 2. Halle.

Mikalson, J. D. 1975. *The Sacred and Civil Calendar of the Athenian Year.* Princeton.

Miller, S. G. 1995. "Old Metroon and Old Bouleuterion in the Classical Agora of Athens." In *Studies in the Ancient Greek Polis,* M. H. Hansen and K. Raaflaub, eds. *Historia* Einzelschrift 95, 133–56. Stuttgart.

Millett, P. 1991. *Lending and Borrowing in Ancient Athens.* Cambridge.

Moles, J. 1993. "Truth and Untruth in Herodotus and Thucydides." In *Lies and Fiction in the Ancient World,* C. Gill and T. P. Wiseman, eds., 88–121. Exeter.

———. 1996. "Herodotus Warns the Athenians." *Paper of the Leeds International Latin Seminar* 9, 259–84.

Momigliano, A. 1966. *Studies in Historiography.* New York.

———. 1971. *The Development of Greek Biography.* Expanded ed. 1993. Cambridge, Mass.

———. 1990. *The Classical Foundations of Modern Historiography.* Sather Classical Lectures. Vol. 54. Berkeley.

Montuori, M. 1992. *The Socratic Problem: The History—The Solutions, From the 18th Century to the Present Time. 61 Extracts from 54 Authors in Their Historical Context.* Amsterdam.

Morris, I. 1992. *Death-Ritual and Social Structure in Classical Antiquity.* Cambridge.

Morris, I., and K. A. Raaflaub, eds. 1996. *Democracy 2500: Questions and Challenges.* Atlanta.

Morrison, J. S. 1941. "The Place of Protagoras in Athenian Public Life (460–415 B.C.)." *CQ* 35, 1–16.

———. 1942. "Meno of Pharsalus, Polycrates, and Ismenias." *CQ* 36, 57–78.

———. 1961. "Antiphon." *PCPhS,* 49–58.

———. 1972. "Antiphon." In Sprague 1972, 106–240.

Morrison, J. S., and R. T. Williams. 1968. *Greek Oared Ships, 900–322 B.C.* Cambridge.

Mosshammer, A. 1975. "Themistocles' Archonship in the Chronographic Tradition." *Hermes* 103, 222–34.

———. 1976. "Geometric Proportion and the Chronological Method of Apollodorus." *TAPhA* 106, 291–306.

———. 1979. *The Chronicle of Eusebius and Greek Chronographic Tradition.* Lewisberg.

Moysey, R. A. 1981. "The Thirty and the Pnyx." *AJA* 85, 31–37.

Murray, O. 1990. "The Affair of the Mysteries: Democracy and the Drinking Group." In *Sympotica: A Symposium on the Symposion,* O. Murray, ed., 149–61. Oxford.

Nagy, B. 1994. "Alcibiades' Second 'Profanation.'" *Historia* 43, 275–85.
Nagy, G. 1990. *Pindar's Homer: The Lyric Possession of the Epic Past.* Baltimore and London.
———. 1996. *Homeric Questions.* Austin.
Nakamura-Moroo, A. 1988. "The Attitude of Greeks in Asia Minor to Athens and Persia: The Deceleian War." In *Forms of Control and Subordination in Antiquity,* T. Yuge and M. Doi, eds., 567–72. Leiden, New York, Copenhagen, Köln.
Nixon, L., and S. Price. 1990. "The Size and Resources of Greek Cities." In *The Greek City from Homer to Alexander,* O. Murray and S. Price, eds., 137–70. Oxford.
North, H. 1966. *Sophrosyne. Self-Knowledge and Self-Restraint in Greek Literature.* Ithaca.
Obbink, D., and P. A. Vander Waerdt, eds. 1991. *The School of Hellas: Essays on Greek History, Archaeology, and Literature, by A. E. Raubitschek.* Oxford.
Ober, J. 1985. "Thucydides, Pericles, and the Strategy of Defense." In *The Craft of the Ancient Historian: Essays in Honor of Chester G. Starr,* J. W. Eadie and J. Ober, eds., 171–88. Lanham, Md.
———. 1996. *The Athenian Revolution: Essays on Ancient Greek Democracy and Political Theory.* Princeton.
Ober, J., and C. W. Hedrick, eds. 1993. *The Birth of Democracy: An Exhibition Celebrating the 2500th Anniversary of Democracy at the National Archives, Washington, D.C.* American School of Classical Studies at Athens.
Oliver, J. H. 1935. "Greek Inscriptions." *Hesperia* 4, 5–32.
Olmstead, A. T. 1948. *History of the Persian Empire.* Chicago.
Orwin, C. 1994. *The Humanity of Thucydides.* Princeton.
Osborne, M. J. 1981–1983. *Naturalization in Athens.* 4 vols. in 3 tomes. Verhandelingen van de Koninklijke Academie voor Wetenschappen, Letteren en Schone Kunsten van België, Klasse der Letteren, issues 43–45, nos. 98, 101, 109. Brussels.
Osborne, R. 1990. "Vexatious Litigation in Classical Athens: Sykophancy and the Sykophant." In Cartledge and Millett 1990, 83–102.
———. 1991. "Pride and Prejudice, Sense and Subsistence: Exchange and Society in the Greek City." In *City and Country in the Ancient World,* J. Rich and A. Wallace-Hadrill, eds., 119–45. London and New York.
———. 1993. "Competitive festivals and the polis: a context for dramatic festivals at Athens." In Sommerstein et al. 1993, 21–38.
Osborne, R., and S. Hornblower, eds. 1994. *Ritual, Finance, Politics: Athenian Democratic Accounts Presented to David Lewis.* Oxford.
Ostwald, M. 1955. "The Athenian Legislation Against Tyranny and Subversion." *TAPhA* 86, 103–28.
———. 1969. *Nomos and the Beginnings of Athenian Democracy.* Oxford.
———. 1973. "Was There a Concept of ἄγραφος νόμος in Classical Greece?" In *Exegesis and Argument: Studies in Greek Philosophy Presented to Gregory Vlastos,* E. N. Lee, A. P. D. Mourelatos, and R. M. Rorty, eds., 70–104. Assen, Netherlands.
———. 1982. *Autonomia: Its Genesis and Early History.* American Classical Studies 11. Scholars Press, Atlanta.
———. 1986. *From Popular Sovereignty to the Sovereignty of Law: Law, Society, and Politics in Fifth-Century Athens.* Berkeley.

———. 1988. "The Reform of the Athenian State by Cleisthenes." In *The Cambridge Ancient History,* J. Boardman, N.G.L. Hammond, D.M. Lewis, and M. Ostwald, eds. Vol. 4, 303–46. 2nd ed. Cambridge.

———. 1991. "Herodotus and Athens." *ICS* 16, 137–48.

———. 1993. "*Stasis* and *autonomia* in Samos: A Comment on an Ideological Fallacy." *SCI* 12, 51–66.

———. 1995. "Public Expense: Whose Obligation? Athens 600–454 B.C.E." *PAPhS* 139, 368–79.

Parke, H.W. 1932. "The Tithe of Apollo and the Harmost at Decelea." *JHS* 52, 42–46.

———. 1977. *Festivals of the Athenians.* London.

Parke, H.W., and D.E.W. Wormell. 1956. *The Delphic Oracle.* Vol. 1, *The History.* Oxford.

Parker, Richard A., and W.H. Dubberstein. 1956. *Babylonian Chronology, 626 B.C.-A.D. 75.* 2nd ed. Providence.

Parker, Robert. 1990. *Miasma: Pollution and Purification in Early Greek Religion.* Oxford.

———. 1994. "Athenian Religion Abroad." In Osborne and Hornblower 1994, 339–46.

———. 1996. *Athenian Religion: A History.* Oxford.

Patterson, C. 1981. *Pericles' Citizenship Law of 451/0.* New York. Reprint Salem, 1987.

Pearson, L. 1939. *Early Ionian Historians.* Oxford.

———. 1942. *The Local Historians of Attica.* Philadelphia. Reprint Westport, Connecticut, 1972.

———. 1987. *The Greek Historians of the West: Timaeus and His Predecessors.* American Philological Association, Philological Monograph no. 35. Atlanta.

Pelling, C., ed. 1997. *Greek Tragedy and the Historian.* Oxford.

Penner, T. 1992. "Socrates in the Early Dialogues." In Kraut 1992, 121–69.

Pesely, G. 1988. "Sokrates' Attempt to Save Theramenes." *AHB* 2, 31–33.

———. 1995. "Andron and the Four Hundred." *ICS* 20, 65–76.

Peters, K. 1942. "Zwei Panathenäischen Preisamphoren des Aristophanes." *JDAI* 57, 143–57.

Pickard-Cambridge, A. 1962. *Dithyramb, Tragedy and Comedy.* 2nd ed. revised by T.B.L. Webster. Oxford.

———. 1968. *The Dramatic Festivals of Athens.* 2nd ed. revised by J. Gould and D.M. Lewis. Oxford.

Plommer, W.H. 1969. "The Tyranny of the Archon List." *CR* 19, 126–29.

Podlecki, A. 1966. "The Political Significance of the Athenian 'Tyrannicide'-Cult." *Historia* 15, 129–41.

———. 1971. "Cimon, Skyros, and Theseus' Bones." *JHS* 91, 141–43.

———. 1975. *The Life of Themistocles.* Montreal and London.

Pollitt, J.J. 1972. *Art and Experience in Classical Greece.* Cambridge.

Pouilloux, J., and F. Salviat. 1983. "Lichas, Lacédémonien, archonte à Thasos, et le livre viii de Thucydide." *CRAI,* 376–403.

———. 1985. "Thucydide après l'exil et la composition de son histoire." *RPh* 59, 13–20.

Pouncey, P.R. 1980. *The Necessities of War: A Study of Thucydides' Pessimism.* New York.

Pratt, L.H. 1993. *Lying and Poetry from Homer to Pindar: Falsehood and Deception in Archaic Greek Poets.* Ann Arbor.

Pritchett, W.K. 1953. "The Attic Stelai: Part I." *Hesperia* 22, 225–99.

———. 1956. "The Attic Stelai: Part II." *Hesperia* 25, 178–328.

———. 1971, 1974, 1985. *The Greek State at War.* Parts 1, 2, and 4. Berkeley.

———. 1975. *Dionysius of Halicarnassus: On Thucydides.* Berkeley.

———. 1980. *Studies in Ancient Greek topography.* Part III *(Roads).* Berkeley.

———. 1993. *The Liar School of Herodotus.* Amsterdam.

———. 1994. *Essays in Greek History.* Amsterdam.

———. 1995. *Thucydides' Pentekontaetia and Other Essays.* ΑΡΧΑΙΑ ΕΛΛΑΣ: Monographs on Ancient Greek History and Archaeology, 1, S.B. Aleshire, ed. Amsterdam.

———. 1996. *Greek Archives, Cults, and Topography.* ΑΡΧΑΙΑ ΕΛΛΑΣ: Monographs on Ancient Greek History and Archaeology, 2, S.B. Aleshire, ed. Amsterdam.

Proietti, G. 1987. *Xenophon's Sparta, an introduction.* Supplement to *Mnemosyne* 98. Leiden.

Raaflaub, K.A. 1979. "Polis Tyrannos: zur Entstehung einer politischen Metapher." In Bowersock et al. 1979, 238–52.

———. 1987. "Herodotus, Political Thought, and the Meaning of History." *Arethusa* 20, 221–48.

———. 1988. "Politisches Denken im Zeitalter Athens." In *Pipers Handbuch der politischen Ideen* vol. 1, *Frühe Hochkulturen und europäische Antike,* I. Fetscher and H. Münkler, eds., 273–368. Munich.

———. 1992. "Politisches Denken und Krise der Polis: Athen im Verfassungskonflikt des späten 5. Jahrhunderts v. Chr." *Historische Zeitschrift* 255, 1–16. Munich.

———. 1994. "Democracy, Power and Imperialism in Fifth-Century Athens." In *Athenian Political Thought and the Reconstruction of American Democracy,* J.P. Euben, J.R. Wallach, and J. Ober, eds., 103–46. Ithaca and London.

———. 1995. "Einleitung und Bilanz: Kleisthenes, Ephialtes und die Begründung der Demokratie." In Kinzl and Raaflaub 1995, 1–54.

———. 1996. "Equalities and Inequalities in Athenian Democracy." In *Dêmokratia: Conversation on Democracies, Ancient and Modern,* J. Ober and C.W. Hedrick, eds., 139–74. Princeton.

———. 1998. "The Transformation of Athens in the Fifth Century." In *Democracy, Empire, and the Arts in Fifth-Century Athens,* D. Boedeker and K. Raaflaub, eds., 15–41. Cambridge, Mass.

Ramsay, W.M. 1890. *The Historical Geography of Asia Minor.* Royal Geographical Society, Supplementary Papers vol. 4. London. Reprint Amsterdam, 1962.

Raubitschek, A.E. 1940/1991. "Two Monuments Erected after the Victory of Marathon." *AJA* 44, 53–59. Reprinted in Obbink and Vander Waerdt 1991, 204–11.

———. 1941/1991. "The Heroes of Phyle." *Hesperia* 10, 284–95. Reprinted in Obbink and Vander Waerdt 1991, 35–44.

———. 1943. "Greek Inscriptions." *Hesperia* 12, 12–88.

———. 1948/1991. "The Case against Alcibiades (Andocides IV)." *TAPhA* 79, 191–210. Reprinted in Obbink and Vander Waerdt 1991, 116–31.

———. 1949. *Dedications from the Athenian Akropolis.* Cambridge, Mass.

———. 1954. "Philinos." *Hesperia* 23, 68–71.

———. 1960/1991. "The Covenant of Plataea." *TAPhA* 91, 178–83. Reprinted in Obbink and Vander Waerdt 1991, 11–15.
———. 1962/1991. "Demokratia." *Hesperia* 31, 238–43. Reprinted in Obbink and Vander Waerdt 1991, 223–38.
———. 1981/1991. "Andocides and Thucydides." In Shrimpton and McCarger 1981, 121–23. Reprinted in Obbink and Vander Waerdt 1991, 292–95.
Rawlings, H. R., III. 1981. *The Structure of Thucydides' History.* Princeton.
Rhodes, P. J. 1970. "Thucydides on Pausanias and Themistocles." *Historia* 19, 387–400.
———. 1972a. *The Athenian Boule.* Oxford.
———. 1972b. "The Five Thousand and the Athenian Revolutions of 411 B.C." *JHS* 92, 115–27.
———. 1981. *A Commentary on the Aristotelian Athenaion Politeia.* Oxford.
———. 1982. "Problems in Athenian *Eisphora* and Liturgies." *AJAH* 7, 1–19.
———. 1985. "What Alcibiades Did and What Happened to Him." Inaugural Lecture, University of Durham.
———. 1991. "The Athenian Code of Laws, 410–399 B.C." *JHS* 111, 87–100.
———. 1994. "The Ostracism of Hyperbolus." In Osborne and Hornblower 1994, 85–98.
Richardson, N. J. 1974a. *The Homeric Hymn to Demeter.* Oxford.
Richter, G. M. A. 1984. *The Portraits of the Greeks.* Revised and abridged by R. R. R. Smith. Ithaca, New York.
———. 1974b. "Homeric Professors in the Age of the Sophists." *PCPhS* 20, 65–81.
Ridgway, B. S. 1977. *The Archaic Style in Greek Sculpture.* Princeton.
———. 1981. *Fifth Century Styles in Greek Sculpture.* Princeton.
Riedweg, C. 1987. *Mysterienterminologie bei Platon, Philon und Klemens von Alexandrien.* Berlin and New York.
Robert, J., and L. Robert. 1984. "Bulletin Épigraphique, no. 314: Thasos." *REG* 97, 468–70.
Roberts, J. T. 1982. *Accountability in Athenian Government.* Madison.
———. 1994. *Athens on Trial: The Antidemocratic Tradition in Western Thought.* Princeton.
Robertson, N. 1980a. "Timocreon and Themistocles." *AJPh* 101, 61–78.
———. 1980b. "The True Nature of the Delian League, 478–461 B.C." *AJAH* 5, 64–96 and 110–33.
———. 1980c. "The Sequence of Events in the Aegean in 408 and 407 B.C." *Historia* 29, 282–301.
———. 1990. "The Laws of Athens, 410–399 BC: The Evidence for Review and Publication." *JHS* 110, 43–75.
———. 1992. *Festivals and Legends: The Formation of Greek Cities in the Light of Public Ritual.* Phoenix supplement 31. Toronto.
———. 1996. "The Ancient Mother of the Gods: A Missing Chapter in the History of Greek Religion." In Lane 1996, 239–304.
Robinson, P. 1985. "Why Do We Believe Thucydides? A Comment on W. R. Connor's 'Narrative Discourse in Thucydides.'" In Jameson 1985, 19–23.
Rogers, B. B. 1904. *The Thesmophoriazusae of Aristophanes.* London.
Roisman, J. 1988. "On Phrynichus' *Sack of Miletos* and *Phoinissai.*" *Eranos* 86, 15–23.
Roller, L. 1994. "Attis on Greek Votive Monuments." *Hesperia* 63, 245–62.

———. 1996. "Reflections of the Mother of the Gods in Attic Tragedy." In Lane 1996, 305–21.
de Romilly, J. 1958. "L'utilité de l'histoire selon Thucydide." In *Histoire et historiens dans l'antiquité.* Fondation Hardt, entretiens sur l'antiquité classique 4, 41–66. Geneva.
———. 1963. *Thucydides and Athenian Imperialism.* Trans. P. Thody from the French edition of 1947. Oxford.
———. 1995. *Alcibiade, ou les dangers de l'ambition.* Paris.
Rosen, R. M., and J. Farrell, eds. 1993. *Nomodeiktes: Studies in Honor of Martin Ostwald.* Ann Arbor.
Rosenbloom, A. D. 1993. "Shouting 'Fire' in a Crowded Theater: Phrynichus' *Capture of Miletos* and the Politics of Fear in Early Attic Tragedy." *Philologus* 137, 159–96.
———. 1995. "Myth, History, and Hegemony in Aeschylus." In Goff 1995, 91–130.
Rösler, W. 1990. "*Mnemosyne* in the *Symposium.*" In *Sympotica: A Symposium on the Symposion,* O. Murray, ed., 230–37. Oxford.
Rouse, W. H. D. 1902. *Greek Votive Offerings: An Essay in the History of Greek Religion.* Cambridge.
Roussel, P. 1925. "La prétendue défense d'Antiphon." *REA* 27, 5–10.
Ruschenbusch, E. 1956. "Der sogenannte Gesetzcodes vom Jahre 410 v. Chr." *Historia* 5, 123–28.
———. 1958. "ΠΑΤΡΙΟΣ ΠΟΛΙΤΕΙΑ: Theseus, Drakon, Solon und Kleisthenes in Publizistik und Geschichtsschreibung des 5. und 4. Jahrhunderts v. Chr." *Historia* 7, 398–424. Reprinted in Kinzl and Raaflaub 1995, 87–124.
Russell, F. 1994. "A Note on the Athenian Defeat at Notium." *AHB* 8, 35–37.
Rutherford, I. C. 1996. "The New Simonides: Towards a Commentary." *Arethusa* 29, 167–92.
Ryan, F. 1994a. "Thetes and the Archonship." *Historia* 43, 369–72.
———. 1994b. "The Original Date of the δῆμος πληθύων Provisions of *IG* I³ 105." *JHS* 114, 120–34.
Ryder, T. T. B. 1965. *Koine Eirene: General Peace and Local Independence in Ancient Greece.* Oxford.
Sahlins, M. 1985. *Islands of History.* Chicago.
de Ste. Croix, G. E. M. 1954/1955. "The Character of the Athenian Empire." *Historia* 3, 1–41.
———. 1956. "The Constitution of the Five Thousand." *Historia* 5, 1–23.
———. 1972. *The Origins of the Peloponnesian War.* Ithaca.
Sansone, D. 1985a. "The Date of Herodotus' Publication." *ICS* 10, 1–9.
———. 1985b. "Theonoe and Theoclymenus." *Symbolae Osloenses* 60, 17–36.
Scanlon, T. F. 1987. "Thucydides and Tyranny." *ClAnt* 6, 286–301.
———. 1994. "Echoes of Herodotus in Thucydides: Self-Sufficiency, Admiration, and Law." *Historia* 43, 143–76.
Schoene, A. 1866. *Eusebi Chronicorum Canonum quae supersunt.* 2 vols. Reprint Frankfurt, 1967.
Schuller, W. 1974. *Die Herrschaft der Athener im Ersten Attischen Seebund.* Berlin.
Schwartz, E. 1889. "Quellenuntersuchungen zur griechischen Geschichte." *RhM* 44 104–93.

Schwarze, J. 1971. *Die Beurteilung des Perikles durch die attische Komödie und ihre historische und historigraphische Bedeutung. Zetemata* 51. Munich.

Scodel, R. 1980. *The Trojan Trilogy of Euripides. Hypomnemata* 60. Göttingen.

Seager, R., and C. Tuplin. 1980. "The Freedom of the Greeks of Asia: On the Origins of a Concept and the Creation of a Slogan." *JHS* 100, 141–54.

Sealey, R. 1967. *Essays in Greek Politics.* New York.

———. 1973. "The Origins of *Demokratia.*" *CSCA* 6, 253–95.

———. 1975a. "Constitutional Changes in Athens in 410 B.C." *CSCA* 8, 271–95.

———. 1975b. "Pap. Mich. Inv. 5982: Theramenes." *ZPE* 16, 279–88.

———. 1976. *A History of the Greek City States, 700–338 B.C.* Berkeley.

———. 1982. "On the Athenian Concept of Law." *CJ* 77, 289–302.

———. 1984. "The Tetralogies Ascribed to Antiphon." *TAPhA* 114, 71–85.

———. 1987. *The Athenian Republic: Democracy or the Rule of Law?* University Park and London.

Segal, C. 1986. *Interpreting Greek Tragedy: Myth, Poetry, Text.* Ithaca and London.

Shapiro, H.A. 1992. "*Mousikoi Agones:* Music and Poetry at the Panathenaia." In *Goddess and Polis: The Panathenaic Festival in Ancient Athens,* J. Neils, ed., 52–75. Hanover, N.H., and Princeton.

———. 1993. "Hipparchos and the Rhapsodes." In Dougherty and Kurke 1993, 92–107.

———. 1994. "Religion and Politics in Democratic Athens." In Coulson et al. 1994, 123–29.

Shear, T.L., Jr. 1970. "The Monument of the Eponymous Heroes in the Athenian Agora." *Hesperia* 39, 145–222.

———. 1984. "The Athenian Agora: Excavations of 1980–1982." *Hesperia* 53, 1–57.

———. 1993. "The Persian Destruction of Athens: Evidence from the Athenian Agora." *Hesperia* 62, 383–482.

———. 1994. "Ἰσονόμους τ' Ἀθήνας ἐποιησάτην: The Agora and the Democracy." In Coulson et al. 1994, 225–48.

———. 1995. "Bouleuterion, Metroon, and the Archives at Athens." In *Studies in the Ancient Greek Polis,* M.H. Hansen and K. Raaflaub, eds. *Historia* Einzelschrift 95, 157–90. Stuttgart.

Shipley, G. 1987. *A History of Samos.* Oxford.

Shrimpton, G.S., and D.J. McCarger, eds. 1981. *Classical Contributions: Studies in Honour of Malcolm Francis McGregor.* Locust Valley, N.Y.

Siewert, P. 1972. *Der Eid von Plataiai.* Munich.

———. 1977. "The Ephebic Oath in Fifth-Century Athens." *JHS* 97, 102–11.

———. 1979. "Poseidon Hippios am Kolonos und die athenischen Hippeis." In Bowersock et al. 1979, 280–89.

Sinclair, R.K. 1988. *Democracy and Participation in Athens.* Cambridge.

Skias, A.N. 1900. "Ἀνασκαφαὶ παρὰ τὴν Φυλήν." *PAAH* 38–50.

Smith, J.O. 1996. "The High Priests of the Temple of Artemis at Ephesus." In Lane 1996, 323–35.

Snell, B. 1938/1971. *Leben und Meinungen der Sieben Weisen.* 4th ed. Munich.

Sommerstein, A.H. 1977. "Aristophanes and the Events of 411." *JHS* 77, 112–26.

———. 1996. "Aeschylus." In *The Oxford Classical Dictionary.* 3rd ed., S. Hornblower and A. Spawforth, eds., 26–29. Oxford.

Sommerstein, A.H., S. Halliwell, J. Henderson, and B. Zimmermann, eds. 1993. *Tragedy, Comedy and the Polis. Papers from the Greek Drama Conference, Nottingham, 18–20 July 1990*. Bari.

Spence, I.G. 1990. "Perikles and the Defence of Attika During the Peloponnesian War." *JHS* 110, 91–109.

———. 1993. *The Cavalry of Classical Greece: A Social and Military History with particular reference to Athens*. Oxford and New York.

Sprague, R.K., ed. 1972. *The Older Sophists. A complete translation by several hands of the fragments in Die Fragmente der Vorsokratiker edited by Diels-Kranz, with a new edition of Antiphon and of Euthydemus*. Columbia, S.C.

Spyridakis, K. 1935. *Euagoras I von Salamis. Untersuchungen zur Geschichte des Kyprischen Königs*. Stuttgart.

Stadter, P.A., ed. 1973. *The Speeches in Thucydides: A Collection of Original Studies with a Bibliography*. Chapel Hill.

Steiner, D.T. 1994. *The Tyrant's Writ: Myths and Images of Writing in Ancient Greece*. Princeton.

Stone, I.F. 1988. *The Trial of Socrates*. Boston.

Strauss, B.S. 1983. "Aegospotami Reexamined." *AJPh* 104, 24–35.

———. 1986. *Athens After the Peloponnesian War: Class, Faction and Policy 403–386 B.C.* Ithaca and New York.

———. 1993. *Fathers and Sons in Athens: Ideology and Society in the Era of the Peloponnesian War*. Princeton.

Strauss, L. 1964. *The City and Man*. Chicago.

Stroud, R. 1968. *Drakon's Law on Homicide*. University of California Publications: Classical Studies 3. Berkeley.

———. 1971. "Greek Inscriptions: Theozotides and the Athenian Orphans." *Hesperia* 40, 280–301.

———. 1978. "State Documents in Archaic Athens." In *Athens Comes of Age, From Solon to Salamis*, 20–42. Archaeological Institute of America. Princeton.

———. 1979. *The Axones and Kyrbeis of Drakon and Solon*. University of California Publications: Classical Studies 19. Berkeley.

———. 1984. "The Gravestone of Socrates' Friend, Lysis." *Hesperia* 53, 355–60.

———. 1993. "The Sanctuary of Aiakos in the Athenian Agora." Abstract in *AJA* 97, 308–309.

———. 1994a. "The Aiakeion and the Tholos of Athens in *POXY* 2087." *ZPE* 103, 1–9.

———. 1994b. "Thucydides and Corinth." *Chiron* 24, 267–304.

———. 1996. "Law Court or Granary? AIAKOS in the Athenian Agora." Paper delivered on the occasion of the publication of *Agora XXVIII: The Lawcourts at Athens*, sponsored by the American School of Classical Studies at Athens, at the Institute of Fine Arts, New York, May 11.

Taplin, O. 1993. *Comic Angels, and Other Approaches to Greek Drama Through Vase-Painting*. Oxford.

Taylor, M.W. 1991. *The Tyrant Slayers: The Heroic Image in Fifth Century B.C. Athenian Art and Politics*. 2nd ed. Salem, N.H.

Thomas, R. 1989. *Oral Tradition and Written Record in Classical Athens*. Cambridge.

———. 1992. *Literacy and Orality in Ancient Greece*. Cambridge.

———. 1994. "Law and the Lawgiver in the Athenian Democracy." In Osborne and Hornblower 1994, 119–33.

———. 1995. "The Place of the Poet in Archaic Society." In *The Greek World,* A. Powell, ed., 104–29. London and New York.

Thompson, H.A. 1937. "Buildings on the West Side of the Agora." *Hesperia* 6, 1–226.

Thompson, W.E. 1964. "Three Thousand Acharnian Hoplites." *Historia* 13, 400–13.

———. 1967. "Andocides and Hellanicus." *TAPhA* 98, 483–90.

Thomsen, R. 1964. *Eisphora: A Study of Direct Taxation in Ancient Athens.* Copenhagen.

Threpsiades, J., and E. Vanderpool. 1964. "Themistokles' Sanctuary of Artemis Aristoboule." *AD* 19, 26–36.

Toepffer, I. 1889. *Attische Genealogie.* Berlin. Reprint New York, 1973.

Tompkins, D.P. 1972. "Stylistic Characterization in Thucydides: Nicias and Alcibiades." *YClS* 22, 181–214.

———. 1993. "Archidamus and the Question of Characterization in Thucydides." In Rosen and Farrell 1993, 99–111.

Toye, D.L. 1997. "Pherecydes of Syros: Ancient Theologian and Genealogist." *Mnemosyne* 50, 530–60.

Travlos, J. 1971. *Pictorial Dictionary of Ancient Athens.* New York and Washington.

Trendall, A.D. 1991. "Farce and Tragedy in South Italian vase-painting." In *Looking at Greek Vases,* T. Rasmussen and N. Spivey, eds., 151–82. Cambridge.

Trendall, A.D., and T.B.L. Webster. 1971. *Illustrations of Greek Drama.* London.

Tsakmakis, A. 1995. "Das Historische Werke des Stesimbrotos von Thasos." *Historia* 44, 129–52.

Tuplin, C. 1985. "Imperial Tyranny: Some Reflections on a Classical Greek Metaphor." In *Crux: Essays in Greek History Presented to G.E.M. de Ste. Croix,* P.A. Cartledge and F.D. Harvey, eds., 348–75. Exeter and London.

Turner, E.G. 1952. *Athenian Books in the Fifth and Fourth Centuries B.C.* Inaugural Lecture, University College, London.

Tyrrell, W.B. 1984. *Amazons: A Study in Athenian Mythmaking.* Baltimore.

Tyrrell, W.B. and F.S. Brown. 1991. *Athenian Myths and Institutions: Words in Action.* Oxford.

Tzachou-Alexandri, O. 1993. "Personifications of Democracy." In Ober and Hedrick 1993, 149–55.

Ullrich, F. 1846. *Beiträge sur Erklärung des Thukydides.* Hamburg.

Underhill, G.E. 1900. *A Commentary with Introduction and Appendix on the Hellenica of Xenophon.* Oxford.

Vedder, U. 1985. *Untersuchungen zur plastischen Ausstatung attische Grabanlagen des 4. Jhs. v. Chr.* Frankfurt.

Vermaseren, M.J. 1977. *Cybele and Attis: The Myth and the Cult.* London.

Vermeule, E. 1970. "Five Vases from the Grave Precinct of Dexileos." *JDAI* 85, 94–111.

Vernant, J.-P. 1969/1988. "Tensions and Ambiguities in Greek Tragedy." In *Interpretation: Theory and Practice,* 105–21. Baltimore, 1969. Reprinted in Vernant and Vidal-Naquet 1988, 29–48.

———. 1970/1988. "Ambiguity and Reversal: On the Enigmatic Structure of *Oedipus Rex.*" In *Exchanges et Communications: Mélanges offerts à Claude Lévi-Strauss,* 1253–79. Paris, 1970. Trans. in Vernant and Vidal-Naquet 1988, 113–40.

———. 1972/1988. "The Historical Moment of Tragedy in Greece: Some of the Social and Psychological Conditions." Originally in *Antiquitas graeco-romana ac tempora nostra,* 246–50. Prague. Trans. in Vernant and Vidal-Naquet 1988, 23–28.

———. 1979/1988. "The Tragic Subject: Historicity and Transhistoricity." Originally published in French in *Belfagor* 6, 636–42. Trans. in Vernant and Vidal-Naquet 1988, 237–47.

Vernant, J.-P., and P. Vidal-Naquet. 1988. *Myth and Tragedy in Ancient Greece.* Trans. J. Lloyd. New York.

Veyne, P. 1988. *Did the Greeks Believe Their Myths? An Essay on the Constitutive Imagination.* Trans. from the French edition of 1983. Chicago.

Vickers, M. 1987. "Alcibiades on Stage: *Philoctetes* and *Cyclops.*" *Historia* 36, 171–97.

———. 1989a. "Alcibiades on Stage: *Thesmophoriazousae* and *Helen.*" *Historia* 38, 41–65.

———. 1989b. "Alcibiades on Stage: Aristophanes' *Birds.*" *Historia* 38, 267–99.

———. 1993. "Alcibiades in Cloudedoverland." In Rosen and Farrell 1993, 603–18.

———. 1994. "Alcibiades and Critias in the *Gorgias:* Plato's 'Fine Satire.'" *Dialogues d'Histoire Ancienne* 20.2, 85–112.

———. 1997. *Pericles on Stage: Political Comedy in Aristophanes' Early Plays.* Austin.

Vidal-Naquet, P. 1973/1988. "Oedipus in Athens." Originally published as the preface to Sophocles, *Tragédies,* trans. P. Mazon, Paris, 1973. Reprinted in translation in Vernant and Vidal-Naquet 1988, 301–27.

Vlastos, G. 1983/1994. "The Historical Socrates and Athenian Democracy." Originally published in *Political Theory* 2, 495–516. Revised in *Socratic Studies,* M. Burnyeat, ed., 87–108. Cambridge.

de Vries, G.J. 1973. "Mystery Terminology in Aristophanes and Plato." *Mnemosyne* 26, 1–8.

Wade-Gery, H.T. 1932/1958. "Thucydides the son of Melesias." *JHS* 52, 205–27. Reprinted in Wade-Gery 1958, 239–70.

———. 1933. "Classical Epigrams and Epitaphs." *JHS* 53, 71–104.

———. 1936–1937/1958. "Themistokles' Archonship." *ABSA* 37, 263–70. Reprinted in Wade-Gery 1958, 171–79.

———. 1945/1958. "Kritias and Herodes." *CQ* 39, 19–33. Reprinted in Wade-Gery 1958, 271–92.

———. 1958. *Essays in Greek History.* Oxford.

Walbank, M.B. 1978. *Athenian Proxenies of the Fifth Century B.C.* Toronto and Sarasota.

Walker, H.J. 1995. *Theseus and Athens.* Oxford and New York.

Wallace, R.W. 1985. *The Areopagus Council to 307 B.C.* Baltimore and London.

———. 1992. "Charmides, Agariste and Damon: Andokides 1.16." *CQ* 42, 328–35.

———. 1993: "Private Lives and Public Enemies: Freedom of Thought in Classical Athens." In Boegehold and Scafuro 1993, 27–55.

Walters, K.R. 1976. "The 'Ancestral Constitution' and Fourth-Century Historiography in Athens." *AJAH* 1, 129–44.

———. 1983. "Perikles' Citizenship Law." *ClAnt* 2, 314–36.

Wardman, A.E. 1960. "Myth in Greek Historiography." *Historia* 9, 403–13.

Weil, R. 1960. *Aristote et l'histoire: Essai sur la "Politique."* Paris.

———. 1975. "Lire dans Thucydide." In *Le monde grec: pensée, littérature, histoire, documents. Hommages à Claire Préaux,* J. Bingen, G. Cambrier, and G. Nachtergael, eds., 162–68. Brussels.

West, M.L. 1983. *The Orphic Poems.* Oxford.

———. 1992. *Iambi et Elegi Graeci: ante Alexandrum Cantati.* 2 vols. Oxford.

———. 1993. "Simonides Redivivus." *ZPE* 98, 1–14.

Westlake, H.D. 1938. "Alcibiades, Agis, and Spartan Policy." *JHS* 58, 31–40.

———. 1968. *Individuals in Thucydides.* Cambridge.

———. 1971/1989. "Thucydides and the Uneasy Peace—A Study in Political Incompetence." *CQ* 21. Reprinted in Westlake 1989, 84–96.

———. 1975/1989. "Paches." *Phoenix* 29. Reprinted in Westlake 1989, 50–59.

———. 1977/1989. "Thucydides on Pausanias and Themistocles—A Written Source?" *CQ* 27, 95–110. Reprinted in Westlake 1989, 1–18.

———. 1980. "*Lysistrata* and the War." *Phoenix* 34, 38–54.

———. 1981/1989. "Decline and Fall of Tissaphernes." *Historia* 30, 257–79. Reprinted in Westlake 1989, 289–309.

———. 1985/1989. "The Influence of Alcibiades on Thucydides Book 8." *Mnemosyne* 38. Reprinted in Westlake 1989, 154–65.

———. 1989. *Studies in Thucydides and Greek History.* Bristol.

Whitehead, D. 1977. *The Ideology of the Athenian Metic. PCPhS,* Supplement 4. Cambridge.

———. 1980. "The Tribes of the Thirty Tyrants." *JHS* 100, 208–13.

———. 1982–1983. "Sparta and the Thirty Tyrants." *AncSoc* 13/14, 106–30.

———. 1984. "A Thousand New Athenians." *LCM* 9, 8–10.

———. 1986. *The Demes of Attica, 508/7—ca. 250 B.C.: A Political and Social Study.* Princeton.

———, trans. and comm. 1990. *Aineias the Tactician: How to Survive Under Siege.* Oxford.

———. 1993. "Samian Autonomy." In Rosen and Farrell 1993, 321–29.

Winkler, J.J. 1985. "The Ephebes' Song, *Tragôidia* and *Polis.*" *Representations* 11, 26–62.

Winkler, J.J., and F. Zeitlin, eds. 1990. *Nothing to do with Dionysos? Athenian Drama in its Social Context.* Princeton.

Wolff, H.J. 1966. *Die attische Paragraphe.* Weimar.

———. 1970. *"Normenkontrolle" und Gesetzesbegriff in der attischen Demokratie. Untersuchungen zur* γραφὴ παρανόμων. *SHAW,* Phil-hist. Klasse 2. Heidelberg.

Woodhead, A.G. 1954. "Peisander." *AJPh* 132–46.

Woodman, A.J. 1988. *Rhetoric in Classical Historiography.* London and Sydney.

Woodward, A.M. 1956. "Treasure-Records from the Athenian Agora." *Hesperia* 25, 79–121.

Worley, L.J. 1994. *Hippeis, The Cavalry of Ancient Greece.* Boulder.

Wycherley, R.E. 1978. *The Stones of Athens.* Princeton.

Wylie, G. 1986. "What Really Happened at Aegospotami?" *AC* 55, 125–41.

Yunis, H. 1988. *A New Creed: Fundamental Religious Beliefs in the Athenian Polis and Euripidean Drama. Hypomnemata* 91. Göttingen.

———. 1996. *Taming Democracy: Models of Political Rhetoric in Classical Athens.* Ithaca and London.

Zeilhofer, G. 1959. *Sparta, Delphoi und die Amphiktyonen im 5. Jahrhundert vor Christus.* Friedrich-Alexander-Universität dissertation. Erlangen.
Zeitlin, F.I. 1990. "Thebes: Theater of Self and Society in Athenian Drama." In Winkler and Zeitlin 1993, 130–67.
———. 1993. "Staging Dionysus between Thebes and Athens." In *Masks of Dionysus,* T.H. Carpenter and C.A. Faraone, eds., 147–82. Ithaca and London.
Zimmerman Munn, M.L. 1986. "The Zeus Sanctuary on Mt. Kokkygion above Hermion, Argolis." *AJA* 90, 192–93.
Zimmermann, B. 1992. *Dithyrambos. Geschichte einer Gattung. Hypomnemata* 98. Göttingen.
———. 1993. "Das Lied der Polis: Zur Geschichte des Dithyrambos." In Sommerstein et al. 1993, 39–54.

GENERAL INDEX

Abantids, 158, 394n12
Abdemon, 144
Abydos, 75, 152–53, 164
Academy, 36, 201
Acamas, 158
Acastus, 31
accounts and accounting, financial, 71, 77, 82–83, 161, 178, 181, 183–84, 338. *See also* Council, Athenian
Acropolis, 27, 30, 39, 100, 134, 166, 180, 229, 252, 254, 262, 309. *See also* dedications
Adcock, F. E., 383n24, 435n65
adeia, 74
Adeimantus, brother of Plato, 49
Adeimantus, Athenian general, 168, 199, 402n18
Adeimantus, Corinthian general, 54
Adkins, A. W. H., 349n2
Adonis, 384n35
Aeacus and Aeaceum, 189, 269–70 (fig. 8), 299–300, 421–22n38, 422n39
Aegina, 49, 197; Aeginetan standard (*see* Pheidon)
Aegospotami, battle of, 192, 195, 198–200, 205, 223, 232, 407n14
Aenesias, 343–44
Aeschines, 8, 202
Aeschylus, 22, 28–32, 34, 35, 38, 41, 43; depicted in Aristophanes' *Frogs,* 188–88, 193, 286, 404n37, 430n33. Works: *Eleusinians,* 38, 359–60n66; *Eumenides,* 34, 358n55; *Glaucus at Potniae,* 30–32, 356n44; *Persians,* 28–30, 32, 43, 354n28, 355nn36–38, 357n49; *Phineus,* 30–32, 356n42. *See also* Index Locorum
Aetolia, 237
Agamemnon, 16, 317–18, 434n60, 435n66
Agariste, 399n42
agathoi, 55, 77, 220, 290, 294–95, 359n62. See also *kaloi k'agathoi*
Agathon, 51
Agesilaus, 317–20, 327
Agis, 97, 124, 160, 197, 201, 205
agonisma, 315, 433n53
Agora, Athenian, xvi (map 4), 17, 19–21, 28, 171–72, 192, 212, 227–29, 240, 262, 269–71 (fig. 8), 302, 313, 331, 351n12, 405n44, 421n37, 427n19
Agoracritus, 173–74, 400n56
Agoratus, 212–13, 215–16, 227, 266
agraphos nomos, 264, 278, 288, 422n40. *See also* laws of Athens
akoei, 114, 306, 315, 385n43, 429n31. *See also* writing
akribeia, 89, 115, 191–92, 296, 385n46. *See also* expertise
Albini, U., 387n64
Alcibiades, 7–8, 49, 54, 59–60, 75–76, 79, 81, 84, 96–127, 129–34, 136, 139–47, 152–55, 160–79, 184, 188, 190–91, 193–94, 196, 198–99, 202–3, 213–14, 216–17, 232–34, 289–91, 296, 304, 308–11, 320, 322, 335–39, 410n46;

Alcibiades *(continued)*
and Argos, 68, 96, 125, 164, 308, 322, 325, 328–29; and the Athenian empire, 7–8, 59, 75–76, 97–99, 129–31, 153–55, 160–66, 170, 175–8, 202, 214, 217, 232, 308–11, 322, 325, 329, 434n58; changing attitudes toward, 97, 99–100, 103–18, 120–27, 129–34, 139, 141, 144–45, 153, 155, 165–69, 175, 178–9, 184, 191, 193–94, 213–14, 216, 223, 304, 310–12, 322, 329, 333, 336, 434n58, 436nn73–74; and chariot racing, 59–60, 96, 122, 368n31, 387n61, 401n10; his death, 234; and the Erechtheum, 398n37; and Eros, 99, 111, 125–26, 133–34, 169, 174, 188; in modern scholarship, 348n7, 431–32n46; and Mysteries, profanation of the, 105–14, 117–18, 120, 122, 125, 131–33, 168–69, 296; and the oligarchy of 411, 127, 131, 139–47; and Pericles 54, 75, 83, 96, 188, 311, 431–32n46; and Persians, 97, 129–31, 139, 143–45, 162–64, 172–73, 175–6, 179, 196, 203, 213, 232–34, 308, 320, 322, 325, 434n58; his *pthoneros daimon,* 168–69, 290; and Socrates 7–8, 54, 111, 289–91, 311–12, 348n8, 425n33; and Sparta, 96–97, 123–24, 129–30, 133–34, 142, 164, 168, 175; and Themistocles, 320, 435n66; and the Thirty, 220, 232–35; in Thrace, 179, 198–99, 203; and tyranny, 111–20, 122, 125–26, 169, 171, 179, 312. *See also* Andocides; Antiphon; Chalcedon; chronology and dating; Cyzicus; Helen; Herms, mutilation of; Hyperbolus; impiety; Lysistrata; Mysteries; Peisetaerus; Pharnabazus; Plutarch; Thrasybulus; Thucydides; Tissaphernes; youth

Alcibiades the younger, 114, 322, 367n24, 399n42, 436n73

Alcmaeonids, 105, 235, 319, 399n42, 430n35

aletheia, alethes, 15–16, 349n2. *See also* history and historians; truth

Alexander. *See* Paris

allies: Athenian, 34–35, 38, 40, 67–71, 74–76, 82, 95, 97–100, 119, 123–24, 129–30, 141–42, 147, 153, 155, 172, 177–78, 180, 194, 199–200, 203, 216, 280–81, 308, 317, 322–23, 332, 380n5; Persian, 128–30, 141, 143, 154, 176–77, 200, 232, 282; Spartan, 35, 47, 68, 76, 118, 123–24, 129–30, 143–44, 147–48, 162, 169, 176–77, 180, 196, 199, 201, 205–6, 216, 219–20, 232, 236, 242, 280–84, 317–18, 336, 341, 390n22

Allison, J. W., 430n33

allotment, 56, 71, 74, 187, 208, 294

Altar of Twelve Gods, 21, 382n21, 384n35, 400n53

Amazons, 28

Ameipsias, *Connus,* 377n52

Amit, M., 387n1, 396n31, 397nn32–33

amnesty of 403, 274, 279–80, 424n11. *See also* reconciliation

Amorges, 128–29

Amphipolis, 44, 99, 134, 304, 307–9

Amphiptolemopedesistratus, 389n13

Anacreon, 49

anagraphein, 264–69, 274, 276, 422n40

Anaxagoras, 192

ancestral constitution, laws. See *patrios nomos, patrioi nomoi; patrios politeia*

Anderson, J. K., 418n8

Andocides: *Against Alcibiades,* the spurious, 380n2, 384n40, 436n73; in exile, 261–62; family of, 59, 116, 128, 423n8; herms and Mysteries, in affair of, 108, 116, 261–63, 278–79, 284, 290, 300, 433n57; laws and decrees, attention to, 149, 159, 255, 262–69, 273, 277, 278, 304, 327; in *On the Peace with Sparta,* 434n62, 435n70, 438n90; as speechwriter, 11, 249, 273, 280, 321, 327; Themistocles, on the remains of, 438n89. *See also* chronology and dating; impiety; Index Locorum; Thucydides

Andrewes, Antony, 333–35, 347–48n5, 380n2, 388n6, 390n23, 392nn45–46, 394n10, 395n18, 395–96n23, 398n34, 402–3n19, 408n25, 411n52, 414n34, 415n40, 428n22, 429n28, 431n42, 438n83, 439n91

Androcles, 139, 167

Andromachus, 399n42

Andron, 209–10, 410n40

Andros, 177

Androtion, 209–10; his *Atthis,* 209, 327, 410n40

Antenor, 351nn11–12, 394n12

Antigenes, 337–39, 401n6, 402n17

Antiochus, 41, 339
Antiphon: and Alcibiades, 112–13, 141, 167–68, 384n38, n40; and the Four Hundred, 103, 141, 146, 151, 186, 210, 272, 289, 302, 404n31; identity of, 381n16; as speech-writer, 2, 71, 100–3, 191, 271, 273, 289, 302, 310, 371n11, 376n45, 403n25. *See also* Index Locorum; Thucydides
Antiphon, half-brother of Plato, 49, 301
Antiphon, Athenian archon, 332
Antisthenes, 384n38
Anytus, 160–63, 209, 217, 235, 254, 282, 290; and Herodotus, 117–18, 334; and Socrates, 254, 285, 290, 425n22, 426n34
Apatouria, 185, 335, 403n24
Aphrodite, 121, 172, 384n35
apographe, 403nn25–26
Apollo, 25, 58, 158, 205–6, 226, 283–84, 286, 288, 300; Daphnephoros, 394n12. *See also* dedications; Delos; Delphi
Apollodorus, 386n51
Arabs, 144
"Archaeology." *See* Thucydides
Archedemus, 183, 190
Archelaus, 153, 203, 316, 405n45, 433n57
Archestratus, 202, 410n44
Archidamus, 68, 321
Archinus, 209, 254, 257–58, 279, 424n11
Archippus, 436n73
archives, 2, 149, 171, 191–92, 267, 278, 284, 327, 399n48
archon: Athenian, 33, 58, 61–62, 89, 104, 247, 256, 265–67, 283, 332, 357n52, 390n25; Basileus, 102, 285; list of, 41, 88–89; Polemarch, 325, 360n67. *See also* Antigenes; Antiphon; Callias; chronology and dating; Eucleides; Euctemon; Hippocleides; Lysagoras; Menon; Phallenius; Pythodorus; Themistocles; Xenaenetus
Arctonesus, 400n54
Areopagus, Council of, 134, 264, 267
Ares, 30
arete, ii, 42, 50–51, 56, 58–59, 72, 77–79, 83, 89, 96, 101, 226, 251, 257, 272, 310; in battle, 53, 56, 83, 182, 236, 239, 251, 314, 367n28, 415n39. See also *aristeia; aristoi*
Arginusae, battle of, 175, 181–84, 187, 190–91, 194, 196, 207, 211, 226, 230, 232, 250, 252, 256, 272, 302, 335–38, 359n62, 407n14, 426n4
Argonauts, 31, 172
Argos and Argives, 34, 38, 40, 56, 96, 99, 116, 122–23, 125–26, 164, 235, 308, 317, 321–22, 385n47, 397n32, 435n70. *See also* Alcibiades; Hera
Aristagoras, 43, 355n35
Aristarchus, 404n31
aristeia, 24–26, 54, 353n23
Aristeus, 54
Aristides, 26, 75–76, 85, 109, 135, 353n24, 354n27; Aelius, 361n72
Aristippus, 282
aristocracy, Athenian, 46, 48–50, 53, 62–63, 64, 66–68, 72–73, 76–77, 90, 100, 103, 106–10, 128, 131, 135, 139–40, 142, 157, 185, 208, 223, 226, 229, 236, 238, 253, 258–60, 271–72, 277–78, 295–96, 307, 310; beyond Athens, 64, 66–69, 142, 235, 307, 308; definition of, 48–50, 62–63, 365n7; Ionian, 69, 130, 142. See also *aristoi*; *aristokratia;* Council, Athenian; *hetaireiai*; oligarchs; *synomosiai*; Thirty, the
Aristocrates, 146–47, 151, 159–60, 181, 365n6, 401n10, 426n4
Aristogeiton. *See* tyrant-slayers, the
aristoi, 48, 60, 62, 66, 78, 81, 138, 186, 188, 190
aristokratia, 365n6
Ariston, 49
Aristophanes, 2, 21, 27, 35, 52, 55, 73, 76–77, 79, 81, 83, 85–87, 90–91, 104, 136, 158–59, 166, 188, 192–94, 210, 296–98, 302–3, 307, 322, 326, 329, 372n17; and Socrates, 190, 286, 288–89. Works: *Banqueters,* 79; *Birds,* 86, 95, 124–26, 131, 172, 223, 297, 387n66; *Clouds,* 79, 81, 288, 367n24, 369n36, 382n24; *Frogs,* 8, 35, 158, 175, 182, 188–90, 193–94, 221, 286, 302, 338–39; *Knights,* 64, 73–74, 77, 81, 85, 90, 98, 119, 128, 202, 302; *Lysistrata,* 134, 391n36; *Peace,* 55; *Thesmophoriazusae,* 117, 133, 333–34; *Triphales,* 104, 202; *Wasps,* 81, 82, 90–91, 98, 223, 302. *See also* Index Locorum
Aristophon, 259
Aristoteles son of Timocrates, 204–5, 221, 225

Aristotle, 2–3, 9, 20, 21, 49, 69, 73, 97, 137, 140, 148, 182, 190, 193, 219, 223, 227, 240, 254, 256, 275, 283, 293, 328–29; *Constitution of the Athenians*, 7, 73, 103, 150, 161, 209, 247, 250, 341, 389n18, 410n40. *See also* history and historians; Index Locorum
Artaxerxes I, 43, 128
Artaxerxes II, 176–77, 195–97, 200, 203–4, 206, 232–34, 281, 316, 320, 327, 405–6n4. *See also* Cyrus the younger; Darius II
Artemis 58, 172, 325–27; Agrotera, 326, 360n67, 438n86; Aristoboule, 24, 325; Boulaia, 326, 438n86; Cybele/Mother of the Gods, syncretism with, 172–73, 400n55, 438n89; of Ephesus, 172, 178, 216, 325–27, 400n55, 438nn87–89; shrine of, in Munychia, 238–39. *See also* Aulis; dedications; Mother of the Gods
Artemisium, battle of, 26–27, 30, 354n31
Asia and Asia Minor, 29, 127–29, 131, 140–41, 144, 152, 154, 163, 172–76, 178, 196, 198, 203–4, 232, 281, 284, 316, 318–20, 325–27. *See also* Ionia; Mother of the Gods; Sardis
Asmis, E., 404n36
Asopos, 21, 31, 352n15
Aspasia, 258, 260
Aspendus, 152
Assembly, Athenian, 34–36, 46, 64–65, 68–74, 76, 78–81, 83, 86, 87, 91, 99–102, 105–6, 111, 113, 134, 137–40, 147–48, 153, 156–57, 159, 166, 168, 170–71, 179, 182, 184–88, 202, 206, 210–12, 215, 217, 244, 251, 253, 255, 257, 260, 263, 270, 296, 298, 302, 304, 307–8, 323–24, 381n12; at Colonus, 140, 148, 253, 255; at Munychia, 212, 215, 217, 219–20, 253, 342–43; at Samos, 144; tribal, 208.
Athena, 30, 34, 121, 156, 165, 167, 216, 252, 312–13, 389n12; Nike, 84. *See also* Panathenaea; Victory
Athenaeus, 166, 171. *See also* Index Locorum
Athenian democracy. *See* democracy
Athenian empire, 1–4, 6–10, 12, 17, 29–32, 36, 38, 40–41, 43–44, 46–48, 54, 58, 64–65, 67–69, 73, 75–76, 78, 80, 82, 85, 91, 95–100, 118–19, 128–31, 134–35, 141–43, 145, 154–55, 156–57, 161, 163, 165, 170, 174, 180, 183, 201–3, 210, 214, 251, 271–73, 296–97, 304, 307–11, 316–17, 322–24, 326, 331–32, 347n2, 430n33, n36; creation of, 22, 27–32, 36, 38, 40–43, 357n49; destruction of, 2, 5–6, 9, 95, 195, 206, 214–17, 281, 310–11; recovery of, 310, 316–17, 322–24, 326–27, 437n81; relationship to Persian empire, 10, 28–32, 36, 38, 43–44, 127–30, 141, 163–64, 173–77, 179, 196, 308, 322, 324, 326–27, 333, 437n81; tyranny of, 70, 76, 119, 122; vulnerability of, 44, 70, 73, 83–85, 87, 90–91, 95, 99–101, 118–19, 121–24, 127, 129–30, 138–43, 147–48, 155, 176–77, 180–81, 191, 193–94, 202, 213, 308, 316, 326–27. *See also* Alcibiades; allies; democracy; imperialism; navy; revenue; Thucydides; tribute
athletes and athletic competition, 23–26, 49, 51, 56, 59–60, 78, 290, 353n24
atimia, 191
Atossa, 29
Atthidographers and *Atthides*, 278, 327, 386n51, 389n17, 410n40, 423n8, 439n91. *See also* Androtion; Cleidemus; Hellanicus; Phanodemus
Attica, 21, 26, 27–28, 32, 36, 38, 41, 47, 52, 58, 89, 108, 116, 121, 145, 147, 151, 154, 205–6, 217, 231, 235, 238, 241, 243–44, 255, 259–60, 265, 288, 301, 316; invasions of, 53, 68, 76–77, 123, 125, 197, 201, 241–42, 321, 438n82. *See also* Atthidographers; Decelea
Attis, 132, 384n35, 388n10
audits. *See* accounts and accounting, financial; Council, Athenian
Aulis, 318, 326–27
Aurenche, O., 383n28
Austin, N., 388n10, 389n12
autokrator, 99, 168, 178
Autolycus, 51, 290–91, 426n34
autonomy, 142, 163, 219, 221, 308, 396–97n31, 418n5
auxesis, 433n56
Avery, H. C., 407n22, 410n40
Axiochus, 75, 168, 177, 410n47
axones, 265, 267, 270

Babylon, 281
Bacchylides, 23
Badian, E., 341, 352n15, 361n70

Balcer, J. M., 387n1
barbarians, 28, 36, 39, 42–43
Basileus. See archon; Stoa
Bean, G. E., 400n55
Beloch, K. J., 335–38, 343, 371n14, 417n54
beltistoi, 66
Bendis, 51, 238–39
Beschi, L., 402n16
Bithynia, 163, 203, 232
Black Sea, 75, 152, 154, 156, 201
Bloch, H., 439n91
Bloedow, E., 322, 348n7
Blumenthal, H., 426n34
Boardman, J., 431n50
Boedeker, Deborah, 356n46, 362n76
Boegehold, A. L., 363n79, 393n49, 399n48
Boeotia and Boeotians, 21–22, 31, 34, 39, 63, 91, 116, 135, 206, 280, 283, 317, 321, 323, 352n15, 360n69, 390n22; support of Athenian exiles, 229, 231–32, 241. *See also* Sparta; Thebes
Boeotius, 338, 394n7, 396n31, 401n1
books, ii, 87, 105, 117, 192, 296–97, 301–4, 323, 427n7, 438n87
Boreas and the Boreads, 26, 30–32, 38, 354n30, 356nn42–43
Bosporus, 154, 163, 203
Bouleuterion. *See* Council-House, Athenian
boulomenos, ho, 70–71, 82, 372n16
Bourriot, F., 365n12
Bowie, E. L., 353n21
Bradeen, D. W., 359n62
Brandwood, L., 348n8, 417n1
Brasidas, 304, 307–9
Brickhouse, T. C., and N. D. Smith, 348n8, 424n21, 426n1
Bruce, I. A. F., 439n91
Brunnsåker, S., 351–52n12
Brunt, P. A., 431n43
Buck, R. J., 352n15, 409n39
Buckler, J., 341
Bugh, G., 368n35
burial, 20, 36–38, 52–53, 56. *See also* funeral oration
Burkert, W., 382n21, 383n24, n26, 400n52
Busolt, G., 335
Byzantium, 32, 154, 163, 164–65, 201, 203, 232, 335–36

Cadoux, T. J., 352n13, 378n65
calendar. *See* sacrifices
Calliades, 211
Callias, Athenian archon, 337–38, 402n18
Callias decrees, 373n25
Callias son of Hipponicus, 51, 112–13, 167, 263, 278–79, 304, 423n8, 423–24n9, 424n10
Callicrates, 56
Callicratidas, 179–81, 196, 336–38, 402n18
Callimachus, 275
Callipides, 166
Callistratus, 339
Callixeinus, 185–87, 192, 207, 266, 272, 410n40, 423n3
Calydnos, 407n14
Camarina, 119
Camp, J. M., 393n49, 421n34
Cardia, 153
Cargill, J., 437n81
Caria, 165, 196–97, 336
Carter, L. B., 371n15, 389n16
Carthage, 98, 203
Cartledge, P., 348n7, 370n8, 424n13, 433n57, 434n58
Casson, L. 364n3
Castriota, D., 354nn32–33, 355nn34–35, n37
Catana, 35
cavalry, Athenian 53, 62–63, 77, 90, 140, 160, 180, 390n24; Boeotian, 63; Peloponnesian, 63; Persian, 31; Syracusan, 56; and the Thirty, 226, 231, 237, 240–41, 249, 284
Cawkwell, G., 380n2, 404n32
Cephallenia, 281
Cephisophon, 417n54
Ceramic Gulf, 165, 197
Ceryces, 278, 423nn8–9
Chaerephon, 288
Chalcidice, 163
Chalcis and Chalcidians, 21, 39, 157–58, 360n69, 394n12
Chalcedon, 79, 154, 163, 201, 335–36; treaty of, 163, 172, 308, 396–97n31
Chamaeleon, 400n50
Chambers, Mortimer, 332, 352n17
Charicles, 122, 204, 221, 224
Charmides, 49–50, 59, 222, 239, 253
Charminos, 334
Charon, boatman of Hades, 158
Charon of Lampsacus, 41, 435n65
Chersonese, 179, 198

Chios and Chians, 129, 142, 160, 165, 180, 189, 196, 336, 388n7, 395n20, 397n32, 404n39 406n12, 431n39
choregia and *choregoi,* 58, 258, 352n18, 355n36, 357n52
chorus, 17–18, 21, 26–27, 33, 35, 37, 55, 58–59, 61, 117, 125–26, 132, 169, 172, 182, 187, 190, 193–94, 286, 313. *See also* dance; dithyramb; drama; poetry; song
chresmologoi. See oracles
chrestoi, 57, 62, 66, 216
Christ, M.R., 383n33
chronology and dating: of accession of Artaxerxes II, 405–6n4; of Alcibiades' career, 335–39, 395n18, 395–96n23, 398n37, 402n15; of Andocides 2, *On His Return,* 407n14; of Aristophanes' *Thesmophoriazusae,* 333–34; of Attic inscriptions, 331–32, 406n11; establishment of, 41, 88–89, 333; of Euripides' *Helen,* 333–34; general problems of, 10, 331–44; of Spartan ephors, 343–44; of Spartan naval commanders, 337–38; of the Thirty, 195, 340–44, 413n15; Thucydides' method of, 343–44; of Thucydides' "Pentacontaetia," 39–40, 331–44, 358n55, 360–61n70; Xenophon's inadequacy in, 335, 340, 343–44. *See also* Apollodorus; archon; Eusebius; Herodotus, time of writing; Hyperbolus; Thucydides, time of writing
Chroust, A.-H., 424n21, 431n49
Chrysogonus, 160
Chrysopolis, 154
Cilicia, 281
Cimon, 27–28, 31, 34, 38, 39, 75, 109, 282, 304, 354–55n34, 408n29, 430n35, n37
citizens and citizenship: Athenian, 36–38, 40, 46, 51, 59, 62–67, 72–73, 77–78, 82, 102–3, 105, 111, 136–40, 146–48, 150, 155–57, 160, 162, 180, 187, 193, 200, 208–10, 220, 223–24, 229–31, 237, 250–61, 263–64, 295, 299, 359n62, 394n15; granted to foreigners, 180, 185, 200, 250–52, 256–58; granted to slaves, 180, 185, 193, 250, 256–57, 337; limitations on, 138–40, 146–48, 150, 156, 225, 229–30, 244, 250–56, 258–61; numbers of, 62, 64, 138–39, 223, 225, 229–30, 254, 258; Periclean law on, 259–60 ; Phormisius' proposal on, 251, 254–56, 258–59. *See also* hoplites; naturalization; *politeia; thetes; zeugitai*
civil war: Athenian, 3–5, 7, 10, 77, 95, 160, 218, 237–44, 247, 249–50, 274, 281, 295, 316; at Colophon, 128; at Corcyra, 5; at Elis, 281; at Samos, 142; at Thasos, 308–9. See also *stasis;* Thirty, the
Clairmont, C., 351n9, 358–59nn61–62, 367n24
Classen, J., and J. Steup, 433n54
Clazomenae and Clazomenians, 399n47
Clearchus, 232–33
Cleidemus, 327
Cleigenes, 422n3
Cleinias, 410n47
Cleinias decree, 371n15, 409n34, n36
Cleippides, 394n15
Cleisthenes: *nomothetes* (?) of late-5th c. (*see* Cleigenes); reforms of, 18, 21, 46, 137, 150, 210, 225, 251, 297, 426n6
Cleitophon, 137, 189, 209–10, 385n45, 390n20
Cleocritus, 341
Cleomenes, 210, 412n13
Cleon, 44, 72–77, 79–85, 90–91, 96, 98, 109, 118–19, 140, 147, 170, 202, 207, 258, 302, 371n14, 372n17
Cleophon, 155–60, 179, 181–83, 188, 190, 202–3, 211, 251, 253, 258, 260, 286, 334, 381n14, 437n80; executed, 207, 210, 221, 223, 266
Cleostratus, 397n32
Clinton, K., 413n22, 421n35, 423n4
Cloché, P., 416n54, 417n2, 418n8, 424n11
Cobet, J., 363n78
Cohen, E.E., 364n3
coinage, 163–64 (fig. 4a[-]b), 180, 183, 309, 331–32, 397n31, 411n52
Cole, T., 349n2, 359n63, 375n39, 376n45, 412n13
Collingwood, R.G., 363–64n80
Colonus, 140, 148, 255
Colophon, 128
comedy, 2, 8, 10, 33, 34, 50, 55, 64, 71–74, 79, 81, 82, 91, 111, 133–34, 158–59, 171, 190, 194, 258, 260, 292, 297, 310, 358n60. *See also* Ameipsias; Archippus; Aristophanes; Cratinus; Eupolis; Pherecrates; Phrynichus; Plato
commissions. *See* Council, Athenian

Connor, W. R., 348n5, 352n13, 355n34, 357n54, 370n3, 372n20, 383n31, 383n33, 424n21
Conon, 179–80, 184, 196, 199–201, 316, 322, 336, 401n10, 402n18, 433n58, 436n73, 437n81
conspiracy:; of 415, 104–7, 109–10, 113, 116; of 411, 131, 135, 138–39, 142–43, 202–3, 207, 211, 213, 262; anti-democratic, 89–91, 219; anti-oligarchic, 212–14, 217; with Persians, 26, 91, 128, 131, 139, 141, 179. See also *hetaireiai; synomosiai*
constitution: Athenian, 65–66, 135–37, 140–41, 148, 150, 206, 209–10, 222–23, 247–55, 257, 263–65, 269–70, 392n45, 393n50; definition of, 136–37, 250–51, 261; Spartan, 226–27, 288, 413n18. *See also* Aristotle; democracy; Draco; Five Thousand, the; Four Hundred, the; history and historians; laws of Athens; *patrios politeia; politeia;* Pseudo-Xenophon; Solon; Thirty, the
Corcyra, civil war in, 5
Corinth and Corinthians, 31–32, 54, 105, 123, 135, 206, 280, 317, 321, 356n46, 428n24, 430n34
Corinthian Gulf, 281
Corinthian War, 317, 319, 323–24, 436n75, 437n81
Cos, 337
Costa, E. A., 391n35, 406n11
Council, Athenian: in 415, 105–6, 122, 139; in 413–11, 134, 140, 145–46, 148–49, 221, 261, 266, 272; in 403, 261–67, 269–70, 272, 274; in 396–95, 319, 323–24; aristocratic tendencies of, 62, 68, 70, 134, 139–40, 208, 211–12, 219, 256, 395n16, 409n37; audits by, 82, 338; closed sessions of, 319, 434n62; commissions and committees of, 62, 71–72, 134, 149, 157, 208, 274; cults of, 267, 326–27; documents, curation of by, 267, 421n33; duties of, 34, 37, 68, 70–72, 74, 79, 134, 159, 184–87, 202, 207, 212, 217, 219, 257, 262–64, 266–67, 278; Four Hundred, under the, 138, 140, 143, 146, 148–49, 159, 334; judicial powers of, 105–8, 151, 159, 184, 207–8, 212, 217, 221–22, 224, 263–64, 278, 409n34, nn36–37; powers of, limited, 159, 270, 409n37; selective allotment to, 208, 256, 409n37; testimony heard by, 91, 113, 116–17, 168, 212, 216, 221, 262, 264, 277, 315, 323, 326, 386n51; Thirty, under the, 207, 222, 224, 229–30, 240, 303. *See also* Areopagus; Four Hundred, the; laws of Athens; *nomothetai; probouloi; syngrapheis;* Thirty, the
Council-House, Athenian, 149, 171–72, 174, 240, 267, 271 (fig. 8), 302; new, 171
courts. *See* law courts
Craik, E. M., 387n66
Cratesippidas, 337, 397n32
Cratippus, 433n55, 437n80, 439n91
Cratinus, 361n70
Crawley, Richard, 306, 431n52
"criminals", 72, 137, 189, 222–25. See also *kakonomia; poneroi*
Critias, 8, 49–50, 59, 108, 166, 190, 204–5, 208, 214, 251, 253, 298, 300, 303–4, 361n70, 376n45, 407n22, 408n29; as poet, 50, 226; and Socrates, 224, 289, 298, 311, 425n33; and Sparta, 204–5, 208, 214, 226–27, 232, 234–37, 387n64; and the Thirty, 220–22, 224–27, 230–32, 234–39, 242, 259, 272, 302–4, 341. *See also* Thirty, the
Croesus, 43, 44, 56, 115, 350n5, 400n55
Ctesias, 176, 282, 436n72, 437n81. *See also* history and historians
Cybele, 132, 172–74, 327, 384n35, 400nn52–55, 438n87. *See also* Kybebe; Mother of the Gods
Cyme, 178, 336
Cyprus, 30, 39, 144, 165, 199–200, 203, 205, 216, 316, 407n14
Cyrene, 201, 407n14
Cyrus the Great, 115, 437n81
Cyrus the younger: arrested by Artaxerxes, 197, 200, 202, 204, 206; attacks Artaxerxes, 195, 281–84, 316, 326; and Spartans, 176–77, 179–80, 194–97, 200, 206, 219, 232–34, 236, 281–83, 316, 336–38, 397–98n33
Cyzicus, 153–54, 164, 309; battle of, 154, 160, 162, 172, 232, 335, 377n54; Mother of the Gods at, 172

dadouchos, 112, 278
daimon. *See* Alcibiades; Socrates

Damastes, 41
dance, 10, 169, 313. *See also* chorus; drama; orchestra
Darius I, 29
Darius II, 128, 141, 143–44, 155, 163–64, 173, 175–77, 179; death of, 176, 195–97, 308, 341, 397n32, 401n3, 405n4–5, 436n72. *See also* Artaxerxes; Cyrus; Parysatis; Persians; Pharnabazus; Tissaphernes
Davies, J. K., 364n3, 365nn6–8, 368n32, 369n36, 378n65, 387n61, 396n25, 423n9, 431n44
Day, J. W., 350–51n9, 361n72
Decelea, 25, 56, 123–24, 128, 140, 147, 150–51, 154, 160, 169, 182, 197
dedications, 26, 56, 88; on the Acropolis, 39, 60, 180, 183; to Apollo, 25, 32, 205–6; to Artemis, 24, 216, 325–26, 438n84, n87; to the Mother of the Gods, 171–74, 327
dekazein, 161–62, 396n25
Delebecque, É., 388nn10–11, 402n16, 414n26, 417n2
Delian League, 30, 75, 355n40
Delium, battle of, 360n66, n69
Delos, 58
Delphi, 25, 40, 86, 205, 253, 283, 286, 300, 353n24, 354n26, 408n29
Demaenetus, 434n62, 437n79
demagogues, 71–75, 77, 81, 85, 91, 96, 98, 106, 109–10, 118, 134–35, 139, 155–56, 158, 160, 162, 166, 202, 210, 253, 295, 310, 372n20, 394n15. *See also* Androcles; Cleon; Cleophon; Hyperbolus
Demaratus, 240
demes, 74, 208, 255–56, 264, 266
Demeter, 105, 112–13, 132–33, 169, 172. *See also* Ceryces; Dadouchos; Eleusis; Hierophant; Mysteries
democracy, Athenian, 1, 3, 5–12, 17–18, 22, 26, 33, 32, 33, 35, 36, 38, 39, 44, 46–49, 51–54, 57, 60, 64–91, 95, 97, 98, 103, 109, 111, 114–19, 120, 131, 138, 139, 142–44, 146, 150–51, 155–60, 170, 179, 180, 183, 187–89, 192, 194, 203, 205–17, 221, 230–31, 235–36, 238, 247–73, 278–80, 287, 289–91, 295–97, 302, 304, 309, 323–25; celebrations of 9–10, 17–18, 27, 36, 39–41, 174, 310, 312–14, 350nn7–8, 369–70n2; creativity, as incentive for, 1–3, 6, 8–12, 47–48, 57, 78–83, 88–89, 95–96, 101–3, 114–17, 135, 137, 149–50, 170, 191–92, 247–49, 259–61, 263–67, 271–72, 278, 296–97, 304, 323–24; criticism of, 3, 47–48, 50–53, 64–67, 72, 76–80, 83, 87, 103, 123, 131, 134–37, 175, 187, 193–94, 225, 236, 243–44, 248, 251, 254–55, 259–61, 272, 287, 297, 310; origins of, 3, 9, 17–18, 46, 137, 157–58, 260, 264–65, 270–71, 313–14; overthrow of, 5–8, 9, 48, 95, 97, 103, 106, 108, 110, 112, 116, 118, 127, 131, 138–40, 142, 159, 192, 202, 206–20, 223, 227–28, 257, 272, 295, 333–34; piety of, 104–5 120–22, 125–26, 157–59, 162, 168, 170, 271, 277–78; restoration of, 6–10, 143–44, 149–51, 153, 155–56, 218, 236, 240, 247–50, 252–56, 261, 265, 272, 273, 279–80, 283, 295–96, 393nn50–51; safeguards of, 68, 70, 72–73, 76, 104, 134–35, 159–60, 170, 179, 188–90, 193–94, 202, 206–8, 210, 255, 257, 261, 265, 269, 272, 284, 290, 312, 323, 409n37, 431n48; tyranny of, 70, 76–77, 118–19, 142. *See also* Athenian empire; citizens; conspiracy; demagogues; *demokratia; demos;* Four Hundred, the; Herodotus; history and historians; law courts; pay; Theramenes; Thirty, the; Thucydides; tyrant-slayers, the; writing
demokratia, 18, 350nn7–8, 365n6, 369n2
Demophanes. *See* Demophantus
Demophantus, 159, 395n17, 422n3
Demophon, 158
demos: Athenian (*see* democracy); Milesian, 197; Samian, 142–43, 215
Demosthenes the general, 64, 73, 77, 81, 381n12
Demosthenes the orator, 265, 439n91
Demus, step-brother of Plato, 49
Detienne, M., 349n2, 382n22
Develin, R., 373n29
Dewald, Carolyn, 350n5, 362n75
Dexander, 69
Dexileos, 313–14 (fig. 11), 431n50, 436n75
Deyhle, W., 351n12, 394n12
diamnemoneusai, 306, 429n31. *See also* writing
Dicaearchus, 193
Dillery, J., 347n4, 439n91

Dindymus, Mount, 154, 172
diobelia, 156–58, 162, 183, 396n26, 403n23, 406n14
Diocles, decree of, 265–67, 420n29
Diocles, son of Zacorus, 278, 423n9
Diodorus, 155, 162, 166, 168, 198–99, 219, 234, 250, 280, 282, 342; confuses Thrasyllus and Thrasybulus, 395n20, n22, 403n29. *See also* Index Locorum
Diodotus, 381n8
Diogenes Laertius, 284, 301. *See also* Index Locorum
Diognetus, 106, 243
Diomedes, horses of, 387n61
Diomedon, 181, 402n18
Dionysia, 21, 23, 33–35, 51, 55, 61, 121–22, 159, 352n13, 357n54, 380n7
Dionysius of Halicarnassus, 251, 433n55
Dionysius of Syracuse, 434n61
Dionysodorus, 211–14, 231, 342, 410n47
Dionysus, 33, 134, 158, 171; in Aristophanes' *Frogs,* 189–90, 193, 338; theater of, 36
Diopeithes, 86. *See also* impiety
Diotimus, 213
Dipylon gates, 20, 36
dithyramb, 21, 27, 33–34, 61, 352n13
Diyllus, 386n51
documents. *See* archives; *syngraphe*; *syngrapheis*; writing
Donaldson, J. W., 356n41
Donlan, W., 365n9
Dougherty, C., 357n51
Dover, Kenneth J., 367n28, 377–78n58, n59, 381n12, 385n43, 405n49, 429n28
Dow, S., 413n22, 421n34
Draco, 102–3, 149–50, 263–65, 267, 270, 272, 297, 426n6; "constitution" of, 382n19
Dracontides, decree of, 220, 253
drama, 3, 10, 33–38, 40, 42, 51, 78, 96, 118 132, 135, 166, 185–88, 191, 292, 294, 328, 333, 357n54, 358n60. *See also* comedy; tragedy
Dubberstein, W. H. *See* Parker, Richard
dunatoi, 57, 62, 138
Dunbar, N., 387n66
Duris, 166, 398n39

Edmonds, J. M., 389n13, n15
Edmunds, L., 428n26, 431–32n52, 435n67
Eetionia, 146–47
Egypt and Egyptians, 34, 132, 144, 155, 165, 200, 281
Ehrenberg, V., 350n4, 351n11, 370n4, 380n8
Ehrhardt, C., 406n9, 409n39
eikoste, 388n3, 394n9
Eion, 27, 31, 39, 282
eisphora, 74, 100, 131, 162, 180, 250, 381n12, 396n26
Elaphostictus, 216, 411nn52–53
Elephenor, 158, 394n12
Eleusis and Eleusinians, 110–12, 117, 133, 168–69, 194, 278, 341, 423–24n9; the Thirty at, 231, 237–38, 240–41, 244, 283–84, 293, 313. *See also* Ceryces; Dadouchos; Demeter; Eumolpidae; Hierophant; Mysteries
eleutheroi, 216
Eleven, the, 71, 222, 230–31, 244, 287
Elis and Eleans, 206, 280–81, 284, 317
Ellis, W. M., 348n7
Empedocles, 78
Endius, 343–44
ephebes, 145
Ephesus, 161, 172–73, 177–78, 196, 216, 232, 325–27, 337, 411n52
Ephialtes, 18, 46, 267
ephors: as committee of Athenian oligarchs, 208, 220; Spartan, 343–44, 412n13
Ephorus, 233–34
Epicerdes, 407n14
Epichares, 424n11
Epigenes, 398n37, 422n3
Epilycus, 128
epistates, 186–87
Eponymous Heroes, 264, 266, 268–70 (fig. 8), 300, 420n26, 421n37, 421–22n38, 422n39
Er, tale of, 239, 416n46
Erasinides, 181, 183–84, 190, 402n18
Erechtheum, 166, 398n37
Erechtheus, 26, 30
Eretria, 21, 43, 158, 172, 394n12
Erianthus, 219
Eros, 7, 99, 111, 125–26, 134, 169, 174, 188, 290, 326, 380–81n8, 384n35, 387n66, 426n34
Etna, Mount, 434n61
Euagoras, 144, 199–200, 316, 391n35

Euboea and Euboeans, 21, 39, 75, 145, 147–48, 153–54, 157–58, 180, 374n30, 394n12
Euboule, 117, 326, 334
Eucleides: Athenian archon, 256–57, 265–66; Athenian general, 158; Megarian, 300
Eucrates, 106, 211, 231
Euctemon, 338
eugeneia, 50
Eumolpidae, 278, 423–24n9
Euphemus, 119
Eupolis, 297, 361n70, 372n17; *Baptae*, 133; *Demes*, 135, 389n13; *Flatterers*, 377n52. *See also* Index Locorum
euporeia, euporein, euporoi, 57, 101, 367n24
Euripides, 2, 8, 35–36, 121–22, 133, 172, 189, 326, 329, 437n80; a character in Aristophanes' *Frogs*, 189–93; his epitaph, 358n60. Works: *Alexander*, 121; *Andromeda*, 297; *Antiope*, 405n45; *Bacchae*, 172, 397n31; *Electra*, 35; *Helen*, 132–33, 172, 333–34; *Hippolytus*, 326; *Orestes*, 133; *Palamedes*, 386n59; *Phoenician Women*, 403n29; *Suppliant Women*, 38, 360n66, 403n29; *Trojan Women*, 121, 385n46. *See also* Index Locorum
Eurybates, 56, 353n24
Eurymedon, 39
Euryptolemus, 176, 186–88, 192, 272, 302, 404nn31–32
Eusebius, 386n51
Euthydemus, 231, 297, 303, 304, 410n47, 414n28
Euthyphro, 286, 289. *See* Plato, *Euthyphro*
Evans, J. A. S., 362n76, 363n78
exile and exiles, 11, 20, 26, 45, 97–8, 106, 112, 116–17, 123–25, 127, 132, 139, 142–44, 151, 153, 164, 166, 179, 191, 194, 204–9, 214, 223, 261–62, 281, 294, 302, 304, 307–10, 344, 397n32, 399n47, 430n35; recalls or returns from, 153, 166, 168, 172, 206–9, 221, 235–36, 244, 249–54, 262, 295, 303, 307, 310, 340, 430n35, 431n42. ; Thirty, fleeing the, 224–25, 230–36, 238, 248, 274, 336, 339. *See also* Alcibiades; Andocides; Critias; Hermocrates; Hyperbolus; Pasippidas; Piraeus; Thrasybulus; Themistocles; Thucydides; Xenophon
expertise, 17, 85, 87–89, 99, 115, 118, 124, 136, 191–92, 203, 276, 278, 285, 286, 289, 293, 303, 310, 318, 323, 327–28. See also *akribeia;* sophists

Favorinus, 284
Fehling, D., 362n74
Ferguson, W. S., 335–38, 394n10, 396n23, 398n37, 421n34
festivals: of Athens, 21, 30, 33–34, 46, 47, 51, 58, 60–61, 63, 116, 133 156, 169, 184, 220, 228 (fig. 7), 262, 357n52. See also *Apatouria; choregia;* Dionysia; Hephaestia; Isthmia; liturgy; Mysteries; Olympia; *Oschophoria;* Panathenaea; *Plynteria;* Pythia
Fingarette, A., 413n22, 421n35
Finley, John, 11, 349n10, 429n28, 430n33, 433n57, 434n59, 435n69
Finley, M. I., 364n3, 374n30, 389n18, 429n28, 439n92
Five Thousand, the, 138, 140, 145–51, 156, 162, 208, 229, 256
fleet. *See* navy
Flory, Stewart, 362n74, 363n80, 437n78
Forde, S., 348n7, 431n46
Fornara, Charles, 332, 338–39, 351nn9–11, 363n78, 373n25, 385n46, 429n30, 431n44
Forrest, W. G., 389n16
Forsythe, G. *See* Graham, A. J.
fortifications, 318–19. *See also* Piraeus; walls
Four Hundred, the, 127, 138, 140, 143–51, 153, 159, 190–91, 221–22, 229, 261, 272, 277, 295, 302, 308–9, 325, 334, 410n40; members of, among the Thirty, 204, 221, 295, 430n35. *See also* Alcibiades, and the oligarchy of 411
Fowler, R., 362n74
Francis, E. D., 361n70, 394n12
freedom. *See* liberation and freedom
French, A., 364n3
Fuks, A., 382n19, 389n18, 409n39, 410n41
funeral oration, 37–39, 47, 79, 186, 192, 359n63
Funke, P., 424n13, 434n58, 436n75

Gabrielsen, Vincent, 61, 368n32, 369n36, 388n7, 402n15
Gagarin, M., 381n16
Gallucci, Ralph, 332
Garland, R., 351n11
Garnsey, P., 408n23

Gaurium, 177
Ge, 172
generation gap. *See* youth
Gentili, B., and G. Cerri, 398n39, 428n26
Gephyraei, 21–22, 108, 352n14
Germaine, G., 388–89nn10–12
Gerousia, 225, 259
Glaucon: brother of Plato, 49, 239; grandfather of Plato, 49
Glaucus, king of Corinth, 31–32, 356n44; of Rhegium, 41
gnome, 25, 320, 354n26, 435n67
gods, 15, 25–27, 29–30, 33, 35, 38, 44, 85–88, 97, 104, 108, 110–11, 114–15, 120–22, 125–26, 131–33, 136, 167–69, 171–74, 176, 178, 189, 223, 228 (fig. 7), 277, 280, 283–85, 288, 290, 299, 325–27, 355n39. *See also* Aeacus; Altar of the Twelve Gods; Apollo; Artemis; Cybele; dedications; Delphi; Demeter; *demos;* Eros; festivals; Ge; Hades; Hera; Heracles; Hermes; ; impiety; Isthmia; Kybebe; Mother of the Gods; Olympia; oracles; piety; Poseidon; Rhea; sacrifices; sacrilege; Victory; Zeus
Gomme, A.W., 319, 358n61, 371n14, 405n49, 429n28, n30, 431n52, 433n54, n57, 434n59, n61, 434–35n63, n65
Goody, J., and I. Watt, 347n1, 399n48
Gordium, 176,
Gorgias, 2, 37, 79, 81–83, 89, 101, 124, 192, 359n63; his *Helen,* 376n45
Gould, J., 437n80
Graham, A.J., 365n6, 398n36, 431n39
Grandjean, Y.G., and F. Salviat, 398n36, 401n6, 408n25, 431nn39–40, n42
grain dole, 147, 157–58, 201, 260, 394n12, 406–7n14
graphe: asebeias, 285; *paranomon,* 102–3, 138, 186, 257, 271–72. See also *paragraphe*
Gray, V., 347n4, 404nn31–32, 414n26, 418n8, 439n91
Great Goddess, Mother. *See* Mother of the Gods
Green, Peter, 340–44
Gregory, J., 385n46
Griffith, M., 349n3
Grote, G., 371n14
Guthrie, W.K.C., 375n37, 417n1
Gylippus, 124
Gytheium, 165
Hades, 132, 158, 189, 403n23, 422n39. *See also* Underworld, the
Hagnon, 134, 146
Haliartus, battle of, 436n73
Hamilton, C.D., 433–34n58, 437n81
Hanfmann, G.M.A., and J.C. Waldbaum, 400n55
Hansen, Hardy, 421n35, 423n4
Hansen, Mogens H., 62, 377n50, 382n17, 394n11, 404n33, 410n46, 422n41, n1, 424n21, 425n30, 431n49
Harding, P.E., 409n39, 410n40, 439n91
Harmodius. *See* tyrant-slayers, the
Harris, E.M., 390n23, n28, 392n45, 393n50
Harrison, A.R.W., 422n41
Harvey, D., 371–72n16
Hatzfeld, J., 348n7, 379n2, 387n65, 395n18
Havelock, E.A., 347n1, 375n38, 404n36
Hecataeus, 16
Hecuba, 121
Hedrick, C., 399n48
Heftner, H., 436n73
Hegemon, 171
Heliaea, 269, 422n38
Helen. *See* Euripides; Gorgias; Isocrates
Hellanicus: *Attike syngraphe,* 89, 277–78, 315, 327, 361n70, 379n67, 423n6, n8, 438n90; other works, 89, 278, 337, 379n67
Hellanis, 69
Hellenica Oxyrhynchia, 413n15, 435n68, 439n91. *See also* Index Locorum
Hellespont, 29, 75, 129, 152–54, 160–65, 170, 198–201, 203, 233, 335, 407n14
Hellespontine Phrygia, 129, 152–54, 232. *See also* Abydos; Cyzicus; Lampsacus; Pharnabazus
Hellenotamiai. *See* treasurers
Henderson, J., 389n13
Henrichs, A., 428n22
Henry, A.S., 332
Henry, W.P., 335, 439n91
Hephaestia, 262
Hera, Argive, 89, 126, 387n66
Heracles, 31, 223
Heraclitus, 326, 438n87
Hermes, 103–5, 132, 158
Hermocrates, 308, 397n32, 430n37, n39
Hermogenes, 287–88
Hermokopidai, 104–5

Herms, mutilation of, 103–7, 110, 112, 114, 116–18, 125, 139, 172, 261–62, 400n53
Herodes, *On the Constitution,* 387n64, 390n22, 407n22
Herodotus, 2, 9, 16–17, 20–22, 24–25, 32, 39, 41–45, 52, 56, 68, 87, 95, 172, 225, 305–6, 433n56; Athenian Council, given award by, 116–18, 315, 326, 386n51; on Athenian democracy, 22; on fate, oracles, and the gods, 42–44, 87, 121, 172; purpose in writing, 42–44, 115, 121, 315–16; sources, 25, 39, 41–44, 56, 350n5, 353n24, 362nn74–75; time of writing, 2, 41, 43–44, 95, 115–17, 315, 363n78; on the tyrant-slayers, 20–21, 115; on tyranny, 115–16, 374n31, 385n47. *See also* Anytus; history and historians; Index Locorum; Plutarch; Thucydides
Hesiod, 15, 17, 111
hetaireiai and *hetairoi,* 90, 106–8, 124–25, 131, 135, 139, 204, 208–10, 220, 248, 379n68. See also *synomosiai*
Hierophant, 108, 168–69, 278, 423nn8–9
Hignett, C., 389n18, 392n46, 393n50, 421n34, 426n3
Hipparchus. *See* tyrant-slayers, the
Hipparete, 112
Hippias of Elis, 41, 89
Hippias of Thasos, 213
Hippias the tyrant, 20–21, 91, 116–17, 357n51
Hippocleides, 357n52
Hippobotai, 360n69
Hippodamian Agora, 238
Hippomachus, 239
Hipponicus, 51, 112–13
historiai, 328, 431n52. *See also* Herodotus; history and historians
history and historians: Aristotle's views on, 328–29, 433n54, 439nn93–94; as classical discipline, 2–3, 7, 9, 12, 16–18, 89, 95, 113, 115, 247, 249–50, 278, 292–94, 303–4, 306, 315–16, 318, 323–24, 327–29, 349n2, 350n7, 360n67, 362n74, 389n17, 433n54, 436n72; constitutional, 2, 73, 88–89, 103, 136–38, 150, 161, 191, 209, 226–28, 248, 250, 259–61, 263–67, 269–74; of Ctesias, 436n72; and democracy, 1–3, 5–6, 8–12, 47, 78–83, 91, 95, 103, 114–18, 135–37, 149–50, 156–59, 191–92, 249–50, 261, 272, 293–97, 302–4, 315–20, 322–23, 325; and destiny, 38–41, 271, 324, 437n77; of Herodotus, 2, 9, 16–17, 22, 41, 43, 95, 115–17, 121, 306, 315, 316, 362n74; as modern discipline, 1, 3–4, 7, 9–12, 16, 38, 40, 41, 209, 248–49, 293–94, 296, 315–16, 318, 321–24; and myth, 16–18, 21–22, 28, 30–33, 38, 40, 47, 91, 349n2, 363n80; and oral tradition, 361n72; as perspective on significant aspects of the past, 3–4, 9, 16, 22–23, 28, 30, 32–33, 38, 40–41, 43, 47, 78, 79, 88, 91, 112, 114–18, 135, 137–38, 148, 157, 195, 248, 295–96, 312, 314, 316–20, 329; and philosophy, 1–3, 6, 248–50, 293–94, 328; and rhetoric, 2–3, 37–38, 81, 83, 102, 112–13, 115, 157, 191, 209, 247–49, 293–96, 303, 305–7, 327, 350n7, 359n65, 360n67, 363n80, 431n52, 433n56; of Thucydides, 2, 4–6, 9, 11–12, 16–17, 20, 41, 43, 45, 95, 109, 114–15, 150, 194, 292–94, 304–7, 314–29, 431–32n52, 433n54; and truth, 15–18, 22, 23, 26, 40, 44–45, 83, 102, 293, 296, 328, 349n2, 357n51, 431n52. See also *akribeia;* Aristotle; Atthidographers; Herodotus; *historiai; logographoi;* myth; research; *syngraphe; syngrapheis;* Thucydides; writing
Hodkinson, S., 364n3
Hölscher, W., 355n34
Homer, 15, 17, 23, 52–56, 90, 305, 349n2, 360n68, 428n27
homonoia, 436n75
hoplites: Athenian, 54–55, 65–66, 76–77, 100–1, 103, 146–48, 150, 157, 160–61, 252, 255, 390n24; serving Persians, 283; Spartan, 237, 243; under the Thirty, 225, 229, 236–37
Hopper, R.J., 364n3
Hornblower, S., 321, 347n3, 363n77, n78, n80, 429n28, 433n57, 434n61, 435n65, n71, 439n91
Hubbard, T.K., 387n66
Hunter, V., 433n54, 434n61
Hyperbolus, 182, 258, 334, 372n17; ostracism of, 96–98, 109–10, 139, 344, 384n40, 390n25, 430n35; supports Sicilian expedition, 98, 109–10

Hypodicus, 21–22, 352nn13–14
hypomnemata, 300, 306. *See also* writing
hypomosia, 404n33

Immerwahr, Henry R., 350n5, 362n75
imperialism, Athenian, 40, 70, 76, 95, 98, 118–20, 123, 128, 131, 141, 155–58, 183, 202, 210, 361n71. *See also* Athenian empire; law courts, Athenian
impiety: Alcibiades, alleged of and others in 415, 105, 107, 110–11, 120, 125, 131, 168, 296; Andocides, alleged of, 262–63, 284; Diopeithes, supposed decree of against, 378n59; Nicomachus, alleged in trial of, 275–76, 284; Socrates, alleged of, 248, 284–91. See also *graphe asebeias;* Herms, mutilation of; Mysteries; sacrilege; Socrates
initiation. *See* Mysteries
inscriptions, 20, 39, 41–42, 56, 100, 142, 159, 167, 170, 200, 227–28 (fig. 7), 249, 255, 258, 260, 265, 267–70, 275–76, 277–78, 297, 309, 331–32, 352n18, 371n15, 373n25, 402n15, 413n22. *See also* Callias decrees; Index Locorum; *kyrbeis;* Themistocles, decree of
Iolcus, 31–32
Ion, 34, 41, 361n70, 366n21
Ionia and Ionians, 44, 176, 350n5, 356n40, 394n12; during Peloponnesian War, 58, 97, 128–31, 139, 141, 143–45, 147, 152, 160–61, 172, 177–78, 180, 196, 203–4, 335–37; following Peloponnesian War, 232; during Persian War, 29–30, 355n35, 437n81; Revolt of 499, 16, 22, 43, 158, 172. *See also* Asia; Chios; Ephesos; Lesbos; Miletus; Mytilene; Pharnabazus; Samos; Tissaphernes
Irwin, T.H., 417n1
isegoria, 22, 26, 354n28
Ismenias, 235
Isocrates: as speech-writer, 57, 247, 249, 275, 279–80, 303, 322, 424n12. Works: 4 *Panegyricus,* 327; 10 *Helen,* 376n45; 16 *On the Team of Horses,* 399n42, 436n73; 18 *Against Callimachus,* 426n3; 20 *Against Lochites,* 426n2, 431n48, 436n73; 21 *Against Euthynus,* 426n3. *See also* Index Locorum
isonomia, 26, 65, 120, 354n28, 370n2, 386n56
isoteleia, 250, 258
Isthmia and Isthmian games, 24, 262
Italy and Italians, 41, 98, 117
Ithome, Mount, 237

Jacoby, F., 350n7, 351nn10–11, 358n61, 362n74, 363n78, n80, 389n18, 431n42, 439n91
Jameson, Michael H., xi, 369n1, 377n54, n57, 392n45, 400n53, 419n14
Jason, 31
Jebb, R.C., 436n73
Jeffery, L.H., 360–61n70
Johnstone, C.L., 410n46
jury. *See* law courts
justice. *See* laws of Athens
Justin, 35, 44, 167

Kagan, D., 335, 342, 348n7, 377n51, 381n8, 388n6, 395n18, 397n32
Kallet (Kallet-Marx), Lisa, 364n1, n4, 366n15, 372–73n25, 377n51, 430n33
kaloi k'agathoi and *kalokagathia,* 10, 52, 56, 73, 76–77, 81, 90, 142, 145, 415n39
kakonomia, 67
katalogaden, 89, 379n67
Kennedy, G., 429n30
Keos, 404n39
Kerameikos, 52
Kierdorf, W., 359n65
"King's Peace," 437n81
Kleine, J., 351n12, 394n12
kleos, 42, 353n25
"Know yourself," 252–53, 418n9
Knox, B.M.W., 357n50
Kokkygion, 387n66
Konstan, D., 363n78
Kourouniotis, K., 410n46
Kraay, C., 397n31, 411n52
Krause, A., 395n18
Kraut, R., 348n8, 417n1
Krentz, Peter, 335–36, 340–42, 408n31, 410n46, 413n15, n17, 416n54, 419n12, n20, 431n44, 439n91
kudos, 25–26, 42, 353n25
Kuhn, G., 421nn35–36
Kurke, L., 352n15, 353n25, 357n51
Kybebe, 400n52. *See also* Cybele
kybernesia, 184
kyrbeis, 265, 267, 270, 276–77, 297, 426n6

Laches, 96, 98
Lamachus, 55–56, 99, 105, 110, 334, 366nn20–21
Lamaxis, 69
Lampon, 86
Lampsacus, 162, 198, 309
Landwehr, C., 351n12
Lang, M., 403n19
Larisa, 282
Lateiner, Donald, xi, 350n5, 362nn76–77, 385n46, 391n35
Lavelle, B. M., 351n11
law, constitutional, 1, 102, 191. *See also* constitution; history and historians; laws of Athens
law courts, Athenian: Anytus' "bribery" of, 161–62, 396n25; democratic nature of, 10, 64–65, 71–72, 76, 82, 91, 113, 118, 137, 146, 156–57, 183, 186, 191, 223, 284–91, 302–4, 307; imperialistic nature of, 47, 68–69, 71, 76, 82, 98, 157; opponents of democracy, used by, 101–3, 191–92, 207, 216, 218, 244, 271; piety in, 104, 113, 274–78, 288–90; restored democracy after 403, under the, 256–57, 264, 267–68, 271, 273–80, 284–91, 295–96, 299, 303–4; sophistic rhetoric in, 79, 81–83, 98, 101, 118, 124–25, 191–92, 223–24, 260, 268, 275–76, 285
lawgivers. *See* Cleisthenes; Draco; Lycurgus; *nomothetai*; Solon; Tyrtaeus
Lawrence, A. W., 435n63
laws of Athens, 2, 10, 18, 26, 38, 46, 78, 101–3, 120–21, 136–37, 149, 159, 169–71, 174, 186, 191–92, 207–8, 210, 222–23, 227–28 (fig. 7), 248–49, 253, 257–74, 277–78, 287, 292, 297–300, 304; "code" of, 267–68, 292–94; *vs.* decrees, 169–71, 186, 269–72, 292, 297, 399n48; defined, 170–71, 186, 227–29, 271, 299; displayed, 227–28, 264–70, 275–78, 297, 299–300; revision of, 10, 148–50, 157, 159, 169–70, 191, 227, 244, 261–72, 273–78, 299; revisions under the Thirty, 220–21, 223, 225, 227, 259, 261, 263, 272; sacred, 275–78, 289–90, 299–300; written *vs* unwritten, 186, 227–28, 259, 261, 264, 266, 269–73, 278, 287–88, 298–300, 422n40. *See also* Antiphon; archives; citizenship; Cleisthenes; Draco; *graphe paranomon;* inscriptions; *isonomia; kakonomia; nomothetai; patrios nomos; patrios politeia;* Socrates; Solon; writing
laws of nature, 97, 119–22, 174, 299
Lawton, C., 350n7
Legon, R. P., 391n31
Lenardon, R. J., 361n72, 428n26, 438n90
Lenormant relief, 180–82, 402n16
Leogoras, 59, 108, 261–6, 382n17
Leon, 287, 290
Leontini, 37, 79, 380n5
Lesbos and Lesbians, 69, 129, 153, 161, 177–78, 180–81, 336. *See also* Methymna; Mytilene
Lesky, Albin, 292–93, 348n8, 389n15, 417n1, 426n1, 437n80
Lévy, Edmond, 348–49n10, 370n3, 436n75
Lewis, David, 331, 335, 349n10, 371n15, 381n12, 387n1, 391n29, 391n35, 395n16, 396n31, 401n3, 405–6n4, n11, 434n58, 436nn71–72, 437n81
lêxiarchika grammateia, 74, 255, 373n26
liberation and freedom: of Athens, 17–20, 22, 39, 67, 115, 118, 127, 138, 153, 251, 261; of Greece, 29, 32, 220, 340, 344; of the Greeks of Asia, 388n6. *See also* slavery
libraries. *See* books
Lichas, 433n57
Lipsius, J. H., 396n25, 403n25, 426n3
liturgies, 57–59, 61–62, 67, 72, 74, 101, 169
Locris, 281, 324
Loening, Thomas, 279, 416–17nn54–55, 422n3, 424nn11–12
logographoi, 82, 315, 363n80, 428n26. *See also* speech writing
logon techne, 224, 231, 303, 412n13
Long Walls. *See* walls
Loraux, N., 359n63, 361n71
Lou Bengisu, R., 400n55
Lycia, 144
Lycomidae, 24, 108, 353n22
Lycon, 51, 285, 290, 426n34
Lycurgus, 225, 227, 288
Lydia, 161, 172, 397n31
Lysander, 177–80, 196–99, 201, 203–6, 211, 214–21, 232–36, 241–42, 244, 309–10, 336–38; at Athens, 215–21, 235, 242, 340–44; and Cyrus, 177, 196,

204, 206, 233–34, 236, 337–38; decarchies established by, 221, 236; at Eleusis, 241–42, 283; Pausanias, compared to, 320, 435n66
Lysias: as manufacturer, 229, 238, 258; as speech-writer, 11, 107–8, 208–9, 211–16, 219–20, 224, 243, 249, 254–55, 274–80, 295, 298, 301–3, 304, 311, 315, 322, 340, 342, 384n41, 424n12. Works: 12 *Against Eratosthenes,* 280, 303, 340; 13 *Against Agoratus,* 212–13, 215–16, 280, 340; 14 and 15 *Against Alcibiades* 1 and 2, 436n73; 16 *In Defense of Mantitheus,* 369n36; 18 *On the Confiscation of the Property of Nicias' Brother,* 342; 20 *For Polystratus,* 391n40; 26 *On the Scrutiny of Euandros,* 426n3; 30 *Against Nicomachus,* 274–78, 422n1; 31 *Against Philon,* 369n36, 426n3. *See also* Index Locorum
Lysagoras, 352n13
Lysicles, 258
Lysimachus, 75
Lysistrata, 134

MacDowell, D. M., 383n28, 387n66, 394n15, 420nn25–26, 422n41, 424n12
Macedon, 152, 203, 316. *See also* Archelaus
Magnesia, 327, 400n52, n55, 438n89
Malea, 161
Mantinea, battle of, 96, 123
Marathon, battle of, 28, 36, 39, 96, 116–17, 325, 351nn11–12, 355n34, 360n67
March, D. A., 434n58
Mardonius, 24, 31
Marinatos, N., 377–78n58, n61
Markle, M. M., 369n1, 394n11
Martin, R. P., 350n4
Masistius, 31
Mattingly, Harold B., 332, 359n62, 361n71, 370–71n9, 371n15, 372–73n25, 374n30, 379n65, 381n12
Mattusch, C. C., 351n12
McCall, M., 357n49,
McCoy, W. J., 390n26, 391n32, 408n31, 409n39
McGlew, J. F., 376n46
McGregor, M. F. *See* Meritt, B. D.
McPherran, M. L., 425n26, n28, 427n15
Media, 155
Megara and Megarians, 49, 206, 239, 300, 360n69; harbor Athenian exiles, 231, 235, 238
Meier, C., 355n37, 357–58n54
Meiggs, Russell: 331, 355n34, 356n45, 360n70, 381n12, 394n9
Melanthius, 361n70
Meletus, 284–86, 288–90, 417n54, 426n34, 428n23
Melissa, 234
Melobius, 221
Melos and Melians, 100, 119–20, 122
memory. See *aletheia; diamnemoneusai; hypomnemata; mnemosyna;* writing
Menelaus, 132–33
Menander, 198
Menecles, 404n33
Menestheus, 39
Meno, 282, 424nn16–17
Menon, 355n36
mercenaries: of Athens, 100, 128, 147, 160; of Sparta, 232–33, 237–38, 242, 281–83
Meritt, B. D., 394n9, 402n15; and H. T. Wade-Gery and M. F. McGregor, 331, 358n55, 394n9
Messenia and Messenians, 154, 226, 237, 280–81
Methymna, 180, 336
metics, 66–67, 180, 185, 229, 242, 250–52, 256–57, 418n4
Meton, 99
Metroön, 171, 173, 267, 284, 327
Meyer, E., 335, 363n78, 393n7, 397n32
miasma, 289
Miletus, 22, 30, 33, 43, 129, 152, 172, 336–37
Millett, P., 364n3
Miltiades, father of Cimon, 27–28, 117, 135, 187, 430n35; companion of Lysander, 431n44
Mindarus, 153–54, 172, 198, 337, 397n32
misthos. See pay
mnemosyna (memoranda), 302, 429n31; *mnemosyne* (memory), 349n2, 353n19. *See also* writing
Mnesilochus, 221
Moles, J., 362n77, 363n78
Momigliano, A., 363n80

money: moneymaking, 57–58, 90, 101, 364nn2–3; of Pelops, 435n66; Persian, 141, 177, 179–80, 196–97, 233, 281–82, 319–20, 435n64; private, 55, 58, 66–67, 71, 83, 112–13, 124, 138, 145, 180, 238, 262; public, 55, 58, 71, 73–74, 77, 82–83, 89, 130, 134, 141, 143, 145, 153, 156, 161–63, 165, 177–78, 183, 252–53, 275, 308, 311; Spartan worries about, 234, 319–20. *See also* pay; revenue; taxes; Timocrates

Montuori, M., 426n1

Morris, Ian, 52, 366n13

Morrison, J. S., 381n16, 387n64; and R. T. Williams, 395n20

Mosshammer, A., 386n51

Mother of the Gods, 132, 171–74 (fig. 5), 267, 290, 327, 438n89. *See also* Artemis; Cybele; dedications; Kybebe; Metroön

Moysey, R. A., 410n46

Munychia, 212, 215, 219; battle of 238–40, 250

Murray, O., 383n26, n28

Mycenae, 317–18

Myronides, 135

mystagogia, mystagogos, 169, 288

Mysteries: Eleusinian, 105–14, 117, 125, 169, 194, 263, 278, 295, 336; Lesser, 282; of the Mother, 174; parodied in comedy, 382–83n24, 384n35, 387n66; private, 105–11, 288, 384n35, 425n30. *See also* Gephyraei; Lycomidae

myth and legend, 15, 21, 27–28, 30, 32–33, 38, 40, 41, 44, 47, 54–56, 125, 132, 158, 172, 227, 277, 324, 349n2, 355n35. *See also* Atthidographers and *Atthides*; drama; history and historians; poetry; song; tragedy

Mytilene and Mytileneans, 69, 71, 180–81, 336–37 ; revolt of, 69, 79, 81, 187

Nagy, B., 399n40

Nagy, G., 349n2, 350n5, 353n25

Nakamura-Moroo, A., 387n1

naturalization, 231, 260, 410n47

Naupactus, 281

navy: Athenian 46–47, 54–55, 60–61, 63, 66, 74, 82, 87, 101, 127, 129–30, 134, 138–39, 141–45, 147, 150, 152–56, 160–61, 165–66, 175, 177–85, 195, 197–202, 206, 215, 219–20, 308, 311, 319, 322, 325, 342, 344, 352n17, 388n7, 395n20, 434n62, 437n81; Persian/Phoenician, 26, 29, 141, 144, 152, 200, 203, 316, 318, 322, 391n35, 437n81; Spartan, 129–30, 143, 147, 152–55, 160, 165, 177–81, 196–99, 201, 203, 219, 241, 281, 308, 325, 337, 393n4. *See also* Aegospotami; Arginusae; Conon; Cyzicus; Notium; trierarch, trierarchy

Nemea, 60, 368n31

neoterismos, 259

nephelokokkygia, 125

Nepos, 167

Niceratus, 55, 231

Nicias, 49, 55, 58–59, 64, 68, 71, 73, 81, 84, 96–97, 99–101, 105–6, 109–10, 123, 134, 211, 231, 243; piety of, 58, 105, 367n28

Nicomachus, 207, 221, 274–79, 284, 422n1; identity of, 422n3, 423n7

Nicomenes, 259

Nicostratus: Athenian general, 96; cavalryman, 237

Nike. *See* Athena; Victory (Nike)

Nixon, L., and S. Price, 364n1

nomoi. See laws of Athens; *patrios nomos*; *patrios politeia*

nomothetai: 411/10, after, 148–50, 157, 159, 169–71, 191–92, 221, 227–28, 261, 263, 265–66, 269, 272, 274–75, 392n46, 422n3; 404, during *stasis* in, 207–8, 210, 266; 403, under restored democracy after, 255–56, 261, 263–69, 272–76, 436n76; the Thirty as, 221, 227–28, 261, 265. *See also* Nicomachus; *syngrapheis;* Thirty, the

Notium, battle of, 177–78, 214, 336–37

oaths, 31, 88, 90, 104, 143, 145, 159–60, 164, 206–7, 213, 251–52, 264, 267, 279–80, 283, 320; of Plataea, 356n45. *See also* reconciliation agreement; *synomosia;* treaties

oath-stone, 104

Ober, J., 357n51

ochlos, 66, 186, 370n4

Odrysians, 179, 198, 203, 232

Oedipus, 189–90

Oenobius, 309–10, 431n42

Oenoe, Attic, 145
Oenoe, Argive, battle of 39–40, 360–61n70
"Old Oligarch." *See* Pseudo-Xenophon
oligarchs and oligarchy, 1; at Athens, 50, 101, 103, 131, 137–46, 159–60, 190–91, 202–3, 205, 207–25, 229–30, 235–36, 240–42, 244, 249, 252–56, 272–73, 295–96, 297, 303, 304, 342, 364–65nn4–5, 410n40; moderate vs. extreme, 146–50, 229–30, 235–36, 240–44, 303, 410n41; outside of Athens, 64–65, 72, 127, 129, 138, 142–43, 153, 197. *See also* Council, Athenian; Critias; Four Hundred, the; Phormisius; Ten, the; Theramenes; Thirty, the; Twenty, the
Oliver, J. H., 413n22
Olorus, 303–4
Olympia and Olympic games, 24, 31, 41, 56, 59–60, 89, 96, 108, 122, 262, 281, 356n44, 368n31
Onomacles, 221
oracles and oracle mongers, 27, 85–87, 91, 104–5, 121, 205–6, 262, 283, 286, 288, 297, 300, 394n12. *See also* Apollo; Delphi; Diopeithes; Lampon; Theonoë
orchestra, 21, 313, 352n13, 405n44
Oreithyia, 26, 30
Orestes, 358n55
Orneae, 361n70
Orpheus and Orphism, 111, 384n35
Oropos, 145
Orwin, C., 430n33, 431n46
Osborne, M.J., 406n11, 411n47, 415n42, 416n44, 419n16, n20
Osborne, R., 364n3, 367n27, 371–72n16
oschophoria, 184, 403n24
ostracism. *See* Hyperbolus
Ostwald, Martin, xi, 335, 342, 351n11, 354n28, 362n75, 363n78, 365n5, 370n2, n3, n6, 382n17, 389n16, n18, 390n23, 391n31, 392nn45–46, 393n50, 395n16, 396n31, 399n48, 402–3n19, 408n31, 409n39, 416nn54–55, 417n2, 419n12, 420n26, 422n40

Paches, 69–71, 187
paideia, 50
Painted Stoa, 28, 32, 39, 354–55n34, 360–61n70
Pamphylia, 39
Panakton, 391n36
Panathenaea, 30, 51, 116, 156, 252, 313, 356n42, 357n52, 431n50
Pangaeum, 31, 356n43
Paphlagon, 64, 73, 77, 90
Paphlagonia, 234
paragraphe, 279
Paralus, 199, 201
paranomia, 120, 287, 386n56. See also *graphe paranomon*
paraskeue, 320
Paris, 121
Parke, H.W., 408n28, 418n7
Parker, Richard A., and W.H. Dubberstein, 387n1, 405n4
Parker, Robert, 325, 386n57, 400n51
Parmenides, 78, 301
Parnes, Mount, 229, 235, 238
Paros, 165, 174, 398n36, 431n39
Parthenon, 47, 52, 54
Parysatis, 176
Pasippidas, 308, 337, 397n32, 430n37
patria, ta, 157, 159, 183, 228, 248, 259, 264, 276–77
patrios nomos, patrioi nomoi: as ancestral customs and laws, 102, 149, 157, 220–21, 244, 254, 264–65, 278; as funerary customs, 38, 359–60n66. *See also* laws of Athens
patrios politeia, 136–38, 141, 148, 206, 209–10, 223, 226, 236, 244, 250, 261, 409n39, 418n5; definition of, 250–51. *See also* constitution; laws of Athens; democracy; Five Thousand, the; Four Hundred, the; Thirty, the
Pausanias, Spartan commander and regent, 25–26, 32, 319–20, 354n26, n29, 355n35. *See also* Lysander
Pausanias, Spartan king, 218, 242–44, 249, 251, 254, 280, 417n54
Pausanias, travel writer, 17–18, 40, 233, 309, 318, 320, 434n60, 435n68. *See also* Index Locorum
pay, 46, 72, 74, 156–58; for jury service, 137, 156–57, 161–62; for military service, 54–55, 58, 65, 74, 77, 99–101, 129–30, 143, 161, 395–96n23; from Persian sources, 129–30, 143, 177, 179, 280; for political office, 74, 137–38, 148, 156–57. See also *diobelia*
Peace of Gela, 44, 358n57, 430n39

Peace of Nicias (421), 55, 68, 76, 91, 123, 134, 163, 206, 243, 308, 321–22, 429n28, 430n37, 435n70
Pearson, L., 389n17, 439n91
Peisander, 139–43, 146, 151, 153, 253, 295, 308, 425n31
Peisetaerus, 124–26, 172, 223, 297, 387n66
Peisianax, 28, 176, 186
Peisistratus and Peisistratids, 17, 46, 114–16, 125, 134, 171, 235, 311, 352n15, 357n52, n54, 379n66. *See also* tyranny
Pelargikon, 86
Pelias, 31
Peloponnesians. *See* Sparta
Pelops. *See* money
peltasts, 160–61
Penner, T., 417n1
"Pentacontaetia." *See* chronology and dating; Thucydides
Pericles, 2, 3, 7, 18, 28, 30, 34, 37–38, 44, 46–47, 49, 51, 54, 64–65, 68, 75, 78, 82–85, 98, 134–35, 140, 187, 251, 258, 270–71, 310–11, 324–25, 355n36, 423n9; building program of, 47, 54, 202; citizenship law of, 259–60, 418n4; as lawgiver, 46, 72, 78, 157, 170–71, 207, 210, 213, 223, 259–60, 277, 278, 297, 310; leadership of at outbreak of Peloponnesian War, 47, 53, 64, 73, 76–77, 84, 118–19, 202, 219, 319; as orator, 3, 34–35, 37, 47, 72, 76, 85, 96, 111, 118–19, 137, 157, 188, 202, 210, 251, 307, 376n50, 381n8, 430n33, 431n52; reputation of, 34, 37, 47, 72, 84, 135, 194, 210, 310–11, 319, 431n45. *See also* Alcibiades
Pericles the younger, 180–81, 183, 187–88, 191, 193, 226, 260, 402n18, 405n44
Perictione, 49
peripoloi, 147
Persephone. *See* Demeter
Persia and Persians: decision-making among, 324–35, 437n81; negotiations with, 10, 49, 91, 97, 127–31, 134, 141–45, 147, 152, 162–64, 176–77, 179, 196–97, 200, 203–4, 213, 281–83, 308, 316, 319–20, 322–25, 436nn71–72, 437n81; war with, 16, 22–24, 26–33, 39, 41–44, 54, 127–29, 135, 158, 172, 197, 206, 284, 305, 318–20, 325, 355nn38–39, 437n81. *See also* Aeschylus; Alcibiades; Amorges; Artaxerxes; Asia Minor; Athenian empire; Conon; conspiracy; Ctesias; Cyrus; Darius; Herodotus; Ionian revolt; Marathon; money; navy; pay; Pharnabazus; Pissouthnes; Plataea; Salamis; Sardis; Sparta; Thermopylae; Timocrates; Tissaphernes; wealth; Xerxes
Pesely, G., 410n40
Phaeax, 98, 109
Phaedrus, 301. *See also* Plato
Phallenius, 104
phallus, 103–4, 202
Phanodemus, 386n51
Pharnabazus: and the Athenians, 162–64 (fig. 4a{-}b), 173, 175–76, 179, 203, 213, 232–34, 308, 319, 322, 325, 338, 388n6, 396–97n31, 437n81; and Cyrus, 176–77, 232–34; and Ionian Greeks, 154, 162–3, 232, 308; and the Persian court, 163–64, 176, 203, 232–34, 308, 316; and the Spartans, 129, 152–55, 162–63, 232–34, 319; Tissaphernes by Diodorus, confused with, 388n6
Pharsalus, 282
Phayllus: Athenian, 417n54; of Croton, 353n24
Pheidias, 400n56
Pheidon and Pheidonian standard, 265, 420n26
Pherecrates, 133
Pherecydes, 42
Philinus, 100, 381n14
Philistus, 56
Philocles, 199, 402n18
Philon, 424n11
philosophy and philosophers, 1–3, 6, 90, 101, 248, 253, 271, 293, 298–300, 326, 328. *See also* Aristotle; Empedocles; Heraclitus; history and historians; Parmenides; Plato; Protagoras; Socrates; sophists; truth
Phineus, 30–31, 356n42
Phocis, 324
Phoenicia and Phoenicians, 144–45, 152, 165
Phormisius, 209, 251, 254–55
phoros. See tribute
Phrygia, 172, 234, 282, 397n31. *See also* Hellespontine Phrygia
Phrynichus, comic poet, 372n17

Phrynichus, tragedian, 41, 352n16; ; *Phoenician Women,* 23, 28–29, 352n18; *Sack of Miletus,* 22–23, 30, 33, 42–43, 352nn16–17, 362n76
Phrynichus, statesman, 131, 141–2, 145–7, 167–68, 186, 213, 272, 295, 310, 404n31, 407n14
Phyle, 235–38, 247, 249, 257–58, 415nn41–42
piety. *See* democracy, Athenian; festivals; gods; impiety; law courts, Athenian; Nicias; oracles; sacrifices; sacrilege; Socrates; Thucydides; truth
Pindar, 23, 27, 31, 50, 59, 349n2, 354n31
piracy, 318
Piraeus, 23, 65, 145, 166, 176, 201, 212–13, 219, 222, 230, 238–44, 340; fighting in, 238–43; partisans from, 238–44, 247, 249–58, 274, 280, 295–96; Themistocles, fortified by, 23, 202, 210–11, 318–19, 352n17; walls of, 23, 202, 206, 211, 220, 235, 243, 319, 340–44, 434n62, 434–35n63. *See also* Munychia
Pissouthnes, 128
plague, 58, 64, 87, 138, 260, 320, 390n24
Plataea: battle of, 25, 29–32, 319, 356nn45–46; captured in 431, 341. *See also* oaths
Plato, 2, 6–9, 11–12, 36, 37–38, 47, 49–52, 54, 57–59, 62, 101, 111, 175, 188, 225, 227, 235, 239, 247–50, 253–54, 256, 265, 279, 285, 290, 292–94, 298–301, 306, 328–29, 350n4, 427n13, n15; and afterlife, 239, 269, 300, 384n35, 425n30, 427n15; and allegory of the cave, 299–300; birth and family, 49–50, 62, 222, 239, 300; and Delphi, 253, 300; dialogues, as composer of, 292–94, 300–1, 306, 328, 427n19; and poetry, 50, 188; politics, personal experience of, 222–24, 239, 247–48, 265, 288, 298, 304. Works: *Alcibiades 1,* 8, 348n8; *Apology,* 90, 250, 269, 285–88 *Charmides,* 49, 54; *Crito,* 250, 298–9, 425n23; *Euthydemus,* 50–51, 410n47; *Euthyphro,* 250, 286, 289; *Gorgias,* 8, 50, 188, 192, 202, 269; *Hippias* 1 & 2, 50; *Laches,* 50, 374n36; *Lysis,* 51; *Menexenus,* 37–38, 47, 247, 359n62; *Meno,* 250, 282, 374n36; *Parmenides,* 300; *Phaedo,* 425n23, n30; *Phaedrus,* 298, 301, 359n63, 426n34; *Protagoras,* 8, 50, 374n36; *Republic,* 51, 239, 299–300, 404n36; *Seventh Letter,* 222–24, 247–48, 265, 294, 417n1; *Symposium,* 7, 51, 54, 290, 292, 306; *Theaetetus,* 300–1. *See also* Index Locorum
Plato the comic poet, 109, 182, 390n26
Pleistoanax, 68, 243
pleonexia, 370n4
Pliny, 21
Plommer, W.H., 379n66
ploutos, ploutein, plousios, 50, 57, 194
Plutarch: on Alcibiades, 97, 99, 104–5, 107, 109–10, 133, 145, 166–69, 199, 214, 398n39; on demagogues, 73; on Euripides, 35; on Herodotus, 117, 357n48; on Lamachus, 56; on Lysander, 197, 214, 340–42; on Nicias, 71, 101, 109–10; on Themistocles, 26, 438n89; on Theramenes, 210. *See also* Index Locorum
Pnyx, 64, 140, 148, 212, 410n46
Plynteria, 167, 336, 399n40
Podlecki, A., 351n11, 354n30
poetry and poets, 1–2, 23–24, 27, 33–37, 40, 49–51, 55–56, 59, 78, 81, 114, 121, 133–36, 159, 166, 171, 182–83, 189–94, 226–27, 292–93, 297–98, 305, 316, 328–29, 349nn1–3, 350n4, 353n19, n25, 357n52, 362n74, 403n22, 404n37. *See also* Aeschylus; Aristophanes; comedy; drama; dithyramb; Euripides; Hesiod; Homer; Phrynichus; Pindar; Simonides; Solon; song; Sophocles; tragedy; truth
Polemarch. *See* archon
Polemarchus, 229
politeia: definition of, 136–37, 250–51; history of, 247–48, 261, 269–72; Phormisius' proposal on, 251, 254–55. *See also* citizenship; constitution; laws of Athens; *patrios politeia*
politike techne, 80, 87, 375n39
polloi, 78
Polus, 82
Polybus, 407n14
Polycrates: Athenian sophist, 312, 425n22, 431nn48–49; Samian tyrant, 350n5
polypragmosyne, 357n49, 370n4
poneroi, 66, 73, 81, 220, 370n4
population, Athenian, 61–63, 369n37, 390n23. *See also* citizens
Poseidon, 24, 121, 140

Potidaea, 54, 55
Potniae, 31
Pouilloux, J., and F. Salviat, 433n57, 434n59, n61, n63
Pratt, L. H., 349n2
Priam, 121
Price, S. *See* Nixon, L., and S. Price
Pritchett, W. K., 332, 356n45, 358n61, 361n70, 362n74, 395n23
proagon, 33
probouloi, 134, 136–37, 221, 334
Prodicus, 404n39
Proietti, G., 387n64
Propontis, 153–54, 162, 164–65
Propylaea, 60
Protagoras, 78–80, 83, 87
proxenia, 68–69, 123, 260
Proxenus the Boeotian, 283, 424n17; the Syracusan, 397n32
Prytaneum, 20, 351n9, 421n37
Prytany, 186–87, 266
psephismata. See laws of Athens, vs. decrees
Pseudo-Xenophon, 65–67, 142, 307, 364n2, 370n3, 430n34. *See also* Index Locorum
Pylos, 44, 154, 161, 202
Pyrilampes, 49, 62
Pyrrolochus, 397n32
Pythia, 60, 166, 288; Pythian games, 368n31. *See also* Delphi
Pythion, 56
Pythodorus, 247, 341

Raaflaub, Kurt, 350n8, 354n28, 355n35, n37, 359n62, 363n78
Raubitschek, Antony E., 350nn7–8, 351n12, 359n62, 380n2, 381n14, 415n42, 438n90
Rawlings, Hunter R., 349n10, 431n46, 435n66, 436n74
reading. *See* books; writing
reconciliation agreement, 244, 249, 251–58, 261, 275, 279, 283, 431nn39–40. *See also* amnesty of 403
Riedweg, C., 384n35
research, 2, 41, 88–89, 103, 116, 118, 137, 149, 192, 277, 297, 327. See also *syngraphe; syngrapheis*
revenue, Athenian, 46–47, 54, 57, 67, 74, 82, 100, 128, 130, 134, 138, 141, 143, 145, 152–58, 161–62, 165, 177, 180, 309, 318, 388n7. See also *eisphora;* money; taxes; treasurers; tribute; wealth
Rhea, 172
Rhegium, 380n5
rhetoric: study of, 1–2, 11, 37, 79–83, 85, 135, 188–89, 191–92, 224, 247, 249, 271, 292, 294, 297, 302–7, 328; styles of, 2, 34–35, 81, 102, 157–59, 167, 175, 181–91, 193, 206, 254, 273, 277, 279, 285–86, 302, 359n63, 376n45, 433n56, 437n80; themes of, 3, 8, 37, 39–40, 47, 77, 81–83, 87, 91, 97, 101, 110–11, 113, 118, 125, 134–36, 155, 157–59, 168, 183, 184–88, 202, 251–55, 257, 268, 271, 279, 285–86, 289–90, 292, 295–96, 304, 307–8, 315–16, 319, 322, 324–25, 328, 430n33, 430n36, 431n52, 433n54, 437n80. *See also* Cleophon; funeral oration; Gorgias; history and historians; *logon techne;* Pericles; sophists; truth
Rhinon, 417n54
Rhodes, 26, 177, 180, 197, 337
Rhodes, Peter J., 334, 342, 348n7, 378n63, 380n2, 389n18, 390n23, 392nn45–46, 393n50, 394n10, 409n37, 410n40, 413n15, n22, 416n54, 420n23, n26, 421n31, n37, 426n3
Ridgway, B. S., 366n13, 394n12
Robert, L., and J. Robert, 433n57
Roberts, J. T., 347n2, 384n41
Robertson, Noel, 335–38, 354n27, 398n35, 400n54, 401n4, 413n22, 420n26, 421n31, n37, 423n7
Rogers, B. B., 334
Roisman, J., 352n16
Roller, L., 388n10, 400n53
de Romilly, J., xi, 348n7, 349n10, 429n28, 430n33, 433n54
Rosenbloom, A. D., 352n16, 355n38, 362n76
Rösler, W., 353n19
Rouse, W. H. D., 438n83, n87
Ruschenbusch, E., 389n18, 409n39
Russell, F., 401n8
Rutherford, I. C., 353n21
Ryan, F., 395n16
Ryder, T. T. B., 437n81

sacrifices, 132, 169, 172, 239, 252, 262, 275–77, 283, 300, 318, 325–27, 357n52; calendar of, 228 (fig. 7), 275–78, 300

sacrilege, 104–5, 111, 116. *See also* Herms, mutilation of; impiety
Sahlins, M., 357n51
de Ste. Croix, G. E. M., 356n46, 370n3, 392n45, 393n50, 418n5
Salamis: battle of, 23–30, 39, 54, 134, 326, 341; celebrated, 220, 341, 343, 354n31, 360n67; community of, 231; Cypriot, 30, 144, 199; Solon and, 403n22; Spartans, plundered by, 197, 201
Salviat, F. *See* Grandjean, Pouilloux
Samons, L. J., 332, 370n3
Samos and Samians, 139, 142–3, 165, 166, 180, 201–2, 211, 214–16, 219; Athenians at, 129, 131, 139, 141–45, 151, 159, 160–61, 165, 177–81, 201, 211, 216, 325, 395n20, 395n23; revolt of, 440, 35, 216; Spartans at, 215–17, 232, 342–44
Sansone, D., 363n78, 388n10, 389n12
Sardis, 22, 128, 163, 172–73, 176–77, 196–97, 204, 232–34, 283, 327, 336–38, 438n89
Sarpedonian Rock, 31, 356n43
Satyrus, 207
Scanlon, T. F., 363nn78–79
Scapte Hyle, 309, 431n43
Schwarze, J., 389n15
Scyros, 27
Seager, R., 387n1, 388n6
Sealey, R., 392nn45–46, 393n50, 422n41, 428n22
seers. *See* oracles
Segesta and Segestans, 99, 109, 122, 332, 380n5
Selymbria, 163, 397n31, 399n47
semata, 350n5
Sestos, 152–53, 160, 198–99
Seuthes, 179, 198, 232, 297
Seven Sages, 16, 350n4. *See also* Solon
Shapiro, H. A., 351n12, 353n20
Shear, T. L., Jr., 382n21, 393n49, 400n51, 421–22n38
Shipley, G., 391n31, 411n51
ships. *See* navy
Sicily and Sicilians, 35, 41, 44, 79, 122, 203, 430n39, 434n61; Athenian defeat of 413 in, 5, 35, 58, 86, 127–29, 131–32, 134, 138, 147, 154, 180, 194, 221, 231, 272, 390n24; Athenian expeditions to in the 420s, 35, 44, 98; Athenian expedition to in 415–13, 10, 45, 55–56, 58, 91, 95, 97–101, 103, 105–6, 110–11, 115–17, 119, 121, 124–25, 150, 161, 168, 177, 198; receptive to Attic poetry, 35, 358n60. *See also* Catana; Etna; Gela; Leontini; Peace of Gela; Segesta; Syracuse
Sickinger, J. P., 393n49, 399n48
Siewert, P., 356n45, 390n27, 391n37
Simon, 301, 427n19; house of, 271 (fig. 8), 422n39
Simonides, 21, 23–26, 30–31, 352n13, 353nn21–22, 354n30
Sinclair, R. K., 409n37
Sisyphus, 31
Skias, A. N., 415n41
skolia, 351n11
slavery: Athenians sold into, 35, 205–6, 219; other captives sold into, 121–22, 165, 197, 216; symbolic, 64–67, 73, 118, 210, 218–19
slaves and servants, 36–37, 54, 64, 66–67, 73, 105, 110, 116, 166, 168, 180, 185, 189, 193, 216, 237, 242, 250, 252, 255–58, 277, 337. *See also* citizenship
Socrates, 6–8, 10–11, 37, 49–52, 54, 59, 62, 78, 83, 87, 90, 101, 111, 175, 183, 186–88, 190–92, 202, 226, 239, 250, 253, 269, 279, 282–94, 296–304, 311–12, 326, 328–29, 427n15; *daimonion* of, 99, 286–88, 290, 425nn26–27; and Delphi, 253, 283, 286, 300; and the laws, 298–300; his *megalegoria*, 285–86, 290; and the Thirty, 224, 287, 289, 304, 311; trial of, 2, 6, 11, 239, 248–49, 254, 274, 284–92, 294, 298–99, 302, 312; at trial of generals, 186–87, 287; and writing, 292–94, 297–302, 306, 328, 427n18. *See also* Alcibiades; Aristophanes; Critias; Plato; Simon; Xenophon; youth
Solon: as lawgiver, 18, 46, 103, 135, 138, 149–50, 159, 210, 223, 225, 255, 258–59, 263–65, 267, 270, 272, 274, 277, 297, 350n4, 395n16, 426n6; laws of, criticized, 223, 225, 227, 297; as poet, 49, 190, 350n4; as sage, 16, 44, 135, 363n77, 403n22
Sommerstein, Alan, 333–34
song, 10, 16–18, 20–28, 42, 50, 55, 69, 193, 313, 353nn19–20. *See also* chorus; dithyramb; drama; myth; Pindar; poetry; Simonides

soothsayers. *See* oracles
Sophanes, 25, 56, 353n24
sophia, 25, 78, 83, 87, 89, 115, 354n26, 375n37
sophists, 2, 8, 11, 78–83, 89, 101, 135–36, 271, 279, 284, 286, 297, 301–2, 375n37. *See also* Antiphon; Gorgias; Hippias; *logon techne;* Lysias; Polus; Protagoras; rhetoric; Socrates; Thrasymachus
Sophocles, member of the Thirty, 430n35
Sophocles the tragedian, 2, 35, 134–35, 362n75; *Philoctetes,* 172. *See also* Index Locorum
sophos, 285–86. *See also* Seven Sages
sophrosyne, 49
South stoa, 269–70 (fig. 8)
Spanos, Pantelis, 332
Sparta and Spartans: Agamemnon's power compared to, 317–18; Athenian civil war, intervention in, 218, 241–44, 251; Athenian surrender negotiated with, 35, 201–2, 205–6, 210–11, 216–17, 219–20, 302; Athenian treaty of 404 with, 206, 209, 213, 215–17, 219–20, 243–44, 251, 304, 320; Athenians admire, 66, 77, 123, 133–34, 142, 145, 147, 202, 204, 207–11, 213, 218–19, 224–27, 230–31, 236–37, 241–44, 253, 259, 288–89, 387n64, 408n29, 414n23; Athenians hold hostages from Sphacteria (Pylos, 77, 123, 237; Athenians receive embassies from, 34, 67–68, 72, 76, 96, 98, 123, 154–55, 160, 161, 175–76, 181–82, 243, 289; Athenians send embassies to, 145–47, 151, 159, 201–6, 225, 236, 241–43, 308, 319; Athens defeated by in 405/4, 2, 35, 195–217, 309–10, 341; Athens garrisoned by, 146, 151, 206, 212, 225, 229, 231–32, 237–38, 240–41, 244, 413n15; Athens, define terms of surrender of in 404, 35, 201–2, 205–6, 210–11, 216–17, 219–20, 302; Athens following the Thirty, 249–54, 280–84; Athens under the Thirty, 218, 220–21, 224–27 229–32, 234–37, 241–44, 260–61; awkwardness abroad, 25, 28, 32, 233–34, 355n35; Boeotians or Thebans and, 34, 116, 205–6, 219, 232, 235, 241, 318, 321; buildings, unpretentious, 317. ; in central Greece, 34–35, 124, 147, 206, 232, 234–35, 281–82, 324; Corinthian War, before outbreak of, 10, 12, 235, 294, 316–24; Corinthian War, during, 313–14, 317, 321; Decelean War, during, 123–24, 128, 147, 160, 169, 201; Ionian War, during, 124, 129–30, 142–4, 152–55, 160–66, 175, 177–82, 194, 196–99, 308–9, 325, 336–38; Peisistratids and, 20, 21, 114, 116; in Peloponnesian affairs, 39, 67–68, 96, 123, 161, 234–35, 280–84, 317; Peloponnesian War, demands before, 47, 73, 76, 118, 130, 220, 319; Peloponnesian War, during, 2, 10, 41, 43, 68, 76–77, 304, 316–18, 320–23, 343–44, 435n69; Persian Wars and, 24, 25, 29, 32, 206, 319; Persians and, 129–30, 141–4, 147, 152, 154–55, 163–64, 176–77, 179–80, 194, 196–97, 200, 202–4, 206, 232–34, 281–82, 284, 308, 316, 318–20, 322–23, 325, 337–38, 397n32, 437n81. *See also* Agesilaus; Agis; Alcibiades; allies; Archidamus; Boeotius; Brasidas; Callicratidas; chronology and dating; Clearchus; Cleomenes; constitution; Critias; Cyrus; ephors; hoplites; Lycurgus; Lysander; mercenaries; Mindarus; money; navy; Pausanias; Pasippidas; Peace of Nicias; Pharnabazus; Pleistoanax; Pylos; Samos; Thirty, the; Timocrates; Tissaphernes; treaties; Tyrtaeus
speech writing. *See* Andocides; Antiphon; Isocrates; *logographoi*; Lysias; rhetoric; Thucydides; writing
Spence, I. G., 368n35
Sphacteria, 237
Spyridakis, K., 391n35, 406n11
stasis, 5, 90, 110, 207, 209, 221, 265, 272, 273, 287, 309; neutrality during, 426n3. *See also* civil war
Steiner, D. T., 350n5, 376n47, 399n48, 405n44, 427n18, 429n31, 438n87
Stesimbrotos, 41, 361n70; *On Themistocles, Thucydides, and Pericles,* 431n45; *Peri Teleton,* 277, 423n6
Sthenelaidas, 412n13
Stoa Basileios (of the Herms), 104, 267–68, 421nn34–35
Stoa of Zeus Eleutherios, 17–18
"Stoa, the," 264, 267–69
Strauss, Barry S., 383n32, 389n16, 390n24, 412n11, 414n30, 418n8, 419n12, 434n58, 436n73, n75

Strepsiades, 288
Strombichides, 211, 213, 342, 411n47
Stroud, Ronald, 268–69, 378–79n65, n66, 399n48, 420n27, 421n38, 423n4, 428n24, 430n34
Strymon, 27, 31, 99–100, 282, 304
Susa, 176, 213, 234
sycophants, 70–71, 169, 191, 223–24
syndikoi, 82
synegoroi, 82
synesis, 320. See also *gnome*
syngramma, 89
syngraphe, 88–89, 115, 276–77, 315, 317, 323–25, 327, 423n6
syngrapheis, 88, 298; in 411, 137–38, 140, 148–49, 220–21, 385n45, 436n76; meaning historians, 439n93, cf. 88–89, 115
synomosiai, 90, 106, 108. See also *hetaireiai*
Syracuse and Syracusans, 35, 41, 55–56, 58, 97–98, 105, 123–24, 164, 203, 308

Tanagra, battle of, 34, 135
Taureas, 49, 51, 54, 59, 108
taxes, 47, 74, 88, 162, 250, 255, 262, 372–73n25; of five percent, 128, 156; *metoikion,* 250; of ten percent, 154, 156. See also *eikoste; eisphora;* liturgies; revenue; trierarch, trierarchy
Taylor, M.W., 350–51n9
Teisamenus, decree of, 264–69, 274, 420n26, n30
Teisias, 60, 122, 167, 387n61, 401n10
tekmeria, 118
Telecleides, 372n17
Tellus, 56
Ten, the: of Athens, 240–44, 251, 253, 275, 341, 417n54; of Piraeus, 222, 238–39
Teos, 336
Tereus, 125
Terpsion, 301
Thasos, 31, 153, 165, 171, 177, 205, 213, 216, 304, 308–10, 397n32, 398n36, 431nn39–42, 433n57
Theano, 133
theater. *See* Dionysus; drama
Theaetetus, 300–1
Thebes and Thebans, 31, 38, 206, 219, 436n72; support of Athenian exiles, 232, 235. *See also* Boeotia
Themistocles, 23–28, 51, 59, 85, 87, 202, 210, 277, 297, 318–20, 352n18, 354nn27–30; archon, 352n17; and Artemis Aristoboule, 24, 325–26, 352n18; decree of, 373n26; foresight of, 23–26, 28, 87, 210, 318–20, 326, 354n29; honors to, 24–25, 353n21, 354n26, n28; and the Mother of the Gods, 327, 400n52, 438n89; ostracism of, 26, 28, 319, 354n28, 355n36; and poets 23–26, 50, 353n21. *See also* Alcibiades; Andocides; Piraeus; Plutarch; Stesimbrotos; Thucydides
Theocritus, 216
Theodorus: geometer, 301; Hierophant, 168
Theonoë, 132–33
Theophrastus, 376n45
Theopompus, 97, 374n35, 439n91
theoria, 58
theorikon, 156
Theramenes: and the Four Hundred, 134, 137, 146–47, 203; his reputation, 203, 205, 209–10, 219–20, 222, 247, 251, 303–4.; and the restored democracy, 151, 153–54, 159–60, 164, 166, 203, 310; and the surrender of Athens, 203–7, 209–11, 215, 219, 302, 340, 343; and the Thirty, 220–22, 225, 230, 236, 238, 242, 302–3, 342; and the trial of the generals, 184–85, 187–91
"Theramenes Papyrus," 407n21, 428n22
Thermopylae, 24
Theseus, 17–18, 21, 27–28, 31, 32, 36, 38, 157–58, 184, 355n34, 394n12
Thessalus, 117
Thessaly and Thessalians, 34, 63, 124, 204, 282, 358n55, 407n22
thetes, 64–65, 74, 100–1, 103, 150, 161, 254–56, 359n62, 369n1, 382n19, 419n12
Thibron, 284
Thirty, the, 8, 9, 207, 211–12, 214–15, 217–18, 220–32, 234–41, 243–44, 249–55, 258–61, 263, 265–66, 272, 274, 279–81, 287, 290, 295, 303, 310, 311–13, 340–44, 404n31, 430n35; appointment of, 215, 220–22, 266; at Eleusis, 231, 237–38, 240–41, 244, 283, 313; fall of, 239–40, 244, 247, 255, 257, 265, 341; followers of, under restored democracy, 244, 250–56, 265, 275, 279, 283–84, 294–96, 303, 426n3; legislative program of, 221, 223–31, 251, 259–61, 263, 265, 272, 287, 297, 303;

Thirty, the, *(continued)*
as *nomothetai,* 220–21, 227–28, 340–44; Spartan customs, emulation of, 208, 218, 220, 225–27, 229–31, 236–37, 259; "tyrants," dubbed as, 311, 431n48. *See also* Council, Athenian; Critias; laws of Athens; *nomothetai; patrios politeia;* Ten, the
Thomas, R., 359n65, 361n72, 379n66, 399n48, 420n24, 422n41, 426n4
Thompson, H.A., 400n52, 410n46, 421nn35–36
Thomsen, R., 371–73n25, 381n12, 396n26
Thorax, 232–33
Thrace and Thracians, 26–27, 29–32, 39, 133, 153, 161, 162–63, 179, 203, 232–33, 297, 304, 308–10, 428n24. *See also* Bithynia; Odrysians; Seuthes
Thrasybulus, 143–44, 153, 160, 165, 177, 184–85, 187; and Alcibiades, 144, 153, 160, 235, 310, 436n73; citizenship, proposes for partisans in Piraeus, 250–51, 256–58, 274; before Corinthian War, 322; democracy, restores, 252–56, 295; Thirty, opposes the, 235–40, 242, 244, 250. *See also* Diodorus
Thrasydaeus, 280–81
Thrasyllus, 143, 153, 160–61, 163, 165–66, 173, 181, 191, 326, 335–36. *See also* Diodorus
Thrasymachus, 2, 79, 135–36
Thucydides, xi, 2–12, 15–17, 20, 30, 32, 36–37, 39, 41–45, 47, 54, 55, 56, 58–60, 69, 72–74, 76, 79, 81, 83, 85, 89–90, 95, 97–99, 101, 105, 109, 114–15, 119, 122, 123, 128–30, 135, 137–40, 144, 147–48, 150–51, 175, 194, 225, 249, 277, 292–94, 302–11, 314–29, 341, 343–44, 350n5; on Alcibiades, 7, 97, 120, 193–94, 310–11, 322–23, 325, 431n46; and Amphipolis, 304, 307–9; and Andocides, 321, 327, 433n57, 438n90; on Antiphon, 101–2, 289, 302, 310, 431n46; "Archaeology," 317–18; on Archelaus, 316, 428n24, 433n57; on the Athenian empire, 4, 6, 12, 30, 32, 44, 97, 175, 194, 307–11, 318–19, 329; Book 1, 305, 317–20; Book 2, 85–86, 137; Book 5, 321–22 324, 435n71, 436n72; Book 6, 20; Book 8, 5, 309, 322, 324, 347–48n5, 436n71; on Brasidas, 307–8, 428n24; on democracy, 4–6, 12, 44, 73, 99, 109, 114–15, 127, 135, 138, 148, 150–51, 175, 194, 256, 310, 314; in exile, 11, 45, 294, 302, 304, 307–10, 428n24, 431n42–44; family of, 303–4, 307; gold mines of, 304, 309–10, 431n41, n43; on Hermocrates, 430–31n39; and Herodotus, 2, 16–17, 20, 41, 43–45, 95, 115, 225, 305, 315–16, 326, 350n5, 363n80, 428n27; incompleteness of his work, 4–6, 9, 45, 150, 194, 324–27, 335, 343, 433n55, 437n78, 438nn83–84, n91; on Nicias, 367n28; "Pentecontaetia," 318; on Persians, 130, 144, 319–20, 322–27, 436n71; piety of, 85–87, 325–27; posterity, views on, 433n55, 438–39n91; purpose in writing, 4–6, 11–12, 43, 115, 293–94, 304–8, 310–11, 314–24, 327–29, 363n80, 431–32n52, n54, 436n72, 437n81; "second preface," 321, 429n28, 435n69; and Thasos, 304, 309, 428n24; on Themistocles, 318–20, 325–27, 354n26; and Theramenes, 304, 309–10; time of writing, 2, 5–6, 11–12, 20, 41, 45, 305–7, 316–23, 327, 433n57, 434n61, 435n69, 438n82; on the tyrantslayers, 20, 114–15, 314, 316, 384n35, 385n43; "unitarian" vs. "analyst" interpretations of, 429n28, 435n67; use of speeches by, 5, 11, 81, 292–94, 305–8, 324–25, 364n80, 429n30, 429–30n32, n33, 431n52, 433n55, 437n80. *See also* chronology and dating; history and historians; Index Locorum; writing; Xenophon
Thucydides of Pharsalus, 282, 424n16
Thucydides son of Melesias, 47, 109, 371n11, 377n50
Thudippus, 75
Thurii, 117, 378n59, 386n51
Timaea, 97
timema, timesis, 257, 419n13
Timocrates, 319–20, 435n64
Timocreon, 26
Timophanes, 69
Timotheus, *Persians,* 438n89
Tissaphernes: and Athenians, 130–31, 139, 141–45, 153, 161, 162–63, 173, 196, 200, 325, 397nn31–32; and Cyrus, 196–97, 200, 202, 282; executed, 327, 438n88; and Ionian Greeks, 128–30, 161, 173,

284, 325–27; and the Persian court, 128, 144–45, 173, 176–77, 196–97, 200, 327; Pharnabazus, confused with by Diodorus, 388n6; and Spartans, 129–30, 141, 143–44, 152, 155, 162–63, 197, 284, 308, 325, 327, 397n32
tomia, 104, 382n21
Tompkins, D. P., 429–30n32
Toye, D. L., 362n74
tragedy, 2, 8, 10, 17–18, 22–23, 28, 30–35, 37, 42–43, 50, 58, 61, 166, 185–86, 188–90, 292, 358n60, 430n35. *See also* Aeschylus; Agathon; Drama; Euripides; Phrynichus; Sophocles
treasurers: of Athena, 167, 262, 309; execution of, 71, 187; of imperial revenue *(hellenotamiai)*, 35, 67, 71, 134, 156, 158, 161
treaties, 88, 91; between Athens and Persia, 128, 143, 163, 173, 200, 213; between Athens and Sparta, 76, 206, 217, 219, 241, 244, 284, 304, 342; between Persia and Sparta, 129, 141, 176. *See also* Chalcedon; Peace of Nicias; reconciliation agreement
trial of the generals, 175, 181, 184–92, 207, 272, 287, 298, 302, 335, 337–38, 402–3n19, 404n31
tribute: Athenian, 34–35, 68–69, 74–76, 88, 98, 100, 127–28, 156, 163, 201, 397n31; assessment of, 68, 74–76, 82, 156, 374n30; Persian, 128, 233, 397n31. *See also* revenue; treasurers
trierarch, trierarchy, 58, 60–61, 101, 130–31, 141, 184; joint, 61, 180
Troy and Trojans, 16, 22, 23, 28, 39, 54, 56, 121, 132, 172, 305, 317–18
truth, 15; and the gods, 15, 86–87, 99, 290, 299, 326, 382n22; and history, 15–18, 22, 23, 26, 40, 44–45, 83, 95, 102, 157, 210, 233, 234, 249, 287, 293, 296, 306, 314–15, 324, 328, 349n2, 350n5; and law, 102, 190, 192, 210, 228, 236, 269, 271–72, 299–300; and myth, 44, 259, 269, 349n2; and philosophy, 83, 90, 192, 249, 253, 289–90, 293, 298–300, 328; and poetry, 15–17, 23–27, 35, 40, 44, 190, 328, 349n2, 363n80; rhetorically constructed, 40, 44–45, 73, 81, 83, 85, 155, 190, 192, 271–72, 287, 289, 295–97, 303, 314, 315, 321, 363n80; and subjectivity, 15–17, 210, 296, 303, 305–6, 349n2, 357n51; and victory, 22, 25–27, 39–40, 83–85, 237, 253; and writing, 16, 192, 228, 297–98, 303. See also *aletheia;* books; citizenship; Helen; history and historians; myth; oracles; *patria; patrios nomos; patrios politeia*; song; writing
Tsakmakis, A., 431n45
Tuplin, C., 387n1, 388n6
Turner, E. G., 427n7
Twenty, the, 244, 257, 263, 417n55, 419n13
tyche, 320, 435n67
Tydeus, 56, 366n21
tyranny and tyrants, 3, 28, 39, 44, 76, 82, 91, 111–12, 115–16, 119, 122, 123, 132, 134–35, 142, 159, 169–70, 311–14, 316, 385n47, 386n51, 387n66; Peisistratid, 17–22, 26, 39, 91, 114–15, 127, 135, 137–38, 311, 360n67. *See also* Alcibiades; Athenian empire; democracy; Herodotus; Thirty, the
tyrant-slayers, the, 9, 18–19 (fig. 1), 20–22, 27, 33, 60, 75, 114–15, 159, 312–13 (fig. 9 and 10), 316, 350–52nn9–13, 394n12, 431nn50–51. *See also* Thucydides
Tyre, 144
Tyrrell, W. B., 354n33
Tyrtaeus, 226–27, 259

Ullrich, F., 429n28, 433n57
Underhill, G. E., 335
Underworld, the, 189, 193–93, 269, 425n31. *See also* Aeacus; Hades; Plato, and afterlife
unwritten law. See *agraphos nomos;* laws of Athens

Van Hook, L., 376n45
Vermaseren, M. J., 400nn51–52, nn54–55
Vermeule, E., 431n50
Vernant, J.-P., 362n76
Vickers, Michael, 334, 348n7 and n8, 361n70, 376n45, 387n66, 388–89nn10–12, 400n53
Victory (Nike), 84 (fig. 3), 183, 380n8. *See also* truth
Vlastos, G., 425n26, 427n13, n15
Vries, G. J. de, 383n24

Wade-Gery, H. T., 352n17, 377n50, 387n64. *See also* Meritt, B. D.
Walbank, M. B., 370n9

Walker, H.J., 354n32, 355n34
walls: of Athens, 76–77, 140, 150–51, 160, 167, 201–2, 206, 210–11, 215, 217, 219–20, 252–53; Long, 202, 206, 211, 220, 340–44, 407n18, 434n62, 434–35n63; wooden, 87. *See also* Piraeus
Walters, K.R., 389n18, 409n39
Warner, Rex, 306, 431n52
Watt, I. *See* Goody, J.
wealth and the wealthy: of Athenian allies, 67–71, 74–75, 82, 128–29, 141–43, 196; of Athens 37, 47, 49–52, 55–63, 66, 70–72, 74, 77, 78, 82, 87, 100–1, 103, 112–13, 138–9, 145, 147, 223, 229, 231, 240, 244, 250–56, 259–61, 271, 311; of Persian king, 130, 141, 145, 196. *See also* money; revenue
Weil, R., 428n26, 439n93
weights and measures: Attic, 264–65, 331; Pheidonian, 265
Westlake, H. D., 348n5, 361n72, 371n14, 389n13, 428n26, 429n28, 431n43, 435n65, 435–36n71, n72
Whitehead, D., 391n31, 409nn37–38, 413n17, 419n14, 439n91
Winkler, J.J., 357n54
Wolff, H.J., 382n17, 424n11
Woodhead, A. G., 390n26
Woodman, A.J., 349n2, 362n76, 375n43, 428n27, 433n56
Worley, L.J., 368n35
writing, 1–3, 8, 12, 41–45, 49–50, 81, 112, 170, 227, 261–69, 272–74, 276–80, 284–85, 290, 292–94, 296–307, 315–20, 323–28, 428n26; documents, 8, 40, 88–89, 102, 136, 169–71, 191–92, 276–77, 284, 292, 296–98, 436n72; and hearing, 103, 112–115, 293, 298, 303, 305–6, 347n1, 429n31; inadequacies of, 169–70, 227–29, 297–301, 303, 427n16, 438n87; laws, 149, 159, 170, 227, 248, 259, 261, 264–78, 292, 297–300, 399n48; letters, 233, 319, 342, 417n1; and memory, 292–93, 298, 300–3, 305–6, 361n72, 379n66, 427n16, 429n31; notes, 11, 81, 294, 296, 300–3, 305–7, 429n31; prose vs poetry, 379n67, 428n26; as safeguard of democracy, 261, 269, 272, 273, 296–97; speeches, 2, 11, 44, 81–83, 88–89, 101–2, 107, 113, 191, 224, 249, 254–55, 271, 273, 277, 279–80, 292–94, 298, 301–3, 305–7, 315, 376–77n50. See also *akoei; anagraphein;* Andocides; Antiphon; archives; books; *diamnemoneusai;* Diocles; *graphe paranomon;* history and historians; *hypomnemata;* inscriptions; laws of Athens; *logographoi;* Lysias; *mnemosyna;* Plato; poetry; Socrates; *syngraphe;* Thucydides; truth

Xenaenetus, 283, 419n20
xenia, 67–68, 282, 372n21
Xenophon, 4–8, 50–51, 65, 160, 164–67, 175–76, 179–80, 183, 185–88, 191–93, 196, 199, 206–7, 216, 247, 249–50, 252, 272, 278, 281–84, 292–93, 297, 303, 323, 326–27, 335–44, 387n64; on Alcibiades, 7–8, 111, 164–67, 170, 335, 339, 348n8; at Athens, 4, 6, 51, 167, 180, 188, 226, 231, 249, 252, 283, 293, 413n15, 415n42; Peloponnesian War, reports length of, 343–44; on Socrates, 283, 285–87, 290, 293, 297, 348n8, 427n13; on the Thirty, 219–20, 224–27, 230–31, 237–40, 243, 340–44; Thucydides, continues, 4–5, 327, 335, 343, 347n4, 438–39n91; writing, time of, 4–5, 8, 327, 347n4, 417n2. Works: *Constitution of the Lacedaemonians,* 226, 413n18; *Hellenica,* 347n4; *Memorabilia,* 8, 183, 191; *Symposium,* 51, 55. *See also* chronology and dating; Index Locorum; Pseudo-Xenophon
Xenophon of Curium, 207
Xerxes, 23–24, 26, 29–30, 32, 36, 38, 43, 115, 127, 206, 319

Yauna, 30, 355–56n40
youth and the young, 28, 41, 49–51, 57, 71, 76, 99, 132, 135–36, 145; of Alcibiades, 54, 75, 79, 96, 106, 111, 112, 136; as radicals, 81, 96, 106, 135–36, 139, 389n16; Socrates and the, 284, 289–90
Yunis, H., 386n57, 429n28, n30

Zacorus, 423n9
Zacynthus, 281
Zeilhofer, G., 408n29
zeugitai, 65, 103, 255, 369n1
Zeus, 17, 30, 31, 111, 121, 126, 133, 172, 387n66
Zimmerman Munn, M. L., 387n66

INDEX LOCORUM

LITERARY TEXTS

Acts of the Apostles
17.16–23 369n37

Aelian
Miscellany
2.9 411n53
2.30 365n11
4.6 408n29
6.1 360n69

Aeschines
1, *Against Timarchus*
scholion to 39 414n30, 420n22
94 363n80
106 409n37
173 348n9, 425n33, 431n49
2, *On the Embassy*
scholion to 31 354n32, 356n43
76 394n10, n15, 407n19
77 414n30
78 437n79
176 418n11, 419n18, 424n11
3, *Against Ctesiphon*
52 384n40
62 409n37
181–82 354n28
184 360n70
185 360n68
187 415n42, 418n11, 419nn18–19
190 419n19
191 419n18
191–92 273
195 and scholion 419nn16–17
235 414n30

Aeschylus
Agamemnon
104–257 438n88
Eumenides
287–98 358n55
576–79 377n50
762–74 358n55
Persians
65–106 29
251 29
274–77 29
284–87 29
302–481 29
345–54 29
402–5 29
474–75 29
562 29, 30
584–97 30
722–24 29
744–50 29
796–820 29
823–26 29
905–6 29

Persians (continued)
950–54 29, 30
975–77 29, 30
1011 29
1025 29
Phineus
Fr. 260 Radt 356n42
Suppliants
726 377n50

Andocides
1, *On the Mysteries*
11–12 399n42
11–24 382n24, 383n28
11–68 383n25
16 399n42
17 382n17
27 390n26
27–28 385n48
36 387n61, 390n26
43 390n26
47 368n30
47–68 385n48
73–79 405n47
77 389n14, 421n33
81 417n55, 419n13
82–83 426n6
82–85 420n26
83 421n31
83–84 392n48
87 422n40
92 364n3
94 426n34
95 426n6
95–102 424n11
96 378n63
96–97 378n64, 395n17
101 387n61
111 426n6
112–32 423n9
116 423n9
132–34 420n24
133–35 364n3
137–39 382n22
144–47 420n24
150 377n50
2, *On His Return*
7–8 385n48
11–16 420n24
14 390n26
17 372n20, 394n11
18, 20–21, 23 407n14
19–22 407n21
20–21 420n24
3, *On the Peace*
2–9 438n90
5, 7 434n62
8–9 435n69
9 402n11
12, 14 434n62
15 402n11, 437n81
17 434n60
21 408n29
22 409n32
23 434n62
29 387n1
31, 36–39 434n62
4, *Against Alcibiades*
4 379n68
8 380n6
9 392n42
10 384n38
11 373nn28–29, 374n30
13 384n39
13–32 384n38
15 384n39
20–21 367n30
22–23 387n60
26–31 368n31
26–29 387n61
39 384n38
42 367n27

Androtion
FGrHist 324
F 38 358n56
F 43 389n120
F 44 398n35, 401n1
F 45 339

Anonymous
Life of Euripides
135W (Edmonds *Elegy* II, 27) 358n60

Antiphon
1, *Prosecution for Poisoning*
18 379n68
First Tetralogy
2.12, 3.8 373n27

Third Tetralogy
3.1 385n46
5, *On the Murder of Herodes*
10, 17 102
14 382n18
36 433n53
69–71 372n18, 404n34
76–77 371n14
81–82 382n22
88 382n21
6, *On the Choreutes*
2 382n18
11–14 367n27
35–37 403n25
35–50 379n68
36, 38 102
On Truth 102, 382n18
Fr. B 6 Maidment (Thalheim 61) 381n12

Apollodorus
1.9.21 356n42
3.15.3 356n42

Apollonius
Argonautica
scholion to 1.211c 356n43
1.216–18 356n43
1.936–1152 400n54
2.178–489 356n42

Aristides
On the Four
156 (260) 360n70
Panathenaicus
scholion to 196.18 408n29

Aristophanes
Acharnians
5–8 and scholion 374n35
104, 106 356n40
393–490 358n57
544–54 398n39
566–98 366n20
600–603 369n1
618 350n8
636–40 354n31
679–718 376n49
692–701 360n67
716 376n45, 380n6, 384n38
1071–1142, 1174–1227 366n20
Banqueters
Fr. 205 *PCG* (198 Kock) 375n41, 376n45
Fr. 244 *PCG* (554 Kock) 382n20
Birds
34, 37–41, 57–59 387n66
114–24 387n66
124–26 395n19
126 365n6
521 377n57
693–702 384n35, 387n66
873–76 400n53
879–80 391n31
904–21 352n13
959–90 377n57, 382n23
988 378n59
1074–75 386n51
1279 381n8
1280–83 425n33
1286–89 426n5
1353–57 426n6
1422–35 372n16
1556–58 390n26
1553–64 425n31
1649–52 420n23
1655–73 412n12
1694–1705 387n66
1706–65 387n66
Clouds
98–99 377n52
138–43 425n31
202–13 374n30
210–13 392n42
250–74 384n35
433–75 377n52
447–48 426n6
873–75 377n52
1187 412n12
1353–1446 376n46
Frogs
52–54 427n7
140–42 394n14
190–91 402n16, 419n16
192 404n40
273–76 403n28
363 364n3, 394n9
416–21 403n23
465–813 422n39

Frogs (continued)
533–41 405n41
588 403n23, 404n40
635–737 405n47
676–77 425n25
678–85 394n15
686–705 403n28, 430n34
693–94 419n16
694 and scholion 337, 402n16
709 423n3
718–20 402n16
718–37 403n28
771–83 403n28, 404n38
943 405n44
965 418n6, n11
967–79 404n39
1058–60 358n56
1039 366n20
1113–14 375n44, 428n20
1195–96 404n40
1403 356n44
1409 405n44
1418–19 404n37
1420–34 405n48
1422–23 338
1422–25 380n3
1428–29 336
1463–65 430n33
1487–99 425n25
1491–99 404n36
1530–32 195
1532–33 403n21

Knights
40–45 64
61 377n57
74–79 407n18
109–220 377n57
136–37 372n22
191 372n20, n23
222–29 374n34, 375n44
435–43 372n24
445–46 382n23
475–79 379nn68–69
478 387n1
565–94 377n53
732–40 381n8
773–76 372n24
781–87, 810–12 360n67
832–35 371n14
923–26 373nn26–27
960–1099 377n57
1085 378n59
1111–14 374n31
1163 381n8
1300–15 380n5
1329 354n31
1358–62 376n49
1373–81 428n20
1375–83 376n46
1377 380n6

Lysistrata
269–70 404n31
387–98 384n35
490 390n26
614–35 360n67
1094 382n20

Peace
395 390n26
1047 377n57
1208–1304 366n18
1289–94 366n21

Thesmophoriazusae
78–79 409n36
805 394n8
806 360n67
808–809 334
809 386n52
850 ff. 333

Triphales
Fr. 556 *PCG* (543 Kock) 382n20
Fr. 556–69 *PCG* (542–57 Kock) 407n18

Wasps
44–46 376n45
197 376n49
240 380n6
240–44 376n49
380 378n59
463–508 379n69
475 430n34
481–84 377n52
522–23 371n14
530–31 428n20
538–39 376n46, 428n20, 429n31
548–631 376n48
548–759 377n51
559 376n46, 428n20, 429n31
576–77 376n46, 428n20
578–87 412n11
596 372n22
682–85 372n20

686–94 376n49
698–724 369n1
700 380n5
715–18, and scholia 374n30, 392n42, 394n12
836–38 380n6
896–97 380n6
1007, scholion 390n25
1075–90 360n67
1094–97 372n16
1104–13 376n48
1122–1264 376n46
1220–64 372n21
1270 382n17

Aristotle

Constitution of the Athenians

4 382n19
6.3–4 419n14
7.3–4 369n36, n1, 382n19
8.5 426n3
10.2 420n28
18.1–3 357n52
18–19 351n10
20–21.2 418n4
21.6 427n15
22.7 352n17
23.1–2 389n14, 421n33
24 370n2
24.3 369n1
25.1 421n33
26.2 369n36
26.3 420n22
27.4 372n20, 394n11
27.5 386n52, 396n25
28.3 372n22, 394n10
28.5 410n39
29.1 388n7
29.2 378n63, 389n14
29.2–3 378n64
29.2–4 389n120
29.3 350n8, 385n45, 390n20, 426n6
29.4 390n27, 419n18
29.4–5 390n21
30–32 390n23
30.1 378n63
30.2 392n44
30.2–31.1 393n50
31.2 392n48
32.1 334
32.3 392n40
33 392n44
33.1 392n43
33.2 391n39, 392n40
34.1 337, 393n50, 394n10, 403n20
34.3 407n22, 408n31, 410n40, 412n2, n4, 415n39, 418n6, nn10–11
35.1 341, 412nn8–9
35.2 412n11, 413n21
35.2–3 412n12
35.3–4 412n14
35.4 414n25, n30, 415n39
36.2 414n24
37.1 414n26, 415n42
37.2 413n15, 414n24
38.1–2 416nn49–50
38.3–4 416n51, n54
39 417n55
39.6 417n56, 419n13, 424n11
40.1–3 418n11, 419n18
40.2 418n3, n7, 419n16, 424n11
40.2–3 419n15
40.4 424n19
41 247, 389n18
41.2 389n14, 393n50, 409n37, 431n48
43.5 383n33
44.4 410n43
45.3 409n37
55.2 409n37
55.3 369n36
55.5 382n21
56.3–5 357n52, 368n33
56.6–7 368n34
58.1 351n9, 438n86
58.1–2 360n67
61.1 410n43
62.1 409n37

Constitution of the Athenians (continued)
62.3 409n37
69.1 404n33
Nichomachean Ethics
1180a 414n23
On the Soul
405b 416n46
Poetics
1451b 439n94
Politics
1253a27–29 380n4
1267b 394n10
1269a-78a 370n2
1278a 390n22
1291a 367n24
1294a21–22, 1301b2–3 365n7
1304a 371n12
1318b 419n13
Rhetoric
1354b 422n2
1360a 439n93
1360a-b 433n53
1367b, 1415b 359n64
1368a 351n12
1375b 403n22, 405n42
1401a 431n48
1419a 389n14

Arrian
Periplous
9 400n56

Athenaeus
3a 405n44
28b 427n16
184d 365n10
187d 358n60, 408n29
218a 337
220c 384n38
233f-34a 415n35
407b-c 400n50
508c-d 427n19
525a 382n20
525b 374n29, 384n38
534b 387n65
534b-c 380n4, 398n39
534c-35e 384n36, 384n38
534d-e 368n31
534e 384n36
534f-535a 374n29
535a-b 389n11
535c-d 398nn38–39
574e 374n29, 384n36, 384n38
574e-f 415n36
577b 420n22
630e 413n20
635e-f 379n67

Cratinus
Fr. 300 *PCG* (274 Kock) 426n6

Cratippus
FGrHist IIA 64
F 1 433n55, 437n80

Critias
DK 88 B 1–29 365n10
DK 88 B 2.10 427n16
DK 88 B 4–5 398n37
DK B 6–9, 32–37 413n18

Ctesias
Persica (epitome)
44–49, 52 387n1
57 401n3, 406n5, 408n24
60 424n17

Deinarchus
1, *Against Demosthenes*
25 415n37
76 419n18

Demosthenes
1, *First Olynthiac*
28 367n24
15, *For the Liberty of the Rhodians*
22 415n37
19, *On the Embassy*
65 408n29
246 363n80
20, *Against Leptines*
11–12 417n56
68–70 437n81
70 351n12
115 374n30, 392n42
139 418n7
21, *Against Meidias* 384n40
127 377n50

147 367n30
22, *Against Androtion*
33–4, 56, 68 410n40
72 437n81
23, *Against Aristocrates*
67–68 382n21
206 377n50
24, *Against Timocrates*
23 421n31, 422n2
42 420n29
125 410n40
135 418n11, 419n15, n18, 424n11
168 410n40
180 437n81
57, *Against Eubulides*
30–32 420n22
58, *Against Theocrines*
66–68 426n4

Dio Chrysostom
21.3 412n7, 413n21

Diodorus
3.55.8 400n54
4.53–4-6 356n44
8.27 413n20
11.29.2–3 356n45
11.33.3 358n61
11.62.3 360n70
11.79.3 389n15
11.81.4–82 389n15
12.13.2 429n31
12.40.2 366n15
12.45.4 377n51, 404n34
12.53.2–5 359n6, 375n40
12.54.1–3 380n5
12.58.6–7 367n28
12.75.4 389n14
12.78–81.3 380n2
13.2.2 381n15
13.2.3–4 382n20
13.5 386n50
13.5.1 385n47
13.9.2 387n61
13.34.1–2 388n4
13.34.2 391n31
13.37.2–5, 38.5 388n6
13.37.3–5 391n33
13.37.5 391n35
13.38.1–2 390n23
13.38.2 393n2
13.38.3 391n32
13.38.3–42.4 393n1
13.38.5 391n35
13.40.4–42.1 391n34
13.40.6 414n32
13.42.2 393n2
13.45.1–46.5 393n1
13.46.6 391n35
13.47.3 392n43
13.47.6–8 393n3
13.47.8 398n36
13.49.1 393n3
13.49.1–3 431n43
13.49.2 335
13.49.2–51.8 393n4
13.51.1–4 414n32
13.52.1 395n20
13.52.4–6 393n6
13.53.2–4 394n8
13.64.1 395n20
13.64.1–3 395n22
13.64.2–4 393n5, 396n29
13.64.4 398n37
13.64.6–7 396nn24–25
13.65.3–4 397n32, 398n36, 406n12
13.66.1 396n27, 396n29
13.66.1–2 396n30
13.66.1–6 393n5
13.66.3 401n11
13.66.4 396n30
13.66.5–6 414n32
13.67.7 398n38
13.68.1–3 398n38
13.68.2–69.1 399n41
13.68.3 398n39, 399n41
13.69.1 399n42, 399n43
13.69.2–3 399nn44–45
13.69.3 399n42
13.69.4–5 401n5
13.70.2–4 401n7
13.70.3 401n4
13.71 401n8
13.72.1 431n43
13.72.1–2 401n6
13.72.7–9 374n34
13.73.3–6 401nn9–10
13.73.3–74.1 401n10
13.74.1 338
13.74.2 401n11

Diodorus *(continued)*
13.74.3–4 387n61
13.76.1 402n12
13.76.2–79.7 402n14
13.76–79 337
13.77.1 402n12
13.80–96 407n20
13.97.1–2 402n16, 419n16
13.97.6 403n29
13.97.2–100.6 402n18
13.98.1 414n32
13.101.2–6 403n26
13.101.5 403n28, 410n44
13.101.6 403n29
13.103.1–2 405n46
13.104.3–4 405nn1–3
13.104.5–8 406n6
13.104.7 398n35
13.105.1 368n32
13.105.2–106.7 406n7
13.105.3 401n11
13.105.3–4 406n8
13.106.6 406n9
13.106.7 406n10
13.106.8 406n13
13.107.1 406n13
13.107.2 407n15
13.107.3 407n16
13.107.4 408n23, n31
13.108.1 341, 405n4
13.108–114 407n20
14.3.2 408n31
14.3.4–7 342, 411n50
14.3.5 411n49, 412n1, 414n32
14.3.5–7 412n2
14.3.6 408n31, 409n32, 412n3
14.3.7–4.1 412n4
14.4.1–2 412n8
14.4.2 412n14, 414n24
14.4.3–4 413n15, 414n25
14.4.5–5.4 414n26
14.5.2–3 415n39
14.5.5–6 414n25
14.5.7 414n27, 426n34
14.6.2 415n37
14.6.3 415nn37–38
14.11.1–2 414n31
14.11.1–4 414n33
14.11–1-5 415n36
14.12.2–9 414n34
14.13.3 408n28
14.17.4–7 424n13
14.17.7–12 424n14
14.19.4–5 424n15
14.27.2 424n17
14.32 415n42
14.32.4 414n24, 414n29
14.32.5–6 415n43
14.32.6 417n3
14.33.2–3 416nn44–45
14.33.5 416n50
14.33.6 415n40, 416nn51–52, 417n55
14.34.1–3 424n14
14.37.7 431n49
14.39 433n58
14.59.3 434n61
14.78.5 424n14
14.79.5–6 433n58
14.80.6–8 438n88
14.84.3–85.3 437n81
14.98.1 391n35
15.63.1 408n29
15.66.3 413n20

Diogenes Laertius
2.22 438n87
2.38 425n22
2.40–41 424n10, n21
2.43 431n49
2.57 438n91
2.60 427n19
2.61–62 427n19
2.122 422n39
3.1–3 365n7
3.5 365n11
4.59 389n11
9.6 438n87
9.52 375n39

Dionysius of Halicarnassus
Demosthenes
3 389n16
Letter to Pompeius
3 433n55
Lysias
32 417n56, 418n6, 419n12
On Thucydides
5 362n73
10–12 433n55

16 437n80
17–18 433n55

Diphilus
67.7–8 *PCG* (66 Kock) 411n53

Eupolis
Fr. 327 *PCG* (304 Kock) 427n7
Baptae
PCG 5.332 389n11
Demes
Fr. 99–146 *PCG* (90–135 Kock)
Fr. 102 *PCG* (94 Kock) 358n56
Fr. 104 *PCG* (100 Kock) 372n20
Fr. 384 *PCG* (117 Kock) 372n20
Fr. 424 *PCG* (424 Kock) 389n13
Flatterers
Fr. 171 *PCG* (158 Kock) 389n11
Goats
Fr. 9 *PCG* (9 Kock) 403n23

Euripides
Andromache
481–82 375n36
Bacchae
13–172 397n31
64–87 400n53
Children of Heracles
379–80 347n2
Helen
1301–68 400n53
1353–68 388n10
Hippolytus
986–89 374n36
1311 438n87
Medea
824–43 347n2
Orestes
129 389n11
Suppliant Women
311 413n23
410–43 375n36
430–41 370n2
526, 563 413n23
671 359–60n66
Trojan Women
884–88 386n58

Frontinus
Strategematon
2.5.44 393n4

Gorgias
DK 82 B 5–6 359n63, 405n45

Hecataeus
FGrHist 1
F 1 349n2

Hellanicus
FGrHist 323a
F 8 423n8
F 25 337, 402n16, 419n16
F 26 402n16

Hellenica Oxyrhynchia
4 401n8
6 434n58
6.1 434n62
6.2–3 418n11
6–7 437n79
7 435n64
7.2, 17 415nn37–38
7.4 430n38
16.1 415n38
16.2–4 390n22
17 415n38

Herodes
On the Constitution
30–31 390n22

Herodotus
1.1 361n72
1.6–71 385n47
1.6.2 350n5
1.30 366n22
1.33 363n79
1.59 360n67
1.59–64 385n47
1.61 385n47
1.65 413n16
1.65.2 370n6
1.92.1 400n55
1.96–100 385n47

Herodotus *(continued)*
1.152 412n13
1.153 437n81
3.14–38 385n47
3.39–45 385n47
3.46 412n13
3.48–53 385n47
3.55 353n24
3.80 385n47
3.80.6 370n2
3.122–25 385n47
3.122.2 350n5
3.142–43 385n47
4.137.6 355n34
4.76 400n54
5.32 357n47
5.36 350n4
5.47 353n24
5.47.6 420n28
5.49–51 355n35, 412n13
5.55–57 351n10
5.55–65 385n47
5.57 352n13, 383n29, 394n12
5.61 352n13, 383n29
5.62–65 351n10
5.63 385n47
5.66.2 427n15
5.67–68 385n47
5.69 418n4
5.70–72 382n23
5.71 353n24, 379n68
5.74–78 352n15
5.77 360n69, 392n42
5.77–78 394n12
5.78 360n67, 418n4
5.79–81 352n15
5.89–91 352n15
5.91 385n47
5.92 385n47
5.93 385n47
5.95 379n68
5.97 412n13
5.97.3 362n76
5.99 394n12
5.102 353n24, 400n52
5.105 400n52
5.125 350n4
6.21 352n17, 362n76, 400n52
6.39 355n34
6.43 394n12
6.52 353n24
6.92 353n24, 366n22
6.96 400n52
6.100 392n42, 394n12
6.101.3 400n52
6.103 385n47
6.104 355n34
6.107 385n47
6.108 352n15
6.109 351n11
6.121 385n47
6.123 351n10
6.126–31 385n47
6.131.1 350n8
6.136 355n34
7.6.3 357n52
7.8b 400n52
7.107 354n32
7.123.1 358n55
7.132.2 356n45
7.139.5 355n39
7.144.1 352n17
7.161 369n37
7.181 353n24
7.189 354n30
7.220–33 353n24
8.3 357n47
8.11 353nn23–24
8.17 353n24
8.26.3 353n23
8.33 400n52
8.47 353n24
8.53 400n52
8.57–58 354n29
8.59 353n23
8.61–62 354n27
8.92 353n24
8.93 353nn23–24
8.94 366n15
8.108–10 354n29
8.111–12 354n29
8.124 353n21, n23
8.125 354n27
9.15 356n45
9.20–25 356n45
9.27 360nn67–68
9.33–35 353n24
9.64 357n47
9.69 356n46

9.71 353n24
9.73–75 353n24, 366n22
9.75 356n43
9.81 353n23
9.85 358n61
9.106.3 355n35

Hesiod
Theogony
27 349n1
120–22 384n35

Himerius
Orations (Colonna)
12.32, 47.14 356n42
36.18 401n10

Homer
Iliad
2.540–43 394n12
Odyssey
1.150–55, 325–72 353n19
4.15–19 353n19
8.43–100 353n19
17.385 353n19
19.203 349n1
22.330–53 353n19

Homeric Hymns
Demeter 383n34
Dionysus
1–8 349n3

Hyginus
Fabulae
250, 273 356n44, 357n48

Hyperides
Fr. 14.1 425n30

Isaeus
5, *On the Estate of Dicaeogenes*
41 368n32
7, *On the Estate of Apollodorus*
38 368n32

Isocrates
2, *To Nicocles*
7, 42 379n67
4, *Panegyricus*
43–46 369n37
61–65 413n20
99–109 438n90
100–102 387n60
108 392n42
110 413n16
113 414n30
119 437n81
154 437n81
5, *To Philip*
64 437n81
7, *Areopagiticus*
12 437n81
60–61 414n23
64 410n42
65 437n81
67 414n27, n30
68 417n56
8, *On the Peace*
105 410n39
123 415n39
9, *Euagoras*
15 422n39
11, *Busiris*
4–6 431n49
5 425n33
12, *Panathenaicus*
62–66 387n60
14, *Plataicus*
31 408n29
15, *Antidosis*
159–60 367n24
166 354n31
231–35 426n6
318–19 413n16
16, *On the Team of Horses*
1–3 387n61
5–11 399n42
6 383n27
6–7 382n24
29 366nn15–16
31 384n39
32–34 368n31
35 367n27
37 412n55
40 411n48, 412n55, 415nn36–37
42–43 387n61, 407n22
45 387n61
47 367n24
50 387n61

18, *Against Callimachus*
1–4 424n11
2 418n11
10 422n3
13–14 422n3
16 414n24
17 417n55
22 424n11
23 418n11
45 416n50, n52
49 416n50, n52, 426n3
59–60 406n8, n13
60–61 407n16
61 407n14
20, *Against Lochites*
2–11 368n30
11 414n30

Justin
4.3.4–7 380n5
4.4.1–2 358n57
4.4.2 380n5
4.5.12 152
5.1.1–3 386n50
5.1.5–8 388n4
5.3.4–6 390n23
5.3.6–9 391n34
5.4.2 393n4
5.4.4 393n6
5.4.6 393n5
5.4.7 399n41
5.4.8 398n38
5.4.9–18 399n41
5.4.10 399n41
5.4.11–12 399n42
5.4.13–18 399nn43–44
5.4.16 399n45
5.5.2–3 401n9
5.5.4–7 401n10
5.6.1–2 402n12
5.7.4–12 406n13
5.8.3 408n23, n29
5.8.4 408n29
5.8.10 414n24, n27
5.8.11 413n15
5.8.12 411n48, 412n55, 414n25
5.8.12–14 415n36
5.9.1–3 414n25
5.9.2 414n26
5.9.4, 8 415n37
5.9.6–15 415n42
5.9.8 415n38
5.9.13 415n43
5.10.1–3 416n47
5.10.4 416n48
5.10.5 416n49
5.10.8–11 424n19
5.11.1–5 406n5
5.11.5 408n24

Libanius
Orations
25.63–64 414n29

Lycurgus
Against Leocrates
80–81 356n45
105–108 413n20
113–14 404n31

Lysias
2, *Funeral Oration*
9 359n66
18–53 360n67
52 389n15
59–60 437n81
66 359n62
6, *Against Andocides*
2 423n9
10 423–24n9, 431n45
21–24 385n48
33 420n24, 423n6
47–49 407n14, n16
50–51 382n24
51 383nn27–28
54 423n9
7, *Defense in the Matter of the Olive Stump*
4 390n26, 393n52
12, *Against Eratosthenes*
4 418n4, 431n45
5 412n14
5–40 414n25
8, 19 364n3
21–22 414n25
35 431n48
40 414n25
43 379n68
43–44 409n38
52 414n29, 415n42

53 416n47
53–55 416n48, n51
54–60 416n50
55–56 416n49
65 389n14
66 390n26
66–67 408n25
67 393n52
68–70 407n21, 408n27
69 428n22
70 410n42
71 410n43, n46, 412n1
71–72 343–44
72 431n44
72–74 412n2
73–76 412nn3–4
73 412n2, 418n10
77 408n25, 428n23
77–78 414n26
92 416n47
94–95 414n24
95 415n37
13, *Against Agoratus*
1–2 411n47
5 407n15
5–8 407n19
7–38 421n32
8 407n17
9–10 407n21
10 405n42
10–16 408n27
11 407n23
12 409n34
13 410n44
13–16 409n32, 410n42, 410n43
13–48 342–44
18–34 409n35
19 411n53
20 409n37, 412n8
31 410n46
33 212
34 411n50, 412n1
34–35 412n5
37–38 412n55
39–48 411n47
44 414n29
47 414n25
48 212, 410n45
51 213, 410n45
53–54 411n47
58–63 411n47
70–76 392n41
77 433n53
77–79 415n42
80–81 418n7
82 418n11
92–97 411n47
14, *Against Alcibiades I*
33 416n50
37–38 401n10, 401n11
38 406n8
41–42 384n41
42 382n24
16, *In Defense of Mantitheus*
7 376n49
31 409n37
18, *On the Confiscation of the Property of Nicias' Brother*
4 410n44
5 342
6 412n8
6–7 414n28
10 371n10
10–12 416n51, n53, 417n55
19, *On the Property of Aristophanes*
25 365n7
20, *For Polystratus*
3 391n40
13 419n14
13–14 390n23, 391n40, 392n43, 409n37
23 373n27
21, *Defense Against a Charge of Taking Bribes*
1–5 367n27, 368n32
3 396n26
6–7 431n47
7 401n10
8 410n44
10–11 406n9
25, *Defense Against a Charge of Subverting the Democracy*
8–10 426n2
9 390n26
21–22 416nn50–51, 417n54
25–27 422–23n3

26, *On the Scrutiny of Euandros*
6, 10 409n37
28, *Against Ergocles*
12 415n42
30, *Against Nicomachus*
2 420n29, 422n1, 423n7, 426n6
2–5 422n3
4 422n1
5 422n2
9–12 422n3
10 407n19
10–13 409n34, 421n32
11–12 412n6
14 410n44, 412n55, 421n32
17–19 423n4
17–22 423n4
19–21 422n3
19–22 423n7
21 421n36, 423n5
24–25 422n3
25 423n4
26 426n6
27 423n7
28 410n41, 426n6, 431n45
30 423n7
31, *Against Philon*
12 367n24
15–16 418n7
17–18 416n50
27 426n3
32, *Against Diogeiton*
5–7 395n22
6, 7, 15 364n3, 402n11
24 402n15
25 364n3
26 402n15
34, *Against the Subversion of the Ancestral Constitution*
passim 417n56, 419nn12–13
1 419n13
3 392n42
4–5 419n13

Marcellinus
Life of Thucydides
5 363n77
14, 19, 25 431n43
28 424n16
47 431n43

Nepos
6.2.2–3 408n25
6.2–3.3 415n40
7.3.2 382n20
7.3.6 382n24
7.4 386n50
7.5.5 399n41
7.5.5–7.1 393n6, 398n38
7.6 399n41
7.6.4 399nn42–43
7.6.5 384n39, 399nn44–45
7.7.1–2 401n9
7.7.2–4 401n10
7.7.4 401–402n11
7.8.2–6 406n8
7.9.3–10.1 414n31
7.10.1 415n36
7.11.2–6 380n4
7.11.3–4 387n65
8.2.1–4 415n42
8.2.5–7 416n45, n47
8.3 417n55

Ovid
Metamorphoses
6.708–21 356n43

Palatine Anthology
7.45 358n60
7.255 361n70
7.614 371n14

Pausanias
1.2.5 382n24
1.3.3 350n6
1.3.5 400n56
1.5.1–4 427n15
1.8.4 354n31
1.8.5 351n12
1.15 355n34
1.15.1 360n70
1.17.1 369n37
1.17.6 355n34, 394n12
1.18.1 356n44
1.22.7 368n31, 383n29
1.23.9 428n24, 431n42

1.24.3 369n37
1.26.4 438n89
1.28.2 360n69
1.29.3 415n42
1.29.4 358n61
1.29.5 353n24, 366n22
1.29.7 359n62
1.29.15 351n9
2.17.4 387n66
2.36.1–2 387n66
3.8.6 408n29
3.9.1 415n35
3.9.2 435n68
3.9.4 434n60
3.9.8 435n64
3.11.6–8 353n24
3.18.3 414n34
3.18.16 356n44
4.1.5 383n29
4.15.6 413n20
5.8.2–4 356n44
6.3.15 411n52
6.14.13 353n24
6.20.19 356n44
7.2.6–8 400n55
7.17.9–12 400n54
8.46.4 400n54
9.8.1–3 356n45
9.27.2 383n29
9.32.8 426n34
9.32.9 406n10
9.32.10 415n35
10.9.2 353n24
10.10.4 360n70

Pherecrates
Fr. 164 *PCG* (155 Kock) 389n11

Philochorus
FGrHist 328
F 30 380n7
F 130 360n69, 394n12
F 140 395n16
F 141 402n16

Philostratus
Lives of the Sophists
1.9.1 375n40
1.9.2–5 359n63
1.15.2 382n16

Photius
Lexicon
s.v. *orchestra* 351n12
Library
377 401n10

Pindar
Isthmian
4.37–45 365n10
5.46–50 353n23
Olympian
7.7–12 365n10
Pythian
1.42–45 365n10
1.75–77 354n31
3.8 358n55
3.68–79 400n54
Paeans
5 394n12
Dithyrambs
Fr. 76, 77 Sandys 354n31

Plato
Alcibiades 1
124a, 129a, 132a 418n9
Apology
19e 375n40
19e-20c 367n25
20a 424n10
21a 425n24
24b 424n21
26b 424n21
26d 428n23
27b-e 425n26
28b-29b 425n23
30b-31a 425n23
31d 425n27
32a 425n23, n27
32b-c 404n30, 405n46
32b-e 425n28
33c 425n24
34a 416n46
36a 425n22
36b 379n68
38e 425n23
39c-42 425n30, 427n15
40b-42 425n23
41a 425n24
Axiochus
368d-e 404n32

Charmides
157e-158a 365n7
164d 418n9
Cratylus
407b 389n12
Crito
50a-e 413n18
51a-b 427n12
Euthydemus
271a-273e 366n17
271b-72b 410n47
Euthyphro
2c 4254n21
3b 424n21, 425n26
3c, 4b-e 377n57
3c-5c 425n32
Gorgias
447a-462b 375n40
452b-e 367n25, 375n39
452d-72b 377n52
455b 378n62
455e 354n26, 407n18
461e 347n2
466b-c 376n49
472a 367n28, 395n19
481d-86c 425n33
482a 379n68
483b 374n36
485d-86c 427n14
486c 368n30
488b-90a 374n36
500–502 404n36
501d-17a 377n52
503b-19b 431n45
503c 354n26
508d 368n30
515c-19b 372n20
515e 364n2, 377n51, 425n33
515e-16a 404n34
516d 354n26, 355n34, 404n34
518e-19a 364n2, 407n18
519a-b 425n33
519a-22e 427n14
521b-27e 425n23
521e 425n24
523a-27e 425n30
523e-24a 422n39
526c 422n39
527a 368n30
Greater Hippias
282b-83d 359n63, 367n25
282d 375nn39–40
285d 379n67
Hipparchus
228b-29d 357n52
Ion
541c-d 411n47
Laches
178a-184c 366n17
184d-e 374n36
Laws
624a-25a 413n16, n18
629a-30c 413n20
630c-31a 413n18
632d 413n16
667a 413n20
704e-705b 364n2, 367n25
705a 420n28
706b-c 374n32
743d 367n25
793a-d 413n18
858e 413n18, 413n20
923a 418n9
Lysis
204d 379n67
205a-e 365n10
211e 367n25
Menexenus
235a-36b 359n64, 377n52
234b 419n18, 424n11
236a 382n16
240a-c 394n12
242b-c 358n61
244a-b 416n47, 419n15
245a 437n81
Meno
70a-71a 424nn16–17
71e-94d 377n52
76e 424n16
78d 424n16
90a 367n25, 396n25, 415n38
90a-b 418n11, 424n16
90b-95a 426n34
92e 424n16
93a-94e 431n45
94e-95a 427n14
95b-c 375nn39–40

Parmenides
126a 416n46
126b-c 365n7
126c 427n18
127d 407n22
Phaedrus
227c-28c 427n18
228a 424n10
229c 354n30
230a 418n9
230d 427n18
235c 379n67
245c-56b 425n30
246b-57a 384n35
257c 363n80
258b-c 413n16
260a-62d 377n52
260d 433n53
266c-72d 377n52
269e-70a 358n56
272b 379n67
275c 427n10
276c 427n9
278c 424n10
278d-e 427n11
278e 379n67
Philebus
48c-49b 418n9
Protagoras
309a-c 384n36
310d-311e 367n25
311a 424n10
312d 375n40
314b-17e 424n10
316c-326c 375n37
318e-319a 375n39
319b-d 378n62
319b-20b 377n52
320c-328c 375n38
323a-29d 377n53
326c 374n36
337c-e 347n2, 369n37
339a 375n37
342da-e 412n13, 413n16
343b 418n9
349a 375n39
Republic
330a-c 367n25
336a 415n38
364b-e 377n57
365d 377n52
368a 365n7
517d 427n14
519c-41b 427n15
562b, 589d-590a 367n25
614b-21d 416n46
Seventh Letter
324b-d 412n10
324c 412n9
324d-325a 412n14, 425n28
325a-26b 417n1
325b 419n15
325d 420n28
325d-e 379n68
341b 418n9
341b-45a 427n16
Symposium
172–73b 416n46
177b 379n67
178a 292
178a-b 384n35
181e 426n35
213c-d 384n36
220d-e 366n16
221c 358n56
Theaetetus
143a 376n47
143a-c 427n17
Timaeus
20e 365n7
Poetry (Edmonds *Elegy* II, 2–11) 365n10

Plato Comicus
Cleophon
Fr. 61 *PCG* (60 Kock) 394n15

Pliny
Natural History
7.111 431n42
34.17 351n12
36.17 400n56
36.28 387n66

Plutarch
[Note: Citations are according to chapter divisions of the Loeb edition.]
Agesilaus
3.1–2 380n4
6.4 434n60

Alcibiades
1.1 353n24
1.2 376n45
1.3–6.2 384n36
1.4 436n73
2–10 384n38
2.2 377n55, 389n11
2.2.3 385n48
3 384n38
4.4–5 396n25
5.2–3 364n3
7.2–3 366n16, 377n51
8.1 367n30, 377n54
8.2 384n39
9 398n39
10.1 398n39
10.3 376n45
11–12 368n31
12.2–3 387n61
13.1 377n54
13.2 383n29
13.3 383n30
13.3–5 380n2
13.4 380n6, 383n32
13.5 383n30
14–15 380n2
14.3 371n10
15.1 371n10
15.2–3 407n18
15.4 391n37
16 384n38
16.1 389n11, 398n39
16.2 384n36
16.4 377n53
16.5 368n31, 387n60
17 380n5
17.2 381n8
17.4–5 381n9
18.3 384n35
18.3–19.1 382n20
19.1–2 382n24
20.2–5 382n20
20.3 382n24
20.3–22 383n25
21.1–5 385n48
21.5–23.1 386n50
22.3 382n24, 399n42
22.4 384n39, 389n12
23 384n38
23.1 371n10, 385n47
23.3–5 380n4
23.5 387n65
23.6 389n11
23.7 384n36
23.7–8 380n4
24.1 388n4
24.5 384n36
25.5–10 388n9
26.1–3 391n33
26.2 390n23
26.3–7 391n34
26.4–27.1 396n28
28 393n4
29.1–2 396n29
29.3–30.1 396n30
30.2–5 396n30, 401n11
31.1 397n32
31.1–2 396n30
31.2–6 398n34
31.4 398n38
32.1 398n38
32.3 399n40
32.4–5 399nn41–42
33.1 398n37
33.2 399n43
33.2–3 399n44
33.3 384n39
34.1 336
34.1–2 399n40
34.3–6 399n46
35.1 399n44
35.1–3 401n5
35.2 395n20, 398n36
35.4–6 401n8
36.1–2 384n38
36.1–3 401n10
36.2–37.2 401n11
36.4–37.3 406nn7–8
37.3–4 407n20, 414n31
38.1–4 411n48
38.2–4 380n3
38.3 218
38.3–39.1 415n36
39.5 384n38
Alexander
34.2 353n24
Aristides
7.2 383n31
7.2–4 380n2
7.4 383n33
10.8 389n15
19.1 353n24

20.1 389n15
24.3 373n28
26.3 371n14, 404n34
27.1 374n30

Artaxerxes
2, 2.3 401n3, 405n2
3 406n5
6.2–3 424n15
18.3 424n17
20.3–4 435n64
23.1 438n88

Camillus
19.3 341

Cimon
4 361n70
4.1–2 428n24
4.2 431n43
4.5 354–55n34
5.4 354n29
7 354n32, 360n68, 360n70
7–8.2 356n43
8.3–6 354n32, 355n34
9 358n56, 361n70
10, 15, 16 361n70
16.8 408n29
17.6–18.1 430n37

Demosthenes
1.1 368n31
12 384n40

Lysander
3.2 401n7
4.5–6.2 401n8
5.3 401n9
6.7 408n30
7 405n2
8.1–3 406n6
9.1–2 405nn1–3
9.2–4 406n6
9.4–11.7 406n7
11.6 406n10
13.1–2 406n10
13.2–14.3 406n13
14.1 407n15
14.3 408n23, 408n23
14.4 412n13
14.4–5 408n30
14.5–6 409n32, 410n42
15 340–41, 344
15.1 409n32, 412n5
15.2 408n29, 411n54
15.2–3 358n59, 412n2
15.5 413n15, 426n34
16–17 415n35
16.1 414n34
18.1–2 408n28
19 415n40
19.4 414nn34–35
20.1–4 414n35
20.5 414n34
21.2 415n40, 416n50
21.3 416n51, 417n55
22.1 408n29, 415n37
22.3 380n4
27.2 408n30
27.2–4 415nn37–38

Nicias
2.4 382n23
3–4.1 367n28
4.2 364n3
4.3–6 372n17
6.1–2 371n14, 372n17, 377n54, 404n34
6.2–4 382n23
7–8 372n21
8.3 372n22
9.3–10.3 371n10
11 380n2
11.3 383n30
11.4 383n32
11.6 383n30
12.2 381n15
13 381n9
13.1 382n23
13.2 382nn20–21, 384n35, 400n53
13.7 384n35
18.2–3 366n20
19.5 366n20
29.2–3 358n58

Pelopidas
6.4 415n37

Pericles
5.3–4 358n56
6.2 378n59
7.6 392n42
8 358n56
8.2–3 372n20
8.4 377n55
8.6 361n71

Pericles (continued)
9 372n20
10.5 376n49
11 364n4
12.1–2, 14 364n4, 372n20
15 358n56
16.3–5 364n3
23.2 360n69, 392n42
26.3–4 411n53
29.5–35 377n54
32.1 378n59
35.4 377n51, 404n34
36.3 375n38
37.3 420n22
Solon
2.3–4 420n21
20.1 426n3
22, 24.2 420n21
25.1 426n6
Themistocles
1.3 353nn21–22, 383n29
2.3 354n27, n29
2.4 354n29
2.6 354n29
5.3 353n22, 354n29
5.4 352n18, 353n21, 354n30
7.5 354n29
8.2 354n31
11.3–5 354n27
14.3 353n24
15.2 353nn21–22, n24
16 354n29
17 353n21
18.3–4 354n27
18.5 354n29
19.4 410n46
20 354n27, n29
21.3 353n22
22 352n18, 354n27, n29
23.3–4 354n27
30–31 400n52
30–32 438n89
Theseus
5.1 394n12
17.5, 22–23 403n24
29.4–5 360n66
35.5 355n34, 394n12
36 354n32
Comparison of Aristides with Marcus Cato
2.2 353n24
Moralia
185f 389n15
236b-c 369n37
349f 417n55
832c-e 376n50, 428n21
832c-34b 381n16
832f 381n14
833c 382n16
833d 382n17
833e-34b 393n52, 404n31
833f 376n49
835f 415n42, 416n44, 418n7
835f-36a 419nn16–17
836a 420n21
836f 415n39
844b 439n91
862b 386n51
867c 354n31
870f-871a 354n29
872c-e 356n46, 357n48

Polyaenus
1.40.9 393n4
1.45.2 406n7
1.45.4 408n25
1.45.5 408n30
1.47.2 398n34
1.48.3 435n64
2.2.5–10 414n32
7.19 415n35

Pseudo-Xenophon
Constitution of the Athenians
1.1–2 418n4
1.2 381n13
1.2–4 369n1, 370nn3–4
1.3 369n36
1.4–5 347n2, 350n8, 370n4, n7
1.5 385n46
1.8 370n6
1.9 370n4
1.10 368n30
1.10–13 347n2, 370n5, 411n53, 418n4
1.11 364n3

1.13 367n23, 368n33, 370n4
1.14 371n11, 372n16
1.14–16 388n3
1.16–19 364n3, 376n48
2.1 374n32
2.7–12 347n2
2.9 366n22
2.10 370n4
2.17 370n4
2.18 357n53
2.20 350n8
3.1 350n8
3.1–3 364n3, 369n37, 370n4
3.1–6 371n15
3.1–9 376n48
3.4 368n32, 368n33, 369n37
3.5–11 388n3
3.10 370n4
3.13 370n4

Simonides
Edmonds *LG*
Fr. 12–16 354n30, 356nn42–43
Fr. 91 353n21
Fr. 92 356n46, 357n48
Fr. 125 354n29
Fr. 132, 132, 171 360n70

Sophocles
Antigone
450–61 422n40
454–55 359n66, 413n23
Philoctetes
391–402 400n53

Strabo
1.2.38 400n54
1.3.1 411n47
8.2.24 356nn44–45
10.5.1 387n60
12.8.11 400n54

Suda
s.v. *Lêxiarchika grammateia* 373n26
s.v. *Simonides* 353n21
s.v. *Timocreon* 354n27

Theopompus
FGrHist 115
F 92 372n21
F 96b 390n25
F 153 356n45
F 155 413n22

Thrasymachus
DK 85 B 1 389n16

Thucydides
1.1 350n5, 428n24
1.1.1 428n27, 431n52
1.1–19 317–18
1.1.2 362n77
1.1.3 361n72
1.4.1 350n5
1.7–8 318
1.9.1 350n5
1.9.2 435n66
1.9–11 317
1.10.2 434n59
1.11–12.1 318
1.13.4 350n5
1.13–15 318
1.18.1 350n5, 370n6, 413n16
1.20–22 350n5
1.20.1 15, 363n80
1.20.2 385n43, 431n51
1.20.2–3 114–15, 351n10, 357n52
1.20.3 431n51
1.21.1 363n80
1.22 305, 428n24
1.22.1 306, 315, 429n28, 431n52
1.22.2 431n52
1.22.4 115, 315, 323, 325, 363n80, 385n45, 430n36, 431n52, 433n53
1.33.1 369n37
1.44.3 380n5
1.56–65 366n15
1.70 355n35, 357n49, 377n53
1.73.4–74 355n39, 360n67

Thucydides *(continued)*
1.74.1 354n26
1.75.2 355n35
1.77.1–5 376n48
1.86 412n13
1.89–93 318
1.89–117 318
1.91.4–7 319, 354n27, 407n18
1.92.5 434n63
1.93.3 352n17
1.93.5 319
1.93.7 407n18
1.94–95 357n47
1.95 355n35
1.96.1 356n40
1.97.2 423n6, 429n31
1.97.2–98 357n49, 361n70
1.98.1 354n32, 356n43
1.98–118 361n70
1.100.2–3 356n43, 364n3
1.100.2–101.3 428n24, 431n41
1.101.3 356n43, 364n3
1.102 415n41
1.102.4–108 358n55
1.103.4 356n46
1.105.4 389n15
1.107.1, 4 407n18
1.108.2 389n15
1.111.1 358n55
1.114.3 392n42
1.118.3 408n28
1.122.3, 124.3 374n31
1.126–27 382n23
1.126–38 319
1.128–33 355n35, 357n47
1.132.2–3 354n26
1.135–38 354n29
1.138.3 354n26, 438n85
1.138.5 438n89
1.139.3 412n5
1.140–41 386n53
1.141.1 412n2
1.144.2–3 386n53
2.1 428n24
2.1–2 341
2.2.1 344
2.13.1 371n10
2.13.3 366n15
2.13.7 418n4, n7
2.14.1 392n42
2.17.2 378n58
2.19.1 344
2.21.2–22.1 374nn32–33, 377n54
2.24.1 388n7
2.24.2 373n27
2.26.1 392n42
2.31.2 366n15
2.32 392n42
2.34 359n62, 359n66
2.34.4 418n4
2.35.2 385n43, 431n52
2.36 360n67, 361n71
2.36–41 364n2
2.37.1 350n8, 369n2
2.37.3 413n23
2.38.1 369n37
2.39–41 418n4
2.40.2–3 375n44, 377n53, 433n53
2.41 357n49, 360n68, 361n71
2.41.4 46
2.43.1 379n1, 381n8
2.54.3 438n82
2.58 366n15
2.59–65.3 377n54
2.61–65 386n53
2.62.2 95, 369n37, 386n54
2.63.1 386n53, 412n2
2.63.2 374n31
2.63.3 377n54, 412n2
2.65.8–9 431n39
2.65.9 358n56, 372n20
2.65.10–12 405n49, 431n46
2.65.11 380n3
2.67.4 367n24
2.67, 70 366n15
2.97 428n24
2.97.4 402n11
2.99–100.2 428n24
2.100.2 316, 433n57
3.1.2 374n33
3.2.3 371n12
3.3.2 394n15
3.10.5 391n31
3.17 366n15, 368n32, 369n37
3.17.2 392n42
3.19.1 372n25

3.32.1 367n24
3.34 387n1
3.36.5 371n13
3.36.6 372n22
3.37.2 374n31
3.37.3–4 370n6, 375n36
3.38.2–7 375n42
3.38.7 427n19
3.40.4 376n46
3.42–43, 48 375n43
3.42.2 430n36, 433n53
3.45.5 381n8
3.50 371n14
3.68.5 352n15
3.80.6 370n2
3.82.1 5
3.82.2–4 348n6
3.82.5 379n68
3.82.8 365n6
3.86 380n5
3.87.3 390n24
3.88 380n5
3.90 380n5
3.93.1 392n42
3.98.4 4
3.94–98 415n41
3.99 380n5
3.103 380n5
3.104.5 429n31
3.113.6 350n5
3.115 380n5
3.115.5 380n5
3.116 434n61
4.1 380n5
4.10.5 385n43
4.21.2 372n22
4.21.3 372n20
4.24–25 380n5
4.27–39 377n54
4.28 377n54
4.31–40 415n41
4.41.1 374n34
4.50.3 387n1
4.58–65 430n39
4.60.2 380n5
4.61.5 380n5, 386n54
4.65 358n57, 363n79, 380n5
4.65.3 380n5, 430n35
4.65.4 377n53, 385n46
4.73.1 385n43
4.80 414n29
4.81.2 428n24, 430n34
4.84.2 430n34
4.97 360n66
4.101.5 402n11
4.102 356n43
4.104.4–107.2 428n24, 431n41
4.105.1 356n43, 364n3
4.109.2–4 428n24
4.118.12 358n55
4.126.4 433n53
5.2–10 372n21, 377n54
5.3.5 391n36
5.4–5 380nn5–6
5.16 416n53
5.16.1 371n10, 382n23
5.17.2 408n29, 415n38
5.18.2 408n28, 418n5
5.18.5 374n30, 396n31
5.20 343–44, 358n55
5.21 430n37
5.23.4 358n55
5.25–26 321, 429n28, 435n69
5.26 428n24
5.26.1 409n32
5.26.1–3 341, 343
5.26.3–4 378n58
5.26.4–5 428n25
5.31 424n13
5.31.6 415n38
5.33 387n62
5.35 430n37
5.35.3 378n63
5.36.1 344
5.38 430n37
5.38.2 390n22
5.41.3 378n63
5.42.1 391n36
5.43 380n2
5.43.2 348n7, 380n6, 431n46
5.43–47 371n10
5.45 380n2
5.46.2 430n37
5.46.5 380n2
5.52.2–56 380n2, 407n18
5.53 371n10
5.55.4–56.3 371n10
5.57–60 387n62
5.61 380n2

Thucydides *(continued)*
5.61.2 371n10
5.64–74 387n62
5.76.3 371n10, 380n2
5.76–81 387n62
5.77.5 418n5
5.79.1 418n5
5.80–116 381n11
5.82.5–6 407n18
5.83.1–2 387n62
5.83.4 430n37
5.84.1 380n2
5.84.3 387n61
5.89 386n55
5.103.2 378n58
5.105.1–2 386n60
5.111.2–5 433n53
5.115 387n62
5.116 386n60
5.116.1 387n62
6.1.1 381n8
6.2.1–2 350n5
6.6.2 380n5
6.6.3 381n12
6.7 381n11
6.7.1 387n62
6.7.2 361n70, 387n62
6.8 381n8
6.8.1–2 380n7
6.8.2 399n44
6.8.4 377n54
6.15 377n54
6.15.3–4 348n7, 380n3, 431n46
6.15.4 386n56, 405n49, 431n39
6.16 431n46
6.16.1–4 367n29
6.16.3–4 386n56
6.16.6 377n55
6.17.1 382n23
6.18.2–3 386n54
6.23.3 382n23
6.24.3 99, 381n10
6.24.4 99
6.27 382n20
6.27.2 385n48
6.27–29 383n25
6.27.3 379n68
6.28.1–2 382n24
6.28.2 384n37, 386n56
6.29.3 106, 385n47
6.31 366n15, n19
6.43 381n13, 393n51, 395n21
6.47 377n54
6.53 383n25, 386n50
6.53.3 114, 384n42, 385n43
6.53.3–59 351n10, 431n51
6.54–59 384n35
6.54.1–2 115
6.54.2 385n43
6.54.5–6 357n52
6.56–57 357n52
6.60–61 383n25, 386n50, 431n51
6.60.1 379nn68–69, 384n42
6.60.2 433n57
6.60.2–5 385n48
6.61.1 384n37
6.61.3 371n10
6.61.3–5 385n47
6.72.2–3 430n39
6.83 360n67
6.85.1 374n31, 386n54
6.87 357n49
6.88.9–10 386n50
6.89 431n46
6.89–92 387n63
6.89.6 370n5
6.100.1 395n21
6.101.6 366n20
6.105 387n62
6.105.2 416n49
7.1.5 395n21
7.18 387n62
7.18.1 435n69
7.20 387n61
7.20.2 381n12
7.26 381n12
7.27 387n61
7.27–28 367n24
7.27.5 364n3
7.28.1 392n42
7.28.2 393n51
7.28.4 388n3
7.29.5 4
7.42, 48–50 377n54
7.57.2 392n42
7.57.4 391n31

7.73.3	379n68
7.75.4	379n68
7.77.2	382n23
7.86.5	4, 367n28
7.87.5	4
8.1.1	378n60, 382n23, 388n9
8.1.2–3	388n7
8.1.3	392n42
8.1.4	389n15
8.4	388n7
8.5–7	388n4
8.5.1	388n7, 391n36
8.5.1–2	392n42
8.5.5	388n2
8.6.3	387n63
8.12	388n4
8.14–48	388n5
8.15	391n31
8.15–17	411n47
8.15.1	388n7
8.17.1	395n21
8.17.4–18	388n5
8.19.2	388n2
8.21	391n31
8.23.4	395n21
8.25.1	395n21
8.28	388n2
8.29	388n7
8.30	411n47
8.36–37	388n5
8.36.1	388n7
8.45.2–3	388n7
8.46.5	388n7
8.47.2–49	388n8
8.48.2	379n68, 388n8
8.48.3	388nn7–8
8.48.4	379n68
8.48.4–7	391n30
8.48.4–54.2	388n9
8.48.5–6	388n3
8.49.1	390n26
8.53.2	388n7, n9
8.53–54.3	388n8, 390n26
8.54.1	390n26
8.54.3	388n2
8.54.4	379n68, 388n8
8.56	391n29
8.57–58	388n7
8.57–59	391n29
8.60.1	391n36
8.60.1–2	392n42
8.62–63.1	411n47
8.63.3–65.1	391n30
8.63.4	388n7, 391n40
8.64	393n3
8.64.2–5	428n24, 430n38
8.65.2	379n68, 411n47
8.65.2–66.5	390n25
8.65.3	388n7, 391n40
8.66.5	392n40
8.67–68.1	390n26
8.67.1–2	378n63, 389n20
8.67.2	419n18
8.67.2–3	390n21
8.67.2–68.1	390n27
8.67.3–70.1	390n23
8.68.1	379n68, 381n16, 390n26, 418n10
8.68.1–2	428n21
8.68.2	393n50, n52
8.68.4	127, 409n39
8.69.1	390n27, 393n51
8.69.4–70.1	334
8.70.2	391n36
8.71.3	391n36
8.72.1	392n40
8.72.2	391n37
8.73	391n32
8.73.2–3	390n25
8.73.3	383n30
8.74.2	392n42
8.74–76	391n32
8.74–77	391n37
8.76.7	391n33
8.78	391n33
8.79	411n47
8.80.1	391n33
8.81–82	391n34, n37
8.81.1	391n33
8.81.3	388n7
8.83–85	391n33
8.84.5	433n57
8.86	391n37
8.86.3	390n26, 392n40
8.86.5–7	348n7, 391n37, 431n46
8.86.6	392n44
8.86.9	391n36, 392n42
8.87	391n33
8.87–88	391n35

Thucydides *(continued)*
8.87.1–3 388n7
8.89–93 391n39
8.89.1 391n37
8.89.2–3 392n40
8.90–93 391n38
8.90.1 390n26, 391n36
8.92.1 392n40
8.92.2 391n36, 392n41, 411n47
8.92.3 392n42
8.92.5–11 392n41
8.92.8 424n16
8.92.11 393n51
8.93.2 392n40
8.95–96 392n43
8.95.2 392n42
8.95.6 394n13
8.95.7 392n42
8.96 392n42
8.97 392n44
8.97.2 4, 392n45, n46, 409n39, 419n15
8.97.3 393n2
8.98 391n36, 393n52, 404n31
8.98.1 390n26
8.98.4 392n44
8.99–109 393n1
8.109 326, 438n83
8.109.1 400n55

Timaeus
Lexicon Platonicum
s.v. *orchestra* 351n12

Timocreon
Edmonds *LG*
Fr. 1.10–12 353n22
Fr. 1–3 354n27

Timotheus
Persians
115–50 400n54
127–73 400n55, 438n89

Vergil
Georgics
3.267–68 356n44

Xenophon
Agesilaus
1.27 438n88
Apology
1, 5–9 425n23
10 424n21
12–13 425n26
12–16 425n29
14 425n24
24 425n22
29 425n22
29–30 426n34
Anabasis
1.1.1–2 405n2
1.1.1–5 401nn3–4
1.1.3–4 406n5
1.1.5–8 408n24
1.1.7–8 414n35
1.1.9 414n34
1.1.10 424n17
1.4.2–3 424n15
1.9.9 406n6
2.5.38 424n17
2.6 424n17
2.6.2 414n32
2.6.2–5 414n34
2.6.16 375n40
2.6.29 424n17
3.1.5–8 424n18, 438n88
3.2.12 438n86
5.3.4–13 438n88
7.2.31–38 402n11
7.3.19 402n11
7.5.14 427n7
Cavalry Commander
7.1 369n37
9.3–7 418n7
Constitution of the Lacedaemonians
1.1–2 413n16, n23
5.1, 8.1–5 413n23
8.5 425n29
10.8 413n23
Hellenica
1–2.4.42 417n2
1.1.1–8 393n1
1.1.8 393n2
1.1.9–10 396n28
1.1.12 393n3, 398n34, 431n43
1.1.20–22 393n5
1.1.22 393n3

1.1.24 395n21
1.1.24–26 393n7
1.1.32 397n32, 430n38
1.1.33–34 395nn19–20
1.1.35 393n5
1.1.35–36 414n32
1.2.1 335
1.2.1–2 395n20
1.2.1–13 395n22
1.2.6 400n55, 438n88
1.2.8 395n21
1.2.13, 15 396n27, n29, 398n38
1.2.15–17 395n22, 396n29
1.2.18 396n24
1.2.19 394n7
1.3.1–8 395n22
1.3.2–7 396n29
1.3.8 401n11
1.3.8–9 397n32
1.3.9 394n9
1.3.10 396n29, 401n11
1.3.12 411n47
1.3.13 401n2, 430n39
1.3.13–14 397n32
1.3.14–22 398n34
1.3.15–19 414n32
1.3.22 398n38
1.4.1 397n32
1.4.2 338, 397n32
1.4.2–4 401n2
1.4.4–7 401n4
1.4.6 397n33
1.4.6–7 402n13
1.4.7 338
1.4.8 398n34
1.4.8–21 335
1.4.9 401n6
1.4.9–11 398n34, n36
1.4.10 398n37, 401n10
1.4.12 398n37, 399n40
1.4.13–16 380n3, 399nn41–42
1.4.17 399n40
1.4.19 401n2
1.4.20 399nn41–42, n44, n46
1.4.21 399n42, 401n10
1.4.2–23 401n5
1.5.1–7 401n4
1.5.1–10 337
1.5.8–9 402n13
1.5.10–15 401n8
1.5.16 338
1.5.17 401n11
1.5.18 401n10
1.5.20 402n12
1.6.1–3 402n12
1.6.1–23 402n14
1.6.6–11 402n13
1.6.7 408n30
1.6.14–15 398n35, 411n53
1.6.24–25 368n32, 402n16
1.6.26–38 402n17
1.6.38 405n1
1.7.2 394n10, 403nn23–24
1.7.3–4 403n25
1.7.4–7 403n26
1.7.8 335, 403n24, n28
1.7.9–10 403n27, 404n33
1.7.9–11 403n29
1.7.12 175, 400n49
1.7.12–15 404n30
1.7.12–33 404n32
1.7.28 393n52, 404n31
1.7.29–32 402n17
1.7.34 404n33
1.7.35 405n46, 409n33, n35, 421n32, 423n3
2.1.6 411n52
2.1.1–7, 10–11 405n1
2.1.8–9 405n2
2.1.10 411n52
2.1.13–15 405n3
2.1.15 398n35
2.1.15–19 406n6
2.1.16 405n1, 406n6
2.1.20 368n32
2.1.20–32 406n7
2.1.25–26 406n8
2.1.28–29 406n9
2.1.30–32 406n10
2.2.1–4 406n13
2.2.3 387n60
2.2.5–9 406n13
2.2.7–10 407n15
2.2.10–11 407n23
2.2.11–15 407n17
2.2.14 407n23
2.2.15 407n19

Hellenica (continued)
2.2.16 407n21
2.2.17 407n22, 408n26
2.2.17–19 408n27
2.2.19 408n28
2.2.19–20 408n29
2.2.20 408n31
2.2.21 407n23
2.2.23 412n1, n5
2.2.23–3.11 340–43
2.3.1–10 412n5
2.3.2 342, 387n61, 412n4
2.3.3 343
2.3.6 411n53
2.3.6–7 342, 411n49
2.3.8 344, 412n1
2.3.9–10 343–44
2.3.11 412n8
2.3.12 412n14
2.3.13 407n22
2.3.13–14 413n15
2.3.15 414n28
2.3.16 414n27, 431n48
2.3.17–19 416n51
2.3.18–20 414n24
2.3.18–56 414n26
2.3.21–22 414n25
2.3.28 428n23
2.3.29–33 408n25
2.3.34 413n21, n23, 415n43
2.3.35 403nn25–26
2.3.35–36 405n42, 407n22
2.3.38 415n39
2.3.38–42 416n51
2.3.39 414n28
2.3.42 412n55
2.3.46 407n22
2.3.48 389n19
2.3.54 412n9
2.4.1 414n25, 415n37
2.4.2 415n41
2.4.2–7 415n43
2.4.8–10 414n29
2.4.10 416n44
2.4.9 404n31
2.4.11–22 416n45
2.4.13–17 417n3
2.4.20–22 416n47
2.4.21 341, 414n30
2.4.23 416n48
2.4.23–24 341, 416n51
2.4.24–28 416n50
2.4.25 418n3, n7
2.4.30–35 416n52
2.4.31 416n53
2.4.35 416n51
2.4.35–36 416n53
2.4.36 417n54
2.4.37 416n50, 417n54
2.4.38 417n55
2.4.40–41 418n8
2.4.42 417n56, 418n10
2.4.43 424n19
3.1.1 424n15
3.1.4 424n20
3.2.2–5 407n20
3.2.21–23 408n29, 424n13
3.2.25–29 424n14
3.4.2 415n40, 418n5
3.4.2–4 434n60
3.4.5 418n5
3.4.25 438n88
3.5.1–2 435n64
3.5.2 434n58
3.5.8 408n29
3.5.16 434n62, 436n75
4.2.1 435n64
4.2.20 438n86
5.2.35 435n64
6.1.8 358n55
6.3.3–6 423n8
6.5.36 408n29
7.2.1 439n93
Memorabilia
1.1.1 424n21
1.1.2–4 425n26
1.1.2–9 425n27
1.1.6–9 425n26
1.1.18 425n28
1.1.32 425n28
1.2.9–47 425n33
1.2.9–61 425n22
1.2.12 348n8
1.2.12–47 431n49
1.2.24 384n36
1.2.31 412n7
1.2.31–37 387n61
1.2.40–42 399–400n49
1.2.62 412n9
2.7 416n50
2.9 403n23

3.1.1 410n47
3.3.12–13 369n37
3.5.3 369n37
3.5.7–8 403n22
3.5.14–16 413n19
3.5.16 405n43
3.6 416n46
3.6.1–18 430n36
3.7 365n8
4.2.1 427n8
4.2–3 414n28
4.2.3–5 411n47
4.2.24 418n9
4.4.15 413n23
4.4.19 414n23
4.5–6 414n28
4.8.1–2, 8–10 437n81

Oeconomicus
1.13–14 367n25
4.3, 5.7, 6.6–7, 6.10 369n1

Symposium
1.5 424n10
1.8–10 384n35
2.14 390n26
3.5 366n17
4.1–2 424n10
4.62 424n10
8.1–9.7 384n35
8.39 426n6
8.40 423n8
9.1 426n34

Ways and Means
2.2–5 418n7

INSCRIPTIONS AND PAPYRI

Fornara
15 420n29
23 378n65
42 360n69
55 373n26, 419n14
57 356n45
81 332
92 371n15, 378n63
93 378n63
97 331, 371n15
98 371n15, 409n34, n36
99 387n1
100 369n1, 378n63
101 366n22
102 374n30
103 374n30, 392n42, 394n12
119 364n3, 373n25, n27
121 378n63
124 380n5
125 380n5
126 411n47
128 371n15
133 371n15, 409n36, 421n31, 422n38
136 371n15, 373n28, 378n63, 409n36
140 378n63
144 373n27, 381n11
146 381n12
147d 399n42
154 394n13, 395n23, 396n26
155 392n41, 411n47
156 374n29, 398n34, 399n42, 401n6, 431n42
161 399n47, 402n15, 405n45, 407n20
162 396n30, 397n31, 399n47
163 398n37, 399n47, 423n3
165 407n20
166 406n13, 407n16, 411n51

Harding
3 416n44
7 415n42, 419n19
9 423n4
19C 431n50
35 437n81

***IG* I²**
1085 366n22

***IG* I³**
11 332, 380n5
14 378n63
21 371n15, 378n63

IG I³ (*continued*)
27 421n33
34 371n15, 409n34, n36
35 378n63
37 387n1
39 374n30
40 374n30, 392n42, 394n12
45 378n63
46 369n1, 378nn63–64
52 364n3, 373n25, n27
53 380n5
54 380n5
61 371n15, 378n59
66 371n14
68 371n15, 409n36, 421n31, 422n38
71 371n15, 373n28, 378n63, 409n36
78 378n59, nn63–64
79 378n63
84 378n63, 421n31
85 380n2, 383n31
93 381n12
96 391n31
99 378n63
101 374n29, 398n34, 399n42, 401n6, 431n42
102 392n41, 411n47
104 420n29
105 395n16
113 391n35, 406nn11–12, 407n14
117 399n47, 402n15, 405n45, 407n20
118 396n30, 397n31, 399n47
119 398n37, 399n47, 423n3
120 399n47
123 407n20
125 407n14
126 407n14
127 406n13, 407n16, 411n51
131 368n31
132 378n63
133 364n3
135 378n63
138 373n26, 419n14
238 378n63
250 378n63
269 358n56
364 411n47
370 373n27, 381n11
375 394n13, 395n23, 396n26
376 399n41, 431n43
379 406n14
402 378n63
418 374n30, 392n42
422 392n42
426 392n42
474–479 398n37
501 360n69
1453 331, 371n15

IG II²
1 411n52
10 415n42, 416n44, 418n3, 419n20
43 437n81
2318 355n36

IG XII
5, 109 398n36
8, 262 401n6

ML
6 378n65
15 360n69
21 394n15
23 373n26, 419n14
37 332
44 378n63
45 331, 371n15
46 371n15, 409n34, n36
47 387n1

49 369n1, 378n63
51 366n22
52 374n30, 392n42, 394n12
58 364n3, 373n25, n27
61 411n47
62 378n63
63 380n5
64 380n5
65 371n15
68 371n15, 409n36, 421n31, 422n38
69 371n15, 373n28, 378n63, 409n36
73 378n63
77 373n27, 381n11
78 381n12
79 399n42
84 394n13, 395n23, 396n26
85 392n41, 411n47
86 420n29
87 396n30, 397n31, 399n47
88 398n37, 399n47, 423n3
89 374n29, 398n34, 399n42, 401n6, 431n42
91 399n47, 402n15, 405n45, 407n20
92 407n20
94 406n13, 407n16, 411n51

Parian Marble
FGrHist 239
F A46 and F A54 352n13

POxy
XI, no. 1364 382n18
XV, no. 1800, frs. 6 & 7 419n17
XVII, no. 2987 421n38

Tod
63 371n14
100 419n20
106 437n81
107 437n81
123 437n81
204 356n45

Text: 10/12 Baskerville
Display: Baskerville
Composition: Impressions Book and Journal Services, Inc.
Printing and binding: Edwards Brothers, Inc.